A Taste of Life

1,000 Vegetarian Recipes from Around the World

Supreme Design Publishing books are printed on long-lasting acid-free paper. When it is available, we chose paper that has been manufactured by environmentally responsible practices. These may include using trees grown in sustainable forests, incorporating recycled paper, minimizing chlorine in bleaching, or recycling the energy produced at the paper mill. Supreme Design Publishing is also a member of the Tree Neutral™ initiative, which works to offset paper consumption through tree planting.

TreeNeutral

ISBN 978-1-935721-10-9

Library of Congress Control Number: 2011924868

Editing by Supreme Understanding and Patra Afrika

Cover Design by Suprem Design Media
Interior Design by Patra Afrika, NIA, New Image Alliance

Acknowledgements

It's not easy to thank the many people who have supported us at Supreme Design Publishing. We're more of a grassroots network than a traditional company, so our "staff" is something more like a family of thousands. Because space prevents us from acknowledging the hundreds of people who contributed recipes, we begin by thanking the people whose names do not appear here for various reasons, including their own modest wishes. Even though the prospects of rewarding someone's generosity with silence is difficult, we know who you are and you know that we are grateful. If you asked, and we failed to credit your contribution, please accept our humblest apologies. Just let us know and we'll fix it, we promise. If we've made any other errors or typos, please feel free to let us know. We would also like to thank everyone who submitted images, ideas and other content, as well as the contributors who wrote pieces for *The Hood Health Handbook,* which have been republished here. And to our readers, we owe each of you a great debt of service for your support.

Supreme Design Publishing is an independent, grassroots company.
You can help support our work by:
Ordering wholesale quantities of our books for resale or charitable donations
Posting pictures of yourself with the book (or a dish you prepared using one of these recipes) online
Discussing this book on your social networks or messageboards
Sharing this books with your friends and family

For more on *The Hood Health Handbook,* visit **www.hoodhealthhandbook.com** or request a copy at your local bookstore or library. For more on Supreme Design Publishing's other nonfiction titles, visit
www.supremedesignonline.com

Table of Contents

Introduction

by SUPREME UNDERSTANDING

This is not your ordinary cookbook. This isn't even your ordinary vegetarian cookbook. While other cookbooks focus on a specific region, or offer only a smattering of selections, this book is filled to the brim with over 1,000 delicious and exotic recipes from the cuisines of over 200 nations. And we've worked countless hours to select recipes that are not only tasty, but affordable and easy-to-prepare, so that just about anyone can change their diet with this book!

We've even included articles that will help a novice cook become a master chef in no time: We'll show you how to set up your kitchen, how to cook using a variety of methods, how to plan your meals, and how to shop so that you can feed more while spending less.

We're doing all this because we know people need alternatives to the diet they're eating nowadays. And it's not that people don't WANT to eat better, it's just that many of us simply haven't figured out HOW. When we published *The Hood Health Handbook*, it was an awakening for thousands of readers who realized just how sick we are here in the Western world, particularly among the poor and people of color. Poor people, especially those in the South, tend to eat worse and die sooner. Yet unlike other groups, Blacks and Latinos tend to eat the same unhealthy diets no matter what income level they're at.

This is why we spent considerable time in *The Hood Health Handbook* discussing the roots of disease, the downright disgusting facts about fast food, and the benefits of eating at home, and eating less meat. After all, studies have shown that a plant-based diet can help reduce the risk of many preventable diseases, and plant-based fiber can actually allow you to eat more without gaining weight. Yet, for many people, this wasn't enough.

It's one thing to WANT to eat differently, and another thing to have the knowledgebase and skillset to actually DO it. This is what led us to publishing *A Taste of Life*. We know this book will change lives in ways few other cookbooks can. By taking considerable time and effort to dig up the healthiest and tastiest of recipes from all over the planet, we're sharing the culinary habits of the majority of the world's inhabitants, most of whom eat very little meat or none at all. Outside of the Western world, we eat a fairly consistent diet, one that is nothing like the one we eat here in the U.S.

As we noted in *Hood Health*:

> "You see, everywhere in the world where you find Black and brown people with some remembrance of their original way of life, we eat similarly. We eat a grain with a legume as our staple dish. In East Asia, it's rice and soybeans. In South Asia, it's rice and lentils. Among Native Americans, it's corn (or quinoa) and beans. In Africa, it's millet (or sorghum, tef, etc.) and lentils. We eat a ton of vegetables with our meals, and we eat fruit separately as a snack or a dessert."

This is why the oldest and healthiest people in the world eat the kinds of foods you'll find in this book. While we know that many people throughout the world also eat meat and fish, we would recommend that you consider the toxic environment and industry practices that affect those items before they make their way to your plate. Your best bet – in our opinion – is to eat a diet heavy in fruits, vegetables, and whole grains, and to buy your ingredients organic as often as possible.

In *The Hood Health Handbook* we provide a nutritional guide to the health benefits of over 100 fruits, vegetables, mushrooms, legumes, and spices, as well as a guide to the essential vitamins and minerals and the foods where they can be found. You'll find abridged versions of those guides here in *A Taste of Life* as well.

Together *with The Hood Health Handbook*, this book has EVERYTHING you need to change the way you and your family eats and lives. Take it one day at a time, and you WILL be able to do it. So let's change our world together. Please share these recipes (and the book you found them in) with your friends and community…and – above all – BE the change you want to see in the world! You owe it to the future!

The Original Diet: Getting Back Down to Earth

by PATRA AFRIKA

One of the most beautiful aspects of a vegetarian diet is you can eat all the pure foods you want, requiring a lot less to satisfy your appetite. Eating at will (whatever and whenever you want) can have serious consequences. However it's only true when the foods you choose to overload your system with are fattening and contain unhealthy substances. But as you begin to incorporate more raw foods and vegetables into your diet, no matter if you're traveling, dining out or cooking at home, a knowledgeable vegetarian can find very creative and soul-satisfying alternatives to unhealthy eating. And there's plenty here to inspire your next great food experience.

Unearthing Naturally Great Tasting Foods. While "non-foods" are things that we consume, whether solid or liquid, that have no nutritional value, nutritional foods are alive and supports the healthy function of the body. When food has been processed to the point where important minerals and vitamins have either been destroyed or removed, food becomes non-food. When we talk about live foods in *A Taste of Life*, we're talking about naturally prepared foods that are minimally processed and having more nutrients to help protect you from free radicals which can later become cancer causing. The less food is tampered with, the healthier it will be for you.

Soul Food, It Doesn't Have to be Unhealthy. As soul food conjures up ideas of "rich" flavors, it doesn't necessarily mean it has to be created with fat, oil and high levels of salty spices, as perceived by many ethnic food surveyors. The term soul food originated in North America during the ethos of the 60's when southern chefs would offer their cooking to soldiers and out-of-towners. This caught on to mainstream America, and became associated with "down home" cooking and Black cuisine. By the mid-1960s, when the Civil Rights Movement peaked, there were terms like soul brother, soul sister and soul music, with the word 'soul' emphasizing the essence and collective experiences of Africans in America. However, the most local examples of soul food is also commonly found deeply-rooted in Southern, Creole, Indian as well as Caribbean cultures.

Today, just about every ethnic group has their own equivalent of soul food, which includes specific dishes that remind them of home, for some it may be iced tea with cheese grits and fish, while for others it could mean a beer, burger and fries with ketchup. Loosely speaking, it's a term meaning deep satisfaction that reminds you of where you come from. Traditionally, many aspects in the preparation of soul foods

tend to be very high in starch, fat, sodium, calories and cholesterol. But soul food does not have to be unhealthy nor does it have to have meat in it to be tasty. As you'll find in the vegetarian culture, herbs and spices are the basics to making any soul food dish.

Because bland and soul food should never be used in the same sentence, the following multi-purpose blend of spices and flavors can be used regularly to prepare robust, vegetarian dishes. Flavors, mostly dried/powdered herbs and spices, often used together in soul food are: Garlic, onion, chili, paprika, sea salt, black pepper corn, red/cayenne pepper, lemon pepper, parsley, thyme, bay leaves, oregano, mint, basil, whole cloves, all spice, chipotle, cumin, turmeric and coriander; to include vegetable and olive oil. So ethnic food does not have to be unhealthy to be rich and flavorful.

Lowering Cholesterol. Basically, cholesterol is a protein which comes from two sources that is either produced in our bodies (mostly the liver); or is found in animals and animal-based products. If what we eat does not come from an animal (like fruits and vegetables), then it does not have cholesterol. Though our body requires cholesterol, only a small amount is needed in the formation of cell membranes and the manufacturing of hormones. The three main factors that raise blood cholesterol level are saturated fats, cholesterol and obesity.

Foods with the highest amounts of cholesterol are eggs and liver. Other high cholesterol foods include: whole (cow's) milk dairy products, butter, cream, ice cream, cream cheese, certain shellfish (such as shrimp), organ meats (such as kidney and brain), duck and goose (which have more cholesterol than chicken or turkey; the skin on these animals is high in cholesterol), beef, veal, pork and lamb. Foods that lower cholesterol are dark leafy vegetables such as *kale and collard greens, blueberries, whole grains, oats, almonds, walnuts, pistachios and flaxseed oil, pomegranate juice, (also avocado, olives and olive oil are a good source of fat and protects against diabetes and heart disease).

Satisfying Your Craving. Have you ever grabbed a pint of ice cream and told yourself you were only going to eat half…but didn't stop until it was all gone? Or ever eaten your way to the bottom of a bag of salt & vinegar potato chips and found yourself still craving? That's because sweets and spices cause an endorphin rush, just like caffeine, fat and an array of other chemical compounds which target the brain's "bliss" system to further reinforce our cravings. But by mastering TASTE, you can actually feel better AND be satisfied, just by adding the proper BALANCE of flavor to your food. Ask yourself, if you're craving a food, what it is you really want? Well we can start by defining the experiences. The word 'taste' is defined as a sense that distinguishes the five basic tastes: sweet, sour, salty, spicy and bitter, plus a distinct smell, texture and flavor. So how do we get the taste we're craving and keep it healthy?

The sources of the *sweet* taste are many, most fruits, many vegetables, nearly every grain (as well as eggs, dairy and meat products), and of course, sugar and honey. Though its essence is cooling and soothing, you can literally become addicted, and the health effects of excessive sugar intake are well-known. *Sour* is the predominant flavor in lemons, limes, vinegar, yogurt and fermented foods which promotes digestion and weight gain in equal measure and is also related to emotions. *Salt* is found in the earth, in sea salts, in seaweed and kelp, and of course in flesh and blood – which is why many of think we're craving meat when we're really just craving a particular taste (or nutrient). Salt is warming to the body, stimulating to the appetite and promotes tissue development. Salt helps the body retain things like calories, fluids, and information. Salt also has an emotional connection, and is said to increase motivation. Most of us get too much of this taste, however. One teaspoon of salt a day is the perfect prescription, while 2 to 3 tablespoons is nine times more than we need. *Bitter*, the flavor most lacking in our diet, is found in green leafy vegetables such as spinach, kale, and mustard greens, as well as in turmeric, coffee and aloe vera. It's a detoxifier with particular benefit to the liver. Bitter is cooling and anti-inflammatory and helps reduce overall body fat. *Pungent* can also be thought of as "spicy" which is your garlic, onion, chilies, ginger, cayenne and other foods tha are hot on the tongue. The pungent taste is heating and stimulating to the body, strengthening metabolism, circulation and digestion. Pungent is also known to fire

us up, but an overdose can cause anger and irritability. Last but not least is a sixth taste, *astringent*, the flavor found in beans, berries, Brussels' sprouts and broccoli. These are anti-inflammatory foods that cool the body and aid the process of detoxification and are great for fostering meditative states. Careful though, as astringents are thought to pull the senses inwards, causing excessive inward focus and feeling of isolation.

The phrase *"A Taste of Life"* could mean anything from experiencing that which nourishes our existence…to becoming acquainted with the savoring of any substance perceived by the senses. Our goal, with this book, is to offer you that wide range of possibilities…with all the best tastes and flavors the world has to offer. Take control of your cravings and you can truly enjoy the best natural foods life has to offer. Our 1,000 flavorful and diverse recipes are gourmet dishes that can be created right in your own kitchen. We'll show you how to incorporate fresh produce in your diet until you've transitioned to where it is you want to be. At the same time you'll be totally eliminating the toxins that your body can't process or isn't meant to digest. Again that's totally up to you as to when and at what pace you want to do that. But you can start now just by incorporating extra servings of vegetables on your plate.

We've also included fresh juices for more satisfying flavors and it's detoxification properties. We imagine after reading it, most people will want to get away from sugary drinks, perhaps to lose weight, while others will simply want to add more years to their lives. For some very excellent tips, techniques and to examine some of the historical food facts around our vegetarian inspired recipes (which are all part of the global vegetarian cuisine) just keep reading, try things out and ENJOY!

How to Cook Ethnic Food

by SUPREME UNDERSTANDING

Cooking food from foreign cuisines isn't as scary as you might think. In fact, if you learn some of the basic staple foods, cooking techniques, and seasonings of your favorite culinary cultures, you can not only reproduce the amazing dishes in this cookbook, but you'll also be able to create your own takes on traditional ethnic cuisine. So here are some basics to some of the world's most popular fares.

Chinese

A balanced Chinese meal involves two elements: (1) the *fan* element made up of starches and grains, normally white rice in the southern provinces, and noodles or

dumplings in the north where wheat is common, and (2) the *tsai* element containing the protein and vegetable element, all cooked in a variety of ingredients and methods (such as sauteing, stir-frying, deep-frying, and steaming), producing a large range of flavors.

Staple Foods. Most Chinese dishes are made with rice or noodles (made from egg, wheat, or rice). Common ingredients include bok choy, Chinese eggplant, Chinese cabbage, Chinese broccoli, bean sprouts, snow peas, white radish, straw mushrooms, bamboo shoots, and bean curd or tofu.

Staple Seasonings. Common Chinese condiments include garlic, ginger, green onions, chilies, cilantro, soy sauce, sesame oil, five spice powder (made of ground peppercorns, star anise, cloves, fennel and cinnamon and sometimes coriander seeds), chili sauce, chili paste, rice vinegar, plum sauce, and black bean sauce.

Thai

Thai cuisine places emphasis on lightly prepared dishes with strong aromatic components. Thai cuisine is known for being spicy. Balance, detail and variety are important to Thai cooking. Thai food is known for its balance of the five fundamental taste senses in each dish or the overall meal: hot (spicy), sour, sweet, salty, and (optional) bitter.

Staple Foods. Thai food typically offers a spicy curry or stir-fry served alongside a plain rice, sticky rice or Thai rice noodles to counteract the spiciness of the dish. Commonly-used Thai vegetables include bamboo shoots, Chinese broccoli, spinach, eggplant, green onion, and mushrooms.

Staple Seasonings. Thai food is often served with a variety of sauces and condiments. These may include sweet chili sauce, sliced chili peppers in rice vinegar, sriracha sauce, or a spicy chili sauce or paste called nam phrik. Common herbs include cilantro, lemon grass, Thai basil, and mint. Some other common flavors in Thai food come from ginger, galangal, tamarind, turmeric, garlic, soy beans, shallots, white and black peppercorn, kaffir lime and, of course, chilies. Thai food is known for its enthusiastic use of fresh (rather than dried) herbs and spices.

Japanese

A typical Japanese meal is based on combining a staple grain, typically rice or noodles, with a soup and okazu (dishes made from fish, meat, vegetable, or tofu). These are typically flavored with dashi, miso, and soy sauce and are usually low in fat and high in salt. A standard Japanese meal generally consists of several different okazu accompanying a bowl of cooked white Japanese rice, a bowl of soup and pickled vegetables. Japense methods of food preparation include raw, grilled, simmered/boiled, steamed, deep-fried (sometimes coated in tempura), pickled, vinegared, or dressed.

Staple Foods. Traditional Japanese dishes are heavy on seafood. Meat-eating has been rare until fairly recently, but strictly vegetarian food is also rare since even vegetable dishes are flavored with dashi stock, usually made with katsuobushi (dried skipjack tuna flakes). Rice is Japan's most common staple. Japanese rice is short grain and becomes sticky when cooked. Noodles are an essential part of Japanese cuisine usually as an alternative to a rice-based meal. Soba (thin, grayish-brown noodles containing buckwheat flour) and udon (thick wheat noodles) are the main traditional noodles and are served hot or cold with soy-dashi flavorings. Common Japanese vegetables include seaweed (there are several kinds, cucumber, daikon (Japanese radish), Japanese eggplant, Napa cabbage, spinach, sweet potato, bamboo shoots, and pickled vegetables. Several mushrooms are also common.

Staple Seasonings. Many Japanese foods are prepared using one or more of the following: Dashi stock made from kombu (kelp), katsuobushi (flakes of cured skipjack tuna, sometimes referred to as bonito) and/or niboshi (dried baby sardines), negi (Welsh onion), onions, garlic, nira (Chinese chives), rakkyō (a type of scallion), sesame, shōyu (soy sauce), miso, wasabi (and imitation wasabi from horseradish), karashi (hot mustard), red pepper, and ginger.

Mexican

When conquistadores arrived in the Aztec capital Tenochtitlan (now Mexico City), they found that the people's diet consisted largely of corn-based dishes with chiles and herbs, usually complemented with beans and tomatoes or nopales. The diet of the indigenous peoples of pre-Columbian Mexico also included chocolate, vanilla, tomatillos, avocado, guava, papaya, sapote, mamey, pineapple, soursop, jicama, squash, sweet potato, peanuts, achiote, huitlacoche, turkey and fish. In the 1520s, while Spanish conquistadors were taking over Mexico, they introduced a variety of animals, including cattle, chickens, goats, sheep, and pigs. Rice, wheat, and barley were also introduced as were olive oil, wine, almonds, parsley, and many spices. The imported Spanish cuisine was eventually incorporated into the indigenous cuisine. Further, it should be noted that "traditional" Mexican food is different from its American relatives, such as Tex-Mex and "Americanized" Mexican food. For example, the chimichanga and chalupa are not authentic Mexican dishes.

Staple Foods. The staples of Mexican cuisine are typically corn and beans. Most corn is used to make the masa dough for tamales, tortillas, gorditas, and other staples. The most common beans used in Mexican cooking are pinto beans and black beans. Many Mexican dishes also incorporate squash, tomatoes, and peppers.

Staple Seasonings. The most important and frequently used spices in Mexican cuisine are chile powder, oregano, cilantro, epazote, cinnamon, and cocoa. Chipotle, a smoke-dried jalapeño chili, is also common in Mexican cuisine. Many Mexican dishes also contain garlic and onions.

Middle Eastern

The so-called Mediterranean diet is really a mix of Greek, Turkish, Middle Eastern, and some Southern Italian cuisine. These cuisines are light on meats, and heavy on greens and lentils. One of the Mediterranean diet's strongest influences, Middle Eastern cuisine, is known for its blend of healthy ingredients and savory flavors.

Staple Foods. Many Middle Eastern dishes are made with a paste called tahini, a sesame paste. Chickpeas are another staple, used to make hummus, falafel, and other common foods. Common grain dishes include couscous and pita bread. Other commonly used ingredients include olives and olive oil, eggplant, onions, nuts, and tomatoes.

Staple Seasonings. Common seasonings include tahini, garlic, sesame seeds, mint, parsley, cumin, black pepper, paprika, mint, dill, lemon juice, honey, oregano and thyme.

Ethiopian

Ethiopian (and Eritrean) cuisine consists of a combination of injera (flatbread) with different wats (stews), yet each diverse cultural group has their unique variation. Most Ethiopian dishes are cooked through simmer or sauteeing the ingredients in a pot. Ethiopians eat with their right hands, using pieces of injera to pick up bites of entrées and side dishes. No utensils are used. Ethiopian cuisine contains many dishes that are vegan.

Staple Foods. Legumes and lentils are common in Ethiopian food. Most vegetarian wats consist of onions and spices simmered with split peas, lentils, potatoes, carrots, or chard.

Staple Seasonings. Berbere, a combination of powdered chili pepper and other spices, is an important ingredient used in many dishes. Also essential is niter kibbeh, a clarified butter infused with ginger, garlic, and several spices.

Indian

Indian cuisine has changed considerably over the past 5,000 years. One thing that's been consistent has been the reliance on grains and lentils, and the limited use of meat, particularly taboo meats like beef and pork. Indian meals typically involve a number of separate dishes that can be eaten together.

Staple Foods. The staples of Indian cuisine are rice or a flatbread made from whole wheat flour, and a variety of pulses, the most important of which are masoor (red lentil), channa (bengal gram), toor (pigeon pea or yellow gram), urad (black gram), and mung (green gram). Most Indian curries are cooked in vegetable oil.

Staple Seasonings. The most important or frequently used spices in Indian cuisine are chilli pepper, black mustard seed, cumin, turmeric, fenugreek, asafoetida, ginger, coriander, and garlic. There are also popular mixes like curry powder and garam masala, a powder that typically includes five or more dried spices, especially cardamom, cinnamon, and clove. Some leaves are commonly used, including bay leaf, coriander leaf, fenugreek leaf, mint leaf, and curry leaf. Sweet dishes are seasoned with cardamom, saffron, nutmeg, and rose petal essences.

Basic Cooking Techniques

by EBONI JOY ASIATIC, from THE HOOD HEALTH HANDBOOK

I understand that if we're going to recommend that you eat less fast food, less processed food, and less microwave meals…many of you will have a hard time because you think you don't know how to cook. The following is a breakdown of basic cooking techniques. Once you know a little about them, you will be much less intimidated to try new things in the kitchen.

Boiling

To boil food all one must do is cook it in liquid, usually water, that is boiling – rapid or "rolling" bubbling and the breaking of the bubbles into steam – at a temperature of 212° F. By putting a lid on the pot that the liquid is in one can bring the liquid to a boil faster, and also prevent evaporation. If a pot of boiling liquid is left uncovered, the liquid will evaporate quicker than it will if covered – creating a greater risk of burning one's food. If the pot is too full the liquid will boil over onto the stove top.

A cook should start with cold water, rather than hot, if using water from the tap. When a starchy food – grains like rice, couscous, or quinoa or potatoes, or meat alternatives like TVP and wheat gluten/seitan – are placed in boiling water they expand by absorbing the water. So, once they're cooked they will take up about twice the space they did (if not more as is the case with rice) before being prepared.

When boiling vegetables, the water/liquid should be brought to a boil first, and once the vegetables are added they should be watched closely. However, boiling vegetables is a sure way to destroy nutrients in your food. Steaming veggies was the method I was raised on.

The advantages of boiling one's food is that it is relatively safe (no chance of a grease fire) and simple, it is the best means to producing a flavored stock, and tough leafy greens (like collards and turnips) become edible and still retain their nutritive value when not boiled for too long. The disadvantages, however, is that generally soluble vitamins are extracted out of the food and into the water it has been boiled in, also boiled foods can become limp and withered looking. When I do boil foods I strive to retain the water turned juice as a broth.

Steaming

Steaming works by allowing water to be heated to its boiling point and maintaining a rolling boil as the water vaporizes into steam. The steam then carries heat to the food that has typically been placed in a circular metal or bamboo steamer basket and a lid placed on top during cooking. By keeping the food separate from the boiling water, it is cooked by the steam and maintains many of its nutrients, enzymes and moist, yet crunchy, texture. The only foods that cannot be cooked by steaming are mushrooms – they will get water-logged. Steaming veggies shouldn't take longer than 5 minutes, including time to sprinkle on a little sea salt and ground black pepper.

Frying

Frying is the technique of cooking food at high temperatures in oil or fat – the difference being their melting point and that fats are solid at room temperature. The crispy surface that develops in fried foods allows for moisture to be retained under the surface so that fried foods are both crispy and juicy.

Technically, shallow frying, deep frying, stir frying, sautéing, and pan searing are all common frying techniques that require more or less oil, and are categorized based on what kind of pan or fryer the food is cooked in – a frying pan, deep fryer, griddle, or wok.

Shallow frying is placing food only halfway covered in pre-heated oil inside a shallow frying pan or skillet. In deep frying, the food is submerged in oil that has been pre-heated in a deep fryer. After deep frying, the cooking the oil can be strained, refrigerated and re-used a couple of times before being discarded. Some fried foods are battered or breaded before frying, allowing the outside to become golden and crispy, yet maintaining tender juiciness underneath.

Both of these frying techniques cooks food relatively fast – but time spent deep frying is less than half that spent pan or shallow frying because the food does not need to be flipped from one side to the other. Another difference between these techniques is that food is not quite as greasy when deep fried. Proper frying temperature depends on the thickness and toughness of the food being prepared (think sweet potato vs. eggplant), but most food is typically fried at 350–375° F.

Stir Frying

This technique involves frying quickly at very high temperatures, requiring that the food be stirred continuously to prevent it from sticking to the wok and burning. This cooking technique originated in China, and by cooking bite-sized chopped tofu and vegetables (or whatever you choose) in a wok very quickly and at high heat, followed by a quick steam-in sauce you can cook a complete one-pot wonder meal. When stir frying, your oil must be heated in the wok first, the foods that take longest to cook should be placed in the wok next – for instance, you would first fry your meat or meat substitute, then add onions and carrots after about 4 to 5 minutes, and then broccoli and squash for the last couple minutes of cooking. And when the food is about two-thirds done, add your sauce, cover the wok, and your food should steam for a minute or two.

Because your food is cooked so rapidly when stir frying, and on high heat, all ingredients must be prepped (washed and cut) before you start cooking to prevent burning and sticking. And because you are cooking at high heat, you will need to use an oil that has a high smoke point like peanut, safflower, corn or canola.

The stir frying sauces I use most are either some spicy concoction I created, teriyaki sauce, or Bragg's liquid aminos. Other stir frying sauces include soy sauce, hoisin sauce, peanut sauce, tamari, and chili sauce – of course you can always create your own too.

Sauté

Sauté in French means "to jump" and the French called this technique "to jump" because you don't want your food sitting too long in the pan due to the very high heat. You've probably seen professional cooks sauté by flipping their food in the air while still in the skillet.

Sautéing and pan frying (or searing) vary only slightly in that in searing you use less heat and cook larger portions of solid food like half an eggplant, a chicken breast, or a fish steak. In searing, you do not have to stir, toss or flip your ingredients as frequently as when sautéing either. Because the heat index is lower when sautéing, you can even prepare foods in butter – or a vegan butter-like product (Earth Balance for instance) – without fear of burning, but foods that require less cooking time must only be prepared with butter because it burns much more easily than oil. Non-stick pans are good for sautéing in light oil or butter, however, if you are creating a sauce a metal pan helps to better create browning.

Common mistakes made when sautéing is that many cooks do not let their pan get hot enough before adding their fat/oil and cold ingredients to it. Not preheating your pan before adding oil and cold foods causes the juices in the food to be released as the pan heats up, and your food becomes dry. Another benefit of pre-heating your pan is that when you add cold butter, you don't have to wait for it to melt, as soon as you add your fat or oil you are ready to start cooking. Also, as fats heat they start to degrade once they reach 140° F.

Baking

In general, the term baking is used in reference to cakes, pies, pastries and breads; and what it means is "immersing the object to be cooked in an environment of still, hot air." This is why we pre-heat our ovens before placing our food in it to bake, so that all of the air in the oven reaches the same temperature and the food being prepared cooks evenly.

In baking, the food is cooked through two processes – the heat transfer from oven to food, and the heat transfer from baking dish to food. Baking in convection ovens require less time and less heat (25-50 degrees less). Baking in high altitudes requires more time and higher baking temperatures.

In preparing your desserts, follow the recipes exactly until you are skilled enough to create your own. It is said that cooking is an art, but baking is a science, so in baking, it is very important to be exact.

Roasting

Roasting is the baking of food – not bread and desserts – in an open pan, uncovered. When roasting meat (which I have never done being that I've been a vegetarian for all of my adulthood) the meat is usually placed on a rack that fits inside a fairly shallow pan, so that the meat does not sit in its "juices." The difference between roasting and baking is that you typically roast food that has structure already, like meats and vegetables. And baked foods are those that require rising, or whose structure changes during the baking process, and you have a different structure once baking is complete, like cakes, pies, breads, and casseroles.

Roasting is often considered a healthier method of cooking foods because of the need for less oil and fat in the preparation process – however, basting is oven required to keep foods from drying out. When I make my vegan soy-fish and roasted root vegetables I put clumps of vegan butter in a small amount of seasoned water to create a juice for that dish. Poultry should be cooked breast down to start and finished on the flip side so that the fat ("juice") drips into the breast meat. Roasting "juices" can also be used to create gravies and sauces.

You must always pre-heat your oven before roasting, and in roasting your thermostat is usually set at a high temperature (375-450° F), this seals the outer layer of your food and prevents the loss of juices while also caramelizing the surface. After about 20 minutes, the temperature can be lowered to about 350° F for the remaining cooking time.

Choosing a roasting pan is of vital importance – if it is too big your food will burn, too small and your food will stick o the pan, too deep and your food will steam (not roast), and too shallow and the juices will splatter all over the oven causing a horrible mess and difficult clean-up job.

Braise

Braising is a cooking technique in which the main ingredient is seared, or browned in fat, and then simmered in liquid on low heat in a covered pot for a relatively long range of time – from 1 to 6 hours – depending on what you are cooking. The best equipment for this process is a crock pot, pressure cooker or Dutch oven, and can be done on the stove top or in the oven. Braising is typically used as a means to cook less expensive, tough cuts of meat. The end result is said to be tender and flavorful. However, since we are building on "hood health" we recommend that you refrain from eating cheap, tough cuts of meat – as inexpensive cuts are almost always higher in fat which causes heart health problems, and tougher meats are harder to digest and begin to decompose in your intestines and colon before they can be digested – leading to colon cancer. Vegetables that are ideal for braising include squash, sweet potatoes, leeks, parsnips, carrots, beets, cabbage and onions.

Stew

People tend to think of stew as a dish rather than a cooking method, but it is actually both, and the dish itself is defined as "meat or fish and vegetables cooked by stewing." Stew, the cooking method, is "a moist heat cooking process by which meat and vegetables are slowly simmered in a flavorful liquid."

There is really very little difference between braising and stewing. In a braise, the meat and/or vegetables are typically left whole. In a stew they are cut in chunks. In a stew the ingredients are completely submerged in their cooking liquid. When braised, the liquid doesn't come further than halfway up the food being prepared.

Did you know that chili is a stew? And French Ratatouille is simply stewed vegetables. Vegetables ideal for stewing include eggplant, tomatoes, celery, celery root, leeks, cabbage, fennel, carrots, potatoes, onions, garlic and almost any tough greens, such as collard greens, chard, kale or mustard greens. I make a great vegan stew – similar to beef or lamb stew – with brown TVP chunks. In a food processor, or with my sick blender in the pot itself, I puree the vegetables that have cooked so thoroughly that they practically dissolve in your mouth. This is how I thicken my stew and also create a vegetable broth; adding fresh vegetables to my pot of stew about 30 minutes (depending on their toughness) before the stewing process is complete adds nutrients to the dish.

Grilling

All too often the terms grilling and barbecuing are used interchangeably, when they are quite different, and true barbecuing is rare. Traditional barbecue is done slowly, with low cooking temperatures, with lots of smoke accumulating over an open (preferably wood fire rather than charcoal) pit. A gas grill cannot accomplish this goal.

Grilling, however, requires a higher temperature to sear what's being cooked in order to preserve the food's juices. In fact, if you are comparing grilling to any other cooking method, the most similar would be broiling – as they both use a high heat source, however the grill's heat comes from below, where as the broiler's heat comes from above. They are both ideal means of cooking tender cuts of red meat, poultry, fish and vegetables – and let's not forget our meat alternatives like seitan, tempeh and tofu. Whatever you're grilling, you want to ensure that it isn't too thick to cook properly on the interior otherwise be stricken with a food borne illness.

Although grilling is considered by many to be a healthier way to cook because the fat drips off of the food and into the fire, inhaling smoke is never good for the lungs, and the charring process isn't particularly good for our intestinal tract or digestive system. When grilling, you must also be careful to avoid flare-ups – don't want to burn your food or yourself!

Vital Notes on Grilling

- ☐ Bring your food to room temperature before placing it on the grill.
- ☐ Start with a clean grill. The best time to clean (remove residue from) a grill is immediately after you finish cooking and the grate is still hot.
- ☐ Brush or spray the grill with oil to prevent food from sticking.

- ☐ The grill must be pre-heated 15 to 30 minutes before food is placed on it.
- ☐ Put all of your cooking utensils, seasonings and sauces near the grill before you put the food on it, and have a spray bottle filled with water on hand in case of flare-ups.

Every grill is different and will have different hot and cool spots. It's important for you to learn where they are and use them to your advantage. Marinating your food to be grilled for as long as possible is the best way to ensure a flavorful meal – but your food must be patted dry before being placed on the grill in order to reduce dripping which prevents flare-ups. Our favorite "hood" marinade – barbecue sauce – which is nothing more than the perfect combination of pureed tomatoes, vinegar, onion, mustard and brown sugar – it is so easy to create your own by also adding your preferred spices (mine are spike, with salt, and powdered jerk seasoning). The time frame for which it takes your ingredients to grill differs – refer to your favorite cookbook for timing guidelines.

Broiling

Broiling is cooking food in the bottom compartment of your oven, and allowing it to be cooked via infrared radiation from the oven's top burner, so your food is being cooked from above rather than below, as in baking and grilling. The downside to broiling is that lots of splattering occurs causing a mess and smoke can repeatedly set off the fire alarm. This is why most people prefer to grill, and why, when broiling, it's imperative to make sure the broiler pan, which catches excess liquid and grease, is in place before you start to broil any food.

The upside to broiling if you are a meat eater is that the broiler does not have to pre-heat, and is a fast method for cooking meats, poultry and fish, and gives it a nice dark char. The broiler is actually located in a compartment beneath the oven, pull the drawer all the way out and it usually folds down for easy removal of the broiler pan or the flipping of food. Every oven's thermostat knob has a "broil" position.

Blanching

Blanching is a cooking term that "describes a process of food preparation wherein the food substance, usually a vegetable or fruit, is plunged into boiling water, removed after a brief, timed interval, and finally plunged into iced water or placed under cold running water (shocked) to halt the cooking process." Many fruits and vegetables can be frozen and preserved once they have been blanched (I have done this with leeks, onions and celery). Blanching literally means "to whiten" but often, its purpose is to so soften a food, remove an overwhelming taste, or even preserve the original vibrant color of a food before cooking it in another manner. Upon blanching nuts, the skin of the nut becomes softened by blanching and can be removed once cooled.

Live/Raw

Yes, you're right, preparing live/raw food is not "cooking." So why mention it? Because it's an important aspect of food preparation, and eating fresh, uncooked vegetables, fruits, grains, nuts, seeds, and sprouts is necessary in bettering health for ourselves and our families. Incorporating raw foods into your diet doesn't require special tools or special knowledge (but a few recipes that go beyond salads can help!). Raw foodists can create amazing meals with a dehydrator that can heat food without cooking it. A seasoned raw foodist will have a frequently used juicer and food processor in their kitchen as well.

Be Prepared

Finally, the last bit of best advice I can give as a professional cook is about *mise en place* (pronounced MEEZ ahn plahs), which translates from French as "to put in place" – which means before you start cooking have all of your ingredients prepared. Have them on hand for one (to avoid running to the grocery store at the last minute), and have them washed, peeled, deseeded, chopped, diced, julienned, etc, etc.

All too often, I've delved into a recipe and halfway through the cooking process I realize I'm missing an ingredient and I have to substitute with another or run to the grocery store in mid process. I have also found my food burning uncontrollably as I cut vegetables while another ingredient is cooking and the entire dish is ruined. Trust me when I say you will save yourself a world of hurt by making a comprehensive list of ingredients before you start cooking, double check to make sure you have them on hand, and prep them as need be before turning on a single burner on your stove. And keep in mind one of the greatest sayings in the culinary world – cooking is an art, so experiment with flavors and textures and turn your favorite recipe into your own unique creation; baking is a science, stick to the blueprint and you can't go wrong!

Tips and Tools for Healthy Eating

by BRYANT TERRY, author of VEGAN SOUL KITCHEN

Look, I won't pretend that I make every meal from scratch. I enjoy eating out and being served as much as the next man. But I do realize the costs (and I'm not just talking about money). Food eaten outside the home ultimately drains our pockets and takes a toll on our overall health. So we up spending too much money and ruining our bodies all while making food corporations, hospitals, and insurance companies rich in the process.

Food eaten outside the home has more salt, more sugar, more fat, and almost twice the calories of meals prepared at home. Why, you might ask? 'Cause salt, sugar, and fat taste good! And most of us are addicted to them. Those ingredients don't cost that much either. So think about it, if you are selling food for mass consumption, overloading your products with inexpensive salt, sugar, and fat makes good business sense. Processed, packaged, and fast food is cheap to make; this type of food can last a long time without rotting once you add preservatives to it; and you can turn major profits by selling a lot of it. That's why you are much more likely to see an advertisement for a 500-calorie hamburger that you can swoop up from the drive-through than for some collard greens and lamb chops that you need to hook up at the crib. It all works out for the four corporations that control most of the food that we eat. They make money and take ours.

The long-term costs of eating out a lot can be extremely high, too. Preventable diet-related illnesses such as hypertension (high blood pressure), heart disease, and certain cancers will end up costing you and your family lots of money if you land in the hospital. And the emotional toll of having loved ones sick or dying is immeasurable. Think about your spouse and kids going bankrupt to pay for your medical bills 'cause you wanted to eat a double cheeseburger 5 days a week. Suddenly that dollar menu isn't looking as appealing, right.

Now cooking at home, on the other hand, is an easy way to save money, particularly if you focus your meals around whole unprocessed ingredients instead of packaged foods: You know exactly what ingredients are going into your meals; making food from scratch is a great way to impress that special someone (especially if you plan the meal and y'all cook it together); and kids love cooking with their parents. The best thing about cooing at home for me, though, is that I get to have my preferred dishes exactly how I like them. When I'm depending on a restaurant to make my favorite meal, they might mess it up and disappoint me. So I do for self.

If you did not spend a lot of time in the kitchen with grandma growing up, I know it can be intimidating. But the best way to get better at cooking is practice. If you love eating, the more you experiment in the kitchen and learn from your mistakes the better home chef you will become. Here are some equipment suggestions that might help you work it out.

Some Equipment to Help You Become a Better Cook

Baking Sheets: Whether you are heating frozen fries, roasting carrots from scratch, or baking canned biscuits, you should keep a baking sheet handy. And a good oven glove will keep you from burning your hands.

Blender: You can find a good blender for less than 20 bucks. Use it for making smoothies before and after workouts and blending soups made from scratch. Remember not to fill it more than halfway if you are blending hot liquids or you will get burned.

Colander: Keep a large colander (12-inch) handy for draining (and washing) vegetables, beans, grains, and pastas after cooking.

Cutting Board: I won't pretend that I have never cut straight onto a counter before. But after getting cursed out by moms for scratching up her surfaces I made sure I used a cutting board after that. In order to avoid getting food poising you should keep at least two: one for preparing fish and meat and one for cutting vegetables. Use woodcutting boards since bacteria can't thrive on them. Plus they won't make your knife as dull as other types of cutting boards.

Grater: These are perfect for shredding cheese for tacos and vegetables for salads.

Knives: If you are serious about throwin' down in the kitchen you should invest in a good chef's knife. If you take good care of it, your knife should last for a couple of generations.

Measuring Cups and Spoons: Unless you already feel comfortable enough to freestyle when you are cooking, owning some plastic or metal measuring cups and spoons (for dry goods) and glass cups (for liquids) will help you follow recipes with ease.

Peeler: A solid Y-shaped swivel peeler is great for peeling the skin off potatoes and other vegetables and fruits.

Pots and Pans: Unless you choose to invest in a set of pots and pans, you should decide what is a priority in your kitchen and slowly build your arsenal. Here are a few options to consider:

- ❏ 10-inch fry pan
- ❏ 4-qt. saucepan with lid
- ❏ 3-qt. sauté pan with lid
- ❏ 7-qt. stockpot with lid

Salad Spinner: Assuming that you will be eating more salads after reading this book…invest in a salad spinner to wash your greens before dressing.

Spoons: Next to the stone axe, a wooden spoon is probably the oldest tool known to man. Get one or two.

Tongs: Think of these as your metal fingers when cooking. Whether on the stove or the grill, a pair of tongs is great for frying, roasting and barbecuing.

Meat vs. Vegetables True/False Quiz

Still not convinced about letting go of meat? Take this quiz and see how much you know. Answers below. Don't cheat!

1	T / F	Millions of people get sick each year from eating contaminated meat and fish, and thousands die. For example, 98% of all broiler chicken carcasses have levels of E. coli bacteria that indicate fecal contamination.
2	T / F	Meat-eaters are more likely to have parasites, worms, and bacterial infections, some of which can survive in even well-cooked meat.
3	T / F	Every product that is put into the animal's system becomes a part of the meat-eater's system, which leads to diseases, chemical imbalances, and hormonal problems, such as how girls are beginning puberty younger and younger each year.
4	T / F	Well-planned vegetarian diets provide us with all the nutrients that we need, minus all the saturated fat, cholesterol, pesticides, dioxins, hormones, antibiotics, bacteria, and other contaminants found in animal flesh and by-products.

5	T / F	Meat-eaters are 9 times more likely to be obese than vegans.
6	T / F	Vegetarians are 50% less likely to develop heart disease than meat-eaters.
7	T / F	Vegetarians have a cancer rate 60% lower than meat-eaters, even if they're smokers.
8	T / F	Scientists haven't yet proven that animal fat and cholesterol cause heart disease, or that animal protein causes cancer.
9	T / F	Consumption of meat, eggs, and dairy products has not been strongly linked to osteoporosis, Alzheimer's, asthma, and male impotence.
10	T / F	Vegetarians have stronger immune systems than meat-eaters, which further reduces their risk of disease.
11	T / F	Vegetarian children grow taller and have higher IQs than their meat-eating classmates.
12	T / F	Older people who switch to a vegetarian or vegan diet cannot prevent and even reverse many chronic ailments.
13	T / F	Experts agree that healthy vegetarian diets support a lifetime of good health and provide protection against numerous diseases, including our country's three biggest killers: heart disease, cancer, and strokes.
14	T / F	Meat-eaters are typically stronger than vegetarians, and better fighters and athletes.
15	T / F	Vegetarians and vegans live, on average, 6 to 10 years longer than meat-eaters.*

*All the statements are true, except numbers 8, 9, and 12.

How to Become Vegetarian (in 8 Steps)

by MENTAL SUN and AIYA ABRIHET of Vegan Hood TV, from THE HOOD HEALTH HANDBOOK

There are many reasons why people decide to transition away from a meat-based diet towards a plant-based one. Whatever your reason, how you transition can determine whether or not you end up sticking to your new diet, or falling off. Transitioning is different for everyone. Some find it very easy to cut meat out of their diet right away, while others need more time to make the transition permanent. Here are some tips and tricks that will help you make the journey a smoother one.

1. Do Your Research

Learn as much as you can about the vegetarian/vegan diet. Study the human body and the immune system. Learn about everything you are now putting into your mouth, as well as all the foods that you're leaving behind. By taking in as much as you can on the topic, the change will become an informed and genuine one and you won't have to worry about relying only on willpower. Don't simply stop eating something because someone told you not to. Get hands-on, do the research and learn the information for yourself. Fortunately, this book should help you with most of that process, but don't stop here.

2. Swap Out Old Choices for New Ones

Transitioning is all about getting healthier, not simply eliminating things. Many people find it easy to transition by eating vegetarian meat alternatives. You can find vegan burgers, vegan hot dogs, and even vegan "chunks" for stir-fry dishes, and those may help you kick the "meat" addiction. However, don't get stuck there, and don't think that eliminating meat is all it takes to be healthy. Other transitions are necessary as well. Instead of white rice, look for brown rice, quinoa or black rice. Instead of white bread and other varieties, look for whole grain bread or spelt bread. And instead of white sugar, try agave nectar or maple syrup. For those transitioning away from dairy, look for a vegan product called Daiya cheese. Replace cow's milk with almond, hemp, coconut or rice milk. If possible, the best thing to do is use a blender to mix up some almonds and water and make your own milk. By swapping out your old choices for new ones, you won't feel like you're missing out or deprived.

It's also important to constantly add new foods to your diet. Meat-eaters typically have very limited food choices (which make it especially ironic when they ask vegetarians, "So what DO you eat?"). As a vegetarian, you'll need to expand your tastes. Not only should you try the cuisines of other cultures (Indian, Thai, and Ethiopian are good places to start), but you should start trying new fruits and vegetables. Add a new fruit, vegetable, or grain to your diet every week. Learn how to prepare it and work it into the new recipes you're learning. To really eat healthy, color-coding can help. Set a goal of eating 4 or 5 different colors (natural colors, not food coloring colors!) at every meal, and you'll be getting the full range of nutrition you need.

3. Don't Be a Starchetarian

People transitioning often make the mistake of becoming starchetarians. Make sure that you don't attempt to make up for the meat you're not eating with more bread, pasta and potatoes (or "veggie meat" made from wheat or soy). A diet overemphasizing starch is almost as dangerous as a meat-based diet. Replace meat with more fruits and vegetables, preferably leafy greens. Remember to be strong like the cow (or bull), don't eat the cow, eat what the cow eats (in its natural environment of course).

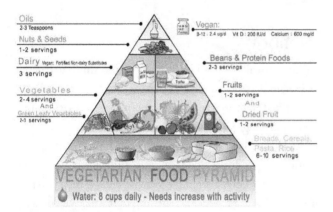

4. Make Smoothies

Get in the habit of starting your day off with a smoothie. Use lots of frozen fruits, bananas, nuts and one of the milk alternatives mentioned above and get busy with your blender. There's no special formula, just mix in your favorites and try to make enough so you can take some with you for your morning commute. Smoothies are a great way to increase your fruit intake and because everything is blended up and easy to digest, you can get a lot of ingredients down that you probably wouldn't be able to eat whole in one sitting. Eventually, if you're feeling adventurous you can even throw in some fresh spinach and some avocado (you won't even be able to taste them if you have enough fruits in there). Get your kids involved and make it a family thing. They will love preparing them and you'll feel good knowing that you're getting closer to your goals and helping your children to be healthy at the same time. Also, look into the benefits of juice fasting. (See "Living the Fast Life")

5. Don't Bring Junk into Your Home

If you control what comes into your kitchen and refrigerator, don't allow unhealthy food to enter your home. What often happens is people end up eating whatever they're surrounded by. Eat apples instead of cookies, get nuts instead of chips, and treat yourself to a non-dairy sorbet/ice cream instead of that scoop of lactose intolerance. Better options make for better choices.

6. Try Not to Go Hungry

It's usually when we're hungry that we're likely to cheat on our diet. This is especially true when you're driving. When you're hungry, the fast food spots you pass on the street look extra tempting. By eating before you go out you will avoid any added temptation to go back to your old eating habits. This also goes for grocery shopping. Junk food items will almost seem to fall off of the shelf into your cart when you go to the grocery store on an empty stomach. With all those options enticing you, it makes it very hard to resist. Try to do all of your shopping after you've had a meal, write out a list before you leave and try your best to stick to it. Same goes for when you're watching television. Watching TV and junk food often go hand-in-hand. Sometimes when you're distracted you don't realize how much you eat and all the food commercials make it even worse. Be sure to always have healthy snacks and lots of fruit around for moments like this.

7. Eat Out

Many people think that they won't be able to eat out like they used to now that they are a vegetarian or vegan. This couldn't be further from the truth. Try out local veggie spots in your neighborhood.* It's a great way to keep you motivated and help you get creative when it comes to repairing your own food. Plan ahead. Research what restaurants offer vegetarian/vegan options. Call a restaurant ahead of time to make sure that they have satisfying choices that you can eat. Learn how to analyze menus when you go out. There are always options, even if you have to get the chef to customize something for you. Read online menus before you go out if you're someone who gets easily tempted. If you know what you're going to order ahead of time, you don't have to even bother opening the menu and will eliminate unnecessary temptation. At first it may be awkward going out with friends and family who might expect you to get "the usual." Surprise them with a healthier option along with info that might help them to eat better as well.

8. Stay Strong

No matter how good you feel or how good you think you're doing, be prepared because there will always be someone there to scrutinize your actions. Usually these people mean well, but for the most part they are usually misinformed when it comes to proper nutrition. Don't let someone who doesn't share your discipline, talk you out of doing the right thing.

Prepare to block out negative responses to your new diet from others. Remember that to some, this diet is strange so you may not always get the support you're looking for from the people around you. If you're used to having burgers and fries with your friends everyday at lunch, understand that they might find it weird that "all of a sudden" you don't want to go with them anymore.

Find as many healthy people in your circle as you can and surround yourself with them. Join online vegetarian/vegan social networks, a great place to meet people with common interests, ask questions and look for new recipes. The greater the support system around you, the greater your chances for success.

Try to think of your transition as a lifestyle change rather than a diet and don't be hard on yourself. You didn't get to where you now are overnight, so don't expect things to change overnight either. Remember, small permanent changes are better than big changes that don't last for very long.

---

* Check out www.happycow.net for a world-wide listing of vegetarian/vegan restaurants, health food stores and more.

A Simple Meal Plan

by JUSTICE RAJEE, from THE HOOD HEALTH HANDBOOK

One of the easiest ways to take control of your diet and get more bang for your buck is make a meal plan. The hard part is developing a habit of sticking to the plan. What we choose to eat has a huge impact on our health, it is deliberate and it should be planned. I am going to provide you a simple method that you can use to get started. On the reverse side of this page, you'll see a template for a weekly meal planner (make copies as needed). For each day of the week, write what you are going to eat. In the ingredients list, write down what you will need to create the meals you have listed. Place the completed chart on your fridge or a kitchen cabinet so you can see it clearly.

Now I know what you are thinking. How will this work? It will work because the first step in changing behavior is creating a means to hold yourself accountable to the new standard. Writing it down allows you to remember what you promised yourself you would do. If you are reading this book, you are more than likely looking for ways to gain control of your health. By changing what you eat into something you plan instead of something you just run out and do, you pull the motivations for your choices out of your subconscious mind to your conscious mind. Instead of choosing food on impulse you will eventually follow the plan you have set for yourself.

When you go shopping with a list and menu, you are less likely to come back with items you did not plan to purchase. Stores are designed to get you buy things you never wanted. The layout, coupons, signs, and even the lighting are all focused on getting you to think with your stomach. When you have a counter to the emotional cues found in the store, you have a better chance of limiting your spending to just what you need. That is also why you include days you intend to eat out. Eating out in our world of fast food dollar menus and cheap processed snacks can quietly lead to far more spending than you may notice. Creating a plan and sticking to it will give you a leg up in changing your eating culture.

Following a meal plan makes it much easier to incorporate modifications to your diet. When you don't have a plan, changes to your eating habits creates a greater feeling of uncertainty because you don't have any gauge of how adjusting to add more fresh fruits or cutting your dairy intake will really affect your life. Since you are operating without a standard it is hard to predict how buying a bag of apples every two weeks will differ from buying a jar of applesauce. When you have a plan and you condition yourself to following your plan you get a better hold of what you are eating, how much you are spending, and how fast you go through those items. With a greater understanding of your eating habits you will be able to make comfortable and sustainable adjustments to meet your ultimate diet goals.

There are far more complex meal planning methods you can use, from Excel spreadsheets to detailed food logs – you name it (you can find many examples online). Whatever you do, start out simple and work your plan.

Meal Planner

Week _____

Sunday

Main Course

Cookbook   Page
A Taste of Life

Side

Dessert

Notes

Monday

Main Course

Cookbook   Page
A Taste of Life

Side

Dessert

Notes

Tuesday

Main Course

Cookbook   Page
A Taste of Life

Side

Dessert

Notes

Wednesday

Main Course

Cookbook   Page
A Taste of Life

Side

Dessert

Notes

Thursday

Main Course

Cookbook   Page
A Taste of Life

Side

Dessert

Notes

Friday

Main Course

Cookbook   Page
A Taste of Life

Side

Dessert

Notes

Saturday

Main Course

Cookbook   Page
A Taste of Life

Side

Dessert

Notes

Special Ingredients

- [ ]
- [ ]
- [ ]
- [ ]
- [ ]
- [ ]
- [ ]
- [ ]
- [ ]
- [ ]
- [ ]

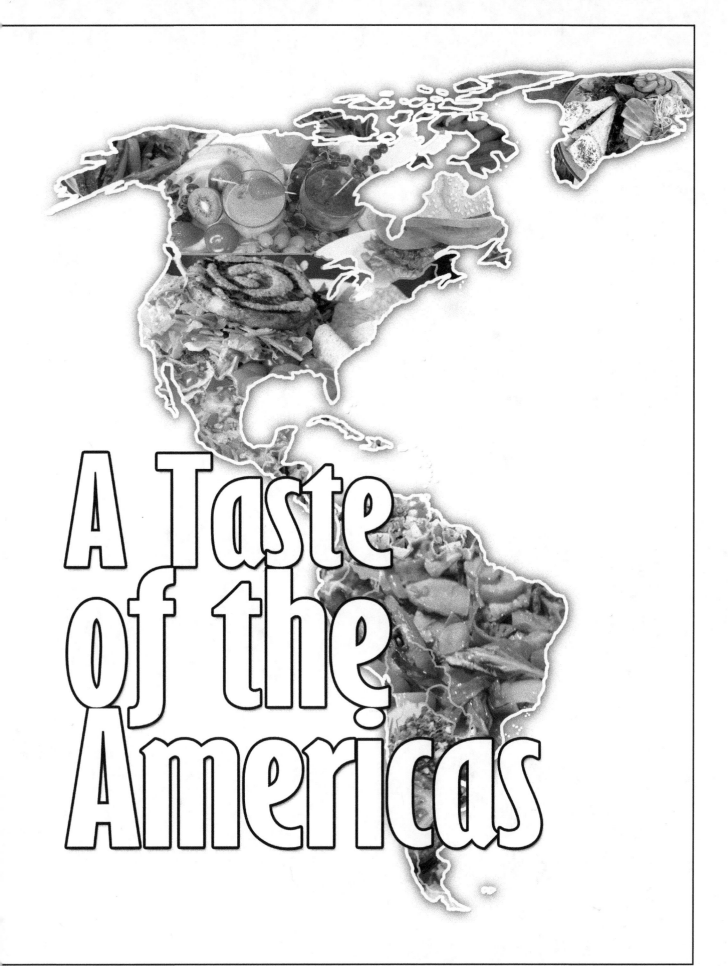

A Taste of the Americas

Appetizers

Spiced Lentil Tacos

1 tablespoon olive oil	1 package (2.25 oz.)
1 cup finely chopped onion	taco seasoning
1 clove garlic, chopped	2½ cups vegetable broth
½ teaspoon salt	8 taco shells
1 cup dried brown lentils, rinsed	1¼ cups shredded lettuce
	1 cup chopped tomato
	½ cup shredded reduced-fat (2%) cheddar

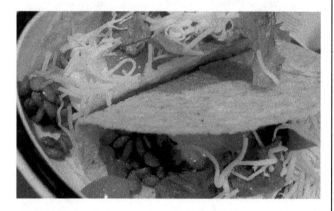

Optional:
½ cup fat-free sour cream
1 chipotle chili in adobo sauce, finely chopped
(use half for less heat)
2 teaspoons adobo sauce

1. Heat oil in large skillet over medium-high heat.
2. Cook onion, garlic and salt until onion begins to soften, 3 to 4 minutes.
3. Add lentils and taco seasoning. Cook until spices are fragrant and lentils are dry, about 1 minute.
4. Add broth; bring to a boil. Reduce heat, cover and simmer until lentils are tender, 25 to 30 minutes.
5. Uncover lentils and cook until mixture thickens, 6 to 8 minutes. Mash with a rubber spatula.
6. Spoon ¼ cup lentil mixture into each taco shell.
7. Top with favorite taco fixings, lettuce, tomato and cheese.
8. **Optional:** Mix sour cream, chili and adobo sauce in a bowl and top lentils with mixture of sour cream, chipotle and adobo

Veggie Pockets

Serves 6-8

1 package of Smart Ground	1 tbsp. Adobo
½ red onion	2 tbsp. basil
1 green bell pepper	1 can black beans
1 red bell pepper	1 package of pita bread (pocketed)
1 tsp. Adobo	olive oil or Smart Balance
	salt and pepper to taste

1. Dice red onion, red and green bell pepper in to quarter inch slices.
2. Coat medium frying pan with Extra Virgin Olive Oil (or Smart Balance) and put on low-medium heat.
3. Once heated add the onions and bell pepper. Cook until onions are transparent.
4. Add basil and 1 tsp. adobo. Increase to medium heat.
5. Add the smart ground and mix in the remain adobo and basil.
6. Drain 1 can of black beans and add salt and pepper to taste.
7. In a separate pan add Smart Balance and heat over high heat.
8. Add the pita bread and continue to turn until brown on both sides.
9. Let cool slightly and stuff with 'meat' mixture. Enjoy!

From *The Hood Health Handbook: A Practical Guide to Health and Wellness in the Urban Community* also available from Supreme Design Publishing.

Tofu-Onion Burgers

Serves 4

½ lb firm tofu, mashed
1 medium onion, minced
2 tbsp. wheat germ
2 tbsp. unbleached, all-purpose flour
2 tbsp. garlic powder
2 tbsp. soy sauce or tamari
pepper to taste

1. Preheat oven to broil. In a medium bowl, mix all ingredients, except oil.
2. Shape mixture into 4 patties; lightly coat each with flour.
3. Place patties on a lightly oiled baking tray and broil 5 to 10 minutes on each side, or until browned.

Yeast Biscuits

Looking for a good biscuit recipe that isn't dry and crumbly, but light and fluffy? They're a little more slightly involved than regular biscuits, but they're worth it. The result is like a cross between a biscuit and a roll. All the taste of a biscuit with a more tender texture and no crumbling.

1 tablespoon yeast
¼ cup water
2½ cups flour
1 teaspoon baking powder
½ teaspoon baking soda
1 teaspoon salt
2 tablespoons sugar
½ cup shortening
1 cup soy milk with 1 tbsp. vinegar (in place of buttermilk)

1. Dissolve yeast in water, set aside.
2. Mix dry ingredients in order given; cut in shortening until the size of small Lima beans.
3. Stir in buttermilk and yeast mixture.
4. Cover bowl with towel and let sit until ready to use. (At least 1 hour, but it is fine if it sits for a couple hours. Dough will be very sticky.)
5. Scrape out onto well floured board.
6. Flip over and knead lightly (4-6 times).
7. Roll out and cut with biscuit cutter.
8. Place on greased pan and let rise slightly (10-30 minutes).
9. Bake at 400°F until light brown
10. Prep. time: 10-12 minutes.

Baked French Fries

4 baking potatoes, sliced into strips
pan spray
salt & pepper, to taste

1. Preheat oven to 450 degrees.
2. Soak potato strips in ice water for 15 minutes.
3. Pan spray two 9 x 13-inch cookie sheets.
4. Drain potatoes, pat dry, and place on cookie sheets.
5. Bake for 30 minutes, or until golden.
6. Salt and pepper to taste.

Pinto Bean Sloppy Joes

Serves 6

½ tbsp. oil
1 med onion, chopped fine
½ bell pepper, chopped fine
16 oz. can pinto or red kidney beans, drained and rinsed
¼ cup wheat germ
1 cup thick tomato sauce (you can mix a 6-oz can tomato sauce with enough water to make a cup)
1 tbsp. soy sauce or tamari
1 tsp. chili powder
1 tsp. paprika
½ tsp. dried basil
6 buns

1. Heat oil, sauté onion and bell pepper 3-4 minutes.
2. Add remaining ingredients [not buns, of course] and bring to a simmer.
3. Mash beans lightly with fork or potato masher.
4. Simmer, loosely covered, 5-7 minutes or until preferred consistency, stirring occasionally.
5. Serve on buns.

Quick Barbeque Sandwiches

1 cup TVP
½ cup water
1 medium onion, chopped fine
1 or 2 cloves garlic, minced
water or other liquid for sautéing
your favorite barbeque sauce or mustard sauce

1. Mix the TVP with the ½ cup water and set aside for 5 minutes.
2. Sauté onion in about 1 tbsp. liquid until almost clear.
3. Then add garlic and cook for another minute.
4. Add the reconstituted TVP.
5. Add the barbeque sauce until the mixture is the right consistency for sandwiches.
6. Heat thoroughly and serve.

Tempeh Tuna Salad

1 lb wild rice organic tempeh
1 cup vegan mayonnaise
2/3 cup diced kosher dill pickles
2/3 cup diced celery
½ cup diced red onion
2 tbsp Nama shoyu
2 tbsp chopped parsley
1 tbsp stone ground mustard
2 tsp raw apple cider vinegar
½ tsp minced garlic
Pepper to taste

1. Steam the tempeh in a steam basket until tender, about 10 minutes.
2. Cut in to 1/8 inch pieces.
3. Combine ingredients and serve.

Vegetarian Mac and Cheese

Serves 4-6

In this recipe, cheese gets replaced with nutritional yeast, butter with Earth Balance spread, and cream with veggie broth. And though it's not exactly like the mac & cheese you'll remember as a kid, it's just as good. If you're not familiar with nutritional yeast, you can find it at most health food grocers in the bulk bins aisle. It's what gives the dish its hearty, cheese flavor, while also loading it with vitamin B12.

4 tablespoons Earth Balance spread
¼ cup flour
3 cups vegetable broth
⅛ cup soy sauce
1½ tablespoons garlic powder
1 tablespoon paprika
1 tablespoon turmeric
salt and pepper to taste
1 cup nutritional yeast
1 pound cooked macaroni pasta

For the topping:
2 tablespoons Earth Balance spread
1 cup breadcrumbs

1. Preheat oven to 350°F. In a medium-size Dutch oven, over low-medium heat, melt the Earth Balance spread.
2. Add flour and vegetable broth. Whisk into a smooth paste.
3. Stir in soy sauce, garlic powder, paprika, turmeric, salt and pepper.
4. Add nutritional yeast and mix until the sauce is smooth and creamy.
5. Add cooked macaroni to the sauce and stir until all the pasta is coated evenly.
6. In a small saucepan, melt the Earth Balance spread and toss the breadcrumbs to coat.
7. Top the macaroni with the breadcrumbs.
8. Bake for 30 min. Let rest for 5 min. before serving.

Tofu 'Fish' Fillet Sandwiches

If you are a vegetarian who doesn't eat fish, yet still have that hankering for a juicy fish sandwich, these bread crumb-crusted tofu 'fish' sandwiches will blow your mind!

1 (12 ounce) package firm tofu –
    (drained, patted dry, and sliced into 4 slices)
1 cup bread crumbs
1 teaspoon kelp powder
¼ teaspoon garlic powder
¼ teaspoon paprika
¼ teaspoon onion powder or flakes
1 teaspoon salt olive oil, as needed

Tartar Sauce:
½ cup vegan mayonnaise
¼ cup dill pickle relish
1 tablespoon fresh lemon juice
4 whole wheat hamburger buns, split

1. Preheat oven to 350°F (175 degrees C).
2. In a bowl, toss bread crumbs together with kelp powder, garlic powder, paprika, onion powder, and salt.
3. Dip tofu slices into olive oil, then bread crumb mixture, patting lightly to coat well.
4. Bake on a cookie sheet in preheated oven for 30 minutes.
5. When first side is golden brown and slightly crispy, turn over, and finish baking.
6. Meanwhile, mix together mayonnaise, relish, and lemon juice until well-blended.
7. When tofu is nearly done baking, brush each bun half with olive oil, and toast in the oven.
8. Serve with tartar sauce and your favorite sandwich condiments.

Sprouted Garbanzo Burgers

1 cup sprouted garbanzo beans
¼ onion, chopped
½ zucchini, chopped
1 tbsp extra-virgin olive oil
1 large organic egg
1 cup micro sprouts
¾ tsp fine grain sea salt
⅛ tsp pepper
1 cup toasted homemade bread crumbs

1. Steam the garbanzo beans until tender, about ten or so minutes.
2. Puree the garbanzo beans in a blender until it's a consistency similar to hummus.
3. At the same time sauté the onions and zucchini until tender.
4. Puree with the garbanzo beans. Don't overdo this, as you want it pretty chunky.
5. Add in eggs, sprouts, salt, and pepper.
6. Add in bread crumbs and stir in a bowl.
7. Form into patties. It should be about four or so, depending on how big that you like them.
8. Add olive oil to a heavy skillet and begin to cook.
9. Cover them up and cook for about 7 minutes, covered, until they have browned. Flip them.
10. When they are cooked through, put on a bun and top with a slather of fresh guacamole.

Grilled Vegetable Sandwich

Servings 8

3 medium zucchini
1 medium-size yellow bell pepper
2 medium-size red bell peppers
1 large onion
⅓ cup balsamic vinaigrette
2 teaspoons molasses
1 (16-ounce) French bread loaf
2 tablespoons vegan mayonnaise

1. Cut zucchini lengthwise into ¼-inch-thick oblong slices.
2. Cut each bell pepper into 6 wedges, and cut onion into ½ inch-thick slices
3. Combine vinaigrette and molasses in a large heavy-duty zip-top plastic bag.
4. Add vegetables; seal bag, and chill 2 hours, turning bag occasionally.
5. Remove vegetables from bag, reserving marinade; place in a lightly greased grill basket.
6. Cut bread loaf in half horizontally, and brush cut sides with 3 tablespoons reserved marinade.
7. Grill vegetables, without grill lid, over medium-high heat (350° to 400°) 5 minutes, basting occasionally with remaining marinade.
8. Turn basket over, and grill, basting occasionally, for 2 minutes.
9. Place bread, cut sides down, on grill rack; grill 3 minutes or until vegetables are tender and bread is toasted.
10. Spread mayonnaise over cut sides of toasted bread.
11. Place grilled vegetables on bottom half of bread.
12. Top with remaining bread half.

Spanish 'Omelets'

1 onion
1 or 2 potatoes (depends on how hungry you are)
1 broccoli (or any other vegetable, but broccoli looks great on it)
chickpea flour (garbanzo flour or gram flour)
salt and pepper
olive oil

1. Make a mixture with water and chickpea flour in such a proportion to get an 'egg-like' batter.
2. Start with ½ cup of water, add the chickpea flour, stirring constantly, and progressively increase the amount of water and chickpea flour until you get about 1 cup of batter.
3. Season it with salt and pepper.
4. Boil the potatoes 'al-dente', then slice.

5. In a pan, stir-fry the onion (sliced) in 1 tsp. of olive oil.
6. Add the sliced potatoes and stir until golden.
7. Add the broccoli florets and pour the batter along the vegetables.
8. Put a lid on top and simmer until the bottom is golden, then turn (a plate can help - if the pan is non-stick it will make the turn a lot easier) and cook the other side.
9. Serve hot or cold.

California Burgers

Makes 8 to 10 burgers.

Sweet bits of fruit will make you dream of sunny California! These burgers are great with sweet-and-sour sauce (recipe below).

3 cups cooked sweet brown rice
1 carrot, grated
½ cup raisins
5 dried apricots, finely chopped
3 tablespoon. finely chopped cilantro
¼ cup (3 tbsp.) toasted sunflower seeds or chopped, toasted almonds
3 tbsp. tahini
3 tbsp. maple syrup
½ cup firm tofu (optional)
bread crumbs or shredded coconut

1. Preheat oven to broil. Process tahini, maple syrup and tofu in a blender until smooth.
2. Mix rice, carrot, raisins, apricots, cilantro, and sunflower seeds in a large bowl.
3. Stir tahini-tofu mixture into rice mixture.
4. With wet hands, shape mixture into 8 to 10 patties, and coat the patties with bread crumbs or shredded coconut, if desired.
5. Place the patties on a lightly oiled baking tray.
6. Broil 5 to 10 minutes on each side, or until browned for 30 minutes, or until golden brown.

Salmon-less Spread: the Raw Vegan Way

It's a requirement for those born in the Pacific Northwest to grow up eating fresh salmon. Salmon in eggs, salmon in pasta, salmon steaks, salmon salad, you name it. The solution: A raw, vegan salmon-less spread that parallels the real deal in both taste and consistency.

¼ cup unhulled rye, presoaked
½ cup carrot pulp
¼ cup onion, minced
¼ cup celery, minced

¼ cup sunflower seeds
⅛ cup water
1 tbsp. lemon juice
1 tsp. dill
½ tsp. kelp granules
½ tsp. salt

This recipe requires a little prep. Presoak unhulled rye for 14 hours to allow sufficient time for softening. You may wait until they begin to sprout to use them in this recipe. You'll also need the pulp from 2-3 juiced carrots.

1. Place ¼ heaping cup of presoaked rye in a grinder, blender, or food processor and pulse to splinter the grains. Stop before it turns into a flour-like consistency.
2. Stir rye and the next three ingredients together in a bowl. Set aside.
3. In a blender, grind the sunflower seeds into a powder. Add lemon juice and seasonings and blend, adding just enough water to get a soft cream-cheese-like consistency.
4. Add sunflower mixture to the ingredients previously set aside. Mix thoroughly by hand. The mixture should be flaky but should also hold together when pressed.
5. Serve Fish are Friends Salmon[less] Spread as an appetizer on cucumber slices, celery sticks, endive leaves, or on raw crackers. Serve on a bed of lettuce for a satisfying main course. Salmon[less] Spread will keep for three days in the fridge.

"Barbecued" Tempeh

1 pound tempeh, cubed
3 tbsp. vegetable oil
1 cup finely chopped onion
2 large garlic cloves, minced
1 tsp. ground fennel seeds

1 tsp. chili powder
1 tsp. ground coriander
1 tsp. ground cumin
⅛ tsp. cayenne
1 green or red bell pepper, chopped

Sauce:
2 tablespoons tamari soy sauce
2 tablespoons fresh lemon juice
3 tablespoons molasses or brown sugar
2 tablespoons cider vinegar
1 tablespoon prepared mustard
6 tablespoons tomato paste (7-ounce can)
1 cup water
4 to 5 dashes Tabasco or other hot red pepper sauce

1. Sauté the onions, garlic, and spices until the onions begin to soften.
2. Add the peppers and tempeh and continue sautéing until the peppers brighten and the tempeh browns.
3. Transfer this mixture to a shallow baking pan.
4. Whisk together the sauce ingredients and pour them over the vegetable-tempeh mixture.
5. Bake covered at 350°F for half an hour and uncovered for another half an hour, stirring frequently throughout.

Super Soy Burgers

Makes 8 4-ounce patties
Pan spray
1½ cups soybeans, cooked and mashed
¾ cup brown rice, cooked
1 egg (substitute)
3 tablespoons soy sauce
5 scallions, minced
1 tablespoon nutritional yeast
1 tablespoon cornstarch
2 tablespoons dijon mustard
2 tablespoons fresh mixed herbs, chopped
salt & pepper to taste

1. Preheat oven to 400 degrees.
2. In a large bowl, thoroughly combine all ingredients.
3. Let rest for 15 minutes.
4. Form mixture into 8 patties.
5. Place on cookie sheet and bake to desired consistency.

Grilled Portobello Mushrooms

4 six-to-eight-inch portobello mushrooms
2 tablespoons stone ground mustard
½ cup champagne vinegar
½ cup balsamic vinegar
½ cup red wine
3 tablespoons garlic puree or eight cloves of peeled garlic
2 cups fresh basil leaves
a pinch each of salt and pepper
1 cup canola oil

1. Rinse mushrooms in cold water and pat dry.
2. Remove stems.
3. Place remaining ingredients, except canola oil, into a blender.
4. Blend on a medium speed, slowly adding canola oil until all is blended.
5. Pour marinade into a sealable, non-reactive container
6. add the mushrooms.
7. Turn to coat well, cover, refrigerate and allow to marinate overnight for ultimate flavor.
8. Grill over a hot fire, two to three minutes per side, basting with remaining marinade if desired.
9. Mushrooms will shrink somewhat when grilled.

Serving suggestions: Mushrooms can be served plain, or they make a delicious sandwich on a whole wheat bun with a bit of mustard. Leftovers from your cookout can be sliced up and tossed in a salad. Or try tossing them with some pasta, add some fresh herbs like basil or cilantro.

Variations: Apple cider vinegar may be substituted for the wine. More or less salt can be added to taste. Hot peppers can be added for flavor and heat. In lieu of marinating overnight, mushrooms can be dipped in the marinade and grilled immediately, and basted while grilling. Feel free to add other vegetables to the marinade to grill, too, such as onions, peppers, etc.

Frozen Vegetables a la Grill

The great smokey flavor will cause the kids to fight over the vegetables, believe it or not so make more than usual.

1. Open bag of frozen vegetables of your choice.
2. Empty into foil pan or other oven type utensil.
3. Sprinkle with seasonings or leave plain.

Vegetarian Cabbage Rolls

Serves 12
2 Cabbage head

Filling:	**Sauce, per batch:**
¾ cup barley	2 cup prego
¾ cup bulgur	¼ tsp. sea salt
6 cup water; salted if desired	¼ tsp. onion powder
1 cup rice	⅛ tsp. garlic powder
1 large onions	⅛ tsp. chili powder
1 tbsp. paprika	1 tbsp. sugar, brown
½ tsp. chili powder	1½ tbsp. wine vinegar
4 garlic cloves, crushed	**Sauce, remaining batches:**
½ cup pine nuts	6 cup prego
10 ½ oz. tofu, firm	¾ tsp. sea salt
½ bunch parsley, chopped	¾ tsp. onion powder
6 tbsp. soy sauce	⅜ tsp. garlic powder
4 tbsp. molasses	⅜ tsp. chili powder
2 tbsp. sesame oil	3 tbsp. brown sugar
	4 ½ tbsp. wine vinegar

1. **Filling:** Precook grains in water until done. Crush tofu. Sauté remaining ingredients in oil until cooked and add cooked grains.
2. **Sauce:** Season tomato sauce with remaining ingredients.
3. **Cabbage:** Core cabbage and cook in boiling water for several minutes.
4. Pull leaves away as they soften. Cut out hard core of leaf. Cut largest leaves in half.
5. Preheat oven to 300 degrees. Oil 9"x13" casserole.
6. Place enough tomato sauce to cover bottom.
7. Fill cabbage leaves with cooked filling and wrap, tucking sides and ends in to form neat rolls.
8. Place rolls snugly in casserole against each other.
9. Spoon remaining sauce over.
10. Cover tightly and bake 2 hours.
11. Leave in oven until serving time.

Grilled Corn on the Cob

Simple and great tasting.

1. Push back husk and remove silk.
2. Pull husk back over the corn.
3. Grill for about 30-40 minutes turning no less than once every 15 minutes.
4. Remove husks and dig in!

Sides

Roasted Rosemary Vegetables

8 medium organic potatoes
6 large organic shallots or small yellow onions, peeled and sliced
3 large cloves garlic, slivered
2 to 3 tbsp. Spectrum organic extra-virgin olive oil salt
⅓ to ½ cup fresh rosemary leaves, stripped from stems

1. Preheat oven to 350 degrees.
2. Wash and cut the potatoes into quarters.
3. Place in a large, glass baking dish.
4. Sprinkle with the shallots and garlic and toss with the olive oil until well-coated.
5. Sprinkle with salt and rosemary, tossing again lightly to combine.
6. Bake for 50 to 60 minutes until potatoes are browned.
7. To have all sides browned, stir once during cooking.

Variations:
1. Add cherry tomatoes and sunburst squash or zucchini, sliced.
2. Wrap in foil and cook on the barbecue.

Lemon and Garlic Potato Salad

Serves 5
2½ pounds red potatoes
½ cup chopped parsley
1 clove garlic, minced
juice of 2 lemons
1 tablespoon vegetable oil
Salt and pepper to taste

1. Boil potatoes, and cool.
2. Add remaining ingredients and mix well.
3. Chill and serve.

Oven Roasted Garlic Vegetables

Serving Size: 6
1 large red onion, sliced into
¼" thick rounds
2 small zucchini sliced into
¼" thick rounds
1 pound mushrooms; sliced
1 small bundle asparagus, trim off white ends
1 red bell pepper, seeded and cut into ½-inch strips
½ cup roasted garlic flavored olive oil
½ teaspoon fennel seed (optional)
½ teaspoon red pepper flakes (optional)
2 tablespoons red wine vinegar or sherry
2 tablespoons flat leaf parsley, finely chopped salt & freshly ground pepper to taste

1. Preheat broiler and place rack 5 or more inches below the heat.
2. Place vegetables in a large bowl.
3. Pour 4 tablespoons of roasted garlic olive oil (from the ½ cup) over vegetables and toss well.
4. Add more oil, if necessary, to coat vegetables.
5. Spread vegetables on one layer on a baking sheet.
6. Place in oven and roast until they are cooked through, about 30 minutes.
7. Stir vegetables occasionally to prevent burning.
8. Vegetables should brown slowly, lower the rack or the heat if they cook too quickly.
9. Heat the remainder of the roasted garlic olive oil in a small sauté pan over medium high heat until hot.
10. Stir in the vinegar, fennel seed, red pepper flakes, and parsley.
11. Whisk well and add salt and freshly ground pepper to taste. Remove dressing from heat.
12. Toss dressing with roasted vegetables and serve.

Apricot Glazed Carrots

Serves 6

2 pounds carrots, sliced
1¼ teaspoons salt, divided
3 tablespoons margarine
⅓ cup apricot preserves
¼ teaspoon nutmeg
1 teaspoon grated orange rind
2 tablespoons fresh orange juice garnish: fresh Italian parsley (optional)

1. Cook carrots.
2. Add 1 teaspoon salt in boiling water to cover in a large saucepan for.
3. 15-20 minutes or until tender; drain.
4. Melt margarine in saucepan; stir in apricot preserves until blended.
5. Stir in remaining.
6. ¼ teaspoon of salt, nutmeg, orange rind, and orange juice.
7. Add carrots and toss to coat.
8. Garnish if desired.

Quick Vegetable Masala

2 potatoes, peeled, cubed	1 tsp. mustard seed
1 carrot, chopped	1 tsp. ground cumin
10 green beans, chopped	1 onion, finely chopped
1 liter cold water	2 tomatoes, blanched,
½ cup garden peas	peeled and chopped
1 clove garlic, crushed	1 tsp. garam masala
1 tsp. salt	½ tsp. ground ginger
½ tsp. ground turmeric	½ tsp. chili powder
1 tablespoon vegetable oil	handful chopped fresh coriander to garnish

1. Place potatoes, carrots and green beans in the cold water. Allow to soak while you prepare the rest of the vegetables; drain.
2. In a microwave safe dish place the potatoes, carrots, green beans, peas, garlic, salt and turmeric. Cook for 8 minutes.
3. Heat oil in a large frying pan over medium heat. Cook mustard seeds and cumin and when seeds start to sputter and pop, add the onion and cook until transparent. Stir in the tomatoes, garam masala, ginger and chili powder. Cook 3 minutes and then add the cooked vegetables. Simmer 1 minute and serve garnished with coriander.

Tempeh in Sauce

2 packages tempeh, cubed
3 or 4 zucchini
1 large onion, chopped ⅚ cloves garlic
2 cups frozen corn
1 red or green bell pepper
1 small can Ortega chilies (mild) extra hot stuff if you want
2 large cans enchilada sauce or chili sauce (or
1 can sauce and one 6 ounce can tomato paste and
2 cups water)

1. Put it all in a large pot and simmer for 30 minutes.
2. Serve over polenta, rice or other grain, or pasta.

Ragout of Summer Vegetables

Serves 8

4 oz. cans vegetable broth or imitation chicken broth
¼ cup butter or margarine
3 shallots, minced
2 cups yellow beans, diced
2 cups zucchini, diced
1 pound baby green beans
½ teaspoon freshly ground pepper
¼ cup fresh Italian parsley, minced

1. Bring broth to a boil in a large saucepan over medium heat, and boil 30 minutes or until reduced to ⅓ cup.
2. Remove from heat and set aside.
3. Melt butter in a large skillet over medium-high heat; add shallots and sauté until tender.
4. Add reduced broth, yellow squash, and next 3 ingredients.
5. Sauté 5 minutes or until vegetables are crisp-tender.
6. Sprinkle with parsley and serve immediately.

Creamy Yams

3 cups cooked, mashed yams
1 cup applesauce
1 tsp. cinnamon
¼ tsp. nutmeg
½ cup Mocha Mix or other creamer

Mix all thoroughly.

Classic Coleslaw

½ head of a medium cabbage (4 cups shredded)
2 medium to big carrots
1 small to medium onion

1. Shred or grate the carrots.
2. Chop or shred the cabbage.
3. Chop or grate the onion.
4. Toss all together in a large bowl.
5. In another bowl or in a container with a lid, mix:

1 cup mayonnaise, vegan, non-fat, low-fat or soy
1 tablespoon sugar
1 tablespoon vinegar (flavored is nice, we like sage, but use what you have)
1 teaspoon celery seed
a grind of black pepper

1. Water or soy milk to thin to desired consistency.
2. If using a jar, put lid on and shake until blended. Otherwise, mix with fork for whip until smooth.
3. Taste to see if you think it needs more vinegar or sugar.
4. If it's too thick, add a little water or milk to thin, a spoonful at a time.
5. Pour dressing over the vegetables, starting with ½ cup, and toss.
6. Add more dressing if this seems too dry.
7. If you don't have celery seed, leave it out.
8. If you don't have any onions, use onion powder in the dressing instead of grated onion in the vegetable portion.
9. This keeps very nicely overnight in the refrigerator and is also good fresh made.

Note: A lot of our mayo in the US no longer contains eggs (the low fat; and some no diary). Soy mayo is easy to find there are several companies that issue catalogues and will ship to your house by mail or other carrier.

Corn Salad with Three-Herb Dressing

¼ cup white wine vinegar
2 tablespoons olive oil
2 teaspoons Dijon mustard
1 teaspoon sugar
2 cups grilled corn on the cob (about 2 ears)
2 tablespoons finely chopped fresh cilantro
2 tablespoons finely chopped fresh marjoram
1 tablespoon finely chopped fresh dill
salt and pepper
1 small avocado, cut into 8 wedges
1 small tomato, cut into 8 wedges
cilantro sprigs

1. In a large bowl combine vinegar, olive oil, mustard, and sugar; mix well until blended.
2. Add corn, cilantro, marjoram, and dill; Stir to combine. Season with salt and pepper to taste.
3. Cover and store in refrigerator for one hour or until chilled. Mound corn salad on platter.
4. Arrange avocado and tomato wedges around salad.
5. Garnish with cilantro sprigs.

Crisp Candied Sweet Potatoes

6 large sweet potato
2 tablespoons margarine
¾ cup dark brown sugar
½ cup water pinch salt pinch ground ginger

1. Place potatoes in a large pan; cover with cold water.
2. Bring to a boil; cook 10 minutes.
3. Plunge potatoes into cold water to stop cooking.
4. When cool enough to handle, peel and discard skin.
5. Cut potatoes into thick slices or chunks; refrigerate.
6. (If desired, this can be done the day before.)
7. In a large nonstick skillet, melt margarine.
8. Add brown sugar, water, salt, and ginger.
9. Bring to a simmer; add half of potato slices in one layer. Cook at a slow boil over medium heat until potatoes are brown and crisp around edges. Turn; brown other side.
10. With a slotted spoon, transfer potatoes to a platter; reserve in a warm place near the stove.
11. Add remaining potatoes to skillet; cook as the first batch. Serve immediately.

Sauté of Sweet Potatoes

Serves 3

4 medium sweet potatoes, peeled
3 tablespoons margarine
1 orange, grated rind and juice
¼ cup brown sugar, may be doubled
2 tablespoons chopped fresh parsley OR chives

1. Cook the sweet potatoes in boiling water for 10-15 minutes or until they are tender.
2. Drain well. Slice them or cut into cubes.
3. Heat the margarine in a frying pan and add the sweet potatoes. Toss over a moderate heat until the potatoes are coveted with margarine, then add the orange rind and juice, the sugar and herbs.
4. Heat, stirring and tossing, and serve immediately.

Note: You can boil sweet potatoes in the same way as ordinary potatoes, as in this recipe. You can also bake them in their jackets (they don't take as long as ordinary potatoes), roast them, or make them into chips to serve with a dip.

Fluffy Garlic Mashed Potatoes

1 large head garlic, split in half horizontally
1 teaspoon olive oil
3 large baking potatoes, peeled & quartered
3 tablespoons low-fat margarine
1 cup low-fat milk or soymilk salt, to taste
¼ teaspoon ground white pepper

1. Preheat oven to 350 degrees. Drizzle garlic with oil.
2. Wrap securely in foil; roast 30 to 40 minutes, or until soft.
3. Cool, then squeeze garlic out of skins; refrigerate.
4. Discard skins.
5. (If desired, garlic can be roasted the day before.)
6. Cover potatoes with water, add salt and bring to a boil. cover; cook 20 to 30 minutes, or until fork-tender.
7. Drain; reserve cooking water.
8. Mash potatoes well. Add garlic, margarine, salt, pepper and milk or soymilk.
9. Whip potatoes, adding reserved cooking liquid ¼ cup at a time until potatoes are fluffy and light but still hold shape.

Black-Eyed Peas with Spinach

1 medium onion, chopped
vegetable broth for sautéing
10 oz. fresh spinach, rinsed, stemmed and coarsely chopped (I think frozen would be fine)
3 cups drained black-eyed peas (or 2 16-oz. cans)
ground black pepper to taste
pinch of cayenne or crushed red pepper flakes.

1. In a large skillet, sauté the onions in the broth for a few minutes, until soft. Add the spinach to the skillet. Stir for a minute or two until it wilts.
2. Add the black-eyed peas, black pepper, and cayenne if desired. Bring to a simmer on medium heat.
3. Serve right away or cover; keep warm on low heat.

Hot Chili Macaroni

Serves 6

2 quarts water
1 cup elbow macaroni
1 tablespoon canola oil
1 medium yellow onion, diced
1 green pepper, seeded & chopped
2 stalks celery, chopped
4 cloves garlic, minced
1 28 oz. can stewed or diced tomatoes
1 15 oz. can kidney beans, rinsed & drained
1 11 oz. can corn kernels, drained
1½ tablespoons chili powder
2 teaspoons dried oregano
1 teaspoon ground cumin
½ teaspoon freshly ground black pepper
½ teaspoon salt or to taste

1. In a large saucepan, bring the water to a boil over medium-high heat.
2. Add the macaroni, stir, and return to boil.
3. Cook over medium-high heat until cooked al dente, about 6-8 minutes. Drain.
4. In a large saucepan, heat the oil over medium-high heat.
5. Add the onion, bell pepper, celery, and garlic and cook, stirring, for about 7 minutes.
6. Stir in the tomatoes, beans, corn, chili powder, oregano, cumin, pepper, and salt, and bring
7. to a simmer.
8. Cook over medium-low heat for 15 minutes, stirring occasionally.
9. Mix in the cooked macaroni and cook for 5 more minutes over low heat.
10. Remove from heat and let stand for about 5 minutes before serving.

BBQ Black-Eyed Peas with Collard Greens

Serves 5-8

4 cups cooked black eye peas
½ teaspoons dry mustard
⅛ teaspoons black pepper
2 cups collard greens
1½ cups tomato puree
1 cup sliced mushrooms
2 cups chopped onion
½ tablespoons garlic powder
1 tablespoon smoke oil or liquid smoke flavoring
1 cup maple syrup
1 teaspoon salt

1. **BBQ sauce:** Mix the above in a large bowl: tomato puree, maple syrup, smoke favoring, mustard powder, garlic powder, black pepper, and salt.
2. Heat until bubbling and simmer for 10 min.
3. Steam the collard greens with the mushrooms and onions, fold in the beans and the BBQ sauce.
4. Simmer all ingredients together for 10-15 minutes.
5. Serve warm, by itself or over rice!

Southern Corn and Limas

1 can whole kernel sweet corn, drained
1 can lima beans, or butter beans, drained
¼ cup red bell peppers
2 tablespoons chopped onions
½ teaspoon salt
1 teaspoon chili powder
¼ teaspoon paprika

1. Combine ingredients in foil pan, oven proof pan, or other- you can even make a pan out of aluminum foil if you want.
2. Grill for 15 minutes, shaking from time to time.

Basic Black Beans

2 cups black beans (cooked or canned)
1 small onion chopped
1 heaping tablespoon minced garlic. (if you want, substitute the minced fresh garlic with
1& ¼ tsp. of granulated garlic
1cup crushed or diced tomatoes
   (fresh or canned/ make sure the skin is removed)
⅛ tsp. cayenne
⅛ tsp. black pepper
1 tsp. ground cumin
¾ tsp. ground coriander seed
1 tsp. basil
¼ tsp. oregano
3 tbsp. extra virgin olive oil

1. Heat the oil in a skillet, add all of the ingredients except for the black beans and tomatoes, sauté until onions are soft but not glassy (clear).
2. using a pot that can hold not only the beans and tomatoes but all of the other ingredients as well, heat and mix the beans and tomatoes until they are just lightly bubbling if you use raw tomato cover the pot once the mixture starts bubbling.
3. Turn the heat low and cover for 10 minutes.
4. Once both mixtures are ready, fold them together in the pot and heat for an additional 2 min., stirring well.
5. Salt to taste and serve hot over rice or cornbread!

Grilled Okra

Serves 4
1 quart salted water
1 pound fresh okra, washed and trimmed
ice water
¼ cup vegetable oil
2 cloves garlic, mashed
1 teaspoon ground cumin
¼ teaspoon salt

Cooked rice:
1. In a 2-quart saucepan bring salted water to a boil.
2. Add okra; blanch for 1 to 3 minutes.
3. Remove okra from boiling.
4. water and plunge into a bowl of ice water to chill.
5. In a small bowl combine oil, garlic, cumin, and salt.
6. Remove okra from ice water, dry and place in bowl or large plastic bag.
7. Pour oil mixture over okra; toss to coat.
8. Place okra in center of cooking grate.
9. Grill 7 to 9 minutes, turning once during cooking time. Serve with cooked rice.

Banana Muffins

3 very ripe bananas (about 1½ cups puree)
½ cup apple juice, frozen concentrate
2 tablespoons apple juice, frozen concentrate
1 tablespoon orange juice, frozen concentrate
2 tablespoons vegetable oil
1 teaspoon fresh lemon juice
1¼ cups whole-wheat flour
¾ cup wheat germ
1½ teaspoons ground cinnamon
2 teaspoons baking powder
¾ cup raisins or chopped dates
½ cup walnuts, coarsely chopped
2 egg whites

1. Preheat oven to 375 degrees.
2. Process the bananas, juice concentrates, oil, and lemon juice in a blender until smooth.
3. Combine the flour, wheat germ, cinnamon, and baking powder in a mixer bowl.
4. Stir the banana mixture into the dry ingredients to make a thick batter; then stir in the raisins and walnuts. Beat the egg whites until stiff.
5. Gently fold into the batter. Spoon the batter into 18 muffin cups coated with vegetable cooking spray.
6. Bake for 20 to 25 minutes.
7. Remove from the tins immediately.

Asian Inspired Marinated Portebello Mushroom Steak

Tangy, aromatic and nutty flavours combine into an Asian taste sensation!
4 large portebello mushrooms
2 tablespoon of sesame oil
2 tablespoons of apple cider vinegar
1-2 cloves of garlic
1 tablespoon of chopped ginger
1-2 tablespoons of tamari or braggs
2 tablespoons of raw, unhulled sesame seeds1

1. Cut the portebello into strips
2. Place into a mixing bowl and add all the ingredients then gently massage the mushrooms until they are evenly covered. Put into the fridge and allow to marinate for 2 hours or more.
3. The longer you leave them the more the flavours will soak into the mushrooms.

Sauces and Dressings

Marinara Sauce

1 ripe tomato
½ cup sun-dried tomatoes, soaked or oil-packed
½ red bell pepper, chopped (about ½ cup)
2 tablespoons extra-virgin olive oil
1 tablespoon minced fresh basil, or 1 teaspoon dried
1 teaspoon dried oregano
½ teaspoon crushed garlic (1 clove)
¼ teaspoon plus ⅛ teaspoon salt (or to taste)
dash cayenne or black pepper (optional)

1. Place all ingredients in a food processor and process until smooth.
2. Stop occasionally to scrape down the sides of the bowl. Keeps for three days in the fridge.

Sweet-and-Sour Sauce

Makes 1½ cups
1⅓ cup (12 fl. oz./ 350 ml) pineapple or apple juice
2 tbsp. Soy sauce or tamari
4 tsp. Arrowroot
1 tbsp. Rice or apple cider vinegar
2 tsp. brown rice syrup or raw sugar

1. In a small saucepan over medium heat, combine all ingredients, stirring with a whisk to dissolve the arrowroot.
2. Bring mixture to a boil, reduce heat to low, and simmer, stirring constantly, until sauce thickens.

Almond Mayonnaise

Makes almost 2 cups

½ cup sprouted almonds, blanched (*check Index under "Almond, Sprouted, Blanched" for sprouting and blanching instructions which will not cook the almonds properly otherwise).
1 tbsp. soaked pine nuts (optional)
1 heaping tbsp. agar-agar flakes
½ clove garlic
½–¾ cup filtered water (put 2 ice cubes in water)
1 cup organic, unrefined oil like extra-virgin olive oil
  -or- use a combination of oils like: ½ extra-EVO,
½ sesame or sunflower oil with 1 tbsp. of flaxseed oil)
3 tbsp. lemon juice
½ tsp. unpasteurized apple cider vinegar
½ tsp. raw honey
¼–½ tsp. Celtic sea salt
1 tsp. freshly minced dill (optional)
⅛ tsp. yellow mustard powder (or 1 tsp. prepared dijon mustard)
⅛ tsp. white pepper (grind fresh in a peppermill)

1. Place a small glass bowl and a wire whisk into the freezer for later use.
2. Put the almonds, pine nuts, agar-agar flakes, garlic and ½ cup of the water into the blender and blend very well, adding more water if necessary. (The ice cubes are in the water to keep it cold, which helps to solidify the mayonnaise when you add the oil.)
3. When the almonds are broken down to a fine cream, start adding in the oil very slowly.
4. Have the blender running on medium or high (depending on your blender).
5. The mayonnaise will start to thicken. If it gets thin, add in an ice cube or two, which will thicken it up again.
6. When all the oil is absorbed into the almond mixture, transfer the mayonnaise to the small chilled bowl and add in the lemon, vinegar and honey slowly, beating constantly with the wire whisk.
7. Then, add in the Celtic sea salt and spices.
8. Taste and adjust the flavors. Store in a glass jar in the refrigerator. Keeps up to 3 weeks in the refrigerator.

Note: If the mayonnaise separates (and gets thin) when you add in the lemon juice and spices, it is usually because you added them in too fast and didn't whisk all the while. Should this happen, put the whole thing back into the blender, add in another ½ tbsp. agar-agar flakes and 2 to 3 ice cubes, and blend again. It should thicken up. If it still doesn't, put the mayonnaise into the refrigerator, and after a while it will thicken from the cold.

Almond Mayonnaise II

½ cup finely ground almonds; 1 cup water.
2 tablespoons cider vinegar or fresh lemon juice.
1 teaspoon mustard powder or French mustard.
1 teaspoon sugar or syrup.
¼ to ½ teaspoon vegetable bouillon powder.
¼ teaspoon powdered ginger; pinch of salt (optional).
¾ cup sunflower, safflower or other light oil (olive oil produces a rather strong taste).

1. Ingredients should be at room temperature.
2. Blend all the ingredients well, excluding the oil.
3. Slowly trickle the oil in through the hole in the top of the blender in a continuous stream.
4. Adding the oil slowly will make it better.
5. Cool in the refrigerator in an airtight jar.
6. The flavor may be varied according to the mustard, bouillon powder or other seasoning used.

Fruit Sauce

Here's an interesting sauce to try for basting tofu, veggie burgers, tempeh, or vegetables. For those of you who don't like tomato based sauces, try this.

1½ cups water
1 cup dried fruit of your choice
2 tablespoons sugar
¼ teaspoon garlic powder
½ teaspoon salt
2 teaspoons ground ginger
½ teaspoon ground turmeric
3 tablespoons soy sauce
¼ teaspoon celery seed
½ cup brown sugar

Simmer the ingredients in a saucepan.

Fiery Classroom Sauce

1 Bermuda Onion minced fine
1 tsp. ground cumin
2 tablespoons liquid sweetener, e.g., maple syrup
2 tablespoons tarragon vinegar
¼ cup brown sugar, well packed
¼ cup freshly squeezed orange juice
2 tablespoons crushed red pepper
1 8 oz. can diced tomatoes.

1. Pulse blend in food processor until desired. consistency. Marinate tofu, veggies, etc. overnight.
2. Grill over slow fire until done.
3. Serve with Basmati rice and a large salad.

Creamy Herb Dressing

Serves 1

½ cup lite soft tofu
2 tablespoons soy milk or skim milk
2 tablespoons olive oil
2 tablespoons to 3 tbsp. lemon juice
1 teaspoon honey (optional)
¼ teaspoon salt
¼ teaspoon garlic powder
2 teaspoons fresh dill or 1 tsp. dried dill

1. Combine all ingredients except the dill in a blender and blend until smooth.
2. Scrape the sides of the blender as needed.
3. Add more milk as needed to get a consistency that is quite thin and pourable.
4. Pour into a bowl and stir in dill.
5. Add more lemon juice if a tangier taste is preferred.

Garlic Dressing

½ lemon, juiced
2 tablespoons wine
 Vinegar, or more to taste
1 teaspoon sea salt
4 lrg garlic cloves, minced
⅔ cup extra virgin olive oil

1. Mix the lemon juice, vinegar, salt and garlic in a bowl and add lots of freshly ground black pepper.
2. Stirring all the time, drizzle in the olive oil so that the dressing thickens as you mix.
3. Drain thoroughly the canned beans and rinse them.
4. Steam the green beans, until just tender, 5 to 6 min.
5. Toss all the beans together with the green onions, then add the garlic dressing and toss again.
6. Sprinkle the chopped parsley over the top.
7. Serve at room temperature.

Cranberry-Orange Relish

Makes 3½ cups

1 pound fresh or frozen cranberries
1 thin-skinned organic orange; no seeds; washed; cut
2 cups sugar

1. Combine cranberries and orange in bowl of food processor. Chop into fine small bits being careful not to over puree.
2. Transfer mixture to a large mixing bowl; add sugar and stir well. Transfer mixture to a jar; cover tightly.
3. Allow to macerate in the refrigerator 2 days before using.

Note: When using unpeeled oranges or zest in recipes, use organic fruit to avoid possible pesticide residue on the fruit skin. If organic oranges are not available, scrub orange thoroughly before using.

Cranberry-Pineapple Relish

Makes 3½ cups

1 pound fresh or frozen cranberries 1
cup pineapple, chopped
2 cups sugar

1. Combine cranberries and pineapple in bowl of food processor.
2. Chop into fine small bits being careful not to over puree. Transfer mixture to a large mixing bowl; add sugar and stir well.
3. Transfer mixture to a jar; cover tightly.
4. Allow to macerate in the refrigerator 2 days before using.

Entrees

Barbecue Tofu

Serves 4

Marinade:

¼ cup soy sauce
1 or 2 cloves garlic, minced
2 tsp. sugar
½ tsp. dry mustard (or 1 tsp. Dijon or prepared mustard)
Barbecue sauce (anchovy-free for vegetarians)

1. Slice tofu ¼ to ½ inches thick and place in shallow dish.
2. In small bowl, combine soy sauce, garlic, sugar and mustard; drizzle over tofu.
3. Let marinate in refrigerator for at least 2 hours or overnight.
4. Drain tofu; grill on lightly greased barbecue rack over low heat for 2 minutes.
5. Carefully turn over using a wide spatula; grill 2 minutes.
6. Brush with barbecue sauce; continue grilling, 2 minutes a side.

Tofu Cutlets Marsala

¼ cup plus 2 teaspoons cornstarch, divided
¼ cup all-purpose flour
¼ teaspoon salt
¼ teaspoon freshly ground pepper
1 14-ounce block extra-firm tofu, drained, rinsed and cut
   crosswise into eight ½-inch-thick slices
4 tablespoons extra-virgin olive oil, divided
2 large shallots, minced
1 teaspoon dried thyme
6 cups sliced cremini or white mushrooms
   (about 10 ounces)
½ cup dry Marsala wine (see Ingredient note)
1 cup vegetable broth
1 tablespoon tomato paste

1. Preheat oven to 300°F. Whisk ¼ cup cornstarch,
    flour, salt and pepper in a shallow dish. Pat tofu with
    paper towel to remove excess moisture.
2. Heat 2 tablespoons oil in a large nonstick skillet over
    medium-high heat.
3. Dredge 4 tofu slices in the flour mixture, add them to
    the pan and cook until crispy and golden, about 3
    minutes per side.
4. Place the tofu on a baking sheet and transfer to the
    oven to keep warm.
5. Repeat with another tablespoon of oil and the
    remaining tofu, adjusting the heat if necessary to pre-
    vent scorching.
6. Add the remaining 1 tablespoon oil, shallots and
    thyme to the pan.
7. Reduce heat to medium and cook, stirring constantly,
    until the shallots are slightly soft and beginning to
    brown, 1 to 2 minutes.
8. Add mushrooms and cook, stirring often, until tender
    and lightly browned, 3 to 5 minutes.
9. Stir in Marsala and simmer until slightly reduced,
    about 1 minute.
10. Whisk the remaining 2 teaspoons cornstarch with
    broth and tomato paste in a small bowl.
11. Stir into the mushroom mixture, return to a simmer
    and cook, stirring constantly, until thick and glossy,
    about 4 minutes.
12. To serve, spoon the hot sauce over the tofu.

Note: Marsala, a fortified wine, is a flavorful and wonderfully economical addition to many sauces. An opened
bottle can be stored in a cool, dry place for months, unlike
wine, which starts to decline within hours of being
uncorked.

Vegetarian Fish

2 pieces of bean curd pockets
3 oz. of golden mushrooms
3 oz. of water chestnuts
1 sheet of purple seaweed
1 sheet of bean curd skin
1 tablespoon flour
1 tablespoon water
1 tablespoon cornstarch
¼ teaspoon salt
¼ teaspoon pepper
1 egg substitute

1. Mix flour and water into a smooth batter.
2. Mince bean curd pockets and water chestnuts.
3. Wash the golden mushrooms, trim off the ends and
    mince.
4. Mix the minced ingredients with cornstarch, salt,
    pepper, and egg substitute until well blended.
5. This is the filling (any sort of bean curd can be a
    substitute).
6. Place the purple seaweed on top of bean curd skin,
    then place the filling on top of the purple seaweed.
7. Roll into a 3 x 2 inch rectangular block.
8. Seal tightly with batter.
9. Steam 10 minutes over high heat.

Cranberry Stuffed Squash

2 med. acorn squashes
1 cup chopped pears
½ cup cranberries
3 tbsp. orange juice concentrate
3 tbsp. maple syrup
1½ tsp. cinnamon
½ tsp. allspice

1. Preheat oven to 400 degrees.
2. Slice squash lengthwise and place cut side up on foil-
    lined baking pan.
3. In medium bowl, combine pears, cranberries, orange
    juice concentrate, maple syrup, cinnamon, and all-
    spice.
4. Spoon mixture into squash cavities.
5. Brush cut edges with any remaining liquid.
6. Bake 45 minutes, or until squash is tender.

Vegetable Kebabs with Parsley Sauce

Serves 4

1 red pepper, rinsed, cored, seeded, and cut into
1-inch pieces
1 yellow or green pepper, rinsed, cored, seeded, and cut
into 1-inch pieces
12-16 button mushrooms, stems trimmed and wiped
clean 8 cherry tomatoes, rinsed with stems removed
12 1-inch-thick slices zucchini or summer squash olive oil
for brushing on vegetables

Parsley Sauce Ingredients:

½ cup fresh parsley leaves, rinsed and patted dry
1 cup fresh cilantro leaves, rinsed and patted dry
1 tbsp. garlic, minced
2 tbsp. red wine vinegar
1 tbsp. fresh lemon juice
½ cup vegenaise salt and black pepper to taste

1. Prepare grill to medium heat.
2. Soak skewers in water prior to preparing kebabs.
3. Make four kebabs by threading the vegetables onto
   eight wooden skewers (using them in pairs to hold
   the pieces more securely).
4. Alternate peppers, mushrooms, tomatoes, and
   zucchini (or summer squash) on each set of skewers.
5. Brush the kebabs all over with olive oil.
6. Grill, turning once or twice, until the vegetables are
   cooked, just about 6 to 8 minutes total.
7. Serve warm or at room temperature with parsley
   sauce.
8. To prepare sauce, place all ingredients in a blender or
   the bowl of a food processor fitted with the steel
   blade.
9. Pulse or process until parsley and cilantro are finely
   minced and all ingredients are thoroughly combined.
10. Tip: The Parsley Sauce can also be used as a dip.
11. Tip II: The double-skewer technique keeps vegetables
    secure. Simply thread the pieces on two skewers held
    parallel to each other to keep from losing vegetables
    to breakage on the grill.

Squash Goulash

Serves 2

¼ cup medium grain rice
½ acorn squash
1 small red potato
1 small carrot
¼ cup chopped onion
1 tbsp. tomato paste
1 small clove garlic, minced
1 bay leaf
½ tsp. coriander
½ tsp. paprika
½ tsp. cinnamon
¼ tsp. tumeric
¼ tsp. cayenne
¼ tsp. pepper
dash cardamom

1. Sauté onion, rice, and all spices except garlic and bay
   leaf in a small amount of oil until rice sizzles.
2. Add 1 cup water, tomato paste, bay leaf and garlic.
3. Simmer for 15 minutes while you prepare vegetables.
4. Scrape out squash, then peel and chop all vegetables
   into bite-sized chunks.
5. Add to rice mixture along with an additional ¾ cup
   water.
6. Simmer over low heat for about ten minutes, or until
   vegetables are soft.
7. A note about the squash: the ridges on acorn squash
   make it difficult to peel; it's easiest to chop the squash
   first and then peel the pieces.

Collard Greens with Aromatic Spice

Serves 4 – 6

1 teaspoon cumin seeds
1 teaspoon minced ginger
1 teaspoon minced garlic
2 Thai chiles, stems removed and minced
1 pound collard greens, ribs removed, coarsely chopped
½ cup vegetable broth or water
1 pound spinach leaves, tough stems removed, coarsely chopped
½ teaspoon salt
1/8 teaspoon Garam Masala, or to taste

1. In a large nonstick sauté pan, heat the ghee over medium heat. When hot, add the cumin seeds and cook until fragrant and beginning to brown, 1 to 2 minutes.
2. Add the ginger, garlic, and chiles and cook 30 seconds longer.
3. Add ¼ of the collards, stirring until wilted, then continue adding the collards in batches until fully incorporated and wilted.
4. Add the vegetable broth and cook, stirring occasionally, until collards are slightly tender, about 5 minutes. Add the spinach in batches, stirring until wilted before adding more.
5. When completely combined, add the salt and continue cooking to the desired degree of tenderness and all liquid has evaporated, 4 to 5 minutes longer. Sprinkle with the Garam Masala, if desired, and stir to combine before serving.

Vegan Dressing

1 medium onion, coarsely chopped
8 celery stalks, coarsely chopped
8 oz. fresh mushrooms, sliced
1 can water chestnuts, finely chopped
poultry seasoning (the vegan kind!)
parsley, sage, thyme, salt & pepper
1 pkg. (7 ½ oz) Love's Seasoned Stuffing

1. Sauté onions, celery, mushrooms, and water chestnuts in water, wine, or beer. Cook until onions are soft.
2. Put stuffing mix in a bowl and add onion, celery, mushrooms, water chestnut mixture.
3. Add poultry seasoning, parsley, sage, thyme, salt and pepper to taste.
4. Heat water and add slowly to stuffing mix and stir till thoroughly moistened.
5. Place in lightly oiled 10 inch covered casserole.
6. Bake in 325 oven for 30 minutes.

Pumpkin & Dressing

Chick'n Flavored Tofu (see recipe below)
3-4 finely minced garlic cloves
¼ cup barley malt

1. Use a small baking pumpkin and cut off top and remove seeds from inside.
2. Save seeds to bake and eat later. Mix garlic and barley malt together and brush approximately half on inside of pumpkin.
3. Fill with corn bread dressing. Pour the rest of the honey/barley malt mixture on top of dressing.
4. Cover with lid and bake 350°F for 1 hr or until pumpkin is tender. Serve with Chick'n flavored tofu.

Chick'n Flavored Tofu:
1 pkg. firm tofu (packed in water)
1-2 tablespoons olive oil (to fry)
2 tablespoons meatless chicken flavoring powder or
1 teaspoon chicken-style bouillon
1 tablespoon nutritional yeast
⅛ cup water

1. Drain and cut tofu into thin slices and fry in oil till crisp. You will need to flip and turn the tofu several times until it becomes brown.
2. Mix meatless chicken flavoring powder or vegetarian bouillon, nutritional yeast and water together till smooth. Pour over tofu and mix well to coat.
3. Cook a short time more to dry out tofu. (WATCH closely! It can burn quickly!)

Cornbread

1 recipe cooked cornbread
1 cup chopped celery
1 cup chopped onion
1 cup chopped whole-wheat bread crumbs (or leftover grains of any type)
2 teaspoons poultry seasoning
1 teaspoon sage
1 tablespoon meatless chicken flavoring powder or
1 teaspoon bouillon salt/pepper to taste
½ pkg. silken tofu
1 cup soy milk

1. In a blender combine tofu and soy milk.
2. Blend till smooth. Break cornbread into crumbs with hands and combine with rest of ingredients.
3. Bake in oven proof dish in 350°F for 35-45 minutes.

Leek and Corn-Stuffed Peppers

Serves 8 to 10

10 medium green or red bell peppers, or a combination
2 tablespoons olive oil
4 large leeks, white and palest green parts only, chopped and well rinsed
2 tablespoons minced shallots
2 cloves garlic, minced
4 cups cooked corn kernels, preferably fresh
¼ cup fine bread crumbs
¼ cup minced fresh parsley
1 teaspoon dried summer savory
1 teaspoon ground coriander salt and freshly ground pepper to taste wheat germ for topping paprika for topping

1. Preheat the oven to 350 degrees.
2. Carefully cut away the top stems of the peppers and remove the seeds.
3. Cut a very thin slice from the bottoms so that the peppers can stand.
4. Arrange, standing snugly against one another for support, in1 or 2 very deep casserole dishes or a roasting pan.
5. Heat the oil with 2 tablespoons of water in a large skillet. Add the leeks, shallots, and garlic.
6. Sauté over medium heat, covered, lifting the lid to stir occasionally, until the leeks are tender.
7. Stir in the remaining ingredients except the toppings.
8. Cook, stirring, another 5 minutes.
9. Distribute the stuffing among the peppers.
10. Top each with a sprinkling of wheat germ, followed by a dusting of paprika.
11. Cover the casserole or roasting pan and bake for 40 to 50 minutes, or until the peppers are tender but still firm enough to stand.
12. Arrange in a circle on a large platter, serve a rice dish in the center. Serve at once.

Seitan Roast with Mushroom Gravy

Serving Size: 6

1 lb Seitan
2 c Sliced mushrooms
2 c Sliced onions
1 1/3 oz Tofu scrambler
4 c Water
1 tb Chopped fresh basil leaves
1 tb Chopped fresh sage leaves

1. Slice seitan into ½" slices & place in a Dutch oven.
2. Layer mushrooms & onions on top.
3. In a bowl, combine dry tofu scrambler with water, basil & sage.
4. Pour over seitan & vegetables.
5. Bring to a boil & simmer gently for 30 minutes, till gravy has thickened.

Pumpkin Curry With Lentils & Apples

Serving Size: 6

1 cup red or brown lentils
6 cups water
½ teaspoon turmeric
1 tablespoon canola oil
1 large onion, diced
2 tomatoes, cored and chopped
3 cloves garlic, minced, up to 4
1½ tablespoons curry powder
2 teaspoons ground cumin
½ teaspoon pepper
½ teaspoon salt
¼ teaspoon ground cloves

2 cups peeled and chopped pumpkin or other winter squash
2 cups white potatoes, unpeeled & chopped
8 medium cauliflower florets
2 medium carrots, peeled and diced (about 1 cup)
2 cups shredded leafy greens (kale, escarole or spinach)
2 apples, unpeeled, cored and diced
cooked basmati or jasmine rice

1. Place lentils, water and turmeric in a saucepan; cook about 45 minutes over medium-low heat.
2. Drain, reserving 2½ cups cooking liquid.
3. Heat oil in large saucepan; add onion.
4. Saute over medium heat 4 minutes.
5. Add tomatoes and garlic; cook 4 minutes more, stirring occasionally.
6. Add curry, cumin, pepper, salt and cloves; cook 1 minute more, stirring frequently.
7. Stir in lentils, reserved cooking liquid, pumpkin, potatoes, cauliflower and carrots; cook over medium-low heat until vegetables are tender, 35 to 45 minutes.
8. Stir in greens and apples; cook about 15 minutes more, stirring occasionally.
9. Transfer to a large serving bowl and serve with basmati or jasmine rice.

Summer Vegetable Tian

Serves 4

5 roma or plum tomatoes
1 torpedo onion or red onion, quartered
4 to 5 small summer squash, one variety or a mixture
2 to 3 small Japanese eggplant
2 to 4 tablespoons virgin olive oil
2 large garlic cloves, thinly sliced
1 tablespoon marjoram leaves or
½ teaspoon dried
1 teaspoon fresh thyme leaves or several pinches of dried
1 lemon wedge, very thinly sliced salt freshly ground
  pepper
extra-virgin olive oil (optional)
lemon wedges

1. Preheat the oven to 400°F.
2. Slice the vegetables into pieces about ¼ inch thick.
3. The zucchini and eggplant can be sliced on a gentle diagonal (not too extreme, or they will be difficult to place).
4. Brush 1 or 2 teaspoons of the oil over the bottom of the baking dish and scatter half the garlic slices and half the marjoram or thyme leaves over it.
5. Build the tian by overlapping layers of the vegetables.
6. Make a layer of zucchini, followed by a layer of eggplant, tomatoes, and so forth; or mix them all together in random fashion.
7. Placing a slice of tomato over each piece of eggplant helps give the eggplant some moisture while it's baking.
8. Don't worry about making the rows even: when you get to the end of the dish, push everything together and insert vegetables where gaps appear.
9. Tuck the garlic slices and the lemon slices here and there among the vegetables then brush them all with the remaining olive oil.
10. Be sure to put a little extra oil on the eggplant as it tends to dry out more than the other vegetables.
11. Sprinkle lightly with salt and scatter the rest of the herbs over the top.
12. Cover the dish and put it in the oven.
13. Check after 25 minutes; the vegetables should be beginning to steam in their own juices.
14. Dip a pastry brush into the juice and brush it over the vegetables; then cover the dish and return it to the oven for 20 minutes more.
15. When they're tender, baste the vegetables again; then cook them, uncovered, for another 7 to 10 minutes.
16. If the vegetables have exuded a great deal of juice by the time they're finished cooking, pour it off into a saucepan and boil until it is reduced to a syrup.
17. Spoon this sauce over the top.
18. Remove the tian from the oven and let it cool.
19. Serve it with freshly ground pepper and extra--virgin olive oil drizzled over the top, if you like, and wedges of lemon.
20. With all the new varieties of summer vegetables on the market you needn't limit yourself to a single type of squash or tomato or to the ingredients in the list.
21. Try whatever comes your way.
22. With a loaf of bread and something fresh and crisp from the garden, this tian makes a simple but perfect summer supper.

Spring Vegetables In A Parcel

1 new potatoes
1 courgettes
1 french beans
1 asparagus tips
1 carrots
1 cauliflower
1 sweet corn
1 oz. toasted hazelnuts, chopped
2 tbsp. extra virgin olive oil
½ tbsp. balsamic vinegar
2 tbsp. chopped fresh herbs

Herbs:

1 part basil
1 part chervil
1 part chives
1 part tarragon

1. Preheat the oven to 400F.
2. Cut circles of baking parchment (one for each serving), 8 inches in diameter, and make a fold down the centre.
3. Trim the vegetables and cut any larger ones into similar sized pieces.
4. Divide between the paper circles and scatter with hazelnuts.
5. Mix the oil, vinegar, herbs and seasoning and sprinkle over the vegetables.
6. Fold over the paper to enclose the vegetables and crimp the edges together to seal.
7. Place on a baking sheet and bake for 25-30 minutes until the vegetables are tender.
8. Serve with the paper just open, accompanied by lemon tagliatelle.

Kind Shepherd's Pie

10 oz. (about) firm tofu: frozen, thawed, drained, squeezed dry and cut into cubes or torn into chunks about ½ inch square (shape and size not really important. Just small enough to mix in nicely and big enough to look like a chunk of something.) The tofu will have turned beige and chewy.

2 tbsp. toasted pine nuts (if using green beans)

3 cup mashed potatoes (make them however you like them. I use instant.)

1 16 oz. can of vegetables, drained and liquid saved for gravy or leftover vegetables if you have them (you can try niblets corn, green peas, green beans).

1 cup gravy (Make your favorite, or buy readymade. Even a can of mushroom soup, thinned down, can work.)

1 tablespoon margarine or oil

2 tablespoons flour

2 cup water or liquid from the canned vegetables above or a combination ½ cup red wine (Optional)

1 med. onion, chopped coarsely

1 clove garlic, pressed or minced

1 small can mushrooms

salt and pepper to taste

1. Turn on your oven to 350°F.
2. If you don't have an oven (for example, when traveling or camping) just assemble the pie, making sure everything is hot.
3. You may need less gravy if making without an oven.
4. Assemble pie for oven baking (about 30 minutes, longer if reheating).
5. Make a gravy by melting the margarine or oil in a skillet.
6. Add onions (and mushrooms if you use them) and then the garlic. Stir frequently to keep from burning.
7. When onions are almost tender and liquid has evaporated from the pan, sprinkle flour into pan and cook and stir until it is slightly brown or is done (about 2 minutes).
8. Now add the water or stock and wine; bring to a boil.
9. Stir slowly and boil until it begins to thicken.
10. If it gets like paste, add more liquid and stir it in.
11. If it's a little too thin, don't worry, just cook it a little longer.
12. The potatoes will absorb some liquid (within reason) while it bakes.
13. Get a baking dish that holds about 2½ quarts.
14. Put in the tofu pieces and pine nuts (if used), add the vegetables; add the gravy and mix a little.
15. Top with the mashed potatoes. Sprinkle a little (1 tablespoon) soy cheese on top if you like.
16. I use Parmesan since I use small amounts of dairy at home.
17. Bake until heated through.
18. This sometimes runs over, so place it on a baking sheet in the oven if you hate to clean your oven.
19. You can assemble this the day before, keep it in the refrigerator and reheat it in either the oven or the microwave.
20. In the oven takes about 45 minutes for chilled, longer for frozen.
21. Microwaves vary a lot so use your own experience.
22. This makes a fair amount, so make in two small dishes and freeze one to use at a later time.

Vegetarian Shepherd's Pie

Serves 4

5 garlic cloves, crushed

1 red bell pepper, chopped

1 green bell pepper, chopped

2 medium zucchini, thinly sliced

1 cup canned tomatoes, crushed

½ teaspoon salt

⅛ teaspoon pepper

1⅓ cups pinto beans, cooked, drained

1⅓ cups black beans, cooked, drained

1⅓ cups chickpeas, cooked, drained

3 cups mashed potatoes

¼ teaspoon paprika

1. Preheat the oven to 375 degrees.
2. Sauté 2 cloves garlic for 1 min.
3. Add the red and green peppers, and zucchini and sauté, stirring occasionally for 4 minutes, or until tender.
4. Add ¾ cup of the crushed tomatoes, salt, and black pepper, and cook uncovered three minutes longer.
5. Place the pinto beans, black beans, chickpeas, remaining garlic and tomatoes in food processor, and puree until smooth.
6. Spoon the puree into a lightly greased 9" pie plan.
7. Top with the skillet mixture. Then spoon the mashed potatoes on top.
8. Bake uncovered for 25 minutes, or until the potatoes are lightly browned. Sprinkle with paprika if desired.

Tofu, Leek & Potato Pie

Serves 4
2 lb potatoes
10 oz. block of firm tofu
1 large leek
1 clove garlic
2 oz. margarine
soy milk
salt (to taste)
black pepper (to taste)
juice of ½ a lemon

Whole Wheat Pastry Flan Case:
6 ounces whole-wheat flour
3 ounces margarine (or substitute)
pinch of salt
little water

1. Peel, boil and then mash the potatoes with a little Soy milk to make them soft and creamy.
2. Meanwhile chop the leek and sauté in the margarine with the crushed garlic until soft.
3. Make a whole-wheat flan case and bake it blind for a few minutes (see below for pastry making).
4. Mash the tofu.
5. Mix the mashed potatoes, tofu, leeks, salt, pepper and lemon juice in a bowl.
6. Pile the potato mixture into the flan case and bake at 400 F for 20 - 30 minutes.
7. Serve hot with peas, carrots and a white sauce or cold with salad.

Whole Wheat Pastry Flan Case:
1. Place the flour in a mixing bowl and add the salt, mix well.
2. Chop the margarine into small pieces and add it to the flour.
3. Rub the margarine and the flour lightly together with your fingers until an even breadcrumb like consistency is reached.
4. Add a little water and mix until the pastry forms into a ball, adding a little more water if necessary.
5. Roll the pastry out on a floured surface to a circle a little larger the diameter of the flan case.
6. Grease the flan tin with margarine and press in the pastry. Trim the edges.
7. Use as described in the recipes requiring a flan case.

Creamy Vegetable Pie

Serves 6
1⅓ cups corn kernels
¾ pound broccoli
¾ pound zucchini
¾ pound carrots
¼ pound french beans
3 small leeks
1¼ cups bechamel sauce
fresh summer herbs, a bunch such as tarragon; thyme; dill chopped
8 ounces puff pastry

1. Steam all the vegetables separately until they are tender or slightly crisp.
2. Leave to cool, reserving cooking liquids, then chop if necessary into bite-size pieces.
3. Thin out the bechamel with about ¼ pint of the reserved liquids. Stir in the vegetables and herbs and pour into a large ovenproof dish.
4. Roll out the pastry to a round or other shape that is 1 inch larger than the diameter of the dish. With the trimmings make a long thin strip of pastry.
5. Moisten the rim of the dish and place this strip on it. Moisten the strip, then place the pastry lid on top and press down with a fork to seal the edge.
6. Bake at 400F for 30–40 minutes or until the pastry is risen and golden.

Shepherd's Beanie Pie

1 can butter beans	2 tomatoes, chopped
3 tbsp. oil	3 tsp. mixed herbs
1 onion, chopped	salt & pepper
1 clove garlic, crushed	3 cups mashed potato
¾ cup mushrooms, sliced	6 tbsp. cheese, grated
2 carrots, sliced	(optional)

1. Preheat oven 400F.
2. Heat oil and fry onion, garlic, mushrooms and carrots for 5 minutes.
3. Add tomatoes, beans, herbs and seasoning.
4. Pour bean mix into dish. Spread potato over top.
5. Sprinkle with cheese and bake 30-40 min.
1. Heat to boiling; reduce heat to medium-low.
2. Cook, uncovered, for 8-10 minutes, stirring occasionally, until hot.
3. Split potatoes and mash slightly.
4. Top each potato with chili mixture.
5. Top with sour cream (if desired) and cilantro.

The Best Raw Pizza Ever

The next two pages are complete with step by step directions to assemble a perfect raw vegan pizza.

The process:
For the *Raw Crust*, there are different flavor raw breads and textures you can find in the health food store or you can make your own gluten free, buckwheat, dehydrated, *Pizza Crust*. Crispy and crunchy, the below *living pizza crust* is thick enough to hold all the wonderful toppings and thin enough not to overpower the other flavors.

Cover each crust with an abundant amount of homemade *Pizza Sauce*. Blended in minutes (everyone's favorite part of this pizza is the sauce.)

Top with *raw cheese nut* recipes as they are creamy and completely different even unique in comparison to heated pizza cheese and yet they offer a familiar Italian flavor.

Top it with *live marinated vegetables* for that delicious heated flavor and texture, without destroying the enzymes, that are key for proper digestion.

Now let's get started!!

Living Pizza Crust

5 ½ cups sprouted buckwheat (soak 3 cups dry buckwheat for 24 hours, sprout 24 hours)
1 date
½ cup basil
1 cup cherry tomatoes or chopped roma tomatoes
¼ cup onion
½ orange juiced
2 cups ground flax seeds (about 1½ cups whole seeds)
1 tea salt
1 celery stick
1 carrot
2 garlic clove

1. Sprinkle with Italian seasoning Mix all veggies in a food processor first, then add buckwheat 1 to 2 cups at a time.
2. Last slowly add ground flax 1/2 cup at a time. Blend well.
3. With olive oil on your hands or put on latex (latex-free) gloves and oil and press dough into a dehydrator with the solid sheet (Tefflex sheets), score into desired shape.
4. Divide them into 7x7 squares.
5. Dehydrate until dry on top flip over, peel off Tefflex sheets and dry until hard around 12 to 24 hours.

Note: This living pizza crust requires advanced preparation, 3 days before you want to enjoy it. Just soak the hulled buckwheat groats 24 hours, sprout them 24 hours and then create the crust and dehydrate around 20 to 24 hours.

This crust will last 4 weeks and will fill around 3 to 4, 14x14 inch dehydrator sheets. I like to create mini pizza by dividing the 14x14 sheets into 4, making around 16, 7-inch mini pizza perfect for personal pizzas. Have fun creating all sorts of shapes and pizza sizes.

Quick, Sweet, Homemade Pizza Sauce

3 cup baby grape tomatoes
1½ cup raisins
1 lemon, juiced
3 garlic clove
½ cup basil or tablespoon of Italian Seasoning or dry basil
sea salt to taste

1. Blend in a blender until smooth.
2. Adjust for enough sweet flavor with a hint of tang from the lemon juice.

It is important to use grape tomatoes, they are so sweet and have less water content then other tomatoes, you want the sauce to be thick and saucy! Adjustments to the flavor may need to be made depending on the type of raisins and the amount of sweet vs. sour with the lemon juice. The recipe should be enough for at least 2, 14X14 pizzas. Although it usually turns out different each time sometimes I am able to make more and sometimes less, fresh ingredients are unpredictable.

This sauce is also delicious over pasta or raw zucchini pasta. If there are leftovers, feel free to add some flax seeds to the sauce, let them soak for an hour and spread it out on dehydrator solid sheets for Italian crackers.

Spreading the sauce on thick with the back of a spoon or small ladle works well. The layer of the thick tomato sauce helps to soften the raw pizza crust and helps keep the pizza moist too.

Also, try using fresh basil as opposed to dry. Fresh, especially from the garden, offers a superb Italian flavor. Use only enough to taste, it can turn the sauce a brown color (unless you don't mind).

Raw Cheese Nut Recipes

Raw nut cheeses are a great healthy alternative for cheese and are easy and quick to make, using less than 5 ingredients. Prep. Time: 10 minutes to create.

For anytime you're in the mood for cheese. Create any cheese recipe from yellow cheddar cheese by adding red bell pepper, or nacho cheese with sun-dried tomatoes and jalapeno to a simple white cheese dip with macadamia or cashew nuts.

Basic Nut Cheese Recipe

2 cups macadamia nuts, cashews, or any other white nut
1 lemon juiced
1 teaspoon salt or 1 celery stalk for a salt-free version
water to blend in a Vita-Mix or your favorite
    blender on high adding just enough water until thick
    and creamy.

This recipe is great for a vegetable dip or any base for any other cheese.

Next you can add:
any type of seasoning or fresh herbs
for a dressing add a bit more water and maybe some fresh garlic
red pepper
sun-dried tomatoes
spice (jalapeno, cayenne, red hot pepper)
something sweet if you like (date, 1 tablespoon raisins,
    Agave Nectar, honey)

Creamy Mac & Cheez

2 cups macadamia nuts
1 lemon juiced
1 chunk of onion
1 teaspoon sea salt
water to blend in a Vita Mix blender until creamy
    adding enough water until thick. I like to put it in a
    pastry bag and create fun designs on to

Walnut Parmesan Cheez

1 cup walnuts chopped until very fine powder
1/2 TB garlic bread seasoning, dried garlic or 4 fresh pressed garlic
1 teaspoon sea salt
4-8 dry tomato slices chopped until very fine, powder Stir together.

Marinated Vegetables (Mix)

Marinated vegetables for any fresh meal time, pasta or raw pizza. No need for cooking, just marinate and enjoy.

Marinate: broccoli, cauliflower, Brussels sprouts, mushrooms, or even Asparagus, in a bit of:
olive oil around 2-3 tablespoons
salt about ½ to 1 teaspoon
1 tablespoon lemon juice (optional)
fresh ground pepper

You can also add a touch of honey or Agave nectar for a light sweet flavor, about 1 teaspoon I just put veggies in a bowl pour on marinating ingredients and toss, then taste for adjustment.

Summer Time Veggie Marinating:

Another fresh tip for marinating vegetables in the summer time is utilizing the heat of the sun.

1. Marinate the veggies
2. then place in a glass container
3. cover with parchment paper or plastic wrap (making sure it is not touching the vegetables)
4. poke a few holes in the top
5. place in the sun for 3 to 5 hours
6. Sun baked, still fresh marinated veggies.

Combination Vegetables:

½ sweet onion sliced thinly
1 red pepper sliced thinly
(optional) 5 mushrooms, sliced thinly
1 head broccoli, chopped into small pieces
½ head cauliflower, chopped into small pieces

Toss together with a bit of olive oil, sea salt, 1 tablespoon lemon juice and 1 crushed garlic clove.

Hawaiian Vegetables:

2 Large Portabella mushrooms or 1 pack of small Portabella mushrooms
⅓ sweet onion
5 to 10 olives
1 tablespoon olive oil
1 garlic clove crushed
1 tablespoon lemon juice
1/2 tea salt
1 pineapple, chopped finely

Be creative. Enjoy the variety cheeses you can create!

Pizza Pie, Vegan Style

1 large homemade base (or you can use Lebanese bread for the base)
½ cup soy cheese (can increase/decrease depending on your preference)
¼ cup fresh basil leaves
4 tbsp. tomato paste
1 vegetarian sausage
10 cherry tomatoes
5 large mushrooms
2 tbsp. pine nuts
salt & pepper to taste

1. Preheat oven to 350°F (180°C). Chop cherry tomatoes into halves, slice vegetable sausage and the mushrooms.
2. Spread the tomato paste evenly around the Lebanese bread base. Then place tomatoes, sausage, basil and mushrooms onto the base.
3. Thinly slice the soy cheese into pieces. (Most soy cheese won't grate but can be easily sliced and then place on top of the pizza.)
3. Sprinkle pine nuts and season with a sprinkle of salt and pepper and cook in preheated oven for 15 minutes.

Grilled Pepper Pizza

2 teaspoons olive oil
¼ teaspoon salt
¼ teaspoon pepper
1 cup yellow bell pepper rings
1 cup green bell pepper rings
1 cup red bell pepper rings
1 cup sliced red onion, separated into rings
cooking spray 2 (10-inch) pizza crusts
any combination of bell peppers can be used.

1. Combine first three ingredients in a small bowl; set aside.
2. Prepare grill. Place bell peppers and onion on grill rack coated with cooking spray; grill 10 to 12 minutes or until tender. Set aside.
3. Place 1 crust on grill rack coated with cooking spray; grill 3 minutes or until puffy and golden.
4. Turn crust, grill-mark side up; brush with half of oil mixture. Top with half of grilled vegetables.
5. Cover and grill 4 to 5 minutes or until crust is lightly browned.
6. Repeat with remaining crust and toppings.

Homemade Pizza Base

1 cup warm water	1½ cup plain flour
¾ teaspoon salt	2 teaspoons caster sugar
2 tablespoons olive oil	2 teaspoons dried active baking yeast

1. Add ingredients in the order suggested by your manufacturer. Set for dough setting and start machine. When the unit signals, remove dough.
2. Pat dough into a greased 8-inch round pizza pan. Let stand 10 minutes. Preheat oven to 400°F. Spread pizza sauce over dough. Sprinkle toppings over sauce. Bake 15 to 20 minutes, or until crust is golden brown.

Green Beans Stewed with Onions, Tomatoes and Dill

Serves 4

1 pound green beans or a mixture of green and yellow wax beans 8 boiling onions, about 1½ inch wide
2 tablespoons virgin olive oil
1 large garlic clove, thinly sliced pinch of cumin seeds or dried cumin salt
1 cup canned tomatoes, chopped, or
2 large fresh tomatoes, peeled, seeded, and chopped
1 tablespoon chopped fresh dill or ½ teaspoon dried
1 tablespoon chopped parsley tomato juice or water

1. Choose beans that are bright and firm.
2. The smaller ones will be less fibrous.
3. Top and tail them, then cut into pieces about
4. 1½ inches long and wash them well.
5. Peel the onions and slice them into rounds.
6. Warm the olive oil and add the onion, garlic, and cumin seeds.
7. Cook over a gentle heat for several minutes, until the onions begin to soften.
8. Salt lightly then add the beans; cover them with the chopped tomatoes and herbs.
9. Add several tablespoons tomato juice or water, cover the pan tightly, and cook over medium heat until the beans are tender, about 15 minutes.

Mushroom Stroganoff Casserole

Serves 6-8

1 pound dry bow-tie pasta (farfalle)
2 tablespoons olive (or vegetable) oil
1 medium yellow onion, chopped
2-3 cloves garlic, minced
1 pound mushrooms, cleaned and sliced
  black pepper, to taste
2 10 ¾ oz. cans Cream of Mushroom soup
1 cup half-and-half
8 ounces mozzarella cheese, grated
¼ cup parmesan cheese, grated

1. Cook the pasta until 'al dente' in a pot of boiling, salted water (or according to package directions).
2. Drain, rinse under cold water and drain again.
3. Set aside. Heat a large skillet and coat with the olive or vegetable oil.
4. Sauté onion and garlic for a few minutes then add the sliced mushrooms and sauté with the onions and garlic for about 7 minutes, or until mushrooms are just cooked through and onion is translucent.
5. Add black pepper to taste. Leave to cool a bit.
6. In a bowl, whisk the two cans of soup with one cup of half-and-half until smooth.
7. Set aside. Coat bottom of a glass 9x13-inch baking dish with non-stick spray oil.
8. Place 1 cup of the soup mixture in the bottom of the dish and spread to coat.
9. Now begin layering the casserole: Start with half of the cooked pasta, and continue layering with half the sautéed mushrooms, half of the remaining soup mixture and half of the grated mozzarella.
10. Repeat with one more layer.
11. Sprinkle the parmesan cheese over the top. (Casserole may be covered and refrigerated at this point, for up to one day.
12. Take out of refrigerator one hour before baking.) Bake at 350°F for 50-60 minutes, until casserole is bubbling and browned on top.
13. Let rest 5-10 minutes before serving.

Artichoke & Kidney Bean Paella

Serves 4

1 tablespoon olive oil
1 medium onion, chopped
2 cloves garlic, minced
1 14.5 oz. can vegetable broth
1 cup uncooked long-grain rice
1 cup frozen peas
½ teaspoon ground turmeric (or ⅛ tsp. saffron)
3 drops red pepper sauce
1 15 oz. can dark red kidney beans, rinsed & drained
1 6 oz. jar marinated artichoke hearts, drained

1. Heat oil in a 12-inch skillet over medium-high heat.
2. Cook onion and garlic in oil 3-4 minutes, stirring frequently, until crisp-tender.
3. Stir in broth and rice.
4. Heat to boiling and then reduce heat.
5. Cover and simmer 15 minutes.
6. Stir in remaining ingredients.
7. Cook uncovered 5-10 more minutes, stirring occasionally, until rice and peas are tender.

Braised Red Cabbage

1 kg red cabbage
2 onions, chopped
2 cooking apples; peeled, cored and grated
1 teaspoon grated nutmeg
¼ teaspoon ground cloves ¼ teaspoon ground cinnamon
1 tablespoon soft dark brown sugar
3 tablespoons red wine vinegar
1½ tbsp. margarine (or ¼ cup olive oil)
fresh thyme sprigs; for garnish

1. Pre-heat oven to 325°F
2. Cut off and discard the large white ribs from the outer leaves of the cabbages then finely shred it.
3. Layer the shredded cabbage in a large ovenproof dish with the onions, apples, nutmeg, cloves, cinnamon and sugar.
4. Pour over the wine vinegar.
5. Cut the butter into cubes and scatter over the mixture.
6. Cover the dish and cook in the oven for about 1½ hours, stirring a couple of times, until the cabbage is very tender.
7. Serve hot garnished with thyme sprigs.

Bulgur Stuffed Cabbage

1 small head green cabbage
1 cup finely chopped parsley
2 onions, chopped
4 celery stalks, chopped
¼ tsp. Italian seasoning
½ tbsp. minced garlic
2 15-oz cans tomato sauce
4 cup water
2 cup dry bulgur
1 8-oz can tomato sauce
½ cup water

1. Remove core from cabbage, place cabbage head in steamer and steam until all leaves are soft and separate easily.
2. Sauté parsley, onions, celery, seasoning, and garlic in oil substitute until onions are soft.
3. Add 2 15-oz. cans of tomato sauce, 4 cups water and bulgur.
4. Cook about ½ hr. over medium heat, stirring occasionally, until bulgur is tender.
5. Remove from heat.
6. To stuff cabbage leaves, place a spoonful of mixture in center of each leaf.
7. Starting at one side, roll leaf up and fold ends under.
8. Place in a deep baking pan.
9. Mix the 8 oz. can of tomato sauce with ½ cup water and pour over stuffed cabbage leaves so they remain moist during baking.
10. Bake at 375°F for about 30 min. until cabbage is hot.

Cabbage with Juniper Berries

Serves 4
1½ tbsp. margarine (or ¼ cup olive oil)
1 medium onion, chopped
1 clove garlic; crushed
6 juniper berries; crushed
1 lb. cabbage; shredded

1. Melt the butter in a large saucepan.
2. Add the onion, garlic and juniper berries and lightly cook for 5 minutes, until the onion is soft.
3. Add the cabbage and stir until well coated with butter.
4. Cover and cook the cabbage in its own juices for 10 minutes, stirring occasionally.
5. The cabbage should be slightly crunchy and not soft.
6. Serve hot.

Cabbage & Carrot Curry

Serves 4 to 6
4 cups of finely chopped green cabbage
2 cups of graded carrots (loosely packed)
1 small onion finely sliced
2 tablespoons of vegetable oil
½ tablespoon of crushed ginger
1 teaspoon of crushed garlic
1 packet of Easy Curry's Veggie Curry spice mix
½ tablespoon of salt
1 tablespoon of water
finely chopped chilies if desired

1. Heat a non-stick pan under medium heat.
2. Add oil and let it get hot. Add onions; stir, cover, and sauté for 2-3 minutes until slightly golden brown.
3. Add garlic, ginger, (chilies), water, Veggie Curry spice mix, stir occasionally, cover and sauté for 3-4 min.
4. Add cabbage, carrots, salt, mix well and cover.
5. Lower heat to medium-low. Simmer for 5-10 min.
6. The curry is now cooked but you can cook it longer if you want crunchier veggies. Turn off heat.
7. Serve curry on bed of rice.

Sautéed Kale

This recipe can be used for any green, leafy vegetable such as Savoy cabbage, collard greens, spinach or any combination of the latter.

1 pound kale, tough stems and center ribs discarded and leaves cut into 1-inch-wide strips (8 cups)
2 tablespoons olive oil
1 small red onion, halved lengthwise and thinly sliced crosswise
1 garlic clove, minced
pinch of dried hot red pepper flakes
1 tablespoon red-wine vinegar, or to taste
¼ teaspoon salt

1. Cook kale in a 6-quart pot of boiling salted water, uncovered, stirring occasionally, until just tender, about 10 minutes, then drain in a colander.
2. Heat oil in a 12-inch heavy skillet over moderately high heat until hot but not smoking, then sauté onion, stirring occasionally, until softened, 6 to 8 minutes.
3. Add garlic and red pepper flakes and sauté, stirring, until garlic is fragrant, about 1 minute.
4. Reduce heat to moderate, then add kale and cook, stirring occasionally, until heated through.
5. Remove from heat and stir in vinegar and salt.

Quick Saucy Vegetables

Serves 2

2 cups frozen mixed vegetables
1 cup water
2 tablespoons soy sauce
1 tablespoon cornstarch or arrowroot
¼ cup water

Seasoning options

½ teaspoon turmeric
½ teaspoon ground cumin
½ teaspoon cajun spice mix -or-
½ teaspoon dried basil
½ teaspoon dried dill
½ teaspoon paprika -or-
½ teaspoon dried thyme
½ teaspoon dried rosemary
½ teaspoon dried marjoram

1. Cook the vegetables in the 1 cup of water until tender, about 8 to 10 minutes.
2. Add the soy sauce and optional seasonings of your choice. Mix the cornstarch or arrowroot in the ¼ cup of water.
3. Add to vegetable mixture while stirring.
4. Cook and stir until thickened.
5. Serve over rice, pasta or potatoes.

Easy Pie Crust

1½ cups fat free cookie crumbs or fat free graham cracker crumbs
3 tablespoons apple juice concentrate

1. Preheat oven to 350 degrees.
2. Make crumbs by processing in a blender or food processor.
3. Combine crumbs and concentrate.
4. Mix well. Press into bottom and sides of a 9 inch non-stick pie pan. Bake for 5 minutes. Cool before filling.
5. If using with a no bake filling, chill and serve.
6. If baking, bake as directed.

Recipe Hint: This crust gets soggy if it sits for longer than 1 day. It can be baked, cooled and filled another day. Other sweeteners may also be used. Try orange juice concentrate with peach or apricot pies. Pure maple syrup also works well.

Soups & Stews

Navy Bean Soup

There are numerous ways to make Navy Bean Soup. By adding other healthy herbs and vegetables, this can be a complete meal providing proper nutrition for the entire family. Here is just one way to prepare Navy Bean Soup.

You can omit/substitute any ingredients you prefer:

2 cups navy beans
8 cups water
4 carrots, sliced
3 tbsp. balsamic vinegar, red wine
vinegar or veggie stock
2 onions, chopped
5 cloves of garlic, minced
1 cup celery leaves and tender, inner stalks chopped fine
1 bell pepper, chopped
2 bay leaves
15 oz. can tomatoes
¼ tsp. ground cloves
½ tsp. powdered mustard
½ tsp. chili powder
½ tsp. black pepper
½ tsp. thyme
1 tbsp. parsley flakes
½ tsp. Salt
1 dash tobasco sauce
2 tbsp. barley miso, optional

1. Wash and pick over beans. Cover with water and soak overnight, or quick soak (quick soak: boil beans for 3 minutes, remove from heat, let sit for an hour, drain) Discard soaking water, rinse beans and put in a large soup pot.
2. Add the 8c of water and bring to a boil. Cover tightly and reduce heat to a low simmer.
3. Add carrots. In a nonstick pan sauté onion in balsamic vinegar until it caramelizes (This takes a while on low heat).
4. Add garlic, celery leaves, and bell pepper. Continue sautéing, adding more liquid as necessary.
5. When the mixture has cooked down somewhat, add it to the beans.
6. Add the remaining ingredients except the miso. Simmer *very* slowly for 2 hours, stirring occasionally.
7. Stir in the miso and simmer from 1 to 2 more hours, until beans are as tender as desired.
8. Remove bay leaves and serve with hard bread and salad.

From *The Hood Health Handbook: A Practical Guide to Health and Wellness in the Urban Community* also available from Supreme Design Publishing.

Asiatic (Navy) Bean Soup

2 cups of navy beans
6 cups water (to cover beans)
1 cup vegetable stock
4 medium onions
1 tablespoon brown sugar
⅓ cup veg. oil or extra virgin olive oil
1 green pepper
2 carrots

2 bay leaves
3 stems celery
3 clove garlic
black pepper
1 tablespoon thyme
2 tablespoon sage
2 tablespoon turmeric
½ can tomato paste
salt

1. Pick and wash beans. Soak beans overnight. Rinse beans.
2. Place in pot, along with vegetables and seasonings and oil. Add water to well cover beans.
3. Cook on moderate flame until beans will mash easy to the touch.
4. Add vegetable stock. When beans are well done you may blend them with a whole food processor or blender.
5. If the soup is still too thick, add a little boiling water.
6. Strain. (You can use a Foley Food Strainer to remove the hull of the bean.)*

* Though many people do not strain their beans to eat them, straining is a process that achieves a smoother texture. But it's fine if you eat them in their hull (skin). Blending does not remove the hull.

Split Pea & Lentil Soup

½ pound green split peas
¼ pound orange lentils
1½ large onions, quartered
4 stalks celery, including leaves, rinsed and chopped
2 tomatoes, peeled
2 leeks, white part only, cut into 1" chunks
5 cups water, (about)
¼ pound soy margarine -or- 3 tablespoons olive oil
crushed black peppercorn / sea salt

1. Place split peas, lentils, onions, celery, tomatoes and leeks in large pot and cover with water.
2. Bring to boil, lower heat and simmer about 1½ hours, until split peas and lentils are soft.
3. Add olive oil and stir until melted. Add peppercorns and sea salt to taste.

Vegetable Stew

⅓ cup olive oil
1 large red onion, chopped
2 celery ribs, cut into ¼-inch-thick slices
3 carrots, cut into ¼-inch-thick slices
4 garlic cloves, finely chopped
1 bunch Lacinato, red or curly kale
½ cup water (from boiled vegetables)
1 (28-ounces) can stewed tomatoes in juice, drained, juice reserved and tomatoes chopped, -or- 1¾ pounds fresh tomatoes, chopped
2 bell peppers (1 red, 1 yellow), cut into ¾-inch pieces
¾ pound green beans, trimmed and cut into 2-inch pieces
1¼ pounds zucchini and/or yellow squash, halved lengthwise and cut into ¼-inch-thick slices
¾ pound red potatoes (about 2 medium), unpeeled and cut into 1 inch pieces

1. Heat oil in a 7 to 8-quart heavy pot over medium-high heat until it shimmers.
2. Add onions, celery, carrots, and garlic and cook, stirring occasionally, until pale golden, about 10 minutes.
3. Stir in tomatoes with juice and bell peppers, then reduce heat to low and cook, uncovered, stirring occasionally, 15 minutes.
4. Meanwhile, cook green beans in a 3- to 4- quart saucepan of well-salted boiling water until crisp-tender, about 5 minutes. Transfer with a slotted spoon to a large bowl.
5. Add zucchini to boiling water and cook until crisp-tender, about 5 minutes.
6. Transfer with slotted spoon to bowl with green beans. Add potatoes to boiling water and cook until just tender, about 10 minutes.
7. Drain and add to beans and zucchini.
8. Add boiled vegetables to stew and simmer with kales and ½ cup of water, stirring, until all vegetables are very slightly tender, about 10 minutes. Season with 1½ teaspoons sea salt and 1 teaspoon pepper.

Green Gumbo

1½ cup veggie stock (or prepared bouillon)
1 bunch kale, chopped
½ lb fresh okra, sliced ¼" thick
2 large portobello (or ordinary) mushrooms,
    diced small (¼")
½ cup fat-free roux (see below)
3-4 ribs celery, sliced across in ¼" pieces
1 green pepper, chopped
1 large onion, chopped Pepper, veggie bouillon

1. Cook the kale in the veggie stock, covered, until tender.
2. Hold in the stock while preparing the other ingredients.

Roux:

Put ½ cup flour in a large-bottom well-seasoned cast iron pot or skillet and stir constantly over medium-low heat until caramel colored and toasty smelling (You could use a non-stick skillet or an old cast iron "gumbo pot").

As soon as it gets to the point you want it, put in the chopped pepper, onion, celery and mushrooms and stir, increasing heat a bit, until the onion is clear (and the whole thing smells wonderful and "cooked").

(If you prepared a couple cups of the toasted roux flour ahead and stored it in the icebox, you should then dry sauté the vegetables until the onion is clear and edges a bit brown, and it smells good.)

1. Add ½ cup of toasted flour and stir in, then proceed with the rest of the recipe.
2. Now add all the other ingredients, including the kale and the stock the kale cooked in.
3. Cook for 20 min. to a half hour, or until the okra is done but still a bit crunchy.
4. Taste for seasoning; if it needs more salt, add veggie bouillon to bring it up and round out the flavor.
5. Serve hot over cooked rice, and pass the Tabasco.
6. If you like, you could also sprinkle a ¼ tsp. of gumbo file over it at the table, but this is not necessary because the okra is in there.

We put a big ring of rice in a flat soup bowl, put a big scoop of fat-free refried beans in the middle, and put the gumbo in a ring over the rice.
On the side we had toasted french bread and a head of roasted garlic to spread on it.
T'was a satisfying fall meal.

Creamy Mushroom Soup

Serves 4 to 6
12 ounces mushrooms
1 pint of soy milk
1 pint of water
1 tablespoon of finely chopped fresh parsley
1½ ounces of Soy margarine
3 tablespoons of unbleached white flour
salt & pepper
garlic salt to taste

1. Slice and chop the mushrooms into small pieces about the size of a garlic clove.
2. Put the mushrooms and the water into a saucepan, bring to boil and simmer for a few minutes.
3. Strain the mushrooms and set aside, keep the stock.
4. Melt the margarine in a large saucepan and stir in the flour and cook gently for a few minutes until a smooth paste is formed.
5. Keep the pan on the heat and add the mushroom stock and the Soy milk to the flour a little at a time continuously to avoid lumps.
6. Add the chopped parsley and the seasonings and simmer for 10 minutes stirring occasionally to avoid sticking.
7. Add the cooked mushrooms and adjust the seasoning to taste. Reheat the soup but do not boil.
8. Serve immediately. If you want a 'creamier' soup stir in some Soy cream before serving.

Pumpkin Soup

Serves 6
1¾ pounds pumpkin, cleaned and cut -or-
    4 cups pumpkin cubes
1½ quarts water
2 tablespoons olive oil
2 onions, chopped
¾ cup chopped parsley
sea salt

1. Add freshly ground black pepper, to taste.
2. In a large saucepan, simmer pumpkin cubes in the water until they are very tender.
3. Meanwhile, heat oil in a frying pay and sauté onions until golden.
4. Puree pumpkin and liquid in a blender or food processor, or press through a strainer, and return to pan. Add the sautéed onions and parsley.
5. Season to taste and heat through.

Roasted Spaghetti Squash with Peas and Lemon

1 2-3 pound spaghetti squash
1 cup frozen petite peas, thawed
4 tablespoons lemon juice
2 tablespoons margarine
1 teaspoon dried marjoram
salt and pepper

1. Place whole spaghetti squash on cooking grate.
2. Cook 35 to 45 minutes or until squash pierces easily with a fork. Turn every 10 minutes.
3. Remove squash from the grill; allow to cool.
4. Cut squash in half lengthwise and scoop out the seeds.
5. Using the tines of a fork, scrape the inside of the squash to remove the spaghetti-like strands.
6. In a Large Foil Pan place the spaghetti squash, peas, lemon juice, butter, marjoram, salt, and pepper.
7. Gently toss all ingredients.
8. Place pan in center of cooking grate and cook about 10 minutes or until heated through.

A Pilgrim's Lentil Pottage

2 teaspoons olive oil
2 cloves garlic, finely chopped
1 medium onion, chopped
8 cups cold water
1½ cups lentils, rinsed and drained
3 tablespoons ketchup
⅛ teaspoon ground cloves 1½ teaspoons salt and pepper, or to taste dash freshly ground black pepper

1. In a large soup kettle, heat oil over medium heat.
2. Stir in garlic, carrots and onion.
3. Cook, stirring constantly, until vegetables wilt but not brown.
4. Add water, lentils, ketchup, cloves and salt; cover and bring to a boil.
5. Reduce heat to low and cook, stirring occasionally, 45 minutes or until lentils are tender.
6. If soup gets too thick, add more water.
7. Reheat before serving, adding pepper.
8. Add vinegar, wine or lemon juice for extra flavor.

Note: For a variation, refrigerate overnight to allow flavors to blend.

Classic Black Bean Soup

1¾ cups black beans, soaked overnight
12 cups water
2 teaspoons olive oil
1½ cups onion, diced
2 teaspoons garlic, minced
½ cup green onion, diced
¾ cup carrot, diced
¾ cup red bell pepper, diced
2 teaspoons ground sage
1 bay leaf
1 teaspoon ground rock salt or salt-free seasoning
2 teaspoons powdered vegetable broth (1 veg. bullion)
dash freshly ground pepper, to taste

1. Discard soaking water from beans.
2. Beans will have swollen to much more than 1¾ cups, so do not re-measure the soaked beans.
3. In large, heavy bottomed soup pot, heat olive oil or water and onion, garlic, green onion, carrot, and red pepper.
4. Add sage and bay leaf and sauté for several minutes or until onions begin to wilt.
5. Add soaked and drained beans and fresh water. Bring to a boil and skim off any scum that may form on the top.
6. Reduce cooking temperature to low, cover soup and allow to cook for 3 hours, stirring occasionally and taking care that heat is low enough so that beans do not stick.
7. At end of cooking time, uncover and allow soup to continue cooking as you stir in salt, if desired, powdered vegetable broth and fresh pepper to taste.
8. Discard bay leaf.
9. Use hand blender to puree soup to desired consistency, breaking down only about half the beans, or transfer half the soup to a blender, puree and return to soup pot. Adjust seasonings.

Meatless Chili

Serves 6

2 tablespoons vegetable oil
1 medium onion, chopped
1½ teaspoons chili powder (or more, to taste)
2 packets TVP Chunks
  -or- (4 ½ ounce vegetable burgers, crumbled
1½ cups vegetable stock or water (¾ when using
  vegetable burgers)
1 can tomatoes (16 ounce) chopped, liquid reserved
1 can red kidney beans (16 ounce) do not drain
2 Mexican green chilies in brine drained, chopped
  (optional).
salt and freshly ground pepper, to taste

1. Heat oil in large saucepan.
2. Add onion, sauté until golden brown.
3. Add chili powder and TVP, sauté 5 minutes.
4. Add vegetable stock, tomatoes, kidney beans, green chilies and reserved liquid from tomatoes.
5. Cover, simmer 20 minutes. Serve with rice, mashed potatoes or an avocado salad.

Black-Eyes & Barley

2 16oz cans black-eye peas, rinsed & drained
⅛ tsp. salt
1c chopped onions
¼ tsp. pepper
½ cup chopped celery
¼ tsp. dried thyme
⅓ cup uncooked barley
¼ tsp. dried rosemary
1 cup water
(You can substitute 2 cups soymilk for 1 cup water)
¼ tsp. garlic powder
1 bay leaf, broken in half

1. Preheat oven to 350.
2. Lightly oil a 1¾ QT casserole, or spray w/ Pam.
3. In large bowl, combine all ingredients.
4. Place in casserole, cover tightly, bake 1¼ hours.
5. Stir once, halfway through cooking time.
6. Discard bay leaf before serving.

Hearty Split Pea Soup with Beans and Barley

14 cups water
2 cups onions, diced
1½ cups carrots, diced
2 cups celery, diced
⅔ cup fresh parsley, minced
4 green onion, thinly sliced
2 cloves garlic, minced
1 medium zucchini, quartered & sliced
⅓ cup green split peas
⅓ cup yellow split peas
2½ tablespoons barley
2 tablespoons baby lima beans or other tiny white beans
3 tablespoons ajuki beans
1 tablespoon powdered vegetable broth
dash seasoned salt or any salt-free seasoning
dash freshly ground pepper.

1. Bring water to a boil in a large soup pot.
2. Add the ingredients in the order given, except for the salt and pepper, which can be added at the end of the cooking time.
3. Return soup to a boil, skimming off any foam or scum that comes to the surface with a large spoon. (Repeat this skimming process several times in the first half-hour of cooking, until no more scum forms.) Cover and reduce heat to medium-low.
4. Simmer soup for 2½ hours, stirring periodically to ensure that the barley isn't sticking.
5. At end of cooking time, adjust seasonings to taste.

Sweet Potatoes w/ Black Bean Chili

Serves 4

4 medium sweet potatoes
2 tablespoons vegetable oil
1 small green pepper, chopped
1 (15 oz.) can black beans w/chili spices (or add), undrained
1 14.5 oz. can Mexican-style stewed tomatoes undrained
¼ cup sour cream (optional)
1 tablespoon fresh cilantro, chopped

6. Heat oven to 350°. Pierce potatoes with a fork to allow steam to escape. Bake for 50-60 minutes.
7. Alternatively, microwave potatoes uncovered on high for 8-10 minutes.
8. While potatoes are baking, heat oil in a 12-inch skillet over medium-high heat.
9. Cook bell pepper in oil 3-5 min., stirring frequently.
10. Stir in beans and tomatoes.

Sweet Bean Soup

1 lb. adzuki beans or black-eyed peas (tofu instructions in text)
¼ tsp. Chinese 5-spice powder -or- ¼ tsp. each ground cinnamon & cloves or your favorite sweet spice.
water
½ cup brown sugar or turbinado sugar or the equivalent in your favorite sweetener

1. Rinse the beans in a colander, then place in a large pan, bring to boil, boil 1 min.
2. Turn off heat, let sit one hour or allow beans to set overnight in water to the top of the pot.
3. The beans will about triple in volume. Drain off water.
4. Add sugar & fresh water to cover and spices.
5. Taste liquid. Add more sugar and/or spice if you think it's needed.
6. Cook until the beans are tender, adding more water if needed.
7. This will vary with the type of bean and their age.
8. Probably 45 minutes to 1½ hours.
9. As the beans are cooling add salt, if you use it, to taste.
10. Also add more sugar or spice if you think it needs it.
11. This is good either hot or cold as a dessert.
12. No time to cook beans? Use canned or make the sweetened liquid, slice soft silken tofu and heat in the hot liquid or just cover with the chilled liquid.
13. Vary the spices and sweetener to get different tastes.
14. Try maple syrup for a portion of the liquid after cooking (use less or no sugar during the cooking process) if you love maple, or just pour it over the tofu.
15. This keeps 4 or 5 days in the refrigerator.
16. Freeze for longer storage.

Stuffed Pumpkin

2 cups raw basmati rice
1 cup raisins
Sherry to cover raisins
Pumpkin (cheese pumpkins are the best, smoother) about 12-14 inches
1 stick margarine
¾ pound apples, peeled and sliced
¾ pound pears, peeled and sliced
¾ cup slivered almonds
½ cup dried apricots, chopped
4 tablespoons rice syrup (optional), or juice concentrate (apple or orange)
1 teaspoon cinnamon
½ teaspoons nutmeg
½ teaspoons mace
½ teaspoons allspice
½ teaspoons cardamom
½ teaspoons freshly ground pepper
salt to taste

1. Cook rice, and while doing so, soak raisins.
2. Preheat oven to 325°F.
3. Cut top of pumpkin and remove all seeds and strings.
4. Using a spoon, carefully scrape out a layer of flesh without breaking the shell (about 1 lb.)
5. Steam pumpkin meat until tender
6. Heat 2 tablespoons margarine, and sauté apples, pears, almonds, and apricots, about 5 min.
7. Add 2 tablespoons rice syrup, spices, cooked rice, steamed pumpkin, and salt
8. Melt remaining margarine, and stir in remaining rice syrup.
9. Add a little cinnamon, and brush inside of pumpkin with it.
10. Spoon filling into pumpkin and replace lid..
11. Place on oiled baking sheet and bake for one hour.
12. Place on large platter, and surround with fall-colored flowers, and leaves.
13. Serve with stuffing, caramel carrots, cranberry sauce, salad, and biscuits.

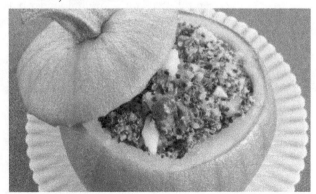

Baked Pumpkin with TVP, Vegetable and Peach Filling

Serves 6

A 10-12 lb pumpkin, or other large winter squash
½ cup butter, softened
2 tbsp. olive oil
2 lbs TVP, cut into 1-inch cubes
1 cup coarsely chopped onions
½ cup coarsely chopped green peppers
½ tsp. chopped garlic
4 cups stock
½ cup Sherry
3 medium tomatoes, peeled, seeded and coarsely chopped, or substitute 1 cup chopped, drained, canned Italian plum tomatoes
½ tsp. dried oregano
1 bay leaf
1 tsp. salt
cayenne pepper to taste
freshly ground pepper
1 lb sweet potatoes, peeled and cut into ½ inch cubes (about 3 cups)
1 lb white potatoes, peeled and cut into ½ inch cubes (about 3 cups)
1 lb zucchini, scrubbed but not peeled, and cut into ¼ inch slices (about 2 cups)
3 ears corn, shucked and cut into rounds 1 inch wide
4 fresh peaches, peeled, pitted and diced

1. Preheat the oven to 375°F.
2. Scrub the outside of the pumpkin under cold running water with a stiff brush.
3. With a large, sharp knife, cut down into the top of the pumpkin to create a lid 6 or 7 inches in diameter.
4. Leave the stem intact as a handle.
5. Lift out the lid and, with a large metal spoon, scrape the seeds and stringy fibers from the lid and from the pumpkin shell.
6. Brush the inside of the pumpkin with the soft butter.
7. Place the pumpkin in a large shallow roasting pan and bake in the oven for 45 minutes, or until tender but somewhat resistant when pierced with the tip of a small, sharp knife.
8. The pumpkin shell should remain firm enough to hold the filling without danger of collapsing.
9. Meanwhile, heat the oil over moderate heat in a heavy 6-8 quart casserole until a light haze forms above it.

10. Add the cubes of TVP and brown them on all sides, turning them frequently with a large spoon.
11. Then with a slotted spoon, transfer the meat to a platter.
12. To the oil, remaining in the pan, add a 1tsp. oil, add the onions, green pepper and garlic, and cook over moderate heat, stirring constantly, for about 5 minutes, or until the vegetables are soft but not brown.
13. Pour in the stock and Sherry and bring to a boil over high heat.
14. Scrape in any brown bits clinging to the bottom and sides of the pan.
15. Return the TVP and any of its accumulated juices to the pan and stir in the tomatoes, oregano, bay leaf, salt and a few grindings of black pepper.
16. Cover the pan, reduce the heat to low, and simmer undisturbed for 15 minutes.
17. Then add the sweet potatoes and white potatoes, cover the pan and cook for 15 minutes; add the zucchini slices, cover the pan again and cook for 10 minutes.
18. Finally add the corn rounds and peaches and cook, still covered, for 5 minutes longer.
19. Pour the entire contents of the pan carefully into the baked pumpkin, cover the pumpkin with its lid again, and bake for another 15 minutes in a 375°F oven.
20. To serve, place the pumpkin on a large serving platter and, at the table, ladle the "veggie carbonada" from the pumpkin onto heated, individual serving plates.

Pumpkin Stew

2-3 onions
4 cups of diced pumpkin or squash
½ tsp. each, cumin, coriander, powdered ginger dash cayenne pepper
2 bay leaves
¾ cup millet or barley
6 or more cups water
3-4 cups of chopped root vegetables, including potatoes, carrots, parsnips etc.
¼ cup soy sauce or miso

1. In a large pot, sauté onions. When golden brown add the other vegetables, spices, and water.
2. Bring all of this to a boil, reduce to a simmer, and cook covered for
3. ½ hour or until pumpkin, vegetables, and grains are soft. The taste is delicious, and it and freezes well.

Winter Casserole

Serves 4

1 red pepper, deseeded and chopped
1 medium onion, chopped
¾ lb root vegetables (parsnips, carrots, etc.) chopped (mix/match!)
1 can mixed bean salad or make your own (marinated green bean, wax bean and kidney bean)
1 12 oz. can tomatoes
as much garlic as you like, crushed
1½ tsp. yeast extract
1 tbsp. tomato puree
2 bay leaves
1 tsp. mixed herbs
½ pint water
olive oil

1. Sautee the onion, pepper and garlic in the olive oil for a few minutes, in a casserole dish.
2. Add the vegetables and cook for about five minutes.
3. Throw everything else into the pan (you may have to adapt the amount of water depending on the size of your dish, and the amount of liquid in your cans, which I drain off.).
4. Bring to the boil, then cover and place into a preheated low to medium oven (about 250 – 300°F).
5. Cook for 1.5 hours, checking every half an hour or so to make sure it is not drying out. Remove the bay-leaves before serving.

Southwestern Stuffed Squash

Serves 4

2 acorn or butternut squash, cut in half, and seeded

Filling:

2 cups tomato juice
1 cup couscous
1 cup salsa
¼ cup chopped black olives
1 4 oz. can chopped green chilies
¼ cup chopped fresh cilantro
2 teaspoons ground cumin
salt & pepper to taste

1. Microwave squash on high for 4-5 minutes until slightly tender.
2. To prepare filling, bring tomato juice to a boil in medium saucepan.
3. Stir in couscous and reduce heat to simmer.
4. Cook about 5 to 8 minutes until couscous in done.
5. Remove couscous from heat and stir in remaining ingredients. Fill squash with about ½ cup of mixture.
6. Place in a large casserole and bake at 325 degrees F for 20-25 minutes.

Salads

Tangerine Frisee Salad with Grilled Sweet Potatoes

2 medium sweet potatoes, peel on
2½ tablespoons vegetable oil
1 tablespoon light soy sauce
1 clove garlic, minced
1 teaspoon sugar
4 sprigs fresh parsley
2 heads frisée lettuce, curly endive, romaine lettuce, or a combination
½ cup olive or peanut oil
5 tablespoons white wine
2 tablespoons honey mustard
1 tablespoon balsamic vinegar
1 tablespoon fresh chopped chervil
1 teaspoon toasted poppy seeds
4 tangerines, peeled and sectioned
salt and pepper

1. Wash sweet potatoes and boil in water until cooked ¾ through, about 20 to 25 minutes.
2. Cool and slice ¼" thick.
3. Do not peel.
4. For marinade, combine oil, soy sauce, garlic, sugar, and parsley sprigs in a resealable plastic bag.
5. Add sweet potato slices, turning to coat.
6. Close bag and marinate 6 to 8 hours or overnight, turning occasionally to distribute marinade.
7. Wash greens and separate from core.
8. Drain and pat dry with paper towels.
9. In large bowl, combine oil, wine, honey mustard, vinegar, chervil, and poppy seeds.
10. Add tangerine slices and toss to coat.
11. Season with salt and pepper to taste.
12. Add greens and toss.
13. Remove sweet potato slices from marinade and place in center of cooking grate.
14. Grill until warm, about 8 minutes, turning once halfway through grilling time.
15. Set aside and keep warm.
16. Arrange salad on large platter and garnish with grilled sweet potato slices.

Cranberry Pecan Salad

1 cup pecan halves
2 tablespoons raspberry vinegar
½ teaspoon Dijon mustard
½ teaspoon sugar
½ teaspoon salt
freshly ground black pepper to taste (optional)
6 tablespoons olive oil
6 cups mixed salad greens, rinsed and dried
¾ cup dried cranberries
1 medium avocado, cubed

1. Preheat oven to 400°F.
2. Spread pecans evenly on a baking sheet.
3. Toast for 8 to 10 minutes, or until lightly browned and fragrant.
4. In a small bowl, stir together the vinegar, mustard, sugar, salt, and pepper; mix until sugar and salt dissolve. Whisk in olive oil.
5. In a salad bowl, toss together the greens, cranberries, pecans, onions, and avocado.
6. Drizzle with vinaigrette, and toss gently to coat.

Mixed Green Salad with Oranges, Dried Cranberries and Pecans

1 cup plus 3 tablespoons orange juice
6 tablespoons dried cranberries
3½ tablespoons olive oil
2 tablespoons white wine vinegar
1 tablespoon grated orange peel
6 cups mixed baby greens
3 oranges, peel and white pith removed, segmented
¾ cup pecans, toasted

1. Bring 1 cup orange juice to simmer in heavy small saucepan.
2. Remove from heat. Mix in dried cranberries. Let stand until softened, about 30 minutes.
3. Drain well; discard soaking juice.
4. Whisk oil, vinegar, orange peel and remaining 3 tablespoons orange juice in small bowl to blend.
5. Mix in cranberries. Season dressing to taste with salt and pepper. (Can be prepared 1 day ahead.
6. Cover and refrigerate. Bring to room temperature before serving.)
7. Place greens in large bowl. Toss with ⅔ of dressing. Divide greens among 6 plates.
8. Add orange segments to bowl; toss with remaining dressing.
9. Top salads with orange segments and pecans.

Fennel Salad

Serves 5

12 radishes, trimmed
3 fennel bulbs, trimmed
2 medium carrots, peeled
1 green apple, cored (not too sour)
1 tablespoon fresh lemon juice
½ cup vegan mayonnaise, or less as needed

1. Make 4 vertical cuts, crossing in the centre, in each radish.
2. Soak in iced water for 2-3 hours or until the petals open; Drain.
3. Cut the fennel bulbs lengthwise in half and cut out the hard core. Slice very finely.
4. Cut the carrots into matchsticks and dice the apple.
5. Mix the lemon juice into the vegetables, and then toss with the mayonnaise.
6. Pile into a salad bowl and garnish with the radishes.

Note: This healthy, crunchy salad of fennel, carrot, apple and radish is dressed in a lemony mayonnaise, which adds to its freshness.

Pasta Salad

1 box pasta (rotini, farfalle)
2 small cucumbers diced into ¼in thick pieces
1 bag of shredded carrots
¾ cup black olives
2 cups broccoli crowns diced
1 cup red onion sliced
1 bottle of Italian dressing
1 tablespoon EVOO

1. Boil pasta until al-dente. While pasta is boiling, chop all vegetables and set aside.
2. When pasta is ready, place into a colander or strainer and rinse with cold water until noodles are cool.
3. Pour EVOO over pasta and toss.
4. Add pasta and vegetables to a large bowl or container. Drizzle with Italian dressing until no pasta is dry.
5. Retain Italian dressing to use once pasta is finished cooling.
6. Chill for 3-5 hours. Best if made in advance and refrigerated overnight.

Vegan Kale Salad

Serves 6-8

2 bunches of fresh kale (or a 1 lb bag), chopped
½ pack (or 2 cups) of shredded carrots
1 pack of Mushrooms (your preference), sliced
2 avocados, de-seeded and sliced
½ red bell pepper, diced
1 pint cherry tomatoes, halved
4 scallion stalks, diced
3 cloves fresh garlic, diced
⅛ cup extra virgin olive oil
⅛ cup Bragg's Liquid Aminos
⅛ cup agave nectar
1 tsp. cayenne pepper
1 tbsp. spike seasoning
1 lime, juiced

1. If using bunches of kale, clean thoroughly (I recommend washing 3 times), pick off stalks, and chop leaves into smaller pieces.
2. If using pre-washed bags, just place the kale in an extra-large salad bowl.
3. Add the shredded carrots, sliced mushrooms, sliced avocado, diced red bell pepper, halved cherry tomatoes, diced scallion and diced fresh garlic.
4. Then drizzle over the vegetables the olive oil, liquid aminos, and agave nectar.
5. Then sprinkle over the salad the cayenne pepper and spike seasoning.
6. Finally, squeeze 1 lime over the salad and mix thoroughly with your clean hands. (If you prefer more salt add a bit more liquid aminos, and if you prefer more spice add a little more cayenne pepper.)

Nicoise Green Beans

Serves 4

1 medium onion, chopped
2 stalks celery, chopped
1 pound green beans
15 ounces canned tomatoes, chopped
4 tablespoons vegetable stock
1 bay leaf
½ cup parsley, chopped
salt and pepper

1. Boil or steam beans until tender, 10 mins; drain and set aside. Heat oil in frying pan; gently sauté onions and celery until lightly browned.
2. Add tomatoes, stock, bay leaf and parsley to sauté.
3. Stir well; simmer 20 mins uncovered. Season to taste.
4. Add beans to sauce and stir well.
5. Bring back to simmer and cook 2 mins.
6. Serve with rice, mashed potatoes, or potato pancakes.

Green Bean Salad

1 lb cooked green beans (French/snap/string)
1 onion, chopped (size is your preference)
1 or more cloves garlic, pressed bottled non-fat, low-fat, or regular Italian dressing to moisten.

1. Let marinate overnight (at least 2 hrs) in refrigerator.
2. Sprinkle with 3 tablespoons chopped, toasted walnuts.

Cabbage Salad – Indian Style

2 cups thinly shredded cabbage
2 cup shredded carrot
½ cup crushed roasted peanuts
¼ cup peanut oil (salad oil is an OK substitute)
1 hot green chili chopped
½ cup chopped cilantro
½ tsp. sugar
lemon juice and salt to taste

Mix everything except salt and lemon; add them only when ready to eat.

Desserts

Fruit with Ginger

1 x 1lb. can of Dole Tropical fruit salad -or-
4 oranges -or-
2 grapefruit, peeled and made into slices or segments
¼ cup candied ginger

1. Cut the ginger into thin slivers with scissors and put in with the fruit
2. Add a little sugar (to taste)if using grapefruit.
3. Let set overnight or all day.
4. Don't freeze.
5. It seems to work best with citrus or Dole Tropical Fruit salad.
6. Use more or less ginger, to taste. It has to be the kind of ginger that is called candied or crystallized. It's cooked with sugar (and a tiny bit of water) to preserve it.
7. If you don't want to use white sugar, use another sweetener, grated or thinly sliced fresh ginger, cooked together until the ginger changes appearance, like candied fruit.

Ambrosia Fruit Salad

1 pummelo*
1 navel orange
1 tsp. Sucanat
¼ cup shredded coconut

1. Peel the pummelo and orange so no white membrane is left.
2. With a sharp knife, section the fruit by cutting it away from the membrane.
3. Mix the fruit in a bowl with Sucanat and coconut.

You can make endless variations of this by adding other favorite citrus fruits, nuts, etc., but this basic recipe is really good.

Note: *Pummelo is a green grapefruit-looking fruit that tastes somewhat like grapefruit but is much milder.

Tofu Pumpkin Pie

1 package firm tofu
2 cups canned pumpkin (or equivalent - see below)
⅔ cup maple syrup (More or less adjust to taste)
1 tsp. vanilla
1½ tsp. cinnamon (or 1 tablespoon pumpkin pie spice)
¾ tsp. ginger
¼ tsp. nutmeg (to taste)
¼ tsp. clove
1 unbaked pie crust (of your choosing)

1. Preheat oven to 400°F.
2. Blend drained tofu in processor or blender until smooth.
3. Add remaining ingredients and blend.
4. Pour into unbaked crust and bake 1 hour or until toothpick comes clean. Cool.

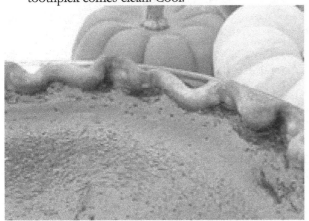

Apple 'Cake'

8 oz. self raising flour
4 oz. soy margarine
4 oz. unbleached sugar
1 lb cooking apples
soy milk

1. Pre-heat the oven to 400 degrees.
2. Grease a shallow baking tray.
3. Rub the margarine into the flour until the mixture resembles breadcrumbs.
4. Peel, core and grate the apples.
5. Mix the apples and sugar with the mixture, add a little milk to make a firm but dry mixture.
6. Spread the mixture in the tray and bake for about half an hour.
7. Let cool, cut into squares and serve as cake.

Champagne Sorbet with Wild Strawberries

2½ cup champagne
1¾ cup granulated sugar
2 cup Soda water
¼ cup lemon juice
¼ cup orange juice
¾ cup wild strawberries or fresh strawberries

1. Bring three-quarters of the champagne to a boil in a saucepan.
2. Remove from heat and let cool.
3. Combine the sugar and water in a pan and stir to dissolve sugar.
4. Bring mixture to a boil, and let cook 20 minutes, stirring frequently, until syrup forms a thread when pulled between your thumb and forefinger. Remove from heat immediately.
5. Stir champagne and fruit juices into the sugar syrup; cool.
6. Freeze mixture in a plastic container until hard, several hours or overnight.
7. In the bowl of an electric mixer, beat sorbet until smooth.
8. Return sorbet to freeze until firm.
9. Serve scoops of sorbet on chilled plates or in glasses, garnished with wild strawberries or strawberry slices.

Lemon Mousse

Serves 2-3
2 cup water
pinch sea salt
3 tbsp. agar flakes
concentrated apple juice and/or malt syrup as sweeteners, to taste.
1 tbsp. finely grated lemon rind
few drops vanilla essence (optional)
2 tbsp. tahini

1. Bring the water to the boil, add all the ingredients and simmer for 10 minutes, until the agar flakes are completely dissolved.
2. Pour this mixture into a glass or ceramic container and leave to cool and set (approx 1 - 2 hours).
3. Blend into a creamy consistency (either by hand or with a blender), adding a little water or fresh apple juice if the consistency is too thick
4. Serve the mousse chilled or at room temperature.

Vegan Apple Cobbler

3-4 Granny Smith apples
1 tsp. ground cinnamon
½ tsp. ground cloves
½ tsp. ground allspice
½ tsp. grated nutmeg
1 cup plus 1 tsp. sugar
½ cup (1 stick) margarine
1 cup unbleached all-purpose flour

1. Preheat the oven to 350°F. Grease a 9-inch pan.
2. Cut the apples into thin slices; place in the pan. Sprinkle the spices and 1 tsp. of the sugar over the apples.
3. Melt the margarine in a medium saucepan over medium heat.
4. Add the flour and remaining sugar. Cover the apples with the flour mixture.
5. Bake for 20 to 30 minutes or until the crust is lightly browned.
6. Prep. time: 15 minutes Baking time: 20 to 30 minutes.

Tofu Ice Cream Parfaits

2 cup soft tofu
2 tbsp. maple syrup
½ ripe banana
1 teaspoon vanilla extract
3 cup sliced strawberries or kiwifruit

1. In a blender or food processor, puree tofu, maple syrup, banana, and vanilla until very smooth and creamy.
2. Pour into a shallow pan and freeze overnight or for 8 hours.
3. Just before serving, cut frozen tofu mixture into small chunks and quickly blend to the consistency of ice cream.
4. Spoon into dessert glasses, alternating layers with sliced strawberries.
5. Serve immediately.

Note: Although the banana is hard to replace since it adds creaminess and masks any telltale soy taste, almost any fresh fruit in season can be substituted for the strawberries or kiwifruit. Try blackberries, peaches, pears, and apricots for variety.

Strawberry-Orange Spread

Makes 4 half pints of spread
20 oz. frozen strawberries; thawed
1¾ oz. fruit pectin; powdered (1 pack)
1 tbsp. orange peel; grated
½ cup orange juice
3½ cup sugar

1. Mix the strawberries, pectin, orange peel and orange juice in a 3-quart saucepan until the pectin is dissolved.
2. Heat over high heat, stirring constantly, to a rolling boil, about 2 minutes.
3. Add the sugar and bring back to a rolling boil, stirring constantly, then remove from the heat.
4. Skim off the foam and immediately pour into hot sterilized jars or glasses or freezer containers.
5. Cover tightly and cool to room temperature.
6. Refrigerate or freeze no longer than 3 months.

Mori-Nu Tofu Pumpkin Pie

1 pkgs mori-nu lite ex-firm tofu (for lighter texture, use mori-nu firm tofu)
2 cups canned or cooked pumpkin ⅔ cup barley malt
1 tsp. vanilla
1 tbsp. pumpkin pie spice, or next
4 ingredients ¾ tsp. ground ginger
¼ tsp. ground nutmeg
⅛ tsp. ground cloves
1 unbaked 9" pie crust

1. Drain tofu and blend in a food processor or blender until smooth.
2. Add remaining ingredients; blend well.
3. Pour into a 9" unbaked pie crust.
4. Bake in a preheated 350 degree oven for approximately one hour.
5. Filling will be soft, but will firm up as it chills.
6. Chill and serve.

Straw PoPs

3 cup soy milk
½ ripe banana
1 cup fresh strawberries or blueberries
⅛ cup maple syrup

1. Blend all ingredients until smooth.
2. Pour into popsicle molds or ice cube trays and freeze.

Raw Vegan Cheesecake

Dried coconut is used as the bottom layer (to replace the graham crackers); macadamia nuts used for the bulk of the "crust" layer; and cashews make the "cheese" portion.

Bottom Layer Ingredients:
¼ cup of dried coconut

Crust Ingredients:
1½ cups of raw macadamia nuts
½ cup of dates
1 pinch of sea salt (optional)

Raw Cashew Cheesecake Filling Ingredients:
3 cups of cashews
¾ cup of lemon juice
¾ cup of raw honey (or other raw sweetener)
¾ cup of coconut oil
1 tablespoon of vanilla

Sauce Ingredients:
2 cups frozen mixed berries (or any frozen fruit)
½ cup of dates

1. Sprinkle coconut on the bottom of cheesecake pan (or any glass 'baking' dish).
2. Blend crust ingredients (you'll see when it starts to get 'crusty') in food processor and spread on top of coconut layer.
3. Blend filling ingredients in food processor and then spread on top of crust layer.
4. Cool in fridge or freezer to firm up a bit. It took about 45 minutes in the freezer when I prepared it.
5. Blend sauce ingredients in food processor and then spread on top of cheesecake layer.

Vegan Chocolate Chip Cookies

1 cup softened margarine (I use Earth Balance Soyless)
¾ cup cane sugar
¾ cup brown sugar
1 teaspoon vanilla extract
egg replacer equal to 2 eggs
2¼ cups unbleached flour
1 teaspoon baking soda
½ teaspoon salt
1½ – 2 cups vegan chocolate chips

1. Cream together margarine, both sugars, vanilla and egg replacer. Add the flour, salt, baking soda and mix well.
2. Lastly, mix in the chocolate chips and spoon onto an ungreased cookie sheet leaving a space between each spoonful.
3. The batter will spread. Bake at 350°F for 15 minutes or until browned. (Makes about 2 dozen cookies)

Vegan Coffee Cake

Cake Batter Ingredients:
2 cups all-purpose flour
1 teaspoon baking powder
1 teaspoon baking soda
¼ teaspoon salt
½ cup vegan butter
1 cup vegan sugar
2 egg substitutes (½ cup apple sauce -or-
¼ cup plain vegan yogurt -or-
¼ cup silken tofu blended until smooth)
1 cup vegan sour cream
1 teaspoon vanilla extract

Topping Ingredients:
¼ cup vegan sugar
⅓ cup brown sugar
2.5 teaspoons ground cinnamon
½ cup chopped pecans or walnuts

1. **Cake** – Cream the vegan butter and sugar in a bowl. Then add sugar.
2. Add the egg replacer, sour cream and vanilla to the mix and mix well.
3. In a separate bowl, mix the flour, baking powder, baking soda and salt.
4. Combine the flour mixture to the sour cream mixture until combined well.
5. Pour half the total batter into a greased 13"x9" baking pan.
6. It looks like there may not be enough batter, but it rises a lot.
7. Mix the topping ingredients all together. Sprinkle half the topping over the batter then add the remaining batter on top.
8. Then add the remaining topping to the top of the 2nd layer of batter.
9. Bake for about 40 minutes or until toothpick comes out dry at 325 degrees.

Note: You can omit/substitute any ingredients you prefer.

From *The Hood Health Handbook: A Practical Guide to Health and Wellness in the Urban Community* also available from Supreme Design Publishing.

Easy Vegan Apple Pie Recipe

Serves 8

4-5 Granny Smith apples, cored and thinly sliced
⅓ cup vegan margarine, softened
⅓ cup packed brown sugar
1 tbsp. ground cinnamon
1 tsp. grated nutmeg

Pastry Dough:

1. Stir together flour and salt.
2. Cut in margarine till pieces are the size of small peas.
3. Sprinkle 1 tablespoon of the water over part of the mixture; gently toss with a fork.
4. Push to side of bowl.
5. Repeat till all is moistened.
6. Form dough into a ball. On a lightly floured surface, flatten dough with hands.
7. Roll dough from center to edge, forming a circle about 12 inches in diameter.
8. Ease pastry into a 9-inch pie plate, being careful not to stretch pastry. Trim pastry.
9. A little soymilk for glazing

Pie Filling:

1. Preheat the oven to 375 degrees.
2. Places the apples in the crust.
3. Dot with half the vegan margarine.
4. Stir the rest of the margarine into the brown sugar and spices and crumble this mixture on top of the apples.
5. Bake for 45 to 50 minutes, or until apples are very soft when pierced with a knife.
6. For a golden glaze, brush the top crust (but not the edge!) lightly with soymilk.
7. Bake pie for 40-50 minutes, until crust is golden. Enjoy!

Vegan Whole Wheat Biscuits

Makes about 12 biscuits

1¼ cup whole wheat flour	1 tablespoon baking powder
¾ cup unbleached all-purpose flour	1 tsp. turbinado sugar
½ teaspoon salt	4 tablespoons vegetable shortening, chilled and diced
	¾ cup rice, almond or soymilk

1. Preheat oven to 425°F. Lightly oil a baking sheet or line it with parchment paper or foil.
2. Combine the flours, salt, sugar and baking powder in a large bowl.
3. Pulse or cut the shortening into the flour, until it resembles coarse crumbs.
4. If you're using a food processor, remove the mixture to a large bowl and stir in the milk to form a ball of dough.
5. Turn the dough out onto a floured surface and knead 5 or 6 times.
6. Roll out to a ½-inch thickness and cut into 2-inch rounds. Place the biscuits on the baking sheet and bake for about 12 minutes, or until the biscuits are brown on top and a tester comes out clean.
7. Cool on a wire rack before enjoying!

From *The Hood Health Handbook: A Practical Guide to Health and Wellness in the Urban Community* also available from Supreme Design Publishing.

Single Crust Pie Pastry

1¼ cups flour
½ teaspoon salt
⅓ cup margarine -or- ¼ cup olive oil
4 tablespoons cold water

1. Stir together flour and salt.
2. Cut in margarine till pieces are the size of small peas.
3. Sprinkle 1 tablespoon of the water over part of the mixture; gently toss with a fork.
4. Push to side of bowl.
5. Repeat till all is moistened.
6. Form dough into a ball.
7. On a lightly floured surface, flatten dough with hands.
8. Roll dough from center to edge, forming a circle about 12 inches in diameter.
9. Ease pastry into a 9-inch pie plate, being careful not to stretch pastry. Trim pastry.

Double Crust Pie Pastry

2 cups flour
1 teaspoon salt
⅔ cup margarine -or- ¼ cup olive oil
7 tablespoons cold water

1. Sprinkle 1 tablespoon of the water over part of the mixture; gently toss with a fork.
2. Follow steps 2-9 above.

Vegan Buttercream Frosting

½ cup non-hydrogenated shortening
  ½ cup margarine
  3½ cups powdered sugar
  1½ teaspoon vanilla
  up to ⅛ cup soymilk

1. Cream together the margarine and the shortening.
2. Add sugar and beat for at least 5 minutes.
3. Add the vanilla then the soy milk 1 tablespoon at a time
4. while continuing to beat.
5. Depending on the weather and the humidity of your kitchen will decide how much liquid you add.
6. Stop adding soymilk when you are happy with the consistency but continue to beat for at least another 5 minutes you want a very fluffy, very creamy consistency.

Vegan Chocolate Ganache

Frosts a 2 Layer Cake
7 to 8 ounces vegan dark chocolate
2 tablespoons vegan butter
⅓ cup vanilla soymilk
1 tablespoon strong coffee
Pinch cinnamon (optional)

1. In the top of a double boiler, place the vegan butter and soymilk.
2. Bring the water below to a very low simmer and whisk. Mix in the coffee and cinnamon. Add the chocolate.
3. Once it looks like it is beginning to melt, whisk until smooth. Remove from the heat immediately.
4. This should all happen quite quickly, as chocolate can burn.
5. Prep. time: 7 minutes. Cooking time: 4 min.

Vegan Cupcakes

1 tbsp. apple cider vinegar
1½ cups almond milk
2 cups all-purpose flour
½ tsp. Stevia* powder
2 tsp. baking powder
½ tsp. baking soda
½ tsp. salt
½ cup coconut oil, warmed until liquid
1¼ tsp. vanilla extract

1. Preheat oven to 350°F. Grease two 12 cup muffin pans or line with 18 paper baking cups.
2. Measure the apple cider vinegar into a 2 cup measuring cup.
3. Fill with almond milk to make 1½ cups. Let stand until curdled, about 5 minutes.
4. In a large bowl, Whisk together the flour, sugar, baking powder, baking soda and salt. In a separate bowl, whisk together the almond milk mixture, coconut oil and vanilla.
5. Pour the wet ingredients into the dry ingredients and stir just until blended. Spoon the batter into the prepared cups, dividing evenly.
6. Bake in the preheated oven until the tops spring back when lightly pressed, 15 to 20 minutes.
7. Cool in the pan set over a wire rack. When cool, arrange the cupcakes on a serving platter.
8. Frost with desired frosting.

Note: Stevia, an herb that is native to Paraguay, is non-caloric and extremely sweet. The product, available in most health food stores. Many holistic physicians are now touting the benefits of using stevia instead of artificial sugar substitutes which many doctors believe create a myriad of health problems. 1 cup of sugar is the same as 1 tsp. liquid stevia or ⅓ to ½ tsp. stevia extract powder.

North America
Appetizers, Snacks & Sides

Mushroom Scrambler

1 pound firm tofu
2 teaspoons oil
2 cloves garlic, minced
4 cups sliced assorted mushrooms
    (brown, button and shiitake)
½ cup chopped green onions
1 teaspoon minced fresh rosemary
8 oz. egg substitute
½ cup grated Fontina cheese
salt and pepper to taste

1. Drain tofu and crumble into cottage cheese sized pieces.
2. Heat oil in large skillet; add tofu; cook over medium high heat until tofu becomes light golden brown.
3. Add garlic and cook three to four minutes more.
4. Add mushrooms and continue to cook until mushrooms begin to brown, then add green onions and rosemary. Cook three to four minutes.
5. Add egg substitute and cook just until liquid begins to set, then add cheese and salt and pepper to taste.
6. Cook just until cheese begins to melt.
7. Do not overcook.

Easy Soybean Patty For One

Home alone? This moist patty can be enjoyed on a bun with all the usual condiments, or by itself drizzled with your favorite sauce. Simply multiply the ingredients to serve a crowd.

½ cup cooked soybeans, mashed well with a fork
1 tablespoon water or vegetable broth
1 tablespoon wheat germ
¼ teaspoon Spike or other all-purpose seasoning
1 to 2 tablespoons fresh bread crumbs or whole-wheat flour olive oil for cooking

1. In a bowl, combine mashed soybeans, water or broth, wheat germ, Spike and 1 tablespoon bread crumbs or flour.
2. Use your hands to mix well and press firmly into a patty shape, adding more bread crumbs or flour if necessary for the patty to hold together.
3. Heat a little olive oil in a skillet. Cook patty until browned on both sides gently turning once.

Wild Rice Pancakes

Makes ten 4-inch pancakes
1¼ cups whole wheat flour
¼ teaspoon salt
2 teaspoons baking powder
¼ teaspoon hot paprika
2 tablespoons brown sugar or other sweetener
2 tablespoons vegetable oil
1¼ cups low-fat soy milk
1 teaspoon lemon juice
½ teaspoon vanilla
1¼ cups wild rice, cooked
⅓ cup finely chopped pecans
½ cup grated carrot

1. Combine dry ingredients in a large bowl and make a well in the center of the mixture.
2. In a separate bowl, combine the remaining ingredients and beat until smooth; quickly pour into the well and combine with a few quick strokes.
3. Meanwhile, heat a non-stick griddle over medium heat; spray with vegetable cooking spray.
4. Pour batter from the tip of a large spoon onto hot griddle.
5. Cook 2-3 minutes until top bubbles and becomes dry.
6. Turn and cook until the second side is done.
7. Serve warm with fresh berries or apple sauce and soy "sour cream" or yogurt.

American "Cheese"

Dissolve ⅓ cup Emis veggie gelatin into 2¼ cups boiled water Combine & liquefy in processor:
1 cup raw cashews (first powder them in a coffee grinder or processor)
4 oz. pimentos (for color, substitute a carrot if you prefer)
3 tbsp. Nutritional yeast flakes
2 tbsp. lemon juice
2 tsp. onion or onion powder
1 tsp. salt
2 tsp. paprika
garlic or garlic powder to taste

1. Lightly oil a round or square container to put it in (makes it easier to get out later) & refrigerate.
2. To use for grating, freeze it.
3. It will also melt very well if heated.
4. For JACK "Cheese" variation: simply omit pimento (or carrot), & double the lemon, yeast & garlic.

Oven Baked Seasoned Fries

Serves 4

1½ pounds baking potatoes (about 7 medium), peeled, cut into thin strips
1 tablespoon canola oil
½ teaspoon garlic powder
¼ teaspoon to
½ tsp. paprika (optional)
¼ teaspoon salt

1. Preheat oven to 450°F.
2. Combine oil and seasonings in a bowl and mix well.
3. Add potatoes and toss well to coat.
4. Arrange potatoes in a single layer on a baking sheet.
5. Bake for 15 to 20 minutes or until golden brown.

Notes: Be sure to use baking potatoes (russet).
Thin skinned potatoes, which have a higher sugar content than baking potatoes, will burn on the outside before the inside is cooked, resulting in soggy fries.

Popcorn Balls

12 cups air popped popcorn
½ cup brown rice syrup
½ cup molasses
1 tablespoon canola oil
1 tablespoon apple cider vinegar
½ teaspoon salt

1. Preheat oven to 325°F.
2. Put popcorn in a large bowl.
3. Mix all of the other ingredients in a saucepan.
4. Heat on medium just long enough for the ingredients to blend.
5. Stir and pour over popcorn, mixing well to coat the popcorn completely.
6. Spread mixture on a greased cookie sheet and bake for about 15 minutes, checking often to prevent burning.
7. (Warning: when I made this it got overdone in about 10 minutes. It took a lot less time than the 15 minutes, although I don't think I used enough popcorn since I didn't measure. It still tasted pretty good as crispy as it was!)
8. Remove from oven and let cool slightly so they're still warm, but cool enough to handle.
9. Grease up your hands (or just use wet hands) and form into balls.

Spinach Balls

2-10oz. pkg. frozen chopped spinach, thawed
1 pkg. Stove-Top stuffing, mixed to pkg. directions
1 cup Parmesan cheese
dash nutmeg
6 eggs, beaten
⅓ cup melted butter

1. Mix all ingredients together.
2. Form into walnut-sized balls.
3. Place on lightly greased cookie sheet and bake 400°F for 10-15 min. until firm or 20 balls can be microwaved on Medium-High for 5 minutes.
4. Serve with mustard sauce, below.
5. The spinach balls may be frozen either before or after baking.

Mushroom Tempeh Pate

Makes 2 cups

1 cup sliced fresh mushrooms (any variety)
1 small onion, minced
1 tablespoon olive oil
2 cloves garlic, minced
1½ cups cooked or canned (and drained) lima beans -or- white beans
8 ounces cooked Marinated Tempeh, crumbled

1. Sauté mushrooms and onion in olive oil for 5 minutes.
2. Add garlic, and sauté 3 to 5 minutes more.
3. Combine sautéed vegetables with beans and Marinated Tempe in a food processor, and blend until smooth.
4. Transfer to a serving dish, and chill thoroughly.
5. Serve garnished with fresh parsley.

Grilled Spring Onions & Asparagus With Lime

4 large spring onions
4 asparagus spears
1 olive or sunflower oil
1 wedges of lime
1 coarse sea salt

1. Brush the spring onions and asparagus with the oil and grill, turning, until patched with brown.
2. Serve immediately with wedges of lime and sea salt.

Vegan Hush Puppies

Yes, vegan hush puppies! No need to use eggs and dairy, as egg replacer and soy milk work just as well in this vegan hush puppy recipe. Made with fresh sweet corn as well as cornmeal, this fried dough balls are soft on the inside, crispy outside and just as spicy as they should be.

1 egg replacer
⅔ cup soy milk
1¼ cup corn meal
½ cup flour
½ tsp. black pepper
3 tsp. baking powder
1 tsp. sugar
½ onion, minced
½ cup sweet corn
4 green onions, diced
1 jalapeno pepper, de-seeded and diced
oil for frying

1. Mix the egg replacer with the soy milk in a large bowl.
2. Add the corn meal, flour, black pepper, baking powder, sugar then stir in the onion, corn, green onion and jalapeno.
3. Mix until well combined, then form into balls.
4. Heat the oil over high heat in a large skillet, and add hushpuppies a few at a time.
5. Cook until firm and golden brown.

Spicy Seitan Buffalo "Wings" with Vegan Tofu Ranch Dressing

Spicy Seitan Buffalo "Wings" are a vegetarian and vegan substitute for traditional pub buffalo wings. Seitan doesn't come with wings any more than buffaloes do, but these meatless buffalo wings are cooked up with hot sauce and margarine for the same spicy flavor.

1 pound seitan, sliced into strips
2 tsp. garlic powder
1 tsp. onion powder
olive oil for frying
⅓ cup margarine, melted
½ cup hot sauce

Coat the seitan with garlic powder and onion powder then lightly fry in olive oil over medium high heat for 5 to 7 minutes, or until done.
In a medium sized bowl, mix together the melted margarine and hot sauce. Place the seitan in the bowl and stir to coat well. Serve with ranch dressing if desired.

Tofu ranch dressing:
1 carton of silken tofu
1-2 tbsp. olive oil
2 tbsp. cider vinegar
1 tbsp. onion powder
2 tsp. garlic powder
1 tbsp. original Mrs. Dash seasoning
2-3 tbsp. fresh parsley
2 tsp. sea salt
enough soy milk for desired consistency

1. Add all inexpedience together in the blender and mix well.
2. Store in a quart jar in the refrigerator.

Soybean and Eggplant Summer Gratin

Serves 4 to 6

1 tablespoon olive oil
1 onion, chopped
3 cloves garlic, minced
3 4-inch baby eggplants or 1 medium eggplant, trimmed and diced in
½-inch pieces
½ teaspoon paprika
¼ teaspoon nutmeg
¼ teaspoon salt
6 plum or Roma tomatoes, chopped
1½ cups cooked soybeans
1½ cups fresh bread crumbs

1. Preheat oven to 350°F.
2. Sauté onion and garlic in olive oil for 1 minute.
3. Add eggplant, and sauté for 5 to 10 minutes, or until eggplant is soft.
4. Stir in paprika, nutmeg and salt.
5. Transfer contents of sauté pan to a 2 ½-quart casserole dish.
6. Add chopped tomatoes and soybeans, and stir to combine.
7. Sprinkle bread crumbs over the top.
8. Bake casserole, covered, for 30 minutes.
9. Uncover, and bake 15 more minutes, or until top is lightly browned.

Roasted Garlic Soybean Hummus

Makes approx. 1½ cups

3 large cloves garlic
1½ cups cooked soybeans
2 tablespoons roasted sesame tahini
1 tablespoon olive oil
1 tablespoon lemon juice
½ cup fresh parsley
salt to taste
1 to 4 tablespoons water or vegetable broth

1. Preheat broiler. Broil garlic cloves for 5 to 10 minutes, or until they just begin to brown and can be pierced easily with a fork.
2. In a food processor, combine garlic with soybeans, tahini, olive oil, lemon juice and parsley.
3. Blend until smooth, adding salt to taste and water or broth to reach desired consistency.

Baked Cabbage Rolls With Garlic and Wild Rice Stuffing

Makes 10 rolls

2½ cups wild rice, cooked
¼ cup finely chopped onion
½ cup finely chopped fresh parsley
2-4 cloves garlic, minced
½ teaspoon sage
1 medium head of cabbage
½ - 1 tablespoon olive oil
¾ cup tomato juice
½ cup soy "yogurt" or "sour cream"

1. Combine the first five ingredients; chill for several hours to develop flavors.
2. Preheat oven to 375 degrees.
3. Cut the stem from the cabbage deep enough to start a separation of the very outer leaves from the core.
4. Dip the head in boiling water.
5. This will loosen several leaves.
6. Dip again and continue to remove the loosened leaves. (1 head of cabbage should yield 10 leaves of usable size.) Blanch the leaves 2 min in the boiling water. Drain and plunge into cold water.
7. Arrange 10 cabbage leaves on damp towel.
8. Fill with approximately ½ cup of the wild rice mixture per leaf.
9. Fold in outer right and left edges and roll.
10. Place in large baking dish.
11. Dip fingers into oil and lightly coat the top of each cabbage roll.
12. Cover the rolls with tomato juice.
13. Bake covered at 375 degrees for about 50 minutes.
14. Serve each roll with a spoonful of the baked tomato juice and a dab of soy "sour cream" or yogurt.
15. Delicious served with brown rice and green salad.

Unyeasted Carrot Rye Bread with Caraway

2 cups rye flour
4 cups whole wheat flour
2 cups carrot pulp
½ cup caraway seeds (or more, to taste)
1½ tsp. salt
2 tbsp. sesame oil (if no sesame oil, use all corn oil)
2 tbsp. corn oil, or other light vegetable oil 3
½ cups boiling water (or slightly less, for carrot puree)

1. Pan roast rye flour in 1 tbsp. sesame oil until darkened. (This creates a heavenly aroma!) Mix flours together with salt. Add caraway seeds.
2. Add oil, rubbing flour between hands until oily. Add carrot pulp, and mix well.
3. Add boiling water, using spoon to mix until dough begins to form, and then hands.
4. Keep hands cool by dipping them in a bowl of cool water. Mix until earlobe consistency.
5. Knead until smooth; i.e., until dough stretches instead of tearing.
6. Shape into two small loaves, and place in oiled pans. Cut tops lengthwise. Proof 2-6 hours, in oven set at 100-150°F, or on countertop overnight.
7. Brush tops of loaves with oil and place damp tea towel over top to prevent drying.
8. Bake at 450F for 20 minutes on middle shelf, and then at 400F for 40 minutes on top shelf.
9. Alternatively, you may bake at 350F for 1½ hours. Crush will be rough but inside tender, and bottom and sides will be dark brown.
10. Cooked bread will sound a hollow thump when tapped with finger.
11. Wait until cool (approx. 1 hour) before slicing, for bread that slices cleanly.

This is one of the recipes I created in order to utilize the carrot pulp left-over from juicing carrots. Carrot puree will work in place of pulp, although you may wish to decrease the liquid ingredients somewhat.

Corn Berry Muffins

1 cup whole-grain cornmeal
½ cup whole-wheat flour
¼ cup wheat germ
1½ teaspoons baking soda
⅔ cup low-fat buttermilk
¼ cup apple juice, frozen concentrate
3 tablespoons apple juice, frozen concentrate
2 egg whites, lightly beaten
¼ cup vegetable oil
1 ⅔ cups fresh or frozen blueberries (or raisins)
vegetable cooking spray

1. Preheat oven to 400 degrees.
2. Combine the cornmeal, flour, wheat germ, and baking soda in a mixing bowl.
3. Beat the buttermilk, juice concentrate, egg whites, and oil in separate bowl.
4. Add the liquid ingredients to the dry ingredients and blend well with a few strokes.
5. Fold in the blueberries or raisins until distributed evenly.
6. Spoon the batter into 12 muffin cups coated with vegetable cooking spray.
7. Bake until lightly browned, about 20 minutes.
8. Remove from the tins immediately.

Yummy Pumpkin Bread
Serves 10-12

Dry Ingredients:
2 cups whole-wheat pastry flour
2 teaspoons non-aluminum baking powder (such as Rumford)
1 teaspoon baking soda
½ teaspoon ground cinnamon
¼ teaspoon ground cloves

Wet Ingredients:
2 cups unsweetened canned or puréed cooked pumpkin
½ cup pure maple syrup
2 tablespoons canola oil
1 teaspoon vanilla extract
½ cup coarsely chopped pecans
½ cup golden raisins

1. Preheat the oven to 350°F.
2. Oil an 8 ½ x 4 ½-inch loaf pan and set it aside.
3. Place the dry ingredients in a large mixing bowl, and stir them together.
4. Place the wet ingredients in a medium mixing bowl, and stir them together until they are well combined.
5. Pour the wet ingredients into the dry ingredients.
6. Mix just until the dry ingredients are evenly moistened.
7. The mixture will seem very stiff and dry.
8. Stir in the pecans and raisins until they are evenly distributed.
9. Spoon the batter into the prepared loaf pan.
10. Place the loaf pan on the center rack of the oven, and bake the bread for about 50 to 55 minutes, or until a cake tester inserted in the center tests clean.
11. Remove the bread from the oven using oven mitts or pot holders.
12. Turn it out of the loaf pan onto a cooling rack, and carefully turn the bread upright.
13. Allow the bread to cool completely before slicing or storing it.
14. Wrap the cooled bread tightly, and store it at room temperature up to 3 days, or refrigerate it up to 7 days.

Shepherd's Pie
Serves 6

Filling:
1½ cups textured soy protein (TSP), also known as textured vegetable protein (TVP)
1½ cups boiling water
2 tsp. tamari
1 tbsp. soy oil
2 medium onions, diced (about 2 cups)
2 cups chopped mushrooms
1 cup peeled, diced carrots
3 tbsp. chopped fresh garlic
2 tbsp. tamari
4 tsp. basil
1 tbsp. thyme
1 tsp. savory
1 tsp. salt
¼ tsp. black pepper
1 cup diced celery
¼ cup unbleached white flour mixed in ½ cup water
chopped parsley for garnish

Topping:
3 medium potatoes, peeled, cubed (about 4 cups)
¼ cup soy milk
1 tsp. soy oil
½ tsp. salt
⅛ tsp. black pepper

1. Topping: Preheat oven to 325°F.
2. Boil the potatoes in salted water until the potatoes are soft. Remove and drain the potatoes.
3. Blend them in a mixer with the soy milk, oil, salt and pepper. Set aside.
4. Filling: Add the TVP and tamari to boiling water, then cover, remove from heat and set aside.
5. Sauté vegetables (except the celery) and seasonings in the oil over medium heat for about 15 minutes.
6. Add the celery and TSP, then cook about 5 minutes longer, stirring occasionally to prevent from sticking.
7. Add the flour mixture and stir until thickened.
8. Transfer the filling to a lightly-oiled baking dish.
9. Cover the top with the potatoes and smooth them with a rubber spatula until flat and even.
10. Bake the pie in preheated oven for 30 minutes, then broil for several minutes or until the top is lightly browned.
11. Remove from oven and serve hot, garnished with parsley.

Vegetable Pot Pie

¼ ½ cup white wine or vegetable stock
1 cup chopped onion
1 cup thinly sliced celery
1 cup diced red bell pepper ⅔ cup thinly sliced carrots ⅔ cup sliced frozen green beans
⅓ cup frozen peas
⅓ cup whole wheat flour
1 cup skim milk or soy milk
2 cup vegetable stock
2 tablespoons chopped fresh parsley
1 tsp. salt or low sodium-soy sauce
½ tsp. dried thyme
¼ tsp. dried sage
¼ tsp. fresh ground pepper
¼ tsp. cayenne pepper

Biscuit Crust:
Serves 6
1¾ cup unbleached or whole wheat pastry flour
½ tsp. salt
2 tsp. baking powder
½ tsp. baking soda
2 tsp. butter or margarine ¾ cup buttermilk or soymilk
2 tsp. honey (I would think rice syrup or maple syrup would make a suitable sub)

1. Preheat oven to 400 degrees. Coat an 8-inch casserole dish with vegetable cooking spray.
2. In heavy saucepan, heat wine or stock over medium to high heat.
3. Add onion and cook, stirring often until soft, about 3 minutes.
4. Add celery, bell pepper, carrot, green beans and peas.
5. If mixture begins to dry out, add ¼ cup more wine of vegetable stock.
6. Cook, stirring often, 3 minutes. Reduce to low.
7. Sprinkle flour over vegetable mixture.
8. Cook, stirring constantly, 2 minutes.
9. In a glass measuring cup, combine milk or soymilk and 2 cups of vegetable stock.
10. Slowly add to vegetable mixture while whisking constantly. Sauce will start to thicken.
11. Add parsley, salt or soy sauce, thyme, sage, pepper and cayenne.
12. Cook stirring constantly, until filling is thickened.
13. Remove from heat, transfer mixture to prepared casserole and set aside.
14. Biscuit topping: In a large bowl, mix flour, salt, baking powder and baking soda.
15. Using a pastry blender or fork, cut butter or margarine into flour until mixture resembles coarse meal.
16. In measuring cup, combine buttermilk or soymilk and honey.
17. Add liquid to flour mixture, stirring with a fork to form a stiff dough.
18. Add more buttermilk or soymilk if dough is too dry.
19. Knead lightly in bowl, 3-5 minutes, until dough is no longer sticky.
20. Turn dough out onto a lightly floured surface.
21. Roll out into shape to cover casserole dish or cut into wedges.
22. Lay biscuit topping lightly over filling.
23. Bake until crust is golden brown and filling is bubbling. Cooks in 20-30 minutes.

Stuffed Peppers

Serves 4
½ cup long grain white rice (uncooked)
4 medium green bell peppers
1 large onion, chopped
4 tablespoons olive oil
1 cup TVP granules
2 tablespoons fresh parsley, chopped
2 cups spaghetti sauce salt & pepper to taste

1. Cook rice per package directions.
2. Preheat oven to 400 degrees.
3. Cut tops off peppers, seed insides, and arrange peppers in a large baking dish.
4. Reserve tops and chop usable portion.
5. Heat oil in a large skillet and sauté chopped peppers with onions until soft.
6. Add TVP granules and stir well.
7. Add parsley and cook over low heat for 5 minutes.
8. Add the cooked rice to the pepper & onion mixture and 1½ cups of spaghetti sauce.
9. Mix well and season to taste.
10. Spoon the mixture into the peppers and top each with remaining spaghetti sauce.
11. Cover and bake about 45 minutes or longer.

Wild Rice, Mushroom and Pepper Pizza

Makes 8 slices

The cheese makes a more traditional pizza but it is delicious with wild rice and vegetables alone.

1 cup pizza sauce
10 ounces Boboli (or your favorite homemade \ pizza dough)
1½ cups cooked wild rice
8 ounces fresh mushrooms, sliced
½ medium onion, thinly sliced
1 red pepper, sliced in thin strips
4 ounces grated low-fat soy cheese (optional)

1. Preheat oven to 450 degrees.
2. Spread pizza sauce evenly over Boboli or pizza dough.
3. Sprinkle wild rice over pizza sauce and top with the remaining ingredients.
4. Bake 12 minutes at 450 degrees for the Boboli crust (or follow the directions of the pizza dough recipe).

Wild Rice, Cilantro and Garlic Pizza

Makes 8 slices

¾ cup pizza sauce
10 ounces Boboli (or your favorite homemade pizza dough)
2 cups cooked wild rice
1 cup packed fresh cilantro
4 cloves garlic, minced
½ medium onion, thinly sliced
2 large or 3 small fresh tomatoes

1. Preheat oven to 450 degrees.
2. Spread pizza sauce evenly over Boboli or pizza dough.
3. Sprinkle wild rice over pizza sauce.
4. Finely chop fresh cilantro, mix with minced garlic, and sprinkle over wild rice.
5. Top with onions and tomatoes.
6. Bake 10 minutes at 450 degrees for the Boboli crust (or follow the directions of the pizza dough recipe).
7. Turn oven to broil, and broil 1-2 minutes to brown onions and tomatoes lightly.

Lentil Barley Shepherd's Pie

2 cups water
½ cup uncooked lentils
¼ cup uncooked barley
1 large carrot diced
1 medium onion chopped finely
8 oz. canned tomatoes diced
1 clove garlic crushed
1 tsp. flour
1 tsp. parsley
1 tsp. herbs du Provence
salt and pepper
3 medium potatoes cooked and mashed

1. Peel, cut up and boil potatoes until soft, then mash
2. Heat 1¼ cups water, add lentils and barley, simmer 30 min.
3. Heat remaining water in a saucepan, add carrot, onion, garlic and cook until tender, then add tomatoes and spices.
4. Mix the flour with a little water and add to sauce pan, stir and cook over low heat until thickened.
5. Combine contents of saucepan with cooked lentils and barley, place in ovenproof baking dish, cover with mashed potatoes.
6. Bake at 350°F for 30 min. (or you can make it ahead of time and bake it for 45 min. with it starting from refrigerator temp.)

Tasty "Toona" Salad

Serves 4

1lb. firm tofu, frozen, then thawed
¼ small green bell pepper, finely chopped
2 tbsp. grated carrot
½ cup vegan mayonnaise, commercial or homemade
2 tbsp. soy sauce
1 tbsp. lemon juice
½ to 1 tsp.
kelp or kombu powder (optional

1. Squeeze the excess moisture out of the thawed tofu and crumble into small pieces.
2. Combine with bell pepper, onion, and carrot.
3. Stir together the mayonnaise, soy sauce, lemon juice, and kelp powder in a small bowl.
4. Add the mayonnaise mixture to the tofu and vegetables and mix well.

Spring Pita Sandwiches

2 pita breads
2 tomatoes, diced
1 avocado, sliced
1 cup kidney beans, canned/drained
1 cup cheddar cheese, grated
1 cup mushrooms, sliced
1 cup alfalfa sprouts
½ cup canola oil
4 tbsp. vinegar
¼ cup roasted cashews
1 salt & pepper to taste

1. Slice pitas in half and fill with remaining ingredients, dividing evenly.
2. Fillings will be overflowing.
3. Simply separate the pita halves and pile up what's left between them.
4. Add oil and vinegar and top with cashews.
5. These sandwiches are colorful, delicious, nutritious, easy to make, and perfect for picnics, too.

Zesty Cranberry Sauce

Serves 8

2 cups fresh or frozen cranberries cup undiluted orange juice concentrate
2 ripe pears, finely chopped
1 medium apple, finely chopped teaspoon ground cinnamon
1 teaspoon grated orange rind cup raw sugar or other sweetener

1. Combine all ingredients except sweetener in a saucepan, and bring to a simmer over medium heat.
2. Continue cooking, uncovered, until cranberry skins pop and mixture thickens slightly, about
3. 10 minutes. Add sweetener to taste if desired.
4. Serve hot or cold.

Grilled Vegetable Medley

Serves 8

2 large yellow squash, cut into 3/4-inch thick, slices
1 large zucchini, cut into 3/4-inch thick, slices
1 large yellow pepper, cut into
1-inch squares
1 large red bell pepper, cut into
1-inch squares
1 pound fresh mushrooms, halved
10 small new potatoes, halved
1 pound baby carrots
½ cup olive oil
1 oz. pkg. dry onion soup mix
1½ teaspoons fresh or dried rosemary

1. Toss together first 8 ingredients.
2. Sprinkle with onion soup mix and rosemary; toss to coat.
3. Tear 8 12x18-inch sheets of foil.
4. Place one-eighth of vegetable mixture in center of each foil sheet.
5. Bring up 2 sides of each foil sheet and double fold with 1-inch wide folds.
6. Double fold each end to form a packet.
7. Grill, covered with grill lid, over medium-high heat (350-400 degrees F) 40 to 45 minutes or until tender.

Sauces

There are five basic flavor categories that each sauce, dressing or marinade should incorporate. In addition to the five basic favors, you'll also need to include a fat ingredient. for a total of six components. Here are some example ingredients for each flavor component.

Sweet - dates, raw honey, agave nectar
Salty - sea salt, soy sauce, miso
Sour - lemon, lime, tamarind
Spicy - hot peppers, garlic, ginger
Bitter - herbs/spices... Basil, parsley, cumin
Fat - avocado, olive oil, coconut oil

This rule applies to all cuisines because flavor profiles are universal.

Tofu Mayonnaise

1 packet firm silken tofu, drained
1tbsp. white wine vinegar or lemon juice
2tbsp. safflower or sunflower oil
1tsp. salt pinch turmeric (optional) little milk or soya milk

Place all the ingredients into a processor and process for 20 seconds or until ingredients are smooth and creamy. Add a little milk at this stage if you require a thinner consistency but not if making any of the following dips. Cover; refrigerate (mayonnaise will keep for 2 to 3 days).

Serving suggestions.
Serve in the usual way or add any of the following seasonings to make into dips:

Avocado
1 well ripened avocado liquidized into the mayonnaise. Add a couple of tbsp. of very finely chopped onion for texture if required.

Cheese and garlic
2 tbsp. grated vegetarian cheese and
2 tsp. powdered or 1 clove minced garlic.

Curry ½ tsp. curry powder.
Chopped onion may be added.

Garlic and herb
1 clove garlic, crushed, and
1 tsp. freshly chopped herbs.

Garlic and dill
1 clove garlic, crushed, and ¼ tsp. dill seeds topped with freshly chopped parsley.

Ginger
1 tsp. grated ginger root and a pinch of chili powder (mild or hot according to taste).

Herb
1 level tsp. of freshly chopped coriander or basil.

Vegan Ranch Dip/Dressing

You can buy the Hidden Valley Ranch original buttermilk mix, which is vegan (strangely enough).

1 package Mori Nu silken tofu
1 packet Hidden Valley Ranch buttermilk mix
½ cup vegenaise
3 tablespoons lemon juice
garlic powder to taste (approx. ¼ to ½ teaspoon)
salt to taste

1. Process it all in a food processor.
2. This turned out pretty good and tasted a lot like the old dressing I remember from my pre-vegan days.
3. I think the mayo had a lot to do with it.
4. Be sure to get a vegan mayo that tastes really good (I think vegenaise is the best I've ever had).
5. To make dressing, you could probably just do soy milk, vegan mayo, and maybe a little lemon juice to get the bite of buttermilk.
6. I haven't tried that yet, though.

Orange Zest Teriyaki

juice of 1 orange (acid)
¼ cup soy sauce (salty)
2 tbsp. raw honey (sweet)
1 clove garlic, crushed (spicy)
1 tsp. sesame oil (fat)
pinch orange zest (bitter)
pinch grated ginger (spicy)

1. In a small bowl add soy sauce and orange juice, and slowly stir in the honey until smooth.
2. Mix in the remaining ingredients and whisk.
3. Pour sauce over a large bowl of your favorite veggies and set aside to marinade for 1-2 hrs before serving!

Soybean and Roasted Red Pepper Sauce

Makes 2 cups

This versatile sauce takes minutes to prepare. Some serving suggestions: Use instead of tomato sauce for pizza. Drizzle on nachos or burritos. Use as a dip for baked tortilla chips. Spread a thin layer on hot cooked veggie burgers.

1½ cups cooked soybeans
1 roasted red bell pepper (about ½ cup jarred roasted red bell pepper)
¼ cup water or vegetable broth
2 tablespoons nutritional yeast flakes
1 tablespoon brown rice vinegar
½ teaspoon salt-free Onion Magic or onion powder
¼ teaspoon salt (or to taste)
pinch of dried red pepper flakes, to taste (optional)

1. Blend all ingredients in a blender at high speed until smooth. Refrigerate until ready to use.
2. If you'd like to serve the sauce warm, heat gently in a
3. saucepan or double boiler (do not simmer or boil).

Mushrooms, Tofu and Snow Peas in Soy Ginger Sauce

Serves 2

1 small onion, halved and sliced thin crosswise
1 tablespoon vegetable oil
¼ pound mushrooms, sliced thin
1 garlic clove, minced
2 teaspoons minced ginger root
¾ teaspoon cornstarch dissolved in 2 tbsp. cold water
3 tablespoons soy sauce
½ pound firm tofu, drained, wrapped in a double thickness of paper towels for 15 minutes and cut into ¼-inch thick slices
¼ pound snow peas, no strings cooked rice

1. Brown onions in a skillet over moderately high heat, stirring occasionally.
2. Add the mushrooms and sauté the mixture, stirring until the mushrooms are tender.
3. Add the garlic and the ginger and sauté the mixture, stirring for one minute.
4. Stir the cornstarch mixture and add it to the skillet with the soy sauce, tofu and ½ cup water, and simmer the mixture, stirring gently and turning tofu to coat with sauce.
5. Add snow peas and stir gently, 30 seconds.
6. Serve over rice.

Vegan White Sauce

Makes 2 cups

1 cup unsweetened soymilk
½ of a 10- to 12-ounce package firm silken tofu
1 tablespoon lemon juice
1 tablespoon Spectrum Naturals Spread
1 tablespoon nutritional yeast flakes ¼ teaspoon salt, or to taste (or use 1 to 3 teaspoons mellow white miso)

1. Blend all ingredients in a blender until very smooth.
2. The sauce can then be warmed gently in a saucepan or double boiler (do not simmer) or refrigerated for up to 2 days.

Roasted Veggie Dressing

Serves 1

¼ cup balsamic vinegar	1 sprig fresh parsley, minced
1 tbsp. Dijon mustard	1 tbsp. fresh rosemary,
1 clove garlic, crushed	minced
	½ cup extra virgin olive oil

1. Combine all ingredients except for olive oil in a bowl.
2. Slowly whisk in olive oil.
3. Makes ¾ cup.

4. Serve on roasted vegetables, sandwiches, salads, etc.

Buttah

1 cup olive oil (extra-virgin)
⅛–¼ tsp. Celtic sea salt
1 tbsp. agar-agar flakes

1. Put ingredients into a blender and blend very well.
2. Pour the mixture into an ice cube tray, filling each cube only halfway, and freeze.
3. Every time you need a butter substitute, take out a cube and let it sit for a couple of minutes before serving.

Entrees

Simple "Sausage" for Pasta

Serves 1
¼ cup TVP (1 part)
⅛ cup Fennel, before crushed

1. Place Fennel in mortar.
2. Crush w/ pestle.
3. Mix crushed Fennel w/ TVP in bowl.
4. Add just enough warm water to cover it.
5. Let sit 15 minutes.
6. Stir into favorite pasta sauce in sauce pan.
7. Cook for 3-5 minutes.

Variation:
1. ½ teaspoons (per person) Crushed Red Pepper.
2. Mix into pasta sauce before adding "Sausage".
3. (I like SPICY/HOT food so I add 1 teaspoon when I'm making it for myself)

Chunky Barbecue Tempe

Serves 4
Serve this dish over noodles or rice, or with thick slices of French bread. For a low- fat version, sauté the onions and garlic in water or vegetable broth instead of oil.

2 tablespoons olive oil
1 medium onion, coarsely chopped
3 cloves garlic, minced
1 14-ounce can unsalted tomatoes, drained and coarsely chopped
2 tablespoons honey, molasses, or maple syrup
2 tablespoons brown rice vinegar or cider vinegar
2 tablespoons tamari
1 teaspoon paprika
1 teaspoon ground cumin
8 ounces temper, steamed for 20 minutes and cut in 1-inch strips
¼-inch thick

1. In a medium saucepan, sauté onion and garlic in olive oil for 5 minutes.
2. Add remaining ingredients and simmer, partially covered, for 15 to 20 minutes, or until sauce thickens.

Vegetable Pot Pie

1 pkg. pie crust
2 tbsp. margarine
2 medium onion
2 tbsp. white flour
2 cup vegetable broth
2 cups cooked vegetables (yellow squash, mushrooms, string beans, diced carrots, etc.)

1. Roast all vegetables in oven for one hour.
2. Melt margarine in a medium saucepan.
3. Add onion and sauté until soft and translucent about 7 minutes.
4. Add flour and stir until it starts to thicken.
5. Stirring constantly, pour vegetable broth in saucepan.
6. Continue stirring until sauce thickens, about 10 minutes.
7. Remove from heat. Preheat oven 425 degrees.
8. Pour vegetables in pie crust and then sauce.
9. Cook about 35 minutes or until done.

Spring Vegetable Cobbler

2 small zucchini cut into 1 ½" pieces
2 small yellow crookneck squash cut into 1 ½" pieces
1 red bell pepper cut into 1 ½" pieces
4 baby carrots; cut in half
8 large mushrooms; cut in half
½ lb broccoli cut into individual florets
2 medium potatoes peeled and quartered
2 cup béchamel sauce; see recipe
2 tbsp. butter
1 large onion; coarsely chopped
4 garlic; minced
½ cup dried lentils
1 tsp. kosher salt
2 tbsp. fresh tarragon
¼ tsp. white pepper

Cheddar Biscuits:
2 cup flour plus flour for dusting
1 tsp. kosher salt
2 tsp. baking powder
1 tbsp. fresh tarragon
3 oz. cheddar cheese; grated
¾ cup milk
3 tbsp. butter; melted

1. Preheat oven to 375°. Place in a 1-quart saucepan and cover with water. Bring to a boil.
2. Reduce heat and simmer until easily pierced with a knife (20 to 25 minutes).
3. Place potatoes and Béchamel Sauce in a blender, food processor, or food mill, and puree. Heat butter in a large skillet. Sauté onion and garlic for 5 minutes.
4. Add zucchini, squash, pepper, carrots, mushrooms, broccoli, lentils, béchamel-potato mixture, salt, tarragon, and pepper. Toss to combine.
5. Pour mixture into a 3-quart casserole. Place Cheddar Biscuits over mixture. Bake until top is golden brown and vegetables are hot (about 1 hour).
6. For each serving, top a generous scoop of vegetables with one or two biscuit tsp.
7. To prepare Cheddar Biscuits, sift together flour, salt, baking powder, and tarragon into a 3-quart mixing bowl. Toss cheese with dry ingredients.
8. Stir together milk and 2 tablespoons of the melted butter.
9. Gently stir milk butter into dry ingredients, mixing only until combined.
10. Place dough on a lightly dusted work surface and pat to ½-inch thick. Cut into 2-inch round disc.
11. Place biscuits on casserole and brush with remaining melted butter.

Californian Style Brochettes

Serves 4
(…as a snack, 8 as a starter; makes 8 12-inch skewers).

1 packet Cauldron Tofu, original or Marinated, cut into 32 cubes
1 small pineapple, peeled and cut into 32 pieces
½ cup large seedless black grapes
1 medium mango, peeled and cut into 4 pieces
½ cup mango chutney
8 sprigs fresh herbs
1 lime, cut into 4 wedges
8 skewers

1. Thread skewers alternately with tofu, pineapple, grapes and mango.
2. Brush with mango chutney.
3. Cook under a pre-heated grill for 5 minutes until very hot and just browning.
4. Serve immediately, scattered with fresh herbs garnished with wedges of lime.

Sherried Wild Rice and Mushroom Casserole

Serves 4
8 ounces fresh mushrooms, sliced
1 tablespoon olive oil
6 tablespoons dry sherry
2 tablespoons flour
¼ teaspoon black pepper
1 cup low-fat soy milk
2½ cups cooked wild rice

1. Preheat oven to 350 degrees.
2. Sauté mushrooms over low heat in olive oil and 4 tablespoons of sherry.
3. Add flour and stir until liquid and flour make a smooth paste.
4. Add black pepper and milk; cook over medium heat until sauce thickens.
5. Stir in remaining sherry and wild rice.
6. Bake in covered dish at 350 degrees for 40 minutes.
7. Delicious served with fresh asparagus, whole wheat bread, orange slices and white wine.

Stewed Okra and Tempeh

Serves 4

4 small onions
pinch turmeric powder
about 1 cup olive oil
1 pound (2 packages) tempeh
1 pound tender young small okra, stemmed but left whole and unpierced
3 tablespoons lemon juice
1½ tablespoons tomato paste
1 pinch saffron threads
(pepper and salt are optional, but some seasoning might liven it up)
basmati rice
1 tomato cut in wedges, for garnish

1. Slice 3 of the onions thinly and put them in a small pan with the turmeric and olive oil to cover.
2. Over medium-high heat, cook the onions, stirring occasionally, to caramelize them, 10 to 15 minutes.
3. When light gold in color.
4. Remove ingredients from the heat to prevent burning; they will continue to cook in the hot oil.
5. When amber in color and cooled, strain the onions and reserve; they will be greatly reduced in volume, to about 1½ tablespoons.
6. Also reserve the oil, which, unless burned, is full of flavor. This much can be done well ahead.
7. In a wide pan over medium-high flame, heat 2 tablespoons reserved oil, or enough to film the pan.
8. Sear the cakes of tempeh, turning to brown all sides.
9. When the moisture has evaporated, add 2 cups of water and the remaining onion, chopped.
10. Simmer the tempeh, uncovered, until it has cooked throughout and imparted its rich soy flavor to the broth, and the liquid has been reduced, about 25 minutes. Meanwhile, in another pan, heat 4 tablespoons reserved oil.
11. Add the okra and gently sauté it, turning it carefully.
12. When it changes from bright green to a mellower color.
13. Add the lemon juice, tomato paste, and saffron.
14. Cook the okra until crisp-tender, about 10 minutes in all. Do not cut or tear it or let it boil, or it will get sticky and limp.
15. Just before serving, add the okra to the tempeh strips or chunks with the reserved caramelized onion.
16. simmer for a few minutes more in order to meld the flavors.
17. Taste for balance of seasoning, and perhaps pepper or salt to taste.
18. Serve the okra-tempeh stew with basmati rice and garnish with tomato wedges.

Pigeon Peas with Tempeh and Rice

2 cups cooked pigeon peas (substitute black eye peas if pigeon peas are unavailable in your area!)
3 cups cooked rice (long grain white or brown)
½ large onion (chopped)
1½ cups stewed sliced tomatoes (canned is ok!)
2 teaspoons ground cumin.
¼ cup diced celery
1 cup very finely chopped cilantro (cilantro is also referred to as Chinese parsley, or fresh coriander leaf)
4 cloves finely minced garlic
⅛ teaspoons black pepper
2 teaspoons paprika
½ lb of tempeh (cut into small cubes, and steamed for 12-15 mins)
2 tablespoons extra virgin olive oil

1. In a large skillet or frying pan, sauté the following in 2 tablespoons of extra virgin olive oil: chopped onion, diced celery, black pepper, paprika, cilantro, and garlic when onions are tender .
2. Add the tempeh and stewed tomatoes.
3. When mixture is reddish color and the tempeh begins to absorb the color, add the beans and bean liquid.
4. Let mixture cook for a few minutes until it bubbles up moderately, making sure to stir frequently to avoid burning it.
5. Salt the bubbling mixture and taste it making sure that it is slightly on the salty side!
6. Fold in rice and stir in skillet until much of the liquid either cooks away or is absorbed by the rice.
7. Serve with a nice tossed salad and enjoy!

Un-Ribs

Serves 5-6

8 oz. dried bean curd (yuba) sticks
 (carried in larger Oriental marts - inexpensive)
¼ cup nutritional yeast
¼ cup peanut butter
2 tbsp. miso
2 tbsp. warm melted margarine
2 tsp. paprika
2 cup barbeque sauce

1. Soak the dried bean curd 4-6 hours or overnight in hot water. Drain and cut sticks into 4-6 inch lengths.
2. Squeeze out excess water and drain.
3. Preheat oven to 350 degrees. Oil cookie sheet.
4. In a large mixing bowl, mix next 5 ingredients together to form a smooth paste.
5. Toss yuba sticks in and mix until all sticks are evenly coated.
6. Lay side by side (touching each other) one layer thick, on the cookie sheet. Bake 25 minutes or until the bottoms are brown and crisp.
7. Remove from oven and put in mixing bowl with barbeque sauce. Toss well.
8. Lay out on baking sheet again and bake at 350 degrees for 10-15 minutes. Messy and good.

If you are vegan, you are probably familiar with nutritional yeast. Nutritional yeast is different than brewer's yeast and can be found in health food stores. It has a savory, somewhat cheesy flavor (which is why vegans use it in cheese substitutes). Yuba is "bean curd skin". When hot soy milk is left undisturbed, it forms a skin on the top that can be removed and eaten, or dried for later use. This "skin" is yuba. It is rich and more flavorful than tofu. It is somewhat chewy. For the ribs you want to purchase dried yuba in stick form as shown. (It is also sold in sheets and other forms.) If you can't find yuba, you can substitute seitan, although cooking time may then vary.

Coconut Vegetable Curry

This is a meal that could please both a vegan and a meat eater. It's rich, hearty, and filled to the brim with flavor.

1 tbsp organic olive oil
1 large onion, minced
2 tbsp curry powder
½ head cauliflower, washed and cut into florets
1 carrot, peeled and sliced
1 yellow pepper, chopped
1 can of coconut milk
½ cup cashews, crushed
Sea salt and pepper to taste

1. Cook the onion in the olive oil.
2. Add curry powder and cook for 1 minute.
3. Add the vegetables and cook for 5 minutes.
4. Stir in the coconut milk and add salt and pepper.
5. Boil and simmer for 10-15 minutes until the vegetables are cooked.
6. Serve with rice.

Make sure that you reduce the coconut milk to add even more richness to the flavor. The cashews make it even more filling. This dish is quite memorable.

Spring Vegetable Paella

1 lb asparagus; cut into 2-inch pieces
3 cup broccoli florets
2 tbsp. olive oil
1 cup red bell pepper, chopped
1¼ cup zucchini, chopped
½ cup onion, chopped
4 cup cooked brown or white-long-grain rice
2 cup tomatoes, chopped & seeded
¾ tsp. salt
½ tsp. saffron threads or ¼ tsp ground
2 garbanzo beans, rinsed &-drained
1 frozen peas, thawed

1. Cook asparagus and broccoli florets in enough boiling water to covering a 2-qt. saucepan, about 4 minutes or until crisp-tender; drain.
2. Heat oil in a 10-inch skillet over medium-high heat.
3. Cook asparagus, broccoli, bell pepper, zucchini, and onion in oil about 5 minutes, stirring occasionally, until onion is crisp-tender.
4. Stir in remaining ingredients.
5. Cook about 5 minutes, stirring frequently, until hot.

Sea Greens

Exceptional Nutrition: As well as containing significant amounts of the major minerals such as calcium, magnesium, potassium, phosphorous and iron, sea vegetables are also a rich source of trace elements such as selenium, chromium, zinc, manganese and iodine, the last of which is often difficult to obtain from food grown on the land.

Sea vegetables are also low in fat and calories and high in protein. They contain substantial amounts of beta carotene (the precursor of the antioxidant vitamin A) and the B complex vitamins. The Health Benefits: The health benefits of Sea Vegetables have been recognized for centuries. Their rich mineral content benefits our nervous system thereby helping to reduce stress, and boosts our immune system. Traditional cultures also valued sea vegetables as beneficial to healthy skin and hair. Sea vegetables have also been shown to reduce tumors, lower cholesterol levels, and generally aid metabolism and digestion.

Protection Against Pollution and Radiation: Research shows that alginic acid in the brown sea vegetables (wakame, kombu, arame and hijiki) binds with heavy metals such as cadmium, lead, mercury and radium in our intestines.

This process renders the metals indigestible - and so they are eliminated. What's more, alginic acid can actually help to draw out similar toxins that are _already stored_ in our bodies. Other studies have shown that the iodine in sea vegetables reduces by 80 per cent radioactive iodine-131 (a by-product of nuclear fission).

A Guide To Popular Sea Vegetables

Nori - is the most popular of all sea vegetables, with a delicate texture and mild flavor. It comes in sheets and is commonly used to make sushi and to wrap a variety of foods. The sheets can also be crumbled or cut to make a tasty garnish for grains, soups and salads. Children often love to munch on a sheet of nori. Apart from sheets you can also buy nori flakes which provide a tasty herb - like garnish for salads or grains.

Dulse - is a purple-red colour and has a pleasing spicy flavor. It is delicious when washed, briefly soaked, and added to salads, soups, and vegetable or pasta dishes. Dulse can also be dry - roasted and crumbled to make a nourishing garnish for cereal grains.

Kombu - contains an abundance of glutamic acid, the substance from which monosodium glutamate was originally synthesized. Kombu can therefore enhance the flavor of soups, stocks, stews and almost any slowly cooked savory dish. Add a small strip of Kombu to beans to help soften them whilst cooking.

Wakame - is a relative of kombu. Like Dulse can be briefly soaked and used in salads and soups, or like nori, it can be toasted and crumbled as a condiment. Because of its mild flavor, wakame is one of the most popular sea vegetables with newcomers.

Arame - comes in delicate black strips. Once soaked, it can be seasoned and added to noodles and salads, or lightly cooked with vegetables, tofu, tempeh or stir fries. It combines especially well with sweet vegetables. It need not always be soaked before use.

Hijiki - looks similar to arame, but it's thicker and has a stronger flavor. Once soaked it can be sautéed with vegetables for salads, or cooked with tofu or other vegetarian proteins. Particularly rich in calcium.

Sea Palm - is succulent, mild and versatile. It needs only light cooking and can be served with stir-fried dishes, vegetables, pasta and salads.

Agar Flakes - make superb vegetarian savory aspics and sweet jellies. The vegetarian's answer to gelatin.

Clear Soup with Spring Vegetables Kombu is especially rich in glutamic acid, which is a natural flavor enhancer, so using it to make a soup stock adds both taste and nutrition.

Kombu

Serves 2 to 3

1 x 4-inch strip kombu
3 cups water
½ onion, finely sliced
1 medium carrot, finely cut into rounds
½ cup sweet corn kernels
pinch sea salt
Shoyu soy sauce, to taste
1 bunch fresh watercress, cut into 1-inch lengths
few fresh bean sprouts
lemon slices, to garnish

1. Place the kombu in a pot with the water, bring to the boil and simmer for 20 minutes.
2. Remove the kombu.
3. (Save it for cooking beans - it helps to soften them.)
4. Add the sliced onions, carrots, sweet corn and a pinch of sea salt.
5. Simmer for 8-10 minutes.
6. Season with the Shoyu soy sauce and simmer for 1 minute.
7. Add the watercress and bean sprout, and serve with the sliced lemon garnish.

Jambalaya

2 teaspoons oil
1 medium onion, chopped
1 red bell pepper, chopped
1 green bell pepper, chopped

2 large cloves garlic, minced
2 cups water

1 (14.5 oz.) can stewed tomatoes with liquid, cut up
1 (15 oz.) can tomato sauce
½ teaspoon dried Italian seasoning
¼ teaspoon cayenne pepper (ground red pepper)
⅛ teaspoon fennel seed, crushed
1½ cups uncooked rice
2-3 (15.5 oz.) cans of various beans of your choice, drained and rinsed, i.e., garbanzos, black beans, kidney beans

1. Heat oil in large skillet or pot w/ lid over medium-high heat.
2. Add veggies and garlic, cook and stir 2 to 3 minutes, or until crisp tender. Stir in water, tomatoes, tomato sauce, and spices. Bring to boil; add rice.
3. Reduce heat to low; cover and simmer (about 45-50 minutes for brown rice, about 25-35 minutes for white rice) until rice is tender and liquid is absorbed. Stir occasionally during cooking time.
4. Gently stir in beans. Simmer another 5 minutes or so, until thoroughly heated.

TVP Bean Burger

1 cup TVP granules (soy protein product)
1 scant cup boiling water
1 tbsp. tomato paste
19 oz. can pinto beans, drained and rinsed (Red kidney beans can be substituted)
¼ cup whole wheat bread crumbs
2 cloves garlic, finely minced
1 tsp. oregano
2 tbsp. tahini paste
1 tbsp. soy sauce
1 tsp. sugar salt and pepper to taste whole wheat flour for dusting

1. Pour boiling water over TVP and tomato paste in a bowl. Stir and let rest for 10 minutes.
2. In food processor, combine TVP mixture and remaining ingredients except for flour.
3. Pulse until mixture is almost a puree.
4. Dust hands with flour and shape mixture into 6 burgers. Dust them lightly in flour.
5. Layer the burgers with sheets of waxed paper and refrigerate for at least one hour.
6. Cook on a grill covered with foil for about 10 min. on each side or fry in pan at med. high for about 5 minutes each side.

Totally Tofu

Tofu is a truly versatile food and if you are looking for an alternative source of high quality protein, look no further! Tofu was originally made in China more than 2,000 years ago and has long been known as the "wonder food of the East".

Made from the soya bean, it is richer in protein than any other food of equivalent weight. It is low in fat, high in calcium and a good source of iron, phosphorus, potassium, essential B vitamins and fat soluble vitamin E.

You can now buy tofu in most supermarkets, wholefood and health food stores. It comes in various forms: silken, firm, exfra firm, smoked and marinated and can be used in both savory and sweet dishes. The firm, smoked and marinated varieties are usually used for savory dishes, curries, stir fries and burgers, while the various types of silken tofu are used in desserts, savory dips, sauces and mayonnaise. Certain types of tofu can be deep frozen, resulting in an interesting change of texture.

This makes it more 'spongy' so that it readily soaks up any flavorings you wish to add. Tofu is a whole food which is very easily digestible and therefore eminently suitable for everyone from the very young to the very old. So don't be put off any longer by first impressions, tackle tofu and discover a world of culinary possibilities.

First-Timer's Tofu Recipe

1 package of extra firm tofu (firm), rinsed and patted dry
Marinade:
1½ cups soy or tamari   1 clove garlic
½ cup water

1. Place all the ingredients for the marinade in small mixing bowl and whisk them together. Pour the marinade over the tofu, spooning it over each slice.
2. Turn the slices over so that all sides are coated well with the marinade. Cover bowl and place in refrigerator. Let tofu marinate for several hours or overnight, turning slices over occasionally.
3. When you are ready to cook the tofu, place the ingredients for coating mix in a shallow mixing bowl, and stir well. Preheat oven to 400 degrees.
4. Mist a baking sheet with nonstick cooking spray, and set aside. Remove each slice of tofu from the marinade and place tofu on baking sheet.
5. Bake the tofu until the bottoms are golden brown, about 15 minutes.
6. Turn slices over, and bake until other sides are golden brown. Place on bun and garnish as desired.
7. It is really good, especially for first time tofuers!

Scrambled Tofu

1 lb extra firm tofu
¼ - ½ cup nutritional yeast (to taste)
2-4 tablespoons of Tamari (again to taste)
1-2 cups of chopped veggies (try onions and carrots)
1 tablespoon of olive oil (or any kind of oil for that matter)

1. Place a pot (or large enough frying pan) over medium-high heat and leave it there until it gets nice and hot (a drop of water on it will immediately sizzle).
2. Immediately add in the olive oil and chopped veggies and stir around until the onions take on a glossy finish (on their way to becoming translucent) and a wonderful strong aroma rises.
3. Then crumble in the tofu (no need to drain it) and stir it around for a minute or so.
4. Then add in the nutritional yeast and tamari and stir around for a few more minutes.
5. You basically just want to heat it through so the time isn't a big deal.
6. Taste it while cooking and adjust flavorings as you see fit.

Tofu Cutlets

1. Cut a pound of tofu in half vertically and then into four horizontal slices each so that you have eight "cutlets" about 1 x 4 inches long.
2. Wrap each cutlet in a paper towel and gently squeeze any excess water out.
3. In a 9 x 13 cake pan or casserole dish, mix the following

Marinade:

4 tbsp. tamari or soy
6 tbsp. water
1 tbsp. olive oil
2 cloves garlic, minced
1 inch of ginger root, peeled and grated or minced very fine

1. Marinate the tofu for at least four hours, up to 12 hours, turning at least once.
2. Heat oven to 425F, remove tofu from marinade and place on a cookie sheet.
3. Bake for about 20 - 30 mins, until firm but not crispy.
4. These tofu cutlets can be combined in a stir fry or (our favorite): served over rice with a little umeboshi paste mixed in, with fresh steamed spinach and mango slices fried for just a minute in maple syrup or rice syrup with a tsp. of margarine.

Stir-Fried Mushrooms with Smoked Tofu and Sea Palm

Serves 2-3

½ oz. sea palm, soaked for 10 minutes and cut into 1-inch lengths.
1½ tbsp. unrefined vegetable oil
1 onion, finely sliced
¼ cup mushrooms, finely sliced
shoyu soy sauce, to taste
¼ cup smoked tofu, cut into small cubes
1 carrot, cut into thin strips
ground black pepper (optional)
finely chopped fresh parsley, to garnish.

1. Place the sea palm and its soaking water in a cooking pot. Bring to the boil, reduce the heat, cover and cook until tender for about 30 minutes.
2. Heat a frying pan and add the oil, onion, mushrooms and a few drops of shoyu soy sauce.
3. Sauté at a medium heat for 5 minutes.
4. Add the cooked sea palm, tofu and carrots and sauté until crunchy and lightly cooked.
5. Add more shoyu soy sauce and pepper, to taste.
6. Serve hot, garnished with the finely chopped parsley.

Tofu Burgers

Once cooked, these tasty burgers freeze well.
Makes 8 burgers

1 block firm tofu
¼ cup bulgar or ½ cup cooked millet or rice
4 tbsp. hot water
1 small onion, very finely chopped
¼ cup mushrooms, very finely chopped
¼ cup carrot, grated
1 vegetable stock cube, crumbled
2 tbsp. soy sauce
1 tsp. dried mixed herbs or 2 tsp. any fresh herb
2 tbsp. whole-wheat flour plus a little extra for coating

1. Break up the tofu with your fingers into very small pieces.
2. Mix all the ingredients together in a bowl and squeeze well to shape into burgers. (As the mixture is very sticky it will help if you dip your hands and utensils in cold water).
3. Refrigerate for an hour or two.
4. For a crisp coating, toss the burgers in a little whole-wheat flour before frying. Deep fry the burgers in oil, a few at a time. Drain well and serve hot or cold.

Note: It is most important to fry the burgers in very hot oil to avoid disintegration.

Peppers with Tofu

Serves 2

10 oz. pack of firm tofu (see method)
1 tsp. sesame oil little garlic powder little sugar little onion power if you have it
¼ cup oil
2 cloves of garlic
2 or 3 tbsp. soy sauce salt and pepper
1 large green pepper
1 cup Spanish onion, cut bite size
1 cup celery hearts, cut bite size
1 tbsp. Corn starch water
1 large tomato, cut in eight
(serve with rice or noodles)

Tofu: This is the slow part, so make lots and use the extra later for Hungarian goulash.

1. Slice the tofu into ⅛" slices Mix sesame oil, garlic powder, onion powder, sugar and
2. 1 tbsp. Cooking oil together in a small bowl.
3. Paint a little oil onto a cookie sheet and lay the tofu on.
4. Paint on a little of the sauce onto the tofu.
5. Bake in a medium oven, turning the tofu occasionally. Paint the other side.
6. Cook until it becomes chewy (Don't let it dry out - take out the pieces that are done.) This process may take about 1 hour.
7. Cut the tofu up into bite size pieces with a knife and set aside in the bowl.
8. **The meal:** Put some oil in the hot frying pan.
9. Add the celery cook a few minutes while you prepare the onion.
10. **Stir fry:** Add the onion and cook while you prepare the garlic.
11. Add the garlic and cook while you prepare the green pepper. Add green pepper; cook 4 or 5 min.
12. Add about 2 teaspoons of soy sauce.
13. Add the tofu. Stir fry 1 minute Add about 1½ cups of water. Add salt and pepper to taste.
14. Cook another 5 minutes covered.
15. Thicken with corn starch and water mixture.
16. You should now have a brown sauce with your vegetables. Add the tomatoes, cover and cook for 5 minutes more. The tomatoes should not go to mush. Add water as needed to the sauce.
17. Serve over rice or noodles.

Options: Add a few chili peppers while cooking Add a little slivered fresh ginger while cooking. Cook lots of rice and use the extra for veggie fried rice.

Stuffed Mushrooms

Serves 4

4 large mushrooms
1 block smoked tofu, mashed with a fork
little vegetable oil
1 small onion, finely chopped
1 clove garlic, crushed
½ tsp. turmeric
1 tbsp. shoyu
dash (⅛ tsp.) nutmeg
pepper to taste
chopped parsley
juice of lemon

1. Wipe the mushrooms carefully. Remove the stalks, chop them finely and keep to one side.
2. Put the mushrooms into a pan large enough to hold them in one layer, add a little water and steam cook until they have softened a little.
3. Remove from the pan and leave to drain.
4. Heat the oil and fry the onion and garlic until golden.
5. Add the chopped mushrooms stalks together with the turmeric, shoyu, nutmeg and pepper and cook for a couple of minutes.
6. Remove from the heat, mix with the tofu and pile on the top of the mushrooms.
7. Put into on ovenproof dish and bake at 375°F/190°C for 20 minutes.
8. Remove from oven; squeeze juice of lemon and garnish with chopped parsley and serve immediately.

Marinated Tempeh

Serves 4 to 8

Make Marinated Tempe on the weekend to have on hand for quick meals throughout the week. The marinade ingredients can be changed to suit your own tastes. Try adding different herbs or spices, nutritional yeast flakes or flavored vinegars.

1½ cups water or vegetable broth
2 tablespoons tamari or soy sauce
1 tablespoon brown rice vinegar or other mild vinegar
2 slices fresh ginger
2 cloves garlic, crushed
1 pound temper, cut into 2-ounce or 4-ounce pieces.

1. Combine all ingredients in a shallow dish, and refrigerate for at least 30 minutes or overnight, turning temper once.
2. Transfer ingredients to a saucepan.
3. Simmer, covered, for 20 minutes, turning temper once.
4. Remove temper, and refrigerate for up to 4 days.
5. The cooking liquid can be strained and used as a sauce for vegetables or rice.

Serving Suggestions: Enjoy hot Marinated Tempe patties as vegetarian burgers in a bun with lettuce and tomato. Thinly slice chilled Marinated Tempe and use in sandwiches, or add to salads. Thin slices of Marinated Tempe can also be browned in oil to serve for breakfast. Cube Marinated Tempe, sauté until browned, and serve with stir-fries. Grate Marinated Tempe to add to casseroles or chili. Crumble Marinated Tempe and simmer gently in your favorite barbeque sauce.

Soups

Winter Vegetable Stew

1 good sized rutabaga
3 turnips
3-4 carrots
1 sweet potato
2-3 white potatoes
1 large onion
½ cup barley, rinsed well

1. Peel and cube all, put into a large stew pot or Dutch oven, add water to cover.
2. Let simmer for an hour or so, until all is nearly tender.

Add:

3. ⅓ cup red lentils and 1 teaspoon dry thyme.
4. Simmer until the lentils have cooked and fallen apart and thickened the stew.
5. Add more water if required.
6. Add salt or veggie broth powder to taste and lots of freshly ground black pepper. Serve.

Carrot, Leek and Olive Stew

Serves 4

Serve this unique stew with whole wheat crackers.

3 cups leeks, scrubbed and chopped in
½-inch pieces
1 clove garlic, crushed
1 tablespoon olive oil
2 cups raw carrots, scrubbed and finely diced
1 cup raw red potato, finely diced
2 tablespoons tomato paste
large pinch dried thyme
large pinch dried oregano
salt and pepper to taste
2 cups vegetable broth (can use water -Matt)
½ cup ripe olives, pitted and chopped

1. Sauté leek and garlic in oil in a 4-quart stew pot.
2. When leeks are soft, add all other vegetables and seasonings.
3. Add broth, cover, and bring to boil.
4. Reduce heat and simmer at least 45 minutes.
5. During last five minutes of cooking, stir in olives.
6. (Note: Thicken with
7. 1 tablespoon whole wheat or rice flour if desired.)

Vegetable Gumbo

1 onion, chopped
½ red, green and yellow bell peppers, diced
2 ribs celery, diced
1 garlic clove, minced
1 lb okra, sliced, fresh or frozen
1 lb tomatoes, fresh or canned
2 cup corn, fresh, frozen, canned
1 teaspoon vegetable bouillon granules
½ cup white grape juice
½ cup water
½ cup vegetable broth
¼ tsp. tabasco sauce
¼ tsp. paprika

1 large yellow onion, chopped
1½ tablespoons minced garlic
3 tablespoons chopped parsley leaves
5 teaspoons salt
2 teaspoons black pepper
1 teaspoon cayenne pepper
5 bay leaves
2½ teaspoons dried thyme
2 tbsp. fresh chopped parsley
1 tbsp. basil or rosemary, minced
5 tablespoons file powder vegetable coating spray

1. Method: In a large heavy stew pot, place bouillon and ½ cup white grape juice, onion, bell peppers, celery garlic, cook until tender, 5-7 minutes.
2. Add other ingredients, cook over low heat, stirring occasionally to keep from sticking to bottom.
3. Cover and simmer gently until corn and okra are done. (or simmer in crock-pot 6-7 hours).
4. Cut fresh corn from cob with a sharp knife, then scrape the remaining corn off the cob

Note:. Four ears will make about two cups. If you use dried herbs, rub them with the palms of your hands before adding to the pot, this releases their aroma and goodness.

Onion Soup

onions (as many as appropriate or to taste)
vegan stock
tomatoes - fine chopped 1 per person
mustard - 1 tsp. per person
1 pint of water per person
salt and pepper to taste
tomato puree - 1 squeeze per person
garlic puree - to taste
provencal herbs
pesto
lemon juice

1. Simply put all into a saucepan and simmer for at least 10 minutes; the longer the better as it intensifies the taste. Very cheap, simple and refreshing for summer!

Holiday Pumpkin Stew

4 cups pumpkin pulp, diced
2 cups dried navy beans, soaked overnight in 5 cups water then drained
2 medium yellow onions, diced
2 large cloves garlic, minced
2 tablespoons olive oil
3 cups fresh corn cut off the cob or
3 cups frozen corn 6 large tomatoes - peeled and diced or
1 28 oz. can tomatoes, diced 6 tablespoons tomato paste
1½ tablespoons dried -or-
3 tablespoons fresh Basil
1½ tablespoons dried or
3 tablespoons fresh Oregano
2 bay leaves ¾ teaspoon black pepper or to taste
1 teaspoon dried or
2 teaspoons fresh Marjoram
1 tablespoon salt, or to taste

To prepare pumpkin: Cut top from pumpkin and scoop out seeds and stringy fibers. With a large spoon, scrape out and reserve pumpkin pulp being careful to leave at least an inch on the sides, so the pumpkin will stand up.

To prepare stew: Sauté onions and garlic until tender in olive oil in a 5 quart heavy pot. Put soaked and drained navy beans, diced pumpkin pulp, and seasonings (except salt) in pot with enough water to cover about 2 inches above ingredients. Bring to a boil, then turn heat to low. Cover and simmer, stirring occasionally, for 2 hours or until beans are tender. Add tomatoes, tomato paste, corn and salt. Bring to a boil, then turn down to a simmer for 30 minutes more.

When ready to serve, place pumpkin shell on serving plate and ladle hot stew into it.

Noodle Soup

1. Sauté onion in oil.
2. Add 1 tablespoon paprika, a dash of cayenne, peas, carrots, parsley root, and salt and pepper (to taste).
3. Add hot water so that you get the desired amount of soup.
4. Boil; add 3 vegetable bouillon cubes.
5. Cook until the vegetables are done to your liking.
6. Add noodles (homemade are best!).
7. Cook until noodles are done.

Baked French Onion Veggies

Serves 4

4 medium potatoes
4 large carrots
1 large onion 6 cloves garlic
1 sweet potato any kind of beans (green, butter)
1 parsnip some whole mushrooms
2 packets of French onion soup mix (check the ingredients!) approx.
1½ cups water mixed herbs

Preheat oven to fairly hot, chop all veggies and put in an oven bag. Mix soup packets with water, pour onto veggies and seal bag. Put in oven for approx. 30 mins or until veggies are tender.

Cool Cucumber And Onion Soup

Serves 2-4

1 cucumber - large
1 onion - also large (though this is dependent on taste)
cold stock substitute (anything not too strong in taste)
condiments to taste

1. Coarsely grate both the whole cucumber and the peeled and topped onion and place in a bowl.
2. Then make up enough of the stock substitute to make two good sized portions of soup. (The amount of stock required is up to personal taste; this recipe could easily stretch to 4 portions if desired.)
3. Next chill the stock substitute and add to the cucumber and onion. Stir and serve, with cucumber rind to garnish.

Garlic Soup

12-15 medium sized garlic cloves
2 big skinned tomatoes or a can
2 tsp. paprika
4-5 cups water
parsley
2 tbsp. vegetable oil
salt and pepper to taste

1. Peel the garlic cloves and cut them in halves.
2. Slice the tomatoes.
3. Heat the oil and warm the garlic lightly in it.
4. Add tomatoes, stir, add paprika, water, salt and black pepper (careful with the pepper).
5. Let simmer 45 minutes. Add parsley on top.
6. Eat with French bread, pasta or to your liking.

Zucchini & Corn Chowder

Serves 6

1 tablespoon margarine
4 shallots, chopped
2 tablespoons plain flour
3 cups soy drink
3 small zucchini, grated
1 can creamed corn
a veggie stock cube
¾ teaspoon salt (or no salt as stock cube is salty)

1. Place margarine and shallots in a saucepan and sauté for 1 minute.
2. Stir through the flour, then cook for further minute
3. Remove from heat and gradually add soy milk, then remaining ingredients.
4. Stir over medium heat until the mixture boils and thickens.

Gypsy Soup

Serves 4

3 – 4 tbsp. olive oil
2 cups chopped onion
2 cloves chopped garlic
2 cups sweet potatoes -or- winter squash, chopped & peeled
½ cup chopped celery
1 cup chopped fresh tomatoes
¾ cup chopped sweet peppers
3 cups stock or water

1½ cups cooked chickpeas
2 tsp. paprika
1 tsp. turmeric
1 tsp. basil
1 tsp. salt
dash cinnamon
dash cayenne
1 bay leaf
1 tbsp tamari soy sauce

1. In a soup kettle or large saucepan, sauté onions, garlic, celery and sweet potatoes in olive oil for about five minutes.
2. Add seasonings, except tamari, and the stock or water.
3. Simmer, covered, fifteen minutes.
4. Add remaining vegetables and chickpeas.
5. Simmer another 10 minutes or so, until all the vegetables are as tender as you like them.

Notes: The vegetables used in this soup are flexible. Any orange vegetable can be combined with green for example, peas or green beans could replace the peppers. Carrots can be used instead of, or in addition to the squash or sweet potatoes, etc.

Garlicky Cream of Celery Soup

Servings 6

12 large celery stalks
2 tablespoons margarine, divided
1 large onion, chopped
8 cloves garlic, minced
2 tablespoons unbleached white flour
3 medium potatoes, peeled and diced
water
2 tsp. salt-free herb-and-spice seasoning mix
¼ cup mixed chopped fresh parsley and dill
¼ cup celery leaves
1 to 1½ cups soymilk, as needed

1. Salt and freshly ground pepper to taste.
2. Chopped fresh dill or parsley for garnish.
3. Trim 10 stalks of celery and cut into ½-inch dice.
4. Trim the remaining 2 stalks, cut them into ¼-inch dice, and set aside.
5. Heat a tablespoon of the margarine in a large soup pot.
6. Add the onion and garlic and sauté over moderate heat until the onion is lightly golden.
7. Sprinkle in the flour and stir it in until it disappears.
8. Add the 10 stalks of celery, the potatoes, and just enough water to cover.
9. Bring to a boil, then add the seasoning mix, fresh herbs, and celery leaves.
10. Simmer over low heat until the vegetables are tender, about 25 minutes.
11. Remove from the heat.
12. With a slotted spoon, transfer the solid ingredients to the container of a food processor or blender and puree, in batches if necessary, until very smooth.
13. Stir back into the soup pot.
14. Return to very low heat and add enough soymilk to achieve a slightly thick consistency.
15. Heat the remaining 1 tablespoon of margarine in a small skillet.
16. Add the reserved celery and sauté over moderate heat until it is touched with golden spots.
17. Add to the soup, then season to taste with salt and pepper.
18. Serve at once, or allow the soup to stand for an hour or so, then heat through as needed.
19. Garnish each serving with chopped dill or parsley.

Split Pea Soup

2 stalks celery, diced
1-2 carrots, diced
1 medium, or 2 small potatoes, peeled & diced
1 onion
3 bay leaves
salt and pepper to taste
1 tsp. marjoram
½ tsp. thyme
¼ cup. fresh parsley, chopped
3-4 tbsp. vinegar (red wine or white)
8-11 cups water
1½ cups split-peas

1. Sauté onion, celery, carrot, and bay leaves in water (or oil) until soft.
2. Add marjoram and thyme, salt, pepper, split-peas, and 7-8 cups water and bring to a boil.
3. Lower to medium-high and cook until split peas are soft, 50-60 minutes.
4. When soup becomes too thick, add additional water to prevent it from burning (and to keep it a soup rather than a stew).
5. Add potatoes and parsley and cook 10 minutes.
6. Remove from heat, add vinegar, mix well, and serve.

Chickpea & Garlic Soup

Serves 3

vegetable stock to sauté (made with 1 OXO stock cube)
4-6 garlic cloves (4-6 tsp)
1 stick celery (¾ - 1 cup)
1 (sweet) red (bell) pepper (¾ cup)
1 small carrot (¼ cup)
1 can (15 oz) chickpeas (garbanzo beans)
¾ cup V8 juice (can substitute tomato juice
freshly-ground black pepper
½ tsp. dried basil (not more!)

1. Finely chop the garlic, celery, red pepper and carrot.
2. Sauté in vegetable stock for about 7-8 minutes until celery is translucent and vegetables are soft.
3. Meanwhile, drain and rinse the chickpeas.
4. Add to the saucepan with V8 juice and 1½ cups water.
5. Season with black pepper and add the basil.
6. Bring to the boil, then cover, reduce heat and simmer for 20 minutes, stirring occasionally.
7. Puree (a hand blender works fine) and adjust consistency by adding more water if necessary.

Spiced Carrot and Orange Soup

Serves 8 to 10

2 pounds carrots, thinly sliced
2 tablespoons fragrant nut oil or canola oil
2 cups chopped onions
2 large celery stalks, diced
1½ cups fresh orange juice
¼ cup dry white wine
1 teaspoon each: ground cumin, coriander, ginger
½ teaspoon ground nutmeg
1 cup low-fat soymilk, or as needed
salt and freshly ground pepper to taste
3 tablespoons minced fresh parsley
3 tablespoons finely minced scallion

1. Reserve and set aside about ½ pound of the carrots.
2. Heat the oil in a large soup pot.
3. Add the onions and celery and sauté over moderate heat, stirring frequently, until golden.
4. Add the carrots (except for the reserved batch), along with 4 cups of water, the juice, wine, and spices.
5. Bring to a boil, then cover and simmer over moderate heat until the vegetables are quite tender, about 30 minutes.
6. Transfer in batches to the container of a food processor or blender and purée until quite smooth.
7. Return to a low heat and stir in enough milk or soymilk to give the soup a medium-thick consistency.
8. Season to taste with salt and pepper.
9. Let the soup stand off the heat for several hours before serving.
10. Just before serving, steam the reserved carrots until crisp-tender and stir into the soup along with the parsley and scallion.
11. Taste to correct consistency and seasonings before serving.

Spring Green Onion Soup

4 cup potatoes, chopped
1½ cup celery, chopped
2 green onions, chopped
2 tbsp. oil
2 vegetable bouillon cubes
3 tsp. tamari
3 tsp. parsley
1 tsp. liquid sweetener
1½ tsp. paprika
1 tsp. sea salt
1 tsp. dill weed
1 tsp. thyme
1 cayenne pepper, dashes
1 sea kelp, several dashes
½ tsp. vegetable broth powder
2½ cup water or stock

1. Steam the green onions and celery until tender.
2. In a large frying pan, sauté the green onion in oil for 1-2 minutes, then add all the seasonings and sauté 1 more minute.
3. Filling the blender twice, blend all the ingredients until fairly smooth, lovely green light green soup is created.
4. Simmer everything on medium heat for 15-25 minutes until the bite is off the onions and the flavors mingle.
5. Serve hot with bread, crackers, or other accompaniments. Keeps 3-6 days refrigerated.

Quinoa Soup With Corn

1 (14.5 oz) can vegetable broth
½ cup quinoa, rinsed and drained
1¾ cup water
¼ tsp. cayenne pepper
2 cloves garlic, minced
1 cup frozen or fresh corn kernels
1½ tbsp. chopped parsley or cilantro
1 tbsp. fresh lime juice

1. Rinse quinoa well in a fine strainer.
2. Place broth, quinoa, water, cayenne and garlic in a small soup pot and bring to a boil.
3. Reduce heat to medium and cook 10 minutes.
4. Add corn kernels and cook 3 minutes.
5. Add parsley or cilantro and cook for 1 minute.
6. Remove from heat and stir in the lime juice.
7. Serve hot or cold.

Mushroom, Squash and Barley Soup

Serves 6

1 tbsp. olive oil
2 medium onions, chopped
3 cloves garlic; minced
1 lb. mushrooms; sliced (approx. 6 cups)
1½ tbsp. all-purpose flour
6 cups vegetable broth
½ butternut squash; peeled and diced (approx. 1½ cups)
1 red bell pepper; diced
1 cup quick-cooking barley
½ medium-dry sherry (non-alcohol sherry or apple juice for substitution)
4 tbsp. fresh dill, chopped

1. Heat oil in a Dutch oven or large pot over medium heat.
2. Lightly sauté onions and garlic, stirring until softened for about 5-minutes.
3. Increase heat to high and add mushrooms.
4. Cook mushrooms, stirring often, until browned and liquid has evaporated, approximately 7-minutes more.
5. Reduce heat to medium and sprinkle flour over vegetables.
6. Continue to cook, stirring constantly until the flour is mixed through, about 1-minute.
7. Add broth, squash, bell pepper, barley and sherry.
8. Bring to a boil and reduce heat to a simmer.
9. Continue to cook, partially covered, until barley is tender, about 15 to 20-minutes.
10. Add half the fresh dill and season with salt and pepper to taste.
11. Ladle soup into serving bowls and sprinkle each portion with the remaining 2 tbsp. fresh dill.

TVP Stew with Parsley Dumplings

Serves 4-5

1 cup TVP
1 tsp. oregano
2 tbsp. olive oil
2 tsp. vegetable stock concentrate
1 tsp. herbes de provence
1 cup boiling water

Combine ingredients and let stand 3 hours:
1 cup turnip, peeled and diced
1 tbsp. fresh parsley, chopped
1 cup chopped onion
2 tsp. light sesame oil
1 cup diced carrot
2 cups water
½ cup sliced celery
5 tsp. tamari
2 bay leaves 2-3 potatoes, peeled and chopped
½ tsp. rosemary, and basil
1 cup frozen peas
1 clove garlic, minced
2 tbsp. cornstarch
2 tbsp. water

1. Sauté TVP, turnip, onion, carrot, celery, bay leaves, rosemary, basil, garlic, and parsley in sesame oil for 8 minutes.
2. Add water, tamari and potatoes.
3. Simmer for 10-15 minutes.
4. Add peas, continue cooking another few minutes.
5. Remove bay leaves.
6. Combine cornstarch and water, add to stew, and stir until thickened.
7. Season to taste with salt and pepper.
8. 1 cup all-purpose flour
9. ¼ cup chopped parsley (or dried herbs)
10. 2 tsp. baking powder
11. ½ cup milk
12. ½ tsp. salt
13. 2 tbsp. vegetable oil
14. Sift dry ingredients.
15. Add parsley.
16. Mix milk with oil, and add to dry ingredients.
17. Stir until moistened.
18. Drop mixture by tablespoonfuls onto stew.
19. Cover and cook for
20. 15 minutes (do NOT lift the lid!).

Tuscan Navy Bean Soup

Serves 6

2 tablespoons olive oil
1 medium onion, chopped
3 cloves garlic, minced or pressed
3 cups vegetable broth
1 16 oz. can peeled tomatoes (undrained), chopped
1 teaspoon dried basil
½ teaspoon dried oregano
salt & pepper to taste
½ cup small uncooked pasta (elbow, shells, etc.)
1 16 oz. can navy beans with liquid

1. Heat olive oil in a large soup pot over medium heat.
2. Add onion and sauté about 1 minute.
3. Add garlic, broth, tomatoes, and spices.
4. Bring to a boil.
5. Stir in pasta.
6. Reduce heat to low and cover.
7. Simmer about 10 minutes, stirring occasionally.
8. Add beans and heat through.

Spring Vegetable Soup with Matzo Balls

2 tbsp. safflower oil	1 cup tomatoes, drained & chopped
1 large onion, finely chopped	½ teaspoon cumin
2 med. celery stalks, diced	2 cup cauliflower, chopped
1 med. potato, peeled and diced	1 salt & pepper
	1 cup lettuce, shredded
2 med. carrots, diced 6 cup water	1 cup peas, steamed
	1 tbsp. dill, fresh, minced
2 ea vegetable bouillon cubes	2 ea scallions, minced
	1 matzo balls
1 handful of celery leaves	

1. Heat oil in a large soup pot.
2. Add onion & celery & sauté over moderate heat until golden.
3. Add potato, carrots, water, bouillon cubes, celery leaves, tomatoes & cumin.
4. Bring to a boil, reduce heat, cover & simmer for 15 minutes.
5. Add cauliflower & continue to simmer for 10 minutes more. Season to taste. Remove from heat & let soup cool. Refrigerate overnight to develop flavor.
6. Just before serving, heat soup & add remaining ingredients. Simmer for 10 to 15 minutes.
7. Add more water if needed. Serve with 3 to 4 matzo balls per bowl.

Salads

Strawberry-Candied Pecan Salad

1 pkg. (5 oz.) mixed baby greens
¾ cup sliced fresh strawberries
¼ cup Kraft Shredded Parmesan Cheese
¼ cup sliced red onions
¼ cup coarsely chopped Planters Pecans, candied
¼ cup Kraft Balsamic Vinaigrette Dressing

1. Combine all ingredients except dressing.
2. Toss with dressing just before serving.

Making Candy Pecans:
Combine nuts and 2 tbsp. sugar in skillet; cook and stir on medium heat 5 min. or until sugar is melted and evenly coats nuts.

Layered Salad

4 cups shredded lettuce (Romaine hearts)
¼ cup sliced water chestnuts
1cup diced tomatoes (remove seeds)
½ cups frozen peas
A few very finely sliced red onions
½ cup diced soy cheddar cheese

1. Layer in a flat Pyrex baking dish, starting and ending with lettuce.
2. Spread enough mayonnaise (use vegan mayo or soy recipe)across the top to prevent air getting to the salad.
3. Cover and refrigerate 6-8 hours before serving.
4. Just before serving top with grated soy cheese and Veggie Bacon Bits.

Seven-Layer Soybean Salad

1. Boiled and sliced red salad potatoes
2. Blanched broccoli florets (to blanch broccoli florets, boil them for 1 minute in water to cover, then drain immediately.)
3. Shredded red cabbage.
4. Cooked soybeans
5. Chopped romaine lettuce
6. A thin layer of soy/vegan mayonnaise dressing
7. Lightlife Fakin' bacon bits (vegan) or sunflower seeds
8. Arrange the ingredients in layers in the order listed above.
9. Do not toss. Chill thoroughly before serving.

Hoppin' John Salad

1¼ cup cooked or canned (rinsed and drained)
  black-eyed peas
⅓ cup chopped onion
6 tbsp. distilled white vinegar
1½ cup cooked brown rice
2 tbsp. water
1 10-oz pkg. frozen chopped spinach
1 spinach, thawed and well
1 drained
¼ tsp. pepper
2 tbsp. baco bits (optional)

1. In a large bowl, toss the black-eyed peas, rice, spinach, and onion until completely combined.
2. In a small bowl, stir together the vinegar, water, and pepper.
3. Pour over the salad and toss.
4. Chill for at least a few hours to let flavors blend.
5. Sprinkle on the Baco Bits (if you use them), toss again, and serve.
6. Note: I've never made this with the Baco Bits and think it is just fine without them.

Crunchy Confetti Salad

Makes 3 cups

Try to cut the vegetables all approximately the same size as the soybeans. Feel free to add or substitute other veggies, depending on what's available (try cucumber, radish, zucchini or celery).

1 tablespoon olive oil (optional)
1 tablespoon balsamic vinegar
1½ cups cooked soybeans
2 bell peppers, trimmed and diced (for the prettiest effect, use two of different colors, such as red and yellow, or orange and green)
½ red onion, diced
½ cup chopped fresh parsley
salt to taste (optional)

1. Whisk together olive oil and balsamic vinegar.
2. Set aside.
3. Combine soybeans, diced peppers and diced onion in a bowl.
4. Add dressing and parsley, and toss to combine.
5. Add salt to taste.
6. Chill thoroughly before serving.

Wild Rice Picnic Salad

Makes six 3/4-cup servings

2½ cups cooked wild rice
2 cups sliced red grapes
8 ounce can water chestnuts, drained and chopped
¼ -⅓ cup soft tofu or plain soy "yogurt"
2 tablespoons eggless mayonnaise
1 tablespoon dill weed
¼ cup slivered almonds

1. In a large bowl combine wild rice, grapes, and water chestnuts. In a separate bowl, beat tofu or yogurt with a fork until smooth.
2. (If the tofu does not beat to the consistency of mayonnaise, add a few drops of water.)
3. Add vegan mayonnaise and dill weed, and stir well.
4. Pour over wild rice mixture and mix thoroughly.
5. Chill for several hours. Toss in almonds before serving.

Live Sweet & Spicy Kale

This kale recipe is one of my favorites of Dr. Sunyatta Amen.. quoting her "full of life, sweet and spicy"! Kale has the highest concentrations of phytonutrients. But not when we cook the greens to death, instead of eating them live. When picking out your kale, pick the deepest colors – they have much greater vitamins and carotenoids.

Kale Prep:
3 bunches of Dinosaur Kale
1 tbsp. olive oil
½ tsp. of Celtic or Himalayan salt

The Sweet & Spicy Marinade:
3 tbsp. Nama Shoyu or Soy Sauce
3 scallion (green onion) thinly chopped
3 tbsp. Agave
juice of 1 lime (the vitamin c helps you absorb all that great iron from the kale)
1 tbsp. toasted sesame oil
1 tsp. Udo's omega 3 6 9 DHA blend (will reduce inflammation in joints, lubricate skin, hair and is a wrinkle killah!)
1 tbsp. black sesame seeds (white will do if you don't have black)
¼ tsp. Chinese mustard powder (or wasabi)
1 pinch of cayenne to taste

1. Chop kale finely. Add olive oil and pinch of sea salt to bowl.
2. Massage kale and leave it to sit for an hour.
3. Mix marinade ingredients together and then pour into Kale bowl.
4. Toss the salad well and serve.

Desserts

Raspberry Tofu Dessert

Serves 4
1½ cup raspberries, fresh or frozen
1 packet firm silken tofu
½ tsp. vanilla essence
2 tbsp. honey

1. If using frozen raspberries allow to thaw completely, retaining a few for garnishing.
2. Combine all the ingredients and press through a sieve to remove the raspberry seeds.
3. (This is made easier if first processed in a liquidizer or food processor).
4. Divide the mixture between four dessert dishes and chill for up to 2 hours.
5. Garnish with reserved raspberries and serve.

Double Chocolate Spice Brownies

Makes 12
¼ cup soy milk
2 tablespoons canola oil
1 tablespoon (packed) Ener-G powdered egg replace
½ cup whole-wheat pastry flour
½ cup Sucanat or sugar
¼ cup cocoa powder
1 teaspoon ground cinnamon
¼ teaspoon ground cardamom
small pinch of salt
1 cup dairy-free chocolate chips

1. Preheat oven to 350°F.
2. Oil an 8-inch square baking pan; set aside.
3. In a small mixing bowl, whisk together soy milk, canola oil, and Egg Replace until thick and foamy.
4. Set aside. In a medium mixing bowl, whisk together flour, Sucanat, cocoa powder, cinnamon, cardamom, and salt.
5. Add soy milk mixture and chocolate chips, and stir to combine.
6. Transfer batter into prepared pan.
7. Use a spatula to spread the batter evenly to the edges of the pan.
8. Bake for 20 min. Cool for 10 min. before cutting.

Strawberry Soup

Serves 4
1 pint fresh or frozen unsweetened strawberries (about 2 cups)
½ cup dry white wine (or apple juice as a non-alcohol substitute)
1 tsp. lemon rind; finely grated
½ cup granulated sugar
1 tbsp. fresh lemon juice

1. Hull the strawberries if fresh. Wash, rinse, and dry.
2. (If using frozen berries, thaw thoroughly and remove any excess liquid prior to preparation.)
3. Slice 3 of the berries and set aside for use as garnish later.
4. Place remaining berries in a blender or food processor.
5. Add wine, lemon zest, sugar and lemon juice and puree until smooth.
6. Pour into a bowl and refrigerate until well chilled.
7. Serve in chilled soup bowls with garnish of reserved strawberry slices.

Tofu with Peaches in Cream and Brandy Sauce

Serves 2

A delightful intimate dinner for two.

1 block firm tofu
little flour, for dusting
1 onion, very finely diced
1 tbsp. vegetable oil
1 tsp. Marigold bouillon powder or
1 vegetable stock cube, crumbled
1 fresh peach, skinned and halved or 2 tinned peach halves
1 tbsp. brandy
½ cup single cream

1. Wash the tofu in cold water and dry carefully.
2. Slice through horizontally and dust with a little flour.
3. Fry the tofu carefully in the oil until golden, turning once.
4. Remove from the pan and keep warm in the oven.
5. Add the peach halves to the pan and cook until just browned on the top.
6. Remove and keep warm.
7. Add the onion and bouillon powder and fry until golden.
8. Return the tofu to the pan, pour over the brandy and flame.
9. Douse the flames with the cream, top with the peach halves and serve at once.

Rich Tofu Crème Cheeze

Cashews contribute their sweet, buttery taste, a flavor often associated with dairy cream cheese, while tofu provides substance to this rich, tempting spread. For tasty vegetarian "lox & cream cheese", top with roasted red peppers.

¼ cup raw cashew pieces
3 tbsp. water
2 tbsp. fresh lemon juice
1 cup firm tofu, patted dry and crumbled

1 tbsp. brown rice syrup, or
2 tsp. pure maple syrup, or
1 tbsp. barley malt syrup
¾ tsp. salt, scant pinch of garlic granules

1. Place the cashew pieces, water, lemon juice, and syrup in a blender, and process several minutes into a thick, smooth cream.
2. Add the salt, crumbled tofu, and garlic granules, and process until very smooth.
3. It is essential to blend the mixture for several minutes in order to pulverize the tofu and achieve a velvety smooth consistency. Chill thoroughly before serving.

Cinnamon Raisin Scones

Makes 12 scones

Serve these relatively low-fat treats for breakfast with fresh oranges and plenty of your favorite hot beverage

1 cup whole-wheat pastry flour
1 cup unbleached all-purpose flour
1 tablespoon baking powder
1 teaspoon ground cinnamon
¼ teaspoon salt
½ of a 10- to 12-ounce block firm silken tofu, crumbled
1 tablespoon canola oil
2 tablespoons Spectrum Naturals Spread
¼ cup soy milk
¼ cup pure maple syrup
½ cup raisins

1. Preheat oven to 425°F. Whisk together flour, baking powder, cinnamon, and salt. Set aside.
2. In a separate mixing bowl, whisk together tofu, canola oil, and Spectrum Naturals Spread until a bit creamy.
3. Whisk in soy milk and maple syrup.
4. Add flour mixture and raisins, and stir until just combined.
5. Turn dough out onto a floured board, and roll or pat to a circle about ½-inch thick (this dough is very soft, so be generous with the flour to prevent sticking).
6. Use a sharp knife to cut dough into 12 triangular wedges.
7. Transfer wedges to an non-greased baking sheet, and bake for 15 minutes, or until scones are lightly browned.

Broiled Coconut Frosting

1¼ cup soy milk
⅛ tsp. xanthan gum
2 tbsp. honey
½ tsp. vanilla
A few drops butter flavoring
A small pinch of sea salt
⅔ cup raw unsweetened coconut
½ cup chopped nuts (optional)

1. Mix the first 5 ingredients.
2. Add coconut and nuts to the milk mixture and beat until smooth.
3. Spread over baked cake while still hot.
4. Return to oven and bake about 10 minutes in 275°.

Carrot Muffins

This easy recipe serves as an appetizer with crackers or pita chips. At dinner, it substitutes for butter as a bread spread.

1½ cups whole wheat flour ¾ cup whole wheat pastry flour
4 tsp. no-alum baking powder
½ tsp. sea salt
2 cups carrot puree
¼ cup maple syrup
⅓ cup soy milk
¼ cup natural light oil
2 tsp. vanilla
½ cup sunflower seeds
½ cup raisins

1. Preheat oven to 400F. Mix wet and dry ingredients separately.
2. Sift dry ingredients slowly into the wet. Add extra liquid only if needed to make a stirable batter.
3. Scoop the batter into a lightly oiled muffin tins.
4. Bake for 20 min., or until lightly browned on top and a toothpick comes out clean.

Carrot Muffins II

2 medium sweet potatoes
1 medium onion, minced
1 tbsp. maple syrup
1 tbsp. Tahini Salt and pepper to taste

1. Preheat oven to 350 degrees. Bake potatoes 30 to 40 minutes, or until soft.
2. While potatoes bake, heat water or veggie broth in a saucepan over medium heat.
3. Sauté onion 15 to 20 minutes or until golden brown.
4. Place cooked onions in food processor; blend a few seconds. Scoop out potato flesh; place in processor with onions.
5. Blend and add maple syrup, tahini, salt and pepper; blend again until smooth. Sample spread, adjusting maple syrup/tahini to taste. Serve warm or cover and refrigerate. Can be made 1 to 2 days ahead. Makes about 3 cups. An alternative to fatty spreads:
2 heads roasted garlic
1 can white beans, drained (save liquid)
6. Squeeze out the good stuff from the roasted garlic and blend until smooth with the drained beans.
7. Add back liquid as necessary for consistency.
8. Put in as pretty dish or crock and serve with good bread.

Vegetarian Strawberry Shortcake

Shortcake:
¼ cup tofu
3 tbsp. sugar
½ cup shortening
1 tsp. salt
1 tbsp. baking powder
½ tsp. cream of tartar
2 cup flour
½ cup water

Topping:
1 strawberries, as needed
1 sugar, optional

1. Preheat oven to 450F. Cream together the tofu, sugar & shortening.
2. Add the remaining dry ingredients in order, mixing well after each addition.
3. Add the water, you may need to add more to ensure that you have a fairly sticky dough.
4. Wet your hands & knead the dough until it is well
5. mixed. Transfer to an oiled 8 ½" round baking dish.
6. Bake in the preheated oven for 15 to 20 minutes.
7. Let cool approx. 5 min.; turning out onto a wire rack.
8. Slice strawberries. If desired, toss with a couple of tablespoonfuls of sugar. Spoon over the still warm shortcake. Serve immediately.

Chocolate Cake

1 cup water
6 tbsp, semolina flour mix Whisk together and set aside.
1 cup natural sugar or ½ cup honey
1¼ cups whole wheat pastry flour or spelt four
⅓ cup cocoa or carob powder
½ tsp. sea salt
1½ tsp. Featherweight Baking Powder
1 cup chopped nuts

Whisk ingredients in mixing bowl. Set aside:
½ cup olive oil
½ tsp. butter flavoring
1 tsp. vanilla
½ cup water

1. Add ingredients to soaked semolina flour mixture, beat until well blended then
2. fold into dry ingredients.
3. Pour into an 8"x8" baking dish.
4. Bake about 45 to 50 minutes in a 275" oven.
5. Spread Coconut Frosting (next recipe) on baked cake.

Caramel Apple Cinnamon Rolls

The Dough:
4½ cups AP flour
2¼ tsp. yeast
½ cup dark brown sugar
1 cup soy milk
1 tsp. vanilla
2 "flax eggs" (2 tbsp. ground flax + ½ cup water)
⅓ cup vegan butter (melted)

The Filling:
2 Granny Smith apples
½ cup brown sugar
2 tablespoons sugar
½ cup vegan butter
2 tablespoons cinnamon

The Glaze:
2 cups powdered sugar
4 tablespoons vegan butter
6 tablespoons apple cider
1 tsp. vanilla

The Drizzle:
(aka caramel)
½ cup sugar
3 tablespoons vegan butter
¼ cup vegan creamer

1. In a small saucepan, heat up the soy milk. Warm it until it's just warm enough to dip your finger in it. Remove from heat once warmed, and pour into a medium-sized bowl.
2. Add the brown sugar, and stir to dissolve. Add the yeast, stir, and set aside to proof.
3. Use a mixer (I can do this now!!) to blend together the ground flax seeds and water.
4. Add the flax mixture, melted butter, and vanilla to the proofed yeast (make sure it sat for about 10 minutes). Stir gently.
5. Grab a large bowl and measure out your flour. Add the wet mixture to the flour, and knead! Knead! Knead! It should be soft and "elastic" -- this will take a bit, but you will get there!
6. Place the dough back into the large bowl, shape into a ball, and cover with a warm, damp cloth. Let rise for about 30 min., or until the dough has doubled in size.

7. While the dough is rising, start your filling! You can either bake your apples, or cook them down on the stove. We chose the stove.
8. Chop your apples into teeny, tiny pieces.
9. Grab a small saucepan, and begin to melt your butter over medium heat. As it begins to melt, add apples and spices. Cook, cook, cook (stirring constantly) until apples are soft (but not mushy!).
10. Once your dough has risen, punch the ball into a disk and throw onto a floured surface.
11. Roll dough into a rectangle (about ¼ inch thick). Once you have a nice rectangle, brush the vegan butter over the dough, leaving 3" naked at one end (to stay sticky- you need to seal those buns somehow!).
12. Spread the filling evenly over the surface of the dough, avoiding the naked edge.
13. Roll that baby up! Cut into slices- you'll get about 8.
14. Line a baking sheet with parchment paper, and place rolls on top, facing up.
15. Cover the rolls with another warm, damp towel, and let rise for another 30 minutes. They should double in size again.
16. Preheat your oven to 400°F.
17. Once buns have risen, place in oven and bake for 10-15 minutes. You're looking to achieve that lovely golden brown color.
18. To make the glaze: Grab a small saucepan and melt butter over medium-heat. Add sugar, cider, and vanilla. Stir to combined, and turn heat to low.
19. To make the caramel: Make sure you have everything pre-measured and ready to go- caramel is fast! Heat the sugar in a medium-sized saucepan over medium-high heat. Stir continuously with a whisk. Once the sugar boils (and smells amazing), add the vegan butter and mix. Once the butter melts, remove from heat. Wait a few seconds, and add the vegan creamer. Wisk to smooth! BE CAREFUL!
20. Once the buns come out of the oven (ha), pour the glaze and caramel over them!

A Taste of Mexico
Appetizers & Snacks

Veggie Burros

Serves 6
2 tablespoons vegetable oil
1 onion, chopped
1 green pepper, chopped
1 zucchini, sliced
1 cup broccoli florets
2 carrots, sliced
1 4 oz. can chopped green chilies
½ teaspoon garlic salt
⅛ teaspoon ground cumin
¼ teaspoon oregano
6 12-inch flour tortillas
½ head lettuce, shredded
1 tomato, chopped
salsa
guacamole

1. Heat oil in a large skillet and sauté onion, green pepper, zucchini, broccoli, and carrots.
2. When vegetables are tender, add chilies and seasonings. Stir and simmer for 6 minutes.
3. Spoon into warmed flour tortillas and roll burro-style.
4. Garnish with lettuce, tomato, salsa and guacamole.

Mole Posole

Serves 8
¼ onion, minced
1 green bell pepper, seeded and diced
1 Serrano pepper, seeded and minced
2 teaspoons vegetable oil
15 ounces chopped tomatoes with juices, (about 2 cups)
15 ounces kidney beans, rinsed, drained (2C)
15 ounces white hominy, canned, rinsed & drained
2 tablespoons prepared mole sauce
1 cup water

1. In soup pot, sauté onion, pepper and chili in oil over medium-high heat until onion is soft, about 4 to 5 minutes.
2. Add remaining ingredients. Bring to a boil.
3. Reduce heat and simmer for 10 minutes, covered.
4. Posole traditionally is served in clay soup bowls and garnished with crisp tortilla strips.

Salsa

The spelling of chili and Chile is deliberate.
Chili is a powder or a dish containing chilies.

1 x 1lb. can ready cut (diced) tomatoes in heavy puree or juice (or 3 big ripe tomatoes, the stem core removed, coarsely chopped, with their juice)
Juice of 1 lime
1 medium onion, chopped
1 medium carrot, grated (big grated pieces, not too small) or diced about ¼")
1 clove garlic, pressed
1 tsp. oregano and/or cilantro

Chilies (use one or more of the following: commercial chili powder, canned chopped green chilies, 2 dried New Mexico or Anaheim Chile and 1 chipotle chili ground in a spice mill into a powder, minced jalapenos or a couple dashes of Tabasco.

1. No amounts are given; it all depends on how spicy you like your food.
2. Start with just a little, ⅛ teaspoon, and add more if needed.)
3. A little sugar, if your tomatoes aren't sweet and ripe.
4. In a medium bowl or container with a cover, place the cut up tomatoes and their juice.
5. Add the rest of ingredients.
6. If you think it needs salt, add some.
7. Taste to see if you are getting a nice sweet/sour taste.
8. If not, add more lime juice or a touch of mild vinegar or more sweetener.
9. Cover and let sit for a while in the refrigerator to let the chili taste develop.

Note: Add more chili if it seems too bland to you. Chiles can take a while to develop on the tongue and different ones give heat to different places in your mouth and lips. Sometimes you don't feel it until the third or fourth bite. Have this with tortilla chips or add it as a flavoring to other things. Sometimes I add it to a can of black or kidney beans, add more onion and garlic, some water, and have CHILI NO CARNE. Sometimes I mix the salsa with sautéed, squished firm tofu to make no egg scrambled eggs (wrap these in a warmed tortilla, put more salsa on top, and you have a good lunch or dinner entree. Even better with a little soy cheese or nutritional yeast mixed in or a little soy cheese on top. This is also a good way to use up any leftover bean mixture). The Salsa keeps about 4 days in the refrigerator.

Tomato Dip Or Salsa

¾ lb red-ripe tomatoes
1 tsp. coarsely grated fresh ginger
2 tbsp. peeled, chopped green mango
1 scallion, finely sliced
¼ - ⅓ tsp. salt or to taste

1. Freshly ground black pepper, to taste
2. Cut the tomatoes into ⅛ inch thick rounds and arrange them in a single layer in a platter.
3. Sprinkle the ginger, green mango, and scallion evenly over the tomatoes.
4. Sprinkle salt and pepper over the top.

Fabulous Salsa

1 small to medium green pepper
1 small to medium red pepper
2-3 green onions
1 small jar red pimentos-drained
1 can Le Suer Small Early Peas-drained
1 can white shoe peg corn-drained

Marinade:
¼ cup oil
¼ cup sugar
¼ cup rice wine vinegar

1. Chop peppers and green onions. Add pimentos, peas, and corn. Mix together marinade ingredients.
2. Add marinade to vegetables and let marinate for a few hours or overnight. Serve with tortilla chips.

Miami Black Bean and Garlic Salsa

Serves 4

1 package black bean soup with spices; made per directions
6 hot pickled garlic cloves, diced
3 medium tomatoes, diced
1 handful of fresh cilantro, diced
2 Jalapeno peppers, diced
2 cups fresh or store purchased Pico de Gallo salsa – medium heat

1. Cook the black bean soup according to directions on package (I recommend Miami brand black bean soup).
2. Continue cooking soup until most of the liquid cooks off and you are left with spiced beans.
3. Using a food processor or hand held chopper, chop all ingredients to a chunky consistency.
4. Squeeze juice of one lemon over the entire mixture.
5. Chill or serve at room temperature with corn chips or your favorite dipping chips. Prep. time: 2 hours.

Tex-Mex Salsa

Serves 6

½ med. red onion, chopped   1 garlic clove, chopped
¼ cup fresh cilantro, minced   juice of 1 lime
6 ripe but firm Roma plum tomatoes, chopped
3 tomatillos (Mexican green tomatoes), peeled and chopped
1 jalapeño chili (roasted, peeled, seeded and chopped) -or-
1 tbsp. canned jalapeño chilies, chopped

1. Place all ingredients in bowl of food processor or blender.
2. Process briefly to just combine; avoid creating a smooth paste. Yield: 3/4cup; 2 tablespoons each.

Black Bean Cakes and Mango Salsa

2-⅔ cup onion, cut   1 jalapeno pepper
1 tbsp. oil   1 tsp. each cumin and coriander
2 cloves garlic   ¼ tsp. hot pepper flakes
¾ cup carrots, cut   2 15 oz. cans black beans

1. Sauté onion until it softens and browns.
2. Add minced garlic and carrots to onions as it cooks.
3. Wash, seed and mince pepper, using about half, add to onion with cumin, coriander and pepper flakes.
4. Rinse and drain beans. When onion mix is well blended and soft, stir in the beans and heat well.
5. Puree the bean mix in a food processor and if it is too thick, add a little water.
6. Brown the cakes on both sides in skillet (or bake) serve with mango salsa

Salsa Mexicana

No brainier, and everyone thinks you're a genius:
Half dozen ripe tomatoes, diced or one large can diced tomatoes

Diced very fine:
Two large stalks celery
Two medium carrots
One medium white onion
One medium red onion
One half each of yellow, green bell pepper
Three or four cloves of garlic
Black pepper, cayenne, dried chili peppers to taste.

Pineapple Salsa

2 cups minced fresh (or canned-in-juice) pineapple
2 medium cloves garlic, minced
2 - 3 tablespoons fresh mint
2 tablespoons fresh lime juice
¼ teaspoon salt
¼ teaspoon cumin
cayenne, to taste

1. Combine everything, cover lightly and refrigerate.
2. This keeps a long time.

Blender Salsa

1 15-16 ounce can of whole tomatoes
2 cloves garlic
¼ cup fresh cilantro leaves
1 fresh jalapeño pepper, seeded with stem removed

1. Place all of the ingredients in a blender or food processor.
2. Process until smooth. Chill.

Watermelon Salsa

Serves 1
2 cups watermelon, peeled, seeded,, and cubed
1 cup nectarine, peeled & cubed
2 to 3 jalapeno peppers, seeded & minced
¾ cup sweet onion, diced
½ cup fresh cilantro, chopped
2 tablespoons lime juice
1 teaspoon grated orange rind
½ teaspoon salt

Stir together all ingredients; cover and chill one hour.

Pineapple Salsa II

½ medium pineapple, peeled, cored and cut into ½ inch dice, juices reserved
1 small red bell pepper, cut into ½ inch dice
3 medium green onions, minced
1 Serrano chili, seeded and minced
1 ½-inch piece fresh ginger, grated
1 tablespoon fresh lime juice
⅛ teaspoon salt

1. Mix all ingredients including reserved pineapple juices in medium bowl.
2. Cover. Let stand at least 1-hr. at room temperature.

Strawberry Salsa

Makes 2½ cups
½ medium red onion, chopped
1 jalapeno pepper, minced
½ each red, yellow, and green bell peppers, stemmed, seeded and chopped
¼ cup fresh cilantro, chopped
½ pint fresh strawberries, hulled and sliced
¼ cup fresh orange juice
2 tablespoons fresh lime juice
2 tablespoons extra virgin olive oil
salt and pepper

1. Place all the ingredients in a large mixing bowl and toss to combine. Cover and refrigerate at least 2 hours or up to 4 hours.
2. Fifteen minutes before serving, remove the salsa from the refrigerator, so it loses some of its chill.

Garbanzo Guacamole

⅔ cup canned garbanzo beans, drained
1 tbsp. lemon juice
1 large clove garlic, halved
¾ cup coarsely chopped onion
½ cup peeled, cubed avocado
2 tbsp. canned chopped green chilies
¼ tsp. salt
¼ tsp. pepper
1 cup seeded, finely chopped tomato
½ cup finely chopped green onion

1. Position knife blade in food processor bowl; add first 3 ingredients.
2. Process 20 secs., scraping sides of processor bowl.
3. Add ¾ cup chopped onion and next 4 ingredients; pulse 5 times or until mixture is chunky.
4. Transfer mixture to a medium bowl; stir in tomato and green onions. Cover and chill thoroughly.

Mango Salsa

2 tablespoons finely minced red onion
2 cups boiling water
1 ripe mango (6 inches long or 1½ cups minced)
2 tablespoons fresh lime juice
1 medium clove garlic, mined
½ teaspoon salt
2 tablespoons fresh cilantro
cayenne to taste (optional)

1. Place minced onion in a small strainer over bowl.
2. Slowly pour boiling water over the onion.
3. Let sit for 5 minutes. This will soften its bite.
4. Combine all ingredients and mix gently.
5. Cover tightly and refrigerate.

Spicy Southwest Salsa

Makes 2 cups
5 medium tomatoes, peeled (5-6)
1 medium onion, coarsely chopped
2 cloves garlic, minced
1 tsp. olive oil
1 tsp. granulated sugar
2 fresh green chilies, diced or 1 small can green
  chilies, drained
juice of 1 lime
2 tbsp. fresh cilantro, chopped

1. Place tomatoes in a pot of boiling water for approximately 30 seconds and remove with a slotted spoon.
2. Let tomatoes cool in chilled water and remove skin.
3. Place all ingredients in the bowl of a food processor and blend until coarsely chopped. Add salt and pepper to taste.
4. Serve with tortilla chips as an appetizer or with grilled tofu. Remember: Wear gloves working with fresh chilies to protect your skin from burning oils.
5. Make sure you clean and clear food surfaces and utensils utilizes on any hot peppers!

Avocado Salsa

1 small green basket of tomatillos (or about 6-7 medium tomatillos).
2 ripe Hass avocados
1 bunch of cilantro
1 cipollini onion
Himalayan sea salt (or Celtic sea salt works fine too, I just like the benefits of the Himalayan)
Pepper

1. Peel the little leaves off of the tomatillos and throw them in the blender and let them do its thing.
2. Then with the blender running, add the avocado (pitted and I just spoon the meat out of the skin) and the onion.
3. Add the salt and pepper (to taste).
4. Add the cilantro; after about 30 sec.; stop blending.

Salsa Verde

10 tomatillos-husked and rinsed
2-4 Serrano chilies and/or some yellow chilies (gueritos)
¼ cup chopped cilantro
some water
pinch salt
¼ cup finely diced white onion

1. You can either boil the tomatillos and chilies in water for about 10 minutes or you can grill them on a Comal until they are a bit charred.
2. each way is good but the flavor will be different.
3. (try them both!)
4. Then blend it all, and stir the onions in afterwards.
5. you could add a bit of spices if you want or experiment with the chilies, maybe some olive oil.
6. I end up making it with whatever I have available.

Fresh Salsa

2 cups finely chopped tomatoes
1 small onion finely chopped
⅓ cup canned green chilies(less if you prefer)
¼ cup finely chopped fresh cilantro
1 tablespoon fresh lime juice
pinch or two cayenne (optional)

1. Combine all of the ingredients, except the cayenne, and mix well.
2. Add the cayenne if it is not spicy enough.
3. This will keep for about one week in the refrigerator.

Yummy Fresh Salsa

6 to 8 ripe tomatoes, chopped
1 bunch cilantro leaves, chopped
1 medium onion, chopped
5 to 7 cloves raw garlic, pressed
3 to 5 (or more) tomatillos (optional), chopped
3 tablespoons lemon or lime juice
1 jalapeño, chopped or a couple dashes of cayenne
  for heat

1. Mix all the ingredients in a large bowl.
2. I press the garlic with a garlic press rather than chop because this allows the maximum flavor of the garlic to come out, with juices, etc.
3. Let it sit in the fridge for a couple hours for the flavors to mingle. Serve with tortilla chips.

Basic Red or Green Salsa

Serves 6
This salsa recipe is a staple with hundreds of variations possible. Try adding fresh corn off the cob or diced carrots after the blending. Serve plain with tostada chips or put on just about anything.

1 tablespoon roasted hot oriental peppers, chopped
1 cup fresh or frozen green or red mild to medium
  chili peppers
1 cup tomatoes, seeded and finely chopped
1 cup white onion, peeled and finely chopped
2 cloves fresh garlic, peeled and finely chopped
2-3 teaspoons vinegar
Salt and pepper to taste

1. Mix the ingredients together in a blender for a few seconds.
2. It should be like a thick juice with some chunkier pieces.

Mango Salsa

2 ripe mangoes
½ jalapeno pepper
1 small red onion
1 tbsp. lime juice
10 sprigs cilantro

1. Dice all ingredients, mix in large bowl.
2. Serve over bean cakes.

Pinto Bean Cakes With Salsa

Serves 4
1½ tbsp. Salad oil
1 small onion, finely chopped
¼ cup red bell pepper, finely chopped)
2 garlic cloves, minced
1 med fresh jalapeno chili, seeded & finely chopped
2 can pinto beans (15 oz. Each), drained & rinsed
⅛ tsp. liquid smoke
¼ cup chopped fresh cilantro
½ tsp. ground cumin
¼ tsp. pepper
⅓ cup yellow cornmeal
cooking spray (optional)
1 cup tomato-based salsa - homemade or purchased

1. In a 12-14 inch nonstick frying pan over medium heat, combine 1½ teaspoons of the oil with the onion, bell pepper, garlic and chili.
2. Stir often until onion is limp but not browned, about 5 minutes.
3. In a bowl, coarsely mash beans with a potato masher until they stick together.
4. Stir in onion mixture, liquid smoke, cilantro, cumin, and pepper, mixing well.
5. Spread cornmeal on a sheet of waxed paper.
6. When bean mixture is cool to touch, divide into 8 equal portions, shaping each into a ½-inch thick cake.
7. Coat cakes with cornmeal.
8. Return the frying pan to medium-high heat.
9. Add remaining 1 tablespoon oil.
10. When oil is hot, add cakes and brown lightly, 8 to 10 minutes; turn cakes over once.
11. Coat pan with cooking oil spray if cakes start to stick.
12. Serve cakes with salsa to add to taste.

Quick Tofu Sour Cream

Serves 6
8 ounces silken or soft tofu drained for 15 minutes, then squeeze out the remaining water through cheese cloth or very fine strainer

2 tablespoons lemon juice
pinch of salt

1. Combine the ingredients and blend with a hand blender or whisk until it is creamy smooth.
2. Use a spatula or spoon to crush any lumps that may remain. Serve over your favorite New-Mex dish.

Black Bean/Butternut Squash Chili

1 small butternut squash, peeled and cubed
2-3 cups black beans (cooked or canned)
1 onion
chopped spices - garlic, chili powder, cilantro, cumin, etc.
tomatoes, fresh or canned
1 lime, zest and juice
chipotle peppers (canned, with adobo sauce)

1. Sautee onion in small amount of oil until limp.
2. Add chopped garlic and spices and let that cook for a few minutes.
3. Add the grated zest of lime and squash cubes, cook for about 10 minutes.
4. Add beans, tomatoes, water if it needs it, and as many chipotle peppers as you can stand (they're hot) and some of that yummy sauce.
5. Cook until the squash is tender, at least a half hour, but it won't hurt it to go longer.
6. Serve with cilantro and lime juice.

Mex-Tex Entrees

Spicy Fat Free Chili

Serves 1
1 cup uncooked hard wheat berries
2 onions chopped
2 cups cooked pinto beans
3 tablespoons (approx.) cinnamon
¼ cup (approx.) chili powder
1 16 oz. jar picante sauce
2 14.5 oz. cans chili tomatoes
1 4.5 oz. can green chilies
1 7 oz. can jalapeno relish

1. Cook the wheat berries in 2½ cups of water (it will take about an hour).
2. Combine the remaining ingredients and simmer while the wheat berries are cooking.
3. Add the wheat berries when they are done and enjoy!
4. If the wheat berries do not absorb all the water, drain them before adding to the chili. They should be a little chewy.

Mexican Chili Burgers

Serves 12
1½ cups water
1 cup seven grain cereal
10 ounces soft tofu, blended
2 teaspoons McKay's chicken-style seasoning
¼ cup fresh cilantro, chopped
3 teaspoons canned chopped green chilies
1½ teaspoons dried oregano
1 teaspoon cumin
1 teaspoon chili powder
2 teaspoons garlic powder
1 cup onion, chopped fine
½ cup shredded carrots
2 cups cooked brown rice
½ cup to 1 cup cracker crumbs
1 cup plum tomatoes, seeded & chopped
cooking spray

1. In a small microwaveable bowl, combine 1½ cups water with the seven-grain cereal.
2. Cover, and microwave on high for 5 minutes.
3. Grains should be softened.
4. Let sit to cool while preparing the remaining ingredients.
5. In a blender container, blend the soft tofu to the consistency of cottage cheese.
6. If tofu is too thick, add a small amount of water.
7. In a large mixing bowl, pour blended tofu or beaten eggs and add McKay's chicken-style seasoning, cilantro, green chilies, oregano, cumin, chili powder, and garlic powder. Mix well.
8. Add the onions, carrots, rice, cracker crumbs, tomatoes, and softened grain mixture. Mix well.
9. If mixture is too thin to form burgers, add additional cracker crumbs.
10. If mixture is too crumbly, add a few tablespoons of water to hold mixture together.
11. Shape into 12 patties that are 4 inches in diameter and about ½ inch thick.
12. Spray a nonstick skillet with cooking spray and place over medium heat.
13. Add patties and sauté for about 5 minutes per side or until golden brown.

Tofu Chili

You may want to use frozen, thawed tofu for this.

1 medium green pepper
1 large yellow onion
4 stalks celery
1 clove garlic, chopped
1 (14 oz) can stewed tomatoes
1 (14 oz) can tomato sauce
1 (14 oz) can red kidney beans
1 (14 oz) can chili beans
1 to 3 tbsp. chili powder (to your taste)
1 cake low fat extra firm tofu (cut into ½ - ¾-inch cubes)

1. Sauté pepper, onion, celery and garlic with a little vegetable stock (or water) in a large pan (You can use a Dutch oven).
2. Then just add all the canned item juice and all to the pot along with the tofu.
3. Bring to a slow boil and simmer covered for at least 45 minutes.
4. Mike, make sure the chili powder you use is pure chili powder and doesn't have added ingredients like oregano, cumin, salt, etc.

Chili

Serves 4
3 tablespoons butter, margarine, or olive oil
2 medium onions, chopped
3 cloves garlic
16 ounces stewed tomatoes, undrained and diced
16 ounces red kidney beans
8 ounces black beans and/or white beans
8 ounces tomato sauce
6 tablespoons chili powder
1 tablespoon sugar
hot sauce, black pepper, white pepper and cayenne pepper to taste

1. In saucepan, cook onions and garlic in butter/margarine/oil until the onions are translucent.
2. Drain off the oil.
3. Stir in tomatoes, beans, and tomato sauce.
4. Stir in the chili powder, sugar, and spices as it cooks.
5. Cover and simmer for 15-30 minutes.
6. Prep. time: 45 min.

Chili Con Cashews

1 clove garlic, minced
1 to 2 carrots, grated
2 onions, chopped
1 to 2 green peppers, chopped
1 to 2 tbsp. oil
1 cup raw cashews
2 to 3 cups kidney beans, cooked
4 cups chopped tomatoes, with their liquid
1 tsp. each basil and oregano
1 tsp. chili powder, or to taste
1 tsp. ground cumin
1 bay leaf
½ tsp. salt or less
dash of pepper
¼ cup raisins
½ to ½ cup sesame seeds
1 recipe cornbread or whole wheat pasta

Optional:
2 tbsp. dry wine or vinegar
½ lb. mushrooms, sliced
1 medium zucchini, sliced

1. Sauté garlic and vegetables (except tomatoes) in oil.
2. Add nuts, beans, tomatoes, seasonings, raisins and wine if used.
3. Simmer for at least 2 hours, until thick, in covered pot or slow-cooker.
4. Serve topped with, over cornbread or pasta.

Vegetarian Chili with Rice

Serves 1
This is typically made in a crock pot. Just add sautéed onions and spices to the rest of the ingredients in a crock pot and let it cook overnight. add the cooked rice the next morning and leave the pot on all day.

3 cans Pinto beans	Cumin
1 large Can crushed tomatoes	2 Packets achiote (annato mix In ethnic section of Grocery)
1 large Onion, chopped	
½ cup Vegetable stock	1 tablespoon Parsley
1 tablespoon Garlic	2 tablespoons Paprika
1 tablespoon	2 tablespoons Hot sauce

1. Sauté onions, cumin, parsley, garlic and paprika in vegetable stock in large stock pot.
2. Add pinto beans, tomato, and achiote and simmer for about 1 hour.
3. Add about 4 cups of cooked brown rice and let stand for about 1 hour.

Vegetarian Chili with Rice

Serves 8

12 ounces dry beans, kidney, chili, or Jacob's cattle (soaked overnight and cooked with ½ teaspoon chili powder and ¼ teaspoon dried chili flakes under 15 lbs pressure for 7 minutes, reserve cooking liquid)

2 teaspoons tamari soy sauce

¼ cup water

3 small onions, chopped (about 1 cup)

3 small carrots, chopped (about 1 cup)

3 small peppers, chopped (about 1 cup)

5 tomatoes, peeled and coarsely chopped (about 2 cups)

1 large can tomato juice, no salt added if possible

½ teaspoon cayenne pepper

1½ teaspoons dried cumin powder

½ teaspoon black pepper (or to taste)

1⅓ cups brown rice, uncooked

1. In a soup pot, heat water and tamari.
2. When water just begins to boil, add onions, carrots, and peppers.
3. "Sauté" until vegetables start to soften.
4. Add tomatoes and cook 3 minutes longer. (If fresh tomatoes are out of season used canned and skip the 3 minutes additional cooking.)
5. Add remaining ingredients and enough of the been cooking liquid to give to appropriate chili consistency.
6. Bring to the boil.
7. Reduce heat and cover.
8. Simmer at least 50 minutes to cook the rice.
9. It can cook much longer, even all day in a crock pot.

Portobello Chili

2 cans of brown beans in tomato sauce

1 can of black beans

1 can of red beans (kidney)

1 cup of water

1 small can of tomato paste (in it mix 2 tbsp. of corn meal, cumin, dried chilies, cayenne peppers, chili powder)

1 can of baby corn

2 cans of mushrooms (one whole/one sliced)

3 stalks celery

chopped onion & garlic (little onion/ garlic mince or press 2) and anything else you like.

1. Place it all in the big pot put it on low heat and let it cook and stir ever 10 minutes or so until it bubbles then take it in the Tupperware to work and re heat it.

Millet Chili

This is a very easy recipe to prep and cook. It is ideal to have children help with or to have them cook supervised.

½ cup millet

¾ cup water

pinch sea salt

1 small onion

1 tablespoon vegetable oil (you can use ½ this amount)

1 teaspoon ground cumin

1 teaspoon oregano

½ teaspoons garlic salt (or garlic powder)

⅛ to ¼ teaspoons chili powder

½ can pinto beans

⅓ cup water

1 tablespoon tomato paste

1. Cover the millet with the water and a pinch of salt.
2. Bring to a boil, then lower heat, cover and simmer for about 20 minutes, by which time the water should be absorbed and the millet tender.
3. Meanwhile, chop the onion and sauté it in the oil for about 3 minutes.
4. Lower heat and add the cumin, oregano, garlic salt, and chili powder.
5. Stir well for a minute or so.
6. Drain and rinse the beans (do this before you cook the onions that way they don't burn while your rinsing the beans).
7. Add them to the sauce pan and stir for another minute.
8. Add the water and tomato paste.
9. Raise heat, bring to a boil, then lower heat and simmer uncovered for about 5 minutes.
10. Add the cooked millet to the beans, stir well, and cook for a minute or two longer.

Note: If you like spice, add a little hot sauce and/or serve with jalapeño cornbread.

Black Bean and Corn Chili

Serves 4

½ cup coarsely chopped onion
2 garlic cloves 1 tablespoon oil
1½ cups cooked black beans
1 cup canned tomatoes with liquid
1 tablespoon tomato paste
1 cup frozen corn
1 tablespoon chili powder
1 teaspoon ground cumin
1 teaspoon sugar
½ cup diced green pepper

1. Sauté the onion and garlic in oil over medium heat for 1-2 minutes.
2. Add beans, tomatoes and their liquid, tomato paste,
3. corn, chili powder, cumin and sugar.
4. Reduce heat, cover pan and simmer for 10 to 20 minutes. Add bell pepper and cook the chili another 5 minutes.

Vegetarian Chili Con Carne

Serves 8

1¼ cups kidney beans
1 medium onion, chopped
2 garlic, crushed
1¼ cups carrots, chopped fine
1¼ cups green beans, chopped
½ cup combined red and green pepper
¼ cup water
½ teaspoon chili powder
½ teaspoon cumin
1 15 oz. can stewed tomatoes
¼ cup tomato paste

1. Preheat oven at 350. Place onion, garlic, carrot, green beans, and peppers in a casserole dish.
2. Add water, chili powder, cumin, tomatoes, and tomato paste to mixture. Bake for 20 to 30 minutes.

Bulgar Chili

Serves 4

1 cup water
¾ teaspoons salt divided
½ cup coarse whole wheat bulgar # 4
2 tablespoons vegetable oil
1 cup chopped onion
1 cup chopped green bell pepper
2 cloves garlic, minced
2½ tablespoons chili powder
2 teaspoons oregano
2 teaspoons paprika
1 teaspoon cumin
2 cans (14 oz.) whole peeled tomatoes, undrained
2 cans (16 oz. each) pinto beans, 1 regular, 1 with jalapeno

1. In a medium-size saucepan, bring water and ¼ teaspoons salt to boil.
2. Add the bulgar, return to boil.
3. Reduce heat and simmer 20 min. or until the water is absorbed. Remove from heat and set aside.
4. In a large skillet, heat the oil over medium-high heat.
5. Add onion, green pepper and garlic and sauté, stirring until onion is soft.
6. Add the chili powder, oregano, paprika and cumin and stir until the oil is absorbed.
7. Stir in the tomatoes and break them up with the back of a spoon.
8. Stir in the beans, bulgar, and remaining ½ teaspoons salt. Simmer, covered, 20 min. or until heated through. Black Beans and Yellow Rice

Rice:

1 5 oz. pkg saffron rice mix
1 15 oz. can black beans
5 tablespoons lime juice
1 teaspoon chili powder
½ teaspoon ground cumin
2 tablespoons chopped fresh cilantro
garnishes: sliced green onions, etc.

1. Cook rice per package directions and keep warm.
2. Meanwhile, drain beans, reserving 2 tablespoons of liquid. Combine beans, reserved liquid, lime juice, chili powder, and cumin in saucepan.
3. Cook over medium heat until thoroughly heated. Stir in 1 tablespoon of cilantro. Serve beans over
4. rice; sprinkle with remaining cilantro. Garnish if desired and serve.
5. **Serving Ideas:** Serve w/tortilla chips & pineapple chunks tossed w/cilantro.

Microwave Vegetable Chili

1 teaspoon olive oil
1 onion, chopped
2 garlic cloves, chopped
2 carrots; sliced
1 cup celery; sliced diagonally
1 zucchini; diced
1 bell pepper
2 jalapeno peppers, chopped
28 oz. tomatoes, chopped
19 oz. kidney beans
1 tbsp. chili powder
1 teaspoon cumin
1 teaspoon oregano
1 pinch salt
1 pinch black pepper
1 pinch sugar

1. In a large 3 quart casserole dish, combine the oil, onion, garlic, carrots and celery.
2. Microwave covered at High for 7 to 8 minutes or until vegetable are almost tender.
3. Add zucchini, peppers, canned tomatoes including liquid, kidney beans chili powder, cumin and oregano.
4. Microwave covered on High for 16 to 18 minutes or until zucchini is tender.
5. Let stand, covered for 5 minutes.
6. Season to taste with salt, pepper and pinch of sugar.
7. Ladle chili into warm soup bowls and serve.

Millennial Chili

2 tbsps olive oil
1 onion, diced
1 green pepper, diced
1 (46 oz) bottle Healthy Request V8 juice
1 can Veggie-burger
1 packet vegan taco seasoning (read ingredients)
2 cups cooked (or 1 can) black beans
1 cup fresh or frozen corn kernels

1. Sauté onion and pepper in oil until onion is translucent. Pour juice into soup pot or crock pot.
2. Add the cooked onion and pepper.
3. In same skillet, empty veggie-burger and taco seasoning mix with ¾ cup water (or according to package directions. When done, add to soup pot.
4. Add beans and corn. Heat through and serve.
5. Can be kept on low in crock pot also.

Black Bean Chili Potatoes

Serves 4
4 large baking potatoes (about 3 lbs)
vegetable cooking spray
1 tablespoon vegetable oil
3 cloves garlic, minced
1 medium onion, chopped
1 14.5 oz. can chili-style chunky tomatoes, undrained
1 15 oz. can black beans, rinsed & drained
1 teaspoon chili powder
½ teaspoon ground cumin
4 green onions, sliced

1. Scrub potatoes and prick each potato several times with a fork.
2. Arrange potatoes 1-inch apart on a microwave safe
3. rack or on paper towels.
4. Microwave on high for 20-25 minutes, turning and rearranging after 10 minutes. Let stand 2 minutes.
5. Meanwhile, coat a large saucepan or skillet with cooking spray. Add oil.
6. Place over medium-high heat until hot.
7. Add garlic and onion; cook, stirring constantly, until tender.
8. Stir in tomatoes and next 3 ingredients; cook over medium heat just until thoroughly heated, stirring occasionally.
9. Remove from heat and stir in green onions.
10. Cut an "X" to within ½-inch of the bottom of each baked potato.
11. Squeeze potatoes from opposite ends to open; fluff
12. pulp with a fork.
13. Spoon bean mixture over potatoes and sprinkle with cheese (if desired).
14. Top each potato with sour cream, if desired, and serve immediately.

Vegetable Chili

Serves 4-6

6 oz. red kidney beans
2 tbsp. oil
1 onion, chopped
2 garlic cloves, crushed
1 tsp. ground cumin
½ tsp. chili powder
   (or 1 small fresh chili, chopped)
2 tbsp. whole meal flour
2 lb. ripe tomatoes, chopped
2 tbsp. tomato puree
vegetable stock cube
1 tsp. brown sugar
salt & pepper to taste
small carrot, diced
small potato, diced
celery sticks, trimmed & diced
4 oz. cauliflower florets
red pepper, deseeded and sliced
4 oz. mushrooms, sliced
1 courgette (zucchini), sliced
to garnish - avocado slices, chopped parsley.

1. If using dried beans, soak overnight, drain, and cook in plenty of water until tender, about an hour. (Otherwise use canned.)
2. Heat the oil, add the chopped onion and cook until transparent.
3. Add crushed garlic, cumin, and chili and cook for a minute more.
4. Stir in the flour, and add the tomatoes.
5. Add tomato puree, stock cube, sugar, salt and pepper.
6. Simmer gently for 5 minutes. The sauce should be quite thick.
7. Add the carrot and potato, cover the pan, and continue to simmer for about 10 minutes until the carrot is almost cooked.
8. Then add the celery, cauliflower and pepper and simmer for 5 minutes.
9. Finally, add the sliced mushrooms and courgette and continue to cook, covered until all the vegetables are tender; 5-10 minutes.
10. Stir in the beans and heat through.
11. Serve topped garnish.

Greg's Vegetarian Chili

Serves 6

1 green pepper
1 large onion (yellow onions work better than Vidalia, but Vidalia can be used)
Olive oil
1 16-oz can frijoles (black beans)
1 16-oz can of dark kidney beans
1 28-oz can tomato puree
1 28-oz can crushed tomatoes
TVP
cumin
black pepper
cayenne pepper sauce
chili powder
salt
coriander or cilantro
parsley

1. Wash the pepper and cut into thin strips.
2. Put pepper strips into large pot.
3. Add a little bit of olive oil and cook on high heat.
4. Stir periodically.
5. While pepper is cooking, cut onion into small pieces (not so small that the pieces are diced).
6. When cut, add onion into pot. Continue to cook the peppers and onions until the peppers get a little soft, and some of the onion pieces start to get brown.
7. Turn heat to the lowest setting possible without the stove being off.
8. Add tomato puree, crushed tomatoes, and both cans of beans.
9. Stir. The mixture will now be very soupy.
10. Stir in TVP. Be sure to do this very slowly. (The TVP absorbs water. If you add in too much TVP, you will get a solid block of chili. You can compensate for a little too much TVP by adding some water, but that can only do so much. If you have added way too much TVP, the only way to salvage the chili is by putting in some more tomato puree. Enough TVP should be added so that once it has absorbed the moisture, the chili has a good consistency - not too watery but not too solid.)
11. Add spices to taste. (Cumin is the most important because it gives the chili its heartiness, and the cayenne pepper sauce gives it a nice tang.)
12. Stir periodically.
13. At low heat, the chili takes just over an hour to heat up to a good temperature for eating.

White Bean Chili

Serves 1
1 pound white beans (like great Northerns)
2 large onions, diced
2 tablespoons ground cumin
1 tablespoon chili powder
1 teaspoon poultry seasoning
2 - 4 oz. cans diced green chiles
1 8 oz. can salsa verde (optional)
7 cups "chicken-like" or veggie Stock
2 bay leaves
½ pound tomatillos, cleaned & quartered
1 cup fresh cilantro, coarsely chopped
salt and pepper to taste
2 tablespoons fresh lime juice
1 cup chopped green onions

1. Soak beans overnight or use quick soak method.
2. Bring beans and water to cover by 1" to a boil for 5 min. Turn off heat and cover. Let sit 1 hour, then proceed.
3. Pour off soaking water and cover beans with fresh water and bring to full boil. Lower heat and simmer.
4. While beans simmer, in a large soup kettle or Dutch oven, sauté onions using your favorite method (you can use a little stock).
5. When translucent, add cumin, chili powder, poultry seasoning, green chilies and salsa verde.
6. Sauté for 5 minutes, adding a little stock if it begins to stick.
7. Then add the rest of the stock, bay leaves, tomatillos and ¾ cup cilantro.
8. Bring to a boil and simmer uncovered while beans continue to cook.
9. When beans are just tender (1-2 hours) add them to the soup pot and simmer everything together for another ½ hour.
10. Season with salt and pepper to taste.
11. Just before serving, add the rest of the cilantro and the lime juice, stir to blend.
12. Ladle into big bowls and top with green onions.

Best Black Bean Chili

4 cups black beans
2 tbsp. cumin
2-3 tbsp. basil, oregano, thyme
2 large chopped onions
1½ cups peppers
2 cloves garlic, minced

½ cup olive oil
1 tsp. cayenne
1½ tablespoons paprika
1 teaspoon salt
3 cups crushed whole tomatoes
⅓ cup finely chopped chili peppers

1. Garnishes: chopped green onions, chopped cilantro.
2. Sauté the onions, peppers, garlic in the oil along with the spices.
3. Add the tomatoes and chilies. Add the beans.
4. Heat until the spices have unleashed their flavor.
5. Serve and garnish.

Vegetarian Chili

1 lb tofu, extra firm, frozen
¾ cup water
¼ cup soy sauce
2 tbsp. olive oil
1 cup pinto or black beans, uncooked
1 onion, chopped
1 green bell pepper, chopped
2 cloves garlic, minced
¼ cup fresh cilantro
3 tablespoons chili powder
1 28 oz. can tomatoes

1. Cook beans ahead of time.
2. Set aside.
3. To freeze tofu, open package and drain water.
4. Place tofu in freezer bag and store until ready to use.
5. To thaw tofu, put freezer bag in microwave on "defrost" for ten minutes.
6. Be careful; edges might be hot.
7. Squeeze excess water out of the tofu, then crush and crumble into a small bowl.
8. Combine water and soy sauce.
9. Add to tofu, and marinate for ten minutes.
10. Heat oil in wide skillet or large saucepan.
11. Sauté green pepper and onion until wilted.
12. Add garlic, parsley, cook one minute.
13. Drain tofu in colander, and add to pan.
14. Add chili powder.
15. Cook 10 minutes.
16. Combine with remaining ingredients.
17. Simmer covered 1 hour, uncovered 30 minutes.

Vegetable Chili II

2 medium sized onions, chopped
fresh garlic, chopped (you decide how much)
2½ tablespoons chili powder
2 teaspoons ground cumin
1 teaspoon dried oregano leaves crushed
¼ teaspoon cayenne pepper
2 cups vegetable stock (or 2 cans)
28 ounces can of peeled tomatoes chopped with juice
1 beer
1 teaspoon sugar
1 teaspoon salt
1 Bay leaf
1 tablespoon cornmeal
2 pounds zucchini cut into 1 inch pieces
2 cans black beans, rinsed and drained
1 can 11 oz. whole kernel corn drained
TVP (optional)

1. Cook onions over low heat until soft and translucent.
2. Add garlic, chili powder, cumin, oregano, and cayenne.
3. Cook a few minutes while stirring constantly.
4. Add vege broth. Add tomatoes and juice, beer, sugar, salt, and bay leaf.
5. Stop here and refrigerate up to two days if you are making this up ahead of time.
6. When ready to finish, bring to gentle simmer and continue.
7. Sprinkle cornmeal over surface slowly while stirring to avoid lumps.
8. Add zucchini and bring to boil.
9. Reduce heat and simmer 5 minutes.
10. Add TVP here if you are using it. Add black beans and corn, simmer 5-15 minutes.
11. I served over brown rice and provided bowls of hot sauce, chopped jalapeno peppers, and chopped onions.
12. I also had a loaf of wheat bread and several people ate their chili with that instead of the rice.

Chili on Baked Sweet Potato

1. Bake a sweet potato, oven or microwave
2. Split it open and top with this chili concoction:
3. Use whatever chili you like, even canned.
4. When you heat it, mix in: 1 can black beans and 1 can Mexican spiced diced tomatoes (w/jalapeno bits)
5. Top the baked sweet potato with the chili mix, then add a dollop of sour cream.
6. "Sweet" potato may seem strange, but the flavor combination really works, and this recipe can be prepared in about 10 minutes.

Veggie Tamales

4 cups masa harina   2½ cups water
1½ salt   1½ cups corn oil

1. Combine masa harina, salt, water and 1 cup oil and knead.
2. Add remaining oil as necessary, to form a smooth dough.
3. A great filling is mixed veggies (carrots, peas, tomatoes, green beans, cauliflower, all chopped and cooked).
4. Sauté onion and garlic in a little oil, add jalapeno or Serrano chilies, then add the veggies and mix till well
5. blended.
6. You can also add olives and black beans, or garbanzo beans as desired.

Dough for Savory Tamales

Serves 16
½ cup vegetable shortening
2 cups masa harina
½ teaspoon salt
¾ cup vegetable stock
¼ cup water
1 teaspoon baking powder

1. Beat shortening in mixing bowl with electric mixer until fluffy.
2. In small bowl mix together masa harina and salt.
3. In separate bowl, mix together stock and water.
4. With electric mixer or wooden spoon, alternately beat in masa mixture and stock mixture, adding just enough stock mixture to make a firm dough.
5. Beat in baking powder.
6. Makes enough dough for 16 to 20 tamales.

Chile Relleno Tamales

Serves 20

2 tomatoes, diced
2 canned chipotle chilies in adobo sauce, minced
2 tablespoons cilantro, minced
2 tablespoons minced onion
1/4 teaspoon salt
5 Anaheim chili peppers
22 corn husks, soaked in hot water until pliable
masa dough for savory tamales (see recipe)
2/3 cup cubed jalapeno soy cheese

1. Combine tomatoes, chipotle chilies, onion, cilantro and salt in medium bowl.
2. Toss until mixed.
3. Cover and refrigerate for at least 1 hour.
4. Cut small slit in each Anaheim chili.
5. Over an open flame or under broiler, roast chilies until their skins turn dark brown.
6. Place chilies in paper bag; allow to steam for 5 minutes.
7. Cool, peel and seed.
8. Cut each chili into 4 pieces.
9. Tear 2 corn husks into 16 long strips for frying tamales; set aside.
10. To assemble tamales, spread 1 to 2 tablespoons masa dough in the center of each husk; spread with fingers to form a rectangle, leaving sides, top and bottom of husk exposed.
11. Place 1 piece of chili and 2 cheese cubes over masa.
12. Spread 1 tablespoon masa dough over filling.
13. Fold corn husk over filling and masa dough, beginning with right and left sides and ending with the non-pointed husk end.
14. Tie the tamale "package" together with corn husk strips.
15. Make sure filling is enclosed and strips are securely knotted.
16. Place tamales not touching each other in steamer over boiling water.
17. Cover and steam for 1 hour over medium high heat, adding more water if necessary.

Squash and Red Pepper Roll-Ups

Serves 6

3 cups yellow squash, cubed
1/4 pound silken low-fat tofu
1 tablespoon barley malt syrup
1 tablespoon corn oil
1 medium yellow onion, minced
1 medium red pepper, diced
1 teaspoon Sea Salt
1/2 cup cilantro, coarsely chopped
6 large whole-wheat tortillas

1. In a large sauce pan, steam the squash just until tender.
2. Combine with the tofu and barley malt syrup in a blender, and puree until smooth.
3. Heat the oil in a medium skillet.
4. Sauté onions, red peppers, and slat until the onions are translucent.
5. Add the onion mixture to the squash mixture.
6. Stir in the cilantro.
7. Cool the mixture well and spread evenly on the tortillas.
8. Roll up tightly and secure with toothpicks.
9. Chill for several hours, then slice 1-inch thick before serving.

Arroz Agua Fresca

Serves 8

1 1/2 quarts hot, not boiling, water
3 cups rice
2 1/4 teaspoons cinnamon, divided
1/2 cup sugar
2 cups rice milk

1. In large bowl, pour hot water over rice and 2 teaspoon cinnamon.
2. Soak 24 hours, covered.
3. Drain liquid from rice, reserving liquid.
4. In food processor or blender, process rice in two batches with about 1 cup of soaking liquid per batch until nearly smooth.
5. Return rice to remaining soaking liquid.
6. Strain mixture through several layers of cheesecloth or coffee filters. (This could take as long as an hour.).
7. Add sugar, rice milk and remaining cinnamon to strained liquid.
8. Refrigerate until chilled. .
9. Before serving, process or shake to thoroughly blend.
10. Helpful Hint: Try making this drink with different varieties of rice.
11. Jasmine rice, for example, creates a different flavor than basmati or other rice.

Eggplant Fajitas

1 medium eggplant, peeled and sliced lengthwise
¼ inch thick
1 tablespoon corn or olive oil
1 teaspoon oregano
½ teaspoon salt 'fajita filling'
2 teaspoons corn or olive oil
1 small Spanish onion, chopped
2 serrano chilies or
1jalapeno chili, coarsely chopped
1 small green bell pepper, chopped
1 tomato, chopped
1 teaspoon dried oregano
½ teaspoon ground cumin
½ teaspoon salt To garnish and serve: 6 flour tortillas
¼ cup prepared salsa

1. Brush the eggplant slices with oil, sprinkle with oregano and salt.
2. Let sit 20 minutes at room temperature.
3. Prepare a gas or charcoal grill to medium heat.
4. Grill the egg plant 3 to 4 minutes on each side.
5. Or preheat an oven broiler element.
6. The eggplant can be broiled approximately
7. 2 inches from heating element 5 to 7 minutes per side. This can be done the day before making the fajita filling.

Fajitas

8oz mushrooms
1 onion
1-2 zucchini
nutritional yeast
margarine/oil
juice of 1 lime
water

1. Slice onion and zucchini into thin strips and coarsely chop the mushrooms.
2. Over high heat, put in as much oil as your diet allows (no more than about ½ tbsp. though) and sauté onion for about 2-3 minutes and add zucchini.
3. Let cook for about 3-5 minutes, adding water if needed so it won't stick. Add the mushrooms and lime juice and sauté for just about 1-2 minutes.
4. Add about 2 tbsp. (more or less to taste) nutritional yeast and water if necessary.
5. Mix to form a "cheesy" sauce and cook down for about a minute or until desired consistency. Enjoy!

Mockamole/Mock Guac

5 or 6 combination of small fresh green zucchinis, patty pan, and scaloppini squashes (patty pans make the guac creamier)
3 garlic cloves, sliced into narrow strips
salt and pepper to taste

Optional seasonings: salsa, lime or lemon juice, cumin, chopped tomatoes, chopped green onions, chopped chilies, chili powder, cilantro

1. Chop the squash into small pieces.
2. Steam the squash, garlic, and salt/pepper together until the squash is completely cooked but still green.
3. Drain the liquid out of the squash and place the squash in a large bowl.
4. With a fork or potato masher, mash the squash until you cannot detect individual pieces of squash.
5. Drain the squash again.
6. Add any of the optional seasonings to taste.
7. Mix together. Chill (to set) or serve immediately.

Broccomole

1½ cups cooked broccoli stems, tough outer layers peeled off
1½ tablespoons fresh-squeezed lemon juice
¼ teaspoon ground cumin
⅛ teaspoon garlic powder
½ tomato, diced
1 scallion, sliced
1 canned green chili, chopped

1. In a food processor, blend the broccoli stems with the lemon juice, cumin, and garlic powder until completely smooth.
2. Add the remaining ingredients and mix well by hand, but do not blend.
3. Chill before serving for best flavor.

Portobello Mushroom Fajitas

Serves 6

1 tablespoon vegetable oil
1 clove garlic, minced
1 teaspoon ground cumin
½ teaspoon salt
¾ pound fresh baby portobello or crimini mushrooms, thinly sliced
2 cups frozen stir-fry bell peppers & onions (from a 16 oz. pkg.)
¼ cup chopped fresh cilantro
2 tablespoons lime juice
6 flour tortillas
salsa, guacamole

1. Heat oil, garlic, cumin, and salt in a 10-inch skillet over medium-high heat.
2. Cook mushrooms and bell pepper mixture in oil for 4 to 6 minutes, stirring frequently, until vegetables are crisp-tender.
3. Sprinkle with cilantro and lime juice.
4. Spoon about ½ cup mushroom mixture onto each tortilla; roll up. Serve with salsa, guacamole, and/or vegan sour cream, if desired.

Baked Tapatillas

Serves 6

Serve with more salsa and tofu sour cream.
6 fresh corn tortillas (containing no animal products)
1 cup refried beans
1 cup mashed avocados
1 cup red or green salsa
1 cup fresh lettuce, sliced very thin
1 cup tomatoes, seeded and chopped

1. Layer the refried beans, mashed avocados, and salsa on the tortillas.
2. Bake for ten minutes at 350 degrees.
3. Remove and layer lettuce and tomatoes.

Tofu Fajitas

Serves 4

1 lb. block firm (or extra-firm) tofu
1 medium yellow onion, sliced into strips
1 red pepper, sliced into strips
1 green pepper, sliced into strips
1 yellow pepper, sliced into strips
5 or 6 mushrooms, quartered
(additional olive oil for frying)
flour tortillas

Marinade:

juice of one lime (or lemon)
¼ cup olive oil
3 tablespoons fajita seasoning ("Spice Hunter" brand is best)

1. Put a medium pot of water on to boil.
2. Salt the water.
3. Drain and rinse the tofu and cut into finger-sized strips.
4. While water is boiling, make marinade in a small bowl.
5. When water is at a rolling-boil, add the tofu, stir to separate and cook until the water has returned to a boil and the tofu is floating on the top, about 5 minutes. Drain.
6. Place cooked tofu in shallow dish (or even a zip-lock bag), pour marinade over and let flavors blend for several hours, or up to 24 hours, turning occasionally.

Frying:

7. In a large (best to use non-stick) skillet, fry the tofu mixture, until the tofu is a little crispy on the outside.
8. Remove to a plate.
9. Add a little olive oil and fry the onions, peppers and mushrooms until bright-colored, 2 or 3 minutes.
10. Add the cooked tofu back to the skillet.
11. Stir to blend and reheat the tofu.
12. Serve in flour tortillas.

Chilaquiles

Two ways of making chilaquiles:

Get some dried red chilies (pasilla or whatever) boil them in some water with about 5 garlic cloves, half an onion, Serrano or yellow chilies, pepper and salt, for about 10 minutes or until soft. Then I blend it all, and strain. Put this sauce aside.

Heat up a pan, then add a good amount of oil, and add torn or cut tortilla strips to fry. After you toss and turn and they are nice and golden, put them in a container and set aside. In the same pan fry some onions and maybe some more chilies. Then put in a block of crumbled tofu and cook for a bit.

1. Add cumin, oregano, pepper, salt and other spices to improve the bland tofu flavor.
2. When the water is almost boiled out add the blended chili sauce, cook for a bit and add the tortillas at the last minute (so they don't get soggy).
3. Serve and enjoy.

The lazy way is to not make the chili sauce and just add a can of tomato sauce to the tofu and onions frying in the pan, then add the tortillas. It's not authentic but it's still quite good. It's all in the spices.

Refried Beans

Use to fill tortillas, adding grated cheese, chopped fresh vegetables and salsa to taste.

2-3 tablespoons olive oil
2 onions, chopped
4 cloves garlic, crushed
1 tsp. ground cumin
1 tsp. ground coriander
chili powder to taste
18 oz. cooked red kidney beans

1. Heat the oil and add the onion, garlic, cumin, coriander, and chili if used.
2. Stir fry 2 minutes.
3. Add the beans and stir until everything is heated through.
4. Mash some of the beans if you wish.
5. Note: I usually fry the onion until it is soft and cooked through.
6. If you fry it for only 2 minutes, it tends to stay
7. undercooked and a bit too strong in flavor.

Go Chu Jang Fajita

Serves 6

Seitan (wheat gluten) can be found in natural foods stores.

1 tablespoon vegetable oil
1 large Spanish onion, peeled and sliced into ½-inch rings
2 green bell peppers, washed, stemmed and seeded, cut into ½-inch-wide x 2-inch strips
1 pound seitan, cut into ¼ inch x 2-inch strips
1 avocado, peeled, pitted, cut into ½-inch chunks
2 tablespoons Korean pepper paste (Go Chu Jang: available in Oriental groceries)
2 tablespoons soy cheese, shredded
6 whole-wheat tortillas
1 cup Tofu Sour Cream

1. Heat the oil in a large skillet.
2. When hot, sauté the sliced onions for about 2 minutes.
3. Add the sliced peppers, sliced seitan strips, and avocado.
4. Sauté 2-3 minutes; then add the Go Chu Jang paste and mix everything together.
5. Sauté for another minute or two, sprinkle the soy cheese on top and let it melt.
6. Serve the hot fajita mixture on a fresh tortilla with Tofu Sour Cream topping.
7. Serve with plain white rice as a side dish to absorb the fajita drippings.
8. For authenticity, roll the fajitas in the tortillas.
9. Have plenty of napkins handy.

Meatless Taco

1 cup rice (white or brown)
6 cloves garlic, minced
2 small onions, minced
1 can stewed tomatoes
1 can chopped green chilies
1 pack taco seasoning

1. Prepare rice as usual. While rice is cooking, sauté garlic and onions in a little water and cooking spray.
2. When onions are slightly translucent, at chilies, and tomatoes.
3. Cook for 30 seconds, then add ¼ cup water and taco seasoning. Cook for a few minutes, then add to rice.
4. Serve with ff tortillas and your favorite taco toppings!

Vegetarian Red Beans and Seven-Grain Dirty Rice

Serves 4

2 cup brown rice
1½ cup red onion, chopped
3 garlic cloves, minced
1 cup carrots, fine diced
½ cup celery, chopped
1 jalapeno pepper, seeded, minced
1 tbsp. cumin
1 tbsp. coriander
2 tsp. chili powder
3 ¾ cup vegetable stock
1 bay leaf
1½ cup red beans, cooked
1½ cup tomatoes, chopped
½ cup corn kernels
½ tsp. salt
3 tbsp. parsley
3 tbsp. cilantro, chopped

1. Place a medium-sized pot over medium heat.
2. Add the first 9 ingredients and heat for 3 to 5 minutes, stirring almost.
3. constantly, until lightly browned.
4. In another pot, bring the stock and bay leaf to a boil and add to the rice mixture.
5. Cover the pan, lower the heat, and simmer for 15 minutes.
6. Add the beans, tomatoes, corn, and salt.
7. Stir, cover, and simmer for 15 more minutes, or until the liquid is absorbed.
8. Remove from the heat and add the parsley and cilantro.

Harbour Special

1 cup of refried beans
sprinkle of garlic powder
sprinkle of cumin
½ of a medium zucchini, thinly sliced
few tablespoons salsa

1. Combine the beans and spices, warm in saucepan.
2. Stir-fry zucchini in a frying pan until lightly browned.
3. Spread beans on a warmed plate, top with zucchini and salsa.
4. Serves. 1 Prep. time: 10 min

Pico de Gallo

Here is a simple salsa called "Pico de Gallo." It can be improved or improvised by adding different types of chilies or by changing the consistency (i.e., blending, mashing, chopping).

4 or 5 medium sized tomatoes (if you can't find ripe tomatoes use Roma type)
1 small onion
2 jalapeno chilies (or whatever you can handle!)
2 cloves of garlic
1 bunch of cilantro
2 small limes, juiced (Mexican or key lime is best, lemon is also okay)
2 tbsp. of olive oil
1 tsp. salt or to taste

1. Chop all ingredients very fine and mix them thoroughly. Add oil, salt and a little water.
2. You can use canned tomatoes if fresh tomatoes are too green.
3. Yellow chilies are also a nice addition because they are very flavorful.

Note: Try Serrano chilies if you want a hotter salsa. You may enjoy making your own salsas, so do lots of experimenting!

Oven Baked Mexi-Fries

Serves 4

1½ pounds baking potatoes (about 7 med), peeled, cut into thin strips
1 tablespoon canola oil
2 teaspoons chili powder
½ teaspoon salt
½ teaspoon dried oregano
¼ teaspoon garlic powder
¼ teaspoon ground cumin

1. Preheat oven to 450°F.
2. Combine oil and remaining ingredients.
3. Add potato strips and toss well.
4. Arrange potatoes in a single layer on a baking sheet.
5. Bake for 15 to 20 minutes or until golden brown.

Note: Be sure to use baking potatoes (russet). Thin skinned potatoes, which have a higher sugar content than baking potatoes, will burn on the outside before the inside is cooked, resulting in soggy fries.

Avocado Chimichurri Bruschetta

Serves 6

2 tbsp. lemon juice
2 tbsp. red wine vinegar
3 cloves garlic, minced (1 Tbs.)
¾ tsp. salt
½ tsp. red pepper flakes
½ tsp. dried oregano
¼ tsp. ground black pepper
¼ cup olive oil
¼ cup chopped cilantro
¼ cup chopped fresh parsley
2 avocados, peeled, pitted, and cubed
6 ½-inch-thick slices whole-grain or ciabatta bread, toasted

1. Combine lemon juice, vinegar, garlic, salt, red pepper flakes, oregano, and black pepper in small bowl.
2. Whisk in oil, then stir in cilantro and parsley. Fold in avocado cubes.
3. Spoon avocado mixture onto toast slices, and serve.

Bagel Nachos

Serves Lots

Bagels garlic (fresh or powdered) - optional
paprika - optional
other seasoning - optional

1. Preheat oven to 350°F.
2. Slice bagels with a food slicer ⅛ - ¼ inch thick (if you work in a restaurant, or have friends who do, it's really GREAT to have them slice a bagful for you.)
3. Stack the slices and cut into quarters.
4. Place in a single layer on baking sheets.
5. Rub with cut garlic or lightly sprinkle with garlic powder or other seasonings.
6. (Paprika adds mainly color, very subtle flavor.)
7. Place in oven and bake just until beginning to brown.
8. Chips will 'dry' and be very crisp - rather than chewy like a sliced bagel.
9. These chips are GREAT with salsa, hummus, 'taco' salad, anything that you would normally eat with nacho or potato chips.
10. Store extras in an airtight container.

Grace's Green Bell or Poblano Peppers Relleno

Serves 6

Serve this dish with tostada chips.

2-3 cups pre-cooked brown rice
1 medium (1½ pounds) eggplant, baked 45 minutes, skin peeled off, then drained in a strainer while mashing
1 red onion, cleaned and finely chopped
1 medium yellow or zucchini squash, carefully washed and finely chopped
½ pound firm tofu, drained approximately 15 minutes and crumbled
½ cup frozen or fresh green chili peppers, finely chopped
¼ teaspoon oregano
1 tablespoon ground cumin
½ teaspoon salt
4-6 whole fresh bell or poblano peppers, stems and seed sacks removed (cut around the stem base; the whole seed sack will come out; then wash and drain the inside of the peppers.)

1. Preheat oven to 375°F.
2. Mix the rice, vegetables, tofu, and seasonings in a bowl.
3. Stuff the hollowed-out peppers with the mixture.
4. Set the stuffed peppers in a non-stick baking pan, preferably on their sides.
5. Put a little water in the pan as well.
6. Cover and bake for about 30 minutes.
7. Be sure to check the stuffed peppers so they don't overcook and dry out.
8. Remove from oven, and cover each pepper with salsa to taste.

Pico de Gallo II

Here's another variation of Pico de Gallo.

3 medium tomatoes (firm to the touch)
1 green onion with the stalk
3 jalapenos or Serrano peppers (depends on the spiciness of the pepper) to taste
½ cilantro bush (about half cup or more chopped)
1 medium sweet yellow onion
1 pinch of salt (you can add a pinch per tomato if you'd like)

Chipotle Salsa

Chipotles are smoked Jalapeno peppers, often available canned in Adobo sauce, which is made with chipotle, vinegar and spices. The chilies are also sold dried in Mexican markets. Dried chipotles keep indefinitely.

4 medium-sized fresh ripe tomatoes
1 small bunch of cilantro (about 8 to 10 long pieces with leaves)
1 fresh lime
1 medium onion
salt & pepper, to taste
2 to 3 chipotle chilies, canned in adobo sauce
Red pepper flakes to taste

1. Wash and core the tomatoes. Wash and dry the cilantro between layers of paper towels. Remove the stems and seeds from the chipotles.
2. Peel onion, now cut the tomatoes and onion in quarters to prepare for the food processor.
3. Place all the prepared vegetables and the chipotles in food processor along with the cilantro. Squeeze lime juice into the blender.
4. Place lid on food processor and blend. For chunkier salsa, pulse the food processor only for a few seconds. For smoother textured salsa, process to your desired consistency.
5. If you don't have a food processor, a blender will work as well or you can chop all ingredients by hand and mix in bowl.
6. For extra zip, add dried pepper flakes. Salt and pepper to taste.
7. You can enhance the smokey flavor of your Chipotle Salsa by adding a tablespoon or two of the adobo sauce the chipotles came in.
8. Allow the salsa to chill for a couple of hours.

Quick Black Bean Chili with TVP

6 cups black beans
5 cloves of garlic
2 tablespoons. cumin
1 tablespoon black pepper
2 tablespoons oil
(olive or other)
1 large onion
½ tsp. of cayenne
1 tablespoon salt
1 10 oz. can tomato paste
¼ to ½ cup of TVP

1. Cook black beans in a sufficient amount of water along with oil and 4 cloves of garlic.
2. When ALMOST done (meaning soft, but not quite done), fry onion and remaining garlic in a pan until translucent.
3. Add onions, seasonings, tomato paste and TVP to beans and cook until done. Season to taste.
4. Add your favorite spices.

Black Bean Enchiladas

1 pkg tortillas (try fajita size or wheat)
enchilada sauce
4 can black beans, cooked
2 can corn
2 can brown rice, cooked
¼ cup onion, chopped fine
2 tsp. chili powder
3 tbsp. tomato paste
garlic powder
black pepper

1. Sauté onions until soft.
2. Mix beans, corn, rice, tomato paste and chili powder.
3. Spoon into tortillas.
4. Roll them up and put into a casserole pan.
5. Pour enchilada sauce over the top.
6. Bake for 15-20 minutes at 350°F.

Smashed Beans

Use for bean nachos, tacos, burritos, casseroles, and dips.
2 cups pinto beans
8 cups water
½ teaspoon onion powder
½ teaspoon garlic powder
½ to 1 cup salsa (mild to spicy, your preference)

4. Soak beans overnight, drain and rinse.
5. Place beans in the water.
6. Bring to a boil, cover, reduce heat and simmer for 3 - 4 hours.
7. Drain reserving the cooking liquid.
8. Mash the beans using a hand masher, beater, or food processor. Return to pan.
9. Add the spices, a little of the reserved liquid and the salsa, stirring until the beans have a softened, smashed consistency. Heat through to blend flavors.

Tofu Enchiladas

14oz. enchilada sauce
14oz. tomato sauce
1½ tablespoons garlic powder
1 medium onion, chopped
2 ounces diced green chilies
4 teaspoons chili powder
½ teaspoon dried basil
16 ounces White Wave Tofu, drained and crumbled
6 ounces Soy-A-Melt, cheddar style, grated
6 ounces Soy-A-Melt, mozzarella style, grated
soy oil
12 corn tortillas
1 ounce black olives, sliced
¼ cup Soy-A-Melt, grated

1. In a medium saucepan combine the enchilada sauce, tomato sauce, garlic powder, onion, green chilies, chili powder, and basil.
2. Bring to a boil then lower the heat and simmer for 15 minutes.
3. Combine the tofu and both Soy-A-Melt cheeses in a bowl for the filling, and mix well.
4. Place soy oil in a medium skillet to a ⅛" depth over medium heat.
5. When the oil is hot, fry the tortillas one at a time just until soft, not crisp.
6. Place some filling in the middle of each tortilla, top it with some sliced olives and roll it up.
7. Place the enchiladas in an oiled 9X13-inch baking dish seam-side down.
8. Preheat oven to 350 degrees.
9. Cover the enchiladas with the sauce and sprinkle with the ¼ cup of Mozzarella Soy-A-Melt.
10. Cover and bake for 15-20 minutes.
11. Serve immediately.

Spicy Tortilla Chips

One serving is 6 chips
2 tablespoons extra virgin olive oil
½ teaspoon chili powder, or cayenne pepper
8 (8 to 10 inch diameter) flour tortillas

1. Preheat the oven to 400 degrees.
2. Mix cayenne pepper (or chili powder) into olive oil.
3. Brush this mixture on one side of tortillas.
4. Cut each tortilla into about 12 wedges.
5. Place on ungreased cookie sheet or a 15 ½ x 10 ½ x 1 inch jelly roll pan.
6. Place uncovered into oven, and bake for 8 to 10 minutes or until golden brown and a little crispy.
7. The chips will continue to get crispy as they cool down so make sure not to burn them in the oven trying to get them crispy!!

Tomato-Poblano Vinaigrette

Serves 1
⅓ cup cider vinegar
3 tablespoons tomato paste
2 tablespoons lime juice (1 lime)
1¾ teaspoons tabasco pepper sauce
½ teaspoon chopped garlic
½ teaspoon salt
1½ cups olive oil
1 medium tomato (about 4 ounces) blanched, skinned, seeded, diced
1 poblano chili or other roasted, seeded, medium-hot green chili, diced
½ teaspoon dried oregano
freshly ground black pepper

1. In bowl of food processor, combine vinegar, tomato paste, lime juice, TABASCO Sauce, garlic and salt; process 30 seconds.
2. With motor running, gradually add oil until mixture is emulsified.
3. Transfer dressing to medium bowl.
4. Stir in tomato and chili pepper.
5. Season with oregano and black pepper.
6. Just before serving, season with additional salt and
7. Tabasco sauce, if desired.
8. Makes 2½ cups.

Spicy Mexican Bean Burgers

Serves 5

1 tbsp. sunflower oil
1 onion, diced
1 tbsp. minced garlic
¼ tsp. oregano
1 tbsp. minced hot pepper
half a green pepper, diced
2 cups cooked, drained, and mashed pinto beans
¼ cup bread crumbs
¼ tsp. ground cumin
½ tsp. Salt
¼ tsp. chili powder
2 tbsp. minced fresh parsley
whole-wheat flour
5 slices jalapeno-pepper-jack soy cheese

1. In a large skillet, or frying pan, over medium heat, warm the oil.
2. When hot, add onion, garlic, oregano and hot pepper, and sauté until the onions just start to brown.
3. Add the bell pepper and sauté for two more minutes.
4. Remove from heat.
5. In a large bowl, mix cooked vegetables with mashed beans.
6. Add the bread crumbs, cumin, salt, chili powder and parsley, and mix well.
7. Shape into 5 patties, lightly coat each with flour.
8. Place the patties on a lightly oiled baking tray.
9. Broil 5 to 10 minutes, or until tops are browned.
10. Flip patties over, top each with a slice of soy cheese, and broil until cheese has started to melt.

Curried Chickpea Burritos

Serves 4

3 large cloves garlic, peeled
1 2-in piece fresh ginger, peeled and quartered
1 jalapeno pepper, with seeds, stemmed and quartered
1 large onion, cut into 8 pieces
1 tablespoon canola oil
1½ tablespoons curry powder
1 tablespoon ground cumin
1 pound potatoes, peeled and diced
1½ cup water
⅓ cup currants or raisins
½ teaspoon salt, or to taste
1 15 oz. can chickpeas
1 cup frozen green peas
¼ cup chopped fresh cilantro
8 flour tortillas (opt for wheat)

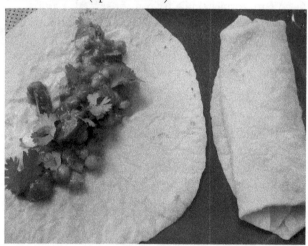

1. In a food processor, process garlic, ginger, and jalapeno until minced. Add onion and pulse until coarsely chopped. In a large non-stick skillet, heat oil over med. heat.
2. Add onion mixture and cook stirring, until softened, and light golden, 10-12 minutes.
3. Add curry powder and cumin, and cook stirring constantly until fragrant, about 1 minute.
4. Add potatoes, water, currants or raisins, and salt.
5. Bring to a simmer. Reduce heat to low, cover and simmer until potatoes are done, about 10 minutes.
6. Stir in chickpeas, green peas, and cilantro.
7. Simmer until heated through, 2-3 minutes.
8. Season with salt to taste. Meanwhile, warm tortillas in a hot skillet or microwave. Wrap to keep warm.
9. To serve, set out warm tortillas, curry filling, and sauces.

Note: For a nice addition, check the index for recipe of "Fresh Mint and Chile Sauce".

Groovy Breakfast Burrito

whole wheat tortillas
firm tofu, crumbled
tamari
curry powder, turmeric, paprika, cayenne, parsley, cumin
fresh crushed garlic
chopped onion
spaghetti squash salad
salsa
nutritional yeast (the yellow flaky kind)

1. Sauté garlic and onions in a little olive oil.
2. Add crumbled tofu, tamari and spices.
3. Sauté until lightly browned.
4. Add spaghetti squash salad (see directions below).
5. Sauté until fully incorporated into tofu mixture and warmed thoroughly.
6. Warm tortilla(s) in a fry pan for several seconds.
7. Remove. Spoon the scrambled tofu/squash mixture in a line down the center of the tortilla.
8. Sprinkle with nutritional yeast.
9. Add salsa, or you can serve it on the top.

Roll it up like a burrito. Add your choice of steamed or fresh veggies, e.g., steamed broccoli florets, grated carrot, chopped fresh mushroom, chopped tomato, to cooked spaghetti squash (removed from the shell, of course). Toss. If you want to use it as a salad, top with your favorite salad dressing. If you want to use it in the breakfast burrito, omit the dressing. You can use green goddess dressing; it's also good in the burrito.

Bean & Vegetable Tostadas

1 can black beans, drained and rinsed
1 can canned corn kernels, drained and rinsed
1 small tomato, cored and chopped (about ½ cup)
2 tbsp. finely chopped red onion
1 small jalapeño or any hot chili, seeded & finely chopped
2 tbsp. chopped coriander
1 tbsp. freshly squeezed lime juice
½ tsp. salt
dash of Tabasco
1 small ripe avocado, stoned, peeled and chopped

1. Preheat oven to 220°C (425°F). Place tortillas in a single layer on a baking tray; coat both sides of each one with cooking spray. Bake until lightly browned and crisp, about 10 minutes; turn them over halfway through. Transfer to wire racks to cool.
2. Combine beans, corn, tomato, onion, chili, coriander, lime juice, salt and Tabasco in a large bowl. Gently fold in avocado. Top tortillas with bean mixture.

Burritos with Potatoes, Pinto Beans and Guacamole

1 lb red potatoes
1 tbsp. oil
1 tsp. dried thyme
1 tsp. dried marjoram
3 medium green onions, minced
1 Cup canned or cooked pinto beans
2 medium avocados, ripe
1 clove garlic, minced
2 tbsp. fresh lemon juice
¼ tsp. salt
pinch cayenne
1 tbsp. red onion, minced
1 medium Roma tomato, chopped finely
1 tbsp. fresh cilantro, minced flour tortillas

1. Finely chop the potatoes and put them in a pan with boiling water.
2. Simmer for 5 minutes and drain in a colander.
3. Put the oil in a large skillet and heat.
4. Add the thyme, marjoram, and green onion.
5. Cook for 2 minutes and add the potatoes.
6. Sauté for 15 minutes, tossing occasionally, until potatoes are browned in places.
7. Add the pinto beans and heat through for 5 minutes.
8. Remove from the heat.
9. In the meantime, cut open the avocado and remove the pit.
10. Scoop the avocado out and place in a bowl.
11. Add the garlic, lemon juice, salt, and cayenne and mash together until fairly smooth.
12. Add the red onion, tomato, and cilantro and stir to mix well. Let the flavors blend at room temp.
13. Warm the tortillas and place on the potatoes mixture and guacamole mixture
14. and roll. Top with salsa if desired.

Corn and Bean Burritos

1 cup corn
2 cups canned black beans, rinsed
1½ canned cooked soybeans, rinsed (you can use any small white bean, if you have trouble finding soybeans)
2 roma tomatoes, chopped
1 tsp. olive oil
5 tbsp. chopped onion
2 oz. fresh chili pepper, minced
1 green pepper, chopped
1 clove garlic, minced
1 tsp. ground cumin
1 tsp. oregano
2 tsp. fresh cilantro
2 tbsp. lime juice
tortillas

1. In bowl, mix corn, beans, and tomatoes.
2. Heat oil in skillet. Add onions, chili peppers, green pepper, and garlic; sauté until soft.
3. Add bean mixture and toss until heated.
4. Add seasonings and juice and cilantro and heat.
5. Wrap in tortillas.
6. I serve this with plain soy yogurt as a condiment.

Burritos

1 cup corn
2 cups canned black beans, rinsed
1½ canned cooked soybeans, rinsed
2 roma tomatoes, chopped
1 tsp. olive oil
5 tbsp. chopped onion
2 oz. fresh chili pepper, minced
1 green pepper, chopped
1 clove garlic, minced
1 tsp. ground cumin
1 tsp. oregano
2 tsp. fresh cilantro
2 tbsp. lime juice

1. In bowl, mix corn, beans, and tomatoes.
2. Heat oil in skillet.
3. Add onions, chili peppers, green pepper, and garlic; sauté.
4. until soft. Add bean mixture and toss until heated.
5. Add seasonings and juice and cilantro and heat.

Bean Tacos

Serves 6

2 tablespoons oil
1 large onion, chopped
2 cloves garlic, minced
19-oz can kidney beans, drained and mashed
1 cup frozen or fresh corn kernels
¼ teaspoon oregano
salt and pepper to taste
taco shells

1. Sauté onion and garlic in oil.
2. Add mashed beans and corn.
3. Add spices and mix well.
4. Heat 5-10 minutes over medium heat, stirring occasionally.
5. Add water if necessary to prevent sticking.
6. Serve in heated taco shells with shredded lettuce and chopped tomatoes.

Soft Vegetable Tacos

Serves 1

1 tablespoon olive oil
1 medium onion, chopped
2 red bell peppers, coarsely chopped
2 large garlic cloves, chopped
1 jalapeño chili, seeded, chopped
2 tablespoons chili powder
1 tablespoon ground cumin
1 teaspoon dried oregano
¾ cup tawny Port
1 to 16-oz. can pinto beans, rinsed, drained
1 to 16-oz. can golden or white hominy, rinsed, drained
2 cups chopped fresh spinach
12 warm corn tortillas

1. Heat olive oil in heavy large saucepan over medium-high heat. Add onion, red bell pepper, garlic and chili.
2. Sauté until vegetables soften, about 10 minutes.
3. Add chili powder, cumin and oregano and sauté 2 min.
4. Add Port and simmer until liquid reduces by half, about 10 minutes.
5. Mix in beans and hominy and heat through.
6. Cover and refrigerate. (Can be prepared 1 day ahead.)
7. Re-warm mixture over medium heat before continuing.) Add spinach and stir until wilted, about 2 minutes.
8. Spoon ⅓ cup vegetable mixture onto each tortilla.
9. Roll up tortilla to enclose filling and serve.

Slow-Simmered Fava Bean Soup with Mint & Pasilla Chile

Serves 10

1 pound hulled dry yellow fava beans (about 2-⅔ cups picked over and rinsed)

8 cups vegetable stock (or water)

6 cloves garlic, unpeeled

1 large white onion, thickly sliced

1½ lbs ripe tomatoes (3 large round or 9-12 plum)

6 medium dried pasilla chilies (about 2 oz. total stemmed and seeded)

2 tablespoons olive oil + extra for garnish

2 tablespoons cider vinegar

3 tablespoons water

¾ teaspoon dried oregano, preferably Mexican

2½ teaspoons salt, or to taste

½ cup chopped cilantro, loosely packed

1 tablespoon chopped fresh mint, up to 2 tablespoons (preferably spearmint)

1. Place beans in large soup pot. Cover with stock or water; simmer over medium-low heat, partially covered, until very tender and falling apart, about 1 hour.
2. While beans are simmering, roast garlic on ungreased griddle or heavy skillet over medium heat, turning occasionally, until blackened in spots and soft, about 15 minutes.
3. Cool then slip off papery skins and finely chop.
4. On piece of foil in same skillet, roast onion slices in single layer, turning once, until richly browned and soft, 6 to 7 minutes per side.
5. Dice onion. Roast tomatoes 4 inches below very hot broiler or in foil-lined skillet until blackened on one side, about 6 minutes.
6. Flip and roast other side. Cool, then peel and chop, saving all juice.
7. Add garlic, onion and tomatoes to beans, Simmer until beans are consistency of a coarse puree, about 30 minutes.
8. While soup is simmering, cut chilies into ⅛-inch slivers using kitchen shears.
9. Heat oil in small saucepan over medium heat.
10. Add chilies; stir for 1 minute.
11. Remove from heat; add vinegar, water, oregano and scant ½ teaspoon of salt.
12. Let stand at least ½ hour, stirring occasionally.
13. Just before serving, add a little stock or water to soup, if necessary, to reach desired consistency.
14. Stir in cilantro and mint. Season with remaining salt to taste. Ladle soup into warm bowls.
15. Spoon about a tablespoon of chili condiment into center, drizzle with oil.

Note: Hulled yellow fava beans are sold in Hispanic markets. They're the same as the brown fava beans found in Italian markets only with the papery brown hull removed. Also known as broad beans Pasilla chili: Dried, brownish-black chili used primarily in sauce and known for its rich flavor. Sold whole and powdered. Also known as chili negro for its color. In its fresh form pasilla chilies are called chilaca.

Taco Filling

Mix together in a saucepan:

1¼ cups cold water

1 tbsp. sun dried tomato bits (dry, not oilpak)

1 tsp. dried minced onions

½ tsp. Garlic powder

1 tbsp. Mild chili powder

1 tsp. Cumin

½ tsp. Sugar or equivalent

2 tbsp. Bragg's liquid aminos (or 1 tbsp. Soy sauce)

1 tbsp. Cornstarch

Stir until cornstarch dissolves.

Then stir in:

½ cup plain TVP granules

1. Bring to a boil, stirring constantly; stir and simmer until it is of the desired consistency for tacos, about 2 to 5 minutes. Put into a taco shell; top with the usual.

Note: If you don't have sun dried tomato bits, chop up some sun dried tomato halves in a food processor. Or make them by cutting Roma or Italian plum tomatoes in half; dry in a dehydrator until they're dry yet still flexible; leave them out for a day to "cure;" store, preferably in the freezer. Don't use any other kind of tomato, as they're too watery and seedy.

Tex-Mex Pinto Soup

Serves 6

1 tablespoon olive oil
½ cup onion, chopped
1 tablespoon garlic, minced
1 large jalapeno, minced
1 teaspoon ground cumin
4 ½ cups water
1 7 oz. pkg Fantastic Foods Instant Refried Beans salt to taste (1 to 1½ tsp)
1 15 oz. can corn kernels, drained
¼ cup minced fresh cilantro

1. Heat oil in a large saucepan.
2. Sauté onions, garlic, jalapeno, and cumin for 1 minute, stirring frequently.
3. Add water and bring to a boil.
4. Whisk in the bean flakes (use a whisk or they will lump up) and salt to taste.
5. Cover, reduce heat, and simmer for 5 minutes.
6. Stir in the corn and cook, uncovered, until heated through, about 1-2 minutes.
7. Stir in cilantro just before serving.

Low-Fat Veggie Tacos

Serves 3

3 tbsp. olive oil
3 chopped onions
fresh mushrooms (as many as you want)
1 green pepper
Fresh Broccoli Crowns (as many as you like)
1 Can Old El Paso no fat refried beans
low fat taco shells

1. Sauté onions, mushrooms, green pepper and broccoli in olive oil until onions are translucent and veggies soft (approx. 15 mins.).
2. Add refried beans and continue to sauté for an additional 15 mins. stirring occasionally.
3. When done, add to taco shells (salt and pepper to taste, add a little garlic powder if desired) and dig in.
4. Prep. time: 30mins.

Yucca Root Soup -or- Manioc Soup

Serves 4

1 yucca root, peeled and cut into pieces
5 teaspoons Organic Gourmet veggie broth
5 cups water (more if needed to cover the veggies)
2 onions, chopped and sautéed in some of the broth
salt and pepper to taste

1. Boil the yucca root pieces in the broth until tender (about 20 minutes) along with the sautéed onion pieces.
2. When tender, put into the blender a portion at a time.
3. It thickens by itself.
4. Add salt and pepper to taste.
5. It made about 4-5 good sized bowls of soup.
6. Serve with some good bread

Green Chile Stew

Serves 6

This stew only gets better and hotter the next day.
I use a large dollop of Tofu Sour Cream to cut the heat.

1 tablespoon vegetable oil
1 medium onion, peeled, finely chopped
2 cloves fresh garlic, finely chopped
2 medium white potatoes cut into ¼ x 1 inch sections
1 pound frozen or fresh roasted green chilies, peeled and chopped
1 cup dried pinto beans, washed, soaked overnight, drained, washed again, and then cooked in 4 cups fresh cold water for approximately 40 minutes or until tender.

1. In a large sauce pan, heat the oil and fry the chopped onions for 2-3 minutes until translucent.
2. Add the chopped garlic and sliced potatoes.
3. Fry together 5-7 minutes, stirring frequently so the mixture doesn't burn.
4. Add the defrosted or fresh green chilies and continue to fry until the mixture is well blended and all the vegetables are soft.
5. Add the cooked pinto beans and bean water.
6. Bring to a boil and then turn down heat to a simmer.
7. Cook semi-covered 15 minutes.
8. Serve with tortillas.

Vegetarian Sierra Stew

1 15oz can of kidney beans (or uncooked beans)
1 large thinly sliced onion
4 chopped garlic cloves 1 coarsely chopped green pepper
1 cup of coarsely chopped green cabbage
½ cup of diced russet potatoes
16 oz. can of tomatoes
1 tbsp. chili powder
½ tsp. cumin
½ cup uncooked brown rice
4 cups of water or veggie broth

1. In a large pot over medium high heat, heat 2 tbsp. of olive oil and sauté onion and garlic until the onion is soft. Add bell pepper, cabbage, potatoes, tomatoes, chili powder and cumin.
2. Continue cooking, stirring frequently for 3 minutes.
3. Add the rice, water or veggie broth, and beans.
4. Cover and cook on a low heat for two hours until stew is thick, and the rice and beans are tender; (if you used canned beans, cooking time will be less).
5. Top with grated cheese if desired.

Spicy Summer Stew

3 cups water or stock
3 cups textured vegetable protein
1 tablespoon ketchup
1 large onion, chopped
6 cloves garlic, chopped
1 cup white wine
4 zucchini, sliced
3 yellow squash, sliced
1 yellow bell pepper, diced
3 Roma tomatoes, chopped
soy sauce to taste
1 Serrano chili, sliced
1½ teaspoons New Mexico ground red pepper
2 teaspoons cumin
1 can corn kernels
a handful chopped fresh cilantro

1. Mix the ketchup in 3 cups water; add TVP.
2. Soak the TVP until liquid is absorbed.
3. Sauté the onions, garlic, Serrano and bell pepper in the wine for five minutes or so (add additional water as needed). Add squashes, tomatoes, soy, and spices.
4. Simmer for 10 minutes or so.
5. Add TVP, simmer for 10 to 15 minutes.
6. Before serving, stir in cilantro.
7. Serve with tortillas.

Southwestern Pasta

Serves 4
¼ cup olive oil
2 medium onions, sliced
1 clove garlic, minced
3½ cup peeled tomatoes, crushed
¾ tsp. Tabasco or other hot pepper sauce
¼ tsp. salt
2-3 tbsp. minced fresh cilantro
¼ tsp. sugar
12 oz. angel hair pasta, cooked al dente and drained

1. Heat the oil over medium heat, stir in onions and garlic and sauté until tender (10-12 min).
2. Add rest of ingredients (except pasta); bring to boil.
3. Reduce heat to low and simmer uncovered until thickened slightly (30 min).
4. Place pasta on platter and top with sauce.

Mexican Potato Salad

2 lbs. red potatoes, cut into chunks
1 cup frz. corn kernels, thawed
1 leg. tomato, chopped
1 bunch scallions, chopped
½ cup salsa
2 tables. fresh lime juice
2 tables chopped fresh cilantro or 1 tablespoon dried freshly ground pepper

1. Place the potatoes in a large pot and cover with water. Bring to a boil, reduce the heat, cover, and cook 30 minutes, or until just tender. Remove from the heat, drain, and place in large bowl.
2. Add the corn, tomato, and scallions. Combine the salsa and lime juice.
3. Pour over the salad and mix well. Add the cilantro and a few twist of pepper. Mix gently and serve at once or chill overnight.

Cucumber Salad

¼ cup rice or white vinegar
¼ cup water
¼ cup sugar
1 tbsp. soy sauce, or salt
1 chili, minced
about 10 inches cucumber
several sprigs coriander, finely minced

1. In a small saucepan, combine vinegar, water, sugar, and soy sauce and bring to boil.
2. Remove from heat and add chili.
3. Let cool. Meanwhile, slice cucumber in ½ lengthwise and slice thinly.
4. Mix all ingredients together when liquid has cooled.

Avocado, Carrot & Tomatoe with Garlic Salad

Serves 6
8 cloves garlic - peeled and mashed
3 cups carrot - grated
3 ripe avocados, chopped
2 ripe tomatoes, chopped
¼ cup olive oil
¼ cup lime juice
sea salt to taste
freshly ground black pepper

1. Combine all ingredients, toss, and let stand for ½ hour before serving.
2. Toss again just before serving.

Raspberry, Avocado & Mango Salad

½ cups fresh raspberries, divided
¼ cup extra-virgin olive oil
¼ cup red wine vinegar
1 small clove garlic, coarsely chopped
¼ teaspoon kosher salt
1/8 teaspoon freshly ground pepper
8 cups mixed salad greens
1 ripe mango, diced (see Tip)
1 small ripe avocado, diced
½ cup thinly sliced red onion
¼ cup toasted chopped hazelnuts or sliced almonds
  (see Tip), optional

Tips:
1. **To dice a mango.** Slice both ends off the mango, revealing the long, slender seed inside. Set the fruit upright on a work surface and remove the skin with a sharp knife.
2. With the seed perpendicular to you, slice the fruit from both sides of the seed, yielding two large pieces.
3. Turn the seed parallel to you and slice the two smaller pieces of fruit from each side.
4. Cut the fruit into the desired shape.
5. **To toast chopped or sliced nuts.** Heat a small dry skillet over medium-low heat. Add nuts and cook, stirring, until lightly browned and fragrant, 2 to 3 minutes.

Salad:
1. Puree ½ cup raspberries, oil, vinegar, garlic, salt and pepper in a blender until combined.
2. Combine greens, mango, avocado and onion in a large bowl.
3. Pour the dressing on top and gently toss to coat.
4. Divide the salad among 5 salad plates.
5. Top each with the remaining raspberries and sprinkle with nuts, if using.

Fresh Fruit Vinaigrette

Serves 6

1 small banana, thinly sliced
½ cup orange juice
1 tbsp. limejuice
½ jalapeno pepper, seeded and mince
¼ teaspoon sesame oil
1 teaspoon rice wine vinegar
1 teaspoon minced fresh ginger root
1 pinch salt and pepper

1. Combine banana, orange juice, lime juice, jalapeno, oil, vinegar, ginger and salt and pepper in a blender or food processor and puree until smooth.
2. Transfer to a container with a tight lid, cover, and refrigerate until ready to serve. Shake before serving.

Caribbean & Latin American
Appetizers

Jamaican Patties

Filling

1 tbsp coconut oil
½ cup, onion, diced
⅛ tsp ground cinnamon
¼ tsp ground allspice
½ tsp ground cumin
¼ tsp red pepper flakes
⅛ tsp cayenne
coarse sea salt
2 large cloves garlic, minced
¾ cup coconut milk
¼ cup carrots, finely diced
¼ cup potatoes, finely diced
½ cup fresh (or frozen) green peas
½ cup fresh (or frozen) corn
½ cup cabbage, shredded
1 tbsp fresh thyme, minced
1 tbsp freshly squeezed lemon juice
½ tsp freshly ground pepper

Pastry

1¾ cups unbleached white flour, chilled
1 cup whole wheat pastry flour, chilled
2 tsp turmeric
½ tsp sea salt
¾ up chilled coconut butter
2 tsp apple cider vinegar
½ cup plus 2 tbsp ice water

For the filling

In a medium-size pan over medium-low heat, combine the coconut oil, the onion, cinnamon, allspice, cumin, red pepper flakes, cayenne and ½ tsp slat. Saute, stirring occasionally for 8 to 10 minutes, or until the vegetables are caramelized. Add the garlic and cook for an additional 2 minutes. Stir in the coconut milk, carrots, and potatoes. Reduce the heat to low, cover, and cook until the carrots and potatoes are tender, 10 to 12 minutes. Stir in the green peas, corn, cabbage, thyme and lemon juice, over and cook for 3 minutes more.

Season with additional salt and pepper to taste and set aside to allow the flavours to marry.

For the pastry

1. Combine 1½ cups of the white flour with the pastry flour, turmeric and salt in a large bowl and mix well. Set the remaining ¼ cup white flour aside. Add the coconut butter to the flour mixture and rub your fingertips until the mixture resembles fine sand, about 10 minutes.
2. Combine the vinegar and water and mix well. Then, without overworking the dough, add the vinegar mixture by the tablespoon while stirring, just until the dough comes to coalesce. Squeeze into a tight ball., flatten, cover in plastic wrap, and refrigerate for at least 1 hour.
3. Preheat the oven to 350F and remove the dough from the refrigerator. With the reserved flour, lightly dust a clean surface, roll out the dough until it is about 1/8" thick. Cut six 6" circles from the dough (use a bowl). Spoon 2 heaping tablespoons of the filling onto the centre of one side of each circle, leaving about 1/8" border. Fold the other half over to make a half-moon, press to seal and make ridges around the edge using a fork.
4. Transfer to patties to a baking sheet and bake until golden brown, about 35 minutes. Serve immediately with some hot sauce.

Mango Pomegranate Guacamole

4 ripe avocados (2 pounds total)
1 cup finely chopped white onion
2 fresh serrano chiles, finely chopped (2 tablespoons), including seeds
¼ cup fresh lime juice, or to taste
3/4 cup pomegranate seeds (from 1 pomegranate)
3/4 cup diced peeled mango
½ cup chopped cilantro
Accompaniment: plantain chips
Garnish: lime wedges

1. Halve, pit, and peel avocados. Coarsely mash in a bowl.
2. Stir in onion, chiles, ¼ cup lime juice, and 1 ¼ teaspoons salt, then fold in pomegranate seeds, mango, and cilantro.
3. Season with salt and additional lime juice.

Note: Guacamole can be made 4 hours ahead and chilled, its surface covered with parchment paper or plastic wrap. Bring to room temperature and stir before serving.

Spinach and Split Pea Patties

Makes 14-16

There are many types of delicious fried snacks that are made and eaten in the Caribbean. They are most sold as street food and as part of the food offerings at festival times such as Hindu and Muslim holidays.

This spinach and split pea patty recipe is a rift of an Indian Vada and the West Indian Phulourie (split peas fritter). Packed with healthy protein, these hearty patties can work as a meal in themselves. Serve them as a snack or breakfast item.

1 cup yellow split peas soaked overnight	2 tsp ground cumin or garam masala
1 tsp chopped garlic	¼ cup water
minced hot pepper to taste	2 packed cups finely chopped spinach (fresh)
½ cup all purpose flour	2 tsp chopped cilantro
1 tsp baking powder	salt to taste
1 tsp cornstarch	oil for shallow frying

1. Drain peas and rinse a few times until the water runs clear. Drain well and then add to a food processor along with garlic and pepper. Puree until the mixture is a fine grainy paste. Set aside.
2. Add flour, baking powder, cornstarch, cumin or garam masala to a large bowl. Mix thoroughly.
3. Transfer the pea mixture along with the water to the flour mixture and stir to incorporate.
4. Add and mix in spinach, cilantro and salt to taste to the flour-pea mixture. Mix thoroughly.
5. Cover and set aside to rest for 1 hour.
6. Rub a little oil on your hands and take a little of the mixture at a time, about the size of a golf ball or larger, and shape into 1/3 to ½ inch thick disks.
7. Repeat until all the patties are shaped. The mixture will be moist, don't worry about that.
8. Heat oil on medium heat and fry in batches until browned on both sides. Total cooking time take about 4 - 5 minutes per batch depending on how thick you make them. Drain on paper towels.
9. Serve warm as is or with a salsa or chutney or pepper sauce.

Roti Bread

1 cup flour
dash baking soda
milk (1 to 4 tablespoons, depending on humidity)
¼ cup vegetable oil
salt to taste
Optional: use combination of flour and ground chick peas), corn meal, bread crumbs, ground chick peas, or flour (for cutting board)
rolling pin and cutting board or similar surface

1. In a big bowl, mix flour, and baking soda (and salt if you want any). Mix with your hands/fingers. Add 1 tablespoon milk and work the mixture with your hands, trying to make a big ball.
2. Once you have the dough in a ball, stop adding milk.
3. Make the dough into 3 balls and let them rest for 10 minutes.
4. Put the oil in a in a bowl (so that you can get to it with your fingers).
5. Roll out the dough on a board covered with bread crumbs or cornmeal or ground chick peas or flour.
6. Each ball should make a circle 8" wide.
7. Don't worry if it's too hard to roll out at this stage; the dough may be tough.
8. Brush a thin layer of oil over the top surface of the circle and then scrunch it back up into a ball.
9. Do this for all 3 balls, then let them sit for ½ hour to rest.
10. The roll them out and oil them again.
11. This time it should be easier, but they may be a little more sticky, so make sure your board and rolling pin are well floured.
12. Now warm a frying pan with a thick, even bottom to medium heat, no oil (there is already oil on the roti).
13. Put one of the roti circles in and cook for about a minute.
14. Turn it and when the hot surface cools a little, wipe it with oil.
15. When there are some golden spots, the bread is done.
16. Keep it between 2 plates or under a cloth to keep it soft and warm.
17. Dump the potato curry mixture on top of the skin and fold the skin around it.
18. You can eat it with your hands, or if it is too messy, silverware.

Potato Curry Filling

¼ sunflower oil
2 tsp. turmeric
1 tsp. cumin
½ tsp. allspice
½ ground ginger
(instead of the above spices, you can use 4 tsp. curry powder)
1 small onion, cut into small pieces
4 cloves garlic, minced or crushed
2 medium sized potatoes, washed, peeled, and chopped into ¼-inch cubes salt to taste

Additional ingredients, (optional-depending on personal taste and what is available in the kitchen):

up to 1 cup chick peas
up to 1 cup sweet potato, Nigerian yam, or plantain (if adding these, then use less potatoes from above)
up to 1 cup red, yellow or green pepper (cut small).
up to ½ cup broccoli or cauliflower (chopped small)
up to ½ cup sliced bok choy or cabbage
½ cup to 1 cup of water

1. Heat the spices in the oil on medium heat, in either a sturdy, deep frying pan, or a heavy-bottomed sauce-pan.
2. Cook stirring for 5 minutes, careful not to burn spices.
3. Then add onion and garlic and cook for 1-2 minutes stirring.
4. You may have to turn down the heat a little bit so that the garlic doesn't burn.
5. Then add the potatoes and fry them up for 1-2 minutes, stirring.
6. This is also the time to add any of the following items: chick peas, sweet potato, Nigerian yam, plantain, peppers, broccoli, cauliflower, bok Choy, or cabbage.
7. Add the water so that it covers the bottom to at least ¼" of liquid, (but not more than ½") Cover the pan and simmer for 15 minutes on medium low heat (the mixture should gently bubble).
8. Taste for salt and be sure that potatoes are soft.
9. Add a little more water if necessary.
10. Serve on rice or scooped onto "roti" bread.

Sides

Cooked Plantains

1 very ripe plantain (black peel),
1 tsp. of butter, margarine or olive oil,
3-6 cloves 1/8 tsp. all-spice (optional)
shredded coconut (vegan version - cheese is traditional).
1 tsp. raw sugar (optional, not necessary at all if the plantain is ripe, but is maybe good if the peel is just yellowish).

1. Preheat the oven at 450 F.
2. Make a longitudinal cut on the plantain peel, open it and cut the plantain in two halves, again longitudinally.
3. Grease a tray, or simple cover the tray with baking paper or aluminum foil.
4. Put the plantain over its peel on the tray.
5. Insert the cloves, distributing them well along the two halves (remember where, to remove them after the cooking).
6. Optionally, sprinkle some all-spice powder and/or a teaspoon of raw sugar.
7. Then put small amounts of margarine or olive oil on the plantain halves and spread the shredded coconut over them.
8. Bake it until the plantain becomes golden.
9. Remove it from the oven and take the cloves out.
10. Another way to make this dish is to put the plantain (without the peel) cut it in halves (across the plantain) on a greased iron pan, with the sugar (optional) and the spices.
11. Slowly cook it until brown and mushy, the natural sugars should caramelized.
12. Then sprinkle the coconut, continue cooking until the coconut browns and remove it from the heat.
13. This dish is traditionally eaten with black beans, rice and shredded meat.

Due to a lack of time, many people in countries fry the plantain slices, pour on some sugar and white wine and simmer. Then, they add the cheese. It's absolutely delicious but not really healthy. As a replacement for the meat, in this traditional "pabellon", vegans use the green plantain peel, shredded and cooked in the same way as the original recipe.

Veggie Venezuelan 'Ham' Bread

mixed-grain or whole meal bread mix
1 garlic clove
1 onion
½ red sweet pepper
4 or 5 calamata olives
4 or 5 green olives
thyme
handful of raisins
olive oil
molasses

1. Prepare the dough as indicated in the package (usually it only needs to add warm water).
2. Extend the dough and cover with a tiny layer of olive oil, rub the garlic clove (chopped), and cover with the rest of the vegetables, finely chopped.
3. Spread the thyme and the raisins, roll it and let it rise for 30 minutes, in a warm place (cover with a damp cloth) and, before putting it into a preheated oven (450 F), cover it with a layer of olive oil and molasses.
4. Bake until brown (about 20 minutes).

Caribbean Rice and Beans

Serves 4

1 tablespoon vegetable oil
1 small onion, diced
1 carrot, peeled and diced
2 cloves garlic, minced
1 Scotch bonnet pepper or other chili pepper, seeded and minced
1½ cups long-grain white rice, uncooked
2 cups vegetable broth
1 cup canned coconut milk
1½ cups red kidney beans, canned, drained
2 teaspoons fresh thyme leaves (or ½ tsp. dried)
¼ teaspoon ground allspice
¼ teaspoon ground black pepper
¼ teaspoon salt

1. Heat the oil in a saucepan and add the onion, carrot, garlic and Scotch bonnet pepper.
2. Sauté over medium heat for about 7 minutes.
3. Stir in the rice, water, coconut milk, beans and seasonings.
4. cover and cook over medium heat for 15 to 20 minutes.
5. When the rice is done, transfer to a serving bowl.
6. Fluff the rice and serve hot.

Aztec Couscous

Serves 4

1 cup couscous
½ teaspoon ground cumin
1 teaspoon salt or to taste
1 cup to 1¼ cup water
1¾ cups black beans -or- 1 15 oz. can
1 cup corn kernels
½ cup red onion, finely chopped
¼ cup fresh cilantro, minced
1 jalapeno, minced
3 tablespoons roasted garlic olive oil
3 tablespoons to 4 tbsp. freshly squeezed lime juice

1. Place couscous, cumin, and salt in a large heatproof bowl or storage container and pour 1 cup boiling water on top.
2. Cover tightly and let sit until all the liquid is absorbed, about 10 minutes. If the couscous is not quite tender, add an additional ¼ cup of boiling water, cover, and let sit for a few minutes longer.
3. Fluff up with a fork. Toss in the beans, corn, onion, cilantro, and jalapeno.
4. Mix in olive oil and enough lime juice to give the salad a puckery edge. Serve warm or at room temp.

Caribbean Coconut Vegetables

Serves 4 to 5

2 tablespoons butter
3 green onions, chopped (about ¾ cup)
1 large onion, chopped (about 1½ cups)
1 tomato, diced (about 1½ cups)
½ pound mushrooms, quartered
1 (14-ounce) can coconut milk
3 carrots, thinly sliced diagonally (about 1½ cups)
1 stalk celery, sliced diagonally
1 cup broccoli florets
½ pound green beans
2 sprigs of fresh thyme (or 1 teaspoon dried thyme)
½ teaspoon finely chopped Scotch bonnet pepper
½ teaspoon salt
¼ teaspoon black pepper

1. In a medium saucepan over medium heat, melt the butter. Sauté the green onions, onions, tomato, and mushrooms until the vegetables are tender.
2. Stir in the coconut milk. Boil for 10 to 15 minutes or until nicely thickened.
3. Stir in the carrots; cook for 2 to 3 minutes. Add the celery, broccoli, green beans, thyme, Scotch bonnet pepper, salt, and black pepper. Simmer until the vegetables are cooked yet still crunchy.
4. If the sauce is too thick, add 1 to 2 tablespoons water. Remove the thyme sprigs before serving.

Traditional Cuban Black Beans

Serves 6

1 pound dried black beans, sorted & rinsed
2½ quarts water
2 large green bell pepper, chopped & divided
2 tablespoons olive oil
1 large onion, chopped
4 cloves garlic, minced
1 teaspoon hot red pepper sauce
¼ teaspoon dried oregano
1 bay leaf
2 teaspoons sugar
3 teaspoons to 4 tsp. salt
2 tablespoons dry white wine
2 tablespoons olive oil
hot cooked white or yellow rice
Garnish: chopped onion

1. Sort and wash beans and place in a Dutch oven.
2. Add water and half of bell pepper and bring to a boil.
3. Reduce heat and simmer, uncovered, 1½ hours or just until beans are tender.
4. (If desired, beans can be presoaked overnight before this process.)
5. Heat 2 tablespoons of olive oil in a skillet over medium-high heat until hot. Add remaining bell pepper, onion, and next 4 ingredients.
6. Cook, stirring constantly, 5 minutes or until tender.
7. Add onion mixture, sugar, and salt to beans, cover and simmer, stirring occasionally, for 45 minutes.
8. Uncover and cook for 15 minutes or to desired thickness. Stir in wine and 2 tablespoons of olive oil.
9. Remove and discard bay leaf. Serve over rice.
10. Garnish with chopped onion, if desired.

Griots

This dish, often sold along the roads of Haiti, is traditionally made with pork but we have substituted tempeh to make it vegetarian.

1 package tempeh, thawed and cubed
1 cup onions, chopped
¼ cup chives, chopped
½ cup lime juice
½ cup water
pinch of thyme
¼ teaspoon salt
¼ teaspoon black pepper

1. Marinate all ingredients in a shallow bowl for several hours.
2. Heat some oil and brown the tempeh, then add the marinade and simmer over low heat for 30 minutes, covered.
3. Remove the lid and cook to eliminate any leftover liquid. Serve hot.
4. If you are making a Haitian meal out of the above, try ending it with tropical fruit such as mangos, bananas, oranges, and pineapple for dessert.

Curried Brown Rice with Mushrooms and Tofu

½ tbsp. Earth Balance Natural Buttery spread
¼ cup, chopped onions, raw
One serving tofu
6 medium, sliced mushrooms, fresh
1 tsp. curry powder
1 cup leftover or precooked organic brown rice
1 tbsp. basil

1. Heat sauté pan with ½ tbsp. Earth Balance.
2. Add onions and cook 3-4 minutes, add tofu and cook another 3-4 minutes, stirring often.
3. Add mushrooms and cook for 2-3 minutes.
4. Add rice and curry powder. Stir well and cook an additional 3-4 minutes.
5. Add 1-2 tbsp. of water if needed for moisture.
6. Top with chopped basil and serve.

Tomato Rice (Caribbean)

Serves 6

2 teaspoons vegetable oil
½ cup onion, finely chopped
3 cloves garlic, finely minced
2½ cups vegetable broth
1 cup brown rice, uncooked
¼ teaspoon salt
2 medium ripe tomatoes, peeled and chopped
⅛ teaspoon pepper
⅛ teaspoon dried thyme

1. Heat oil in a medium saucepan over medium heat.
2. Add onion and garlic. Cook, stirring frequently, 5 minutes.
3. Add broth and bring to a boil. Add remaining ingredients. Reduce heat to medium-low, cover, and simmer 45 minutes, until rice is tender and most of the liquid has been absorbed.
4. Remove from heat and let stand covered, 5 minutes.
5. Fluff rice with a fork before serving.

Jamaican Jerk Tofu

Serves 6

This is the kind of miracle dish that can convert anyone to tofu. The Jamaican "jerk" seasoning is sure-to-please. It's sort of like barbeque and sort of like curry, savory and sweet at the same time. Just make sure you allow plenty of time for the pressing and marinating. The drier the tofu gets before you put it in the marinade, the better. It will soak up more flavor and be nicely chewy.

1 lb extra firm tofu, drained, sliced and pressed (see directions)	3 tbsp. pure maple syrup
	1 tbsp. dried thyme
½ large sweet onion, roughly chopped	2 tsp. allspice
	½ tsp. cayenne
4 cloves garlic	1 tsp. nutmeg
2 tbsp. fresh ginger, grated	½ tsp. cinnamon
juice of 2 limes	2 jalapeno peppers, seeded and chopped (you can cut back to one or omit entirely if you like spicy)
zest of 1 lime	
2 tbsp. soy sauce	
2 tbsp. olive oil	

1. Slice the tofu into thick slabs then lay the slices on several layers of paper towels or on a clean dish towel and place a heavy plate or skillet on top.
2. Let it sit for an hour or two. Pressing the tofu is a way to get the extra moisture out - and the drier you can get the tofu, the more of the flavorful marinade it can absorb.
3. Puree all the rest of the ingredients in a blender or food processor to create the marinade.
4. Place the tofu slices in a bowl, pour in the marinade, making sure to coat all the slices, and cover.
5. Let it sit for an hour or two, flipping the slices about halfway through Heat a skillet with a small amount of olive oil over medium high heat.
6. When the pan is hot, lay the tofu slices in a single layer and sauté until crispy and browned. That will take 8-10 minutes on each side.

Banana Nut Bread

3/4 cups all purpose flour	equivalent of 2 eggs using egg replacer
2 tsp baking powder	
¼ tsp baking soda	2-3 ripe bananas mashed
½ tsp salt	1 tsp vanilla extract
1 cup demerera sugar	½ cup chopped pecans or walnuts
½ cup vegetable oil	

1. Preheat oven to 350°F. Sift together dry ingredients.
2. Stir in nuts, egg replacer, bananas, oil and vanilla.
3. Mix well. Pour into greased loaf pan and bake for 45-60 mins (until knife comes out clean).
4. Cool for 5 mins before removing from pan. Cool on wire rack.

Cranberry – Walnut Pumpkin Bread

(Ingredients separated into groups A-D)

A:
- 2/3 to 3 cups bread flour
- 1 teaspoon cinnamon
- ½ teaspoon grated nutmeg
- ½ teaspoon salt

B:
- 2 tablespoon tepid water (80°F to 90°F)
- 2 teaspoons active dry yeast

C:
- 5 tablespoons unsalted butter, at room temperature
- 1/3 cup sugar
- 1 cup pureed cooked pumpkin (or butter nut squash)
- 1 egg equivalent, using egg replacer

D:
- ¾ cup walnut pieces, toasted
- 1 cup plump golden or dark raisins
- 2/3 cup cranberries (if frozen, thaw & pat dry)

1. Take A & mix together. In a mixing bowl attach a paddle and mix B. Add C to the bowl & let mix slowly so the mixture is evenly mixed.
2. Add A gradually on slow speed to let the dough form. Once all ingredients are mixed, turn the paddle on high speed for 4 minutes.
3. Turn on low speed & add D gradually & let mix until all is incorporated.
4. Remove from mixer & proof in an oiled bowl covered with saran wrap for 1 hour & half.
5. Measure 5 oz. pieces & form into any small shaped bread rolls. Proof for additional 45 minutes
6. Brush with egg wash & bake in a pre-heated oven at 400 degrees for 45 minutes.
7. When out of the oven, let cool on perforated trays

Note: Great for making French Toast or perfect just toasted for breakfast. Add some havarti & roasted red peppers for a lunch sandwich.

Sauces & Spices

Island Jerk Marinade

medium onion, peeled
6 scotch bonnet peppers,
  seeded
1 bunch scallions
  (green parts only)
1 oz. fresh ginger, peeled

1 tbsp. ground allspice
  berries
1 tbsp. dried thyme
1 c. white wine vinegar
12 c. soy sauce

1. Combine all ingredients in a food processor and
    blend to a fine puree. Refrigerate in an airtight con-
    tainer for (up to) several weeks.
2. Marinade meat substitute for 24 hours before
    cooking over hot coals.

Caribbean BBQ Sauce

1 teaspoon vegetable oil
3 slices bacon, diced
1 medium onion, finely chopped
1 cup tomato sauce

½ cup black rum
1 lemon, juiced
1/3 cup brown sugar
1 dash chili sauce

1. Place vegetable oil, bacon, and onion in a medium
    skillet over medium high heat. Cook until bacon is
    evenly brown and onion is tender.
2. Stir tomato sauce and rum into the skillet with bacon
    and onion, and reduce heat. Simmer about 2 minutes.
3. Mix in lemon juice, brown sugar, and chili sauce.
    Continue to simmer about 8 minutes.

Curry Powder Mixture

8 tbsp cumin powder
7 tbsp coriander powder
2 tbsp ginger powder

4 tbsp turmeric powder
½ tbsp cayenne pepper

1. Combine all the ingredients and store in an airtight
    container.

Jamaican Jerk Spice Mixture

2 tsp ground thyme
1 tsp dried parsley
1 tsp ground allspice
¼ tsp ground cinnamon
1 tsp ground black pepper
¼ tsp red pepper flakes

1 tsp paprika
¼ tsp ground cumin
2 tsp salt
¼ tsp ground nutmeg
2 tsp fine grain sugar
2 tsp dried chives

1. Mix ingredients together.

Ti malice (hot sauce)

Ingredients:
1 small hot pepper, finely diced
1 large chopped onion
½ cup chopped green onions
3 cloves of garlic, minced
½ cup lime juice
¼ cup olive oil
salt and pepper to taste

1. Pour the lemon juice over the onions and let marinate
    for about 2 hours.
2. Place all ingredients in a pot, bring to a boil and cook
    until the pepper is soft (about 10-15 minutes).
3. Let the mixture cool and refrigerate to store.

Entrees

Smoked Tofu Paella

Serves 4

1 packet Cauldron Smoked Tofu, cut into 32 triangles
5 tbsp olive oil
18 oz mixed vegetables, cut into 1-inch vegetable pieces
  (e.g., peppers, baby sweet corn, broccoli, mushrooms)
5 oz onion, chopped
5 oz carrot, cut into 1-inch batons
2 tsp. garlic crushed
½ mild green chili, finely chopped
1 oz brown rice
1 pint white wine
1 pint light vegetable stock, double strength
5 oz tomatoes, peeled and chopped
3 oz pitted black olives, sliced
2 bay leaves, 2 tbsp chopped fresh tarragon (or 1 tsp.
  dried), 1 tbsp chopped fresh sage
2 tbsp chopped parsley, salt and black pepper
1 lemon, cut into 8 wedges

1. In a non-stick pan, fry tofu in oil over a medium heat
    until light brown. Remove from pan.
2. Increase heat and add the mixed vegetables to the
    same pan. Cook until browned slightly.
3. Remove from pan. Place onions and carrots in same
    pan. Cook gently until softened.
4. Add the garlic, chili and rice. Cook for 1 minute.
5. Add wine, stock, chopped tomatoes, olives and bay
    leaves. Simmer, covered until the rice is cooked
    (about 25 min.).
6. Add more liquid if necessary during the cooking time.
7. Remove bay leaves. Add the tofu, vegetables and
    fresh herbs. Season with salt, black pepper and lemon
    juice. Garnish with lemon wedges.

Caribbean Baked Tofu Cutlets

Serves 4

1 pound firm tofu, sliced 1-inch thick
8 ounces tomato sauce
2 tablespoons lime juice
1 tablespoon grated onion
¾ teaspoon dried oregano
¼ teaspoon garlic powder
⅛ teaspoon salt
⅛ teaspoon pepper
1¼ teaspoons coconut extract

1. Press tofu slices between two pans for one to two hours to squeeze out the water and compress the tofu. While tofu is draining, combine remaining ingredients.
2. Mix well and set aside. Preheat oven to 350°F.
3. Lightly oil a 7 x 11-inch baking pan or spray with a nonstick cooking spray.
4. Spoon about a third of the sauce into prepared pan.
5. Place pressed tofu on sauce and top with remaining sauce. Bake uncovered, 45 minutes.
6. Serve hot with Tomato Rice, or cold in sandwiches.

Stuffed Collard Greens with Jamaican Jerk Tempeh

Serves 4

5 tablespoons garlic, minced
4 tablespoons coconut oil, melted
1 small red onion, diced
1 fresh jalapeno, seeded and minced
3 tablespoons fresh ginger, peeled and minced
1½ teaspoon ground allspice
1½ teaspoon dried thyme
½ teaspoon ground cinnamon
½ teaspoon ground nutmeg
Salt
freshly ground black pepper

juice from ½ of a lemon
¾ cup orange juice
2 tablespoons agave nectar
16 oz. tempeh, cut into bite-size chunks
About 10 large, broad collard leaves, washed
1 15 oz. can diced tomatoes
1 15 oz. can coconut milk

1. Preheat the oven to 350 degrees. To make the marinade for the tempeh, combine 3 tablespoons of the garlic, 2 tablespoons of oil, and the next 12 ingredients (through agave nectar) in a medium bowl. Mix thoroughly.
2. Pour half of the marinade into a 2-quart baking dish. Put the tempeh chunks in the dish and arrange so that they are in a single snug layer.
3. Pour the rest of the marinade on top of the tempeh. Bake, uncovered, for 35-40 minutes, until most of the marinade has been absorbed and the tempeh is nicely browned.
4. While the tempeh cooks, cut each half of each collard leaf off the stems; reserve the stems. Be careful to keep the leaves intact so you have at least 18 long, wide collard ribbons. Roughly chop the stems.
5. Put the remaining 2 tablespoons of the oil in a deep skillet or casserole with a tight-fitting lid over medium-high heat.
6. Add the remaining 2 tablespoons of garlic and the chopped collard stems and sprinkle with salt and pepper.
7. Cook, uncovered, stirring occasionally until the collar stems are just beginning to soften, about 5 minutes. Remove from heat.
8. Lay out a collard ribbon, top with a few pieces of the baked tempeh (be careful not to overfill) and roll it up loosely. Put it in the skillet on top of the garlic and stems.
9. Repeat until all of the ribbons and the tempeh are used, nestling the rolls in next to each other in a single layer.
10. Combine the diced tomatoes and coconut milk in a medium bowl and season with salt and pepper. Pour the tomato-coconut milk mixture over the stuffed collard greens.
11. Return the skillet to medium heat. When the liquid starts to boil, cover and turn the heat down to medium low.
12. Cook, undisturbed, for 10 minutes, or until the collard leaves are tender. To serve, carefully scoop the rolls out and top with the coconut-tomato gravy and bits of collard stems.

Rasta Pasta (British Virgin Islands)

3 tablespoons olive oil
2 cloves garlic, minced
1 large onion, sliced
2 yellow and/or red peppers, cored, seeded and
  cut in lengthwise julienne slices
1 pound fettuccini
1 tablespoon olive oil
2 cups cooked drained black beans
2 cups cooked broccoli floweretes (just the top
  portion of small broccoli)
¼ cup chopped fresh basil or 1 teaspoon dried
2 teaspoons fresh chopped oregano or ½ teaspoon dried
parmesan cheese

1. Heat oil in a large skillet and sauté garlic, onions and
   peppers just until limp. Add drained, cooked black
   beans. Cook fettuccini in rapidly boiling salted water
   just until cooked. Drain and toss with olive oil.
2. Combine cooked pasta with pepper mixture, broccoli
   and seasonings. Sprinkle generously with freshly
   grated Parmesan cheese.

Note: This can be served hot or at room temperature as a
salad or main dish.

Soups

Callaloo Stew

¼ cup sunflower oil or canola oil
1 cup chopped green onions
2 garlic cloves, chopped
1 large fresh thyme sprig
½ Scotch bonnet chile or habanero chile, seeded, minced
4 cups low-salt vegetable broth
2 cups ¾-inch cubes seeded peeled sugar pumpkin or
butternut squash (about 3/4 pound)
½ pound veggie "ham," cut into ½-inch cubes (about 1½
cups)
1½ cups ½-inch-thick rounds trimmed okra
1 pound fresh callaloo or 10 ounces spinach, stalks
trimmed and discarded, leaves chopped

1. Heat oil in heavy large pot over medium-high heat.
   Add green onions, garlic, thyme, and chile. Sauté until
   soft, about 2 minutes.
2. Add broth, pumpkin, ham, and okra. Bring to boil;
   reduce heat to medium and simmer until vegetables
   are tender, stirring occasionally, about 10 minutes.
3. Add callaloo; cook until wilted and leaves are tender,
   stirring frequently, about 3 minutes. Season to taste
   with salt and pepper.

Caribbean Black Bean Soup

Serves 4

2½ cups dry black beans
6 cups water 3 tablespoons olive oil
2 onions, chopped
3 cloves garlic, chopped
6 stalks celery, chopped, with leaves
2 cups water
8 cups vegetable broth
½ teaspoon ground cayenne pepper
1½ teaspoons ground cumin
2 tablespoons balsamic vinegar
¼ cup sherry
1 tablespoon soy sauce
½ teaspoon ground black pepper
¼ cup sour cream
¼ cup chopped green onions

1. In a medium-size stock pot, add dried black beans
   and 6 cups of water, cover and let soak overnight.
2. In another large stock pot, heat olive oil and add
   onion, minced garlic and chopped celery. Saute
   until vegetables are softened.
3. Drain and rinse soaked black beans. Add presoaked beans or drained and rinsed canned beans
   to vegetable mixture along with 2 cups water and
   broth. Bring to boil; reduce heat and simmer.
4. Add cayenne pepper and ground cumin. Partially
   cover the pot and simmer over low heat for 2 to
   2½ hours, or until beans are soft.
5. Puree soup in batches in food processor or blender.
   Return pureed soup to stock pot and simmer.
6. Add vinegar, sherry, soy sauce and pepper. Serve
   hot with a dollop of sour cream or yogurt and
   chopped green onions.

Abobora Refogada
(Brazilian Stewed Pumpkin)

1 lb pumpkin, seeded,   1 clove garlic, minced
  peeled and cut into   2 scallions, minced salt and
1 in square pieces   pepper to taste
2 tablespoons cooking oil

1. Place the pumpkin, butter, garlic and scallions in a
   saucepan.
2. Cook over medium heat, stirring, until the butter
   melts.
3. Cover, reduce the heat and cook until the pumpkin is
   fork tender.
4. Stir the mixture occasionally so that it does not stick.
5. Season and cook for 3 more minutes. Serve warm.

Brazilian Bean Soup & Pineapple/Mango Salsas

2 cups dry black beans, soaked
6 cups water
1 tablespoon olive oil
3 cups chopped onion
10 medium cloves garlic, crushed
2 teaspoons cumin
1 teaspoon salt
1 medium carrot, diced
1 medium bell pepper, diced
12 ounces orange juice
cayenne pepper to taste
2 medium tomatoes, diced (optional)
4 cups brown rice, cooked
optional topping: cilantro, salsa

1. Providing the beans have soaked 8 hours or overnight, drain.
2. Then place soaked beans in a kettle or Dutch oven with 4 cups water.
3. Bring to boil, cover, and simmer until tender (about 1¼ hours).
4. Heat oil in a medium-sized skillet.
5. Add onion, half the garlic, cumin, salt, and carrot.
6. Sauté over medium heat until carrot is tender.
7. Add remaining garlic and bell pepper.
8. Sauté until everything is very tender (another 10-15 minutes).
9. Add the sautéed mixture to the beans, scraping in every last morsel.
10. Stir in orange juice, cayenne, cooked rice and optional tomatoes.
11. Puree' all or some of the soup in a blender or food processor, and return to kettle.
12. Simmer over very low heat 10 to 15 minutes more.
13. Serve topped with an artful arrangement of cilantro and/or salsa.
14. I've used different salsas each time I've made it.

Dominican Black Bean Soup

2 lbs. washed black beans
1 lbs. diced white onions
1 oz. clean diced garlic
4 oz. chopped celery
1 lb. white rice
.5 lbs. cuban or anaheim peppers
.5 bunch of fresh cilantro

1. Wash beans well and let soak overnight. Lightly saute garlic, onions, celery and Cuban Peppers. This is referred to as a Sofrito.
2. Bring beans to boil, add "sofrito", fresh cilantro and gently simmer for 4 hours. To make a cream of Black bean soup puree until smooth.
3. This soup is traditionally served with boiled white rice and diced onions.

Brazilian Vegetable Feijoada

Serves 6

2 whole dried red peppers or ¼ tsp. crushed red pepper flakes
1 tsp. ground cumin
2 tsp. dried leaf thyme or 1 tsp. ground thyme
2 medium sweet potatoes, peeled, sliced lengthwise into quarters and then into ¼-inch thick slices
1 large or 2 medium leeks (white parts only), rinsed and sliced lengthwise into ½-inch thick slices
1 red bell pepper, seeded and sliced lengthwise into ½-inch wide slices
1 yellow bell pepper, seeded and sliced lengthwise into ½-inch wide slices
1 medium yellow onion, peeled and sliced lengthwise into ½-inch thick slices
2 tbsp. fresh-squeezed lime juice 1 large tomato, sliced into ¼-inch thick slices
2 16-oz cans black beans
1 thin lime or orange slices, and cilantro sprigs for garnish
cooked rice (optional)

1. Heat a little veggie broth or water and add dried red peppers or crushed red pepper flakes, cumin and thyme; lower heat and cook 1 minute.
2. Add sweet potatoes; cook 5 minutes.
3. Add leeks; cook 5 minutes more.
4. Stir in bell peppers and onion, cook 5 minutes.
5. Add lime juice, combine well and cook 5 minutes more.
6. Add tomato slices.
7. Coat saucepan with nonstick cooking spray; set over low heat.
8. Add beans and cook, stirring, until hot, about 3 minutes; drain.
9. Place beans in a casserole or serving bowl; add vegetables.
10. Garnish with lime or orange slices, cilantro sprigs; serve at once.
11. Serve over rice if desired.

Caribbean Vegetable Stew

2 cups chopped onions
vegetable broth for sautéing
3 cups chopped cabbage
1 fresh chili, minced (seeded for a milder "hot") or ¼ tsp.
cayenne 1 tablespoon grated fresh ginger root
2 cups water
3 cups diced sweet potatoes, cut into ½ to ¾-inch
  cubes
salt to taste
2 cups undrained fresh or canned tomatoes
2 cups fresh or frozen sliced okra
3 tbsp. fresh lime juice
2 tbsp. chopped fresh cilantro
chopped peanuts (optional)
sprigs of cilantro (optional)

1. In a non-reactive pot, sauté the onions in the broth on medium heat for 4 or 5 minutes.
2. Add the cabbage and the chili or cayenne and continue to sauté, stirring often, until the onions are translucent, about 8 minutes.
3. Add the grated ginger and the water, cover the pot, and bring to a boil.
4. Stir in the sweet potatoes, sprinkle with salt, and simmer for 5 or 6 minutes, until the potatoes are barely tender.
5. Add the tomatoes, okra, and lime juice.
6. Simmer until all of the vegetables are tender, about 15 minutes.
7. Stir in the cilantro and add more salt to taste.
8. Sprinkle the stew with chopped peanuts.
9. Top with a few sprigs of cilantro, if you like.

Gazpacho Soup

Serves 4

You will need a blender to make this soup; and you'll need to start it in advance to allow time for chilling. If you're using a stock cube or powder, blend it in with the vegetables to make sure it's well-distributed. Add a drizzle of extra-virgin olive oil at the end if you like; but I don't think it's necessary for either flavor or thickening.

3 large tomatoes
⅓ cucumber
1 small green sweet bell pepper
1 small red bell sweet pepper
½ small onion
2 garlic cloves
1¾ cup tomato juice
½ cup vegetable stock
3 tbsp. red wine vinegar
salt and freshly-ground black pepper
1 tbsp. chopped fresh chives or mint or both

1. Dice the tomatoes, cucumber and bell peppers.
2. Reserve about a quarter of each for garnish, and put the rest into the blender.
3. Finely dice the onion and garlic, and add these to the blender too.
4. Pour the tomato juice into the blender and blend until smooth.
5. Stir in the stock and wine vinegar, and chill for 30 minutes.
6. Mix in the reserved vegetables and the herbs. Serve with croutons or French bread if desired.

Avocado and Green Chili Soup

2 ripe avocados
3 cup Soy milk
4 oz. canned green chilies
1 medium onion, chopped
Salt and pepper; to taste
2 tablespoon lemon juice
2 tablespoon dry sherry

Garnish: chopped chilies -or- fresh parsley

1. Cut the avocados in half and remove the pits.
2. Scoop out the avocado pulp and puree in a blender.
3. Add the remaining ingredients except garnish to the blender and puree until evenly smooth.
4. Pour the mixture into a serving bowl, garnish, and serve immediately.

A Taste
of Europe

A Taste of Italy and the Mediterraneans

Appetizers

Roasted Vegetable Sandwich

2 med eggplant
1 zucchini
1 red bell pepper
1 yellow pepper
1 yellow onion
1 red onion
1 tablespoon olive oil
3 cloves garlic (change to taste)
fresh basil

1. Slice vegetables/finely chop garlic and put in 9x13 pan.
2. Drizzle with olive oil.
3. Place in preheated oven (350-375) and roast for about an hour, turning contents every 15 minutes.
4. Vegetables should be soft and can be dark in spots.
5. Serve on bread with fresh basil.

You make these with Teese Vegan Cheese (or any mozzarella vegan cheese) and a Tabasco Non-dairy Yogurt Dipping Sauce (you could mix a few drops of Tabasco in with the yogurt to make a spread). Teese tastes, melts, and stretches better than any other dairy-free cheese alternative on the market. The vegetables (especially the peppers and onions) get very sweet and taste delicious cold as well as hot. You can also put roasted vegetables on top of humus spread in sandwiches as well.

Stuffed Mushrooms

Serves 4
20-30 small/ medium fresh mushroom
bread crumbs
spinach
soy sauce
green onions
celery
soy oil
garlic, chopped

1. Clean and separate mushroom caps from stems.
2. Save stems for later.
3. Place caps in shallow baking dish and drop a small amount of butter or soy oil and soy sauce in caps.
4. Place in oven at about 350 degrees to soften.
5. Chop and blanch spinach with small amount of water until dark green.
6. Drain. In same pan, (with little spinach broth left) add chopped garlic and oil to sauté.
7. Chop green onions and add to garlic and spinach broth.
8. Chop mushroom stems and add to sautéed mixture
9. Chop celery and add to sautéed mixture.
10. Let cook for 10 minutes.
11. Add bread crumbs to cover mixture and create enough stuffing for the mushroom caps.
12. Add water and soy sauce to loosen and flavor.
13. Fill mushroom caps with stuffing and rebake at 350 degrees for 10-15 minutes (until stuffing gets brown).
14. Serve warm. Prep. time: 25 min

Stuffed Mushrooms 2

20 large white mushrooms (about 2 inches diameter)
2 cups cubed bread crumbs
2 cloves garlic, minced
1 medium onion, finely minced
¼ cup wine for sautéing
2 ribs celery, finely minced
2 tbsp. finely shredded carrot
1½ tsp. salad herbs (mix of parsley, marjoram, etc.)
salt/pepper to taste

1. Remove mushroom stems. Chop and reserve stems.
2. Bring a large pot of water to boil and add mushrooms.
3. Cook for a couple minutes or until they start to shrink.
4. Drain and place the mushrooms into a pan of cold water for a minute to stop cooking.
5. Drain mushrooms. Preheat oven to 350F.
6. In a large non-stick sauté pan, sauté the onions, mushroom stems, garlic and celery in the wine.
7. When vegetables are tender, add the carrot and herbs.
8. Add bread crumbs and mix well.
9. Add salt/pep and adjust seasonings to taste.
10. Fill mushrooms with a heaping tablespoon of the mixture, place on a lightly sprayed baking sheet and cook for 10-12 minutes or until lightly browned on top.

Italian Vegetable Kababs

Serves 4

8 small new red potatoes (about ½ lb.), halved or quartered 8 fresh or frozen Brussels sprouts
1 green or red pepper, quartered and cut in half crosswise
½ red onion, quartered and cut in half crosswise
⅓ cup Italian salad dressing

Grilling Directions:
1. Heat grill.
2. In medium saucepan, combine potatoes and Brussels sprouts.
3. Add enough water to cover by
4. 2 inches.
5. Bring to a boil.
6. Reduce heat; cover and cook
7. 10 minutes or just until Brussels sprouts are tender.
8. Drain.
9. Alternately thread all vegetables onto four
10. 12-14-inch metal skewers.
11. Brush vegetables with salad dressing.

When ready to grill, place Kababs on gas grill over medium heat or on charcoal grill
4 to 6 inches from medium coals.
Cover grill and cook 8-10 minutes or until vegetables are browned and tender, brushing with salad dressing and turning occasionally.

To broil:
1. Place Kababs on broiler pan; broiler 4-6 inches from heat using time above as a guide.

Italian Tofu Balls

About the ingredients:

Tofu: Don't use tofu in a box, even if it says firm, and don't use anything but firm or extra firm (or a block of each), fresh tofu. It should be possible to hold one end of the block without it breaking in half immediately.
Rinse it and squeeze as much of the water as you can out of it right before you start.

Bread crumbs: You can make your own from your favorite toasted bread, but any crumbs should work.
Some people like chunks of bread in the mix, and that works ok. Pre-season the crumbs with a little salt (vegetable salt is nice), basil, (considerably less) oregano, granulated garlic or garlic powder, and pepper. The amount of bread crumbs required will greatly depend on the texture and wetness of the tofu.

Granulated garlic: If you've never had it, you're missing a great seasoning. look for it in natural foods stores.

Dried onion flakes: You can substitute fresh minced onion, but you should probably partially cook it in the microwave or in a saucepan, if you do. Ditto minced garlic, if you use it.

Dry egg replacer: Ener-G makes one; you can probably substitute arrowroot flour or cornstarch.
I've used cornstarch.

Tamari: Yes, you can use soy sauce.
If you use soy sauce or regular tamari, use a bit less.

Nutritional Yeast: Adds vitamins, micronutrients and a mild "cheesy" flavor.
Don't use brewer's yeast, which is bitter.

** Means optional but strongly suggested for best results.
(makes about 22 1 ½" balls):

2 x 16oz blocks of firm or extra firm tofu (or one of each)
1½ cups of preseasoned bread crumbs
1 heaping tablespoon powdered egg replacer
1½ tablespoons (six to ten shakes) low sodium tamari
vegetable or sea salt to taste (or potassium salt substitute)
pepper to taste
2 tablespoons dry flaked onion.
Soymage Parmesan substitute to taste
1 teaspoon basil
¼ teaspoon oregano
granulated, minced or garlic powder to taste
1 tablespoon nutritional yeast
1½ quarts pasta sauce

1. Lightly oil a full-size baking sheet, and begin preheating oven to 350. Rinse, drain, and squeeze dry the tofu, crumble it into a large mixing bowl, then mash it into an even - but not extremely fine - consistency, using a sturdy fork.

2. Sprinkle on the tamari, and mix it in with the fork.

3. Add the other seasonings and the yeast, while continuing to mix the tofu without mashing it further.

4. Taste it several times; you want it to taste mildly salty, and for the flavor of the seasonings to be present, but not overwhelming.

5. Stir in the flaked or minced onion, and the egg replacer. Then add about ⅔ of the bread crumbs, first mixing them in with the fork, then with your (slightly moistened) hands. First squeeze it through your fingers repeatedly, then press the mixture firmly into the bottom of the bowl with your knuckles. While doing this, add enough bread crumbs to make the mixture form readily into firm balls, without being wet or dough like. If you add too much bread and it gets dry and crumbly, sprinkle in a little water. If it's still a little wet and you are out of bread, add a little more egg replacer or some cornstarch or potato starch.

6. Form the mixture into balls. They can be small (about 1") or medium size (about 1 ½"). Larger ones are possible, but are likelier to end up underdone in the middle. Place them on the baking sheet. They can be close together, but not touching.

7. Bake at 350 degrees for about 45 minutes (small) to 1 hour (medium). The tofu balls should be well browned, especially if you are omitting the last two steps, but not burned looking. You can turn them after ½ hour, but it isn't absolutely necessary.

8. **Let the tofu balls cool for about 20 minutes, then place them in a large *covered* frying pan that has been coated with canola oil, olive oil, or a mix of the two; preheated. Gently sauté them for about 15 minutes, turning them frequently.

9. **Add enough tomato sauce to completely cover the balls, then cover and simmer them for one hour, gently stirring them occasionally. They are ready to eat at this point, but for the best flavor, let them sit in the sauce, in a glass bowl or steel pan, in the refrigerator overnight. They freeze fairly well.

A Touch of Spice–So Nice

Serves 4

Elena's Black Pepper Linguini (12 oz)
Garlic Survival Company Pasta Sauce (16 oz)
1 bag or bunch of fresh spinach
large handful of snow peas
1 large tomato - roughly chopped
2-3 tbsp. roasted pine nuts

1. Bring water to a boil, add pasta, cook until al dente.
2. Heat sauce in a separate pot, med-low.
3. Add the snow peas 2 minutes before draining.
4. Add spinach 30 seconds before draining.
5. Drain pasta, toss with vegetables and sauce.
6. Sprinkle tomatoes and pine nuts over top.

Simply Spinach Fettuccine

Serves 2

Savoia Spinach Fettuccine
one-quarter lb fresh parsley or basil
1-2 cloves garlic
one-quarter cup extra virgin olive oil

1. Bring water to a boil, add pasta, cook until al dente.
2. Rinse the chosen herb. Roll in paper towels or clean dish cloth to dry. Chop. Chop the garlic.
3. Heat the oil and garlic over medium heat.
4. After 2-3 minutes (careful to not burn the garlic) add the herb. Combine toss pasta with oil.
5. Pasta cooks in 2 minutes. Serve with a salad on side.

Smooth and Easy

Serves 4-6

Fattora Stortoni Pasta
Timpone's Roased Peppers Sauce
Broccoli - bite-sized pieces
1 yellow zucchini cut into half-circles
1-2 tomatoes - roughly chopped

1. Bring water to a boil, add pasta, cook until al dente.
2. Add broccoli to boiling water 2 minutes before draining, add zucchini, 1 minute before draining.
3. Heat sauce in separate sauce pan, medium heat.
4. Gently toss sauce, pasta, vegetables and tomatoes into a shallow baking dish. 5. Serve immediately.

Bruschetta

4 slices of toasted French or Italian bread
(any good firm bread)
4 chopped tomatoes, big ripe ones
fresh sweet Basil leaves, chiffonade or chopped (to taste)
2 garlic cloves, peeled and minced small or pressed
1 tablespoon Olive oil 2 tablespoons Balsamic vinegar

1. Mix the chopped tomato with the basil, garlic, oil, balsamic vinegar, and salt to taste.
2. (If you don't have oil, etc.; use Italian dressing. Not as good, but OK).
3. Let set while you toast the bread.
4. When camping or grilling you can toast it on the fire or grill and get a really smokey flavor.
5. Put the bread slices on plates and divide the tomato mixture, placing some on each slice of bread.
6. Let all the juice soak into the bread (make sure you start with a really firm bread).

Stuffed Portabella Mushrooms

Serves 4 as a main course or 8 as an appetizer

2 tsp. olive (preferably extra virgin)
1 carrot, peeled and finely diced
1 medium onion, finely diced
¼ green pepper, finely diced
1 clove garlic, minced
1 tsp. basil
1 tsp. oregano
1 cup cooked brown rice
Salt and pepper to taste
4 medium Portabella mushrooms

1. Heat 1 tsp. olive oil in nonstick pan over medium heat.
2. Add carrot, onion, green pepper and garlic.
3. Sauté until crisp-tender.
4. Stir in basil and oregano.
5. Remove from heat and combine with rice.
6. Add salt and pepper to taste.
7. Remove stems from mushrooms.
8. Place mushrooms in lightly oiled casserole dish, stem side up.
9. Top with rice mixture, packing down slightly.
10. Brush lightly with remaining 1 tsp. olive oil.
11. Bake at 400 degrees for 20 minutes.

Mushroom Ragout

Serves 8-10 as an appetizer

1 oz. dried porcini mushrooms (see note)
2 tbsp. diluted balsamic vinegar
1 large red onion, finely minced
2 small garlic cloves, finely minced
1 lb fresh brown mushrooms, such as cremini or
  portobello, well-cleaned and sliced
3-4 small ripe plum tomatoes, chopped
1 tbsp. chopped flat leaf parsley
salt
freshly ground pepper

1. Soak dried mushrooms in warm water to cover for at least 45 minutes or until softened.
2. Remove from liquid carefully and rinse well under cold running water to remove any sand clinging.
3. Chop mushrooms roughly and drain thoroughly.
4. Strain soaking liquid at least twice through a sieve lined with cheesecloth and reserve.
5. Heat a couple of teaspoons of reserved mushroom liquid and diluted balsamic vinegar in a heavy skillet and sauté onion until translucent and tender, 10-15 minutes.
6. Use additional mushroom liquid if onions start to stick.
7. Add garlic and all mushrooms, turn heat to low and cook, stirring intermittently, for up to 20 minutes, until tender.
8. Add tomatoes, parsley, salt and pepper to taste.
9. Continue cooking another 5 minutes.
10. Serve over slices of polenta.

Note: the dried porcini are expensive but integral. They have an incredible woodsy flavor and odor.

Marinated Mushrooms 1

Serves 2

1 cup oil
1 tsp. dry mustard
⅔ cup vinegar
½ tsp. salt
1 clove garlic
½ tsp. paprika
1 tsp. vegetarian Worcestershire sauce

1. Put mushrooms in boiling water for 2-3 minutes.
2. Drain. Drop mushrooms in marinade and refrigerate for 48 hours.

Marinated Mushrooms 2

Makes 2 cups

⅔ cup olive oil
2 cloves garlic, bruised with knife
½ cup water
6 peppercorns
2 lemons, juiced
½ tsp. salt
1 bay leaf
1 lb small mushrooms

1. Combine everything but the mushrooms in a 10 or 12 inch enameled or stainless-steel skillet and bring to a boil over moderate heat.
2. Reduce heat, cover and simmer for 15 minutes.
3. Strain the marinade through a sieve and return it to the skillet; bring to a simmer over low heat.
4. Drop in the mushrooms and simmer, turning mushrooms over from time to time, for 5 minutes.
5. Let the mushrooms cool in the marinade.
6. Serve at room temperature or let cool and refrigerate and serve cold.
7. They will keep in refrigerator for 2 days.

Mushroom Marinara

3 portabella tops
1 cup white mushrooms, sliced
1-2 tablespoons (3-6 cloves) garlic, minced
1 teaspoon brown sugar
1 jar of your favorite plain pasta sauce
1 cup brown onion, chopped
¼ to ½ bottle red wine
2 tablespoons extra virgin olive oil
½ teaspoon dried oregano (you can also use fresh if you
  have it on hand)
½ teaspoon dried basil (you can also use fresh if you have
  it on hand)
¼ teaspoon salt and pepper
freshly grated Romano or Asiago (or parmesan if
  you're not that exciting)
1 can crushed tomatoes (you can also use 1 lb. of fresh
  tomatoes crushed)
1 can diced tomatoes (you can also use 1 lb. of fresh
  tomatoes diced)

1. Chop mushrooms into fairly large chunks, ½ to 1-inch pieces. Finely chop the garlic, sauté in about 3 tablespoons olive oil in a large pan.
2. When it has diffused most of its flavor, but before it starts to turn brown, add in the mushrooms.
3. Stir CONSTANTLY or else they will burn.
4. Keep the heat up pretty med-med/high.
5. When the mushrooms have absorbed all the garlic oil, add in about a half cup of the red wine.
6. Keep cooking the mushrooms, stirring constantly and adding wine when they soak up the previous addition, until they are just about thoroughly cooked.
7. Dump in the cans of tomatoes and herbs, salt and pepper, bring to a simmer and cook for 25 minutes, with the lid ajar, stirring every few minutes. The heat on your stove will probably need to be at low to medium-low, and your kitchen will be smelling even better at this point.
8. After 25 minutes, add the sugar, stir well, and cook for another five minutes. Why are we adding sugar, you ask? Because its sweetness will help counter some of the acidity from the tomatoes and balance the flavor. Taste the sauce and make any final adjustments, such as adding more salt and pepper or, for some heat, some red-pepper flakes.
9. Here's the key: Turn the heat off and let it sit uncovered for 5-10 minutes so that it thickens a little bit, stirring occasionally, before you are ready to serve
10. If you don't, it will be chunky and runny--yuck! Serve over shaped Pasta–Rotini or penne with the Romano.
11. Savor the mushrooms; they are divine.

Mediterranean Tofu Casserole

Serves 4

4 oz. tofu
¼ lb. aubergine, diced ½-inch
4 tbsp. olive oil
4 oz. onion chopped
2 tsp. garlic, crushed
½ mild green chili, finely chopped
15 oz. tinned tomatoes, chopped
1½ cup white wine
1½ cup light vegetable stock or water
1 tbsp. tomato purée
2 oz. uncooked pasta (e.g. shells)
4 oz. fennel, cut into ½ inch, diced
4 oz. cauliflower, broken into small florets
4 oz. courgettes, cut into ½ inch, diced
2 oz. broad beans
2 oz. pitted black olives, quartered
2 tbsp. mixed chopped fresh basil and thyme (or 1 tsp.
  dried mixed herbs)
salt

1. Drain tofu, cut into 36 pieces.
2. In a non-stick pan, fry tofu and aubergine gently in the oil, until evenly browned. Remove from pan.
3. Add onion to the same pan and cook gently until softened.
4. Add garlic and chili and cook for a further minute.
5. Add remaining ingredients, and the cooked tofu and aubergine.
6. Simmer gently until pasta and vegetables are just cooked (about 7 minutes). Season to taste.

Grilled Mediterranean Vegetables with Couscous

Serves 4

2 baby or Japanese eggplants, ends trimmed, halved
   lengthwise
2 small zucchini, ends trimmed, halved lengthwise
2 small yellow squash, ends trimmed, halved lengthwise
1 large red bell pepper, quartered
1 large yellow bell pepper, quartered
2 to 3 tbsp. garlic infused olive oil
1 14.5 oz. can vegetable broth
1 cup couscous
salt & freshly ground pepper to taste
1 tablespoon porcini, basil, or rosemary infused olive oil
   (optional)

1.   Preheat grill.
2.   Brush both sides of eggplants, squash, and bell
     peppers with garlic oil.
3.   Arrange vegetables on grill rack over medium-hot
     coals.
4.   Grill until tender, turning once, about 10-12 minutes.
5.   Meanwhile, bring broth to a boil in a medium
     saucepan.
6.   Stir in couscous; remove from heat.
7.   Cover and let stand until liquid is absorbed, about 5
     minutes.
8.   Spoon couscous onto 4 serving plates and top with
     grilled vegetables.
9.   Season with salt & pepper to taste.
10. Drizzle with flavored oil if desired.

Note: If garlic infused olive oil is not available, substitute
3 tbsp. olive oil combined with 2 cloves of minced garlic.

Mediterranean Fusilli

Serves 6

1 16-oz package fusilli pasta
¼ cup olive oil (or other veg. oil)
1 tablespoon capers
3 cloves garlic, finely chopped
2 28-oz cans Roma (Italian pear-shaped) tomatoes,
   drained and chopped
1 small red chili pepper, seeded and chopped
½ cup sliced black olives
½ cup sliced green olives
1 tablespoon chopped fresh oregano (or 1 teaspoon dried)
1 tablespoon chopped fresh basil (or 1 teaspoon dried)
   freshly ground pepper

1.   Cook and drain pasta per package directions.
2.   Heat oil in 4- to 6-quart pot over medium-high heat.
3.   Cook capers and garlic in oil, stirring constantly, until
     garlic is golden.
4.   Stir in tomatoes and chili pepper.
5.   Heat to boiling.
6.   Reduce heat, cover and simmer 20 minutes, stirring
     occasionally.
7.   Stir in pasta, olives, and herbs.
8.   Cover and simmer 20 minutes.

Fusilli with Radicchio and Pancetta

Serves 6

3 tablespoons olive oil
4 ounces bacon substitute (e.g., Baco Bits), diced
½ cup sliced onion
2 teaspoons minced garlic
1 head radicchio, thinly sliced (6 oz)
½ cup vegetable broth
2 tablespoons balsamic vinegar
⅛ teaspoon salt
⅛ teaspoon freshly ground pepper
1 pound fusilli or linguine, cooked according to package
directions

1.   Heat oil in medium skillet over medium heat.
2.   Add bacon substitute and cook, stirring occasionally,
     5 minutes.
3.   Add onion; cook 5 minutes, until softened.
4.   Add garlic and cook 30 seconds.
5.   Stir in radicchio, broth, vinegar, salt and pepper.
6.   Cook until radicchio is just wilted, about 30 seconds
     more.
7.   Toss sauce with hot pasta in large serving bowl.

Mediterranean Potato-Stuffed Onions

4 large Vidalia or yellow onions (2 pounds), trimmed
olive oil
3 medium red potatoes (¾ lb.), peeled and quartered
1 tablespoon margarine
1 tablespoon soy milk
2 teaspoons dry white wine
2 teaspoons chopped fresh rosemary

1. In 9 X 13-inch foil pan place onions upright; brush with oil. Place pan on center of cooking grate uncovered; cook onions 1¼ hours or until centers are tender.
2. Meanwhile, in 9 X 13-inch foil pan place potatoes; cover tightly with heavy-duty aluminum foil.
3. Place pan on cooking grate next to onions; cook potatoes 30 minutes or until tender when pierced with a fork.
4. Remove onions to cool. In foil pan used for onion, combine margarine, soy milk, and wine.
5. Heat until warm; stir to dissolve brown bits from bottom of foil pan.
6. In large bowl, with mixer at low speed, beat potatoes until fluffy. Gradually add in milk mixture until smooth, adding more milk if necessary.
7. Hollow center of onions, leaving two or three outer layers; chop onion from centers.
8. Add ¼ cup chopped onions to potatoes; save remaining onions for another use.
9. Add rosemary to cooked potatoes; mix well.
10. Fill onions with equal amounts of potato mixture.

Note: Stuffed onions may be prepared up to this point, covered and refrigerated one day before serving.

Pasta Arrabbiata

Serves 4
1 tablespoon olive oil
½ cup finely chopped onion
1 tablespoon minced garlic
1 teaspoon red pepper flakes
½ teaspoon salt
1 can tomatoes, chopped (28 oz.)
1 pound linguine, cooked according to package directions
¼ cup chopped fresh parsley

1. Heat oil in large skillet over medium heat.
2. Add onion; cook 5 minutes until softened.
3. Stir in garlic, red pepper and salt; cook 30 seconds.
4. Add tomatoes and their liquid; cook 15 minutes.
5. Toss sauce with hot pasta and parsley in large serving bowl. Serve with parmesan cheese, if desired.

Stuffed Cabbage

Instead of meat, use walnuts, mushrooms, and tomatoes. It has a wonderful interplay of sweet and sour. Make plenty; you'll eat more than you realize, and can always freeze the leftovers.

2 heads of cabbage
1½ cups brown rice (I used brown basmati), uncooked ¾ cup raisins
1 cup maple sugar or syrup
2 cans stewed tomatoes
½ pound oyster mushrooms (sliced into small chunks) ¾ cup walnuts, chopped coarse
2 large onions, chopped
1 cup lemon juice
1 cup water salt and pepper to taste

1. Bring a large pot of water to a boil. Core the cabbage.
2. Take the pot off of the heat, drop in a cabbage, and let sit 10-15 minutes.
3. Drop the cabbage into a colander to cool a few minutes, then carefully pull off whole leaves and set them aside. (You should get 12-16 leaves per head.)
4. Repeat with the second head.
5. Set aside the remainder of the cabbage.
6. Combine rice, raisins, mushrooms, walnuts, brown sugar, ½ cup of lemon juice, ⅔ of the onion, and one can of tomato (drain off the juice and reserve it).
7. Place approximately 2-3 tablespoons of the mixture onto the thick end of a cabbage leaf, fold in the sides, and roll towards the tip. Place seam-side down in a Dutch oven. Repeat until all of the cabbage leaves are stuffed (they will stack up to nearly fill the pot).
8. Chop up the remaining cabbage (sometimes called this the 'shmatas', which means 'rags') into a bowl. Dump in the second can of tomatoes, the juice from the first, the remaining lemon juice, onion, salt and pepper, and any remaining filling.
9. Mix, and dump on top of the rolls in the pot. Add about 1 cup of water (won't quite cover it). Heat on medium until the mixture boils, then cover and reduce heat to medium-low.
10. Cook 3-4 hours, reducing heat to low if necessary.
11. The rolls steam in the juices, and shrink down as the cabbage cooks. Don't stir!
12. You can then serve immediately, or reheat the next day. It reheats and freezes well.
13. To serve, spoon 2-3 rolls onto a plate, add some shmatas and juices, and serve with Russian rye bread (to mop up the juice). Eat, and repeat until unconscious.

Russian Sauerkraut Soup

Serves 8

The broth for this soup is a combination of tomato puree, vegetable broth, and sauerkraut juice.
Add caraway seeds for flavor, and the end result is absolutely delicious.

15-ounce can tomato puree
8 cups vegetable broth
16-ounce can or jar of sauerkraut
1 onion, peeled and finely chopped
2 turnips, peeled and cubed (about 1 pound)
3 carrots, peeled and finely chopped
1 teaspoon caraway seeds
Salt and pepper to taste

Place all the ingredients in a large covered pot and bring to a boil. Reduce heat; cook for 1 hr. Serve with bread.

Tempeh Reubens

8 oz. tempeh
5 tbsp olive oil
1 clove garlic, minced
¼ cup Vidalia onions, diced
4 slices rye bread
2 tbsp Thousand Island dressing (recipe below)
¼ cup sauerkraut
4 slices vegan Swiss cheese

1. Slice the tempeh so that it's about ½ inch thick.
2. Heat the olive oil up to medium and add garlic and onions. Cook until softened and add in tempeh. Fry tempeh for about 4 minutes on each side.
3. Toast the rye bread on each side. Add a slather of Thousand Island Dressing on both pieces of bread. Top with tempeh, onions, sauerkraut, and cheese. Melt under the broiler and serve immediately.

Easy Thousand Island Dressing

1 cup vegan mayonnaise
1/3 cup ketchup
¼ cup hot pickle relish

1. Combine ingredients and serve.

Black Bean & Key Lime Bow Ties

Serves 6

12 ounces bow tie pasta, uncooked
6 cloves to 8 garlic, minced
¼ cup olive oil
⅔ cup fresh Key lime juice*
½ cup dry sherry
2 cups green onions, sliced
1 pound plum tomatoes, chopped
2 15 oz. cans black beans, rinsed & drained
1 teaspoon salt
½ teaspoon freshly ground pepper
1½ teaspoons freshly grated Key lime rind
½ cup fresh Italian parsley, chopped

1. Cook pasta according to package directions.
2. Drain and keep warm.
3. Sauté garlic in oil in a skillet until tender.
4. Add lime juice and sherry; cook over high heat for 5 minutes or until mixture is reduced to ¼ cup.
5. Add green onions and chopped tomato; cook over medium heat, stirring occasionally, 5 to 8 minutes.
6. Stir in black beans and next 3 ingredients; pour over pasta, tossing to coat.
7. Sprinkle with parsley and serve immediately.

Note: * Or use Nellie & Joe's brand in a bottle

Sautéed Peppers

Serves 1

3 tablespoons olive oil
1 small red onion, or ½ Vidalia
3 bell peppers (any color or colors)
2 garlic cloves, sliced (or powder)
¼ cup tomato sauce
1 tablespoon balsamic vinegar
1 tablespoon marjoram (or 1 teaspoon dried)
salt and pepper, to taste

1. Quarter onion and slice thinly.
2. Slice peppers to desired thickness.
3. Sauté onions, over high heat, in olive oil for 4-5 minutes until edges are browned.
4. Add peppers and garlic, and continue to sauté over high heat for 10 minutes, until peppers start to get browned.
5. Lower heat to medium, add tomato sauce.
6. Cook for another 10 minutes.
7. At the end, add vinegar, salt and pepper to taste, and marjoram.
8. Serve over pasta, rice, or polenta.

Garbanzo-Nut Burgers

Makes 6 burgers

16-oz. can garbanzo beans (chick peas), drained
1 medium green or red bell pepper, roasted and minced
1 carrot, grated
¼ cup toasted-cashew pieces
1 tsp. basil
½ tsp. garlic powder
½ tsp. salt
1 tbsp. dill weed
juice of 1 lemon (2 to 3 tbsp.)
½ cup (2 oz) whole-wheat flour

1. In a food processor or blender, process beans until finely chopped.
2. Mix beans and remaining ingredients, except flour, in a large bowl.
3. Mix in flour; the mixture should be moist but stiff.
4. Shape into 6 patties, lightly coat each with flour.
5. Place patties on a lightly oiled baking tray.
6. Broil 5 to 10 minutes on each side, or until browned.

Pesto Pizza

1 pkg. active dry yeast
1 teaspoon sugar
1 cup warm water
¾ teaspoons salt
1½ cup whole-wheat flour
1 cup bread flour
2 tablespoons olive oil
1 cup loosely packed basil leaves

3 tablespoons extra virgin olive oil
juice of ½ lemon
1 clove garlic, crushed
2 tablespoons pine nuts
add tomatoes, mushrooms, red peppers, olives, onion (anything else you like)

1. Dissolve yeast and sugar in warm water.
2. When it's foamy add whole wheat flour and salt.
3. Mix vigorously until well blended and set aside for 20 min. Beat in the 1 cup bread flour.
4. Knead until smooth, then place in a grease bowl in a warm place for about 1 hour.
5. Punch down the dough and roll out.
6. Place on oiled pan, poke holes in it with a fork, let rise another 20 min and Preheat oven to 450*F.
7. Par-bake crust for 20 min.
8. Make pesto by combining the basil, olive oil, pine nuts, garlic, and lemon juice in a blender.
9. Add a tablespoons water or olive oil as needed to make a smooth but thick sauce.
10. Spread Pesto over crust and top with veggies.
11. Bake another 15-20 min.

Sides, Sauces & Standalone Items

Pasta Sauce Raphael

2 (6 oz.) jars marinated artichoke hearts in oil
¼ cup olive oil (you can easily get away with just 2 tablespoons if you want it to be a little less fattening)
2 cups chopped onions
2 tablespoons minced garlic
½ tsp. dried oregano
½ tsp. dried basil
1 tablespoon coarsely ground black pepper
½ tsp. salt
pinch of red pepper flakes
1 (28 oz.) can plum tomatoes, with their juice
¼ cup chopped Italian flat leaf parsley

1. Drain the artichoke hearts reserving the marinade (you can leave the artichoke hearts whole or chop them if you prefer).
2. Heat the olive oil in a large saucepan.
3. Add the onions, garlic, spices, and reserved marinade.
4. Sauté over medium-low heat until onions and garlic are soft and translucent, about 10 min.
5. Add the tomatoes and simmer for 30 min.
6. Add the artichoke hearts and parsley.
7. Stir gently, and simmer for another 5 min.
8. 6 portions, enough for 1 pound pasta (this may work for more like 1½ pounds pasta)

Note: If you're not sure about the red pepper, try 1 to 1½ teaspoons, unless you're really used to it.

Tofu Pesto

Serves 8

1 cup fresh basil leaves
¼ cup raw cashews
3-4 teaspoons minced fresh garlic
10.5 ounce pkg lite silken tofu
1-2 tablespoons soy parmesan cheese, optional

1. Place the basil, cashews, and garlic in a food processor. Process until smooth.
2. Add the tofu and cheese, if desired, and process until smooth and creamy. You can substitute nutritional yeast for the soy cheese.

Pasta Puttanesca Sauce

½ cup green olives, chopped
½ cup black olives, chopped
1 clove garlic, crushed
1 large can plum tom's.
(crushed between fingers)
olive oil
black pepper
salt only if needed

1. Heat olive oil (I use about 2 tablespoons) in sauté pan (note that good olive oil is really crucial for flavor here).
2. Add garlic, cook about 2 min., or until just turning color. Add tomatoes, cook for about 5 min.
3. Add olives, cook another 3 min. or so.
4. Sauté briefly after combining with cooked (al dente, please!) pasta.
5. Serve this with a Gemelli or Rigatoni

Light Spaghetti Sauce

Serves 12

2 tablespoons extra virgin olive oil
2 large garlic cloves, minced
½ cup onion, chopped
2 28 oz. cans crushed tomatoes
1 teaspoon salt
½ teaspoon black pepper
¼ cup fresh basil, chopped

1. Heat olive oil in a 3- to 4-quart saucepan.
2. Add garlic.
3. Cook and stir constantly over medium-low heat for about 2 minutes, making sure the garlic doesn't brown.
4. Add onion and, stirring frequently, continue cooking for about 8 minutes
5. or until the onion is soft and golden.
6. Add tomatoes, salt, and pepper, and bring to a boil.
7. Reduce heat to low and simmer for 25 minutes, stirring occasionally.
8. Add fresh basil and simmer 5 minutes longer.
9. This recipe yields about 6 cups.

Garlic and Onion Tomato Sauce

Serves 2

28 ounces plum tomatoes, pureed
½ teaspoon ground thyme
1 teaspoon fresh basil, minced
1 garlic clove, minced
1 small onion
black pepper, to taste
4 teaspoons olive oil
use plum tomatoes canned in tomato puree if available.

1. Chop onion; peel garlic and mince.
2. In heavy skillet, place the olive oil and heat over medium heat.
3. Add onion and garlic; stir occasionally and cook for 5-6 minutes until onion is tender.
4. Drain tomatoes through a sieve placed over a bowl.
5. Add thyme, basil and tomatoes to skillet.
6. Use large spoon to crush tomatoes.
7. Scrape the puree from the sieve and add to the
8. skillet.
9. Do not use the remaining tomato juice for this recipe.
10. Bring the mixture to a simmer over medium heat, stirring often.
11. Continue to crush tomatoes with wooden spoon.
12. Simmer for about 10-15 minutes; sauce will thicken.
13. Remove from heat, add fresh ground black pepper to taste, salt also if you wish.
14. Serve this sauce with baked souffles, and pasta, or refrigerate and use as needed by reheating slowly.

Garlic Sauce

6 to 8 cloves garlic, thinly sliced
1 onion, sliced
one 8.45 ounce package low-fat plain soy milk
1 heaping tablespoon cornstarch
1 heaping tablespoon brewer's yeast
garlic powder to taste (optional)

1. Sauté' the garlic and onion in a small amount of water for 3 to 5 minutes.
2. In another pot, mix the soy milk, cornstarch, and yeast.
3. Add the garlic, onion and any water remaining in the sauté' pan.
4. Bring to a boil and cook, stirring constantly, until thickened.

Note: For a stronger garlic flavor add garlic powder. Serve over pasta.

Arrabbiata Sauce

Serves 3

1 teaspoon olive oil
1 cup chopped onion
4 garlic cloves, minced
½ cup dry red wine or 2 tablespoons balsamic vinegar
1 tablespoon sugar
1 tablespoon chopped fresh or 1 teaspoon dried basil
1 teaspoon crushed red pepper
2 tablespoons tomato paste
1 tablespoon lemon juice
½ teaspoon dried Italian seasoning
¼ teaspoon black pepper
2 cans diced tomatoes, undrained (14.5-ounce)
2 tablespoons chopped fresh parsley

1. Heat oil in a saucepan or large skillet over medium-high heat. Add onion and garlic; sauté 5 minutes.
2. Stir in wine and next 8 ingredients (wine through tomatoes); bring to a boil.
3. Reduce heat to medium, and cook, uncovered, about 15 minutes. Stir in parsley.

Pesto

Makes 1 Cup

2 tbsp. olive oil, almond butter
¾ cup vegetable soup stock
2 tbsp. brown rice vinegar
2 to 3 cloves garlic, finely minced
½ tsp. salt or 1 tbsp. Umeboshi plum vinegar
2 cup fresh basil leaves or fresh parsley and
1½ tbsp. dried basil
½ cup crushed rye or wheat cracker crumbs
5-oz can water chestnuts drained and finely minced

1. In a food processor or blender, combine all ingredients except water chestnuts.
2. Add more water as needed to make a creamy mixture.
3. Put in a medium bowl.
4. With a wooden spoon, stir in minced water chestnuts.
5. Adjust seasoning to taste.

Vegan Pesto

1 bunch fresh basil (a nice full handful)
¾ cup pine nuts
5 whole cloves garlic
½ tsp. salt
several fresh grinds of black pepper, or ½ tsp. already ground
2 oz. tofu
¼ cup yeast and/or soy parmesan
¾ cup extra virgin olive oil

1. Combine all ingredients EXCEPT OIL in the bowl of a food processor. Process until semi-smooth.
2. With processor running, add oil in a continuous stream.
3. Toss with pasta, serve on toasted bread with tomatoes, etc.
4. All of these amounts are approximate. Adjust them to your own taste. It's pretty hard to mess up.
5. I often use other herbs besides basil. Right now there's a cilantro pesto in the fridge, and last week was basil-mint.
6. Walnuts or almonds can be used in place of the pine nuts, which are awfully expensive. I prefer walnuts.
7. If you like tons of garlic, add as much as you want, but the more garlic you add the longer you should let it sit before eating. Pesto keeps very well and is delicious the next day. It freezes well, too.
8. A dash of Dr. Bronner's liquid aminos is nice in pesto.

Balsamic Dressing

Makes ½ cup

6 tablespoons olive oil
2 tablespoons balsamic vinegar
1 teaspoon minced garlic
½ teaspoon sugar
¼ teaspoon salt

1. Place all ingredients in lidded jar. Close jar; shake thoroughly.
2. Chill until ready to serve. Shake again before using.
3. Helpful Hint: Dressing is best if made at least 30 minutes ahead of time.

Focaccia

Serves 16

1½ teaspoons active dry yeast
2½ cups bread flour
1 teaspoon salt
2 tablespoons vegetable oil
1 cup water
1 tablespoon cornmeal
1 tablespoon olive oil
1 teaspoon coarse salt (kosher)
2 teaspoons dried rosemary

1. Add the yeast, flour, salt, vegetable oil, and water in the order suggested by your bread machine manual and process on the dough cycle according to the manufacturer's directions.
2. At the end of the dough cycle, remove the dough from the machine.
3. Preheat the oven to 450 degrees.
4. Cut the dough in half. Press out each half into a circle about 9 inches in diameter.
5. Transfer to a pizza tray or cookie sheet dusted with the cornmeal.
6. Cover with a clean kitchen towel and let rise 5 minutes.
7. Press fingers into dough to create dimples.
8. (You can also make one large focaccia that will cover a whole 11-by-16-inch pan.)
9. Drizzle half the olive oil over each focaccia and sprinkle half the salt and half the rosemary on each.
10. Bake for 15 minutes, or until golden.

Note: Focaccia is a great snack; it can be cut up and served as an hors d'oeuvre, and it goes well with soups and pasta. Instead of rosemary, try basil or thyme, or top the bread with olives.

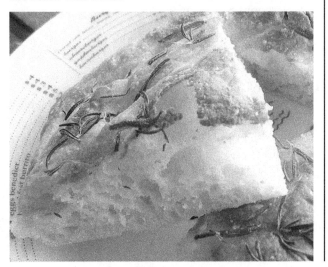

Spinach Pasta Dough

1 cup semolina flour
¾ cup a purpose flour
½ tsp. salt
⅓ cup warm water
¼ cup cooked spinach, chopped and well drained.
1 tablespoon olive oil

Follow your machine's directions for further preparation.

Stromboli Dough Recipe

3 cups flour
3 tablespoons sugar
⅛ teaspoon salt
1 package yeast dissolved in 1 cup lukewarm water
¼ cup vegetable oil

1. Mix all ingredients, cover, and let stand until double in size, about 45 minutes to an hour.
2. Cut dough in half.
3. Roll out into flat into 1 foot squares.
4. Add filling. Roll in jelly roll fashion starting at sides.
5. Fold each end under, lay folded ends down on greased cookie sheet.
6. Cover and let stand 30 minutes before baking.
7. Bake at 350°F for 20 to 30 minutes.

Parmazano

1 cup nutritional yeast flakes
½ cup raw almonds, blanched and patted dry
½ teaspoon salt

1. To blanch almonds, place them in enough water to completely cover.
2. Bring to a boil and simmer for 1-2 minutes.
3. Drain and allow to cool, or rinse under cold tap water for rapid cooling.
4. Pinch skins between thumb and forefinger at the base of each almond.
5. Skins will slip off readily.
6. Place all the ingredients in a food processor, and process for several minutes until the almonds are very finely ground.
7. Store in a tightly sealed container in the refrigerator.

Tofu Ricotta

1½ packages silken tofu (12.3 oz)
1 teaspoon garlic powder
1 teaspoon onion powder
1 teaspoon salt
2 teaspoons energy egg replacer (without liquid)
5 cups shredded zucchini
3 cups mashed firm tofu
1 small onion, diced
1½ teaspoons Italian seasoning
1 teaspoon garlic powder
1 teaspoon salt
2 teaspoons basil

1. Place onion and shredded zucchini in a saucepan with 2 tablespoons water and simmer for 5 minutes.
2. Meanwhile, mash tofu and add seasonings.
3. Stir in the zucchini and onion.
4. Makes approximately 6 cups.

Pomodoro Fresco Alla Romona Spaghetti Sauce

1 lb. cherry tomatoes
salt (coarse is best)
6 tbsp extra virgin olive oil
5 cloves garlic, thinly sliced
pinch cayenne pepper
12 fresh basil leaves, torn into pieces

1. Fill sauce pan boil tomatoes for 1 minute drain and peel tomatoes.
2. At the same time in a small sauce pan warm olive oil, don't let smoke.
3. Add garlic and cayenne pepper.
4. Reduce heat to very low and cook very slowly stir for about 5 minutes.
5. Serve pasta; add tomatoes and basil, toss; pour oil mixture over mixture and toss again. Eat at once.

Entrees

Capellini with Salsa Cruda

Serves 4

1½ pounds ripe tomatoes, seeded & chopped, juice reserved
2 teaspoons minced garlic
2 tablespoons chopped fresh basil
⅓ cup olive oil
1 tablespoon red wine vinegar
salt & freshly ground pepper to taste
12 ounces capellini

1. Cook the capellini according to package directions.
2. In the meantime, in a large bowl, combine the chopped tomatoes, tomato juice, garlic, basil, olive oil, vinegar, and salt & pepper.
3. Toss well to mix and set aside.
4. When pasta is done, drain and immediately pour into the bowl with the tomato mixture.
5. Toss to mix and coat all the pasta. Serve at once.

Chunky Vegetable Sauce Over Pasta

Pasta with Greens and White Beans
1½ lb Greens, washed but not dried
2 tbsp. Olive oil
6 cloves Garlic
¼ tsp. Crushed red pepper flakes
⅓ cup Vegetable stock or water mixed with 1 tsp. broth powder
1½ cup cooked cannellini or other white beans, rinsed & drained
¼ tsp. Salt
12 oz. Uncooked pasta--penne, ziti, etc.
Salt & ground pepper to taste
2 tablespoons Soy Parmesan (opt.)

1. Bring 3 quarts of water to boil. Prepare greens by ripping leaves off stems. Tear or cut leaves into bite-size pieces. You should have about 12 cups.
2. Heat oil in large skillet over med-high heat.
3. Add garlic and red pepper flakes; sauté for 2 minutes.
4. Stir in greens and stock; cover pan. Cook until greens are wilted and tender yet still bright green, about 7 minutes. Gently stir in beans and salt; keep warm.
5. While greens are cooking, drop pasta into boiling water; cook until al dente, about 10 minutes.
6. Drain; stir into greens mixture. Top with soy cheese.

Pasta with Picante Tomato Sauce

Serves 1

1 tablespoon olive oil
2 large cloves garlic, minced or put through a press
3½ pounds tomatoes, fresh or canned, seeded
  and coarsely pureed.
3 tablespoon chopped fresh basil or 1 tablespoon, dried
1 teaspoon crushed or minced dried red pepper
salt
1 tablespoon safflower oil
1 pound small shell or tube macaroni

1. Heat the olive oil in a large, heavy bottomed sauce-pan or skillet and sauté garlic gently until it begins to color, 1-2 minutes.
2. Add tomatoes, basil and red pepper and bring to a simmer stirring.
3. Cook uncovered, over moderate heat, stirring occasionally, for 20-30 minutes, until the sauce thickens, Season to taste with salt.
4. Meanwhile, bring a large pot of water to a boil.
5. Add salt and a tablespoon safflower oil and add pasta.
6. Cook al dente.
7. Remove from the boiling water with a slotted spoon and place in a warm serving dish.
8. Toss with half the sauce.
9. Pour the rest of the sauce on top of the pasta or place the remaining sauce on individual servings.

Note: I omitted the safflower oil all together and.
If you do that you might want to omit the salt in your cooking water and rinse the pasta with cool water to prevent a longer cooking time or sticky cooked pasta.

Easy Spinach Lasagna

½ lb fresh mushrooms, sliced
2 tsp. olive oil
2 28-oz jars of spaghetti sauce (or your favorite
  homemade sauce)
9 lasagna noodles
10 oz. frozen chopped spinach, thawed
1 lb tofu
1 tsp. salt
1-2 tbsp. nutritional yeast
1 tsp. oregano
¼ tsp. garlic powder
½ tsp. basil
⅛ tsp. cayenne pepper
soy parmesan (optional)

1. Sauté the mushrooms in the olive oil until tender; remove from heat and add the spaghetti sauce.
2. Place the tofu and thawed spinach in the food processor and process briefly.
3. Add the remaining ingredients--except the noodles--to the processor and blend until smooth.
4. Preheat the oven to 375 degrees.
5. Spread half of the sauce in the bottom of a 9x12-inch pan.
6. Place a layer of noodles over the sauce, using three dry noodles and leaving a little space in between them.
7. Spread half of the tofu mixture on the noodles.
8. Cover with another layer of 3 noodles and then spread the remaining tofu mixture over them.
9. Top with a final layer of noodles, and pour the remaining sauce over this.
10. Cover the dish tightly with foil, and bake for 30 minutes.
11. Then, remove the foil and bake for another 15 minutes.
12. Remove from the oven and sprinkle with soy parmesan if you want.
13. The lasagna will cut better if you allow it to cool for 15 minutes before serving.

Vermicelli with Chunky Vegetable Sauce

Serves 6

16 ounces vermicelli pasta
1 red bell pepper, chopped
1 medium onion, chopped
2 stalks celery, chopped
2 small zucchini, sliced
4 cloves garlic, minced
4 cups diced tomatoes
1 6 oz. can tomato paste
salt to taste
1 tablespoon sugar or honey
1 tablespoon lemon juice
¼ cup fresh basil or 2 tbsp. dried basil, chopped
2 tablespoons fresh oregano or 2 tsp. dried oregano

1. Cook pasta per package directions.
2. Drain and pour into a wide serving bowl.
3. In a nonstick skillet over medium-high heat, stir red peppers, onion, and celery until tender, about 5 minutes.
4. Add zucchini and garlic; cook until zucchini is tender.
5. Add tomatoes, tomato paste, salt, sugar or honey, and lemon juice.
6. Stir until tomato mixture comes to a boil, about 5 minutes.
7. Add basil and oregano and cook an additional minute.

Lemon Basil Vermicelli

12 ounces vermicelli
1 cup scallions, chopped
1 cup lemon basil, chopped
½ teaspoon freshly ground black pepper
3 tablespoons fresh lemon juice
2 tablespoons soy sauce
5 drops hot chili oil
2 teaspoons corn oil
2 teaspoons sesame oil

1. Cook pasta per package directions.
2. Drain.
3. Toss vermicelli with scallions, lemon basil, pepper, lemon juice, soy sauce, and hot chili oil.
4. In a wok or large frying pan, heat the corn oil with the sesame oil over medium heat.
5. Stir-fry vermicelli mixture in the hot oil for about 5 minutes, tossing often to prevent sticking.

Spaghetti Tempezzini

Serves 3-4

1 pound spaghetti
4 tablespoons (½ stick) soy margarine
1 small yellow onion, peeled and chopped
1 small sweet green pepper, cored, seeded, and chopped
2 stalks celery, chopped
½ pound mushrooms, chopped
1 cup soy milk
1 cup cubed tempeh, optional
¼ teaspoon salt
¼ teaspoon black pepper

1. If using tempeh, sauté lightly in skillet with your favorite oil, then remove to plate and set aside.
2. Cook the spaghetti according to package directions.
3. Meanwhile, melt the margarine in a heavy.
4. 12-inch skillet over moderate heat.
5. Add the onion, green pepper, and celery, and cook, uncovered, for 3 minutes.
6. Add the mushrooms, and cook.
7. 2 or 3 minutes longer, or until they are just tender.
8. Add the soy milk to the skillet, raise the heat to high, and boil for 6-8 minutes, or until the sauce thickens.
9. Stir in the salt and pepper and, if using, the tempeh.
10. Cook for another minute, until the tempeh is heated through.
11. Drain spaghetti thoroughly in a colander, and toss with the sauce in the skillet.
12. Ready in 20 minutes.

Vegetable Pine Nut Pasta

Serves 5-6

1 green zucchini
1 yellow zucchini
1 tomato
a big handful of snow peas(or some other pea pod I suppose)
1 green pepper
1 yellow pepper
1 green pepper
¼ pound pine nuts (or a little over ¾ of a cup. Could be substituted with almond slivers, but pine nuts make it taste great!)
1 small onion or a section of a larger one
a few broccoli stalks and cauliflower segments
fresh mushrooms (packaged sliced, or whole ones chopped up)
about ⅓ cup olive oil
salt, pepper, garlic powder, oregano-add as desired
angel hair pasta works good (but you can omit/substitute)

1. Chop up the peppers into long strips, and place in a large bowl.
2. Add snow peas(or other pods).
3. Next, chop up mushrooms(if needed), cauliflower, & broccoli into bite size pieces. Place in bowl.
4. Cut a little onion up for flavor into very tiny pieces.
5. Add onion to bowl. Cut the Green zucchini in about ½ inch slices, then cut them in half.
6. For yellow zucchini, leave slices in circles. (You can designe them with cuts, flower patterns, and other shapes, but that takes time. It works fine just sliced.)
7. Mix the veggies in the bowl together well.
8. Peel and clean out the tomato, and slice into very tiny peices, about 3 mm in width.
9. Do not put in bowl, keep separate.
10. Put oil in a medium sized pan for sautéing and heat.
11. Place pine nuts in pan. Cook until slightly brown.
12. Add the bowl of veggies to the pan and mix.
13. Boil a pan of water while veggies cook.
14. When pan reaches boil, add angel hair pasta.
15. Cook veggies for another 3-10 min(I'm not sure) depending on how they look.
16. Add spices and tomato pieces and taste occasionally to get the desired flavor.
17. If veggies are taking a while to cook, lower the pasta's heat to low and let sit.
18. It should be fine if kept warm.
19. Drain pasta, and serve veggies over the pasta.

Baked Macaroni with Béchamel Sauce

Serves 4

1 pound (whole wheat) macaroni, cooked
3 tablespoons light oil (sunflower, safflower, etc.) -or- sesame oil
2 medium onions, chopped
1 large (organically grown) carrot, julienne cut
3 tablespoons whole wheat pastry flour or regular unbleached flour
2½ cups water
½ pound firm, drained tofu, crumbled
4 tablespoons tamari soy sauce, or to taste
1 tablespoon toasted sesame seeds, optional

1. Preheat oven to 350°F.
2. Heat the oil in a large, heavy saucepan.
3. Over medium heat, sauté the onion and carrot until the onion is transparent and lightly browned, about five minutes.
4. Lower the heat and stir in the flour.
5. Brown lightly for about 30 seconds, stirring constantly to prevent burning.
6. Slowly pour in the water, about a half-cup at a time, stirring constantly to prevent lumps (a whisk is helpful).
7. When all the water has been added, return to medium heat and cook, stirring constantly, until smooth and thickened. Stir in the tofu.
8. Season with soy sauce to taste.
9. Place cooked macaroni in a 2-quart casserole dish.
10. Stir in the vegetables and sauce, mixing well to coat.
11. Sprinkle top with sesame seeds, if desired.
12. Bake covered for 20 minutes, then uncovered for another 20 minutes.
13. Remove from oven and allow to rest for ten minutes before serving.
14. Serve hot; leftovers are tasty when reheated.

Vegan Lasagna

Serves 6-8

1 cup chopped onion
1 tablespoon minced garlic
2 teaspoons basil
1 teaspoon oregano
2 bay leaves
2 teaspoons salt
29-oz. can tomato purée
6-oz. can tomato paste
2 tablespoons dry red wine
1 cup fresh chopped tomatoes
¼ teaspoons pepper
1 tablespoon honey
½ cup fresh chopped parsley

2 cup reduced-fat firm tofu (not silken)
egg replacer to equal 2 eggs
salt
pepper
6-8 cloves garlic, pressed
2 cup TVP or crumbled veggie burgers
2 tablespoons Bragg's Liquid Aminos or soy sauce
4 tablespoons catsup or tomato purée
12 lasagna pasta strips, half cooked

1. Present oven to 375°F.
2. Sauté onion, garlic, basil, oregano, bay leaves, and salt in a large pan with ¼ cup water.
3. When onions are clear and very soft, add tomato purée, tomato paste, wine, tomatoes, pepper, and honey.
4. Turn heat way down, cover, and simmer at least 45 minutes, stirring occasionally.
5. Stir in parsley.
6. Mix together tofu, egg replacer, salt, pepper, and garlic.
7. If using TVP, mix with Bragg's, catsup, and 1½ cup boiling water; let sit 15 minutes.
8. To assemble lasagna, spread a little sauce over bottom of 9 x 12-inch pan.
9. Cover with ⅓ the pasta, ½ the tofu mixture, ⅓ the remaining sauce, ½ the TVP mixture, ½ the remaining pasta, remaining tofu mixture, ½ remaining sauce, remaining TVP mixture, remaining pasta, and remaining sauce.
10. Bake 45 minutes. Let stand 10 minutes before serving.

Fusilli Terni

3 large marjoram sprigs
2 bay leaves
Strip of lemon rind
2 tsp coriander seeds
½ cup white wine
8 tbsp. olive oil
6 oz small button mushrooms, halved
Salt and pepper
8 oz fusilli (corkscrews), cooked 'al dente'

1. Put the marjoram, bay leaves, lemon rind and coriander seeds in a pan with the white wine and simmer gently for 10 minutes.
2. Strain and stir into the oil.
3. Return to the pan.
4. add the mushrooms and simmer for 4 minutes.
5. Add salt and pepper to taste and allow to cool.
6. Toss the mushroom mixture into the warm, drained fusilli, Serve cold, sprinkled with fresh coriander leaves. Garnish with fresh coriander leaves

Rosemary-Scented Polenta

Serves 4

3 cups water
3 cups vegetable broth
½ teaspoon crumbled rosemary
2 cups yellow cornmeal
½ cup chopped black olives
½ cup chopped sweet pepper
1 teaspoon olive oil (optional)
homemade or prepared tomato sauce

1. Coat a 9 x 13-inch rimmed baking pan with vegetable cooking spray. Set aside.
2. In a large saucepan, combine water, broth, and rosemary. Heat to a boil.
3. Slowly whisk in cornmeal and cook about 20 minutes over low heat, stirring constantly until thickened and bubbly.
4. Stir in olives and red pepper.
5. Pour mixture into greased baking pan.
6. Let cool several hours or overnight.
7. Heat oven to 400°F. Cut cooled polenta into 8 pieces.
8. Leave in baking pan. Brush with half of the olive oil.
9. Bake 25 to 30 minutes, turning once and brushing with remaining olive oil until golden brown.
10. Serve heated with tomato sauce.

Rosemary Lemon Orzo Pilaf

Serves 4

1½ cups orzo (rice-shaped pasta)
1 tablespoon unsalted butter
1 teaspoon chopped fresh rosemary leaves
1 cup vegetable or imitation chicken broth
1½ cups water
1⅓ tablespoons fresh lemon juice
½ teaspoon salt

1. In a 1-quart heavy saucepan sauté orzo in butter over moderately high heat, stirring, until browned lightly and stir in remaining ingredients.
2. Bring liquid to a boil and cover.
3. Reduce heat to low and cook 15 minutes, or until liquid is absorbed.
4. Remove pan from heat and let stand, covered, 5 minutes. (Can be prepared in 45 minutes or less.)

Italian Vegetable Broth
(Brodo Di Verdure)

Serves 12

2 tbsp. extra virgin olive oil
1 large unpeeled onion, quartered
2 tomatoes, chopped
2 unpeeled carrots, chopped
1 leek, cleaned and sliced
6 stalks Italian parsley
¾ cup kale or Swiss chard stems
1 tsp. fennel seeds
1 bay leaf
4 qt water

1. In a large, heavy bottomed pot, heat olive oil over medium heat.
2. Add all the vegetables and cook, stirring frequently, for 6 to 7 minutes, until they begin to soften.
3. Add fennel seeds, bay leaf, and water.
4. Bring to a boil, then reduce heat to low.
5. Cover and simmer for 1 hour, stirring occasionally.
6. Strain all solids from the liquid, discarding solids and reserving broth.
7. Broth can be kept in the refrigerator for 1 week or frozen for up to 2 months.

Baked Bean and Pasta Casserole

Serves 6

19-oz can pinto or kidney beans, drained (or 2 cups cooked pinto or kidney beans)
3 tablespoons molasses
small onion, finely minced
4 cups cooked pasta, drained
dash of salt (optional)

1. Preheat oven to 350 degrees.
2. Mix all the ingredients together.
3. Pour into casserole dish and bake at 350 degrees for
4. 15-20 minutes. Serve hot.

Fagioli E Radicchio
(Cannellini Beans with Radicchio)

Serves 6

1½ cup dried cannellini beans, soaked overnight
5 cup water
1 16 oz. can plum tomatoes, chopped
3 tbsp. extra virgin olive oil
1 sprig fresh rosemary
3 fresh sage leaves
1 bay leaf
2 cloves garlic, peeled
3 small head of radicchio, halved
salt and pepper, to taste

1. Drain and rinse beans.
2. In a large pot combine beans, water, tomatoes, 2 tbsp. of the olive oil, rosemary, sage, bay leaf, and whole garlic cloves.
3. Bring to a boil, then reduce heat to low and cook, stirring occasionally, for 1 to 1½ hours, until beans are tender. Prepare grill or preheat broiler.
4. Lightly brush each radicchio half with remaining olive oil, then salt and pepper to taste.
5. If using a grill, cook over medium-hot coals for 3 to 5 minutes per side, or until the thick base can be easily pierced.
6. If using a broiler, place the seasoned radicchio on a cookie sheet lined with foil and broil 4 to 6 inches from the heat for 4 to 5 minutes on each side.
7. When the beans are done, discard the rosemary, sage and bay leaf.
8. Season beans to taste with salt and pepper.
9. Divide grilled or broiled radicchio between 6 plates and top with beans.
10. Drizzle with more olive oil, if desired.

Fusilli with Garden Vegetables and Tarragon

Serves 4

3 ripe tomatoes
3 slender carrots, peeled and thinly sliced, into rounds
4 small summer squash, thinly sliced, or cubed
½ cup peas or a handful of sugar snap peas
1 small red onion, quartered and thinly, sliced crosswise
1 yellow or red bell pepper, quartered and, thinly sliced crossways
2 cloves garlic, minced
2 tablespoons chopped fresh tarragon
3 tablespoons extra virgin olive oil
salt and freshly ground pepper to taste
12 ounces fusilli pasta

1. Bring a large pot of water to a boil.
2. Blanch the tomatoes for about 10 seconds, the peel, seed, and neatly dice them.
3. Put them in a large bowl.
4. Blanch the carrots and summer squash for 2 minutes and the peas for 1 minute.
5. As they finish cooking, scoop them out with a strainer, shake off the excess water, and add them to the tomatoes along with the onion, bell pepper, garlic, tarragon, and oil.
6. Add salt to the water and cook the pasta until al dente.
7. Scoop it out, add it to the vegetables, and toss well.
8. Season with salt & pepper and serve.

Vegan Lasagna

Serves 12

Tomato Sauce:
2 tbsp. olive oil
1 cup chopped onion
3 cloves garlic, minced
6 oz. can tomato paste
Three (28-oz.) cans peeled plum tomatoes, chopped with juices reserved
½ cup chopped fresh basil
½ cup chopped fresh parsley
1½ tsp. dried oregano
½ tsp. crushed red pepper flakes (optional)
Salt and ground black pepper to taste

Lasagna:
1 tbsp. salt
1 lb. dry uncooked eggless lasagna noodles
2 (16-oz.) packages firm tofu, drained
2 cloves garlic, minced
¼ cup chopped fresh basil
½ cup chopped fresh parsley
Salt and ground black pepper to taste

1. For the sauce, in large, heavy saucepan, heat oil over medium heat.
2. Add onion and garlic and cook, stirring frequently, until onion is soft, about 5 minutes.
3. Add tomato paste and cook, stirring, for 1 minute.
4. Add tomatoes with juice, basil, parsley, oregano and red pepper flakes.
5. Cover and simmer over low heat about 1 hour.
6. Season with salt and pepper.
7. Meanwhile, bring large pot of water to boil.
8. When water boils, add salt and noodles.
9. Cook until al dente, about 12 minutes, stirring occasionally. Drain, rinse with water and drain again.
10. Preheat oven to 400 degrees.
11. Crumble tofu into medium bowl.
12. Add garlic, basil, parsley, salt and pepper.
13. Stir until well blended. To assemble, spoon about 1 cup sauce over bottom of 13- by 9-inch baking dish.
14. Add layer of noodles and top with one-third tofu mixture. Spoon over about 1½ cups sauce and top with another layer of noodles.
15. Cover with one-third tofu mixture and top with 1½ cups of sauce and another layer of noodles.
16. Top with remaining tofu mixture and 1 cup sauce.
17. Cover with foil and bake 30 minutes.
18. Remove from oven; let stand about 15 min. before cutting and serving. Serve with remaining sauce.

Vegetarian Lasagna

2 tablespoons olive oil
1½ cups chopped onion
3 tablespoons minced garlic
4 (14.5 ounce) cans stewed tomatoes
⅓ cup tomato paste
½ cup chopped fresh basil
½ cup chopped parsley
1 teaspoon salt
1 teaspoon ground black pepper
1 (16 ounce) package lasagna noodles
2 pounds firm tofu
2 tablespoons minced garlic
¼ cup chopped fresh basil
¼ cup chopped parsley
½ teaspoon salt ground black pepper to taste
3 (10 ounce) packages frozen chopped spinach, thawed
    and drained

1. Make the sauce: In a large, heavy saucepan, over
    medium heat, heat the olive oil.
2. Place the onions in the saucepan and sauté them until
    they are soft, about 5 minutes. Add the garlic; cook 5
    minutes more.
3. Place the tomatoes, tomato paste, basil and parsley in
    the saucepan. Stir well, turn the heat to low and let
    the sauce simmer covered for 1 hour. Add the salt
    and pepper.
4. While the sauce is cooking bring a large kettle of
    salted water to a boil. Boil the lasagna noodles for 9
    minutes, then drain and rinse well.
5. Preheat the oven to 400 degrees F (200 degrees C).
6. Place the tofu blocks in a large bowl. Add the garlic,
    basil and parsley.
7. Add the salt and pepper, and mash all the ingredients
    together by squeezing pieces of tofu through your
    fingers. Mix well.
8. Assemble the lasagna: Spread 1 cup of the tomato
    sauce in the bottom of a 9x13 inch casserole pan.
    Arrange a single layer of lasagna noodles, sprinkle
    one-third of the tofu mixture over the noodles.
9. Distribute the spinach evenly over the tofu. Next
    ladle 1½ cups tomato sauce over the tofu, and top it
    with another layer of the noodles.
10. Then sprinkle another ⅓ of the tofu mixture over the
    noodles, top the tofu with 1½ cups tomato sauce,
    and place a final layer of noodles over the tomato
    sauce.
11. Finally, top the noodles with the final ⅓ of the tofu,
    and spread the remaining tomato sauce over every-
    thing. Cover the pan with foil and bake the lasagna
    for 30 minutes. Serve hot and enjoy.

Potato Gnocchi

3 large baking potatoes
1-2 cups unbleached white flour
salt to taste
dash paprika
dash grated nutmeg
2 tablespoons chopped fresh parsley

1. Peel the potatoes, cut in quarters, cover with cold
    water, bring to a boil, reduce heat, cover, and cook
    until tender. Drain and mash.
2. To make the gnocchi, for each cup of mashed potato
    put 1 cup minus two tablespoons unbleached white
    flour in a bowl, and mix with salt (to taste) dashes of
    paprika and nutmeg, and the chopped parsley.
3. Add the warm potatoes and knead on a floured
    surface just until dough is well mixed and not sticky.
4. Let rest for 15 minutes.
5. Roll chunks of dough on floured board into logs
    about 1 inch thick.
6. Cut into diagonal slices about ¾ inch thick.
7. Bring a large pot of water to the boil.
8. Add gnocchi.
9. After they rise to the surface, adjust heat and simmer
    for 10 minutes, uncovered.
10. Drain well and cover with your favorite pasta sauce.

Gnocchi (pronounced "nyo-kee" is derived from the
German word for "knuckle") are tasty little dumplings,
one of Italy's oldest pastas dating back to the 12th century.
Traditional ingredients vary from region to region, with
recipes including potatoes, flour, semolina, spinach and
even bread crumbs. My favorite base for gnocchi is the
Idaho potato. Potatoes are packed with complex carbohydrates, plenty of potassium, vitamins cup and B6, and
lots of great minerals.

Potatoes convert to glucose in your body fairly quickly,
triggering the release of insulin, which leads to increased
levels of relaxing serotonin in your brain. When making
gnocchi (a relaxing activity in itself), to get a better surface
for holding sauce, press each one into the curved cup of a
fork, letting it fall to the floured surface once you've made
an indentation. Handle the gnocchi as little as possible
and cook them right away if you can. Toss the dumplings
into the bubbling water and drink in the scented steam.
They will emerge light and delectable.

Grilled Polenta with Red Chile Sauce & Black Beans

Serves 6
1 teaspoon extra virgin olive oil
2½ cups stone ground yellow cornmeal
3 cups cold water
¾ teaspoon salt
2 ¾ cups cold water
2 tablespoons margarine, melted
½ teaspoon olive oil for grilling

Red Chile Sauce:
5 cloves garlic, pressed
2 tablespoons extra virgin olive oil
2 tablespoons yellow cornmeal
½ cup ground New Mexico red chili
2½ cups vegetable stock or water
¼ teaspoon freshly ground black pepper
2 tablespoons margarine
¾ teaspoon salt (or to taste)

Black Beans:
2 cups dried black beans, sorted and washed
5 cups to 7 cups water
2 cloves garlic, minced
⅛ teaspoon peeled and grated fresh ginger
⅛ teaspoon New Mexico red chili
1 teaspoon ground cumin
pinch nutmeg
1 teaspoon salt

For Polenta:
Oil a 4x8 loaf pan with the 1 tsp. olive oil.
Set aside.

1. Toast the cornmeal over medium heat in a heavy skillet until it is fragrant but not browned.
2. Immediately pour the cornmeal into a bowl and let cool.
3. In a medium heavy-bottomed saucepan, bring the 3 cups water and the salt to a boil.
4. Whisk together the cooled cornmeal and the 2 ¾ cups water.
5. Pour this mixture into the boiling water, stirring constantly.
6. When the polenta begins to boil, cover the pot and reduce the heat to low.
7. Cook the polenta until it is very thick and soft, about 45-55 minutes.
8. Stir in the melted margarine, then spoon the polenta into the oiled pan, pressing it down firmly into the pan using either your hand or a spoon dipped in cold water.

9. Sprinkle on the ½ tsp. olive oil and rub it over the surface of the polenta. Let the polenta cool, then cover it with waxed paper or plastic wrap and store in refrigerator until ready to grill.
10. Can keep in refrigerator for up to 2 days.
11. To grill the polenta, invert the pan onto a cutting board and tap firmly.
12. The polenta may come out the first time but, if not,
13. simply run a knife around the edge of the pan and try again.
14. Slice the polenta into 12 ½-inch pieces.
15. Rinse or wipe the knife between each cut.
16. In a heavy skillet over medium-high heat, grill the polenta slices in the 2 to 4 tbsp. oil until golden and crisp on both sides.
17. Serve immediately with Red Chile Sauce and Black Beans.

To prepare Red Chile Sauce:
18. In a medium saucepan over medium heat, sauté the garlic in the olive oil until golden.
19. Add the cornmeal and cook 1 minute, stirring constantly.
20. Add the red chili and continue cooking only until fragrant. Do not let the chili brown or the sauce will taste bitter.
21. Remove the pan from the heat and slowly whisk in the stock, then bring the sauce to a boil over medium heat.
22. Reduce the heat and simmer 10-15 minutes.
23. Add the black pepper, oregano, butter, and salt and simmer until the flavors mingle 5-10 minutes more.
24. This sauce will keep covered in the refrigerator for up to 4 days. Makes 3 cups.

Note: Flavor will be much richer when the sauce is made with vegetable stock instead of water. To Prepare Black

Beans:
1. Soak the beans in the water overnight before cooking or bring the beans and water to a boil, cook for 5 minutes, then let stand for 1 hour before proceeding.
2. Cook the beans in a large saucepan or Dutch oven until they are very tender but still whole, about 1 to 2 hours.
3. Make sure beans are done before seasoning them because salt will inhibit further softening. Add remaining ingredients to the cooked beans and stir well.

Risotto with Vegetables

Serves 6

1 medium purple onion
1 medium yellow squash
3 medium yellow, red, or green bell peppers
2 medium carrots
2 cloves garlic, minced
1 tablespoon olive oil
1 tablespoon chopped fresh rosemary

1 16 oz. pkg uncooked Arborio rice
4 14.5 oz. cans veg. broth
½ teaspoon salt
½ teaspoon freshly ground pepper
¾ teaspoon ground white pepper
fresh rosemary sprigs for garnish

1. Cut onion, squash, bell peppers, and carrots into thin strips. Sauté vegetable strips and garlic in hot oil in a Dutch oven over medium-high heat until tender; stir in chopped rosemary.
2. Remove mixture from pan and set aside. Add rice to Dutch oven, and sauté 5 minutes.
3. Reduce heat to medium.
4. Add 1 cup of vegetable broth and cook, stirring constantly, until liquid is absorbed.
5. Repeat procedure with remaining broth, 1 cup at a time (cooking time is approximately 30 minutes).
6. Stir in salt and black and white pepper.
7. Spoon into a serving dish; top with vegetable mixture.
8. Garnish, if desired.

Vegetarian Muffaletta

Serves 8

1 large round Italian loaf of bread (10")
Filling: Use as many of the ingredients as you like and can fit into your sandwich!
1 eggplant, about 1 lb. cut into ¼ inch slices & broiled
Hummus
1 sweet red pepper, roasted, peeled, cut into chunks
1 sweet yellow pepper, roasted, peeled, cut into chunks
1 bunch fresh arugula or bitter greens (cress will do)
1 thinly sliced onion
1 thinly sliced avocado
broiled zucchini slices
chopped black olives (brined)
thinly sliced roma tomatoes
⅓ cup pesto sauce

1. Cut top off of bread and scoop out some of the insides (save for croutons or bread crumbs).
2. Layer ingredients thinly,
3. starting with hummus on the bottom, ending with pesto sauce on the top.
4. Add top of bread and wrap tightly.
5. Let sit 2 hours or more; Cut into wedges & serve.

Roasted Red Potato Salad with Parsley-Pine Nut Pesto

For the pesto:

⅓ cup pine nuts
2 cups loosely packed, flat-leaf parsley
2 medium cloves garlic, peeled
1 tbsp mellow white or yellow miso
½ cup extra virgin olive oil
½ tsp coarse sea salt

For the salad:

2 lbs small red potatoes, cut into 1" chunks
1 tbsp extra virgin olive oil
3 large red bell peppers, seeded and cut into 1" pieces
coarse sea salt
freshly ground black peppers

1. Place pine nuts in a small skillet; toast over low heat until golden brown, taking care that they don't burn.
2. In the bowl of a food processor fitted with a metal blade, combine the pine nuts, parsley, garlic, miso, and lemon juice and puree.
3. Slowly add the olive oil and process until smooth Add ½ tsp salt and set aside.
4. Preheat the oven to 400°F. In a large bowl, combine the potatoes and the olive oil. Toss to coat.
5. Transfer the potatoes to a parchment lined baking sheet and roast for 20 minutes, stirring after 10 minutes.
6. Add the peppers to the baking sheet and stir to combine.
7. Roast for 1 hour, stirring every 15 minutes, until the potatoes are tender and the peppers are roasted.
8. Transfer the potatoes and peppers to a large bowl, add ½ cup plus 3 tbsp pesto, stir well and season with salt and pepper to taste.
9. Serve at room temperature. Cover the remaining pesto with a film of olive oil in a tightly sealed container and refrigerate for up to two weeks.

Simply Italian/Pasta Dishes

Spaghettini Con Le Melanzane

Serves 4

1 medium eggplant (about 1 lb.)
salt
olive oil
1½ tsp. finely chopped garlic
3 tbsp. olive oil
2 tbsp. finely chopped parsley (I use Italian, broad-leafed parsley)
one 28-ounce tin of Italian plum tomatoes, drained and coarsely chopped
⅛ tsp. finely chopped hot red pepper, fresh if possible (I use dried red pepper seeds)
¼ tsp. salt
1 lb. spaghettini

1. Cut eggplant (length-wise or cross-wise) into ⅜" slices.
2. Sprinkle slices liberally with salt and arrange upright in a colander.
3. Drain 30-40 minutes over a dish or in the sink.
4. Rinse well with paper towels.
5. Pre-heat oven broiler to 400°F.
6. Brush both sides of eggplant slices with olive oil, place on cookie sheet (or something similar) and broil on each side until nicely browned. Cool and reserve.
7. In a medium-size saucepan, sauté the garlic in the 3 tbsp. olive oil over moderate heat just until the garlic begins to color slightly.
8. Add the parsley, tomatoes, pepper and salt and cook 25 minutes or until the tomatoes have separated from the oil and turned to sauce.
9. Stir frequently. Cut the eggplant into slivers ½" wide, add to the sauce and cook 2-3 minutes more.
10. Taste for salt. Drop the spaghettini into 16 cups rapidly boiling salted (1 tbsp.) water.
11. Cook rapidly 3-5 minutes.
12. The spaghettini should still be somewhat firm.
13. Put a small quantity of sauce in a warm serving bowl.
14. Add drained spaghettini, mix. Serve immediately, topping each serving with additional sauce.

Summer Tomato Pasta

Serves 4

1 pound very ripe tomatoes, chopped
6 large cloves garlic, minced
¼ cup fresh basil, chopped
2 tablespoons extra virgin olive oil
salt & freshly ground pepper to taste
pinch red pepper flakes
12 ounces linguine or cappelletti

1. Place tomatoes in a large bowl and add the remaining ingredients except pasta.
2. Mix well and set aside for about 3 hours at room temperature.
3. Cook pasta per package directions.
4. Drain and add to tomato mixture.
5. Toss well and serve immediately.

Pasta with Three Herb Pesto

Serves 6

3 cups fresh basil leaves
½ cup fresh parsley sprigs
¼ cup fresh oregano leaves
2 tablespoons toasted pine nuts
¼ teaspoon salt
4 cloves garlic
2 tablespoons to 4 tbsp.
olive oil
8 cups mixed hot cooked pasta

1. Place first 6 ingredients in a food processor and process until smooth.
2. With processor on, slowly pour oil through food-chute; process until well blended.
3. Toss with pasta.

Linguine with Asparagus, Lemon and Spring Herbs

Serves 6

2 tablespoons olive oil
2 tablespoons margarine
1 large bunch scallions, including half of the greens, thinly sliced
2½ teaspoons grated lemon zest
1 tablespoon fresh thyme, sage, -or- tarragon, finely chopped
salt and freshly ground pepper to taste
2 pounds fresh asparagus, tough ends removed
1 pound linguine
4 tablespoons pine nuts, toasted
3 tablespoons fresh parsley, chopped
2 tablespoons fresh snipped chives, plus blossoms, if available

1. While water is heating for the pasta, heat half the oil and butter in a wide skillet over low heat.
2. Add the scallions, lemon zest, thyme, and a few pinches of salt and cook slowly, stirring occasionally.
3. Meanwhile, slice 3-inch tips off the asparagus, the slice the remaining stalks diagonally or make a roll cut.
4. When the water boils, salt it, add the asparagus, and cook until partially tender, about 3 to 4 minutes.
5. Scoop it out, add it to the scallions, and continue cooking.
6. Cook the pasta, then add it to the pan with some of the water clinging to the strands.
7. Raise the heat and stir in the remaining oil, the pine nuts, parsley, chives, pepper to taste, and a few table-spoons of cheese, if desired.
8. Divide among pasta plates, grate a little cheese over each portion, and garnish with the chive blossoms (if available).

Garden Sauté w/Penne

Serves 4

6 cloves garlic, minced
3 tablespoons olive oil
1 large yellow bell pepper, cut into thin strips
8 plum tomatoes, seeded, cut into thin strips
1 cup loosely packed fresh basil, cut into thin strips
¼ cup fresh parsley, minced
8 ounces penne, cooked

1. Sauté garlic in hot oil in a large skillet 1 minute.
2. Add bell pepper and sauté 2 minutes.
3. Add tomato, basil, and parsley, and sauté 1 minute.
4. Stir in hot cooked pasta; cook, stirring occasionally, 2 minutes or until thoroughly heated.
5. Serve immediately.

Linguine w/Red Pepper Sauce

Serves 6

vegetable cooking spray
2 teaspoons olive oil
3 cups chopped sweet red pepper
2 cloves garlic, minced
⅓ cup chopped fresh basil
¼ cup balsamic vinegar
¼ teaspoon salt or to taste
⅛ teaspoon freshly ground pepper
6 cups hot cooked linguine

1. Coat a nonstick skillet with cooking spray.
2. Add olive oil.
3. Place over medium heat until hot.
4. Add sweet red pepper and garlic; cook, uncovered, 30 minutes, stirring occasionally.
5. Set aside and cool slightly.
6. Place pepper mixture in container of blender or food processor.
7. Add chopped basil and next 3 ingredients.
8. Cover and process until smooth, stopping once or twice to scrape sides.
9. For each serving, top 1 cup of pasta with ¼ cup of pepper sauce.
10. Garnish if desired. Serve immediately.

Creamed Broccoli and Pasta

1 pound pasta
4 stalks broccoli, chopped
2 cups soy milk
½ cup nutritional yeast
½ teaspoon basil
½ teaspoon onion powder
¼ teaspoon black pepper
1 tablespoon soy margarine
salt to taste

1. Cook pasta in water.
2. Steam chopped broccoli in separate pot.
3. Mix soy milk, yeast, spices, and margarine together in a small pot.
4. Heat over medium heat until mixture begins to bubble. Drain pasta and mix with broccoli.
5. Pour heated sauce over pasta and broccoli. Serve.

Notes: You can add 3 cloves of fresh garlic, pressed, instead of the onion powder. This recipe is also really good with fresh salsa substituted for the broccoli.

Baked Rigatoni & Teese (Vegan)

1 tablespoon Earth Balance margarine
1 garlic clove, minced
¼ cup all-purpose flour
1 tablespoon all-purpose flour
1 cup water
¼ cup nutritional yeast
1 tablespoon soy sauce
¼ teaspoon turmeric
¼ teaspoon sweet paprika
1/8 teaspoon black pepper
1/8 teaspoon cayenne pepper
1 teaspoon prepared yellow mustard
1½ cups Teese vegan mozzarella cheese or 1½ cups teese vegan mozzarella cheese, shredded
1 -2 slice whole wheat bread, toasted and crumbled into pieces
½ lb rigatoni or shell pasta

1. Preheat oven to 350 degrees. Cook pasta until it is almost al dente but still slightly undercooked.
2. Melt Earth Balance in small saucepan and add 1 Tbsp flour. Cook until it gets bubbly, about 2 minutes.
3. Add garlic and cook until fragrant, about 1 minute.
4. Whisk in remaining flour, water, nutritional yeast, soy sauce, turmeric, paprika, pepper, and cayenne, and cook, whisking often, until the sauce thickens but is still runny enough to drip off of the whisk.
5. Mix in mustard. Add sauce and Teese to cooked macaroni in a casserole dish (I used an 8 x 6 ½ inch Pyrex dish) and mix until well combined.
6. Top with breadcrumbs and cook for about twenty minutes, with a couple of minutes under the broiler if you want the breadcrumbs extra crunchy.

Pasta with Roasted Peppers & Spinach

3-4 Peppers (I like red and yellow, they look good in this dish)
3-4 cloves garlic minced
½ lb baby spinach
1½ cup veg. broth
½ cup dry white wine (If you prefer sub. veg. broth)
1 teaspoon olive oil
1 lb pasta (I prefer rigatoni)

1. Roast the peppers and cut into strips.
2. Wash and shake water from spinach leaves (If you don't have baby spinach you may want to course chop the spinach also).
3. Put the olive oil into a large skillet and heat.
4. When hot add ½ of the minced garlic, some salt and the spinach.
5. Cook until the spinach is wilted then remove pan from heat and remove spinach to a plate with a slotted spoon.
6. Leave the liquid in the pan.
7. Return pan with liquid to heat and add the remaining garlic, wine, veg. stock and peppers.
8. Bring to a simmer and allow to cook until the liquid reduces by a little more than half.
9. Add the previously cooked spinach and garlic.
10. Meanwhile cook and drain your pasta, reserving 1 cup of pasta cooking water.
11. I like to under cook the pasta about 1 minute.
12. Return it to the cooking pan after draining and then add the spinach and roasted pepper mixture and cook over a low heat for about 1 minute.
13. Season to taste with salt and pepper (you might try red pepper flakes).
14. Serve in pasta bowls.

Roasting peppers: The easiest way IMO is to cut in half lengthwise, remove seed then smash them flat with my hand onto a sheet of foil paper. Put the peppers under the broiler until they are charred - make sure they are really black. Remove them from the broiler and fold the foil into a little package and let them sit at room temp. until they are cool enough to handle. If you really charred them well, the skin will just slip off.

Pasta w/ Fresh Tomatoes & Basil

Serves 4

3 tomatoes, seeded & chopped
2 cloves garlic, minced
2 tablespoons chopped fresh parsley
2 tablespoons chopped fresh basil
2 tablespoons lemon juice
½ teaspoon sugar
½ teaspoon salt
¼ teaspoon pepper
¼ olive oil
8 ounces angel hair pasta, cooked

1. Sauté first 8 ingredients in hot oil in a large skillet over low heat, stirring constantly, 1 minute or until thoroughly heated.
2. Spoon over hot cooked pasta.

Creamy Mushroom and Tomato Pasta

cooking oil
2 cloves garlic, crushed
1 onion, diced
¾ lb. mushrooms, diced
½ red capsicum, diced
¼ cup plain whole meal flour
1 cup of soy milk
2 tbsp. of tomato paste
½ cup fresh parsley (or equivalent dried)
1 tomato, diced
1 lb. spiral pasta, cooked

1. Heat oil in wok (or large saucepan) & sauté garlic, onion, mushrooms & capsicum for five minutes.
2. Stir in flour & cook for a further 2 minutes.
3. Add soy milk all at once and stir until mixture thickens slightly.
4. Add tomato, stir thoroughly.
5. Add tomato paste & parsley until well combined.
6. Add pasta to wok (or add sauce to paste if using a saucepan) and stir
7. through until heated thoroughly.

Spaghetti with Garlic and Oil

Serves 4

⅓ cup olive oil (extra virgin preferred)
2 to 3 cloves garlic, chopped fine
12 oz. (300 g) spaghetti
2 tbsp. finely chopped parsley
salt and freshly ground black pepper to taste

1. Cook the spaghetti according to package directions.
2. While spaghetti is cooking heat the oil in a pot large enough to hold the spaghetti when it is cooked.
3. Add the garlic and cook over low heat, stirring frequently, until the garlic is golden (do not brown).
4. Add the cooked, drained spaghetti to the oil and garlic.
5. Add the salt, pepper, and parsley and toss to
6. thoroughly coat the spaghetti.

Zucchini (Green Squash)

Serves 4

1 or 2 lemons
salt
black pepper
chopped parsley
1 tsp. extra virgin olive oil
1 clove garlic, chopped

1. Wash well the zucchini.
2. Thinly slice them.
3. Prepare a marinade with the juice and pulp of 1 or two lemons (depends on their dimensions), salt, black pepper, garlic, parsley and olive oil.
4. Put a layer of zucchini slices in a bowl and pour a little of the marinade at the top, do the same for all the layers of zucchini slices.
5. Keep the bowl in a cool place and let it rest for 6 to 8 hours, occasionally pouring some of the lemon marinate at the bottom on the top layers of the zucchini.
6. Grill the zucchini for a couple of minutes (till they become tender).
7. Keep the marinade and use it as a dressing for the grilled zucchini.

Tofu-Spinach Lasagna

½ lb. lasagna noodles
2 10-oz. packages frozen chopped spinach,
    thawed and drained
1 lb. soft tofu
1 lb. firm tofu
1 tbsp. raw sugar
¼ cup soy milk
½ tsp. garlic powder
2 tbsp. lemon juice
3 tsp. minced fresh basil
2 tsp. salt
4 cups tomato sauce

1. Cook the lasagna noodles according to the package directions.
2. Drain and set aside.
3. Preheat the oven to 350°F.
4. Squeeze the spinach as dry as possible and set aside.
5. Place the tofu, sugar, soy milk, garlic powder, lemon juice, basil, and salt in a food processor or blender and blend until smooth.
6. Stir in the spinach.
7. Cover the bottom of a 9-inch-by-13-inch baking dish with a thin layer of tomato sauce, then a layer of noodles (use about one-third of the noodles).
8. Follow with half of the tofu filling.
9. Continue in the same order, using half of the remaining tomato sauce and noodles and all of the remaining tofu filling.
10. End with the remaining noodles, covered by the remaining tomato sauce.
11. Bake for 25 to 30 minutes.

Vermicelli with Tomato-Basil Sauce

Serves 6

8 ounces vermicelli, uncooked
vegetable cooking spray
2 cloves garlic, minced
1 medium onion, thinly sliced
5 cups tomatoes (about 5 medium), peeled & chopped
¼ cup fresh basil, minced
¼ teaspoon salt or to taste
⅛ teaspoon freshly ground pepper
1 8 oz. can no salt added tomato sauce

1. Cook pasta according to package directions.
2. Drain. While pasta is cooking, coat a Dutch oven with cooking spray; place over medium heat until hot.
3. Add garlic and onion and cook, stirring constantly, 5 minutes or until onion is tender.
4. Stir in tomato and next 4 ingredients.
5. Bring to a boil. Reduce heat and simmer, uncovered, for 15 minutes, stirring occasionally.
6. Add cooked pasta to tomato mixture.
7. Cook, uncovered, until mixture is thoroughly heated, stirring occasionally. Sprinkle with cheese if desired.
8. Serve immediately.

Mushroom Pasta

Serves 4

16 ounces fresh mushrooms, halved
3 cloves garlic, minced
3 tablespoons olive oil
⅔ cup dry white wine
4 to 5 plum tomatoes, cut into chunks
½ cup green onions, sliced
½ cup firmly packed fresh basil leaves
½ teaspoon salt or to taste
¾ teaspoon freshly ground pepper
8 ounces spaghetti, cooked

1. Sauté mushrooms and garlic in hot oil in a large skillet 4 minutes or until tender.
2. Add wine and bring to a boil.
3. Boil, stirring occasionally, 6 minutes or until mixture is reduced by half.
4. Stir in tomato, green onions, and next 3 ingredients.
5. Cook, stirring occasionally, until thoroughly heated.
6. Spoon over hot cooked pasta.

Pasta E Fagioli Marinara

Serves 6

2 tablespoons olive oil
½ cup minced onion
½ cup minced carrots
¼ cup minced celery
1 tablespoon minced garlic
¼ teaspoon red pepper flakes
2 cups vegetable broth
1 cup prepared marinara sauce
1 can cannellini beans, drained and rinsed, (19 oz.)
¼ teaspoon salt
¼ teaspoon freshly ground pepper
1 pound ditalini, cooked according to package directions

1. Heat oil in large skillet over medium-high heat.
2. Add onions, carrots and celery and cook for 4 minutes.
3. Add garlic and red pepper flakes; cook for 15 seconds.
4. Add vegetable broth and marinara sauce; bring to a boil.
5. Reduce heat and simmer for 10 minutes.
6. Add the cannellini beans and simmer 5 minutes more. Stir in salt and pepper.
7. Toss sauce with the hot pasta and optional Parmesan cheese in a large serving bowl.

Pasta Provencal

Serves 6

1 tablespoon olive oil
3 cups sliced zucchini
1 cup sliced fresh mushrooms
½ cup chopped green bell pepper
¼ cup chopped onion
2 cloves garlic, minced
1 14.5 oz. can stewed tomatoes, undrained & chopped
1 teaspoon chopped fresh basil or ½ tsp. dried
½ teaspoon chopped fresh oregano or ¼ tsp. dried
¼ teaspoon salt or to taste
¼ teaspoon freshly ground pepper
2 cups hot cooked rotini

1. Heat olive oil in a Dutch oven over medium heat.
2. Add zucchini and next 4 ingredients and cook, stirring constantly, 5 minutes.
3. Add tomato and next 4 ingredients; bring to a boil, and remove from heat.
4. Add cooked pasta and toss gently. Serve immediately.

Black Bean Lasagna

Sauce:

In a large bowl, mix together:
1 (15 oz.) can black beans, drained, rinsed, and slightly mashed
1 (28 oz.) can crushed tomatoes with liquid
1 cup chopped onions
1 green bell pepper, chopped
½ cup salsa
1 teaspoon cumin
½-1 teaspoon chili powder

Mock Ricotta:

In a food processor or blender, mix together:
1½ (12.3 oz.) packages silken tofu, firm or extra firm
1 teaspoon garlic powder
1 teaspoon onion powder
1 teaspoon salt
2 teaspoons egg replacer (without liquid)
12 uncooked lasagna noodles
your favorite soy cheese or Melty Nutritional Yeast Cheese
chopped tomatoes, green onions, and/or olives to top (optional)

Spray pan and layer as follows:

1 cup of sauce
6 noodles
half of remaining sauce
mock ricotta mixture
grated soy cheese or drizzle with melty cheese, to taste
6 noodles
remaining sauce soy cheese (if using melty cheese, hold off until after baking) desired toppings

1. Bake at 350 degrees for 45 minutes.
2. Drizzle with more melty cheese to taste and broil for a few minutes, watching
3. carefully just until it's a cheesy consistency.

Spinach and Eggplant Lasagna

1 tablespoon olive oil
1 clove garlic, minced
1 medium eggplant, diced
20 ounces spinach, frozen, defrosted
8 cups tomato sauce
1 pound lasagna noodles

1. Preheat the oven to 375 degrees.
2. Heat the olive oil in a medium frying pan over medium heat.
3. Sauté the garlic for 2 minutes, then add the eggplant and stir.
4. Cover the frying pan and cook until the eggplant is just tender, about 5 to 7 minutes.
5. Cover the bottom of a 9 X 12-inch baking pan with 2 cups of the tomato sauce, then cover the tomato sauce with 4 or 5 uncooked noodles.
6. Cover this with a thin layer of sauce, then add the cooked eggplant and another thin layer of sauce.
7. Add another layer of noodles followed by a thin layer of sauce, then add the spinach and another thin layer of sauce.
8. Add the remaining noodles and sauce.
9. Cover tightly with foil and bake for 45 to 50 minutes.
10. Noodles are done when they can be pierced with a fork.

Pasta Sauce with Capers and Olives

4 or 5 vine ripened tomatoes, peeled and cut into bite sized pieces.
¼ cup extra virgin olive oil
5 large cloves of garlic, chopped coarse
1 very large handful of fresh basil, stems removed and chopped fine (this recipe will not work with dried basil).
2 tablespoons of capers
12 large Sicilian green olives pitted and coarsely chopped (optional).
sea salt and pepper to taste,

1. Mix all ingredients and let marinate for at least two to three hours.
2. Toss with hot pasta.
3. Traditionally, this dish is best
4. without the addition of cheese.

Pasta E Fagioli

Serves 6
3 tbsp. extra virgin olive oil
1 med onion, chopped
1 large carrot, peeled and sliced
1¼ cup dried borlotti (cranberry) beans, soaked overnight
1 16 oz. can plum tomatoes, chopped
7 cup Italian Vegetable Broth
1 bay leaf
¼ tsp. crushed red pepper
6 oz. small pasta (ditalini or elbow macaroni)
salt and pepper, to taste
2 cloves garlic, minced
6 slices day-old Italian country bread

1. In a large heavy-bottomed pot, heat 2 tbsp. of the olive oil over medium heat.
2. Add onion and carrot and sauté for 4 to 5 minutes, stirring frequently.
3. Drain and rinse beans.
4. Add to pot along with tomatoes, vegetable broth, and bay leaf.
5. Bring to a boil, then reduce heat to simmer.
6. Cook partially covered for 1½ - 2 hours, stirring occasionally, until beans are tender.
7. Add kale and red pepper flakes.
8. Cook for an additional 30 to 45 minutes, stirring occasionally.
9. Bring a small pot of water to boil.
10. Stir in pasta, and cook for 6 to 8 minutes, until just tender.
11. Drain and add to the soup.
12. Add the salt and pepper to taste.
13. Turn on broiler.
14. In a small bowl, mix garlic with remaining olive oil.
15. Divide between the six slices of bread, spreading on one side.
16. Toast the garlic-covered sides under the broiler.
17. To serve, place one slice of bread, garlic side up, in a deep soup bowl.
18. Ladle soup over bread.
19. Drizzle with additional olive oil, if desired.

Linguine w/Sautéed Cabbage & Lentils (Pasta Con Cavolo & Lenticchie)

Serves 6

½ cup dried lentils, rinsed and sorted
3 cup vegetable broth
2 sprigs fresh thyme
1 bay leaf
1 lb linguine
6 cup Savoy cabbage, shredded
2 tbsp. extra virgin olive oil
3 cloves garlic, minced
red pepper flakes, to taste
salt and pepper, to taste

1. Place lentils in a pot with 2 cups of the vegetable broth, the thyme and the bay leaf.
2. Bring to a boil, then reduce heat to low and simmer until lentils are soft but not falling apart, 20 to 25 minutes.
3. Bring a pot of salted water to boil and cook the linguine according to package directions.
4. While pasta is cooking, heat olive oil in a large skillet over medium heat.
5. Add garlic and chili and sauté for 30 seconds, stirring constantly.
6. Add cabbage and toss to combine.
7. Add remaining vegetable broth, cover, and steam over medium-low heat for 5 to 7 minutes, until the cabbage is tender but not mushy.
8. Drain pasta and add to skillet.
9. Add cooked lentils, discarding thyme stems and bay leaf.
10. Toss well and season to taste with salt and pepper.
11. Serve with Parmesan, if desired.

Tuscan-Style Pasta And Cannellini

Serves 4

¼ cup extra virgin olive oil
4 cloves garlic
¼ pound curly escarole or 1 small bunch
  arugula, sliced
1 14.5 oz. can pasta ready diced tomatoes
1 16 oz. can cannellini (white kidney beans),
  rinsed & drained
⅔ cup dry white wine
¼ cup basil leaves, thinly sliced
12 ounces spaghetti
salt & pepper to taste

1. Cook pasta according to package directions.
2. Drain, keep warm, set aside.
3. To make sauce, heat oil in a large skillet, add garlic and cook over medium-low heat for 1 minute.
4. Add escarole or arugula, stir occasionally until wilted, about 2 minutes (1 min. for arugula).
5. Add undrained tomatoes, beans, and wine.
6. Simmer 5 minutes, stirring occasionally, then stir in basil and simmer 1 minute.
7. Toss sauce with hot spaghetti, season with salt & pepper, toss again, and serve immediately.

Fresh Tomato Sauce

3 cups peeled, finely chopped tomatoes (about 1½ lbs)
4 tablespoons olive oil
2 cloves garlic, finely minced
¾ teaspoons salt (or to taste)
1 teaspoon minced fresh basil
pinch oregano
freshly ground black pepper
several drops lemon juice
1 lb. angel hair pasta

1. Place tomatoes in a large bowl and mix with olive oil, garlic, salt, basil, oregano and pepper.
2. Allow to marinate at room temp for two hours.
3. Add lemon juice. Serve over hot pasta.

Note: Sauce can be prepared in advance, but be sure to let it come to room temp before serving.
Somehow, though, to me it never tastes the same after it's been refrigerated.

Risotto

1 cup arborio rice (important to use this kind), unrinsed, unwashed
2.5 cup vegetable broth
2 tbsp. olive oil
2 cloves garlic, minced
½ onion, finely chopped
2-3 cup any vegetable you like

1. You need two pots for this dish, and one should be a deep non-stick pot.
2. First, heat the broth until hot (not boiling, but steaming).
3. In the non-stick pot, heat the olive oil over medium heat. Sauté the garlic and onion in the olive oil until translucent.
4. Add the rice, and cook, stirring frequently, until rice is well-coated, and translucent (about 2 minutes).
5. Add ½ cup of hot broth to rice, and stir until broth is absorbed.
6. At this point, add the vegetable of choice (I'll usually use a head of chard, or broccoli, or a can of white beans, red bell pepper, and zucchini).
7. Continue adding broth in ½ cup increments, stirring until it is absorbed between each addition.
8. Once all broth is absorbed, risotto is done.

Pasta D'Cyriletti

Serves 4
2 cloves garlic, chopped
1½ pounds plum tomatoes, peeled & chopped
½ cup dry white wine
2 tablespoons capers, drained & rinsed
½ cup pitted black olives, chopped
1 small dried chili pepper or ¼ tsp. red pepper
1 teaspoon fresh oregano, finely chopped
⅓ cup Italian parsley, chopped
16 ounces linguine

1. Heat oil in a deep frying pan. Sauté garlic lightly.
2. Add tomatoes, wine, capers, olives, chili pepper, and oregano. Cook over medium heat for about 20 minutes, stirring often.
3. Add parsley, lower heat, and cook gently for a few minutes. Discard chili pepper.
4. While sauce is cooking, cook pasta in boiling salted water according to package directions.
5. Drain and place in a large bowl.
6. Top with sauce.

Sorta Putanesca

Serves 2
1 can diced tomatoes, Muir brand
½ onion, chopped
2 cloves garlic, pressed
¼ cup capers
½ cup kalamata olives
2 tbsp. olive oil
2 tbsp. red wine
salt, to taste
freshly ground black pepper, to taste

1. Heat olive oil in a skillet over medium heat.
2. Sauté onions and garlic until onion is translucent.
3. Add a can of organic diced tomatoes (Muir is really good), the capers, olives, and red wine.
4. Add salt and black pepper, as copiously as your taste can tolerate. Simmer for about 10 minutes.
5. Serve over a pasta large enough to handle it, spaghetti or linguine are tasty.
6. Top with grated Parmesan or vegan parmesan substitute.

Portabella Bruschetta

Serves 5
3 big portabella mushrooms
olive oil
4 to 6 cloves garlic, coarsely chopped
salt
2 tablespoons lemon juice
1 baguette, sliced

1. Clean the portabellas by wiping them with damp paper towels.
2. Remove their stems, reserve them and chop them.
3. Sautee the stems and garlic in olive oil and season to taste with ½ teaspoon of the lemon juice and salt.
4. Brush the tops of the portabellas with olive oil.
5. Place them directly over coals on a barbeque for about ten minutes, until their edges show browned grill marks.
6. Turn the mushrooms over and spread the stem and garlic mixture over their tops, and drizzle with olive oil.
7. Grill for another five to ten minutes.
8. Remove the mushrooms from the grill, drizzle them with the remaining lemon juice and let them cool to room temperature.
9. Cut them into quarters, place the quarters on toasted baguette slices, and serve.

Tofu Spaghetti Balls

1 pound tofu
¼ cup walnuts, chopped or ground in dry blender.
2 medium onions, minced
½ cup quick cooking oats
2 tablespoons chopped parsley
1 teaspoon dry basil
½ teaspoon dill weed
½ teaspoon garlic powder
½ teaspoon thyme
2 tablespoons soy sauce
1 tablespoon corn starch
½ cup whole wheat flour
vegetable oil, for browning
2 cups tomato or spaghetti sauce

1. Wrap tofu in cloth or paper towels for a few minutes to remove excess water.
2. Mash. Mix well with all ingredients except oil and tomato sauce.
3. Form into 24 small balls and flatten slightly as you place them in oiled baking dish.
4. Sprinkle a little oil on each.
5. Bake at 375 for 20-25 minutes, turning once to brown both sides.
6. Spread tomato sauce over balls.
7. Bake at 350°F for another 15-20 minutes.
8. Serve over pasta or on a sandwich.

Spaghetti Sauce with Lentils

1. Boil about ½ to 1 cup of lentils red and green.
2. until nearly tender (about 20-30 minutes).
3. In the meantime, fry a medium-sized onion and a crushed garlic clove in a medium sized skillet in olive oil.
4. Add mushrooms and capsicum, Add your own home made spaghetti sauce to the fried veggies or use bottled. (I use Paul Newmans.
5. Stir and simmer with the cooked lentils until the lentils are soft.
6. Add spices of your choice.
7. cumin, basil and oregano, plus salt and pepper.
8. If you like hot food, chili powder is also add cubed tofu to mine, and simmer on very low heat until the spaghetti water boils and is cooked.
9. So I guess this takes about 20 minutes all together.
10. If you decide to use tofu, if you wrap the tofu in a clean dish towel while the veggies are cooking, it will dry out a bit and soak up more of the ingredients as it rehydrates when added to the sauce.

Spinach Ravioli

Serves 6

1 cup tomatoes, peeled, seeded, diced
1 small onion, oven roasted
1 cup mushrooms, minced
2 teaspoons garlic, minced
½ pound spinach leaves, blanched, chopped
¼ cup nonfat cottage cheese
¾ cup tofu, mashed
2 tablespoons fresh basil, minced
freshly ground black pepper
salt, to taste
48 eggless pot sticker skins

1. In a large saucepan, combine the tomatoes, onion, mushrooms and garlic.
2. Cook over medium heat until the liquid from the mushrooms completely evaporates and the mixture is somewhat dry.
3. Be careful not to burn it.
4. Set aside to cool.
5. In a large bowl, combine the tomato mixture, spinach, cottage cheese, tofu, and basil.
6. Season to taste with pepper and salt.
7. On a cutting board, lay out a single layer of potsticker skins.
8. Using a pastry brush, moisten the edges with water.
9. Place 1 tablespoon of the spinach mixture onto
10. the center of each skin.
11. Cover with a second potsticker skin and press the edges together with the tines of a fork to seal.
12. Cook the ravioli in boiling water or vegetable stock for 3 minutes, or until the potsticker skin is al dente.
13. Serve hot.

Mushroom and Seitan Stroganoff

Serves 4

8 ounces fettuccine
1 tablespoon oil
1 medium onion, chopped
2 cloves garlic, minced
4 cups mushrooms, thinly sliced
3 tablespoons lemon juice
1 teaspoon tarragon
½ teaspoon sweet paprika
2 cups vegetable broth
2 tablespoons tahini
½ teaspoon pepper
1 tomato, peeled, seeded and diced, optional
2 tablespoons fresh minced parsley
½ pound dried shiitake mushrooms
12 ounces seitan, cut into strips

1. Heat oil in a large skillet and sauté the onion, garlic and seitan, until onions are translucent.
2. Add mushrooms and continue cooking until mushrooms soften.
3. Add lemon juice and spices and mix well.
4. Mix broth and tahini and add to mushroom mixture, and cook until it thickens.
5. Add tomato.
6. Remove from heat.
7. Season to taste with pepper.
8. Spoon mixture over hot noodles.
9. Garnish with parsley.

Soups & Stews

Veggie-Mac Soup

Serves 8

3 14.5 oz. cans vegetable broth or imitation chicken broth
1 16 oz. pkg frozen mixed vegetables
1 14.5 oz. can Italian stewed tomatoes, undrained and chopped
1 8.5 oz. can whole kernel corn, drained
2 tablespoons dried onion flakes
¼ teaspoon pepper
2 cloves garlic, minced
½ cup elbow macaroni, uncooked

1. Combine first 7 ingredients in a Dutch oven.
2. Cover and bring to a boil.
3. Stir in pasta, reduce heat, and simmer, uncovered, 20 minutes or until pasta is tender.

Vegetable Minestrone Soup

Serves 1

½ cup Chopped onion
1 Leek, white part only Chopped
2 Cloves garlic
1 can (28 oz) tomatoes, crushed
4 Red potatoes, quartered
2 Carrots, sliced
1 Celery stalk, sliced
½ cup Barley
1½ cups Corn
1 cup (frozen) peas
1 can (16 oz) white beans (drained)
1 teaspoon Basil
1 Bay leaf
1 tablespoon Salt
1 teaspoon Black pepper

1. Sauté garlic, onions and leek.
2. Add tomatoes and one can water, potatoes, celery and carrots and cook 25 minutes.
3. Add barley and cook 10 minutes.
4. Add remaining ingredients and cook 20 minutes or until barley is done.
5. Makes about 1 gallon.

Tuscan Chickpea Soup

One and a half pints vegetable stock
¼ teaspoon rosemary
1 tablespoon tomato puree
1 lb. Passatta or 1 can tomatoes
1 tin chickpeas (drained)
4 tablespoons olive oil
3 cloves garlic
2 ozs soup pasta (any small pasta will do - tiny macaroni works well)

1. Make vegetable stock and put rosemary and tomato puree in jug with it.
2. Blend chickpeas and passatta/tomatoes
3. together so you get a smoothish mixture.
4. Fry garlic in olive oil for 30 seconds, then add the stock mixture and chickpea mixture to it.
5. Bring to boil, cover and simmer for five minutes.
6. Add pasta, stir, cover and simmer for 10 minutes, stirring occasionally to separate the pasta.
7. Season to taste.
8. Serve with ciabatta bread, or whatever comforts you most.

Meat eaters and veggies alike adore this recipe! Remember the more Rosemary you put in the saltier it will taste - so take it gently.

Garlic Soup

2 tablespoons margarine
1 tablespoon olive oil
12 garlic cloves, quartered
6 slices Italian bread, cut into 1-inch cubes
½ cup dry red wine
6 cups vegetable stock, canned or use my favorite homemade stock
1 tablespoon chopped fresh parsley
salt and pepper to taste

1. In a heavy pot, melt butter with olive oil over low heat.
2. Add garlic and cook 2 minutes; be careful not to burn. Add bread to pan and toss.
3. Add wine, stock, and parsley.
4. Bring to a boil over medium heat, reduce heat to low, and cook 10 minutes.
5. Season with salt and pepper. Serve.

Tomato Garlic Soup with Tortellini

6 cups simple garlic broth
(8 cups vegetable stock, or 8 cups of water and 2 cubes vegetable bouillon
3 tablespoons minced garlic - 1 large head
2 tablespoons olive oil
½ teaspoons paprika
1 sprig fresh sage
1 sprig fresh thyme
several sprigs fresh parsley
salt and pepper to taste

1. Sauté garlic in olive oil and add boiling stock.
2. Stir in the paprika.
3. Tie the sprigs together to form a bouquet.
4. Simmer for up to 30 minutes for the most intense flavor.
5. Remove the bouquet and add salt and pepper to taste.)
6. 2 cups undrained canned tomatoes or 4 medium fresh tomatoes 9 ounces fresh or frozen tortellini (filled with chopped greens such as endive, chard, escarole, spinach, kale or watercress - simmer 2 to 3 minutes until wilted)
7. In a saucepan bring the garlic broth to a simmer.
8. While the broth heats, chop the tomatoes.
9. Add the tomatoes to the broth, return it to a boil and simmer for 10 to 15 minutes.

Note: I always add more tomatoes (I've used 10 or more before) and I cook it all day.
The recipe says to cook the tortellini separately, but I find that it cooks just fine in the soup and they get the flavor of the tomatoes all the way through.

Italian Vegetable Stew

Serves 8

2 tablespoons olive oil
1 large onion, chopped
2 stalks celery, chopped
2 cloves garlic, minced
1 28 oz. can diced tomatoes with juice
1 14.5 oz. can diced tomatoes w/garlic and
  onions, with juice
3 cups vegetable broth
1 16 oz. pkg frozen Italian green beans
1 15 oz. can cannellini beans, rinsed & drained
2 teaspoons dried basil
2 teaspoons Italian seasoning
salt & pepper to taste

1. Heat oil in a Dutch oven.
2. Cook onion and celery until soft, about 5 minutes; add garlic, and cook about 2 additional minutes.
3. Add tomatoes, vegetable broth, frozen green beans, and seasonings to taste.
4. Bring to a boil; reduce heat, and simmer about 15 min. Add cannellini beans and cook 10 more min.

Irish Seitan Stew

2 cups seitan, diced
1 cup carrots, roll-cut
1 cup parsnips, roll-cut
1 cup onion, diced
1 cup potatoes, peeled and diced
2 bay leaves
½ teaspoon rosemary, whole
½ teaspoon garlic, minced
½ teaspoon basil
1 tablespoon parsley, fresh, chopped
2 cups water
5 teaspoons tamari soy sauce
½ cup celery, flaked
4 tablespoons water, cold
4 tablespoons cornstarch

1. Put seitan, veggies (except celery), and herbs and spices in a large pot (Dutch oven or small stock pot will do).
2. Sautee in a little water or veggie broth at medium heat for about 8 minutes, stirring to prevent burning.
3. Add water and tamari and bring to a simmer.
4. Cook about 10 more minutes or until veggies are soft.
5. Add celery (add at end to help retain color and texture). Mix the 4 tablespoons cold water with the cornstarch. Turn off heat under stew.
6. Vigorously stir in cornstarch solution. Turn heat back on under stew and stir until thickened.
7. Serve with a good brown bread.

Chunky Italian Soup

Serves 8

1 tablespoon olive oil
1 medium onion, chopped
2 14.5 oz. cans Italian tomatoes
1 10.75 oz. can tomato soup with basil, undiluted
4 cups water
2 cloves garlic, minced
2 teaspoons dried basil
2 teaspoons dried oregano
1 teaspoon salt
½ teaspoon freshly ground black pepper
1 tablespoon chili powder, (optional)
2 16 oz. cans kidney beans, rinsed & drained
1 16 oz. can Italian green beans, drained
1 carrot, chopped
1 zucchini, chopped
8 ounces rotini pasta, cooked

1. Heat olive oil in a Dutch oven over medium heat and cook onion until tender.
2. Stir in tomatoes, next 7 ingredients, and, if desired, chili powder.
3. Bring to a boil.
4. Reduce heat and simmer, stirring occasionally, 30 minutes.
5. In the meantime, during last few minutes of simmering soup, cook pasta per package directions, drain, and set aside.
6. Stir in kidney beans and remaining ingredients.
7. Simmer, stirring occasionally, for 15 minutes.
8. Stir in pasta.
9. Sprinkle with cheese if desired.

Salads

Pasta Salad II

Serves 4

Dressing:
1 tablespoon olive oil
2 tablespoons balsamic vinegar
1 teaspoon dijon mustard, up to 2
½ teaspoon salt
freshly ground black pepper to taste

Salad:
½ pound uncooked spiral shell or elbow pasta
water for boiling
1 teaspoon olive oil
¼ pound fresh asparagus
¼ pound carrots
2 tablespoons capers
¼ cup chopped fresh parsley

1. Combine oil, vinegar, mustard, salt and pepper to make a dressing.
2. Cook pasta according to package directions.
3. While pasta is cooking, slice asparagus lengthwise in quarters, then across in 1 ½-inch pieces.
4. Cut carrots in similar-size julienned pieces.
5. Steam or blanch vegetables for a few minutes.
6. Drain pasta well.
7. Stir in oil to prevent pasta from sticking together.
8. Combine with vegetables, dressing, capers and parsley.
9. Adjust flavor with more vinegar or salt, and serve warm or at room temperature.
10. Makes 4 servings.

Linguine, Roasted Garlic Cloves and Wilted Greens Salad

Serves 4
1 whole head garlic, unpeeled
2 teaspoons olive oil
1 tablespoon minced garlic
7 firmly packed cups hardy greens (such as kale, collard, chard, mustard greens or a mixture), rinsed, shredded, stems cut into 1-inch strips
½ teaspoon salt
8 ounces linguine
1 tablespoon dark sesame oil, up to 2
2 tablespoons fresh-squeezed lemon juice
1 tablespoon sesame seeds, toasted (see note), up to 2

1. Preheat oven to 350°F. Place garlic on baking sheet.
2. Bake 15 to 20 minutes, or until garlic feels soft when squeezed.
3. Peel, discard skin and separate cloves.
4. Heat olive oil in large skillet until sizzling.
5. Add minced garlic; stir.
6. Add greens.
7. Cover, lower heat and cook until greens are tender to taste but still retain color, 5 to 7 minutes.
8. Add salt; cover again.
9. Cook linguine according to package directions; drain.
10. Add to skillet along with garlic.
11. Reduce heat to low; stir 1 minute.
12. Remove from heat; add sesame oil and lemon juice.
13. Adjust salt.
14. Serve garnished with sesame seeds.
15. Makes 4 servings.

Note: To toast sesame seeds, place in single layer in small skillet over low heat. Toast until slightly dark, turning often to prevent burning.

Bowtie Pasta and Black Bean Salad

Serves 4

8 ounces bowtie pasta (farfalle)
¼ cup balsamic dressing (recipe follows), up to ½
5 ½ cups cooked black beans
   (or 14-oz. can black beans, drained)
1 large red bell pepper cut into chunks
6 kalamata olives pitted and thinly sliced, up to 12
1 tablespoon drained and minced capers
salt (optional)
chili oil (optional)
chopped basil and chopped parsley
   (or a mixture of both, for garnish)

1. Cook and drain pasta according to package directions.
2. Plunge into cold water to stop cooking.
3. Add ¼ cup of dressing; toss well.
4. Add black beans, bell pepper, olives and capers.
5. Before serving, stir in remaining dressing to taste.
6. Add salt and sprinkle with chili oil if desired.
7. Garnish with basil and parsley.

Mediterranean Mixed Salad

Serves 2-3

½ oz. wakame or dulse, soaked 3-4 minutes, finely cut
½ lettuce, shredded
¼ cucumber, finely sliced
1 punnet mustard cress
5-6 radishes, finely cut
¼ cup small pickled onions, gherkins or olives

For the dressing:
1 block fresh tofu
pickled or olive water (amount as desired)
1 tsp. corn or olive oil
2 tbsp. finely cut chives or salad onions

1. Mix the salad ingredients in a large serving bowl.
2. To prepare the dressing, bring a small amount of water to the boil, add the tofu and boil for 5 minutes.
3. Blend with the pickle water and oil, to your chosen consistency.
4. Add some chives, to taste.
5. Serve the dressing separately from the salad.

Quick Artichoke Pasta Salad

Serves 6

The liquid from marinated artichoke hearts turns into a zingy dressing for this marvelously simple macaroni salad.

4 ounces (about 1 cup) salad macaroni or other
   medium-sized pasta
1 jar (6 ounce) marinated artichoke hearts
¼ pound mushrooms, quartered
1 cup cherry tomatoes, halved
1 cup medium-size pitted ripe olives
1 tablespoon chopped parsley
½ teaspoon dry basil leaves
salt and pepper

1. Cook macaroni according to package directions; drain well, rinse with cold water, and drain again.
2. Turn into a large bowl. Add artichokes and their liquid, mushrooms, cherry tomatoes, olives, parsley, and basil; toss gently. Cover and refrigerate for at least 4 hours or until next day.
3. Before serving, season with salt and pepper to taste.

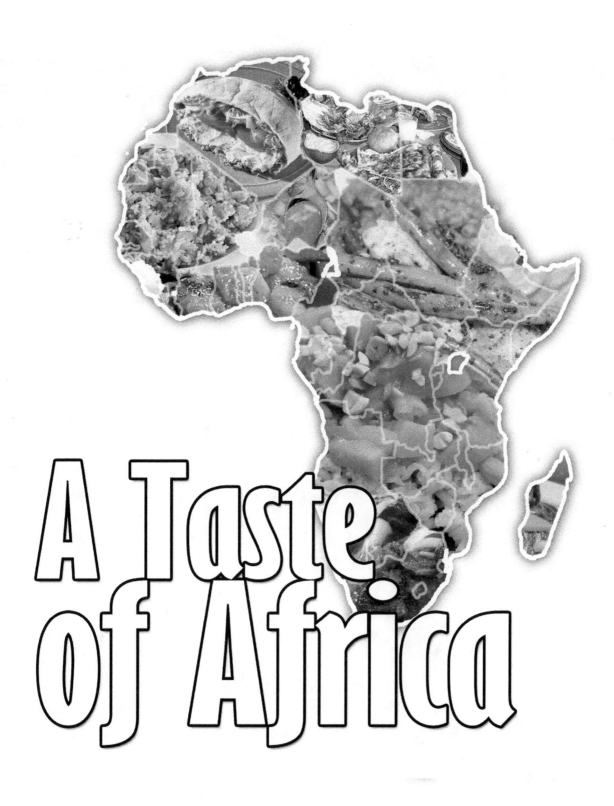

A Taste
of Africa

A Taste of Africa
Appetizers, Sides & Small Items

Uji (Fermented Porridge)

½ cup maize meal or corn meal flour
¼ cup millet flour
¼ cup sorghum flour
water
sugar to taste

1. Put all of the flour into a plastic container and mix well. Pour enough water into the mixture to make a paste.
2. Mix well, cover and leave the mixture at room temperature for 2 days so it can ferment.
3. Skim out the froth that has formed on top of the water, stir the mixture and pour it into a cooking pan.
4. Cook at medium to high heat, stirring continuously until it thickens.
5. You can add more water as needed until the uji cooks into a smooth, runny consistency.
6. Add sugar to taste.

Note: You can skip the fermentation process by buying ready-to-cook fermented uji flour available from Kenyan grocery stores and supermarkets.

Kenyan Cabbage

Serves 4
2 medium tomatoes, chopped
½ medium onion, chopped
2 tbsp. vegetable oil
1 small green cabbage, chopped

1. Fry the tomatoes and onions in the oil until the onions are brown.
2. Add the cabbage and stir over low heat. Cook for 2-3 minutes.
3. The cabbage should be a bit crisp when served.
4. Serve with rice, ugali and a meat of your choice.
5. *You can substitute the cabbage with sukuma wiki or spinach

Harissa (Hot Pepper Sauce)

8 oz. fresh hot chilies
½ teaspoon yellow asafoetida powder (or garlic to your taste)
1 tsp. ground caraway seeds
1 tsp. salt
1½ tsp. fresh ground pepper
1½ tsp. ground cumin
1 tsp. ground coriander

1. Place the chilies in a processor and chop until coarsely ground.
2. Add the other ingredients (except oil) and process until smooth.

Caramelized Ripe Plantains

Serves 6-8
Plantains turn up everywhere in West African cooking. They're nibbled as street snacks, pounded into mashes and Foofoos, added to soups and stews, and served as dessert. Plantains are used at virtually every stage of their maturing process.
The green ones are peeled, sliced, and deep-fried as chips. The ripe yellow ones are used as a starch to accompany main dishes, and the super ripe black ones in which the starch has turned to sugar appear as desserts. This is one way to serve plantain that appeals to everyone.
4 ripe plantains
1 tablespoon margarine or oil
1 tablespoon sugar

1. Peel the plantains and slice them into ½-inch rounds.
2. Heat the oil or margarine to foaming in a heavy skillet over medium heat.
3. Add the plantain slices to the heated oil or margarine and cook for 5 to 8 minutes, or until they are lightly browned and slightly caramelized.
4. Sprinkle the plantain slices with the sugar, allow the sugar to caramelize slightly, then remove the plantains from the skillet. Serve warm.

These plantain slices are also particularly good when served over rice cream, topped with the caramelized oil or margarine from the pan. Not in the least bit healthful, but traditional soul "comfort" food.

Jollof Rice

Serves 6

1 tablespoon olive oil
1 large onion, sliced
2 (14.5 ounce) cans stewed tomatoes
½ (6 ounce) can tomato paste
1 teaspoon salt
1/4 teaspoon black pepper
1/4 teaspoon cayenne pepper
1/2 teaspoon red pepper flakes
1 tablespoon Worcestershire sauce
1 teaspoon chopped fresh rosemary
2 cups water
2 packs of firm tofu
1 cup uncooked white rice
1 cup diced carrots
½ pound fresh green beans, trimmed and snapped into 1 to 2 inch pieces
¼ teaspoon ground nutmeg

1. Pour oil into large saucepan. Cook onion in oil over medium-low heat until translucent.
2. Stir in stewed tomatoes and tomato paste, and season with salt, black pepper, cayenne pepper, red pepper flakes, Worcestershire sauce and rosemary. Cover, and bring to a boil.
3. Reduce heat, stir in water, and add tofu.
4. Simmer for 30 minutes.
5. Stir in rice, carrots, and green beans, and season with nutmeg.
6. Bring to a boil, then reduce heat to low. Cover, and simmer until the the rice is cooked, 25 to 30 minutes.

Fufu

2-4 lbs. yams (use large, white or yellow yams; not sweet potatoes, not "Louisiana yams"); or equal parts yams and plantain bananas
1 teaspoon butter (optional)

1. Place yams in large pot and cover with cold water. Bring to a boil and cook until the yams are soft (maybe half an hour).
2. Remove pot from heat and cool yams with running water. Drain. Remove peels from yams. Add butter.
3. Put yams in a bowl (or back in the empty pot) and mash with a potato masher, then beat and stir with a wooden spoon until completely smooth. This might take two people: one to hold the bowl and the other to stir.
4. Shape the fufu into balls and serve immediately with meat stew or any dish with a sauce or gravy.
5. To eat it, tear off a small handful with your fingers and use it to scoop up your meat and sauce.

Githeri (Dry Maize & Beans)

Serves 4

½ pound dried red beans
1 pound dried maize (corn)
3 medium onions, chopped
1 tbsp. vegetable oil
salt

1. Cover the red beans and maize with water and soak overnight.
2. Drain. Cover again with water, add salt to taste and boil for 2½ hours or until the maize and beans are soft.
3. Drain and set aside. Fry the onions in the vegetable oil until golden brown.
4. Mix in the maize and beans and simmer for 5 minutes before serving.

Odessa's Candied Yams

Serves 8 to 10

In Africa there are fifty-nine varieties of yellowy white-fleshed yams, but only five of them are eaten. There is no similarity between the yams found in Africa and what we call yams outside Africa, because the yams here are really sweet potatoes. Candying the potatoes is one way to eat them. They can also be baked, fried, or eaten raw.

6 medium yams
1 teaspoon nutmeg
1 teaspoon cinnamon
1 cup water
1 cup sugar
8 tablespoons margarine, salted or unsalted
2 teaspoons vanilla extract

1. Peel the yams and slice them lengthwise.
2. Place the yams in a large pot, cover with water, and bring to a boil.
3. Drain half the water and place the yams and remaining water in a large skillet or pan.
4. Sprinkle with half the nutmeg, cinnamon, and sugar.
5. Bring to a boil and cook for approximately 3 minutes.
6. Add the remaining nutmeg, cinnamon, sugar, and the vanilla extract.
7. Spoon the mixture over all the yams and allow to simmer slowly for 15 minutes until the yams have absorbed all the syrup.
8. Remove from the heat until ready to serve. Cooking time: 25 minutes

African Beans and Potatoes

Serves 8

2 cups dried pinto beans
3 large potatoes, peeled and chopped
2 stalks celery, chopped
salt to taste
large sweet onion, sliced

1. Cook beans until tender.
2. That's about 20 minutes in the pressure cooker (what a marvel of technology!).
3. Obviously, a lot longer if you don't have one.
4. You could use canned beans too, if you wanted to be quick about it.
5. Add potatoes and celery and cook until potatoes are tender.
6. In the pressure cooker that takes anywhere from 2-8 minutes, depending how finely you chop the potatoes.
7. I cut mine into large cubes and it took about 4 minutes (but I live at 5500, so adjust accordingly).
8. Salt to taste.
9. Sauté onion until browned.
10. Mix in with beans and potatoes.
11. If you like it hot, a shot or two of hot sauce would be good.

Mataha (Dry Maize, Beans & Potatoes)

Serves 4-6

½ pound dried red beans
1 pound dried maize (corn)
salt
8 medium potatoes, peeled and cubed
10 pumpkin leaves(or spinach), coarsely chopped

1. Soak the beans and maize overnight in enough water to cover.
2. Drain, cover again with water, add salt and boil for 2½ hours.
3. Drain and set aside. Cover the potatoes with water and boil until soft.
4. Add the pumpkin leaves and cook until tender. Drain.
5. Add the mixture to the maize and beans and mash it all together.
6. The mixture should be thick and firm.

Irio (Maize & Peas Mash)

Serves 6

4 green maize cobs (green corn)
4 medium sized potatoes
2 cups fresh green peas
2 bunches pumpkin leaves (or spinach)
Salt

1. Remove the maize from the cobs and boil with peas until soft.
2. Peel potatoes, wash them and add them to the grain mixture.
3. Add the pumpkin leaves and boil together until potatoes are cooked.
4. Drain, add salt and mash.

For a tastier variation, sauté one medium sized onion in vegetable oil (or butter), add a teaspoon of curry powder and mix it into the mash, stirring well until it is a smooth, soft mixture. Serve with stew.

Sukuma Wiki

Serves 2

8 cups sukuma wiki (kale or collard greens), chopped
2 tablespoons vegetable oil
1 medium onion, chopped
1 tomato, chopped
½ cup water
salt

1. In a cooking pan, add the vegetable oil and onions.
2. Sautee the onions until they are golden brown.
3. Add tomatoes and cook until they soften into a paste.
4. Add the sukuma wiki, salt to taste and ¼ cup water.
5. Let the mixture cook on low heat for approximately 5 minutes or until the sukuma wiki has reached a desired tenderness, and still crunchy.
6. Serve with ugali, rice or chapati and any meat of your choice.

Wali (Coconut Rice)

Serves 6

2 cups rice
pinch salt
4 cups thin coconut milk
2 tablespoons thick coconut milk

1. Put the rice, salt and 4 cups of thin coconut milk in a pot.
2. Bring to a boil, reduce heat, and simmer very gently until the rice is done, about 20 minutes.
3. Watch the pot carefully and add more thin coconut milk if the rice becomes dry before it is done.
4. Just before serving, add thick coconut milk and stir.
5. Serve with meat-substitute stew and vegetables of your choice.

Rice Pilau (Rice Pilaf)

Serves 6

1 pound veggie ham or veggie burger (cut in cubes)
4 garlic cloves
Salt
9 cardamom pods
4 tbsp. vegetable oil
1 large onion, chopped
3 cups rice
10 whole black peppercorns
8 whole cloves
8 cinnamon sticks
1 tsp. ground ginger
¼ cup cumin seed powder
4 small tomatoes
6 cups water

1. Boil the "meat" in salted water until tender.
2. Crush the garlic and cardamom together with 2tbsp. water using a mortar and pestle.
3. Sautee the onion until it is golden brown.
4. Add the rice, meat, garlic and cardamom mixture, peppercorns, cloves, cinnamon, ginger and cumin seed powder.
5. Cook covered over medium heat until all are nicely brown, about 10 minutes.
6. Add the tomatoes. Cook and stir until the tomatoes are thoroughly cooked down to the consistency of a sauce.
7. Add the 6 cups water to the rice mixture, bring to a boil and then cook over very low heat, (while covered) for another 15-20 minutes, until all water is absorbed and the rice is cooked through.
8. Serve with kachumbari.

Pickled Black-Eyed Peas

Serves 8

Black-eyed peas are a part of our African legacy. In this recipe they are marinated with vinegar and hot chili to create a savory dish that is also known as Texas caviar. The black-eyed peas can be eaten as a condiment or a side dish. Here, they are served in a lettuce cup as an appetizer. To save time during the busy holiday, this recipe calls for canned black-eyed peas, though the dish can also be made with fresh or frozen peas. Black-Eyed Peas take on a festive air with the addition of dark purple, red, and green bell pepper.

2 cans (1 pound each) black-eyed peas, drained
  (Note: dried black-eyed peas must marinate overnight.)
¼ cup minced dark purple bell pepper
¼ cup minced red bell pepper
¼ cup minced green bell pepper
1 tablespoon finely minced garlic
1 small onion, minced
2 tablespoons red wine vinegar
1 tablespoon balsamic vinegar
⅓ cup olive oil
2 branches fresh thyme, crumbled
1 head Boston lettuce, separated into 8 leaves

1. Pour the drained black-eyed peas into a medium-sized bowl and add the bell peppers, garlic, and onion.
2. In another bowl, combine the vinegars, olive oil, and thyme to form the marinade.
3. Pour the marinade over the black-eyed pea mixture, cover with plastic wrap, and refrigerate overnight so that the flavors blend, stirring occasionally.
4. When ready to serve, place the lettuce leaves on individual plates, spoon the black-eyed peas onto the lettuce, and serve.

A Taste of Ethiopia & East Africa

Appetizers

Meser Wot (Lentil Wot)

2 yellow onions finely minced
2 tablespoon fresh garlic finely minced
2 tomatoes minced
½ cup olive oil
4 cups of water
1 teaspoon ground cardamom
1 teaspoon black pepper
½ cup berbere powder
1 lbs of organic split lentils

1. In a heavy enamel or iron stewpot, sauté the garlic in the olive oil do not burn or brown and the add the tomatoes and cook over moderate heat for about 5 minutes. Add the onions and continue cooking for 10 minutes or until translucent. Do not let burn. Add the Berbere and the rest of the spices; continue to sauté for 5 more minutes, adding water as needed.
2. Add lentils and cook for 5 minutes stirring frequently. Add about 3 cups of water as needed and bring to boil. Reduce heat and cover let the sauce thicken stirring frequently (you can add water if necessary). Salt to taste. Let cool and serve.

Kik Alicha Recipe

2 yellow onions finely minced
3 tomatoes chopped as finely as you can
3 tablespoon fresh garlic finely minced
3 tablespoon fresh ginger finely minced
½ cup olive oil
4 cups of water
1lbs of yellow split peas
2 teaspoons turmeric
1 teaspoon bessobela
1 teaspoon black pepper
1 teaspoon cardamom
Salt to taste

1. Wash split peas in warm water, drain, and set aside.
2. In a heavy enamel or cast iron pot, cook onions over medium heat for about 5 minutes or until translucent, adding water as needed. Add tomatoes and garlic, cooking for five minutes, being sure to not let them brown or burn. Add the ginger and continue to cooking for 5 more minutes, adding more water as needed. Do not let the mixture get soupy just yet.
3. Add olive oil and stir until well blended. Cook briskly, uncovered, for about 5 minutes stirring occasionally, adding more water as needed. Add split peas and cook for 20 minutes stirring frequently and adding hot water as needed (sauce must be thick, not watery). Add turmeric, bessobela, pepper, and cardamom, or more to taste after about 10 minutes. Salt to taste. Let cool and serve.

Note: Traditional injera is made with teff as the only flour in the recipe, and I've heard that the reason that American restaurants add wheat flour is because US humidity messes with the fermentation process. Preparing injera from scratch is a bit of a scary undertaking if you're not comfortable with fermenting your own food, and I'll warn you – it's a process that can take a week or more.

Injera (Ethiopian Flat Bread)

Serves 1

1¾ cup flour; unbleached white
½ cup self-rising flour
¼ cup whole wheat bread flour
1 pack dry yeast
2½ cup water; warm
½ tsp. baking soda
½ tsp. salt

1. Combine the flours and yeast in a ceramic or glass bowl.
2. Add the warm water and mix into a fairly thin, smooth batter.
3. Let the mixture sit for three full days at room temperature.
4. Stir the mixture once a day.
5. It will bubble and rise.
6. When you are ready to make the injera, add the baking soda and salt and let the batter sit for 10-15 minutes.
7. Heat a small, nonstick 9-inch skillet.
8. When a drop of water bounces on the pan's surface, take about ⅓ cup of the batter and pour it in the skillet quickly, all at once.
9. Swirl the pan so that the entire bottom is evenly coated, then return to heat.
10. The injera is cooked only on one side and the bottom should not brown.
11. When the moisture has evaporated and lots of "eyes" appear on the surface, remove the injera.
12. Let each injera cool and then stack them as you go along.
13. If the first injera is undercooked, try using less of the mixture, perhaps ¼ cup, and maybe cook it a bit longer. Be sure not to overcook it.
14. Injera should be soft and pliable so that it can be rolled or folded, like a crepe.

Injera II (100% Teff)

Makes about 4 to 6 injera

For the best results, it's perhaps better to strart with a (previously made) starter batch. Some folks/restaurants in the US substitute mixtures with wheat and self rising wheat flour to save time but it's not authentic. The key is allowing it to ferment (long enough) to the point that it develops the distinctive flavor of Injera; otherwise it's flat and pasty. Tempature is also key.

The starter:

* Takes five days. If you want to have some starter left over to make injera again, wait seven days.

3/4 cup water, room temp.   ¼ cup teff starter
 (70°F)*   1-3/4 cups water, at room
½ cup teff flour   temperature
A pinch active yeast (about   1-3/4 cups teff flour
1/8 tsp)   ¼ tsp salt

For the Injera / Begin with the starter first:

1. **Day 1:** Combine ingredients for the starter in a bowl.
2. Loosely cover the starter with the lid/cloth and ferment for two days on the counter or someplace that is about 70 degrees. You should see some rising in about four hours. Let alone for 2 days.
3. **Day 3:** Stir the starter. This is when the funk begins. The starter has a very yeasty and grassy smell. You will also notice that small bubbles on the surface now.
4. Feed the starter 1/3 cup teff flour and ½ cup water and loosely cover with the lid. Let alone for 2 days.
5. **Day 5:** Starter should have separated into distinct layers. You would think that something has gone wrong with it – what's with watery layer on top and dense muddy flour at the bottom! But that's exactly what we are looking for Stir starter, it should be slightly fizzy and have a very strong grassy aroma. Feed with 1/3 cup teff flour and ½ cup water. Loosely cover and allow to sit alone for at least 4 hours before using to make Injera. You should have about 2 cups of starter by now.

Note: If you go to Day 7, follow Day 3 instructions for Day 5. You will have left over starter to make Injera again in the future this way.

Now lets go to the Injera recipe:

For the Mix.

6. Place the starter in a bowl. Pour the water over the starter and stir to dissolve.
7. Add the teff flour and mix until the batter is smooth. It will have the consistency of thin pancake batter.
8. Ferment. Cover and let stand for 5 to 6 hours at

room temperature. Reserve ¼ cup of the starter for the next batch.

9. **Add the salt and stir to dissolve.**
10. **Heat a 10- or 12-inch skillet over medium heat (you'll also need a tight-fitting lid).** Using a paper towel, wipe the skillet with a thin layer of vegetable oil. Pour about ½ cup (for a 10-inch skillet) or 3/4 cup (for a 12-inch skillet) of batter in the center of the skillet.
11. Tilt and swirl the skillet immediately to coat evenly.
12. Let the bread cook for about 1 minute, just until holes start to form on the surface.
13. **Cover the skillet with the lid to steam the injera.**
14. Cook for about 3 minutes, just until the edges pull away from the sides and the top is set.

The first 1-2 Injera's might be a slight disaster (like pancakes) augh – Don't worry. The rest of them will be pillows, promise! You don't have to turn the Injera. Just cook it on one side. It does not get the spongy texture immediately. But let it rest for 3-5 minutes and it suddenly gets that amazing texture. There is no muddy, bitter taste of Teff either. Serve it with any spicy dish. Enjoy!!

Ethiopian Cabbage Dish

½ cup olive oil
4 carrots, thinly sliced
1 onion, thinly sliced
1 teaspoon sea salt
½ teaspoon ground black pepper
½ teaspoon ground cumin
¼ teaspoon ground turmeric
½ head cabbage, shredded
5 potatoes, peeled and cut into 1-inch cubes

1. Heat the olive oil in a skillet over medium heat. Cook the carrots and onion in the hot oil about 5 minutes.
2. Stir in the salt, pepper, cumin, turmeric, and cabbage and cook another 15 to 20 minutes.
3. Add the potatoes; cover. Reduce heat to medium-low and cook until potatoes are soft, 20 to 30 minutes.

Injera III
Servings: 8
Here is an alternative to the previous recipes for injera. It's quicker and much less complicated.
4 cup Self-rising flour
1 cup Whole wheat flour
1 tsp. Baking powder
2 cup Club soda

1. Combine flours and baking powder in a bowl.
2. Add club soda plus about 4 cups water.
3. Mix into a smooth, fairly thin batter.
4. Heat a large, non-stick skillet.
5. When a drop of water bounces on the pan's surface, dip enough batter from the bowl to cover the bottom of the skillet, and pour it in quickly, all at once.
6. Swirl the pan so that the entire bottom is evenly coated, then set it back on the heat.
7. When the moisture has evaporated and small holes appear on the surface, remove the injera.
8. It should be cooked only on one side, and not too browned.
9. If your first one is a little pasty and undercooked, you may need to cook a little longer or to make the next one thinner.
10. But, as with French crepes, be careful not to cook them too long, or you'll have a crisp bread that may be tasty but won't fold around bits of stew.
11. Stack the injera one on top of the other as you cook, covering with a clean cloth to prevent their drying out.

Ethiopian Vegetable Bowl

Serves 8

This satisfying Ethiopian vegetable stew is extremely fragrant, and is often served over a grain dish called ingera. If ingera is not available, steamed basmati rice makes a great substitute.

¼ cup vegetable oil	3 large onions, chopped
½ tsp. ground ginger	4 large carrots, cubed
½ tsp. ground turmeric	4 large potatoes, cubed
½ tsp. ground blk pepper	¼ head cabbage, chopped
1 tsp. ground cloves	2 cups tomato puree
1 tsp. fenugreek seeds	2 cups water salt and
1 head garlic, minced	pepper to taste
1 tsp. salt	

1. Heat the oil in a large skillet over medium-high heat. Stir in the ginger, turmeric, black pepper, cloves, fenugreek, garlic, and one teaspoon salt.
2. Continue to stir until the spices and garlic are well coated in oil, about 30 seconds. Stir in the onions; cook, stirring, until translucent, about 5 minutes.
3. Add the carrots, potatoes, and cabbage; cook, stirring frequently, until the vegetables begin to soften, about 3 minutes.
4. Stir in the tomato puree and the water. Continue to cook over very low heat, until vegetables are soft and the tomato sauce thickens, about 30 to 40 minutes.
5. Taste for seasoning and add additional salt and pepper, if needed.

Atar Allecha (Ethiopian)

Serves 4

⅓ cup Onion, chopped
2 cloves Garlic, finely chopped
1 tablespoon Corn oil
1 cup Split green peas; soaked, cooked and drained
½ teaspoon Tumeric, ground
½ teaspoon Salt
3 teaspoons Hot green pepper, finely chopped
1 cup water

Atar Allecha is a spiced green pea puree.

1. Soak peas for one hour.
2. Cook for ½ hour. Drain. Mash.
3. Set aside. In dry pan over moderate low heat, stir fry the onion and garlic for 2 mins.
4. Add oil and stir fry one minute more.
5. Add the mashed peas, turmeric, salt, and chili.
6. Mix well. Add the water and cook 3-4 mins longer to reduce the mixture to a thick, green, well spiced puree. Serve with warm Injeera.

Tasty Couscous Summer Dish

Serves 1

½ aubergine
½ squash
½ onion
½ yellow or red paprika (bell pepper)
½ peeled tomato

1. Cut the vegetables into thick (about finger thick) slices and put in a big bowl (chop tomatoes into quarter segments).
2. Pour a few tablespoons of olive oil over, some pressed garlic (optional) and some salt.
3. Mix so all the vegetables are lightly covered with oil.
4. Grease a pan with olive oil and grill vegetables in a hot oven for 30-40 minutes, until they are lightly brown but still juicy.
5. Take out and let cool to room temperature.

Part 2: Make the cous-cous in a big bowl (about ⅓ of a cup per person). Let cool to room temperature.

Part 3: "False" Harissa sauce
⅓ cup olive oil
2 tbsp. cummin (the brown kind used in among others Indian cooking)
3 tbsp. tomato paste (pure pureed tomato)
4 tbsp. lime juice (about 2 limes)
salt

1. Mix well, using a whisk is helpful.
2. Taste and add more tomato paste or oil if it is too sour.

Part 4:
Iceberg salad
firm plain tofu
black onion seeds

1. Cover the cous-cous with about an inch of cut iceberg salad.
2. Cube feta cheese or firm tofu and sprinkle over the salad.
3. Place the grilled vegetables on top and pour some of the dressing over.
4. Sprinkle black onion seeds over.
5. Serve with extra dressing on the side.

Amhari Mesir Wat–Ethiopian Lentil Bowl

Serves 8

½ cup red lentils	1 garlic
2 large onions	½ tsp. ground ginger
½ cup oil	¼ tsp. black pepper
3 tbsp. tomato paste	1 tsp. salt
½ tsp. paprika; sweet or hot	3 cup water

1. Sort the lentils and soak in tap water for 30 minutes.
2. Rinse in running water and drain. Peel and finely chop the onions. Peel and mash the garlic.
3. Heat the oil in large pan and sauté the onion until golden. Add tomato paste and paprika and mix.
4. Add half the water and the garlic, ginger pepper and salt. Stir well and then add the rest of the water, stir again, cover and bring to boil.
5. When the water boil, add the lentils, lower the flame and cook 20-30 minutes, until the lentils soften.
6. Serve hot.

Tunisian-Style Greens And Beans

You need: 30 minutes; Large skillet
3 tablespoons vegetable oil
1 medium onion, sliced
2 or 3 cloves garlic, minced
1 teaspoon ground coriander
½ teaspoon salt
¼ teaspoon crushed chili flakes
4 cup chopped greens, such as beet greens or Swiss chard
1 cup diced tomatoes with juices
1 cup cooked beans (garbanzos work well)
approx. ½ cup bean cooking water

1. Stew the onion and garlic in a little oil until the onion is soft.
2. Stir in the salt and spices.
3. Chop the greens and stir them in.
4. (A little water left on the greens from washing them is good, it helps steam them done.)
5. When the greens wilt, add the tomatoes, beans and some of the bean cooking water.
6. Cook for 10 or 15 minutes.
7. The finished dish should be a little saucy, but not soupy. Add bean water or plain water accordingly.

Garbanzos And Swiss Chard

Serves 4

In the style of the Tunisian Sahel. Cooking time will vary.

¾ pound Swiss chard leaves, stemmed, rinsed and torn into large pieces
2 large cloves garlic, peeled
½ teaspoon coarse salt
1 teaspoon ground coriander
1 small dried red chili
2 tablespoons olive oil
½ cup minced onion
2 teaspoons tomato paste
1 cup Cooked Garbanzos, with ¾ cup cooking liquid
1 lemon, cut in wedges, optional

1. In pot steam, parboil or microwave chard leaves until tender, about 5 minutes. Set leaves in colander to drain.
2. Squeeze out excess moisture and shred coarsely.
3. Crush garlic in mortar with salt, coriander and chili until thick, crumbly paste forms.
4. Heat olive oil in 10-inch skillet and sauté onion until pale-golden.
5. Add garlic paste and tomato paste and stir into oil until sizzling.
6. Add chard, Basic Cooked Garbanzos and cooking liquid and cook, stirring occasionally, 10 minutes.
7. Remove from heat and let stand until ready to serve.
8. (Contents of skillet should be very moist but not soupy. For looser texture, stir in more garbanzo cooking liquid.)
9. Serve warm, at room temperature or cold with lemon wedges.

Note: Broccoli rabe, dandelion leaves, mustard greens, kale or turnip tops may be substituted for Swiss chard. Discard any yellow or damaged leaves and cook like chard.

Algerian Couscous

1 large onion, chopped
½ teaspoons turmeric
¼ teaspoons cayenne
½ cup vegetable stock
1½ teaspoons black pepper
½ teaspoons salt
1 small can tomato paste
3-4 whole cloves 3 medium zucchini
4 small yellow squash or yellow zucchini
¾ large carrots
4 medium yellow or red potatoes, skins on
1 red or green bell pepper
1 15-oz. can garbanzo beans

1. Sauté onion in vegetable stock over med. low heat until translucent.
2. Add all spices and cook for a few more minutes, stirring as needed.
3. Add tomato paste, stir and simmer 2 minutes.
4. Cut the vegetables in large chunks and add all (not the beans) and a dash of cinnamon; add water to cover.
5. Bring to a boil, then reduce heat and simmer, covered, for an hour or so. (This can cook slowly for 2-3 hours, if desired.)
6. Add the drained garbanzos about 5 minutes before you take the veggies off the heat.
7. Put couscous in a bowl. Pour boiling water over couscous and wait about 5 minutes. Fluff with fork.
8. (Ratio of about 1½ to 1 of water to couscous.) For added flavor, add some of the liquid from the veggie stew to the couscous in place of some of the water.
9. Serve the stew over the couscous. Enjoy!

Moroccan Vegetables

2 tsp. margarine
2 cup coarsely chopped cabbage
2 cup chopped onions
5 cup cubed eggplant (1-inch pieces)
1 tsp. turmeric
5 tsp. cinnamon
5 tsp. ground ginger
⅛ tsp. all spice
⅛ saffron threads
2 cup vegetable broth or water
5 cup carrot chunks (1-inch pieces)
5 cup cubed rutabaga (1-inch pieces)
1 cup chopped tomatoes
2 cup chickpeas, drained and rinsed
5 cup golden or dark raisins

1. In a 6-qt. saucepan, melt butter or margarine over medium-high heat.
2. Add the cabbage and onions; cook stirring until the vegetables are softened, about 4 minutes.
3. Add the eggplant; cook stirring until softened, about 3 minutes.
4. Stir in the turmeric, cinnamon, ginger and all spice, and saffron until absorbed.
5. Add the broth and bring to a boil.
6. Add the carrots, rutabaga, tomatoes and bay leaf; cook, covered stirring occasionally, for 40 minutes or until vegetables are tender.
7. Add the chickpeas and raisins; cook covered, 20 minutes longer or until stew is slightly thickened. Discard bay leaf.

Note: This dish is best served with couscous or white basmati rice.

Moroccan Pickled Lemons

1 big glass jar
enough lemons to fill the jar
fresh water
lots of rock salt

1. Rinse lemons well. The idea is to then put long vertical slits in the lemons, without actually slicing them apart into pieces.
2. So, holding the lemons upright, make about 6 or 8 longitudinal cuts, which should end just a centimeter or so before the tips of the lemon.
3. Then, take the rock salt and generously stuff the lemons in the jar and VERY GENTLY completely cover with cold water.
4. Place loosely covered jar in a cool, dark place for about 2 or 3 weeks or so (it might begin to smell sort of funny, but don't worry).
5. Then, drain the jar of its evil-looking liquid contents and start over with fresh salt and water.
6. Let sit in its quiet corner for 2 or 3 more weeks.
7. Finally, you're ready to eat!
8. Drain them one final time, and remove any lingering pieces of fruit from the rind.
9. Eat ONLY the well-rinsed rind slices and enjoy!!

Soups & Salad

African Pineapple Peanut Stew

1 cup onions, chopped
2 garlic cloves, minced or pressed
1 tbsp. vegetable oil
4 cups kale, sliced
½ cup peanut butter
2 cups pineapple, canned crushed and undrained
1 tbsp. tabasco or hot pepper sauce
½ cup cilantro, chopped
taste of salt

1. In a covered saucepan, sauté the onions and garlic in the oil for about 10 minutes, stirring frequently, until the onions are lightly browned.
2. While the onions sauté, wash the kale.
3. Remove the stems. Stack the leaves on a cutting surface and slice crosswise into 1-inch-thick slices.
4. Add the pineapple and its juice to the onions and bring to a simmer.
5. Stir in the kale, cover, and simmer for about 5 minutes, stirring a couple of times, until just tender.
6. Mix in the peanut butter, hot pepper sauce, and simmer for 5 minutes. Add salt to taste.
7. You can use spinach instead of the kale but you may wish to use more as the spinach shrivels up considerably more than the kale does.

African Bean Soup

3 tbsp. margarine or soy spread
2 cups carrots thinly sliced
12 cups boiling water
1 cup black eye peas dry
1 cup navy beans dry
1 cup green pepper diced
3½ tsp. salt
⅛ tsp. crushed red pepper
1 cup salted peanuts chopped
2 tbsp. onion powder
1 tbsp. basil leaves crushed
1½ tsp. ground coriander

1. Melt margarine in large stock pot.
2. Add carrots. Cook for 5 minutes.
3. Add water, Black-Eyed peas, navy beans, green pepper, salt, and crushed red pepper (add more water, if necessary, to cover).
4. Cook, covered, until ingredients are tender, 1½ - 2 hours.
5. Add peanuts, onion powder, basil, and coriander during last 10-15 minutes of cooking.
6. Taste to correct seasonings. Soup should be thick.

Note: If you want more of a peanut flavor, add peanut butter (any kind) to taste during step 4. You can use about ½ of a cup. Time: 15 minutes preparation, 2 hours cooking.

African Bean Soup

Serves 4-6

2-3 medium onions
2 red bell peppers
7 oz. mushrooms
2 cups kidney beans (soak in water overnight - cooked in water - the water is used later)
1-1½ pk. cream of coconut
2 cups hot water
2 cans tomatoes
4 tbsp. tomato puree
2 large broccoli heads
curry powder
pepper and vegetable salt
grated coconut

1. Onions, bell peppers and mushrooms are sautéed in a large frying pan. Set aside.
2. Put next 6 ingredients in a pan and simmer for about 20 minutes.
3. Add the curry powder, salt and pepper.
4. Then add onion, bell pepper and mushroom mixture.
5. Put grated coconut over and serve with bread.

African Vegetarian Stew

Serves 8

4 small kohlrabies, peeled and cut into chunks
½ cup couscous -or- Bulgar Wheat
1 large onion, chopped
¼ cup raisins, dark or golden
2 Sweet potatoes, peeled and cut into chunks
1 tsp. ground coriander
½ tsp. ground cinnamon
½ tsp. ground ginger
½ tsp. ground turmeric
¼ tsp. ground cumin
2 zucchini, sliced thick
5 tomatoes, fresh -or- 16 oz. can tomatoes
15 oz. can garbanzo beans (chick peas with liquid)
3 cup water

1. Combine all the ingredients in a large saucepan.
2. Bring to a boil, lower the heat, and simmer until the vegetables are tender, about 30 minutes.
3. Note: Serve the couscous separately, if desired.
4. Parsnips may be substituted for the kohlrabi.

African Vegetable Stew

Serves 4

1 onion (very large), chopped
1 swiss chard bunch
1 can garbanzo beans, (known also as chickpeas, ceci, etc.)
½ cup raisins
½ cup rice, raw
2 yams
several fresh tomatoes (or large can)
1 garlic clove (or more to taste)
salt and pepper, to taste
tabasco sauce, to taste

1. Fry onion, garlic and white stems of chard until barely limp.
2. Add chopped greens and fry a bit.
3. Either peel the yams or scrub them well with a vegetable brush, then slice them into thick slices.
4. Add garbanzos, raisins, yams, tomatoes, salt and pepper. Cook a couple of minutes.
5. Make a well in the center of the mixture in the pot.
6. Put the rice in the well and pat it down until it's wet.
7. Cover and cook until rice is done, about 25 minutes.
8. Add Tabasco sauce to taste.
9. Note: This is meant to be a spicy vegetable stew. You should add enough Tabasco to make the stew seem spicy to you.

Ethiopian Mixed Vegetable Stew

4 Servings
1 large onion, chopped
4 cloves garlic, chopped
1 teaspoon ginger
3 medium serrano pepper, chopped
2 tablespoons olive oil
2 medium potatoes, chopped
2 medium carrot, chopped
2 cups french-style green beans
1 large bell pepper, chopped
1 teaspoon salt
pepper, to taste
½ teaspoon cayenne
1 teaspoon cinnamon
1 teaspoon cardamom
¼ teaspoon nutmeg
¼ teaspoon cloves
1 can tomatoes, chopped
8 ounces spinach, chopped
rice, cooked

Saute onion, garlic, ginger and chiles in oil for 10 minutes. Add potatoes, carrots, green beans, bell pepper, salt, pepper, cayenne, cinnamon, cardomom, nutmeg and cloves. Saute for 2 minutes.
Add tomatoes and simmer for 45 minutes.
Stir in spinach and simmer for 15 minutes. Serve over rice or with the flat bread injera.

Kachumbari Salad

Serves 6
4 medium tomatoes, sliced
2 medium onions, finely chopped, washed with salted water, anpfd drained
½ cup fresh squeezed lime or lemon juice
1 cup finely chopped cilantro, Dhania or parsley
3 grated carrots

1. Arrange the tomatoes on a serving platter with onions on top.
2. Sprinkle the parsley (or cilantro) over the top.
3. Place the grated carrots to one side.
4. Splash the lemon juice over all.
5. Do not toss. Serve cold with nyamachoma or pilau.

A Taste of Egypt
Appetizers & Side Items

Fool Medemmas (Fava Beans)

Serves 4
This is way of preparing fava beans, which are commonly eaten as a breakfast food in Egypt. The ingredients tend to be common for the dish but may be varied in their quantities.
1 16-ounce can cooked fava beans
1 large onion, chopped
1 large tomato, diced
1½ tablespoons olive oil
1 teaspoon cumin powder
¼ cup parsley, chopped
juice of 2 lemons
salt, pepper, and red chili pepper to taste
pita bread (optional)

1. Pour the beans into a pot and bring to a boil.
2. Mix them well and add remaining ingredients.
3. Bring to a boil again, then reduce to medium heat and cook for about 5 minutes.
4. This dish is usually eaten with pita bread.

Spinach with Dill

Serves 4
1 medium onion, chopped
1 tablespoon vegetable oil
2 garlic cloves, chopped
2 tablespoons chopped fresh dill
1 15-ounce can tomato sauce
10 ounces frozen, thawed spinach
½ cup water
salt and pepper to taste

1. Sauté onions in oil.
2. Add garlic and dill to saucepan and continue to sauté for two minutes.
3. Add tomato sauce and bring to a boil.
4. Simmer for 10 minutes on low heat.
5. Add spinach and water, then bring to a boil again.
6. Cover and simmer on low heat for 15 minutes.
7. Serve warm over cooked rice.

Niter Kebbeh

Servings: 1

1 lb butter; unsalted
¼ cup onions, chopped
2 cloves garlic; minced
2 tsp. ginger; grated, peeled, fresh
½ tsp. turmeric
4 cardamom seeds; crushed
1 cinnamon stick
2 cloves; whole
⅛ tsp. nutmeg
¼ tsp. ground fenugreek seeds
1 tbsp. basil; fresh -or- (1 tsp. dried)

1. In a small saucepan, gradually melt the butter and bring it to bubbling.
2. When the top is covered with foam, add the other ingredients and reduce the heat to a simmer.
3. Gently simmer, uncovered, on low heat.
4. After about 45 to 60 minutes, when the surface becomes transparent and the milk solids are on the bottom, pour the liquid through a cheesecloth into a heat-resistant container.
5. Discard the spices and solids.
6. Covered tightly and stored in the refrigerator, Niter Kebbeh will keep for up to 2 months.

Note: A good quality olive or other oil may be substituted for the butter.

Mchuzi Wa Biringani
(Eggplant Curry)

Serves 4

3 medium sized eggplant vegetables
3 medium sized tomatoes
2 medium sized potatoes
1 bulb of onion
3 table spoons of ghee
1 teaspoon salt or less, for testing

1. After washing (peel potatoes) and cut eggplant, tomatoes and potatoes into small slices.
2. Put in frying pan and add ghee.
3. Fry and continuously keep stirring.
4. When tomatoes and egg plant are well done, add some water and stir until thick curry is formed.
5. Check for readiness of potatoes.
6. If cooked, then all is ready.

Supu Ya Maharage Na Nazi
(Coconut Bean Soup)

Serves 8

½ cup onions finely chopped
½ cup green peppers (capsicum) chopped
1 tea spoon curry powder
1 tea spoon salt
¼ tea spoon hot pepper
3 table spoons margarine or butter
1 cup fresh tomato, cut into ½ inch pieces
2&½ cups kidney beans
2 cups coconut milk
3 cups water
½ cup cooked rice
10 table spoons coconut

In a 3-quart saucepan:

sauté: ½ cup onions, chopped finely
½ cup green peppers, chopped finely
1 tsp. curry powder
1 tsp. salt
¼ tsp. pepper in
3 tbsp. margarine or butter until soft but not brown.

1. Add 1 cup fresh tomato cut in ½-inch pieces.
2. Simmer for two minutes longer.
3. Add: 2½ cups kidney beans (24-oz. Can with liquid), 2 cups coconut milk, 3 cups water.
4. Simmer gently for 10 minutes.
5. Add ½ cup cooked rice.
6. Correct the seasonings to your taste.
7. Serving: serve one-cup portions in attractive soup bowls.
8. Garnish each bowl with 1 tsp. shredded coconut tablespoons

Note: In Tanzania, as in other African countries, soups and sauces are served in a consistency that is as thick as our stews. Coconut Bean Soup would be used there as a meatless main dish by increasing the quantities of beans and rice. However, in adapting this recipe in our test kitchen we thinned it to soup consistency with additional water and served it as a delightful soup course. Any dried beans such as black-eyed peas or pea beans can be used in this soup. Just cover with water and cook until tender before combining them with the other ingredients. Coconut milk and the delicate use of curry give the soup its unusual flavor.

Maharage Ya Nazi (Coconut Creamed Red Kidney Beans)

Serves 4

1 cup red kidney beans, soaked over night
2 cups coconut milk (fresh if possible)
1 onion - large shredded bulb
2 tomatoes sliced in small pieces
1 teaspoon salt or less, for testing
2 green peppers (chilies)

1. Boil beans in 2 cups of water until half cooked, if necessary add more water. (Some beans are so hard that you may have to add water 3 times.)
2. When half cooked, throw out all water, wash under running cold water and put on low fire.
3. Add all other ingredients now, i.e., coconut milk, onion, tomato, green pepper and salt.
4. Stir occasionally with wooden spoon.
5. Use knife or fork, poke the beans to check for softness in order to a certain level of cooking.
6. Your best indicator should be when the beans start to split. Eaten with rice, 'Ugali' or bread like curry.

Ugali (Cornmeal Mush)

Serves 8

1 quart water
1 tea spoon salt
1 cup white cereal (e.g. farina)

Directions – In a 2-quart saucepan:
Boil rapidly 1 quart water or vegetable broth.

1. **Add:** 1 tsp. salt and 1 cup any fine white cereal.
2. Swirl the cereal into the boiling water and cook according to package directions to a thick heavy mush.
3. Keep warm over hot water (in a double boiler) until ready to serve.
4. **Serving:** Put in a big glass or plastic bowl then cover with a big plate.
5. Turn upside down so that 'ugali' which is now bowl shaped gets in the plate.
6. Take a smaller dish and press on the top of 'ugali' to form a hole.
7. Pour coconut cream red kidney beans or tapioca leaves, or duckling into the hole and serve.
8. Usually every one eats together.
9. In case someone wants to eat separately, serve a portion of 'ugali' in their plate and pour any of the above mentioned soups onto it.

Toasted Couscous Vite Vite

Serves 2-4

Regular couscous has a pasta like flavor while this method gives the grains a nutty and smoky taste. If you want to make regular couscous simply read the instructions on the package.

For this recipe, the ratio of couscous to water is always 1:1.5, so you can make any amount using this formula.

1 cup medium size couscous
1.5 cups boiling water

1. Toast the couscous over a low flame in a medium weight frying pan without oil or shortening, stirring and shaking vigorously so the granules don't stick to the bottom.
2. When you smell the rich flavor of the semolina, now slightly darkened and tanned, drop the contents into a deep, covered casserole dish.
3. Add the boiling water immediately.
4. Cover and let the couscous steam for ten minutes.
5. **Warning:** Do not lift the top of the casserole dish for a peek as this seemingly innocuous action will make for lumpy couscous.
6. After 10 minutes remove the cover from the casserole dish, then fluff it with a wooden fork or chopsticks until the mixture is ready to serve.
7. Serve hot under the "face" of the stew in the following recipe.

Kisamvu Na Karanga (Casava Leaves With Peanuts)

Serves 4

1 kilo freshly cut tapioca spinach
2 large tomatoes freshly sliced
2 table spoons crunchy peanut butter or 3 heaped spoons crushed roasted peanuts
1 bulb of onion nicely sliced
1 teaspoon salt or less, for testing

1. Best tasting tapioca spinach consists mainly of the 3 leaves at the tip (near shoot), collect these and cut them from twigs, wash them and grind them well.
2. Cook the spinach adding salt to taste.
3. Make sure that spinach is 'very well' cooked.
4. Once you are certain that it is well cooked, add the sliced tomatoes and onions.
5. Keep stirring and at this point add the grounded peanuts or the peanut butter and stir to mix well.
6. Allow to cool a little and serve.

Manaaeesh (Lebanese Thyme Bread)

1 tbsp.(1 envelope) active dry yeast (or ½ oz. compressed yeast)
1 tsp. sugar
1¼ cup lukewarm water
3 ¼ cup all-purpose flour
½ tsp. salt
6 tbsp.extra virgin olive oil
4 tbsp.zaatar (= 2 heaped tsp. dried thyme + 1 heaped tsp. dried marjoram + 3 tbsp.sesame seeds)

1. Proof the yeast in a few tablespoons of the warm water, with the sugar mixed in.
2. Sift the flour and salt into a large bowl and make a well in the center.
3. Add the yeast mixture and remaining water and knead until you have a firm dough.
4. Transfer to a floured work surface and continue to knead for 10-15 minutes or until smooth and elastic.
5. During this time, knea in 1 tablespoon olive oil into the dough - this will make it softer.
6. Wash and dry the mixing bowl and grease with a little oil.
7. Add the dough and roll around in the bowl until well oiled.
8. Cover with a clean cloth and leave in a warm place to rise for about 2 hours or until doubled in bulk.
9. Punch down the dough and knead for a few minutes.
10. Divide into 10 portions and roll each between your palms until smooth and round.
11. Flour a work surface.
12. Flatten each round with a rolling pin until it is circular, even, and about ¼ inch thick.
13. Cover and leave in a warm place to rise for 20 more minutes. Preheat the oven to 450F.
14. Put 2 large oiled baking sheets in the oven to heat.
15. Brush the tops of the rounds with a little of the olive oil, Mix the remaining oil with the zaatar and spread the mixture over the surface of each round.
16. Slide the bread onto the hot baking sheets and bake for 8-10 minutes.
17. Remove from the oven and place on wire racks to cool.

Flour Tortillas

2 cups all-purpose flour
½ teaspoon salt
¼ cup shortening
½ cups warm water

1. Mix flour and salt together.
2. Rub shortening into flour with fingertips until mixture has a fine, even texture.
3. Stir in water until dough forms.
4. Knead on a floured surface until smooth, about 2-3 minutes.
5. Wrap in plastic and let rest at room temperature for 20-30 minutes.
6. Knead a few times and divide into 8 pieces (for 10-inch tortillas), or 12 pieces (for 8-inch tortillas).
7. Roll each into a ball and cover with plastic to keep from drying out.
8. Roll each ball out on a floured surface, turning over frequently.
9. Stack between sheets of waxed paper.
10. Heat an ungreased heavy skillet over medium high heat until a water droplet flicked onto it dances in tiny droplets.
11. Place a tortilla in the pan and cook until the top is bubbly and the bottom is flecked with brown (about 30 seconds).
12. Turn it over and cook the other side about 20 seconds.
13. If it puffs up during cooking, just flatten it back down with the spatula
14. Cook the rest the same way.
15. Tortillas can be refrigerated up to 3 days or frozen up to two weeks. Reheat before using.

Warah Enab (Stuffed Grape Leaves)

Makes 40 leaves

1 cup uncooked basmati brown or traditional white rice
(traditionally prepared with white)
2 large tomatoes, chopped
1 medium onion, chopped
¼ cup chopped parsley
1 tablespoon vegetable oil
juice of 1 lemon
½ teaspoon salt
¼ teaspoon pepper
¼ teaspoon allspice
1 16 oz. jar of grape leaves
1 cup tomato sauce
2 cups water
round sliced carrots, frozen or fresh
(enough to cover the bottom of a 3 quart pot,
approximately 15 carrot slices, depending on their size)

1. Mix all ingredients except grape leaves, tomato sauce, water, and carrots in a bowl.
2. Remove grape leaves from jar, unfold, and rinse with water.
3. Place grape leaves with the rough side up, one at a time, on a large, flat plate.
4. Be sure that the pointy parts of the leaf are directed away from you and the flatter edges and stem are towards you.
5. Place one teaspoon of the mixture on the bottom of the leaf, near the stem, and arrange it lengthwise using your fingers.
6. First roll the flat edges near the stem upwards and tuck them slightly under the filling.
7. Then applying pressure to keep the leaves rolled tightly, tuck one side at a time of the two parts of the leaf pointing outwards.
8. Now, roll the rest of the way upwards still applying pressure to keep the leaf tight.
9. Cook sliced carrots in water until tender.
10. Cover the bottom layer of a large pot with these carrots.
11. Begin layering the stuffed leaves above the carrots and be sure that they are packed tightly together; otherwise they may fall apart during cooking.
12. Each layer of leaves should be in varying directions across the pot.
13. Pour the tomato sauce and water over the leaves and bring the sauce to a boil.
14. Reduce heat to medium, and place a flat plate (glass or stoneware) upside down over the
15. top layer of leaves, and press down as hard as you can.
16. Leave the plate in place during cooking.
17. Cover the pot with its cover as well, and cook for 40-45 minutes.
18. Check one leaf to see if rice has cooked fully.
19. Serve warm.

Kosheri (Lentils and Rice with a Tangy Tomato Sauce)

Serves 6

This is a typical dish prepared during fasts.
You can substitute one layer of cooked elbow macaroni for a layer of rice.

2 cups uncooked brown or white rice
1 pound lentils
2 tablespoons vegetable oil, divided
1 tablespoon crushed garlic
2 16-ounce cans of tomato sauce
½ cup water
¼ cup vinegar
1 medium onion

1. Cook rice according to directions.
2. Rinse lentils and put them in a pot, covering them with water, and bring to a boil.
3. Then simmer on low heat until almost all water is absorbed and lentils are well cooked.
4. Add extra water if longer time is needed.
5. To make the sauce, first sauté the garlic in 1 tablespoon oil until golden.
6. Add both cans of tomato sauce and simmer 10-15 minutes.
7. Add water and vinegar and bring to a boil.
8. Remove from heat immediately and add salt to taste.
9. Finally, slice onion in thin, small pieces and sauté in remaining 1 tablespoon oil until brown and crispy.
10. This dish should be arranged as a layer of lentils (on the bottom), followed by a layer of rice, then another layer of lentils and another layer of rice.
11. Sprinkle the onions and the sauce on top before serving.

Spice Blends

Berbere

Servings: 1
2 tsp. Cumin seeds
4 whole cloves ¾ tsp. cardamom seeds
½ tsp. whole black peppercorns
¼ tsp. whole allspice
1 tsp. fenugreek seeds
½ tsp. coriander seeds
8-10 small dried red chilies
½ tsp. grated fresh ginger root or
(1 tsp. dried)
¼ tsp. turmeric
1 tsp. salt
2½ tbsp. sweet hungarian paprika
⅛ tsp. cinnamon
⅛ tsp. ground cloves

1. In a small frying pan, on medium-low heat, toast the cumin, whole cloves, cardamom, peppercorns, allspice, fenugreek, and coriander for about 2 minutes, stirring constantly.
2. Remove the pan from the heat and cool for 5 minutes. Discard the stems from the chilies.
3. In a spice grinder or with a mortar and pestle, finely grind together the toasted spices and the chilies.
4. Mix in the remaining ingredients.
5. Store Berebere refrigerated in a well-sealed jar or a tightly closed plastic bag.

Tabil

This spice mixture is used in couscous stews, salad dressings, and dips. Of course there are many variations according to country, region and family history. Try it in the other recipes if you like it in Mechouia.

This makes 3-4 tablespoons:
2 tbsp. ground coriander seeds
2 tsp. ground caraway seeds
¼ tsp. garlic powder
½ tsp. cayenne
¼ tsp. crushed fennel seeds
¼ tsp. crushed aniseed
¼ tsp. ground cumin
¼ tsp. ground turmeric
½ tsp. ground black pepper

Mix well and store in a tightly sealed container. Use in dishes for an authentic taste of North Africa.

1 package store bought seitan, or homemade
1 jar of palm nut sauce(sauce Nyembwe)from a Latino/African grocery
1 medium onion
1 clove garlic
2 habanero or other hot peppers
salt

1. Slice and fry the onions and garlic in a little oil until transparent in a 3qt saucepan.
2. Add the seitan and brown for a few minutes.
3. Add 8oz of palm nut sauce and an equal amount of water, or enough to cover if using more seitan.
4. Bring to a simmer and add the habaneros whole, or chop one if you want it more hot.
5. Serve Nyembwe with Feuille de Manioc (cassava leaves) and steamed manioc and plantain.
6. This is typical village fare for much of Gabon, Congo and the former Zaire.

Soups, Stews & Salad

Nile River Lentil Soup

Serves 4

1 tablespoon olive oil
1 onion, finely chopped
1 clove garlic, minced
1 cup red lentils, rinsed
2 teaspoons ground ginger (I used minced fresh ginger)
2 teaspoons ground cumin
2 teaspoons ground coriander
4 cup water or vegetable stock
2 slices of lemon (¼ inch thick or so)
½ cup canned (or fresh) tomatoes, chopped
¼ cayenne or to taste
salt and pepper to taste
3 tablespoons finely chopped fresh coriander leaves (cilantro)

1. Heat oil in heavy pot on medium high heat.
2. Sauté onion and garlic until softened.
3. Stir in lentils, ginger, cumin and coriander and coat with onion/garlic mixture.
4. Add lemon slices, stock, tomatoes, cayenne, salt and pepper (you can add salt and pepper later, but like to put it in now).
5. Bring to boil, reduce heat to low, cover pot and simmer for about 45 minutes (it may only take 30 minutes) or until lentils are tender.
6. If you like your soup thin, add more stock.
7. Take the pot off the burner, discard lemon slices, and puree soup in blender or food processor.
8. Season if you have not already added the salt and pepper.
9. Sprinkle with coriander (cilantro leaves).
10. Alternatively, you can add the cilantro before you put the soup in the food processor.

Harira - Moroccan Lentil and Garbanzo Soup

Serves 8

2 tablespoons olive oil
2 onions, sliced
1 x 28 oz. can whole tomatoes
¼ teaspoon ground ginger
¼ teaspoon ground cinnamon
¼ teaspoon ground turmeric
¼ teaspoon ground cumin
8 threads Spanish saffron, crushed
20 sprigs fresh cilantro
10 sprigs parsley, flat leaf
salt, to taste
black pepper, freshly ground
1 cup lentils, rinsed & picked over
8 cups water
1½ cups garbanzo beans, cooked, with liquid
1½ cups fava beans, cooked, with liquid
½ cup capellini, (thin, dried pasta)
lemon wedges, as desired/garnish

1. In a soup pot over medium high heat, heat the oil and cook the onions, stirring occasionally, until tender, 6 to 8 minutes.
2. In a blender or food processor, combine the tomatoes, ginger, cinnamon, turmeric, saffron, cilantro, parsley, salt, and pepper.
3. Puree the mixture, in batches if necessary, until fairly smooth. Add to the onions and bring to a boil.
4. Add the lentils and water. Cover tightly and reduce heat to low. Simmer the soup until the lentils are tender, 30 to 35 minutes.
5. Add the undrained garbanzo beans and the favas and bring the soup back to a low boil.
6. Add the pasta and cook until tender, 6 to 8 minutes.
7. Ladle the soup into bowls and serve with lemon wedges.

Note: Canned fava beans, called foul mudammas, are available in Middle Eastern and Italian markets, and sometimes in the specialty section of large supermarkets.

Shurit Ads (Egyptian Lentil Soup)

Serves 6

2 cups dried, hulled split red lentils
2 quarts vegetable stock
1 medium sized onion, peeled and quartered
1 medium sized tomato, quartered
2 tsp. coarsely chopped garlic
4 tbsp. non-dairy butter (or vegetable oil or olive oil)
1 tbsp. finely chopped onions
2 tsp. ground cumin
1 tsp. salt
freshly ground black pepper
lemon wedges

1. Wash the lentils in a large sieve or colander set under cold running water, until the draining water runs clear.
2. In a heavy 4- to 5-quart saucepan, bring stock to a boil over high heat.
3. Add lentils, quartered onion, tomato and garlic, reduce heat to low and simmer partially covered for 45 minutes or until lentils are tender.
4. Meanwhile, in a small skillet, melt 1 tablespoon butter (or oil of your choice) over moderate heat.
5. Add chopped onions and, stirring frequently, cook for 10 minutes until they are soft and deeply browned. Set aside off the heat.
6. Stir in cumin, salt and pepper, and taste for seasoning.
7. Just before serving, stir in the remaining 3 tablespoons butter (or oil of your choice).
8. To serve, ladle the soup into a heated tureen, sprinkle lightly with reserved browned onions and serve the lemon wedges separately.

Yemiser W'et (Spicy Lentil Stew)

Servings: 8

1 cup dried brown lentils	½ cup tomato paste
1 cup onion; finely chopped	1 cup vegetable stock -or- water
2 cloves garlic; minced	1 cup green peas; fresh -or- frozen
¼ cup niter kebbeh	
1 tsp. berbere	salt to taste
1 tsp. cumin seeds; ground	fresh black pepper to taste
1 tsp. paprika (sweet Hungarian)	3 batches injera bread plain yogurt
2 cup tomato, finely chopped	-or- cottage cheese

1. Rinse and cook the lentils. Meanwhile sauté the onions and garlic in the niter kebbeh, until the onions are just translucent.
2. Add the berbere, cumin, and paprika and sauté for a few minutes more, stirring occasionally to prevent burning.
3. Mix in the chopped tomatoes and tomato paste and simmer for another 5 to 10 minutes.
4. Add 1 cup of vegetable stock or water and continue simmering.
5. When the lentils are cooked, drain them and mix them into the sauté.
6. Add the green peas and cook for another 5 minutes.
7. Add salt and black pepper to taste.

Note: To serve Yemiser W'et, spread layers of injera on individual plates. lace some yogurt or cottage cheese alongside a serving of w'et on the injera and pass more injera at the table. To eat, tear off pieces of injera, fold it around bits of stew, and, yes, eat it with your fingers.

Yetakelt W'et
(Spicy Mixed Vegetable Stew) II

Servings: 6

1 cup onions; finely chopped
2 garlic cloves; minced
1 tbsp. berbere
1 tbsp. sweet Hungarian paprika
¼ cup niter kebbeh
1 cup green beans; cut into thirds
1 cup carrots, chopped
1 cup potatoes; cubed
1 cup tomatoes, chopped
¼ cup tomato paste
2 cup vegetable stock
salt and black pepper to taste
¼ cup parsley; fresh, chopped
2 batches injera
Plain yogurt or cottage cheese

Note: Try making this dish and Yemiser W'et for the same meal. In Ethiopia, it is customary to offer several stews at one time, and people eat some of each kind.

1. Sauté the onions, garlic, berbere, and paprika in the Niter Kebbeh for 2 minutes.
2. Add the beans, carrots, and potatoes and continue to sauté for about 10 minutes, stirring occasionally to prevent burning.
3. Add the chopped tomatoes, tomato paste, and the vegetable stock.
4. Bring to a boil and then simmer for 15 minutes, or until all of the vegetables are tender.
5. Add salt and pepper to taste and mix in the parsley.
6. Serve with injera and yogurt or cottage cheese following the same serving and eating procedure as for Yemiser W'et.

Lubia (Bean Stew)

Serves 4-6

You can mix the beans in this spicy stew for a variety of tastes and textures. You can drain off the water by serving up the stew through a slotted wooden spoon.

1 lb. beans (kidney, navy, white, cannellini) soaked and cooked until soft, or 3 cans of these types.
1 large onion peeled and quartered
1 head of garlic peeled
1 head of garlic peeled and minced
1 quart of cold water
¼ cup of parsley, chopped
1 tsp. crushed red pepper flakes
1 tbsp. sweet red paprika
2 laurel leaves
2 tsp. salt
1 tbsp. olive oil
2 cups crushed tomatoes
1 tsp. ground cumin

1. In a stew pot boil one quart of water with beans, whole garlic cloves, and onion until vegetables are tender.
2. Drain off 2 cups of the liquid.
3. In a sauce pan heat the oil and sauté the minced garlic, chopped parsley, hot pepper flakes, paprika, laurel leaves, and salt for 3-5 minutes.
4. When seasonings are slightly smoking add crushed tomatoes ground cumin and one cup water.
5. Bring this mixture to a boil, then add to the bean pot.
6. Serve with pita or over rice.

Tadjeen Gnaoua (Berber Style Vegetable Stew)

Serves 4-6

1 quart boiling water
½ tsp. sea salt
4 tspns mock chicken soup vegetable broth (available at health food stores)
1 cup small white turnips, peeled and cut into 1" cubes
1 cup carrots, peeled and cut into 1" cubes
1 cup zucchini, washed, trimmed and cut into 1" cubes
1 cup white potatoes, washed and cut into 1" cubes
1 large onion, peeled and cut into 1" cubes
1 head of garlic, peeled and trimmed
1 can of chickpeas, drained
1½ cup fresh coriander, chopped
1 tsp. ground black pepper
1 tsp. cayenne
1 tsp. ground ginger
¼ tsp. pulverized saffron
1 tsp. ground cinnamon
1 tsp. ground cumin
1 tsp. ground nutmeg
1 tsp. ground allspice
1 cup black raisins
1 tbsp. olive oil
½ cup almond slivers, blanched then toasted

1. Bring 1 quart of salted water to a boil.
2. Add four tspns of vegetable broth, then the turnips, carrots, potatoes, zucchini, onions, garlic, coriander leaves and chickpeas.
3. Let them cook together until water comes back to a boil, then add the spices and raisins.
4. Cook until vegetables are tender, stirring occasionally.
5. Serve over couscous with toasted almond slivers, or as a stew with whole wheat pita.

Mechouia

Serves 4-6

(Mixed roasted vegetables with capers & twabil spice mixture). This is a nice change from hummus and babaganouj as an appetizer or side dish. Use in dishes for an authentic North African flavor.

¾ -1 lb. mild chili peppers
(Anaheims or poblanos are very good for this recipe)
2 lbs mixed or separate green, red, yellow bell peppers
½ a head of garlic
3-5 small or plum tomatoes
2-3 tsp. twabil spice mixture
Juice of a fresh lemon
1 tbsp. extra virgin olive oil
2 tsp. drained capers

1. Grill or roast the peppers and chili until the skins break and be removed easily.
2. Remove seeds and stems.
3. Chop the peppers well and finely.
4. Broil the garlic and tomatoes.
5. When garlic is cool, slip it out of the skins.
6. Peel, seed, and drain the tomatoes if watery.
7. Mash or puree the garlic and tomatoes.
8. Combine tomato puree, chopped peppers, twabil (see below) salt and lemon juice.
9. Mix well and slowly drizzle in the olive oil.
10. Spread onto a plate and drop the capers on top.
11. Serve with pita.

Algerian Green Beans with Almonds

Serves 4

1 lb fresh green beans
4 cups water, salted
3 tbsp. peanut oil
1 clove garlic, mashed
½ tsp. ground cumin
¼ tsp. paprika
¼ tsp. ground cloves
1 tbsp. slivered almonds

Clean and trim green beans.
Simmer in lightly salted water until just tender, about 30-45 minutes. Drain and put in serving dish.
Put remaining ingredients (except almonds) in a saucepan over medium heat and cook for two minutes, stirring constantly. Add the almonds and stir briefly to coat.
Pour the oil mixture over the green beans and toss gently until beans are thoroughly coated. Serve warm.

Notes: Canned green beans are not an acceptable substitute in this recipe.
Powdered garlic is probably OK.

African-Inspired Yam and Peanut Soup

Serves 4-6

2 large garnet yams, scrubbed and split in half, lengthwise
6 teaspoons olive oil, divided
1 yellow onion, diced
4 cups vegetable or mock chicken stock
2 tablespoons light brown sugar
½ cup creamy salted peanut butter
2 teaspoons smoked pimentón (paprika)
¼ teaspoon cayenne pepper
1 cup cream (or substitute buttermilk)
juice of 1 lime (about 1 tablespoon)
¼ cup fresh chopped cilantro, plus extra for garnish
sea salt, to taste
2 tablespoons chopped salted peanuts, for optional garnish

1. Preheat oven to 400 degrees F. Line a baking pan with tinfoil (for easy clean up).
2. Brush the flesh of the sweet potatoes with 2 teaspoons olive oil and roast, flesh side down, for 40-45 minutes, or until tender when pierced with a fork. Cool. Scoop out the flesh, and discard the skins.
3. In a deep pot over medium heat, sauté onion in remaining 4 teaspoons olive oil until lightly browned. Add cooked potato flesh and broth.
4. Bring to a boil; reduce to low, and add brown sugar, peanut butter and cayenne.
5. Cook 7-8 minutes. Turn off heat, and cool slightly before pureeing.
6. Working in batches, puree the soup in a blender or food processor until smooth.
7. Return to the pot over low heat. Add the cream (or buttermilk), lime juice and cilantro.
8. Stir occasionally until soup is hot, 8-10 minutes.
9. Season to taste with salt.
10. If you prefer a thinner soup, simply add a bit more broth until desired consistency is reached.
11. To serve, place in individual bowls and garnish each with minced cilantro and chopped peanuts.

Butternut Peanut Soup

Pair this rich soup with some good sourdough bread for a soothing, simple lunch. The recipe is also very good with almond butter or hazelnut butter instead of peanut butter, or, for a low-fat soup, omit the peanut butter.

1 3-pound butternut squash
2 cups vegetable broth
¼ cup smooth peanut butter
1 teaspoon curry powder or to taste
2 cups unsweetened soy milk
salt to taste
(optional garnishes: finely chopped peanuts, chopped scallions)

1. Remove the peel and seeds from the squash, and cut the flesh into large chunks.
2. In a large saucepan, simmer squash in 2 cups vegetable broth, covered, until squash is tender; (about 15 to 20 minutes, depending on the size of the squash pieces).
3. Allow squash to cool for a few minutes, then transfer squash and cooking broth to a blender container.
4. Add peanut butter and curry powder, and blend until very smooth.
5. Add a little more liquid if necessary to facilitate blending.
6. Return mixture to saucepan.
7. Add soy milk, and heat through (do not boil).
8. Salt to taste. Serve immediately.

Greek and Middle Eastern Dishes

Appetizers

Falafel

Serves 4

1 15 oz. can garbanzo beans, drained
½ cup onion, chopped
¼ cup fine dry bread crumbs
1 tablespoon fresh parsley, chopped
1 teaspoon ground cumin
½ teaspoon ground coriander
¼ teaspoon salt
⅛ teaspoon black pepper
⅛ teaspoon ground red pepper
2 cloves garlic, minced
vegetable cooking spray
2 teaspoons olive oil, divided
2 6-inch pita rounds, cut in half
4 curly lettuce leaves
Tahini Sauce (recipe follows)

1. Position knife blade in food processor bowl; add first 10 ingredients and process until smooth.
2. Divide mixture into 8 equal portions, shaping each into a 3-inch patty.
3. Coat a large nonstick skillet with cooking spray; add 1½ tsp. of oil and place over medium heat until hot.
4. Add 4 patties to skillet; cook 2 minutes on each side or until lightly browned.
5. Repeat procedure with remaining oil and patties.
6. Spread about 2 tablespoons of Tahini Sauce evenly into each pita half.
7. Fill each half with 1 lettuce leaf and 2 falafel patties.

Taboullah

Serves 6

bulgur 8 oz. (225 g)
medium-sized onion 1
fresh mint, chopped (or dried mint) 1 tbsp. (15 ml)
chopped parsley 6 tbsp. (90 ml)
piquant dressing (see below) ¼ pt (150 ml)

1. Place the bulgur in a basin and pour over sufficient boiling water to cover. Leave to soak for ½ hour.
2. Drain and rinse well. Finely chop the onion.
3. Combine all the ingredients together and toss well into the dressing.
4. Cover and chill until required.

Note: This will keep for several days in a refrigerator.
Tip: you can also add 2 tomatoes and/or 1 cucumber (chopped).

Falafel II

1 19 oz. can chickpeas, drained & rinsed
2 cloves garlic, minced
¼ cup packed fresh parsley
¼ cup packed fresh cilantro (if you dislike cilantro, just double the parsley)
2 tbsp. chopped onion
salt & pepper to taste
¼ cup fresh lemon juice
¼ tsp. baking powder.

1. Combine all ingredients except baking powder in a food processor & process until the texture of ground nuts.
2. Add baking soda & pulse a couple times.
3. Form into small patties and fry until golden brown.
4. (Traditionally, they are deep-fried; I do mine in a non-stick pan).

Serve with Sesame Sauce:
Whisk ¼ cup lemon juice, ¼ cup water, 2 tbsp. Tahini (sesame paste), salt & hot pepper sauce to taste until smooth.

Falafel balls will have complex spiced flavors, usually fried, sometimes baked - made from a base of ground chickpeas and/or fava beans. In Arab countries, Falafel is also used to describe something with a fluffy or crunchy texture.

Vegetarian Gyro with Tzatziki Sauce

For seitan:
½ cup of chickpeas
1 tbsp. olive oil
1 cup vegetable broth
1 tsp. kosher salt
1 tsp. paprika
1 tsp. onion powder
1 tsp. dried mustard
½ tsp. minced garlic
1 tsp. sage
1 tsp. ground black pepper
¼ tsp. turmeric
½ tsp. ground fenugreek seed
1 tbsp. red wine
¼ tsp. all spice
2 tbsp. soy sauce
1 tbsp. tomato paste
¼ cup nutritional yeast flakes
1¼ cup vital wheat gluten flour*
10 cups vegetable broth
½ cup soy sauce

Tzatziki sauce:
½ package vegan sour cream
½ lemon, squeezed
1 clove garlic, minced
1 tbsp. olive oil
½ tsp. kosher salt
ground pepper, to taste
1½ tbsp. fresh dill, minced
¼ tsp. paprika
4 tbsp. cucumber, minced
2 tbsp. fresh parsley, minced

Gyro filling:
pita bread
white onion, chopped
lettuce, shredded
tomato, sliced

*Note: Wheat gluten/seitan is a great addition to the vegetarian protein arsenal. As for "whole" gluten flour or seitan, as long as you don't have Celiac's disease or other gluten sensitivities, it's fine. It's just a natural wheat protein.

1. Combine wheat gluten and nutritional yeast flakes in a bowl. Set aside.
2. Combine all the rest of the ingredients in a blender.
3. Add wet ingredients to the dry ingredients in the bowl. Mix well. Let the wheat gluten mixture rise for a few minutes.
4. While you wait, add the vegetable broth and soy sauce into a big pot. Mix. Do not turn on stove yet.
5. Form the wheat gluten mixture into a log. Cut this log into three equal pieces.
6. Put the seitan into the pot and now turn on the stove to medium heat.
7. Place pot cover on, but allow some room for the steam.
8. Cook for 2 hours, rotating the seitan here and there.
9. To store, keep the seitan in the broth mixture and refrigerate. Prep Time: 30 minutes. Cook Time: several hours.

Note: For this recipe, slice up the seitan and fry it on a skillet over medium heat. Sprinkle the salt on the skillet, allow to heat, add olive oil, then seitan. Fry both sides.

Tzatziki sauce:
1. Combine all ingredients. Mix well.
2. Set aside.

Building sandwich:
1. Split the pita bread in half and open it.
2. Add lettuce, tomato, onion, fried seitan, and sauce.

Tabouleh with Lentils

Cook 1.5 cups of lentils in a large pot of boiling water for 20 minutes, drain. Put cooked lentils in a large bowl.

Add:
1-2 chopped tomatoes
1-2 chopped onions (like vidalas or a couple of bunches of green onions)
½ cup of coarsely chopped olives (green, black, kalmata, or a mix)

The dressing:
½ cup olive oil
salt and pepper to taste
3 tbps of parsley
3 tbsp. of mint
1 tbsp. of basil

1. Toss gently, keeps extremely well for picnics, stores well overnight for consumption the next day.
2. Omit tomatoes until last moment for extremely hot day potlucks (so that they retain that fresh flavor).

Optional ingredients:
Any combination of cooked or raw vegetables such as:
zucchini (courgettes)
green or red peppers
broccoli
green peas
grated carrots, etc.

Spanakopita

3 pkg.
chopped frozen spinach, thawed & very well drained in a sieve
½ lb. butter, melted
4 eggs
pinch of parsley
½ lb. feta cheese
½ lb. cottage cheese
salt (optional)
minced onion for flavor
1 teaspoon dill
½ lb. phyllo leaves
melted butter for phyllo

1. Mix first 8 ingredients together.
2. Butter the bottom of a 9" x 13" pan.
3. Place 4 phyllo leaves on the bottom, buttering after each.
4. Place ½ spinach mix on phyllo leaves, then place 4 more phyllo leaves on top, buttering each leaf.
5. Place remainder of spinach and place 4 more leaves on top, buttering each layer.
6. Turn edges of phyllo under, toward the rim of the pan. Butter top layer.
7. Bake moderately hot 375°F oven for 30 minutes or until golden.

Greek Spinach Pie

The dough:

3 cups all purpose flour
1 cup warm water
2 tbsp. spoons oil
½ spoon oregano
dash of salt

1. Mix ingredients; knead for about 2-3 minutes.
2. Add flour to until it doesn't stick to the hands; separate into equal parts.

The filling:

about one pound of thawed frozen spinach chopped leaves kind
a couple of chopped green shallots (can replace with ⅓ white onion)
½ cup finely chopped parsley
salt, pepper, thyme
Mix ingredients.

The assembly:

1. Roll out the 3 dough balls - so that each one is a bit bigger than your baking pan (8 x 12 in. works well) - the amount of dough, for that size will give you the right thickness.
2. Place the first layer on the greased pan, with ends hanging over the pan rim - add half the filling
3. Follow on with the second dough layer - add the rest of the filling. Finish off with the last dough layer; fold the dough layers together.
4. Pluck a few holes, making sure you go through the second layer of dough.
5. Bake for ¾ hour at around 400°F.

Vegan Moussaka

Serves 2

Tomato Sauce:
1 medium onion
1 medium carrot
1 stock cube
½ pack plain firm tofu
2 tbsp. red wine vinegar
½ can (15 oz can) green lentils
4 oz cooked green lentils
5 tbsp. tomato puree

Aubergine layer:

1 medium aubergine

Creamy topping:

3½ oz. soy milk
2 tbsp. nutritional yeast flakes
¼ pack (2½ oz) tofu (firm works well, can also try silken)

1. Peel and finely chop the onion and carrot.
2. Sauté in stock made with the cube (or use oil if you prefer) until vegetables are softened.
3. Meanwhile, grate or finely chop the drained and rinsed tofu.
4. Drain and rinse the lentils.
5. Add the tofu to the pan with the vinegar and stir for another 5 minutes.
6. Add the drained lentils and the tomato puree, and about ½ cup water.
7. Stir well, lower heat and simmer for 10-20 minutes.
8. Season to taste.
9. Meanwhile, to prepare the creamy topping, liquidise together the soy milk, nutritional yeast and the tofu.
10. Season to taste.
11. For the aubergine layer, slice the aubergine in ¼ inch round slices.
12. To assemble, use a square baking dish, about 5 x 5 inches.
13. Put half the tomato sauce in the bottom and cover with half the aubergine slices.
14. Repeat these 2 layers and finally pour the creamy topping over.
15. Bake at 400°F for about 1 hour until topping is set and aubergines are soft.

Easy Baklava

Serves 12

safflower oil, for coating pan
1 cup ground almonds
1 cup ground walnuts
1½ teaspoons cinnamon
8 sheets filo
¼ cup melted margarine
1¼ cups date sugar
2 tablespoons grated lemon rind
¼ cup lemon juice
2 tablespoons maple syrup

1. Preheat oven to 350°F.
2. Lightly oil a deep 9- by 12-inch baking pan.
3. In a small bowl combine almonds, walnuts, and cinnamon. Set aside.
4. Cut each sheet of filo in half. Stack cut sheets on counter.
5. With a large pastry brush, dot top sheet with about 1 teaspoon margarine, then spread evenly to coat as much heat as possible. Lay evenly in baking pan.
6. Sprinkle lightly with nut mixture.
7. Repeat with remaining sheets, stacking evenly.
8. To cut baklava make 4 evenly spaced vertical cuts through the entire stack of filo.
9. Then cut diagonally to form diamond shapes.
10. (Four evenly spaced diagonal cuts will yield 15 to 20 pastries.)
11. Bake for 20 minutes, then lower heat to 300°F and bake for 30 minutes more.
12. In a small saucepan over medium-high heat, simmer date sugar, lemon rind, lemon juice, and maple syrup until thickened.
13. Pour over cooked baklava as soon as it comes out of the oven. Let cool and then serve.

Note: This traditional Greek dessert alternates sheets of thin filo pastry with a mixture of ground almonds, walnuts, and cinnamon. When the pastry comes out of the oven, it soaks in a lemon-flavored honey glaze.

Spicy Vegetable Couscous

Serves 4

2 tablespoons olive oil
½ cup zucchini, cubed
½ cup yellow squash, cubed
½ cup red bell pepper, seeded, cut into 1" squares
½ cup carrots, sliced
½ onion, chopped
2 cloves garlic, minced
½ teaspoon ground cumin
½ teaspoon curry powder
¼ teaspoon dried red pepper flakes
freshly ground pepper to taste
salt to taste
3 cups instant cooked couscous
½ cup vegetable broth
¼ cup fresh parsley

1. Heat oil in a large skillet and sauté zucchini, squash, red bell pepper, carrots, onion, and garlic for 5 minutes over medium heat.
2. Stir in spices and cook 5 more minutes.
3. Add couscous and broth and cook 5 additional minutes.
4. Garnish with parsley.

Lentil Loaf

1. Cook 1½ cup of rinsed lentils in 3½ cup of water until tender.
2. Partially mash lentils and mix with 2 medium onions that
3. have been sautéed in ¼ cup oil (you can use less).

Add to the onions and lentils:
2 cup cooked rice
1 tsp. garlic powder
1 tsp. salt
¼ cup catsup or barbecue sauce
1 tsp. sage
½ tsp. marjoram

1. Press into an oiled loaf pan and spread catsup or barbecue sauce over the top.
2. Bake for 1 hour.

Grilled Tofu and Vegetable Pita Pockets

Serves 2

Purchased tabbouleh spooned onto whole romaine lettuce leaves is ideal with these Mediterranean-inspired sandwiches. Follow with baklava and fresh grapes.

½ cup bottled Italian dressing
3 tablespoons finely chopped fresh mint
4 3/4-inch-thick slices firm tofu (from 14-ounce package), drained well on several paper towels
2 medium-size green bell peppers, quartered lengthwise, seeded
1 cup mushrooms
8 green onions, all but 3 inches of green tops trimmed
2 7-inch-diameter pita breads, cut in half crosswise

1. Prepare barbecue (medium heat).
2. Whisk dressing and mint in small bowl to blend.
3. Arrange tofu, bell peppers and green onions on small platter; brush with some of dressing mixture.
4. Wrap pita bread in foil; place at edge of grill to warm through.
5. Grill vegetables and tofu until lightly charred and heated through, occasionally turning and brushing with some dressing mixture, about 8 minutes for vegetables and 5 minutes for tofu.
6. Cut tofu and peppers into ¼-inch pieces.
7. Fill each pita half with ¼ of tofu and peppers.
8. Top each with 2 green onions.
9. Drizzle with any remaining dressing mixture and serve.

Baba Ganouj

Serves 12

4 Medium-small eggplants
Juice from two lemons
1 cup tahini
6 cloves of garlic
1 cup finely chopped parsley
2 teaspoons of salt
½ cup finely minced scallions
black pepper
2 tablespoons olive oil

1. Cut off and throw out the stem-ends of the eggplants.
2. Prick the eggplants all over with a fork.
3. Place them directly on an oven rack (preheated to 400 degrees), and roast them slowly until they pop (about 45 minutes). When they are sagging,
4. wrinkled, crumpled and totally soft, they are ready.
5. Remove them from the oven and wait for them to cool enough to handle.
6. Scoop out the insides and mash them.
7. Combine will all other ingredients except the olive oil.
8. Chill completely.
9. Drizzle olive oil on just before serving.
10. Prep. time: 90 min (prepare a day in advance)

Tabbouleh Pitas

Serves 6

1 cup boiling water
¾ cup bulghur
1½ cups fresh parsley, chopped
3 medium tomatoes, diced
½ medium green or red bell pepper, chopped
½ cup green onions, sliced
3 tablespoons fresh mint leaves, chopped
⅓ cup lemon juice
2 tablespoons olive oil
1 teaspoon salt
¼ teaspoon pepper
leaf lettuce
6 pita bread rounds

1. Pour 1 cup of boiling water over bulghur.
2. Let stand for 15 to 20 minutes or until water is absorbed. Stir in parsley and next 8 ingredients.
3. Cover and chill for 1 hour.
4. Place leaf lettuce on bread rounds.
5. Top evenly with tabbouleh and roll.
6. Alternatively, place inside pita pockets.

Veggie-Rice Burgers

Makes 6 burgers

1 tbsp.
sunflower oil
1 carrot, diced
half an onion, diced
¼ cup diced zucchini (or, 1 small courgette, diced)
¼ cup (about 1 stalk) chopped celery
2 large garlic cloves, minced
¼ tsp. dried thyme
¼ tsp. dried dill weed
2 cups cooked brown rice, mashed slightly
¼ tsp. salt
1 tsp. tamari
1 tbsp. tahini
whole-wheat flour
6 slices soy cheddar cheese (optional)

1. Preheat oven to broil.
2. In a large skillet, or frying pan, over medium heat, warm the oil.
3. Add carrot, onion, zucchini, celery, garlic, thyme, dill weed; sauté until vegetables are tender.
4. Remove from heat.
5. Mix vegetables and rice in a large bowl.
6. Mix in salt, tamari, and tahini.
7. Shape into 6 patties; lightly coat each with flour. Place patties on a lightly oiled baking tray.
8. Broil 5 to 10 minutes, or until tops are browned.
9. Flip patties over and top each with a slice of soy cheese, if desired.
10. Broil 5 to 10 more minutes, or until cheese has started to melt.

Note: Dress up these burgers with a creamy tahini sauce, or try a sweet-and-sour sauce for extra zesty taste. For a nice savory sauce addition, check the following pages or the index for recipes of sauces.

Lentil Shepherd's Pie

2 tablespoons vegetable oil
¾ cup chopped onions
1 clove minced garlic
2 tablespoons flour
1⅓ cups vegetable broth
¼ teaspoon dried thyme (or more)
⅛ teaspoon salt or to taste
⅛ teaspoon pepper
2 cups cooked lentils (or canned)
1 10 oz. package frozen mixed vegetables (equally good with only corn and perhaps some fried mushrooms)
2 cups mashed potatoes

1. Preheat the oven to 350°F.
2. Grease a 9x5x3 loaf pan 9x14 glass cake pan.
3. In a med sized saucepan, heat oil and add onions and garlic. Cook, stirring until softened, about 2 minutes.
4. Stir in the flour until absorbed.
5. Add the broth, thyme, salt and pepper.
6. Cook, stirring until mixture comes to a boil.
7. Stir in lentils and vegetables.
8. Spoon into pan.
9. Place potatoes in a pastry bag and pipe them on top.
10. You can use a spoon to put little scoops of potatoes on top and then spread them.
11. You can make the potatoes creamy with some soy milk so they will spread easily.
12. Leave a hole in the centre so steam can escape or it tends to bubble out.
13. Bake 40 minutes or until potatoes are browned a bit on top.

Snacks & Sides

Arabic Pizza

This is a vegetarian version of Lahma wa Ajeen. These are small pizzas the size of saucers. It takes a bit of time but worth the work!

Whole-Wheat Crust:
1 cup whole-wheat flour
2 cups unbleached all-purpose flour
1 tablespoon active dry yeast
1¼ cups warm water (about 110 degrees F)
2 tablespoons honey

1. Sift the flours together in a medium sized bowl.
2. Place the yeast in a separate bowl and pour the warm water over it; let stand for about 5 minutes.
3. Combine all ingredients in the bowl of a stand mixer with the dough hook attachment, mixing for approximately 5 minutes.
4. Set the dough aside to rise for approx. 2 hours.

½ to 1 lb vegetarian mince
4 ripe peeled tomatoes (or use canned)
6 cloves of garlic, crushed
2 tbsp. chopped parsley
¾ cup black olives, sliced
salt, pepper, cayenne pepper

1. Mix mince, tomatoes, parsley, garlic, sumac and salt & pepper to taste, and cayenne pepper (be generous) together.
2. Knead dough again and divide into egg size balls (about 20).
3. Pat each ball into a flat patties about 6" diameter.
4. Spread mix on each one (not edges), place on a greased tray and cook in a 400F/200C hot oven for 15 minutes at most (watch it!)

Nut Pate

1 cup almonds, soaked 12-48 hours and blanched
1 cup sunflower seeds, soaked 6-8 hours and rinsed
¼ cup sesame seeds, soaked 8 hours and rinsed
1 red bell pepper, finely chopped
3 stalks celery, finely chopped
1 small leek, finely chopped
1-2 tsp. powdered kelp
1-2 tablespoons Bragg Liquid Aminos or to taste
2 tablespoons lemon juice

1. Using a champion juicer process almonds, sunflower seeds, sesame seeds using the solid plate.
2. Add red bell pepper, celery, leek, lemon juice, kelp, Bragg and mix well.

Spicy Lentil Patties

Makes 12 patties
(depending on the size you make them)
1 cup dry green lentils
1 large raw potato, grated very fine
1 onion minced fine
2-3 garlic cloves, crushed
¼ cup mild salsa -or- ¼ cup canned, chopped tomatoes and 1 fresh jalapeno, minced
¼ cup homemade bread crumbs
salt to taste

1. Cook lentils for ½ hour in about 2 cups of water.
2. While the lentils are cooking, mix all other ingredients except bread crumbs in a medium-sized mixing bowl.
3. Drain lentils quickly, and add to the rest of the ingredients.
4. Add homemade bread crumbs, and let the mixture sit for about 10 minutes. It should NOT be really thick.
5. It should be very moist.
6. Don't worry about the patties falling apart, as the starch from the raw potato will bind the burger together as it cooks.
7. Form into patties and either bake on cookie sheet or fry in a non stick pan until done.
8. Use very little olive oil to fry them in.

Baba Ganoush

Serves 1

2 large eggplants
¼ cup tahini
1 small onion
7 cloves garlic
1 tablespoon cumin
1 teaspoon ground coriander
1 teaspoon vinegar
2 tablespoons lemon juice
1 tablespoon olive oil
salt, to taste
red pepper, for garnish

1. Pierce the skin of the eggplant and placed on foil lined baking sheet under boiler.
2. Broil, turning once, until they are oozing and the skin is black on both sides.
3. Throw the eggplants in cold water and peel.
4. Drain the flesh and pop into a blender.
5. Add a *conservative amount of all ingredients and blend on low, for a minute or two (until creamy and well-blended) you may have to add water to achieve desired consistency.
6. Adjust the seasoning by adding ingredients and blending and tasting.
7. Pour into a serving bowl and drizzle with some more olive oil and garnish with red pepper or paprika and a sprig of parsley.

Black Bean Hummus

1½ cup cooked black beans
⅓ cup tahini paste
¼ fresh lime juice
3 tablespoons olive oil*
2 cloves garlic, minced
¼ cup thinly sliced scallions (white and green)
¼ teaspoons ground cumin

1. drain and rinse beans.
2. Instead of using oil use drained liquid from the can.
3. Place beans, tahini, lime juice, oil and garlic in food processor or blender.
4. Cover and process until pureed.
5. Add scallions, and cumin.
6. Cover and process until just combined.

Black Bean Hummus II

2 cups cooked or canned black turtle beans or black beans
2 tbsp. liquid from the beans
2 tbsp. lemon juice
1 tbsp. tamari sauce
2 clove garlic, chopped
½ tsp. ground cumin
pinch cayenne pepper
2 tbsp. chopped fresh parsley

1. Combine beans, liquid, lemon juice, tamari, garlic, cumin and cayenne in a bowl of food processor, or blender, and puree until smooth.
2. Add parsley and blend for 5 seconds.

Hummus I

1½ cups drained canned chick-peas
¼ cup water
3 tablespoons lemon juice
1 tablespoon tahini (sesame-seed paste)
1 teaspoon olive oil
¾ teaspoon garlic powder (or fresh cloves)
½ teaspoon ground cumin
pinch of ground red pepper
½ cup chopped coriander leaves (cilantro)

1. In a blender or food processor, puree all ingredients, except the coriander leaves, until smooth.
2. Transfer to a bowl.
3. Stir in coriander leaves.
4. Yields 1½ cups.

Hummus II

4 cups chick peas
½ cup tahine
⅓ cup warm water
⅓ cup olive oil (but you can cut that a bit if you want to avoid the fat) juice from two or three lemons
4 garlic cloves
1½ teaspoon salt
2 teaspoons cumin (a bit more cumin will add to the authentic "Middle Eastern" taste) pepper to taste

Just put it all in a food processor, sit back, and enjoy the results.

Roasted Vegetable Pitas w/ Creamy Herb Dressing

Serves 2

1 cup yellow squash, cut into, ½-inch diagonal slices
1 red bell pepper, cut into wedges
1 small onion, cut into 8 wedges
2 cloves garlic, thinly sliced
1 large tomato, cut into 8 wedges
½ cup spinach leaves, torn into, bite size pieces
2 teaspoons olive oil
1½ teaspoons fresh chopped oregano or ½ tsp. dried
1½ teaspoons fresh chopped basil or ½ tsp. dried
¼ teaspoon salt
⅓ cup Creamy Herb Dressing (recipe follows)
2 to 4 pita pocket halves

1. Prepare and cut vegetables.
2. Combine in a mixing bowl all of the above ingredients except the tomatoes, spinach leaves, dressing, and pita halves.
3. Toss vegetable mixture to lightly glaze the vegetables with olive oil.
4. Spoon vegetable mixture onto a broiler pan or cookie sheet coated with nonstick cooking spray.

5. Broil 5 minutes, add tomatoes and spinach leaves to vegetable mixture and stir.
6. Baste with additional marinade and broil for an additional 5 minutes or until vegetables are just tender and lightly browned.
7. Tomatoes and spinach should be just warmed; if you prefer the tomato softer, add with vegetable mixture at the beginning.
8. Prepare the Creamy Herb Dressing while vegetables are broiling.
9. Divide the vegetable mixture evenly between pita halves.
10. Drizzle with Creamy Herb Dressing. Serve.

Kasha (Cracked Buckwheat Groats)

2 cups kasha
2 tablespoons egg replace
1 tbsp. miso
1 tsp. black pepper
4 cups water
1 medium onion, chopped
1 clove garlic

1. Brown the onion and garlic in a little oil in the bottom of a medium sized pot.
2. Beat the egg replace loosely and mix thoroughly with the kasha and a little extra water, and place in a dry pan over medium heat.
3. Stir constantly until the egg replace looks dry.
4. Add to the onion, add water, miso, and pepper, and bring to a boil.
5. Immediately cover and reduce heat to low; the kasha will absorb the water in about 10 minutes, and is ready to serve right away.
6. For kasha varnishkes, add 1-2 cups of cooked bowtie noodles before serving.

Northeast African Millet Patties

Makes 6 Patties

3 cups cooked millet
½ cup nut butter (tahini, almond peanut etc)
1 tbsp. onion powder
1 tbsp. tamari
1 tsp. celery seed
1 tbsp. oil

1. Mix all ingredients together.
2. form into patties, brown on both sides in lightly oiled skillet.
3. To cook millet: boil 2½ cups water.
4. add 1 cup millet, cover and simmer 15 minutes.
5. let sit uncovered 20 minutes.
6. Makes about 3 cups.

Greek Lentil Soup (Fakes Soup)

Serves 6

1 lb. of lentils
1 cup of oil
1 onion
1 tbsp. of concentrated tomato pulp

2-3 gloves of garlic
3 laurel leaves
half a small tumbler of vinegar
salt, pepper

1. Fill a pot with plenty of water. Add the lentils and bring to the boil. Drain the lentils.
2. Brown the finely chopped onion in the oil, add the lentils, the garlic, the tomato concentrate dissolved in water, salt, pepper, the laurel leaves, and more water if needed.
3. Cook the lentils and a little before they are ready put it the vinegar.

Greek Garlic Dip

Makes 2 Cups

2 large potatoes
5 garlic cloves, up to 6
1 cup parsley leaves
½ cup olive oil
3 tablespoons vinegar
salt and freshly ground black pepper

1. Boil potatoes with skin on.
2. Peel garlic and crush with a pestle and mortar.
3. When potatoes are tender, peel and cut into small pieces.
4. Place potatoes, garlic, parsley, half the oil and vinegar in blender or food processor.
5. Blend for 3 minutes, stop and adjust taste by adding more oil, salt and pepper. Blend until smooth.

Chickpea Soup, Hasa Al-Hummus

Serves from 6-8

1 cup chickpeas, soaked in water overnight, then drained
8 cups water
1 tablespoon olive oil
2 medium size onions, chopped
8 cloves garlic, chopped into small pieces
1 small hot pepper, finely chopped
½ cup finely chopped coriander leaves
2 teaspoons salt
1 teaspoon pepper
1 teaspoon ground mustard seeds
¼ cup lemon juice

1. Place chickpeas and water in a saucepan and bring to boil.
2. Cover and cook over medium heat for 1 hour.
3. In the meantime, heat oil in a frying pan; then stir-fry onions, garlic, and hot pepper until they begin to brown.
4. Add frying pan contents with the remaining ingredients to the chickpeas.
5. Cover and cook over medium heat for 1 hour or until chickpeas are well-cooked.

Tomato and Chickpea Soup, Hasa Al-Tamatat Maa Hummus

Serves from 8-10

Enjoy another version of chickpea soup.
1 tablespoon olive oil
2 medium onions, chopped
4 cloves garlic, crushed
4 tablespoons finely chopped coriander leaves
2 cups cooked chickpeas
2 cups tomato juice
6 cups water
¼ cup white rice, rinsed
2 teaspoons salt
1 teaspoon pepper
1 teaspoon allspice
⅛ teaspoon cayenne

1. Heat oil in saucepan; then sauté onions and garlic over medium heat for 10 minutes.
2. Add remaining ingredients and bring to boil.
3. Cover and cook over medium
4. heat for 25 minutes or until rice is cooked.

Greek Dried Beans Stewed with Tomato (Fayola Xera Yachnista)

Serves 6
1 lb. of beans
1 onion
1 cup of oil
1-2 tbsp. of concentrated tomato pulp
2-3 sprigs of celery
half a small bunch of parsley
2-3 medium size carrots
salt, pepper

1. Soak the beans in water overnight.
2. Next day, boil them in a pot until half-cooked: then drain them.
3. In another pot brown the minced onion with the oil and add the celery and the parsley finely chopped, the carrots cut in round slices or diced and the tomato concentrate diluted in water, salt and pepper.
4. When all this comes to boil, add the beans and simmer.

Betta Feta

1 lb. regular tofu (or firm), cut into ¼ - ½-inch cubes
2 cup water
2 tbsp. all season blend (recipe to follow)
¼ cup red wine vinegar
¼ cup water
2 tbsp. tahini
2 tbsp. fresh lemon juice
1 tsp. salt
1 tsp. dried basil leaves
1 tsp. dried oregano
½ tsp. garlic granules

1. Place the tofu cubes, the 2 cups of water and the all season blend in a sauce pan.
2. Bring to a boil, reduce the heat to medium, and simmer uncovered for 20 minutes, stirring occasionally.
3. Drain and place in a bowl.
4. In a separate bowl, whisk together the remaining ingredients until well blended.
5. Pour over the tofu and toss carefully.
6. Cover and chill several hours, stirring occasionally to make sure tofu cubes are evenly coated.
7. Store in the refrigerator for up to 1 week.

All Season Blend

1½ cup nutritional yeast flakes
3 tbsp. salt
1 tbsp. onion granules
1 tbsp. paprika
2 tsp. garlic granules
1 tsp. dried parsley
½ turmeric
¼ tsp. dried thyme
¼ tsp. marjoram leaves
¼ tsp. ground dill seed

1. Place all ingredients in a blender
2. blend until finely ground.
3. Store in a covered container at room temp.

Butter Beans w/ Mint and Tomatoes

In Greece, this is made with ¼ pint of olive oil! Whilst the taste does suffer very slightly with the omission of the oil, the addition of a very strongly flavoured vegetable stock (¼ pint) redresses the balance well.

1 lb of cooked butter beans
3 large onions, finely chopped
2 cloves of garlic, crushed
¼ pint of strong veg. stock (or olive oil)
1 x 14 oz. can of tomatoes
2 tbsp. fresh mint or 1 dried

1. Sauté onions and garlic in a little of the stock until starting to soften.
2. Add the tomatoes and the cooked beans and the mint. Season to taste.
3. Simmer gently, covered, for about 20 minutes to allow the flavors to blend.
4. Serve as a supper dish with whole meal bread rolls and a green salad.

Entrees

Vegetable, Raisin and Pine Nut Pilaf

Serves 4

This is a quick, delicious and colorful meal that will appeal to almost all kinds of vegetarians.

1 medium eggplant, peeled and cut into ½-inch cubes
1 large yellow bell pepper
1 large red bell pepper
8 mushrooms
1 small zucchini, cut into ¼-inch cubes
1½ cups uncooked wild rice blend
½ cup olive oil
1 tablespoon pine nuts
¼ cup golden raisins
1 garlic clove, minced
Salt to taste

1. Sprinkle the diced eggplant with salt and set aside.
2. After 30 minutes, rinse with cold water and pat dry with paper towels.
3. Stem and seed the peppers and cut into thin strips.
4. Slice mushrooms and dice zucchini.
5. Begin cooking rice according to package directions.
6. Heat olive oil in a large skillet on medium high.
7. Sauté the garlic and eggplant until lightly browned on each side, about 3 minutes.
8. Lower heat and stir in peppers and zucchini and sauté for 3 more minutes.
9. Add mushrooms, pine nuts and golden raisins and stir-fry until the mushrooms are tender.
10. Spoon mixture over .

Greek-Style Cannellini and Vegetables

Serves 4

2 quarts water
2 cloves garlic, minced
1 onion, chopped
3 tablespoons olive oil
2 to 3 carrots, diced
1 red or green bell pepper, chopped
1 cup orzo
1 zucchini, diced
1 tablespoon fresh minced mint (1 tsp. dried)
1 tablespoon fresh minced dill (1 tsp. dried)
½ teaspoon fresh marjoram (sprinkling of dried)
5 artichoke hearts (14 oz. can), drained and chopped
2 cups cannellini beans (15 oz. can), rinsed & drained
1 14.5 oz. can Italian-style stewed tomatoes
salt & freshly ground pepper to taste
red wine vinegar

1. Bring the water to a boil in a large covered pot.
2. While the water heats, sauté the garlic and onions in 2 tablespoons of the oil in a large skillet on medium-high heat.
3. Add carrots and bell pepper.
4. When the water boils, add the orzo, return to a boil, and simmer for about 10 minutes, until al dente.
5. Dice the zucchini and stir it into the skillet of vegetables. Add the mint, dill, and marjoram.
6. Add the artichoke hearts and gently stir the beans and the stewed tomatoes.
7. Simmer for several minutes, stirring occasionally.
8. When the pasta is al dente, drain and stir in the remaining tablespoon of oil.
9. When the beans and vegetables are hot, add the orzo.
10. Season with salt & pepper to taste.
11. Serve with red wine vinegar.

Green Beans Braised with Mint & Potatoes

Serves 4

3 tbsp. olive oil & margarine, mixed
1 cup tomato juice or sauce
1 lb fresh green beans; trimmed, cut
1 tbsp. chopped fresh parsley, opt.
2 med potatoes; peeled
Salt & freshly ground pepper
chopped fresh mint

1. Heat the fat in an enameled pan and mix in the tomato juice or sauce.
2. Add the green beans and parsley to the pan with
3. enough water to almost cover.
4. Tuck the potato slices in between, partially cover the pan, and simmer for 25 minutes, the stir and season with salt, pepper, and 2 tablespoons chopped mint.
5. Cook uncovered until the beans and potatoes are fork tender, about 10 more minutes.
6. If the sauce has not thickened, pour it into a small pan, and boil down to one cup, then combine with the beans and potatoes in a warm serving bowl.
7. Sprinkle with a little additional fresh mint and serve warm.

Basil Roasted Vegetables Over Couscous

Serves 4

¼ cup fresh basil, minced
2 tablespoons lemon juice
1 tablespoon olive oil
¼ teaspoon salt
2 cloves garlic, minced
2 medium zucchini, cut into 1" slices
1 medium red bell pepper, cut into 1" pieces
1 medium yellow bell pepper, cut into 1" pieces
1 medium red onion, cut into 8 wedges
1 cup whole mushrooms, halved
3 cups hot cooked couscous (w/salt)

1. Preheat oven to 425°F. Combine first five ingredients in a large bowl and stir well. Add zucchini, bell peppers, onion, mushrooms; toss well to coat.
2. Arrange vegetables in a single layer on a shallow roasting pan. Bake for 25 to 30 minutes or until tender (stir every 10 minutes or so).
3. Spoon roasted vegetables over couscous.
4. Garnish with fresh basil sprigs if desired.

Eggplant Stuffing

Serves 6

3 med eggplants (1 lb ea.)
¼ cup olive oil
⅓ cup chopped scallions -or- Shallots
1 garlic clove; sliced (opt.)
¼ cup chopped fresh parsley
2 tbsp. chopped fresh fennel or dill
½ tsp. allspice; more if necessary
¼ cup dry white wine
2 tbsp. tomato paste; mixed with:
½ cup water
salt & freshly ground pepper
½ cup bread crumbs

1. Cut the eggplants in half lengthwise.
2. With a small knife, cut away the eggplant flesh from the skin without breaking the skin (if planning to stuff the shells, leave ¼-inch of the flesh with the skin as a firm base) and set the shells aside.
3. Dice the eggplant flesh and push through the medium blade of a meat grinder as quickly as possible to avoid discoloration. (Or the eggplant may be pureed in a blender or food processor.)
4. Heat the oil in a frying pan and sauté the scallions and garlic.
5. Add the parsley, fennel, allspice, wine, and the diluted tomato paste.
6. Stir in the eggplant pulp, season with salt and pepper, and simmer for 20 minutes. Taste to adjust seasonings.
7. Add the bread crumbs to absorb excess liquid.
8. Stuff the eggplant shells, if desired, and place in an oiled baking dish.
9. Bake in a moderate oven (350°F) for 35 minutes.

Turkish Pilaf

Serves 6

This Turkish pilaf consists of brown rice, dried fruit, chopped nuts, and a touch of cinnamon.
Try different types of dried fruit and nuts.

1½ cups brown rice
4 cups water
2 tablespoons slivered almonds
2 tablespoons shelled pistachio nuts
¼ cup dried prunes, chopped
¼ cup dried apricots, chopped
1 teaspoon cinnamon

1. Cook the brown rice in boiling water in a covered pot for 45 minutes.
2. Stir in remaining ingredients and serve warm.

Tabbouleh

2 cups raw bulgur
4 cups water
Simmer 20 minutes, cool, refrigerate overnight.

Dressing:
¼ cup cold-pressed, extra-virgin olive oil
Juice of 1 large, juicy lime
1 ounce dry sherry
2 ounces shoyu
1 tbsp. sesame oil
1 tsp. dry mustard
2 tbsp. minced onion
2 large cloves garlic, crushed or minced
Handful of fresh basil leaves, chopped
A few sprigs of lemon basil, chopped
1½ tsp. thyme
½ tsp. cayenne
½ tsp. sea salt
1 tsp. ground black pepper
2 tbsp. grated fresh ginger root
Combine the day before, and refrigerate overnight.

Veggies:
2 medium carrots, shredded
2 medium cucumbers - dice 1½ in ½-inch dice, and save the other ½ for garnish
2 or 3 tomatoes, diced or cut in wedges
several handfuls each bean sprouts and alfalfa sprouts
one handful radish sprouts
(These are especially good. If you don't have any, use some very thinly sliced radishes)

1. Place bulgur in a large bowl and break up fine.
2. Add veggies and dressing and toss well.
3. Slice the ½ cucumber, and cut slices into half circles.
4. Stand them up around the edge of the bowl, flat side down, to create a 'scalloped' edge.
5. Put together just before serving, as the veggies tend to leach liquid.
6. If you do this too far ahead, you'll have a 'soup' at the bottom of the bowl.

Tabouli
Serves 6
1 cup bulgur
1½ cups boiling water
1½ teaspoons salt
¼ cup fresh lemon juice, and/or lime juice
1 teaspoon garlic, crushed
½ cup chopped scallions, include greens
½ teaspoon dried mint flakes
¼ cup olive oil, (good quality)
fresh black pepper
2 medium tomatoes, diced
1 cup fresh parsley, chopped and packed

Optional:
½ cup cooked chickpeas
1 chopped green bell pepper
½ cup coarsely grated carrot
1 chopped cucumber, or summer squash

1. You should begin to soak the bulghar at least 3 hours before serving time.
2. It needs to thoroughly ma rinate and chill.
3. Combine bulghar, boiling water, and salt in a bowl.
4. Cover and let stand 15-20 minutes, or until bulghar is chewable.
5. Add lemon juice, garlic, oil, and mint, and mix thoroughly. Refrigerate 2-3 hours.
6. Just before serving add the vegetables and mix gently.
7. Correct seasonings. Garnish with olives.

Mangoes' Roasted Garlic Chickpea Puree

2 cups soft-cooked garbanzo beans
¼ cup roasted garlic
¼ cup tahini (sesame paste)
2 tablespoons lemon juice or more to taste
1 teaspoon olive oil
½ teaspoon cumin
¼ teaspoon cayenne pepper
¼ teaspoon coriander
¼ cup fresh parsley
Salt and black pepper to taste

1. Combine all ingredients in a food processor and process on medium high until smooth and creamy in texture.
2. Taste and adjust seasoning according to preference.
3. Note: One elephant garlic bulb will yield just the right amount of roasted garlic for this recipe.
4. This extra-large garlic is slightly sweeter than its smaller counterpart, but is perfect for this recipe.
5. To roast, trim the top of the bulb; do not separate cloves.
6. Drizzle with olive oil and bake for 15 to 20 minutes at 350 degrees.
7. Test with a wooden pick to ensure softness and then allow to cool before proceeding with the recipe.

Tabouli

1 cup bulger
boiling water
4 tomatoes, chopped
2 cups fresh parsley, minced
1 cup fresh mint leaves, minced
1 bunch (about 8) scallions, finely chopped
1 tsp. ground cumin
salt & pepper to taste
⅓ cup fresh lemon juice
⅓ cup olive oil
romaine lettuce

1. Place bulger in a large bowl and pour in boiling water until well-covered. Let stand at least 20 minutes.
2. Drain in sieve & press out excess moisture.
3. Return to bowl and add vegetables & herbs.
4. Stir in spices. Whisk lemon juice & oil together &
5. add to salad, tossing to coat.
6. Serve with romaine lettuce at room temp.

Taboilu with Millet

Millet, cook one half cup millet until soft.
Set aside to cool.
1 - 2 bunches of parsley
2 bunches small scallions
a handful of mint leaves
2 tomatoes
juice of one lemon
2 - 3 tbsp.
extra virgin olive oil
salt to taste

1. Wash and chop vegetables finely (remove stems).
2. Mix all ingredients together. Chill.

Tabouli with Bulgur Wheat

2 bunches parsley
3 tomatoes
½ dozen green onions
2 garlic cloves
1 cup couscous or 1 cup bulgar wheat
3 tablespoons curry
juice of 2 lemons
¾ cup olive oil
black pepper

1. Soak (don't ever boil) the bulgar or couscous in same amount water with curry powder mixed in.
2. Stir occasionally for the first ten minutes.
3. It will be ready in 30 minutes!
4. Clean juice and seeds from tomatoes.
5. Chop parsley, tomatoes, green onion very fine.
6. Send garlic through a press (more if you like)
7. Mix couscous/bulgar, lemon juice, oil and pepper to taste - Ready to eat!

Sweet-Spicy Roasted Yams

Serves 8

4 large garnet yams
4 ounces pancetta
2 tablespoons olive oil
1 tablespoon maple syrup
1 teaspoon red pepper flakes
1 teaspoon sea salt

1. Preheat oven to 400 degrees.
2. Peel yams and cut into ½" cubes.
3. Cut pancetta into small dice.
4. Combine yams and pancetta in a large bowl and toss well with remaining ingredients.
5. Spread this out on a sheet pan or large casserole. It's important that it be in a single layer as this promotes faster cooking and better caramelization.
6. Roast in the oven for about 25 minutes or until nicely browned and sizzling, stirring 2-3 times.

Sweet Potato Casserole

Serves 8

4 large sweet potatoes (about 3½ pounds)
1 8 ounce can of unsweetened crushed pineapple
2 tbsp. of Earth Balance or other vegan buttery spread
¼ to ½ teaspoon cinnamon (to taste)
½ tsp. sea salt (or to taste)
¼ cup raw pecans, chopped

1. Preheat oven to 400 degrees.
2. Wash sweet potatoes and place them on a foil lined shallow roasting pan. Do not peel.
3. Bake for 1½ hours or until a fork easily pierces the potatoes.
4. Let cool enough so that you can handle and remove potato skin.
5. Drain the pineapple but reserve the juice in case you need more moisture for the casserole.
6. Add crushed pineapple, buttery spread, cinnamon and salt to the potatoes and mash until smooth.
7. If needed, add some or all of the reserved pineapple juice.
8. Place in a lightly greased casserole dish and warm (covered) in a 350 degree oven for 20 to 30 minutes. Or, you can cover and refrigerate and warm it the next day.
9. Garnish with pecans right before serving.

Red Onion Tian

Serves 3-4

In August, when the red Spanish or torpedo onions are pulled, you'll always find among the large ones some small onions, which are particularly delectable. Farmers' markets are a likely place to find them. They are wonderful in this dish, bathed with olive oil and baked slowly with sweet red and yellow peppers and tomato. If torpedo onions aren't available, use red onions cut into quarters. The juices that flow out of the vegetables are boiled with vinegar until they've reduced to a syrup, making a naturally sweet and tart sauce.

This colorful tian is delicious with slices of grilled polenta. It's also wonderful piled on top of grilled bread that has been spread first with a layer of garlic mayonnaise. Serve the tian hot, tepid, or even chilled, as part of a plate of small salads or with the main part of the meal.

1 pound small torpedo onions or red onions
1 small red bell pepper
1 small yellow bell pepper
2 medium-sized ripe tomatoes
1 to 2 tablespoons virgin olive oil
5 to 6 thyme branches or several pinches of dried
6 small garlic cloves, peeled and left whole
salt
freshly ground pepper
balsamic vinegar

1. Preheat the oven to 350F. Quarter the onions, leaving the base intact, and peel them.
2. Halve the peppers both crosswise and lengthwise, remove the seeds and veins, and cut them into pieces roughly ½ inch wide. Remove the core from the tomatoes and cut them into sixths.
3. Brush a film of olive oil over the bottom of a gratin dish [or just use an oblong tempered glass dish which works fine too], scatter the thyme over it, and add the vegetables, including the garlic, in an attractive (it can't help but be attractive), easy fashion.
4. Brush the remaining oil over the vegetables, being sure to coat the onions and peppers.
5. Season with salt and pepper. Cover the tian and bake for 1½ hours. The vegetables should be very soft, the tomatoes melting into a jam.
6. Remove it from the oven and carefully pour the liquid that has collected into a small saucepan.
7. Add a teaspoon of vinegar, bring the liquid to a boil, and reduce until it is thick and syrupy.
8. Taste for vinegar and salt; then pour or brush this syrup over the vegetables.

Lentils and Rice (Saudi Arabia)

Serves 8

4 medium yellow onions, peeled
1 tablespoon olive oil
1 cup lentils
3½ cups cold water
1 cup long-grain rice
2 teaspoons salt

1. Dice 3 of the onions.
2. Heat a large frying pan and sauté onions in water or broth.
3. Sauté until tender and set aside.
4. In a 4-quart covered pot place the lentils and water.
5. Bring to a boil, covered, and then turn down to a simmer. Cook for 15 minutes.
6. Add the cooked onion to the lentils, along with the rice and salt.
7. Cover and simmer 20 minutes until rice and lentils are soft.
8. Remove from heat and let stand, covered, 5 minutes.
9. Slice the remaining onion into rings.
10. Heat frying pan again and sauté rings in olive oil.
11. To serve, top the lentils with the sautéed onion rings.

Tabbouleh

Serves 6

2 cups bulgur (cracked wheat)
1 large bunch parsley
½ cup packed fresh mint leaves
4 green onions
¾ pound tomatoes, seeded, chopped
6 tablespoons fresh lemon juice
2 tablespoons olive oil
¾ teaspoon ground cumin

1. Place bulgur in large bowl.
2. Pour enough warm water over to cover generously.
3. Let stand until bulgur softens, about 15 minutes.
4. Drain well, pressing out excess water.
5. Return bulgur to same large bowl.
6. Meanwhile, finely chop parsley, mint and green onions in processor. Add bulgur.
7. Mix in tomatoes, then lemon juice, oil and cumin.
8. Season generously with salt and pepper.
9. (Can be made 3 hours ahead.
10. Let stand at room temperature.)

Greek Vegetable Medley

Serves 6

2 tablespoons olive oil, divided
3 medium onions, sliced
2 cloves garlic, minced
2 pounds medium potatoes, peeled & sliced, into ¼" rounds
2 pounds large zucchini, sliced, into ⅓" rounds
1 large red bell pepper, seeded &, cut into thin rounds
1 large green bell pepper, seeded &, cut into thin rounds
salt & freshly ground pepper to taste
1½ cups plum tomatoes, coarsely chopped, drained of juices
½ cup chopped parsley
1 teaspoon dried oregano
water

1. Heat oven to 350°F.
2. Heat 1 tablespoon of oil in a large nonstick skillet and cook onions and garlic until onions are softened or about 5 minutes.
3. In a large shallow baking dish coated with cooking spray, place potatoes, zucchini, and peppers in one overlapping layer, alternating them.
4. Season with salt and pepper and sprinkle with sautéed onions and garlic.
5. Pour tomatoes evenly over layered vegetables, season with parsley and oregano, and add remaining 1 tablespoon of olive oil.
6. Add enough water to come halfway up the vegetables.
7. Bake for 1 to 1½ hours or until all the vegetables are tender.

Vartabit

1 to 2 loaves French bread, cut into 1" cubes
1 cup Tahini (sesame paste)
1 clove garlic, crushed
juice of 1 lemon
1 teaspoon salt
1 can (15 oz.) great Northern beans
2 tablespoons Sumac
(small amounts of black pepper, cayenne, cumin)
1 stick margarine
¼ teaspoon cayenne or paprika

1. Place bread cubes in a 9"x13" baking pan (preferably glass).
2. Broil bread until golden brown.
3. Mix the tahini with crushed garlic, salt, and lemon juice.
4. Add enough water to this paste to bring the consistency of pancake batter.
5. Drain the beans, wash well.
6. Stir the beans into the tahini mixture.
7. Spread the beans mixture over the toasted bread cubes.
8. Sprinkle with the spices starting with black pepper and ending with sumac.
9. Melt margarine until golden brown.
10. Stir in either cayenne or paprika according to taste.
11. Drizzle over the prepared dish.
12. Serve immediately.

Greek Roasted Potatoes

Serves 6
16 small Yukon Gold potatoes (or small red potatoes
4 tablespoons olive oil
2 tablespoons lemon juice
1 tablespoon dried Greek oregano (or regular oregano)
2 teaspoons Greek seasoning
½ teaspoon salt
¼ teaspoon freshly ground pepper

1. Heat oven to 450.
2. Cut unpeeled potatoes into large chunks.
3. Toss with olive oil, lemon juice, oregano, Greek seasoning, and salt & pepper.
4. Place potatoes on baking sheet or roasting pan.
5. Roast 10 minutes, then turn potatoes.
6. Continue roasting until potatoes
7. are browned, crisp, and tender, turning twice (every 10 minutes), about 30 minutes.

Soups from the Middle East

To the peasants of the Middle Eastern lands, they are a necessity of life. To vegetarians in other countries who have gourmet tastes, they are a very healthy and mouth-watering addition to their daily menu.

Broad Bean Soup, Fool Nabed

Serves from 8-10
Fresh broad beans are best for this recipe, but pre-cooked fava beans can also be used.

2 cups large broad beans, soaked for about 24 hours
8 cups water
1 tablespoon olive oil
2 tablespoons grated ginger
2 cloves garlic, crushed
2 teaspoons salt
1 teaspoon pepper
1 teaspoon cumin
¼ cup lemon juice
2 tablespoons finely chopped parsley

1. Rain beans and remove skins.
2. Place beans in saucepan with water and bring to boil.
3. Cover and cook over medium heat for 1½ hours or until well-cooked.
4. Allow to cool.
5. Puree in a blender; then return to saucepan and bring to boil, adding more water if necessary.
6. Stir in remaining ingredients, except parsley, and bring to boil.
7. Cook over medium heat for 5 minutes, stirring a few times.
8. Place in bowls; then garnish with parsley before serving.

Note: Cooked fava beans (another name for broad beans) in cans can be substituted for the dry broad beans. The fava in cans are usually cooked with their skins, and hence the soup will be much darker in color.

Substitute 4 cups of the canned fava for the 2 cups of the dried. Combine with remaining ingredients, except parsley, and purée; then bring to boil and cook for 5 minutes over medium heat.

Shawrbat 'adas Maa Banadoura (Lentil and Tomato Soup)

Serves from 8-10

1 cup lentils, rinsed
7 cups water
1 tablespoon olive oil
2 medium size onions, chopped
4 cloves garlic, crushed
2 cups stewed tomatoes
2 teaspoons salt
1 teaspoon cumin
1 teaspoon ground coriander seeds
½ teaspoon pepper
⅛ teaspoon cayenne
¼ cup white rice, uncooked
¼ cup lemon juice

1. Place lentils and water in a saucepan and bring to boil.
2. Cover and cook over medium heat for 25 minutes.
3. In the meantime, in a frying pan, heat oil and sauté onions and garlic until they turn golden brown.
4. Stir in remaining ingredients, except lemon juice, and sauté for another 5 minutes.
5. Stir the frying pan contents into the lentils and bring to boil.
6. Cover and cook over low heat for 20 minutes or until rice and lentils are well-cooked.
7. Stir in lemon juice and serve hot.
8. Enjoy this delicious soup.

Shawrbat 'Adas Maa Sh'Ireeya (Lentil and Vermicelli Soup)

Serves from 8-10

The fresh coriander and cooked vermicelli add an interesting touch to this version of lentil soup.

1 cup lentils, rinsed
8 cups water
2 teaspoons salt
1 teaspoon pepper
1 teaspoon ground cumin
1 tablespoon olive oil
2 medium onions, chopped
4 cloves garlic, crushed
1 small hot pepper, finely chopped
½ cup finely chopped coriander leaves
⅓ cup vermicelli, broken into small pieces

1. Place lentils, water, salt, pepper, and cumin in a pot and bring to boil.
2. Cover and cook over medium heat for 25 minutes.
3. In the meantime, heat oil in frying pan; then sauté onions, garlic, and hot pepper over medium heat for about 10 minutes.
4. Add coriander and stir-fry for 3 more minutes.
5. Add frying pan contents and vermicelli to lentils and bring to a boil.
6. Cover and simmer over low heat for about 30 minutes or until vermicelli and lentils are well-cooked.

Vegetable Soup, Hasa Al-Khadr

Serves 8-10

2 tablespoons olive oil
2 medium carrots, peeled and chopped into small pieces
1 large onion, chopped
2 cloves garlic, crushed
2 tablespoons grated fresh ginger
2 medium potatoes, peeled and diced into ½-inch cubes
4 medium tomatoes, chopped
1 cup finely chopped coriander leaves
7 cups water
2 teaspoons salt
1 teaspoon pepper
1 teaspoon cumin

1. Heat oil in a saucepan; then stir-fry carrots, onion, garlic, and ginger over medium heat for 8 minutes.
2. Add potatoes, tomatoes, and coriander leaves and stir-fry for another 5 minutes.
3. Add remaining ingredients and bring to boil.
4. Cover and simmer over medium-low heat for 1 hour or until vegetables are well-done.

Lentil and Leek Risotto

Serves 4

2 cups well-scrubbed leeks, chopped
1 clove garlic, minced
½ cup red pepper, finely chopped
1 tablespoon olive oil
3 cups vegetable broth or water
1¼ cups brown rice
Salt and pepper to taste
Pinch of basil
1 cup pre-cooked lentils
¼ cup freshly chopped parsley
¼ cup finely grated carrots

1. In a 4-quart deep pot with cover, sauté, leeks, garlic, and red pepper in oil.
2. When soft, add broth or water, and stir in rice along with seasonings.
3. Reduce heat and simmer covered for about 40 minutes or until rice is done.
4. Uncover, stir in cooked lentils and re-heat until piping hot.
5. Garnish with parsley and grated carrot before serving.

Shawrbat `adas Majroosha (Pureed Lentil Soup)

Serves from 8-10

1 tablespoon olive oil
2 large onions, chopped
1 small hot pepper, finely chopped
8 cups water
1 cup split lentils, rinsed
2 teaspoons salt
1 teaspoon cumin
1 teaspoon ground coriander seeds
½ teaspoon pepper
pinch of saffron
2 tablespoons white rice, uncooked
¼ cup lemon juice

1. Heat oil in a saucepan and sauté onions and hot pepper over medium heat for 10 minutes.
2. Add remaining ingredients, except lemon juice, and bring to boil.
3. Cover and cook over medium heat for 25 minutes.
4. Puree then return to saucepan and reheat.
5. Stir in lemon juice; then serve.

Lentil and Five Vegetable Stew

Serves 4

1 large leek stalk, finely chopped
1 large carrot, shredded
2 cups water
1½ cups canned crushed tomatoes
1 cup yellow corn kernels
½ cup broccoli
florets, lightly steamed
1 cup pre-cooked lentils
1 tablespoon dried red pepper flakes
Salt and pepper to taste

1. In a stew pot, boil well-cleaned chopped leek and shredded carrot in water until tender.
2. Drain well and add remaining ingredients.
3. Cook until well heated.
4. You may want to add a bit of pre-cooked brown rice or your favorite herb seasoning.

Lentil Soup I

Lentils are a staple in Middle Eastern and Indian cooking and make a thick, rich, and delicious soup. They're also a good source of calcium, iron, and vitamins A and B. With bread and a salad, it's a whole meal cut up some tofu wieners in it near the end of cooking. On a cold night, a filling soup like this is perfect nourishment for warming body and soul.

1 pound green (regular) lentils
bay leaf
3 large carrots
2 stalks celery
1 large yellow onion
2 cups crushed tomatoes
2 tablespoons olive oil
vinegar (red wine, cider, or balsamic), optional
Salt and pepper to taste

1. Pick over lentils to remove any stones, dirt, and other foreign objects. Wash them well in cold water and place in a large pot with enough cold water to cover lentils by 6 inches.
2. Add ⅓ of the bay leaf. Bring to a boil, skim off foam, lower heat, boil gently, partially covered, until lentils are just tooth-tender, about 45-60 minutes.
3. Add carrots, peeled and sliced, celery, sliced, and the onion, halved and thinly sliced.
4. Cook partially covered till carrots are tender, about 20-30 minutes.
5. Add olive oil, salt and pepper, and crushed tomatoes.
6. Simmer, partially covered, until lentils become very creamy and soft, at least 1 hour more.
7. Stir occasionally and add boiling water if necessary to prevent sticking.
8. Add more pepper if desired, along with some vinegar.
9. Remove bay leaf before serving.

Lentil Soup II

Serves 4
2 shallots, finely chopped
1 small yellow onion, finely chopped
2 teaspoons olive oil
3 cups water
1 cup dry green lentils
1 red potato, peeled and finely diced
1 large tomato, peeled and diced
1 small stalk celery, diced
1 small carrot, slivered
¼ cup freshly chopped parsley
Salt and pepper to taste
dry croutons or chopped chives

1. In a deep soup pot, sauté, shallots and onions in heated oil. Add water and lentils and bring to a boil.
2. Reduce heat and simmer, adding more water if needed to keep the three-cup level of liquid.
3. Cook lentils until barely tender.
4. Add all other vegetables and seasonings.
5. Continue cooking at least 20 minutes longer.
6. Fork-mash or puree mixture.
7. Serve warm, garnished with croutons or chives.

Spicy Lentil and Pepper Sauce For Rice

Serves 4
A healthy and unusual gourmet treat.
1 tablespoon olive oil
1 large onion, finely chopped
2 cloves garlic, minced
1 cup green and red bell pepper, finely chopped
1 large tomato, diced
1 cup vegetable juice
1 cup pre-cooked lentils
2 cooked, peeled hot chilies, finely minced (canned or fresh)
pinch of basil
salt and pepper to taste

1. In a deep pot, sauté, onions, garlic, and peppers in heated olive oil. Stir often.
2. Cover and reduce heat to low, add tomato and juice, and simmer for 20 minutes.
3. Add cooked lentils and seasonings (including chilies). Heat thoroughly before serving.
4. If the mixture seems too dry at any time, add a few
5. spoonfuls of water. Serve sauce over cooked pasta or brown rice.

Lentils Curried With Rhubarb and Potatoes

Serves 4

1 cup dry "orange" lentils
1 very large sweet potato, peeled and sliced
1 tablespoon oil
1 cup rhubarb, diced
2 tablespoons liquid sweetener
1 tablespoon curry powder
1 teaspoon ginger root, grated
1 teaspoon hot red chili powder
salt and pepper to taste
¼ cup shredded coconut

1. Cover lentils with water in a deep pot.
2. Bring to a boil, reduce heat and add raw sweet potato slices.
3. Simmer until soft (about an hour).
4. Remove from heat, drain, and set aside.
5. Preheat oven to 400 degrees.
6. Heat oil in a skillet. Once hot, add rhubarb.
7. Reduce heat and cook until tender.
8. Stir in sweetener and seasonings.
9. Mix with drained cooked lentils and potatoes that have been mashed together with a fork.
10. Pour into a oven-proof dish and bake at 400 degrees until piping hot (about 20 minutes).
11. Garnish with coconut.
12. Serve with chutney and a big bowl of brown rice.

Parsnip Curry

Serves 4

½ cup chopped onion
1 tablespoon oil
½ teaspoon cumin
1 teaspoon chili powder
1½ teaspoons turmeric
½ teaspoon cayenne, more for spicy curry
½ cup water
½ teaspoon salt
1 pound parsnips, peeled and cubed
⅓ cup green peppers, cut into thin strips
¼ cup chopped peanuts

1. Sauté onion in oil in a 1½ quart pot for 5 to 8 minutes until golden.
2. Add spices and cook, stirring, for 1 minute.
3. Add water, salt, and parsnips, bring to a boil, cover, and simmer over low heat for 20 to 30 minutes until vegetable is tender but not mushy.
4. Sauce will become quite thick. Garnish with pepper strips and peanuts before serving.

Broad Bean and Vegetable Soup, Shawrbat Fool

Serves from 8-10

2 cups large broad beans, soaked for about 24 hours
1 tablespoon olive oil
2 medium onions, chopped
4 cloves garlic, crushed
1 hot pepper, finely chopped 2 medium tomatoes, chopped into small pieces
1 medium carrot, finely chopped
1 medium potato, diced into ½-inch cubes
½ cup finely chopped coriander leaves
2 teaspoons salt
1 teaspoon pepper
1 teaspoon cumin
8 cups water

1. Drain beans, remove skins, and set beans aside.
2. Heat oil in a saucepan; then sauté onions, garlic, and hot pepper for 10 minutes.
3. Add remaining ingredients and bring to boil.
4. Cover and cook over medium heat for 1 hour or until broad beans are well-cooked, stirring a few times and adding more water if necessary.

Note: 4 cups of pre-cooked fava beans can be substituted for the 2 cups of dry beans. If the cooked fava beans are used, cook the soup for only about 40 minutes.

Lentil-Spinach Stew

Serves 5

1 medium onion
5 cloves garlic
1 cup split red lentils
1 (14 oz) can chopped tomatoes (with juice)
4 tsp. stock powder (or equivalent stock cube)
1 tbsp. vegan Worcestershire sauce, or dark soy sauce
½ tsp. salt
1 tsp. dried thyme
½ tsp. ground fennel seed
1 bay leaf
2 medium carrots
9 oz fresh or frozen chopped spinach
1 tbsp. balsamic vinegar or red wine vinegar

1. Chop the onion.
2. Sauté until soft but not browned.
3. Meanwhile, chop the garlic and rinse the lentils.
4. When the onion is soft, add the garlic, lentils, tomatoes, stock powder, Worcestershire / soy sauce, salt, thyme, fennel and bay leaf to the pan, along with 4 cups water.
5. Bring to a boil, then reduce heat, cover pan, and simmer for about 20 minutes, until the lentils have started to break up.
6. Stir occasionally.
7. Meanwhile, peel the carrots and chop into ¼ inch cubes.
8. If using fresh spinach, wash, remove large stalks and chop roughly.
9. Add the carrots and spinach to the pan.
10. Stir until mixed, and until frozen spinach has defrosted.
11. Cover and simmer a further 15 minutes, or until lentils and vegetables are cooked.
12. Remove bay leaf and stir in vinegar.

Notes: This ends up tasting fairly tomato-ey. Use only ½ can if you're not too fussed on tomato flavor. It also ends up fairly soupy - if you want it thicker, leave it until the next day to thicken, or use less water, or remove the lid for the last 10 minutes to allow water to evaporate. Using frozen chopped spinach gives a more homogeneous texture, fresh spinach will be in larger pieces. You may like a mixture of the two.

Greek Lentil Stew

Serves 8 to 10

1 carrot
1 onion
l large leek
2 cups sweet corn (2 cobs)
2 cups chopped tomatoes
2 tablespoons olive oil
2½ cups dry lentils
8 cups water or light vegetable stock
 (-or- 5 cups veggie stock 2 cups water)
3 whole garlic gloves
2 teaspoons salt
½ cup balsamic vinegar

1. Finely chop carrot, onion and leek.
2. Remove corn off cob is using fresh corn.
3. Sauté onions, leek, and carrots in olive oil 3 minutes then add corn and tomatoes and sauté on low heat around 5 minutes.
4. Mix in lentils then add the water or vegetable stock, whole garlic gloves and salt, simmer on low heat 45 minutes stirring occasionally.
5. Season at the end with the vinegar.
6. Garnish with fresh chopped parsley.

Eggplant Stew (Jewish)

Serves 8-10

2 medium eggplants (2 pounds)
1 tablespoon olive oil
1 medium onion, chopped
14- to 16-ounce can diced tomatoes, undrained
Juice of ½ to 1 lemon, or to taste
1 teaspoon sugar
¼ to ½ cup chopped fresh parsley, to taste
Salt and freshly ground pepper to taste
Cooked rice (optional)

1. Preheat the oven to 450 degrees. Prick the eggplants in several places with fork; place on a foil-lined baking sheet.
2. Bake until softened and collapsed, about 45 to 55 minutes. Cool, slice open and scoop the pulp from the skin. Discard the skin and chop the pulp.
3. In a large, heavy saucepan, heat the oil over medium heat. Add the onion; sauté until golden, five to seven minutes.
4. Add eggplant, tomatoes, lemon juice and sugar.
5. Simmer gently, covered, 20 minutes.
6. Add the parsley, then season with salt and pepper.
7. Simmer 10 minutes more. Serve alone or over rice.

Passover Spinach Squares (Jewish – Pareve)

Serve these nibbles as an appetizer with the main course. You can replace the fresh spinach with 3 packages (10 oz. each) frozen and thawed chopped spinach.

1½ lbs fresh spinach, stemmed and washed
1½ tsp. canola oil
1 leek, thinly sliced (white part only)
2 cloves garlic, minced
2 tsp. lemon juice
¾ tsp. dried oregano
⅛ tsp. ground black pepper
egg substitute for 3 egg whites

1. Preheat the oven to 350°F.
2. Coat an 8" X 8" no-stick baking dish with pareve no-stick spray and set aside.
3. In a large pot, bring a small amount of water to a boil.
4. Add the spinach, cover and cook over medium heat for 5 minutes, or until the spinach is wilted.
5. Squeeze the spinach dry, chop and place in a large bowl.
6. In a small, no-stick skillet over low heat, warm the oil.
7. Add the leeks and garlic. Sauté for 10 minutes, or until tender but not browned.
8. Add the leek mixture to the bowl with the spinach.
9. Stir in the lemon juice, oregano and pepper.
10. In another clean large bowl, using an electric mixer, beat the egg white substitute until foamy.
11. Fold into the spinach mixture.
12. Pour the mixture into the prepared pan and bake for 35 minutes, or until set.
13. Remove from the oven and set aside to cool slightly.
14. Cut into 16 squares and serve warm.

Greek Okra Stew

Serves 4

Here I've substituted seitan (or wheat gluten) for meat to create a delicious vegetarian alternative.

1 onion, peeled and chopped
2 teaspoons oil
1 pound okra, chopped
8-ounce package seitan, drained and cubed
2 tomatoes, chopped
2 tablespoons wine vinegar
2 tablespoons lemon juice
½ teaspoon garlic powder
½ teaspoon coriander
Salt and pepper to taste

1. Stir-fry onion with oil in a large frying pan over medium heat for 3 minutes.
2. Add okra and remaining ingredients.
3. Stir-fry 10 minutes longer.
4. Serve hot over cooked brown rice.

Israeli Wheat Berry Stew

Serves:8
5 cup Trader Joe's marinara and the rest water
1½ cup Great northern beans
1 cup wheat berries
6 small potatoes, cut in half
1 large onion, sliced
4 clove garlic, minced
5 tsp. cumin, ground
3 tsp. turmeric
½ tsp. black pepper, ground
2 green peppers

1. Mix together all ingredients in crock-pot.
2. Cook at high 8 to 10 hours.

Salads

Tabbouleh Salad

¾ cup Bulgar wheat
1½ cup boiling water
4 tbsp. olive oil
4 tbsp. lemon juice
2 cloves garlic, chopped/crushed
handful parsley, handful coriander (cilantro), bit less mint,
  all chopped up
1 lb. tomatoes chopped
½ cucumber diced

1. Pour the boiling water over the bulgar wheat, leave it
    for about 20 minutes to absorb the water.
2. Mix oil, lemon juice and garlic together, pour over the
    bulgar wheat and leave overnight if possible.
3. Add the herbs, tomatoes and cucumbers, mix
    together and eat.
4. You can vary the herbs to taste but don't stint.

Jicama & Orange Salad

Serves 6
1 small jicama, peeled & halved
2 navel oranges
6 scallions, thinly sliced
2 tablespoons chopped fresh cilantro
1 tablespoon fresh lime juice
¾ teaspoon salt

1. Quarter each jicama half and thinly slice.
2. With a paring knife, peel oranges, removing all white
    pith.
3. Halve oranges lengthwise and thinly slice crosswise.
4. In a large bowl, toss jicama, oranges, scallions,
    cilantro, lime juice, and salt.
5. Cover and chill for at least 15 minutes. Toss again
    and serve.

Greek Salad

½ pound reduced fat regular tofu (firm), rinsed and patted
dry (press if time permits)

Marinade:
2 tablespoons red wine vinegar
1 tablespoon fresh lemon juice
4 teaspoons olive oil
½ teaspoons dried basil leaves
½ teaspoons dried oregano leaves
½ teaspoons salt
¼ teaspoons garlic granules
¼ teaspoons ground black pepper

Salad:
4 cup romaine lettuce, torn into bite-size pieces
1½ cup cucumber, sliced horizontally and cut into half-
moon shapes (peel if waxed or thick-skinned)
1 ripe medium tomato, cut in half and thinly sliced into
  half-moon shapes
⅓ cup whole black olives or Greek olives
¼ cup chopped red onion

1. Cut the tofu into ¾ inch cubes, and place it in a wide,
    shallow ceramic or glass mixing bowl.
2. In a small measuring cup or mixing bowl whisk
    together the ingredients for the marinade.
3. Pour the marinade over the tofu chunks, tossing
    them gently so that they are evenly coated.
4. Cover, marinate in fridge several hours or overnight.
5. (Highly recommend is 18 to 24 hours, and give them a
    stir whenever you go in the kitchen so they marinate
    evenly.)
6. Just before serving prepare the salad ingredients and
    place them in a large mixing bowl.
7. Add the tofu and marinade to the salad ingredients,
    and toss gently but thoroughly.
8. Serve at once, with salt and pepper on the side to
    season as desired

Desserts

Syrian Wheat Pudding

Serves 8

This unique Syrian pudding traditionally would contain more nuts, and thus more fat.

1½ cups bulgur (cracked wheat)
4 cups water
1 cup raisins
½ teaspoon caraway seeds
1 tablespoon shelled pistachio nuts
1 tablespoon shelled walnuts, chopped
¼ cup maple syrup

1. Place bulgur, water, raisins, and caraway seeds in a covered pot.
2. Cook over medium heat for 30 minutes.
3. Stir occasionally.
4. Add nuts and syrup. Simmer 5 minutes longer.
5. Serve warm. Cold leftovers are good, too.

Easy Vegan Sweet Potato Pie

The secret to the perfect vegan pumpkin pie is to use plenty of spices for maximum flavor. Using tofu instead of eggs for a vegan pumpkin pie also means that this recipe is much lower in fat than other pumpkin pies, and is also cholesterol free. Plus, because it uses tofu to carry the sweet potato flavor, you're getting a healthy boost of soy protein too! Plus, this sweet potato pie recipe uses a pre-made crust so it's very quick and easy to make. However you can substitute it for our pie crust recipes from found in the index. You can have it in the oven in ten minutes flat, five if you're quick!

1 14 oz. container soft (silken) tofu
1 14 oz. container firm or extra-firm tofu
1 24-oz can sweet potatoes in syrup
2 tsp. cinnamon
1 tsp. ginger
½ tsp. nutmeg
1 tsp. salt
2 tsp. vanilla extract
½ cup sugar
1 pre-made or store-bought pie crust

1. Preheat oven to 350°F.
2. Blend all the ingredients (except the pie crust!) in a blender or food processor until free of lumps.
3. Pour into the pie shell and bake for 1½ hours, or until toothpick inserted in the center comes out clean.

Vegan Cheesecake with Hemp

Serves 8

3/4 cup shelled hemp seed
1 cup warm water
½ cup raw honey
16 oz. firm tofu
1 tsp vanilla
½ tbsp lemon juice
1 tbsp Arrow root
1 organic graham cracker crust
Top with fresh berries or a drizzle of honey

Preheat oven to 350°.
1. In blender, puree shelled hemp seed with water until smooth.
2. Add remaining ingredients and blend.
3. Pour mixture into graham cracker pie shell, and bake for about 30 minutes.
4. Once cooled, top with your berries or honey.

Strawberry Tabouli

Serves 8

1½ cup bulgur wheat
1-2 teaspoons salt
2 cup boiling water
¼ cup extra virgin olive oil
¼ cup freshly squeezed lemon juice
2 cup finely chopped fresh parsley
¾ cup finely chopped fresh mint
4 cup chopped strawberries
1 cup toasted pecan pieces

1. In large bowl, combine bulgur and salt.
2. Add boiling water, cover and let sit for 30 minutes.
3. Remove cover and fluff with fork.
4. Stir in lemon and oil. Add parsley, mint and strawberries. Cover and refrigerate.
5. When ready to serve, add toasted pecans and toss to mix, or serve with pecans sprinkled on top.

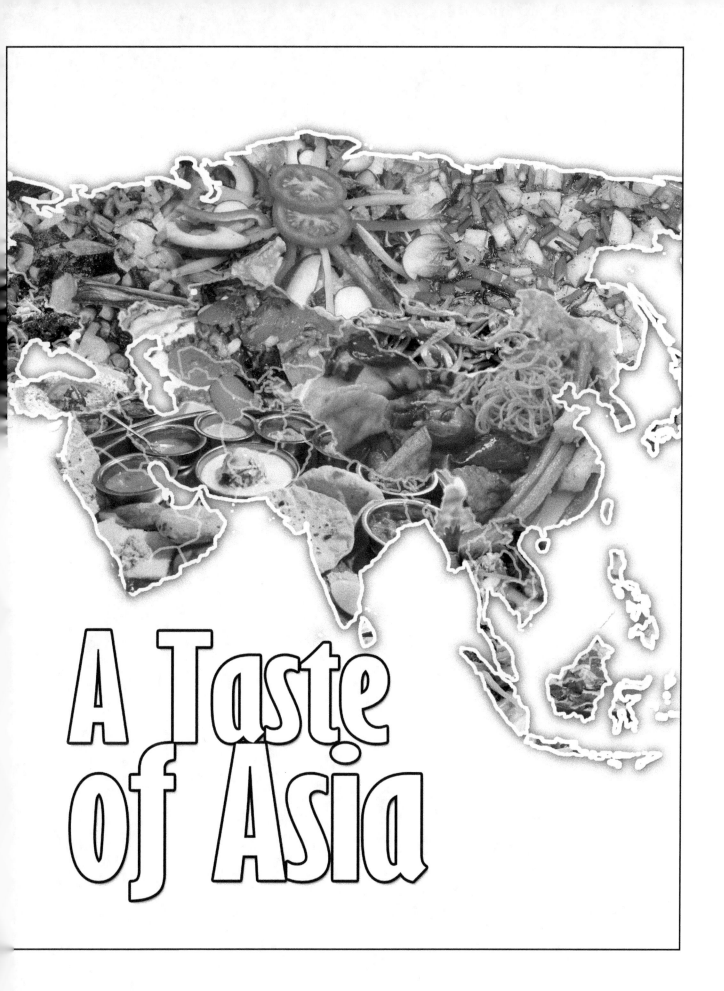

A Taste of Asia

A Taste of Asia

Appetizers

Spring Rolls

Makes 12 Rolls

12 spring roll wrappers (rice paper)
6 oz. firm tofu (not silken)
2 tablespoons or more soy sauce, tamari, or
 Bragg's liquid aminos
6 oz. thin rice noodles (vermicelli)
48 fresh mint leaves
¼ head leaf lettuce
3 shredded carrots (optional)
spring roll sauce

You can get the spring roll wrappers at an oriental grocery store, and they will keep on your shelf indefinitely.
They are fragile; keep them flat and handle them gently. Be sure they are made of rice.

You CANNOT substitute egg roll wrappers in this recipe. The round ones, about 8 ½ inches in diameter, are the easiest to work with.

1. Slice the tofu into ½ inch slices.
2. Pat dry with paper towels.
3. Press it for an hour or so if you have time.
4. Put the tofu slices on a nonstick cookie pan.
5. Add the soy sauce, trying to keep it on the tofu as much as possible.
6. Bake at 325 for about 45 minutes, turning occasionally and adding more soy sauce if they look like they can absorb more.
7. When they are nice and brown and dry, cut them into strips, about the size of French fries.
8. Add one strip per spring roll.
9. (If you don't have time to bake the tofu, cut it into strips and fry it with the soy sauce on a nonstick skillet for a few minutes, carefully turning each strip, trying to crisp it up a little on each side.)
10. Set aside. Wash and dry the lettuce.
11. Tear it into 3 or 4 inch pieces, removing stems and crisp veins. Your lettuce needs to be on the limp side.
12. Any crisp pieces will tear the spring roll wrappers when you try to roll them.
13. Wash and dry the mint. Remove all stems! Set aside. (If you can't get fresh mint, you can substitute fresh cilantro, but the spring rolls will taste completely different.)
14. Shred or grate the carrots. Again, they need to be small enough pieces that they are not crisp.

15. You may prefer your spring rolls without the carrots.
16. Throw the rice vermicelli into boiling water and cook until just done, about 2 or 3 minutes.
17. Pour into a colander, and rinse with cool water.
18. The noodles need to be well drained and cool enough to handle. Set aside.
19. Put an inch or two of water in a pan that is big enough to hold the spring rolls.
20. (Cool water works fine).
21. Separate the wrappers, and stack them in the water, making sure each one is completely covered with water before putting in the next one.
22. Leave the wrappers in the water until they are flexible (about 2 or 3 minutes).
23. Remove the whole stack at once, and place them on a clean wet kitchen towel, covering them with another damp towel.
24. Now you are ready to assemble them. Carefully remove one wrapper and put it on another surface (You can use a bamboo sushi mat, or you could easily use another damp towel. If you use a plate, dump off the excess water between each spring roll.)
25. Working quickly, put onto the wrapper 3 or 4 small pieces of lettuce, 4 leaves of mint, a handful of rice noodles, one strip of tofu, and a few tablespoons of carrots if desired.
26. Quickly fold the bottom of the wrapper over the pile, fold in the sides, and continue to roll up
27. After four or five, wrap each in plastic wrap to keep them from drying out too much.
28. If one of them is falling apart, wrap it in plastic wrap immediately.
29. Have a piece of plastic wrap cut and ready in case one is falling apart. (If you are serving them to company, start over with a new wrapper on the ones that are falling apart.)
30. If a lot of them are falling apart, then something may not be drained well enough, or you may be trying to fill them too full, or some of your wrappers may be defective with too many tears and holes, or too thin.
31. Serve cold or room temperature with sauces of your choice.

Note: Do not EVER cook these spring rolls.

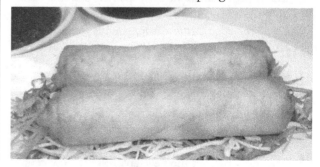

California Nori Rolls

5¼ cups sushi rice (or any short-grain, sticky rice)
1 cup rice vinegar
½ cup sugar
1 tablespoon salt
1 package (ten sheets) nori (a type of seaweed)

Vegetables of your choice: cucumbers, carrots, avocado.
Optional: soy sauce substitute, pickled ginger, wasabi (Japanese horseradish).

1. Combine rice with 5 ½ cups water and bring to a boil.
2. Reduce heat and simmer, covered, for 20 minutes or until water is absorbed.
3. Let cool for at least 10 minutes.
4. In a non-reactive bowl, combine the vinegar, sugar, and salt. Mix until the sugar and salt are dissolved.
5. Drizzle over the rice and gently mix. (You may have to experiment with the amount of vinegar, sugar, and salt that you like.)
6. Slice the vegetables in long thin strips. (Try cucumbers, carrots, celery, avocado, red or green peppers and/or green onion. It's nice to have several different colors.)
7. Now you are ready to roll! If you want to, you can use a bamboo mat (available at your local Asian grocery) to help you roll, but its fairly easy without one.
8. Lay a sheet of nori out on a large plate or cutting board.
9. Then spread on about 1½ cups rice, pressing firmly until the rice is evenly distributed across the sheet.
10. Leave the edge farthest from you uncovered.
11. Lay the vegetables in a line from left to right across the center of the rice.
12. Now starting with the edge nearest to you, roll up and over enclosing the vegetables.
13. Wetting the far edge helps seal the roll.
14. You should end up with a long roll, with the nori on the outside and the rice and vegetables in the middle.
15. The idea is to get the vegetables in the very center, but don't worry too much about it. (In Japan, presen-

tation is very important, but you may not be as concerned about this.) Repeat with the remaining nine sheets.

To serve, slice crosswise into about eight pieces. You can eat them with soy sauce with a little wasabi mixed in. Wasabi comes in paste or powdered form, is light green and very hot. It's really good, but be careful at first. Japanese cuisine would normally also offer pickled ginger, which is not as hot, but very tasty.

The amount you make depends on the number of people and whether you're going to eat the rolls as an appetizer or main course. These rolls are great to bring to parties, as everyone with be impressed with how beautiful and yummy they are. They are also very low fat. Also, using brown rice can make it more nutritious.

Bok Choy with Baby Portabellas and Tofu

1 lb tofu (You can used extra firm and press it to get out as much water as possible)
1 large head bok choy (leaves thinly sliced/Stalks cut into large chunks separate leaves and stems into two bowls)

1 small package baby portabella mushrooms (sliced)
1 carrot julienned
2 tablespoon soy sauce/tamari/shoyu
2 tablespoon oil (for stir frying)
1-2 tbsp. grated fresh ginger (or 1½ tbsp. dried)
1 tsp. dark sesame oil

1. Cut tofu into large cubes and mix with 2 tsp. soy sauce.
2. Set aside. Heat wok and add 2 tablespoons oil.
3. Add carrots and ginger, stir fry for 1 minute.
4. Add mushrooms, stir-fry for 30 seconds.
5. Add bok choy stems and tofu, stir fry for 1 minute.
6. Add bok choy leaves and stir-fry for an additional 2 minutes (cover occasionally to produce some steam) until wilted.
7. Finish by adding 1 tsp. sesame oil.
8. Season with additional soy sauce if necessary.
9. Serve with brown rice.

Spinach-Filled Won Tons

Serves 60
10 ounces fresh spinach
1 tablespoon peanut oil
1 garlic cloves, minced
¼ cup onion, minced
10 water chestnuts, minced, rinsed drained
1 pound won-ton wrappers (about 60)
salt & pepper, to taste

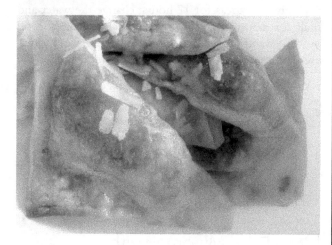

1. Wash the spinach thoroughly and trim any tough stems.
2. Drain, then dry with paper towels or a salad spinner.
3. Coarsely chop and set aside.
4. Place a wok over medium-high heat.
5. When it begins to smoke, add the peanut oil, then the garlic and onion. Stir-fry 30 seconds.
6. Add the spinach and water chestnuts and stir fry until the spinach is dry, about 3 minutes.
7. Transfer the vegetables to a bowl and season with salt and pepper.
8. When the filling has cooled slightly, from the won tons.
9. Dip you fingers in warm water and moisten the entire surface of a wrapper.
10. Place 1 teaspoon of filling in the center of the wrapper and fold it in half. Press the edges to seal.
11. Bring the ends together and moisten with water; press to seal.
12. Cover. Set aside the finished won tons while shaping the remainder.
13. Cook the won tons following the directions in the recipe, boiling water or soup stock until they are just tender, or deep-fry them in 3 to 4 cups of peanut oil until golden brown, about 3 minutes on each side.

Note: Makes 60 won tons. Won tons may be frozen after being shaped. Place on cookie sheet with sides not touching in the freezer. When completely frozen place in plastic air tight bag.

Cashew Tofu

1 block (approx. 14 oz. of tofu)
1 jar Hoisin sauce
1 tbsp. soy sauce (or tamari)
4-5 green onions sliced thin (green and white part)
3 large cloves fresh garlic minced
about the same amount of fresh minced ginger
¾ cup cashews
2 tsp. sesame oil
optional vegetables (water chestnuts, snow peas, bean sprouts, broccoli, etc)
rice

1. Start by putting on some rice to cook
2. To prepare the tofu, slice it into about ½ inch thick slices and press it between paper towels or a kitchen towel to get as much of the water out of it as you can.
3. Add a few tablespoons of oil in a non-stick fry pan and cook the tofu on med-high until it's browned and crispy on the outside.
4. This makes it taste much better than mushy tofu.
5. Sometimes we substitute soy chicken for the tofu.
6. They is also another meat substitute called Quorn, which is excellent.
7. After the tofu is cooked, add the garlic, ginger, cashews onions, soy sauce, and sesame oil.
8. Cook them on med-low to med for a minute to let the flavors come out.
9. Then add enough hoisin sauce to cover everything.
10. Depending upon how thick the hoisin is, you can usually add a little water to thin it out.
11. And add any other vegetables you want now and stir it up. Just cook until it's hot.
12. You don't have to follow a strict recipe with this. Just throw things in, and it usually turns out pretty good.
13. You can add some hot chilies for flavor.
14. Adjust the ingredients as you like.

Cold Fruit Sushi with Honey-Style Dipping Sauce

Serves 4

Pineapple matchsticks are rolled up in paper-thin slices of melon for a spare, cool dessert that is prepared in the same fashion as sushi rolls. It's important that the fruit be perfectly ripe, and the presentation graceful.

Wrap cool slices of melon around pineapple matchsticks, squeeze some fresh lemon juice over the pieces, wrap tightly, and refrigerate until it is time to serve dessert.

1 small honeydew melon
1 small cantaloupe
1 small pineapple
2 tablespoons honey-type sweetener
  (e.g. maple syrup, rice syrup)

1. Place the fruit on a cutting board lined with parchment.
2. Trim the tops and bottoms of the melons and pineapple and sit them upright on the cutting board.
3. Using a very sharp knife, cut away the rind, slicing lengthwise, working your way around the fruit.
4. Cut about 24 very thin slices of melon in the same fashion, slicing from the top to bottom, allowing the juices to collect on the parchment paper.
5. Slice the pineapple lengthwise into ⅛-inch slices.
6. Pile and cut into matchsticks.
7. Pour the juices that have collected into a small bowl.
8. Stir in the sweetener and set aside.
9. To assemble the fruit sushi, lay the melon slices vertically on the cutting board.
10. Place 3 pineapple matchsticks horizontally at the base of the melon.
11. Roll the melon around the matchsticks, wrapping tightly.
12. Trim the base of the roll and slice it into individual pieces.
13. Squeeze some fresh lemon juice over the pieces, and refrigerate until it is time to serve dessert.

Raw Vegan Sushi Rolls

Untoasted Nori Sheets
Alfalfa Spouts
Avocado diced
Cucumber diced into strips
Sundried Tomatoes diced
Tomato Hummus

Tomato Hummus:
Soak raw chickpeas for 12 hours, change the water and soak for a further 12 hours. Place chickpeas in food processor and process with chopped garlic, fresh tomatoes and sundried tomatoes until thick and chunky.

1. Place sheet of nori flat on a kitchen surface and then add raw hummus, alfalfa sprouts, avocado, cucumber and sundried tomato in a horizontal strip reaching from one end to the other.
2. Roll the nori sheet into a tube, dip your finger in water and wet the edge of the nori sheet which will allow it to stick closed.
3. Cut into pieces. Serve with fresh ginger.

Deep Fried Mushroom with Xanthoxylon Salt

1 pack fresh mushroom
¾ tsp. xanthoxylon salt
1 tbsp. minced parsley

Seasonings:
½ tsp. ginger juice
1 tsp. wine
¾ tsp. xanthoxylon salt
pinch of pepper
batter 1 cup self-raising flour
¾ cup water
2 tbsp. oil to be added later on

1. Blend ¾ cup water with 1 cup self-raising flour and stir into batter. Let stand for 5-10 minutes.
2. Add in 2 tbsp. oil and minced parsley.
3. Remove stalks form mushrooms and rinse.
4. Then blanch in boiling water for a while.
5. Take out and soak in cold water.
6. Drain. Marinate with seasonings for a while.
7. Dust marinated mushrooms with flour, then dip in batter.
8. Soak mushrooms in very hot oil and fry until slightly brown and crispy. Take out and drain.
9. Arrange on plate.
10. Serve with tomato ketchup or Worcestershire sauce.

Spinach-Filled Won Tons

Serves 60

10 ounces fresh spinach
1 tablespoon peanut oil
1 garlic cloves, minced
¼ cup onion, minced
10 water chestnuts, minced, rinsed drained
1 pound won-ton wrappers (about 60)
salt & pepper, to taste

1. Wash the spinach thoroughly and trim any tough stems.
2. Drain, then dry with paper towels or a salad spinner.
3. Coarsely chop and set aside.
4. Place a wok over medium-high heat.
5. When it begins to smoke, add the peanut oil, then the garlic and onion.
6. Stir-fry 30 seconds.
7. Add the spinach and water chestnuts and stir fry until the spinach is dry, about 3 minutes.
8. Transfer the vegetables to a bowl and season with salt and pepper.
9. When the filling cools slightly, form the won tons.
10. Dip you fingers in warm water and moisten the entire surface of a wrapper.
11. Place 1 teaspoon of filling in the center of the wrapper and fold it in half.
12. Press the edges to seal.
13. Bring the ends together and moisten with water; press to seal.
14. Cover and set aside the finished won tons while shaping the remainder.
15. Cook the won tons following the directions in the recipe - either in boiling water or soup stock until they are just tender, or deep-fry them in 3 to 4 cups of peanut oil until golden brown, about 3 minutes on each side. **Note:** Makes 60 won tons.
16. Won tons may be frozen after being shaped.
17. Place on cookie sheet with sides not touching in the freezer.
18. When completely frozen place in plastic air tight bag.

Chinese-Style Spring Rolls

1 pack wrappers (or phyllo pastry cut to size?)
1 sheet usu-age (thin deep-fried tofu)
2 large fresh shiitake (or other mushrooms)
2 thin-skinned green peppers (or spring onion?)
similar quantity of bamboo shoot (or bean sprouts?)
Salad oil for cooking and deep-frying

Seasonings:

1½ tbsp. Japanese-style soy sauce (maybe less, if Chinese-style)
1 tablespoon sesame oil
1 tablespoon sake/sherry/Chinese wine
1 tablespoon sugar
¼ tsp. toubanjian (Chinese chili paste) or a good shake of chili powder
pepper if liked

1. Mix together all the seasonings.
2. Pour boiling water over the usu-age, drain.
3. cut in half lengthways, then slice finely across the width. Slice veggies into julienne strips.
4. Heat a little salad oil in a wok or fry pan, and fry all the solid ingredients together until wilted.
5. Add seasonings, stir in well, then set aside to cool a little.
6. Separate the spring-roll wrappers (it's easiest to divide them into twos or threes, then peel off individual wrappers).
7. Place them under a damp towel, easily accessible.
8. Have a small bowl of clean water ready.
9. Place one wrapper on the work surface so that it looks diamond-shaped (if there's a difference between the two sides of the wrapper, put the rougher side downwards).
10. Lay about 1/10 of the filling in a row near the lowest corner.
11. Flip the lowest corner up over the filling, then roll the filling and that corner of the wrapper loosely upward once.
12. Fold in the outer corners so they overlap at the center, then continue overlap at the center, then continue rolling up the spring roll loosely.
13. Just before the uppermost corner disappears, dip your fingers in the water and dab a few drops onto that corner.
14. It won't stick immediately, but if you then place the completed roll on a wire rack with the damp corner underneath, it'll dry sealed.
15. Deep-fry or freeze the spring rolls as soon as you've finished rolling.
16. Test the frying oil by dropping in a tiny piece of wrapper, if the oil is the right temperature, the piece will sink and then immediately rise and make cheerful frying noises.
17. In too-cold oil, it'll just sit on the bottom sullenly; in too-hot oil, it'll skitter across the surface.
18. Fry only about 3 rolls at a time, to prevent the oil cooling suddenly, and turn when they start to color underneath.

Note: If you're frying deep-frozen ones, "French-fry" them: fry them lightly for a minute or so, remove from the oil, let them stand for a couple of minutes to allow the heat to penetrate, then re-fry them.

Chinese Steamed Buns
(Mauna Pua)

1 package active dry yeast
1 cup warm water (not boiling)
1 tbsp. sugar
2 tbsp. vegetable oil
1 tsp. salt
About 2¾ cups whole wheat flour or white flour
mushroom-cashew filling (recipe follows)
1 tbsp. margarine (for baked buns)

1. In a large bowl, dissolve yeast in the warm water; blend in sugar, oil and salt.
2. Let stand until bubbly (about 15 minutes).
3. Add flour and mix until dough holds together.
4. Place dough on a lightly floured board and knead until smooth and elastic (about 8-10 minutes).
5. Turn dough over in a greased bowl; cover and let rise in a warm place until doubled (about 1 hour).
6. Meanwhile prepare the following mushroom-cashew filling; let cool and set aside:

Mushroom-Cashew Filling

¼ lb. chopped mushrooms
1 small onion, chopped
1 clove garlic, minced or pressed
1 tsp. minced fresh ginger
½ cup coarsely chopped bamboo shoots
¾ cup coarsely chopped cashews
2 green onions including tops, thinly sliced
1 tbsp. vegetable oil
1 tsp. sesame oil

In a bowl, combine the following:

3 tbsp. soy sauce
1 tbsp. dry sherry
1 tsp. sugar
¼ cup water
1 tbsp. cornstarch

1. Heat oil in wide frying pan over high heat.
2. Add mushrooms, onion, garlic and ginger and stir-fry for 3 minutes.
3. Add bamboo shoots, cashews, and green onions and cook for 2 minutes.
4. Pour in soy sauce mixture and cook, stirring, until sauce bubbles and thickens. Stir in sesame oil.
5. Remove pan from heat and cool.
6. Turn dough out onto a lightly floured board and knead for 1 minute.
7. Cut dough into 12 equal pieces.
8. Roll each piece into a round about 4½ inches in diameter.
9. Press outside edge of round to make it slightly thinner than the rest of the dough.
10. Place about 2 tablespoons filling in center of each round.
11. Pull edges of dough up around filling and twist to seal. You can steam or bake the buns.

For steamed buns:

1. Place each bun, twisted side down, on a 2 inch square of foil and place on a cookie sheet.
2. Cover with a towel and let rise in a warm place until puffy and light (about 30 minutes).
3. Set with foil, in a single layer in a steaming basket over boiling water.
4. Cover and steam for 15 minutes.
5. Serve warm; or let cool, then wrap and refrigerate or freeze.
6. To reheat, steam buns until hot (about 5-10 minutes).

For baked buns:

1. Place buns about 2 inches apart on a greased cookie sheet.
2. Cover and let rise in a warm place until puffy and light (about 30 minutes).
3. Melt margarine, brush over tops.
4. Bake in a 350 degree oven until bottoms of buns turn golden brown (about 15 minutes).

Entrees

BBQ "Ribs"

8-10 oz. dried yuba (bean curd sheets, found in Chinese groceries)
¼ cup nutritional yeast flakes
¼ cup smooth peanut butter (or other nut butter) [Tried with tahini, but definitely prefer peanut butter]
2 tablespoons dark miso
1 tablespoon melted margarine
1 tablespoon water [If you use more water, the mixture is more the consistency of a gravy than a paste]
2 teaspoons paprika

1. 2 cup BBQ sauce (Ron Pickarski's sauce from Eco-Cuisine is to die for)
2. Soak yuba in water 4-6 hours.
3. Cut off and discard any pieces that remain hard.
4. Drain, cut into 4-6" lengths.
5. Squeeze out as much water as you can.
6. Mix next 6 ingredients in a bowl.
7. Add yuba sticks, coating well.
8. Lay yuba sticks right up against each other on a greased cookie sheet one layer thick.
9. Bake at 350F for 25 minutes, until bottoms are crisp and browned.
10. Remove from oven, mix with 2 cups BBQ sauce.
11. Return to cookie sheet (in one layer) and bake at 350F for 10-15 minutes.

Stir-Fried Spinach with Tofu

Serves 6
1 pound fresh spinach
2 tablespoons peanut oil
1 clove garlic, minced
½ teaspoon salt
½ pound firm tofu, in ½-inch cubes
1 tablespoon rice wine or dry sherry

1. Wash and thoroughly dry the spinach.
2. Remove any tough stems.
3. Place a wok over medium-high heat.
4. When it begins to smoke, add the peanut oil and the garlic.
5. Stir briefly, then add the spinach and salt.
6. Stir-fry just until the spinach is wilted.
7. about 1 minute.
8. Gently stir in the tofu and sprinkle with rice wine.
9. Cook until the tofu is heated through, about 1 minute. Serve immediately.

Cabbage Kimchi

Makes 2 quarts
1 lb. Chinese cabbage (about ½ a large head)
1 lb. white radish
3 tablespoons salt
2 tablespoons finely minced ginger (fresh is *much better!)
1½ tablespoons minced garlic
5 scallions, cut into fine rounds, including green tops
1 tablespoon cayenne -or- hot Korean red pepper
1 teaspoon sugar.

1. Slice cabbage in either bite-sized chunks or strips about 2 inches in length.
2. Peel radish, cut in half lengthwise then crosswise into ⅛ inch slices.
3. In a large bowl, put 5 cup water and 2 tablespoons plus 2 teaspoons of the salt. Mix.
4. Add cabbage and radish and dunk a few times, as they have a tendency to float.
5. Leave in the salty water, cover loosely and set aside for 12 hours, turning veggies over a few times.
6. After the soak period, take the ginger, garlic, scallions, cayenne, sugar and remaining 1 teaspoon salt in another large bowl. Mix well.
7. Take the cabbage out of the soaking liquid with a slotted spoon (save the liquid) and add to the bowl with the seasonings and mix well.
8. Put this mixture in a 2 quart jar or crock.
9. Pour enough of the salt water over to cover veggies.
10. Leave (at least) 1 inch space at top of jar.
11. Cover loosely with a clean cloth and set aside for 3 to 7 days to ferment. Stir/turn veggies over daily.
12. In summer, kimchees ferment quickly; the process slows down in winter.
13. Taste the kimchee after 3 days to check on the sourness.
14. When done to your liking, cover jar and refrigerate.
15. This is really good and is pretty easy to make.

Simple Lo Mein

Serves 4

3 dried Chinese mushrooms
½ pound Chinese noodles
3 tablespoons peanut oil
1 onion, chopped
2 cups shredded cabbage
1 crown broccoli, sliced
1 yellow onion, sliced into half rings
2 carrots julienned
1 small zucchini, in ½-inch cubes
3 tablespoons light soy sauce
½ cup reserved mushroom soaking liquid
1 teaspoon honey
½ teaspoon salt

1. Soak the Chinese mushrooms in 1 cup of hot water for 30 minutes.
2. Meanwhile, bring 4 quarts of water to boil in a large pot. Stir in the noodles and cook 3 minutes, just until tender.
3. Drain, rinse in cold water, and toss with 1 tablespoon of peanut oil.
4. Set aside. Remove the mushrooms, but strain and reserve ½ cup of the soaking liquid.
5. Trim and discard the mushroom stems.
6. Coarsely chop the caps and set aside.
7. Combine the ingredients for the sauce in a small bowl. Stir to dissolve the sugar and set aside.
8. Place a wok over medium-high heat.
9. When it begins to smoke, add the mushrooms, onion, cabbage, carrots, broccoli and zucchini.
10. Stir-fry for 2 minutes.
11. Pour the sauce over the vegetables.
12. Add the reserved noodles and stir until heated through, about 3 minutes. Serve immediately.

Spicy Vegetable Lo Mein

Serves 6

8 ounces soba noodles (or other flat Asian noodle)
2 teaspoons hot chili oil
2 teaspoons ginger root, grated
2 cloves garlic, minced
3½ ounces shiitake mushrooms, pkg, caps thinly sliced
1 medium red bell pepper, in short thin strips
2 cups bok choy, chopped
½ cup canned vegetable broth
6 ounces sugar snap peas or snow pea pods
2 tablespoons tamari or soy sauce
2 tablespoons seasoned or regular rice vinegar
1 tablespoon dark-roasted sesame oil
¼ cup chopped peanuts or cashews, optional

1. Cook noodles according to package directions.
2. Meanwhile, heat oil in large deep skillet or wok over medium heat.
3. Add ginger and garlic; cook 30 seconds.
4. Add mushrooms, bell pepper and bok choy; cook 3 minutes, stirring occasionally.
5. Add broth and sugar snap peas; simmer until vegetables are crisp-tender.
6. stir occasionally, 3 to 5 minutes.
7. Add tamari or soy sauce, and vinegar.
8. Drain noodles; add to skillet with vegetables.
9. Add sesame oil; cook 1 minute, tossing well.
10. Sprinkle with peanuts or cashews, if desired.

Note: You can add, omit/substitute any ingredients you prefer.

Mandarin Noodles

Serves 6

4 dried Chinese mushrooms
½ pound fresh Chinese noodles
¼ cup peanut oil
1 tablespoon hoisin sauce
1 tablespoon bean sauce
2 tablespoons rice wine or dry sherry
3 tablespoons light soy sauce
1 teaspoon sugar or honey
½ cup reserved mushroom soaking liquid
1 teaspoon chili paste
1 tablespoon cornstarch
½ red bell pepper, in ½ inch cubes
½ 8 ounce can whole bamboo shoots, cut
   in ½in cubes, rinsed and drained
2 cups bean sprouts
1 scallion, thinly sliced

1. Soak the Chinese mushrooms in 1¼ cups of hot water for 30 minutes. While they are soaking, bring 4 quarts of water to a boil and cook the noodles for 3 minutes.
2. Drain and toss with 1 tablespoon of peanut oil; set aside.
3. Remove the mushrooms; strain and reserve ½ cup of the soaking liquid for the sauce.
4. Trim and discard the mushroom stems; coarsely chop the caps and set aside.
5. Combine the ingredients for the sauce in a small bowl and stir well to dissolve the sugar; set aside.
6. Dissolve the cornstarch in 2 tablespoons of cold water; set aside.
7. Place the wok over medium-high heat.
8. When it begins to smoke, add the remaining 3 tablespoons of peanut oil, then the mushrooms, red pepper, bamboo shoots, and bean sprouts.
9. Stir-fry 2 minutes.
10. Stir the sauce and add it to the wok, and continue to stir-fry until the mixture begins to boil, about 30 seconds.
11. Mix the dissolved cornstarch and add it to the wok.
12. Continue to stir until the sauce thickens, about 1 minute.
13. Add the noodles and toss until heated through, about 2 minutes.
14. Transfer to a serving platter and sprinkle with the sliced scallion. Serve immediately.

Note: Because of the chili paste in the sauce, this is a rather hot dish. If you prefer less spicy food, cut down on the chili paste or leave it out entirely...the noodles are still delicious without it.

Hunan Chow Mein

Serves 6

1 medium onion, chopped
3 cloves garlic, minced
1 tablespoon peanut oil
2 tablespoons soy sauce
1 teaspoon dried mustard
2 stalks celery, sliced diagonally
2 cups baby bok choy, chopped
1 red bell pepper, chopped
8 ounces water chestnuts, sliced
1 cup vegetable stock
1 cup mushrooms, sliced
4 cups white rice, cooked

1. In a wok or large skillet over high heat, cook onion and garlic in oil for 3 minutes, or until they begin to soften.
2. Add soy sauce, mustard, celery, bok choy, bell pepper, water chestnuts, vegetable stock, and mushrooms.
3. Continue cooking, stirring frequently, until vegetables are crisp-tender, about 5 minutes.
4. Serve over rice.

Vegetables with Spicy Peanut Sauce

¼ cup natural-style peanut butter
3 tbsp. tamari soy sauce
3 tbsp. Chinese rice wine or sherry
1 tbsp. toasted sesame oil
enough water to make a creamy sauce

1. When the squash is ready, scoop it onto a plate of rice and pour the peanut sauce on top.
2. (You can try this recipe with spinach, broccoli, squash, and zucchini, and it will always be delicious.)

Steamed Vegetable Fried Rice

Serves 6

¼ cup light soy sauce
3 tablespoons rice wine or dry sherry
½ teaspoon salt
6 tablespoons peanut oil
2 eggs, lightly beaten
1 carrot, in ½-inch cubes
1 red bell pepper, in ½-inch cubes
½ cup frozen peas
4 cups cold cooked rice

1. Combine the ingredients for the sauce in a small bowl. Mix to blend well and set aside.
2. Place a small skillet over medium heat.
3. When it begins to smoke, add 2 tablespoons of peanut oil and the lightly beaten eggs.
4. Stir until the eggs are firm but moist.
5. Transfer the eggs from the skillet to a small bowl and break them into small curds. Set aside.
6. Bring 1 quart of water to a boil in a small saucepan.
7. Add the carrot and boil 1 minute.
8. Drain and rinse in cold water.
9. Drain again and reserve.
10. Place a wok over medium-high heat.
11. When it begins to smoke, add the remaining ¼ cup of peanut oil and the garlic. Stir briefly.
12. Add the carrots, celery, red pepper, and peas.
13. Stir-fry 1 minute. Stir in the rice and stir-fry 1 minute.
14. Pour in the sauce and cook until the rice is heated through, about 5 minutes, stirring frequently. Serve hot.

Sweet and Sour Sauce

⅓ cup vinegar
⅓ cup sugar
2 tbsp. water
1 tbsp. cornstarch
dash cardamom or ¼ tsp. fresh ginger

1. Combine all ingredients in a small saucepan, stirring to dissolve cornstarch.
2. Stir over high heat until mixture bubbles and thickens.
3. Serve as a dipping sauce for spring rolls or fried tofu.
4. Prep. time: 10 min

Sweet Sauce For Spring Rolls

Makes 3 dozen

4 tablespoons sugar
¼ cup soy sauce
1 cup broth or water
2 tablespoons corn starch

¼ cup cold water
1 clove garlic, crushed with ¼ tsp. salt

1. Combine sugar, soy sauce, and broth.
2. Bring to a boil.
3. Add corn starch mixed smoothly with the cold water, and stir until the mixture thickens some.
4. Simmer, stirring for 1 minute.
5. Stir in garlic. Serve any temperature.

Fat-free Potstickers

Serves 6

2 packages of prepared potsticker or gyoza skins (find ones without egg).
They are about 3" in diameter, round.

Prepare filling:

in a large pot, 'sauté':
6 large carrots, grated
¼ - ½ small head of cabbage, sliced thinly
¼ cup unsweetened rice wine

1. When carrots and cabbage have softened, place about ½ of the carrot/cabbage mixture in a food processor and process with:
2. 1 can (small, 10 oz?) bamboo shoots
3. 1 handful of dried shiitake mushrooms, soaked (10-20+ mushrooms, to taste)
4. Mix blended stuff with unblended cabbage and carrots and add:
5. 1 cup TVP, hydrated with some mushroom-soaking water, then drained
6. 2 tablespoons white or yellow miso, mixed until smooth with about ¼ cup water soy sauce to taste
7. white pepper to taste chopped scallions (optional)
8. 2 tablespoons cornstarch, mixed until smooth with about ¼ cup water
9. The filling should be moist and cohesive, but not drippy, so adjust water amounts.
10. Place a small blob of filling in the center of each potsticker wrapper.
11. Fold the wrapper in half, using water to seal.
12. Join the points of the resulting half circle together, which will result in a little round 'hat'; it looks sort of like a tortellini (tortellini's?).
13. Or do the traditional potsticker fold if you know how (it's harder to explain).
14. Place several potstickers on a bed of cabbage leaves in your bamboo steamer over a pot of boiling water.
15. Cover, and do something else for about 7 min.
16. Eat potstickers immediately with a sauce of:
17. 1 part soy sauce
18. 1 part rice vinegar some grated fresh ginger or chopped scallions

Shui Mai

Serves 24

2 tablespoons peanut oil
1 garlic cloves 1 teaspoon ginger, minced
1 scallion, chopped
1 onion, coarsely chopped
½ small cabbage, coarsely chopped
2 teaspoons thin soy sauce
½ teaspoon sesame oil
1 teaspoon rice wine or dry sherry
1 teaspoon cornstarch dissolved in 1 tsp. cold water
24 dumpling wrappers, 3 inch diameter
½ cup parboiled or frozen green peas
10 lettuce leaves

1. Place a wok over medium-high heat.
2. When it begins to smoke, add the oil, then the garlic, ginger, and scallion.
3. Stir-fry 15 seconds.
4. Add the onion and cabbage and stir-fry 2 minutes.
5. Add the soy sauce, sesame oil, rice wine, and dissolved cornstarch.
6. Stir constantly until the sauce thickens, about 30 seconds.
7. Remove the wok from the heat and set aside to cool.
8. Place a dumpling wrapper on the work surface.
9. With your fingers, completely moisten the surface of the wrapper with water.
10. Place 1 tablespoon of filling in the center.
11. Pull up the sides of the wrapper around the filling, tucking the wrapper in tiny pleats around the filling.
12. Lightly tap the dumpling on the work surface to flatten the bottom.
13. Gently squeeze the center of the dumpling to make a slight indentation and force the filling to bulge a bit at the top.
14. Finally, place a green pea in the center indentation of each dumpling for a garnish.
15. Cover the dumplings as they are finished and fill the remaining wrappers.
16. Bring water to boil under a steamer.
17. Place the lettuce leaves on a heat-proof place and arrange the dumplings on the lettuce.
18. Cover and steam for 10 minutes.
19. Serve immediately with Spicy Soy Dipping Sauce.

Szechuan Shiitake Risotto

Serves 4

2 tablespoons Szechuan peppercorns
2 14.5-ounce cans veggie stock
1 ounce dried shiitake mushrooms, stemmed
2 tablespoons (¼ stick) margarine
⅓ cup minced shallots
¾ cup Arborio or medium-grain white rice
¼ cup dry wine (medium sweet)
1 tablespoon low-sodium soy sauce

1. Heat peppercorns in medium saucepan over high heat 1 minute.
2. Add broth and mushrooms and bring to boil.
3. Cover, remove from heat and steep 30 minutes.
4. Transfer mushrooms to bowl.
5. Strain broth.
6. Thinly slice mushrooms (cut off the hard bits of the stems at this point).
7. Melt margarine in heavy medium saucepan over medium heat.
8. Add mushrooms and shallots; sauté 3 minutes.
9. Stir in rice.
10. Mix in wine and soy sauce and bring to boil.
11. Add all but ½ cup broth.
12. Simmer uncovered 20 minutes, stirring occasionally.
13. Continue cooking until rice is tender and mixture is creamy, adding remaining ½ cup broth if necessary to make creamy, stirring occasionally, about 5 minutes longer. Season with salt and serve.

Congee

Serves 6

1 cup short-grain rice
8 cups cold water

1. Combine the rice and water in a large saucepan with a tight-fitting lid.
2. Bring to a boil, cover, and reduce heat to simmer.
3. Cook for 1½ hours. Serve hot.

Congee with Vegetables

Serves 6

1 recipe Congee
½ pound spinach
1 egg substitute
1 tablespoon ginger, finely shredded
1 scallion, thinly sliced
1 medium tomato, coarsely chopped
salt and pepper, to taste

1. Prepare congee following the basic recipe.
2. Meanwhile, wash the spinach, trim any tough stems, and pat dry. Lightly beat the egg.
3. When the congee is cooked, stir in the egg, ginger, scallion, spinach, and tomato.
4. Cook just until the spinach is wilted and the tomato is heated through, about 3 minutes.
5. Season to taste with salt and pepper.
6. Serve immediately.

Tofu, Cashews, and Vegetables

Serves 4

1 tablespoon light soy sauce
1 tablespoon water
½ teaspoon cornstarch
2 teaspoons honey
1 teaspoon hot bean sauce
2 teaspoons sweet bean sauce
3 tablespoons peanut oil
1 carrot, in ½-inch cubes
1 zucchini, in ½-inch cubes
2½ ounces bamboo shoots, in ½-inch cubes
8 ounces tofu, in ½-inch cubes
½ cup frozen green peas
½ cup roasted unsalted cashews

1. Combine the ingredients for the sauce in a small bowl. Stir to dissolve the sugar and cornstarch and set aside.
2. Place a wok over medium-high heat.
3. When it begins to smoke, add the peanut oil, then the carrot. Stir-fry 30 seconds.
4. Add the zucchini, bamboo shoots, tofu,
5. and peas; stir-fry 30 seconds. Stir in the cashews.
6. Pour in the sauce and stir until it thickens, about 1 minute. Serve immediately.

Mushroom Sui Mei with Piquant Dipping Sauce

1 oz. bean thread (cellophane) noodles
lb white or brown mushrooms w/stems, trimmed and minced
2 scallions, trimmed and minced
1 tbsp. minced cilantro leaves
1 tbsp. tamari
1 tsp. sesame oil
1 tsp. finely grated fresh ginger
1 pkg prepared wonton wrappers, 3 ¼ inches round or square

1. Place bean thread noodles in bowl, cover with boiling water and soak five minutes.
2. Drain well, snip with scissors into ¼ inch lengths.
3. Place in bowl.
4. Add mushrooms to bowl, toss to mix.
5. Add all remaining ingredients except wonton wrappers, mixing well.
6. If using square wrappers, cut into rounds with a cookie cutter.
7. Place one rounded tsp. filling in center of each wrapper.
8. Gather up edges, pleat and pinch, leaving top open.
9. Steam about 10 minutes.
10. Makes 3 to 4 dozen dumplings.

Note: To make it super easy, just dump the mushrooms, scallions, cilantro, and ginger into the food processor for instant mincing. Add to the snipped noodles and mix. Then add the tamari and oil. Also, vegan wonton wrappers are still hard to find, but you can make your own pasta (try Ener-G Egg Replacer for the eggs, or you can probably do without). The filling is also good on rice; just heat it in the wok or frying pan.

Broccoli and Tofu in Spicy Almond Sauce

Sauce:

½ cup hot water

½ cup almond butter (original recipe was for peanut butter - I use almond cause I'm allergic to peanut)

¼ cup cider vinegar

2 tablespoons tamari sauce

2 tablespoons blackstrap molasses

¼ cup cayenne (this is a HUGE amount - I use 1-2 tsp.)

Sauté:

1 lb. broccoli

2 tsp. ginger

4 cloves garlic

1 lb. tofu, cubed

2 cup onion, thinly sliced

1 cup chopped cashews

2-3 tablespoons Tamari Sauce

2 minced scallions

Sauce:

1. In small saucepan, whisk together almond butter and hot water until you have a uniform mixture.
2. Whisk in remaining sauce ingredients and set aside.

Sauté:

1. Stir-fry half the ginger and half the garlic in 1 tablespoon oil.
2. Add tofu chunks, stir-fry for 5-8 minutes.
3. Mix with sauce.
4. Wipe wok clean, sauté remaining ginger & garlic in 2 tablespoons oil.
5. Add onions and fresh pepper, sauté for about 5 min.
6. Add chopped broccoli, cashews and tamari; stir-fry until broccoli is bright green.
7. Toss sauté with sauce, mixing in the minced scallions as you toss. Serve over rice.

Stir Fry Dishes

Sweet-n-Sour Stir-Fry

Serves 2

¼ cup chopped scallions

2 cloves garlic, minced

canola oil (sesame oil would work well too)

1 cup Snow pea pods, de-stringed

1 small yellow zucchini squash, sliced

1½ cup broccoli (florets and stems, cut into small pieces)

12 oz. straw mushrooms

½ cup bean sprouts

½ cup water chestnuts

½ cup bamboo shoots

¼ cup chopped red bell pepper

1 small can pineapple chunks (unsweetened, be sure to save the juice)

1 small can mandarin orange slices

1 ripe mango, peeled, seeded, and sliced

Sauce:

1½ cup tamari

pineapple juice (leftover from the can)

3 tbsp. cornstarch (or enough to make desired thickness)

2 tbsp. water

2 tsp. grated fresh ginger

1. First to go in the wok was the oil, scallions, and garlic.
2. Oil and coat all the veggies.
3. Heat these ingredients until the garlic starts to turn brown. Then add the pea pods, squash, and broccoli.
4. Cook about 3-5 min.
5. Then add the bean sprouts, water chestnuts, bamboo, and peppers.
6. Cook for a few more minutes, until veggies are slightly tender but still sort of crisp.
7. Then add the pineapple, oranges, and mango.
8. Cook about a minute, then add the sauce.
9. When the sauce starts bubbling, the stir-fry is done.
10. Serve over rice.

Spring Vegetable Stir-Fry

1 tbsp. oil
1 garlic clove, sliced
1 in pinch ginger root, finely chopped
4 oz. baby carrots
4 oz. patty pan squash
4 oz. green beans, topped and tailed
4 oz. sugar snap peas, topped and tailed
4 oz. young asparagus, cut into 3 inch pieces
8 scallions, trimmed and sliced down the middle
4 oz. cherry tomatoes

Dressing:
juice of 2 limes
1 tbsp. honey
1 tbsp. soy sauce
1 tsp. sesame oil

1. Heat the oil in a wok or large frying pan.
2. Add garlic and ginger, stir-fry over med-high heat for 1 minute. (Don't burn the garlic though!)
3. Turn the heat to high. Add the carrots, squash, beans, and stir-fry 3-4 min.
4. Add the peas, asparagus, scallions, tomatoes for 2 more min.
5. Add the dressing and fry 2-3 minutes more or until just crispy tender. Serve with brown rice.

Curried Stir-Fried Noodles With Vegetables

Serves 4
½ pound dried rice-stick noodles (rice vermicelli)

Veggies:
2 medium carrots (about ½ pound), thinly sliced
1 bunch broccoli, cut into small 1½-inch-long flowerets (about 3 cups)
1 small zucchini, cut into small strips
1 medium red onion, sliced thin lengthwise (about 2 cups)

For sauce:
½ cup veg. broth
1 teaspoon cornstarch
4 tablespoons soy sauce
2 tablespoons dry sherry or white wine
1 tablespoon sugar
1 teaspoon salt
1 teaspoon Asian sesame oil

For sautéing:
2 teaspoons vegetable oil
1½ tablespoons minced garlic
1½ tablespoons minced peeled fresh gingerroot
1 tablespoon curry powder
4 scallions, cut lengthwise into 2-inch-long julienne strips

1. In a large bowl soak noodles in boiling water to cover 5 to 10 minutes, or until opaque-white and tender, and drain well in a colander.
2. Steam veggies in steamer rack over boiling water (or in the microwave) until just tender. Drain.
3. **Make sauce:** In a small bowl stir together sauce ingredients in order given until cornstarch is dissolved.
4. Heat a wok over med-high heat until hot and add oil.
5. Stir-fry garlic and gingerroot until fragrant, about 5 seconds.
6. Add curry powder and stir-fry 5 seconds.
7. Stir sauce and add to curry mixture.
8. Bring curry sauce to a boil, stirring.
9. Add noodles, scallions, and steamed vegetables to curry sauce and gently toss until noodles are coated well with sauce.

Broccoli Stir-Fry

Serves 4
1 bunch broccoli, chopped
1 carrot, thinly sliced
2 stalks celery, chopped
1½ tablespoons sesame seeds
1 tablespoon oil
½ cup water

1. Stir-fry ingredients over medium-high heat for 8 minutes. Serve with rice.

Stir-Fried Wild Bamboo Shoot with Chili Sauce

12 oz wild bamboo shoot
1 green bell pepper
1 red chili
1 tsp. mashed ginger
1 tsp. mashed garlic
½ tbsp. fried white sesame

Seasonings:
1½ tbsp. light soy sauce
2 tsp. sugar

1. Skin wild bamboo shoot and rinse.
2. Slant. Scald in boiling water until done.
3. Take out and drain.
4. Cut green pepper and red chili into pieces.
5. Heat 1 tbsp. oil and sauté green pepper and red chili.
6. Dish up. Sauté mashed ginger and garlic with ½ tbsp. sesame oil. Add in seasonings and stir.
7. Put in bamboo shoot, green pepper and red chili.
8. Stir well. Dish up and serve.

Marinated Tempeh Stir-Fry w/Broccoli & Red Bell Pepper

Serves 4

4 ounces soy tempeh or 3-grain tempeh, cut into ½-inch, pieces
¼ cup light soy sauce
1 tablespoon rice vinegar
3 garlic cloves, minced
2 teaspoons minced peeled fresh ginger
⅛ teaspoon dried crushed red pepper
12 ounces broccoli, stems peeled and cut into ½-inch pieces, florets cut into 1-inch pieces
2 tablespoons water
1 teaspoon honey style sweetener
1 teaspoon cornstarch
1 tablespoon vegetable oil
½ cup chopped red bell pepper
2 tablespoons thinly sliced green onion

1. Stir tempeh, soy sauce, vinegar, garlic, ginger and crushed red pepper in medium bowl to blend.
2. Let marinate 1 hour at room temperature.
3. Steam broccoli until crisp-tender, about 3 minutes.
4. Set aside. Strain marinade from tempeh into small bowl; set tempeh aside. Whisk 2 tablespoons water, honey and cornstarch into marinade.
5. Heat oil in large nonstick skillet over high heat.
6. Add marinated tempeh and bell pepper and sauté, 4 minutes.
7. Add broccoli and marinade mixture and sauté until broccoli is heated through and sauce thickens, about 3 minutes.
8. Transfer to bowl. Sprinkle with green onion and serve.

Marinated Tofu Stir Fry

Serves 1

1 package firm or extra-firm tofu
¼ cup soy sauce
1 teaspoon garlic powder
1 teaspoon ginger
2 teaspoon red pepper flakes
½ teaspoon salt
2 tablespoon roasted sesame oil
1 tablespoon chili oil
1 head broccoli, chopped
2 carrots, sliced
1 bell pepper, your choice
½ onion, chopped
1 clove pressed or chopped garlic

1. Slice the tofu into ½-inch thick strips and place in contained.
2. Cover with soy sauce, garlic powder, ginger, pepper flakes, salt, and oils.
3. Make sure all the tofu is able to soak up the ingredients, then cover and let marinate in the fridge for at least 2 hours.
4. When the tofu is done marinating, put a drop of oil in a frying pan and cook the tofu until browned on both sides, approximately 10 minutes.
5. Save the marinade.
6. In a wok, heat the garlic in a drop of oil and add the vegetables.
7. Sauté for about 5 minutes and then add the tofu, using the spatula to break it into bite sized pieces.
8. Add a spoonful or so of the marinade to the mixture and watch it sizzle.
9. When the vegetables are as soft as you want, serve hot over rice, drizzling on more of the marinade to taste.

This recipe is especially easy to make with two people in the kitchen, one can work on cooking the tofu, the other can do the vegetables. The tofu is also good to fry and eat by itself, I've found.

Simple Spinach and Garlic Stir-Fry

Serves 1

1 tablespoon vegetable oil
8 cloves garlic, minced
3 bunches spinach, washed and cut in
2 inch piece
½ cup vegetable dry sherry
1 teaspoon sugar, (or 2 teaspoons brown rice syrup)
1 tablespoon sesame oil
1 tablespoon ginger, minced
3 tablespoons green onion, minced
14 ounces firm tofu, cubed
1 tablespoon hot chili paste
1 cup vegetable stock
1 tablespoon cornstarch mixed well with 2 tablespoons cold water
6 cups rice, cooked Cilantro to garnish

1. In a small bowl, mash black beans with garlic, soy, wine, and sugar.
2. In a wok or large skillet, heat oil on high and add black bean paste, ginger, and green onion.
3. Add tofu and turn gently.
4. Add chili paste and stock.
5. Cover and cook for 3 to 4 minutes.
6. Stir in cornstarch mixture and cook until sauce thickens.
7. Serve over rice, and garnish with cilantro.
8. Makes about 6 servings.

Tofu Stir Fry

1 lb extra-firm tofu, cut into 1" cubes
½ cup sake
2 tablespoons sesame oil
4 tablespoons soy sauce
4 cloves garlic, minced
2 teaspoons grated ginger
1 onion, chopped
1 red bell pepper, chopped
2 cups Chinese broccoli, sliced
8 oz. snow peas

1. Bring soy, garlic, ginger and sake to a boil in wok.
2. Add tofu, cover and simmer for 5 minutes.
3. Remove tofu; set aside.
4. Reserve marinade.
5. Heat oil in wok and stir fry vegetables for 3 minutes.
6. Add tofu and reserved marinade.
7. Thicken with a little cornstarch, if desired.
8. Sprinkle with peanuts or cashews, if desired.

Stir-Fry Veggie w/ Tofu

Serves 6

1 cup red bell pepper, thinly sliced
½ cup green bell pepper, thinly sliced
⅓ cup yellow bell pepper, thinly sliced
2 teaspoons safflower oil
1 tablespoon arrowroot powder
½ cup rice vinegar
½ cup pineapple juice
½ cup lemon juice
⅓ cup honey style sweetener
½ teaspoon herbal salt substitute
½ teaspoon grated gingerroot
1 pound firm tofu
2 tablespoons low-sodium soy or tamari sauce
¼ teaspoon cayenne pepper, or to taste

1. In a wok over medium-high heat, sauté bell peppers in the safflower oil until shiny (about 5 minutes).
2. In a large bowl combine arrowroot, vinegar, pineapple juice, lemon juice, honey, salt substitute, and ginger.
3. Pour over peppers and cook, stirring, until mixture thickens slightly.
4. Cut tofu into thin slices.
5. Add to wok, cover, and steam 3 minutes.
6. Add soy sauce and cayenne.
7. Toss well and serve.

Note: Crunchy, brightly colored bell peppers complement the white cubes of protein-rich tofu in this entree. The sweet-and-sour sauce is slightly spicy. The vegetables and tofu can be marinated ahead of time in sesame oil for added flavor. Cook the dish the night before and reheat for lunch the next day-it gets better as it sits and the flavors blend. You can add, omit/substitute any veggie you prefer.

Broccoli-Tofu Stir-Fry

Serves 4

3 tablespoons hoisin sauce
⅔ cup water
3 tablespoons rice vinegar
3 tablespoons soy sauce
1 tablespoon cornstarch

Stir-fry:

2 tablespoons vegetable oil
2 garlic cloves, pressed
1 small fresh chili, seeded and minced
18 ounces tofu, cut into 1" cubes
5 cups broccoli florets
⅓ cup dry sherry
1 bunch scallions, cut into 1" pieces
1 red bell pepper, cut into strips, optional

1. Combine the sauce ingredients in a small bowl.
2. Before beginning to stir-fry, prepare the vegetables and have all the ingredients at hand.
3. In a wok or large skillet, heat 1 tablespoon of the oil on medium-high heat.
4. Add the garlic and chili and stir-fry for just 30 seconds before adding the tofu.
5. Continue to stir-fry for 3 or 4 minutes, until the tofu is lightly browned.
6. Remove the tofu and set aside.
7. Add the other tablespoon of oil to the wok, heat for a few seconds; then add the broccoli.
8. Stir-fry for a minute and pour in the sherry.
9. Stir-fry for 3 minutes.
10. If the broccoli begins to scorch, add a tablespoon of water.
11. Add the scallions and optional bell pepper, continue to stir-fry for a minute, and them the tofu and the sauce.
12. Stir carefully and bring to a simmer.
13. Simmer for 3 or 4 minutes, until the sauce thickens.
14. Serve immediately.

Vegetable Stir-Fry

Serves 6

3 tablespoons peanut oil
2 cloves garlic, minced
1 pound fresh green beans
4 large carrots, cut diagonally into, ¼" thick slices
1 1-inch piece fresh ginger
½ small red cabbage, cut into, ½-inch thick slices
1 leek, sliced
¼ cup vegetable broth
½ teaspoon salt
2 tablespoons lime juice
2 teaspoons hot chili sesame oil
chopped dry-roasted peanuts for garnish
cooked rice or noodles if desired

1. Heat peanut oil in a large skillet or wok over medium-high heat until hot.
2. Add garlic and stir-fry 1 minute.
3. Add green beans, carrots, and ginger, and stir-fry until crisp-tender.
4. Add cabbage and next 5 ingredients, and stir-fry 1 minute.
5. Discard ginger.
6. Garnish, if desired.
7. Serve immediately (over cooked rice or noodles if desired).

Sweet Onion-Asparagus Stir Fry

Serves 2

¾ pound fresh asparagus
2 medium sweet onions (such as Vidalia)
1 tablespoon vegetable oil
1 clove garlic, minced
¼ cup vegetarian mushroom "oyster" sauce
¼ cup chopped pecans, toasted
rice or noodles

1. Snap tough ends off asparagus; remove scales from stalks w/a vegetable peeler, if desired
2. Cut diagonally into 2-inch pieces.
3. Cut onions into ¼-inch thick slices and separate into rings.
4. Heat oil in a large skillet or wok at medium-high heat for about 2 minutes.
5. Add asparagus, onion, and garlic, and stir-fry for 4-5 minutes or until tender.
6. Remove from heat; pour in "oyster" sauce, and toss.
7. Sprinkle with toasted pecans and serve over rice or noodles.

Spicy-Sweet Bean & Noodle Stir Fry

½ cup chickpeas (garbanzo beans) or other beans
2 to 4 ounces Chinese noodles or spaghetti
1 tablespoon soy sauce
1 tablespoon Szechuan stir-fry sauce
2 tablespoons hoisin sauce
1 to 2 cloves chopped garlic
ginger or ginger powder
2 cups frozen veggie stir fry blend (broccoli, red pepper, water chestnuts, green beans, carrots, celery, sugar snap peas)
½ tbsp. oil

1. Soak and cook beans until tender
2. Drain beans and save ¼ cup broth
3. Boil noodles for 9-10 minutes.
4. Meanwhile, lightly fry garlic and ginger in oil in wok or frying pan.
5. When the garlic starts to sizzle, add vegetables to pan and cook for 1 minute
6. Mix sauces and broth together, and add to pan.
7. Cook vegetables for 2 more minutes or until tender
8. Add beans and remove from heat.
9. When pasta is done, drain and rinse with cold water.
10. Add pasta to frying pan and reheat.
11. Add any additional sauce to taste (I like a thick sauce).
12. Substitutions: Kidney beans or some other beans would probably be pretty good.
13. It's easy to find hoisin and Szechuan sauces in the grocery store, but if you must substitute here are some ideas.
14. If you only have 1 of these, just use twice as much of that kind.
15. Hoisin can probably be substituted with some other sweet-and-sour type sauce like duck (an apricot-based sauce with a misleading name), sweet & sour, and maybe black bean(?), or you can use a mix of peach or apricot sauce, vinegar, corn-starch, sugar, and dry sherry or Chinese cooking wine.
16. Szechuan is a hot-and-spicy sauce that can probably be approximated with soy sauce, sherry or wine, sugar, corn starch, red hot pepper (cayenne), and sesame seed oil.

Veggie Stir-Fry with Soy Sauce

several kinds of veggies (see below for suggestion)
bit of oil
1 tbsp. cornstarch
1-2 tsp. water
1-2 tbsp.soy sauce
cooked rice

1. Fry veggies in a wok or skillet with a bit of oil, adding the hard, long-cooking ones first and the soft, fast-cooking ones last, until all are cooked to your taste.
2. Mix water and cornstarch until starch is dissolved.
3. Add this, the soy sauce and cook until sauce is slightly thickened.
4. Serve over rice.

For a very colorful stir-fry, try these veggies together: Red pepper or tomatoes, carrots, yellow pepper, green leafy veggie or broccoli, purple cabbage, brown mushrooms, cauliflower

Five-Spice Stir Fry

Serves 4
8 ounces vermicelli, spaghetti, or linguine
Sauce:
½ cup orange juice
1 tablespoon corn starch
¾ teaspoon Chinese five-spice powder
¼ teaspoon crushed red pepper flakes
2 tablespoons soy sauce
2 teaspoons liquid sweetener

Stir-fry:
12 ounces mushrooms, cut into ¼" slices
1 cup fresh baby carrots, quartered lengthwise
1 medium onion, cut into thin wedges
2 cloves garlic, minced
3 cups broccoli florets (about 6 oz.)

1. Cook pasta per package directions.
2. Drain and cover to keep warm.
3. Meanwhile in a small bowl, combine all sauce ingredients and mix until blended. Set aside. Spray a nonstick skillet or wok with nonstick cooking spray.
4. Heat over medium-high heat until hot.
5. Add mushrooms, carrots, onion, and garlic.
6. Cook and stir 4-5 minutes.
7. Add broccoli, cover, and cook 2-4 minutes or until vegetable are crisp-tender, stirring occasionally.
8. Add sauce, cook and stir 2-3 minutes or until bubbly and thickened. Serve over pasta.

Simple Vegetable Stir-Fry

Serves 1

½ teaspoon ginger root, finely chopped
2 3 cloves garlic finely chopped
½ teaspoon crushed red pepper (optional)
1 medium onion, sliced
20-25 snow peas
2 medium carrots, sliced on diagonal
1 medium green bell pepper, cored and sliced
2 small zucchini (one green, one yellow) sliced on diagonal, thicker than the carrots
1 cup bean sprouts
6-8 mushrooms, quartered
ground pepper to taste

1. Heat wok over med-high heat, toss in first seven ingredients, (thru bell pepper) along with a tablespoon or two of water.
2. Stir fry constantly until onion is becoming limp, then add zucchini and bean sprouts.
3. As zucchini is softening, add mushrooms, stirring continually (takes 6-10 minutes - depending on how crisp you want the vegetables) The trick is to add the quicker-cooking vegetables last, so they don't overcook.
4. Serve over rice, with soy sauce to taste.
5. A variation is to use the wok as a steamer: Heat wok as above, and toss together all ingredients, along with about ½ cup of equal parts soy sauce and water.
6. Quickly stir for a minute or so, then push vegetables up onto side of wok, and cover.
7. When steam escapes from under cover, vegetables are done. Remove from heat, toss together into a large bowl; serve over rice. Some of our favorite variations are:
8. **Peas & Carrots Stir Fry:** use only snow peas and sliced carrots.
9. **Mushroom & Onion Stir Fry:** use only onion slices and quartered mushrooms.
10. You can also try yakisoba noodles, instead of rice.

A note about wok cooking: I use a hammered steel wok, which might make the second method possible: the ingredients will stay up on the sides, away from the very hot bottom, where the liquid is boiling. With a machine-made, or electric wok, this may not be possible. I use only water and a brush to clean the wok, never soap, as this will cause sticking. When clean, I place the wok over heat source to dry, and wipe the inside with about 1 tsp. of olive oil, using a paper towel. Let cool, and put away. The oil will prevent rusting, and is all the oil required for your next cooking.

Stir-Fried Broccoli and Chinese Mushrooms

Serves 4

6 dried Chinese mushrooms
1 bunch fresh broccoli
½ cup mushroom soaking liquid
2 tablespoons light soy sauce
1 tablespoon rice wine or dry sherry
1 teaspoon honey
3 tablespoons peanut oil
1 tablespoon cornstarch

1. Soak the Chinese mushrooms in 2 cups of hot water for 30 minutes. Strain and reserve ½ cup of the soaking liquid for the sauce.
2. Trim and discard the mushroom stems, and cut the caps in half.
3. Set aside. Rinse the broccoli and cut the tops into florets. Peel the stems and diagonally cut them in ½-inch slices.
4. Mix the ingredients for the sauce in a small bowl, stirring to dissolve the sugar.
5. Place a wok over medium-high heat.
6. When it is almost smoking, add the peanut oil.
7. When the oil begins to smoke, add the broccoli and the mushrooms.
8. Stir-fry 2 minutes, then pour in the sauce and bring to a boil. Cook 1 minute.
9. While the vegetables are cooking, dissolve the cornstarch in 2 tablespoons of cold water.
10. Pour into the wok and stir constantly until the sauce thickens, about 30 seconds. Serve immediately.

Chinese Stir-Fry

Serves 4

32 ounces Asian-style frozen mixed vegetables (sometimes labeled Oriental- or Japanese-style)
¼ cup bottled stir-fry sauce or to taste
1 pound firm or baked tofu drained and cut into strips

1. The interesting Asian-style vegetable mélanges in the frozen vegetables section are great to have on hand when you crave a quick stir-fry but don't feel like chopping.
2. Serve with hot cooked rice or noodles and raw carrot and celery sticks.
3. Steam vegetables in a stir-fry pan or wok with about ½- inch of water, covered, until completely thawed.
4. Drain well and transfer back to stir-fry pan.
5. Stir in sauce and stir-fry over medium-high heat until vegetables are tender-crisp.
6. Add tofu strips and toss gently.
7. Cook just until heated through, then serve right away.

Vegetable Stir-Fry With Tropical Vinaigrette

Serves 6

2 tablespoons rice vinegar
2 tablespoons thawed pineapple-orange juice concentrate
2 teaspoons shallots, minced
2 teaspoons lemon juice
1 teaspoon cornstarch
1 teaspoon vegetarian Worcestershire sauce
1 teaspoon liquid sweetener
2 cloves garlic, minced
1 teaspoon olive oil
cooking spray
¾ cup green onions, chopped
1 cup carrots, ¼-inch, diagonally sliced
1 cup yellow bell pepper, julienned
1 cup red bell pepper, julienned
3 cups small broccoli florets
1 cup fresh bean sprouts

1. Combine the first 8 ingredients in a blender; process until smooth. Heat oil in a wok or large nonstick skillet coated with cooking spray over medium-high heat until hot. Add onions, and stir-fry 1 minute.
2. Add carrot and bell peppers, stir-fry 1 minute.
3. Add broccoli; cover and cook 2 minutes.
4. Add vinegar mixture and sprouts; bring to a boil, and cook, uncovered about 30 seconds, stirring constantly.

Broccoli Chow Mein

Serves 3

3 stalks broccoli, chopped
1 tablespoon oil
½ cup water
½ pound mung bean sprouts
½ cup slivered almonds or sunflower seeds (optional)
1 tablespoon arrowroot or corn starch
½ cup water
1½ tablespoons soy sauce or tamari
1 teaspoon sesame oil (optional)

1. Stir-fry broccoli in oil and ½ cup water for 3 minutes over medium-high heat.
2. Add bean sprouts and almonds or seeds.
3. Stir-fry for 2 more minutes.
4. Dissolve starch in ½ cup water.
5. Add to broccoli and sprout mixture along with tamari or soy sauce and sesame oil if desired.
6. Stir, then heat covered for 1 minute longer. Serve hot.

Wok This Way: Raw Stir no-Fry

Stir no Fry Sauce:

1 tbsp. olive oil
2 tbsp. nutritional yeast
1½ tsp. of shoyu (or soy sauce/shoyu is just unpasteurized soy sauce)
½ small or medium lemon - juiced/squeezed
1 small clove of garlic- pressed through garlic press (use juice and pulp)
½ to 1 inch nub of ginger, pressed through garlic press (use juice and pulp)
½ tsp. of agave nectar

Don't Fry These:

3 cups of an herb variety green mix
1 red bell pepper, sliced thin with the mandoline
⅛ of a purple cabbage, sliced thin
a small amount of red onion (only use a little as it's very potent, alternately you could chop green onion)
2 Shiitake mushrooms (fresh), sliced thin (include stem)
¼ lb of sugar snap peas, remove the peas and add to the veggies. Take the remaining shells, pick out the nicest looking ones, tear in half and add half of them to the veggie mix

1. Place the 'no-fry sauce' ingredients in a blender and whip up. Alternately place in a small bowl and use a hand frother/cocktail mixer to blend.
2. Stir, not fry!
3. Put veggies in a large mixing bowl. Coat the veggies with the sauce. Roll up your sleeves, take off your rings, and gets your hands in the bowl. Massage the sauce into the veggies well until they wilt a bit and are completely covered.

Tofu And Vegetable Stir-Fry

Serves 4

Marinade:
1 pound block tofu, cut into 1" cubes
1 clove garlic, minced
1 tsp. fresh ginger, minced
¼ tsp. pepper
2 tbsp.
soy sauce
⅛ to ¼ tsp. red pepper flakes
1 tbsp.
sesame oil
2 tbsp.
dry sherry
¼ cup hoisin sauce

Vegetables:
2 tbsp.
oil
1 medium onion, chopped
1 carrot, thinly sliced
2 celery stalks, sliced
1 cup small cauliflower or broccoli florets
1 cup peas or snow peas
⅓ cup red pepper, slivered
1 tin sliced water chestnuts, drained
1 tbsp. cornstarch

1. Combine marinade ingredients in a large bowl (garlic-sherry).
2. Gently stir in tofu cubes, cover and refrigerate 4 hours or overnight.
3. Heat oil in frying pan and add onion, cooking 'til softened.
4. Add other veggies (in usual stir-frying order from slow-fast cooking veggies) and fry until desired cookness. Add tofu to the veggies.
5. Stir 1 tbsp.
6. cornstarch into marinade and pour over vegetable mixture. Reheat 'til tofu is hot.

Stir-Fried Tofu Cubes with Assorted Vegetables

2 pieces of tofu	2 tbsp. sliced straw
½ cup of diced tomato	mushroom
	¼ cup diced vegetable stalk
	½ tsp. mashed garlic

Seasonings:

| ⅓ tsp. salt | 2 tsp. sugar |
| 1½ tbsp. light soy sauce | ½ cup water |

dash of corn flour solution to thicken sauce

1. Cut tofu into cubes. Then soak in hot oil and fry until golden brown.
2. Take out and drain. Sauté sliced mushroom and diced vegetable stalk with dash of oil.
3. Dish up. Heat 1 tbsp. oil and sauté mashed garlic and diced tomato. Add in seasonings and bring to boil.
4. Put in tofu cubes and all ingredients.
5. Coddle for a while. Thicken sauce with corn flour solution. Dish up and serve.

Tofu & Tempeh Dishes Stir-Fried

Rice with Tempeh

The secret to this simply, tasty stir-fry is speed. Have all the ingredients prepared before you heat the pan, and work quickly.

Serves 3-4
5-6 ounces tempeh
3 tablespoons oil
2 cloves garlic, minced
1½ cups cooked brown rice, well cooled or chilled
½ cup chopped scallion
2 teaspoons natural soy sauce

1. To prepare the tempeh, cut it into pieces each about
2. ½-inch by 1 inch.
3. Soak the pieces briefly in salted water (in a bowl combine 1 teaspoon sea salt with 1 cup cool water), pat dry, and deep- or pan-fry them in any light oil until golden. Drain on paper.
4. Place a wok or skillet (same one used for tempeh is fine) over medium heat and add the 3 tablespoons oil.
5. Add garlic and sauté for 15 seconds.
6. Add the rice and stir-fry for 2 minutes.
7. Add the scallion, fried tempeh pieces, and the soy sauce, stir-frying until just heated through.
8. Serve immediately. Ready in 20 minutes.

Note: If you wish, you may scramble one egg replacer after sautéing the garlic but before adding the rice

Fried Rice with Tempeh and Peanuts

2 cups cooked, cold long-grain white rice
¼ cup canola oil
1 clove garlic, minced
1 seeded and diced green bell pepper
¼ pound chopped mushrooms
½ pound cooked tempeh
½ cup salted and roasted peanuts
2 tablespoons soy sauce
1-2 tomatoes, in wedges cucumber, in slices egg replacer, equivalent of
2 eggs, or scrambled tofu, optional

1. Before starting, cook and chill rice.
2. If using scrambled tofu, prepare beforehand.
3. Cube and sauté tempeh.
4. Rub cooked rice with wet hands so all grains are separated; set aside.
5. If using egg replacer, in a small bowl, lightly beat with salt. Place wok over medium heat; when hot, add 1 tablespoon oil.
6. When oil is hot, add egg replacer and cook, stirring occasionally, until soft curds form; remove from wok and set aside.
7. If using scrambled tofu, use your favorite recipe.)
8. Heat wok to medium-high; add
9. 1 tablespoon oil to wok (this will be the second tablespoon of oil if you cooked the egg replacer in the wok). When oil is hot, add onion and garlic.
10. Stir fry until onion is soft; then add bell pepper, mushrooms, tempeh, and peanuts.
11. Stir fry until heated through, about 2 minutes.
12. Remove from wok and set aside.
13. Pour remaining 2 tablespoons oil into wok.
14. When hot, add rice and stir fry until heated through, about 2 minutes. Stir in tempeh and soy.
15. If using scrambled tofu or egg replacer, stir into mixture until curds are in small pieces.
16. Garnish with tomato and cucumber slices.

Ginger Orange Tofu

Serves 3-5
1 block firm tofu, pressed

For marinade:
½ cup orange juice
¼ cup soy sauce
3 cloves minced garlic
1 tbsp. grated fresh ginger (about a ½ in cube)
¼ tsp. red pepper or red pepper flakes, to taste
1 tbsp. brown sugar or honey
2 tsp. sesame oil

For cooking:
2 tbsp. canola oil
4-6 cups fresh or frozen veggies (carrots, broccoli, onion, peppers, spinach, summer squash, bok choy, etc.)

1. To press tofu, place block of tofu on cookie sheet, cover with foil, and weigh it down with a heavy pan (I use a large cast iron skillet).
2. Let press for about ½ hour, and add a few more pounds of weight - cans of beans or veggies work great.
3. Let press for at least another ½ hour. This will drastically improve the texture of your tofu.
4. Cut tofu into small (¼ in) cubes and place in sealable container.
5. Mix remaining ingredients except canola oil well, and pour over tofu. Stir or shake to coat.
6. Marinate tofu at least 2 hours, or overnight, mixing at least once.
7. Heat a wok or large frying pan with 2 tbsp. canola oil. Add tofu (reserving liquid) and cook over high heat until lightly browned, stirring occasionally, about 5 minutes. Add veggies as desired and remaining liquid.
8. Cook, stirring often, until veggies are just cooked through. Serve with rice or noodles.

Tempeh with Curry Peanut Sauce

Serves 3-4; Time: 30 minutes
1 cup uncooked bulgur wheat

The Sauce:
1½ tablespoons creamy peanut butter
2 tablespoons freshly-squeezed lemon juice
1½ tablespoons brown rice syrup
1 tablespoon light-colored miso
½ cup hot water
1 teaspoon low-sodium soy sauce

The Stir-fry:
1 large carrot
2 ribs celery
2 tablespoons canola oil
2 cloves garlic, minced
1 medium red onion, chopped 8 ounces tempeh, cubed
1 tablespoon curry powder
1 tablespoon dried oregano
1 teaspoon chili powder
4 fresh lemon wedges

1. Bring 2 cups of water to a boil.
2. Stir in the bulgur, cover, reduce heat to low, and steam 15 minutes.
3. Let stand an additional 5 minutes, then fluff with a fork before serving.
4. Meanwhile, whisk together the sauce ingredients in a bowl and set aside.
5. Cut the carrot and celery into 1-inch matchsticks and set aside.
6. Heat the oil over medium heat in a wok or heavy skillet and add the garlic, onion, carrot, celery, tempeh, curry powder, oregano, and chili powder.
7. Stir-fry 2 minutes.
8. Pour in the peanut sauce and increase the heat a little to bring it to a simmer.
9. Cover and continue to cook, stirring frequently, for about 7 minutes, until the vegetables are tender but still crisp.
10. Divide the bulgur among warmed serving plates and top with the stir-fry.
11. Serve immediately, with lemon wedges.

Vietnamese Tofu

1 cake of firm or extra firm tofu
fresh ginger juice - 3 tablespoons
5 large cloves sliced garlic
3-4 large shallots sliced
hot chili pepper paste (sambal olek) to taste
fresh ground black pepper
finely chopped scallions
fresh squeezed lime juice - from one lime
1 stalk of lemongrass chopped very fine

1. Slice tofu lengthwise in half and then into bite sized cubes.
2. Drain very well on cloth towels or paper towels for a few hours pressing very lightly every so often.
3. Marinate the tofu in hot sauce, ginger juice, and chopped lemon grass for a few hours.
4. Heat some oil in a non stick pan.
5. Add shallots and garlic and sauté until golden-brown.
6. Remove and reserve.
7. Add a little more oil if necessary and fry the tofu (drain and reserve marinade) until browned on all sides. Add the garlic/shallots and cook for several minutes.
8. Add the reserved marinade and cook for a few minutes until somewhat dry.
9. Serve over jasmine rice with a squeeze of fresh lime juice and a generous helping of chopped scallions.
10. You can add slices of fresh Thai chili peppers and fresh ground black pepper if you wish.

Tofu Pepper Pot

3 firm tofu squares.
1 vegetable stock cube dissolved in 1 cup hot water.
1 large stick celery, thinly sliced
¾ cup button mushrooms.
1 large dill pickle (cucumber)
2-3 tablespoons cranberry or raspberry jelly.
salt/freshly ground black pepper.
2 tablespoons freshly chopped herbs,
  e.g. parsley, basil.
2-3 tablespoons margarine or oil.

1. Cut each bean curd square into three long strips and each strip into diagonal ¼ inch slices.
2. Fry tofu slices in fat until brown (fry longer if a more chewy texture is preferred). Drain. In the same fat, fry celery and then mushrooms until soft.
3. Sprinkle with flour and cook until slightly brown.
4. Add stock and boil before adding jelly and tofu.
5. Season to taste. Serve with rice or pasta garnished with herbs.

Noodles, Tofu and Wakami

1 lb. firm tofu, cut into 1 in.
cubes and patted very dry
3 cup thinly sliced mushrooms (8 oz.)
1½ tsp. minced gingerroot
2 cup vegetable stock
¼ cup tamari soy sauce
½ oz. wakami

Bring a large pot of water to boil and drop in the buckwheat noodles. Cook about 10 min. Drain well.

1. Meanwhile, heat the oil in a large skillet over high heat until hot but not smoking.
2. Add the tofu and stir - fry until golden, about 10 min.
3. Remove from the pan and set aside.
4. Reduce the heat to medium and add the mushrooms. Stir-fry until the mushrooms are brown and tender, about 7 min.
5. Meanwhile, put the wakami in a bowl and soak about 5 min. Remove from bowl and chop, removing and discarding the tough rib.
6. Return the tofu to the pan and add the ginger.
7. Stir-fry 1 min. Add the vegetable stock, tamari, and wakami and boil 2 min.
8. Place some noodles in each soup bowl.
9. Spoon equal portions of the tofu mixture and broth over each serving. Enjoy!

Tofu Hoisin With Broccoli, Red Pepper and Walnuts

Serves 3-4

⅓ cup hoisin sauce
2 tbsp. Chinese rice wine or dry sherry
1 tbsp. oriental sesame oil
1 tbsp. tamari soy sauce
2 tbsp. vegetable oil
1 lb extra-firm tofu, sliced, patted very dry, then cut into 2 x ½-inch logs
6 garlic cloves, minced
⅛ tsp. crushed red pepper flakes
1 red bell pepper, cut into 3x½-inch strips
1 bunch broccoli, cut into small florets, stalks peeled and sliced (about 5 cups)

½ cup walnut halves ⅓ cup water

1. Combine the first four ingredients in a small bowl and set aside.
2. Heat the oil in a wok or large skillet over high heat until it is hot but not smoking.
3. Make sure the tofu is patted very dry to prevent sticking.
4. Add the tofu and stir-fry until lightly golden all over.
5. Remove to a platter and reduce the heat to medium-high.
6. If there is no oil left in the pan, add a teaspoon or so.
7. Add the garlic and crushed pepper flakes and cook 1 minute.
8. Stir in the red bell pepper, broccoli, and walnuts and toss to coat with the garlic.
9. Pour in the water, toss, then cover the pan.
10. Cook 5 minutes, or until the vegetables are tender yet still crunchy.
11. Stir in the tofu, then pour on the sauce mixture.
12. Stir-fry 1 minute, or until the sauce coats everything and is thickened.
13. Serve on rice.

To organize yourself cook 1½ cups rice before you begin stir-frying and keep it warm on the back burner; the stir-frying will take only a few minutes.

Sauces, Spreads and Dips

Sweet and Sour Sauce

Serves 4

2 tablespoons oil
3 tablespoons finely grated fresh ginger
1½ tablespoons corn flour
2½ cups water
3 tablespoons cider vinegar
3 tablespoons tomato paste
3 tablespoons soy sauce
a cup apple juice concentrate

1. Gently fry the ginger in oil.
2. Mix with the water and corn flour.
3. Add remaining ingredients.
4. Boil, stirring continuously, until thickened.
5. Pour over stir-fried vegetables and/or tofu.
6. Serve with rice.

Bean Curd Dip

Serves 6

½ pound bean curd
¼ cup plum sauce
2 teaspoons prepared Chinese mustard
1 teaspoon salt

1. Mash the bean curd.
2. Then mix with the other ingredients with a whisk or an electric mixer.
3. The dip should have the consistency of sour cream.
4. To prepare in a blender or food processor.
5. combine the ingredients and process until smooth.
6. Refrigerate until ready to serve.
7. Stored in a sealed container, the dip can be kept in the refrigerator for up to a week.
8. Makes 1½ cups.

Easy Sweet & Sour Sauce

Serves 6

¼ cup pineapple juice   1¼ teaspoons soy sauce
1½ tablespoons oil   ½ teaspoon pepper
1 tablespoon brown sugar   2 tablespoons milk vinegar

1. Combine all ingredients in small bowl.
2. Serving Ideas:
3. Use as dipping sauce or to stir-fry vegetables

Manchurian Sauce

Serves 1

½ cup soy sauce
½ cup vegetable stock
½ cup green onion, thinly sliced
1 teaspoon fresh ginger root, minced
1 teaspoon garlic, minced
½ teaspoon wasabi (or ½ tsp. minced jalapeno pepper)

1. In a medium-sized bowl, combine all the ingredients and whisk until well blended.
2. Refrigerate for at least 30 minutes before serving.

Note: If you are watching your sodium intake, substitute one of the low-sodium varieties of soy sauce, but keep in mind that these may still be quite high in salt.

Soy Ginger Dipping Sauce

⅓ cup tamari
¼ cup rice vinegar
1 Tbsp. water
1 tsp. each sugar, grated fresh ginger, sesame oil
and thinly sliced scallion on top.

1. In bowl, mix tamari, vinegar, water and sugar to dissolve.
2. Add ginger and sesame oil.
3. Stir to mix.
4. Serve in dipping bowls garnished with scallions.

Peanut Miso Sauce

Makes 1 cup sauce

½ cup white or yellow miso, (fermented bean paste)
2 tablespoons packed brown sugar
2 tablespoons creamy or crunchy peanut butter
3 tablespoons sake
1 tablespoon reduced-sodium soy sauce

1. In small bowl whisk together miso, brown sugar, peanut butter, sake, and soy sauce.
2. Cover and store in refrigerator until ready to use.

Spicy Soy Dipping Sauce

Serves 24

¼ cup vegetable stock
½ cup light soy sauce
1 tablespoon rice wine or dry sherry
2 tablespoons sesame oil
2 tablespoons rice vinegar
1 tablespoon sugar or honey
1 teaspoon hot oil

1. Combine the ingredients in a small boil.
2. Stir to dissolve the sugar, then cover and refrigerate until serving.

Hoisin Dipping Sauce

Serves 1

2 tablespoons hoisin sauce
2 tablespoons tomato catsup
1 teaspoon rice vinegar
1 teaspoon honey
1 teaspoon black soy sauce

1. Combine the ingredients in a small bowl and mix well.
2. Refrigerate until ready to serve.

Ume Su Pickles

Ume Su is a Japanese vinegar (great for a variety of stomach problems!) (This recipe is best with radishes, the thin slices turn a beautiful pink)

1. Slice squash thinly. Mix 1 part Ume Su with 3-4 parts water to cover slices
2. Store in fridge – ready to eat after 24 hours.

Sweet and Sour Dipping Sauce

Serves 6

½ cup bottled Major Grey's Chutney
¼ cup apricot preserves
¼ cup crushed pineapple
¼ cup applesauce
½ teaspoon ginger, minced
1 teaspoon rice vinegar

1. Combine the ingredients for the sauce in a saucepan and heat just to blend, stirring often.
2. Cool to room temperature and serve.
3. Makes 1¼ cups.

Japanese Carrot Dressing

1 small carrot, shredded
2 tablespoons mirin (Japanese sweet cooking wine)
2 tablespoons rice vinegar or cider vinegar
1 tablespoon soy sauce
2 drops dark sesame oil - *see note
1 tablespoon prepared mustard
1 tablespoon grated fresh ginger root (optional)

Note: You can add, omit/substitute any ingredients you prefer. Original recipe calls for ½ teaspoon of sesame oil. whirl all ingredients in a blender until smooth. Another option would be to add the shredded carrots after blending the other ingredients together. You can also add the ginger for a more enhanced flavor. 1 English cucumber, sliced in half length-wise and sliced
Salt to taste. Well covered, it keeps in the refrigerator for about a week.

Dressing:
1 tablespoon sesame oil
1 teaspoon chili oil (or to taste)
1 tablespoon rice vinegar

Garnish:
Chopped dried chilies to taste
Place sliced cucumbers in serving bowl and sprinkle with salt to taste.
Mix dressing ingredients in a small bowl and pour over cucumber slices. Stir to coat.
Sprinkle with dried chilies to taste.
Stir. Serve cold.
(This dish can be made several hours ahead.)
*the same chilies you use at the pizza parlor!

Soups

Carrot Ginger Soup

Serves 4

Combine all ingredients in a high-power blender such as a Vita Mix and blend well until completely smooth.

¾ lb carrots (about 2½ carrots), roughly chopped
1 cup coconut meat, roughly chopped
1½ tbsp. shallots, diced
½ cup coconut water
½ cup orange juice
½ clove of garlic
1 tbsp. minced ginger
1 tbsp. miso
Pinch of cumin

Combine all ingredients in a high-power blender such as a Vita Mix and blend well until completely smooth.

Thai Coconut Corn Soup

Serves 6

1 tablespoon light olive oil
3 cloves garlic, minced
4 to 5 scallions, white and green parts, thinly sliced
1 medium red bell pepper, cut into short, narrow strips
Two 15-ounce cans light coconut milk
1½ cups rice milk
One 16-ounce bag frozen corn
2 teaspoons good quality curry powder
¼ teaspoon Thai red curry paste, more or less to taste
1 teaspoon salt, or to taste
½ cup minced fresh cilantro

1. Heat the oil in a small soup pot. Add the garlic, the white parts of the scallions, and the bell pepper. Sauté over medium-low heat until softened and golden, about 2 to 3 minutes.
2. Add the coconut milk, rice milk, corn, curry powder, the green parts of the scallions. If using the curry paste, dissolve it in a small amount of water before adding to the soup.
3. Bring to a rapid simmer, then lower the heat. Cover and simmer gently for 5 minutes. Season with salt and remove from the heat.
4. Serve, passing around the cilantro for topping.

Salads

Minced Mushroom Salad

10 dried mushrooms
1 cup fresh mushrooms, diced
juice of 1 lime
4-5 squirts soy sauce
1 tsp. sugar
1-2 tbsp. dried coarsely ground chilies
2 tbsp. roasted ground rice
1 stalk lemon grass, finely chopped
2 shallots, finely chopped
2-3 green onions, finely chopped
4-5 bunches coriander, chopped
20 fresh mint leaves, chopped

1. Soak dried mushrooms in boiling water for 10 mins.
2. Cut off and discard stems; dice heads.
3. In a small saucepan, combine dried and fresh mushrooms with a few tablespoons water, lime juice, soy sauce, and sugar, and cook 2 mins over high heat.
4. Turn heat down to medium, add dried ground chili, ground rice, and lemon grass and cook another minute, until mixture begins to thicken.
5. Remove from heat; add shallots and stir.
6. Let sit until cool, then add green onions, coriander, and mint and stir well.

Nutty Asian Salad

10 oz. snow peas or sugar snap peas, washed, topped and tailed
5 oz. snake beans, trimmed and cut into ½ inch lengths
7 oz. broccoli, cut into small florets
¼ lb. bean sprouts
2 small carrots, peeled and cut into thin strips
1 teaspoon red wine vinegar
½ small red onion, finely chopped
black pepper, freshly ground
1 tablespoon cashew nuts
2 teaspoons ginger, freshly grated
1 tablespoon peanut oil or macadamia nut oil
½ teaspoon sesame oil
1 tablespoon lemon or lime juice
2 tablespoons lemon or lime, grated or rind

1. Separately steam, boil or microwave the snow peas (or sugar snap peas), beans, and broccoli until just cooked.
2. Refresh and cool under cold running water, drain and pat dry with paper towel.
3. In a salad bowl mix vinegar, onion, pepper, cashews, ginger, oils, lemon or lime juice and rind.
4. Gently toss lightly cooked vegetables, bean sprouts and carrots in dressing and serve immediately.

A Taste of Indonesia

Entrees

Pecal (Veg Salad w/ Peanut Sauce)

Serves 6

½ pound water spinach (kangkung), cut into
  3-inch pieces
1 bunch of watercress, coarse stems discarded
¼ pound Chinese long beans, cut into 2-inch pieces
½ pound shredded cabbage
½ pound bean sprouts
3 garlic cloves, sliced
3 or 4 hot chilies, sliced and seeded
1 tablespoon corn oil
1 cup water
1 stalk of lemongrass or a 1-inch piece of lemon rind
2 teaspoons sugar
½ teaspoon salt
1 cup dry roasted peanuts, crushed

Note: Use at least 4 of those vegetables. Blanch the vegetables, separately, in boiling water for 2 minutes each. Drain and let cool in separate dishes.

1. In a food processor, blend the garlic and chilies to form a paste.
2. Heat the oil in a skillet or wok and in it stir-fry the paste over moderate heat for 1 minute.
3. Add the water, lemongrass, sugar, and salt and bring the mixture to a boil.
4. Add the peanuts and cook for 5 minutes, or until the sauce is thickened slightly.
5. In a serving bowl or on a platter arrange the water spinach and cover it with the watercress, then the long beans. Arrange the cabbage and the bean sprouts on top. Serve at room temperature.
6. Pour the sauce over all. Serve with krupuk (chips).

Gado Gado (Mixed Vegetable Salad with Peanut Sauce)

Serves 8-10

½ pound small potatoes, boiled in their skins until tender, peeled and sliced
1 cup shredded cabbage, boiled for 2 minutes and drained
½ pound carrots, sliced thin, boiled for 2 minutes and drained
½ pound bean sprouts, boiled for 3 minutes and drained
¼ pound green beans, cut into 2-inch lengths, boiled for 3 minutes and drained 1 cucumber, halved lengthwise, seeded and sliced (about 1 cup)
1 cup sliced jicama (optional)
Peanut Sauce (see first recipe above)
2 squares of Chinese soybean curd, boiled for 10 minutes, drained, and cut into ½-inch cubes
3 tablespoons Crispy Fried Shallots

Note: Vegetables may be added to the ingredients or substituted for the ones listed here

1. Chill all the vegetables separately in individual containers.
2. In a large serving bowl or on a platter, arrange the vegetables in layers as follows:
3. Potatoes on the bottom, then the cabbage, carrots, bean sprouts, green beans, cucumber, and jicama.
4. Pour the warm Peanut Sauce over the salad
5. Scatter the soybean cubes and the Crispy Fried Shallots on top.
6. Serve at room temperature.

Tahu Goreng
(Fried Soybean Curd)

Serves 6

¼ pound green beans, cut diagonally in 2-inch pieces
4 firm soybean curd squares
½ cup corn oil for deep-frying
3 shallots, sliced
2 garlic cloves, sliced
2 fresh hot red chilies, sliced
½ teaspoon salt
2 tablespoon Kecap Manis (sweet soy sauce)
1 tablespoon tomato paste

1. Blanch the green beans in boiling water for 5 minutes.
2. Drain. Cut the bean curd into slices 1 inch long and ¼ inch thick.
3. Drain the slices on paper towels, patting them dry.
4. Heat the oil in a wok or deep skillet and fry the slices over moderate heat for 3 minutes, or until light brown.
5. Remove and set aside.
6. Remove all but 1 tablespoon oil.
7. In a food processor, blend the shallots, garlic, chilies, and salt to form a paste (bumbu).
8. Heat the oil in the wok and stir-fry the bumbu over moderate heat for 2 minutes.
9. Add the beans, bean curd, Kecap Manis, and tomato paste.
10. Stir-fry the mixture for 3 minutes.
11. Serve warm.

Eggplant Delight

2 medium eggplants (cut in ½-inch circles)
Salt (for taking bitterness out of eggplants)
olive oil
2 tablespoons of oil
1 red pepper (diced)
1 tablespoon basil
½ tablespoon oregano
dash of cayenne pepper
1 palm full of chopped cilantro (Chinese parsley)
2 garlic (minced)
2 tablespoons dry cooking sherry
2 packages of Yves 'like ground' (TVP already prepared)
2 14 oz. cans of tomato sauce
1 package of Soymage's "soychunks cheddar cheese" (lactose, rennet, and casein free)
1 French bread

1. Sprinkle salt over sliced eggplants for 10 minutes, pat dry.
2. Brush eggplant slices on both sides with olive oil, Place in oven on broil for about 5-10 minutes, make sure not to burn, until tender, turn over once.
3. While this is being cooked: In a saucepan, heat oil over medium heat an sauté garlic and red pepper and "Like Ground" for about 3-5 minutes adding the basil, oregano, cayenne and cilantro.
4. Add tomato sauce and cooking sherry, simmer for about another 10-15 minutes.
5. Place eggplant slices when cooked in a 13" dish, layer the slices, empty the "Like Ground" sauce over the eggplants - grate the Soymage cheese over it and bake in oven at 350 degrees for about 20 minutes, serve with garlic bread or french bread.

Seitan, The Vegetarian 'Wheat Meat'

I get blank stares when I ask my vegetarian cooking students if they've ever eaten seitan (say-tahn). Yet, hands go up when I ask if anybody has ever eaten mock chicken, beef, or pork in a Chinese vegetarian restaurant. The name is foreign but you may be more familiar with the product than you think. According to Barbara and Leonard Jacobs in their excellent book Cooking with Seitan, The Complete Vegetarian "Wheat-Meat" Cookbook, "seitan has been a staple food among vegetarian monks of China, Russian wheat farmers, peasants of Southeast Asia, and Mormons. People who had traditionally eaten wheat had also discovered a method to extract the gluten and create a seitan-like product." Seitan is derived from the protein portion of wheat. It stands in for meat in many recipes and works so well that a number of vegetarians avoid it because the texture is too "meaty." Wheat Meat /Seitan is a great addition to the vegetarian protein arsenal. It's perfectly healthy, unless you are sensitive to gluten. As to "whole" gluten flour. As long as you don't have Celiac's disease or other gluten sensitivities, it's fine. Just a natural wheat protein.

Gluten can be flavored in a variety of ways. When simmered in a traditional broth of soy sauce or tamari, ginger, garlic, and kombu (seaweed), it is called seitan. I refer to all flavored gluten as seitan. Making gluten the traditional way is time consuming. It calls for mixing 8 cups of flour with 3 to 5 cups of water and forming a dough. The dough is then kneaded and rinsed under running water to remove the wheat starch. After about 20 to 30 minutes of kneading and rinsing, which to me seems like a considerable amount of time, the resulting 2 or so cups of stretchy gluten is evident. At that point the gluten needs to be simmered in broth for at least 1 hour and up to 2 hours or more.

Luckily there are some shortcut methods for making gluten (see recipe) that make it a convenient food to prepare. I have had the most luck using high gluten flour or vital wheat gluten, although I have found that until you become familiar with the texture you are aiming for during the mixing and kneading process, the results will vary somewhat. The added benefit of using this method is that you can flavor the gluten during the kneading process by adding herbs and spices of your choosing other than the traditional ginger and garlic.

You can use poultry seasoning or chicken flavor broth powder to make a "chicken" flavored seitan, or a blend with paprika, cayenne, fennel, garlic, and Italian seasoning for a "sausage" flavor. Flavoring is limited only by your imagination. For some, a safer first step is to purchase one of the commercially available mixes. Arrowhead Mills'

Seitan Quick Mix or any of the Knox Mountain products, which include Wheat Balls, Chicken Wheat, and Not-So-Sausage, yield a tasty product. Just be sure to follow the box directions exactly. Gluten containing more water or which has been kneaded less tends to get puffy instead of being dense. Some people prefer the less dense result. I like gluten to be quite firm, as it substitutes more easily for animal foods in recipes.

Commercially prepared seitan is produced by White Wave and Lightlife Foods as well as regional manufacturers. You will find it in tubs or vacuum packs soaking in marinade in either the refrigerator or the freezer section of many natural food stores. You may also find frozen or fresh gluten in Asian markets by the name Mi-Tan. Other ready-to-eat forms on the market include Ivy Foods' burgers, sausage-style and chicken-style Wheat of Meat Products, lunch-style "meats," fajita strips, and slices. (Ed. note: Ivy Foods products are now being manufactured by White Wave.)

Gluten seems to be cropping up in more products these days and is often a key ingredient in "not-dogs." Once made, seitan can be stored in broth in the refrigerator for up to about a week. Individually-wrapped cutlets can be frozen for up to a month or more without a loss in texture or flavor. It is best to thaw them before using.

Seitan's versatility lies in the myriad forms it assumes during the cooking process. I find simmering to be the most effective and efficient preparation method. But it can be oven-braised, baked, cooked in a pressure cooker, or deep fried. Each version yields a different texture. Oven braising produces a texture similar to the chewy texture derived from simmering. Baking produces a light texture that works well when grinding or grating seitan. Pressure cooking, according to the Jacobs, "will produce a softer-textured seitan." Fried gluten turns soft and slippery when cooked with a sauce and absorbs flavor well. As gluten is a low sodium and extremely low fat protein (containing around 10 mg. sodium, 0 g. fat, and 7.5 g. protein per ounce in its raw state), additional processing is what may add unhealthy attributes. Most of the commercially prepared seitan contains a considerable amount of sodium (up to 100 mg. per ounce). If you choose to deep-fry the gluten, the fat content will jump from virtually zero to the number of grams in whatever oil is absorbed (at 4.5 grams per teaspoon).

Making seitan and gluten will open up a new horizon for you in the world of vegetarian cooking. It is terrific in stir-fries and paired with noodles in Asian-style dishes, yet also works well in traditional American fare like stew. Try substituting it for animal products in former favorite recipes or those of non-vegetarian friends and relatives. Then get your creative juices flowing and experiment when making seitan by varying the flavorings and cooking methods.

Quick Homemade Gluten

(Makes 1¼ to 1½ pounds or 2 to 2½ cups)
This is the basic recipe for gluten.

2 cups gluten flour
1 teaspoon garlic powder
1 teaspoon ground ginger
1¼ cups water or vegetable stock
3 tablespoons lite tamari, Braggs liquid amino acids, or soy sauce
1-3 teaspoons toasted sesame oil (optional)

1. Add garlic powder and ginger to flour and stir.
2. Mix liquids together and add to flour mixture all at once.
3. Mix vigorously with a fork.
4. When it forms a stiff dough, knead it 10 to 15 times.
5. Let the dough rest 2 to 5 minutes, then knead it a few more times.
6. Let it rest another 15 minutes before proceeding.
7. Cut gluten into 6 to 8 pieces and stretch into thin cutlets.
8. Simmer in broth for 30 to 60 minutes.

Broth:
4 cups water
¼ cup tamari or soy sauce
3-inch piece of kombu (a type of seaweed)
3-4 slices ginger (optional)

1. Combine all ingredients in a large saucepan.
2. Bring broth to a boil.
3. Add cutlets one at a time.
4. Reduce heat to barely simmer when saucepan is covered.
5. Seitan may be used, refrigerated, or frozen at this point.

Barbecued Seitan

Serves 4
1 medium onion, diced
8-12 ounces seitan cutlets, cut into strips
¼ cup barbecue sauce
4 whole wheat buns, optional

1. Spray a skillet with cooking spray.
2. Add the onion and sauté over medium heat for about 5 minutes, adding water 1 tablespoon at a time if onion begins to stick.
3. Cook until onion is translucent.
4. Add the seitan strips and sauté for 1 to 2 minutes.
5. Add barbecue sauce and stir to combine.
6. Sauté until barbecue sauce is hot.
7. Serve on whole wheat buns, if desired.

Seitan-Squash Sauté

Serves 4
Here's another terrific seitan dish.
2 teaspoons vegetable oil
1 medium onion, sliced
2 small carrots, peeled and sliced on the diagonal
½ pound of seitan, marinated in tamari broth, cut in small chunks
1 medium-size yellow squash, diced
1 medium-size zucchini, diced
1 gray or roly-poly squash, diced
2 cloves garlic, minced
1 teaspoon grated ginger
½ cup pineapple juice
1 large tomato, pureed
1 tablespoon seitan marinade -or-
2 teaspoons tamari with 1 teaspoon water
1 tablespoon arrowroot (starch) mixed with 1 tablespoon water

1. Heat oil in large sauté pan over medium-high heat.
2. Add onion and carrots.
3. Cook for about 5 minutes until onion starts getting translucent.
4. Add seitan, squash, garlic, and ginger and sauté for about 5 more minutes.
5. Add the pineapple juice, pureed tomato, and marinade. Stir and cook for a couple of minutes.
6. Remove pan from heat.
7. Add the arrowroot mixture, stir well.
8. Return to heat and stir until sauce thickens.
9. Serve hot over rice or noodles.

Ginger Braised Seitan

An absolute favorite! Ginger braised seitan has become one of the most popular main dish around the world. Though ginger braised seitan originally belongs to the fusion cuisine, today it's a part of the global taste. Braising is the primary method of making ginger braised seitan. No matter whether you are an iron chef or a novice, you will find ginger braised seitan easy to prepare. It is a favorite vegetarian choice of many.

1 8 oz. package seitan (such as White Wave brand), cubed
2 tbsp. freshly grated ginger
2 tbsp. garlic, minced
3 shallots, minced
2 tbsp. brown sugar
1 tbsp. Thai hot sauce (Sriracha sauce) more or less to taste
¼ cup cilantro stems and roots (save leaves)
¼ cup soy sauce
1 cup coconut milk
1 tsp. seasame oil
2 tbsp. vegetable oil
1 tbsp. corn starch
2 tbsp. vegetable oil
1 cup carrots, cut on the bias
1 cup broccoli stems, cut to 2"
2 cup bok choy, sliced
1 cup onion, sliced

Garnish:
Cilantro leaves
Thai hot sauce

1. Marinate seitan in first ingredients for 3 hours. remove seitan but reserve liquid.
2. Heat wok on medium high heat. Add oil. Add vegetables and stir-fry 3 minutes.
3. Add seitan and stir-fry another 3 minutes.
4. Add marinade and corn starch and stir fry all ingredients until sauce has thickened slightly.
5. Serve with rice, cilantro leaves and Thai hot sauce.

Seitan Stew

Serves 4
1 cup of water plus ½ cup water
1 ounce dried wild mushrooms such as morel, shiitake, or porcini
1 tablespoon oil
1 large onion, chopped
2 carrots, diced
3 small turnips, peeled and cut in quarters
4-5 small potatoes, cut in half
½ pound mushrooms, halved
3 dried tomatoes, made into powder
8 ounces seitan, cut in small chunks
1 teaspoon dried rosemary
1 teaspoon dried thyme
1 teaspoon dried sage
1 tablespoon miso
1 tablespoon arrowroot plus additional if needed
2 tablespoons fresh chopped parsley
freshly ground black pepper to taste

1. Boil one cup of the water and soak the dried mushrooms (if they are morels or shiitake) for 30 minutes.
2. Save soaking water.
3. If using porcini add when recommended.
4. Heat oil in pan over medium heat.
5. Add onion, carrot, turnips, and potatoes.
6. Sauté for 3 to 5 minutes until onion begins to soften.
7. Add fresh mushrooms, tomato powder, and ¼ cup water.
8. Cook for 5 more minutes.
9. Then add seitan chunks, dried herbs, and rehydrated mushrooms that have been cut in pieces.
10. Cook for 5 more minutes.
11. Add soaking water drained of any debris and porcini
12. Add the miso and stir.
13. Cook for about 10 more minutes until vegetables are almost tender.
14. Combine the remaining ¼ cup water with the arrowroot and add to the pan over medium heat, stirring until thickened.
15. If too thick add water 1 tablespoon at a time.
16. If too thin add arrowroot 1 teaspoon at a time.
17. Season with black pepper.
18. Add parsley just before serving.

Seitan and Shiitake Mushroom Stroganoff

Serves 4

savor this hearty dish.

vegetable cooking spray
1 tablespoon oil
1 onion, chopped
8-12 ounces seitan cutlets, cut into chunks
1 carrot, finely cut or shredded
1 clove garlic, minced
1 cup sliced button mushrooms
6 to 10 dried or fresh shiitake mushrooms (If dried they need to be soaked for at least 30 minutes and then drained.), sliced
1 tbsp. Bragg liquid amino acids, lite tamari, or soy sauce
5 ounces silken lite firm or extra firm tofu
1 tablespoon lemon juice
1 tablespoon arrowroot
1 teaspoon sweetener
freshly ground pepper, to taste
¼ cup chopped parsley, for garnish

1. Spray a wok or large sauté pan with cooking spray.
2. Add the oil and heat.
3. When the oil is hot, add the onion and seitan and sauté for 2 to 3 minutes.
4. Add the carrot, garlic, and mushrooms.
5. Cook until mushrooms release their water.
6. Add liquid aminos and cook until almost all absorbed.
7. While the mushroom mixture is cooking blend the tofu, lemon juice, arrowroot, and sweetener in a blender or food processor until smooth.
8. Turn off heat and add the tofu mixture.
9. Stir to combine.
10. If heat is too high the tofu mixture will break apart and curdle.
11. Add freshly ground pepper.
12. Top with parsley and serve over hot noodles.

Mock BBQ Pork

Serves 4

Have as an appetizer or used in a stir-fry.
1 tablespoon toasted sesame oil
2 tablespoons lite tamari or soy sauce
2 tablespoons water
1 tablespoon minced ginger
1 tablespoon minced garlic
1 tablespoon sweetener
2 teaspoons five-spice powder
vegetable cooking spray

1. Form gluten into a cylinder and lightly simmer in water for at least 30 minutes until quite firm.
2. Let cool and cut in small pieces in the Chinese "roll-cut" style.
3. (Cut off one corner, turn the cylinder, cut again and continue.)
4. Combine the remaining ingredients make a marinade.
5. Marinate the gluten pieces for 15 to 30 minutes.
6. Preheat the oven to 300 degrees.
7. Spray a baking sheet with cooking spray.
8. Drain gluten from marinade.
9. Put on baking sheet and bake for 20 to 30 minutes.
10. If gluten seems to be getting too dry, baste with the marinade.
11. Eat as is, use in a stir-fry, or as a filling for mock-pork buns.

Seitan Fusion Sauté

Serves 4

1½ teaspoons oil
1 medium onion, chopped
2 cloves garlic, minced
1 tablespoon garam masala
8 ounces seitan, finely chopped or coarsely grated
2 cups shredded zucchini
1 cup chopped fresh tomato
½ can crushed pineapple in juice, undrained (20 oz. can)
2 tablespoons peanut butter
½ cup lite coconut milk
salt and pepper to taste
¼ cup chopped fresh cilantro
dash of tabasco (optional)
chopped peanuts for garnish (optional)

1. Heat the oil in a large skillet.
2. Add the onion and sauté for 5 minutes.
3. Add the garlic and garam masala.
4. Stirring, cook for another 1 to 2 minutes.
5. Add the zucchini,
6. seitan, and tomato and cook for 1 to 2 minutes.
7. Add the remaining ingredients, except cilantro and simmer over medium heat for 10 minutes until sauce begins to thicken slightly.
8. Add Tabasco to taste. Stir in cilantro.
9. Top with chopped peanuts.
10. Serve hot over rice.

Sekihan

Serves 6-8

½ cups azuki (small red beans)
about 3½ cups water
3 cups sweet glutinous rice (mochi gome) **Regular rice isn't sticky enough**
well rinsed, soaked for ½-1 hour, drained
3½ cups water
1 tablespoon black dry-roasted sesame seeds
Shiso or watercress leaf for garnish, if desired
In a medium saucepan, combine beans and water; bring to a boil.

1. Reduce heat to low; simmer 45 minutes to one hour or until beans are soft but not completely cooked.
2. Cool to room temperature.
3. Drain beans, reserving the liquid.
4. Mix the beans, drained rice and water with 3 tablespoons of the bean's cooking liquid.
5. Cook in rice steamer in the usual manner.
6. Spread the cooked beans and rice into a decorative shallow dish or lacquer tray.
7. Sprinkle with the sesame seeds, garnish and serve.

Home Made Seitan

Here's a recipe for homemade Gluten (aka Seitan).
You can also buy it prepackaged in some areas.
1 cup Instant gluten flour or "vital wheat gluten" (NOT just regular high gluten flour, it's just gluten powder)
1 cup water

1. Stir gluten powder & water together.
2. Add more water if necessary.
3. Knead to make the gluten elastic
4. squeeze out the excess water.
5. Break in small (1") pieces
6. Simmer in a vegetable broth at least ½ hour.

Note: The longer you knead and simmer the gluten, the tougher it will become, so you can pick your own texture. 10 cups of flour and after rinsing end up with about 1 cup of gluten. Beginning with pure gluten powder is a bit easier if you can get it. You can buy it bulk at the health-food store.

Home-Made Seitan II

6 cups stone-ground whole wheat bread flour or high-gluten unbleached white flour
3 cups water (or more, depending on the amount of gluten in the flour)
½ cup tamari
12 slices fresh ginger, each ⅛ inch thick,
1 piece of kombu, about 3 inches long.

1. Mix the flour and water by hand or in a machine to make a medium-stiff but not sticky dough.
2. Knead the dough by hand on a breadboard or tabletop, until it has the consistency of an earlobe (!), or by machine until the dough forms a ball that follows the path of the hook around the bowl.
3. You may need to add a little extra water or flour to achieve the desired consistency.
4. Kneading will take about 10-12 minutes by hand or about 6-8 minutes by machine.
5. Allow the dough to rest in a bowl of cold water for about 10 minutes.,
6. While the dough is resting, prepare the stock.
7. In a large pot, bring to boil 3 quarts of water.
8. Add the tamaari, ginger, and kombu, and cook for 15 minutes. Remove from heat and allow to cool.
9. This stock must be cold before it is used.
10. (the cold liquid causes the gluten to contract and prevents the eseitan from acquiring a "bready" texture.) You will be using this stock to cook the seitan later.
11. To wash out the starch, use warm water to begin with.
12. Warm water loosens the dough and makes the task easier.
13. Knead the dough, immersed in water, in the bowl.
14. When the water turns milky, drain it off and refill the bowl with fresh water.
15. In the final rinses, use cold water to tighten the gluten.
16. If you wish, save the bran by straining the water through a fine sieve: the bran will be left behind.
17. Save the starch, which you can use for thickening soups, sauces, and stews.
18. When kneading, remember to work toward the center of the dough so that it does not break into pieces.
19. After about eight changes of water, you will begin to feel the dough become firmer and more elastic.
20. The water will no longer become cloudy as you knead it.
21. To make sure you have kneaded and rinsed it enough, lift the dough out of the water and squeeze it. The liquid oozing out should be clear, not milky.
22. To shape the seitan, lightly oil a one pound loaf pan.
23. Place the rinsed seitan in the pan and let it rest until the dough relaxes.
24. (after the dough has been rinsed for the last time in cold water, the gluten will have tightened and the dough will be tense, tough, and resistant to taking on any other shape.)
25. After it has rested for 10 minutes, it will be much more flexible.
26. Seitan is cooked in two steps.
27. In the first step, the dough is put into a large pot with about 3 quarts of plain, boiling water.
28. Boil the seitan for about 30-45 minutes, or until it floats to the surface.
29. Drain the seitan and cut it into usable pieces (steaks, cutlets, 1-inch chunks, or whatever) or leave whole.
30. Return the seitan to the cold tamari stock.
31. Bring the stock to a boil, lower the temperature, and simmer in the stock for 1½ to 2 hours (45 minutes if the seitan is cut into small pieces).
32. This second step may also be done in a pressure cooker, in which case it would take between 30-45 minutes.
33. To store seitan, keep it refrigerated, immersed in the stock.
34. Seitan will keep indefinitely if it is brought to a boil in the tamari stock and boiled for 10 minutes twice a week.
35. Otherwise, use it within 8 or 9 days.

Variations:
Instead of boiling the seitan in plain water and then stock, let the seitan drain for a while after it has been rinsed.
Slice it and either deep-fry or sauté the slices until both sides are brown.
Then cook it in the stock according to recipe.
Seitan also may be cooked (at the second step) in a broth flavored with carrot, onion, celery, garlic, tamari, and black pepper, which will give it a flavor similar to that of a pot roast.
Shiitake mushrooms may also be added to the stock.

Seitan and Tempeh

Seitan is a cooked form of vegetable protein derived from wheat gluten which is simmered in soy, kombu and herbs, and spices to tenderize it. Makes a great substitute for stewing beef.

The old fashioned way:
Take 4 cups of whole wheat bread flour and dump it in to a large mixing bowl, add enough water to make a nice firm ball of dough. Let water run into the bowl (gently) from a tap and knead the dough in the bowl under the running water. Holding the ball together, knead until the water in the bowl stops getting cloudy. Roll the very firm dough into a log and cut into thin steaks or tear off into small pieces (about ½ the size of a golf ball) in a large (7-quart) stock pot bring the following to a boil:

4 quarts water
3 cups soy sauce
1 6-inch piece of kombu (sea vegetable)
1 tablespoon peppercorns
2 tablespoons ground ginger
2 tablespoons granulated garlic

1. Once boiling add the steaks or balls which you previously cut.
2. Lower heat, cover and simmer for about 1-1½ hours depending on how tender you want the final product to be.
3. Poke and stir occasionally to keep the gluten from sticking to the bottom or sides.
4. Once done, let the seitan cool and store either refrigerated or frozen in broth .
5. Makes a great, low fat source of protein for people who are not wheat or gluten sensitive

Seitan Fajitas

1 med onion, sliced
1 sweet bell pepper, sliced
½ lb seitan
½ tsp. cumin
½ tsp. chili powder
4 tortillas

1. Sauté onions and peppers in a little oil until tender.
2. Add the seitan, cumin and chili powder, and cook until seitan is hot.
3. Fold into a hot tortilla.

Seitan Pepper Steak

Serves 4
1 lb of seitan in broth
1 large onion
2 large peppers
¼ teaspoons black pepper
¼ cup soy sauce
⅛ cup olive oil
1 tablespoon starch mixed with 1 cup water

1. Core and slice peppers into ⅙-⅛ inch wide strips.
2. Peel and slice onion into ⅙-⅛ inch wide strips.
3. Slice the seitan into ⅛ inch thick strips.
4. Sauté the seitan, peppers, and onions in olive oil in a large skillet until the peppers and onions are tender.
5. Add black pepper, seitan broth, and soy sauce.
6. Quickly stir ingredients in skillet until the liquid bubbles.
7. Add Starch/water mixture and continue to stir until thickened, Remove from heat and serve over rice.

Tempeh Ala King

2 cups tempeh, (cut into small cubes)
1 medium onion (chopped)
1 green pepper (chopped)
1 cup green peas
1 cup chopped carrot
1 cup cut corn
1 cup sliced mushrooms
2 cups soymilk,
¼ cup nutritional yeast.
¼ cup Starch (corn, arrowroot or potato)
1t garlic powder
¼ teaspoons black or ⅛ teaspoons white pepper
½ stick of vegan margarine (optional) (about 4 tbsp.)
   enough salt to taste

1. Steam the tempeh for 15 minutes (very important, tempeh must be cooked) at the end of 15 minutes
2. add all of the vegetables to the tempeh and continue steaming for another 10 to 12 minutes.
3. Whisk together the soymilk, garlic powder, pepper, and nutritional yeast, start heating the Soymilk mixture. bring to a low boil, then reduce to a simmer.
4. Once simmering remove the steamed veggies and tempeh from the heat,
5. add 1 cup of the steaming water into the mixture.
6. Mix starch with one cup of water.
7. Add to simmering mixture.
8. Mixture should thicken to a soup like consistency, if too thick add a little more of the steaming water into it. Fold the vegetables and tempeh into the mixture.
9. Salt to taste. Serve over rice, biscuits or toast and enjoy!

Stir-Fry Recipes

Szechuan-Style Stir Fry

1 lb. tofu, cubed
½ lb. snow peas
⅓ cup teriyaki sauce
3 tablespoons Szechuan spicy stir-fry sauce
2 tsp. cornstarch
1 onion, chopped
3 cup chopped bok choy
2-3 tablespoons cooking oil
1 cup broccoli florets
1 red bell pepper
1 7-oz. can straw mushrooms
1 14-oz. can baby corn

1. Combine teriyaki, stir-fry sauce and cornstarch; set aside.
2. Cut bell pepper in strips. Cut snow peas and baby corn in half.
3. In wok stir-fry onion & bok choy in 1 tablespoon oil for 2 minutes. Add broccoli & bell pepper; stir-fry 2 minutes.
4. Remove from wok. Stir-fry cubed tofu in 1 tablespoon oil for 2 minutes; add more oil if necessary.
5. Stir sauce mixture and add to tofu; cook until bubbly.
6. Add all vegetables; heat through. Serve over hot rice.

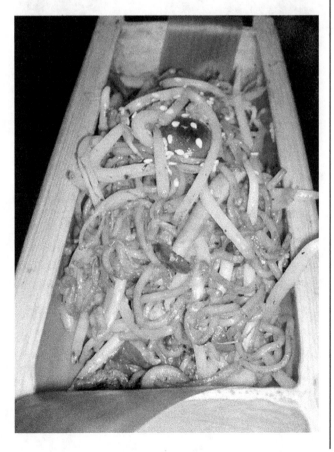

Chinese Stir-Fry

32 ounces Asian-style frozen mixed vegetables (sometimes labeled Oriental- or Japanese-style)
¼ cup bottled stir-fry sauce or to taste
1 pound firm or baked tofu drained and cut into strips

1. Steam vegetables in a stir-fry pan or wok with about ½- inch of water, covered, until completely thawed.
2. Drain well and transfer back to stir-fry pan.
3. Stir in sauce and stir-fry over medium-high heat until vegetables are tender-crisp.
4. Add tofu strips and toss gently.
5. Cook just until heated through, then serve right away.

Marinated Tempeh Stir-Fry w/Broccoli & Red Bell Pepper

Serves 4

4 ounces soy tempeh or 3-grain tempeh, cut into ½-inch, pieces
¼ cup light soy sauce
1 tablespoon rice vinegar
3 garlic cloves, minced
2 teaspoons minced peeled fresh ginger
⅛ teaspoon dried crushed red pepper
12 ounces broccoli, stems peeled and cut into ½-inch pieces, florets cut into 1-inch pieces
2 tablespoons water
1 teaspoon honey style sweetener
1 teaspoon cornstarch
1 tablespoon vegetable oil
½ cup chopped red bell pepper
2 tablespoons thinly sliced green onion

1. Stir tempeh, soy sauce, vinegar, garlic, ginger and crushed red pepper in medium bowl to blend.
2. Let marinate 1 hour at room temperature.
3. Steam broccoli until crisp-tender, about 3 minutes.
4. Set aside. Strain marinade from tempeh into small bowl.
5. Set tempeh aside..
6. Whisk 2 tablespoons water, honey and cornstarch into marinade.
7. Heat oil in large nonstick skillet over high heat.
8. Add marinated tempeh and bell pepper and sauté, 4 minutes.
9. Add broccoli and marinade mixture and sauté until broccoli is heated through and sauce thickens, about 3 minutes.
10. Transfer to bowl. Sprinkle with green onion and serve.

Stir-Fry Veggie W/Tofu

Serves 6

1 cup red bell pepper, thinly sliced
½ cup green bell pepper, thinly sliced
⅓ cup yellow bell pepper, thinly sliced
2 teaspoons safflower oil
1 tablespoon arrowroot powder
½ cup rice vinegar
½ cup pineapple juice
½ cup lemon juice
⅓ cup honey style sweetener
½ teaspoon herbal salt substitute
½ teaspoon grated gingerroot
1 pound firm tofu
2 tablespoons low-sodium soy or tamari sauce
¼ teaspoon cayenne pepper, or to taste

1. In a wok over medium-high heat, sauté bell peppers in the safflower oil until shiny (about 5 minutes).
2. In a large bowl combine arrowroot, vinegar, pineapple juice, lemon juice, honey, salt substitute, and ginger.
3. Pour over peppers and cook, stirring, until mixture thickens slightly.
4. Cut tofu into thin slices.
5. Add to wok, cover, and steam 3 minutes.
6. Add soy sauce and cayenne.
7. Toss well and serve.

Note: Crunchy, brightly colored bell peppers complement the white cubes of protein-rich tofu in this entree. The sweet-and-sour sauce is slightly spicy. The vegetables and tofu can be marinated ahead of time in sesame oil for added flavor. Cook the dish the night before and reheat for lunch the next day-it gets better as it sits and the flavors blend. You can add, omit/substitute any ingredients you prefer.

Sweet-n-Sour Stir-Fry

Serves 2

¼ cup chopped scallions
2 cloves garlic, minced
canola oil (sesame oil would work well too)
1 cup Snow pea pods, de-stringed
1 small yellow zucchini squash, sliced
1½ cup Broccoli (florets and stems, cut into Small pieces)
12 oz. straw mushrooms
½ cup bean sprouts
½ cup water chestnuts
½ cup bamboo shoots
¼ cup chopped red bell pepper
1 small can pineapple chunks unsweetened, save juice
1 small can mandarin orange slices
1 ripe mango, peeled, seeded, and sliced

Sauce:

1½ cup Tamari
pineapple juice (leftover from the can)
3 tbsp. cornstarch (or enough to make desired thickness)
2 tbsp. water
2 tsp. grated fresh ginger

1. First to go in the wok was the oil, scallions, and garlic.
2. Use enough oil so that it'll coat all the veggies but not make them slimy (I'd say about ½ - ⅔ cup).
3. Heat these ingredients until the garlic starts to turn brown. Then add the pea pods, squash, and broccoli.
4. Cook about 3-5 min. Then add the bean sprouts, water chestnuts, bamboo, and peppers.
5. Cook for a few more minutes, until veggies are slightly tender but still sort of crisp.
6. Then add the pineapple, oranges, and mango.
7. Cook about a minute, then add the sauce.
8. When the sauce starts bubbling, the stir-fry is done.
9. Serve over rice. Yum!

Simple Spinach and Garlic Stir-Fry

1 tablespoon vegetable oil
8 cloves garlic, minced
3 bunches spinach, washed and cut in
2 inch piece
½ cup vegetable dry sherry
1 teaspoon sugar, (or 2 teaspoons brown rice syrup)
1 tablespoon sesame oil
1 tablespoon ginger, minced
3 tablespoons green onion, minced
14 ounces firm tofu, cubed
1 tablespoon hot chili paste
1 cup vegetable stock
1 tablespoon cornstarch mixed well with 2 tablespoons cold water
6 cups rice, cooked Cilantro to garnish.

1. In a small bowl, mash black beans with garlic, soy, wine, and sugar.
2. In a wok or large skillet, heat oil on high and add black bean paste, ginger, and green onion.

1. Add tofu and turn gently.
2. Add chili paste and stock.
3. Cover and cook for 3 to 4 minutes.
4. Stir in cornstarch mixture and cook until sauce thickens. Serve over rice, and garnish with cilantro.

Kung Pao Tofu

Serves 4

1 pound extra-firm tofu, cubed into small bite-sized pieces
⅓ cup unsalted, skinned peanuts
2-10 dried red chilies (I use 10)
4 green onions, trimmed and sliced into 1-inch pieces, (white & green parts)
oil for frying - canola, vegetable or peanut oil preferred.

Sauce:

4 tablespoons water
1 tablespoon corn starch
4 tablespoons soy sauce
3 tablespoons rice wine, mirin or dry sherry (I use sherry)
1 teaspoon sugar

1. Put a medium pot of salted water to boil.
2. Rinse the block of tofu and cube it into bite-sized pieces and place the tofu into the rapidly boiling salted water.
3. Let the tofu remain in the water until it returns to a boil and the tofu cubes rise to the top.
4. Drain and put on a plate in a single layer to cool a bit.
5. Make the sauce.
6. In a bowl, mix the cornstarch into the water. Add the soy sauce, sherry and sugar. Stir to blend.

To cook the dish:

7. Heat the skillet and pour enough oil to coat bottom of skillet.
8. Keep the flame pretty high throughout the approx. 5-7 minutes it takes to complete the dish.
9. Fry chilies until they begin to turn brown.
10. Remove with slotted spoon to plate.
11. In same oil, fry peanuts until they begin to turn brown and remove with slotted spoon to plate.
12. In same oil, fry tofu cubes.
13. Let the tofu cook until brown and crispy-looking, turning to brown all sides, about 3-5 minutes. Pour sauce over all.
14. Sauce with thicken very quickly – 30 seconds. (This is not a runny-sauce dish!)
15. Add green onions, cook together less than a minute.
16. Add chilies and peanuts back to re-warm for a few seconds and serve! Serve with a nice Asian rice.

Warning: Do not eat the chilies! Just push them aside!

Sweet & Sour Tofu II

1 lb. tofu
¼ cup lemon juice
¼ cup tamari sauce
6 tablespoons water
¼ cup tomato paste
2 tablespoons honey
1 tsp. ginger
4 cloves of garlic
8 scallions, minced
1 green & 1 red bell pepper, sliced in strips
1 lb. mushrooms
1 cup toasted cashews

1. Cut tofu into small cubes; set aside.
2. Combine lemon juice, tamari, water, tomato paste, honey, ginger, and garlic; mix until well blended.
3. Add tofu to this marinade, stir gently, and let marinate for several hours (or overnight).
4. Stir-fry scallions, bell peppers, and mushrooms in 2 tsp. of oil.
5. After several minutes, add tofu with all the marinade.
6. Lower heat, continue to stir-fry until everything is hot and bubbly.
7. Remove from heat and stir in cashews.
8. Serve over rice.

Broccoli and Tofu in Spicy Almond Sauce

Sauce:
½ cup hot water
½ cup almond butter (or peanut butter)
¼ cup cider vinegar
2 tablespoons tamari sauce
2 tablespoons blackstrap molasses
2 tsp. - ¼ cup cayenne (depending on your sensitivity to heat!)

Sauté:
1 lb. broccoli
2 tsp. ginger
4 cloves garlic
1 lb. tofu, cubed
2 cup onion, thinly sliced
1 cup chopped cashews
2-3 tablespoons tamari sauce
2 minced scallions

1. **Sauce:** In small saucepan, whisk together almond butter and hot water until you have a uniform mixture.
2. Whisk in remaining sauce ingredients and set aside.
3. **Sauté:** Stir-fry half the ginger and half the garlic in 1 tablespoon oil.
4. Add tofu chunks, stir-fry for 5-8 minutes.
5. Mix with sauce. Wipe wok clean, sauté remaining ginger & garlic in 2 tablespoons oil.
6. Add onions and fresh pepper, sauté for about 5 min.
7. Add chopped broccoli, cashews and tamari; stir-fry until broccoli is bright green.
8. Toss sauté with sauce, mixing in the minced scallions as you toss. Serve over rice.

Vegan Stir-Fry "Meat"

1 cup vegetarian meat chunks (This can be purchased from most Asian markets. You can also use TVP chunks).

Mixture 1:
4 tbsp. flour
1 tbsp. cornstarch
1 tbsp. Sugar
¼ tsp. baking powder or soda
½ tsp. salt
½ tsp. pepper
egg replacer to make 1 egg
oil for deep frying
1 tbsp. sesame oil

Mixture 2:
3 tbsp. ketchup
¼ tsp. salt
¼ tsp. sugar
1 tbsp. water

Mixture 3:
Total of ¼ pound sliced carrot, green bell pepper, and pineapple.

1. Combine "meat chunks" with mixture.
2. Heat oil for deep-frying.
3. Fry the "meat" over high heat until brown.
4. Remove.
5. Heat 1 tbsp. sesame oil.
6. Add mixtures 2 and 3. Bring to a boil.
7. Add the vegetarian meat.
8. Stir to mix well.

Stir-Fried Noodles with Mushrooms (Mi Xao Voi Nam Rom)

4 tablespoons vegetable oil
4 cloves garlic, crushed and chopped
3 shallots, finely chopped
½ inch fresh root ginger, crushed and chopped
3 red chilies, finely sliced
6 dried shiitake mushrooms, soaked and sliced
4 dried black fungus, soaked and sliced
6½ oz canned straw mushrooms, drained
1 lb. egg noodles, cooked and set aside
2 tablespoons chopped coriander (cilantro) leaves

1. Heat the oil in a saucepan.
2. Stir fry the garlic, shallots, ginger and chilies for 40 seconds.
3. Add the shiitake mushrooms, black fungus and straw mushrooms.
4. Stir fry for 2 minutes.
5. Run hot water over the noodles to separate them.
6. Add the noodles to the saucepan and stir fry quickly to warm them through.
7. Toss, add the coriander leaves and serve.
8. You can add, omit/substitute any ingredients you prefer.

Dessert

Rujak Medan (Spiced Fruit Salad)

Serves 6
1 small cucumber, sliced thin
1 cup thinly sliced jicama
1 cup cubed firm ripe papaya
1 star apple (carambola), sliced
1 to 2 cups cubed fresh or canned ripe pineapple
1 firm green pear, cubed
1 firm tart apple, cubed

For the Sauce:
3 tablespoons dry roasted peanuts
1 or 2 hot red chilies, sliced and seeded
½ cup brown sugar
1 tablespoon tamarind paste, dissolved in ½ cup water and strained 1 small green banana, sliced (optional)

1. Arrange the cucumber and any 3 or more of the fruits in separate heaps on a serving platter.
2. In a food processor chop fine the peanuts, then blend in the chilies, brown sugar, tamarind, liquid, and banana (if used) to form a paste.
3. It is traditional to serve the sauce and fruit separately.

Each diner may then select the fruit and dip it into the thick sauce. The modern method is to toss the fruit and sauce together and serve the salad at room temperature.

Halua Kenari

Serves 20
1 cup palm sugar or brown sugar
2 tablespoon water
½ cup blanched almonds, toasted lightly

1. In a skillet, melt the palm sugar in the water over low heat.
2. Add the almonds all at once and mix together quickly.
3. Remove the skillet from the heat, drop heaping teaspoonfuls of the "fudge" onto an ungreased tray, and let the sweets cool.
4. Store in a jar with a tight cover.
5. Note: This recipe uses blanched almonds, halved and lightly toasted for about 3 minutes, instead of Java almond (kenari).

Es Cendol (Cold Dessert)

Serves 6

1 pack (12 oz.) of frozen "Banh Lot" (available at oriental store)
1 can of coconut milk, preferably one made for dessert
¼ lb. of Coconut sugar or "Gula Jawa" (brownish colored)
Ice cubes
Cold Water

1. Thaw the 'Banh Lot' in cold water, rinse once or twice afterwards
2. Boil the coconut milk with coconut sugar until they are completely mixed together
3. In an individual serving glass (or dessert bowl), put in:
   - 3 to 4 tbsp. of Banh Lot
   - 4-5 tbsp. of the mixing of coconut milk and coconut sugar.
4. Add cold water (1 tbs) and ice cubes (can be crushed, if wanted)
5. Serve immediately, more of the ingredients can be added to taste.

Kue Mangkok (Cup Cakes)

1½ cup rice flour
10 tbsp. all purpose flour
¾ cup fermented cassava / tapioca (tape singkong)
1 cup sugar
1 cup warm water
2 tsp. baking soda
1¼ club soda
1 tsp. vanilla
food coloring (your choice of 3 or 4 colors)
salt to taste

1. Add enough water to the rice flour so that its weight increases to 1 pound.
2. Add the all purpose flour to the rice flour mixture and stir well. Add the fermented tapioca and sugar.
3. Mix well.
4. Add the warm water and work the dough for about 10 minutes.
5. Add the baking soda, the club soda and vanilla.
6. Mix until everything is evenly distributed.
7. Finally, add the food coloring and blend until smooth.
8. Warm the cup molds for about 5 minutes and fill it to about 4/5th full.
9. Put in a steamer with the water already at a rolling boil. Steam for about 20 minutes.

Green Tea and Vanilla Cake, Vegan

Equipment:
8 or 9 inch springform pan
2 mixing bowls
baking spatula
cup and spoon measures
sieve for sifting dry ingredients

If you can't find matcha, you can boil the soymilk and use 4-5 high quality (i.e., not too bitter) green tea teabags or a couple of spoonfuls of loose green tea. The color won't be as good, but the flavor should be similar.

Dry Ingredients:

1 cup whole wheat pastry flour	2 tsp. baking powder
1 cup all purpose flour	½ tsp. baking soda

Wet ingredients:
¾ cup agave (or ½ cup plus 2 tbsp. sugar and 2 tbsp. soy milk or water)
4 tbsp. canola oil
¼ cup vanilla soy yogurt
¾ cup unsweetened soy milk
2 tbsp. matcha (green tea powder), sifted before adding to other ingredients.
½ cup dried cherries or cooked adzuki beans

Topping:

⅓ cup brown sugar	1 tsp. vanilla
	2 tsp. sifted matcha

Alternatively, you can use a glaze instead of the topping.

Glaze ingredients:
1 tbsp. melted Earth Balance shortening (regular Earth Balance might work, just eliminate the salt from the recipe)
1½ cups confectioner's sugar
⅛ tsp. salt
1 tbsp. sifted matcha
2 tbsp. soymilk
1 tsp. vanilla

1. Mix all ingredients together; you may need a little more soymilk to get it to a slurry-like consistency for drizzling. Drizzle or spread over mostly-cooled cake.
2. Preheat oven to 350 F. Grease pan. Sift dry ingredients together.
3. Stir wet ingredients together, making sure to sift matcha before adding. Add wet to dry, stir until just combined. Add cherries or adzuki beans and combine.
4. Pour into pan and use spatula to even out top. Mix topping ingredients and spread on cake (or if using glaze, don't use topping.) Bake for 35 minutes (check it after 30) or until knife in center comes out clean.

Taste of Thailand
Appetizers

Nori Bundles with Spicy Peanut Dip

Serves 2-3
pinch sea salt
1 medium carrot, cut into long strips (6mm thick)
8 string beans, cut lengthwise
1 sheet nori

For the dip:
2 tbsp. peanut butter
½ garlic clove
1 tsp. prepared mustard
5 tbsp. orange juice
1 tsp. miso
3 tbsp. finely chopped fresh parsley

1. Bring a small pot of water to the boil, add the pinch of sea salt and boil the carrot sticks for 2-3 minutes.
2. Remove, rinse under cold water and drain.
3. Repeat the process if you're using string beans, with the same water.
4. Toast the sheet of nori by holding it horizontally 1 inch above a gas flame, rotating it for 3-5 seconds, until its color changes to bright green.
5. Be careful not to scorch.
6. Cut the sheet with scissors into 4 equal-width strips.
7. Combine a quarter of each of the vegetable sticks into a bundle (making sure they are well drained and dry), then wrap one nori strip tightly around this bundle.
8. If necessary, use a drop of water to stick down the end of the nori.
9. Repeat the process with the rest of the Vegetables and nori strips.
10. Arrange the bundles attractively on a serving dish.
11. Prepare the dip by blending all the ingredients together to give a thick consistency.
12. Serve on the side.

Sweet Potatoes in Coconut Milk, aka "Shoop Shoop"

Purple Okanawian Sweet Potatoes (or other firm type sweet potatoes. (White sweet potatoes are great, too.)
Thai brand Coconut Milk. (Thai Brand specify because it is
   the only canned coconut milk without preservatives.)
Bragg's Liquid Aminos or soy sauce or salt to taste.

1. Use any amount of sweet potatoes you want.
2. Cut in large pieces and steam. Let cool.
3. Peel (can also peel before steaming but this is much easier and you lose less food when you slip the peels off after steaming).
4. Place sweet potatoes in a cooking pot with coconut milk to cover. Mush sweet potatoes with fork.
5. Does not have to be smooth. Some chunks are fine.
6. Cook on medium-low heat until bubbly.
7. Add salt or Bragg's to taste.
8. This is a pudding like treat yet makes a hearty breakfast or dinner dish.

Thai/Chinese Spring Rolls

1-2 oz. cellophane noodles (bean thread)
1 cup TVP
1 teaspoon soy sauce
¼ teaspoons pepper
2 green onions chopped
1 carrot shredded
1 smallish chunk cabbage, chopped
¼ cup chopped mushrooms
1 teaspoon succanat
2 packages spring roll wrappers

1. Mix tvp with 7 oz. hot water, let sit.
2. Soak noodles in warm water, let sit.
3. Five minutes later, chop noodles, and mix everything together.
4. The wrapper package should explain how to roll them, though you can cut wrappers into fourths first to make very small rolls, about 80 of them.
5. Fill a plate with water and dissolve the succanat (or sugar) in it, dip each piece of wrapper in it, add a small amount of filling, and roll according to package directions.
6. The noodles are a pain, because they stick out all over the place.
7. Then fry over medium heat, half-submerged in oil, until sort of golden brown.

Vegetarian Thai Spring Rolls

12 oz. tofu 5 ea fresh shiitake mushrooms
1/4 lb green beans
1 ea celery stalk
1/2 med. carrot
2 ea green onions
3 tbsp. vegetable oil

1 tbsp. garlic, chopped
1/2 teaspoon pepper
2 tbsp. red curry paste
2 tbsp. soy sauce 30 ea spring roll wrappers
3 cup vegetable oil, for deep frying

1. Cut the tofu, mushrooms, beans, celery & carrot into large julienne slices. Chop the green onions. Set aside.
2. Put the 3 tbsp. vegetable oil into a wok over medium heat. When the oil is hot, stir-fry the garlic until it begins to brown.
3. Add the soy sauce, tofu & all the vegetables except the green onions. Stir-fry for 10 minutes.
4. Turn the heat off & add the green onions.
5. Separate the roll wrappers.
6. Place the wrapper with the narrow side facing you.
7. Place a scant 1/4 cup filling about 1/3 of the way over from the closest edge.
8. Fold the closest edge to you over the filling, fold over the left & right edges & then roll.
9. Seal the end using just a touch of water.
10. Place the finished roll seam side down on a baking sheet until all the rolls have been filled in this way.
11. Heat the oil for deep frying in a wok until hot.
12. Deep-fry the rolls on each side until golden.
13. Drain & serve hot with cucumber pickle.
14. Note: Freezing tempeh can change its texture.

Entree

Rice Noodles with Peanut Sauce

8 ounces uncooked rice stick noodles
1/2 cup creamy peanut butter
2 tablespoons soy sauce
1 teaspoon grated gingerroot
1/2 teaspoon crushed red pepper
1/2 cup water
4 ounces bean sprouts
1 medium red bell pepper, cut into fourths and sliced thinly crosswise
2 green onions, sliced
2 tablespoons chopped fresh cilantro

1. Heat 2 quarts water to boiling in 3-quart saucepan.
2. Break noodles in half and pull apart slightly; drop into boiling water.
3. Cook uncovered 1 minute; drain.
4. Rinse in cold water; drain and set aside.
5. Mix peanut butter, soy sauce, ginger root, and red pepper in same saucepan until smooth.
6. Gradually stir in broth.

7. Add noodles, bean sprouts, bell pepper, and onions; toss. Sprinkle with cilantro.
8. Personally, I prefer this recipe to one I got from a friend that is supposed to be "superb" and "authentic."

Sweet & Sour Tofu

4 servings

1 cup pineapple juice
1/4 cup soy sauce
1/4 cup vinegar
1/4 cup crushed tomato
1 tablespoon arrowroot powder
1 teaspoon ginger
2 pounds firm tofu
2 teaspoons sesame oil, and 3 tablespoons vegetable broth
2 green bell peppers, sliced in 2-inch strips
1 carrot, thinly sliced
1 20 oz. can canned pineapple chunks
2 cups cooked brown rice

1. Drain pineapple, reserving 1 cup of the juice, and set aside. In a bowl, mix the pineapple juice, soy sauce, vinegar, tomatoes, arrowroot, and ginger.
2. Drain the tofu, pat dry, and slice into 1-inch cubes.
3. Heat oil & broth and sauté tofu for 10 minutes.
4. Add peppers and carrots and sauté for 3 more minutes.
5. Add sauce to the sauté mixture and cook, stirring, until sauce thickens but carrots are still somewhat crisp, about 5 minutes.
6. Add pineapple chunks and heat through. Serve over cooked brown rice.

Sweet & Sour Pomegranate Tofu

Sauce:

2 tablespoons canola oil
1 cup chopped onions
3 cloves minced garlic
1 tablespoon minced gingerroot
¼ teaspoon ground turmeric
2 teaspoons ground cumin
½ cup walnuts, ground to a coarse powder
2 teaspoons sugar
2½ teaspoons pomegranates, syrup (can be found in an Iranian food store)
½ teaspoon salt
dash cayenne pepper
½ cup water
¼ cup water

Tofu:

1 16 oz. package firm Chinese-style tofu, cut into 1-inch cubes
½ cup frozen or fresh peas, defrosted
Garnishes
Chopped fresh cilantro

1. Sauté onion in hot oil in large skillet until richly browned, but not burned, 8 to 12 minutes, stirring often.
2. (If necessary sprinkle a little water to keep the onions from burning.) Stir in garlic and gingerroot.
3. Add turmeric, cumin and ¼ cup water.
4. Cover and cook 3 to 5 minutes.
5. Remove from heat.
6. Process onion-garlic mixture, walnuts, and ½ cup water in a food processor until thick and creamy, adding a little extra water if mixture is too thick.
7. Remove to a medium bowl and add sugar, pomegranate syrup, salt and red pepper.
8. Mix well and transfer to the same skillet.
9. Bring mixture to a simmer.
10. Add tofu and peas.
11. Simmer, covered, 5 to 7 minutes.
12. During this time, uncover once and gently turn the tofu pieces.
13. Taste and adjust the salt and cayenne.
14. Serve garnished with cilantro.
15. Best served with plain steamed Basmati rice

Super Sweet and Sour Tempeh

½ cup water
2 teaspoons salt
½ teaspoon ground coriander
1 clove garlic, minced
10 oz. tempeh
¼ cup cornstarch or arrowroot powder
oil for deep frying

1. Mix water, salt, coriander, and garlic in a bowl.
2. Cut tempeh into chunks, 1 x 1 x ½ inch thick, and dip quickly in mix.
3. Drain in a colander or on paper towel.
4. Coat tempeh pieces with cornstarch.
5. Heat oil in a wok, skillet, or deep fryer and deep-fry tempeh until golden brown, 3 to 4 minutes.
6. Drain briefly on a paper towel.
7. Put on rice.

Tempeh with Curry Peanut Sauce

1 cup uncooked bulgar wheat
The sauce:
1½ tablespoons creamy peanut butter
2 tablespoons fresh-squeezed lemon juice
1½ tablespoons brown rice syrup
1 tablespoon light-colored miso
½ cup hot water
1 teaspoon low-sodium soy sauce
16 frozen vegetarian dumplings (Assi brand Korean chive dumplings)

1. Boil the water and add the Wakame soup mix, the garlic, the sesame seeds, and the soy sauce.
2. Allow the Wakame to rehydrate for about one minute.
3. Add the Soba noodles and the dumplings, and cook for an additional 5 minutes, turning the heat down as needed to prevent over boiling.

Stir-Fried Vegetables (Pad Pak)

1 broccoli head, cut into thin 2" long sections
½ red pepper, cut into thin 2" strips
1 clove garlic, minced
3-4 squirts soy sauce
2-3 shakes fermented soy bean sauce

1. Heat a little oil in a wok (try sesame oil) and toss in garlic, stirring briskly for 30 secs.
2. Quickly add veggies and sauce and a little water and stir fry for about a minute.

Variations:

1. Use any fairly firm vegetable with this style of stir fry, like zucchini, cauliflower, asparagus, carrots, or green beans.
2. Quartered mushrooms are also nice.
3. Be sure to slice vegetables thinly and of similar sizes so they all cook at the same time.
4. You can also add softer vegetables like bean sprouts or coarsely chopped greens in the last 20 or so seconds of cooking.

Spicy Long Beans and Tofu

1 or more tbsp. red curry paste
2-3 lime leaves, torn into 3 or 4 pieces
2 cup long green beans, cut into 1" sections
1 cup firm tofu, cubed

1. In a heavy saucepan, heat a little oil and add curry paste and lime leaves.
2. Stir for about a minute to release flavors, then add beans.
3. Add ¼ cup water and turn heat to medium.
4. Cook, covered, stirring occasionally, for about 5 mins.
5. Watch that mixture doesn't dry out; add water as needed.
6. Mix in tofu cubes and cook about 2 more minutes.

Thai Basil Eggplant

1 long Asian eggplant, cut into thin 2" x 1" rectangles
½ red pepper, cut into thin 2" strips
1 clove garlic, minced
3-4 squirts soy sauce
25 fresh basil leaves

1. Heat a little oil in a wok.
2. Add garlic; stir fry for 30 secs, then add eggplant, 2 squirts soy sauce, and a little water; stir fry for 2 mins.
3. Add red pepper, rest of soy sauce, and a little water and cook for 1 min.
4. Add basil leaves and cook, adding water if necessary, for another minute.

Variations:

In Thailand this is made with 5 or 6 large fresh chilies thrown in with the garlic, so it's spicy. Be warned: it gives off a pungent, choking smoke!

Thai-Style Spirals

Serves 6

2 tablespoons sesame oil
1 red bell pepper, seeded & diced
2 teaspoons garlic, minced
½ cup scallions, thinly sliced
1 teaspoon minced fresh ginger
1 cucumber, peeled, seeded & diced
½ teaspoon Thai chili paste
2 tablespoons minced fresh basil
2 tablespoons minced fresh cilantro
1 tablespoon minced fresh mint
½ cup dry roasted peanuts, finely chopped
salt & pepper to taste
16 ounces spiral pasta, cooked
¼ cup freshly squeezed lime juice
1 tablespoon lime zest
1 tablespoon toasted sesame oil
tamari or soy sauce to taste

1. In a large sauté pan or wok, heat the sesame oil.
2. Add the pepper, garlic, and scallions, and cook over high heat for 2 minutes, stirring frequently.
3. Add the ginger, cucumber, and chili paste and cook for 2 additional minutes.
4. Remove from heat, and stir in basil, cilantro, mint, and peanuts.
5. Season to taste with salt and pepper.
6. Toss in the cooked pasta, lime juice, lime zest, and toasted sesame oil.
7. Add tamari or soy sauce to taste.
8. Serve warm or at room temperature.

Thai-Style Stir-Fry

Serves 4

3 tablespoons peanut or vegetable oil
1 large or 2 medium leeks, rinsed well and
   cut into ½-inch dice
1 small red or green bell pepper, seeded, cut into strips
3 cloves garlic, minced
¼ pound mushrooms, thinly sliced
3 teaspoons red chili paste or 4-6 fresh hot chilies, minced
3 tablespoons hot water
1½ tablespoons yellow bean paste
4 tablespoons soy sauce
1½ tablespoons rice wine vinegar
1½ teaspoons sugar
salt
3 tablespoons coarsely chopped cilantro
cilantro sprigs for garnish
rice or noodles

1. Heat the oil in a large skillet or wok over medium heat and sauté leeks for a minute.
2. Add the eggplant and cook for 3 minutes, stirring well.
3. Add the bell pepper and garlic and stir for a few minutes more.
4. Add the mushrooms, stir, and sauté for about 2 minutes. Cover the pan, reduce the heat to medium low, and let cook for a few minutes.
5. Meanwhile, combine the red chili paste or chilies with the hot water and stir with a fork until the paste is dissolved.
6. Stir in the bean paste, 3 tablespoons soy sauce, vinegar, and sugar.
7. Add this sauce to the pan and toss well to distribute evenly.
8. Cover for a minute or two, then add the cilantro, stir, and cover for 1 minute more.
9. Taste and add salt, soy sauce, or vinegar to taste if necessary. Serve over rice or noodles.

Vegan Thai Curry

Serves 3

3 small onions
4 pieces of garlic
1 dl herb broth
4 dl coconut milk
2 teaspoons red curry paste
3 teaspoons coconut paste (santen)
1 lb. tofu
1 lb. mixed vegetables (mushrooms, mangetouts,
   zucchini or whatever you desire).

1. Heat up a little vegetable oil, and throw in the roughly chopped onion.
2. Stir 'till it gets a little brownish, then add the finely chopped or mashed garlic.
3. Stir a little, then add vegetables.
4. Stir-fry until the vegetables are slightly cooked.
5. Add tofu in small cubes and stir-fry until they're a little brown.
6. heat the coconut milk and mix with the broth and the curry paste.
7. Stir and wait until everything is thoroughly mixed.
8. Wait until the coconut milk mixture boils and add to the vegetables and onions.
9. Add coconut paste to thicken the curry.
10. Leave on fire for a while and mix regularly.
11. Add fresh coriander leaves and serve with rice.

Spicy Noodles w/ Ginger and Fresh Vegetables

Serves 4

2 carrots, peeled
1 large zucchini
3 green onions
1 tablespoon vegetable oil
4 tablespoons matchstick-size strips fresh ginger
3 teaspoons chopped garlic
1 teaspoon oriental sesame oil
1¼ cups water
1 cup canned unsweetened coconut milk, (light is available)
1 tablespoon reduced-sodium soy sauce
1½ teaspoons Thai red curry paste
9 ounces somen noodles or rice noodles
½ cup finely chopped toasted peanuts
½ cup finely chopped fresh mint leaves

1. Cut carrots, zucchini and green onions into matchstick-size strips.
2. Heat vegetable oil in large skillet over high heat.
3. Add 2 tablespoons ginger and 1½ teaspoons garlic; sauté until fragrant, 30 seconds.
4. Add carrots, zucchini, half of green onions and sesame oil; sauté 2 minutes.
5. Add remaining ginger and garlic; sauté until vegetables are crisp-tender, about 1 minute longer.
6. Using slotted spoon, transfer vegetables to bowl.
7. Reduce heat to medium.
8. Add 1¼ cups water, coconut milk, soy sauce and curry paste to same skillet. Stir until smooth. Simmer until sauce is reduced to 1¼ cups, about 6 minutes.
9. Add sautéed vegetables and remaining onions.
10. Meanwhile, cook somen in large pot of boiling salted water until just tender, about 2 minutes.
11. Drain. Transfer to large bowl.
12. Add vegetable mixture. Toss to coat.
13. Sprinkle nuts and mint over.

Curry Pastes

Thai Green Curry Paste

2 fresh green chilies	1 stalk lemon grass
1 small onion	1 clove garlic
1 tsp. ground coriander	1 tsp. soy sauce
1 lime, juice and rind	1 tsp. ground cumin
¼ cup fresh coriander, stalks & leaves	1 tbsp. grated fresh ginger
	2 tbsp. oil (vegetable)

1. Place all ingredients in a food processor and grind into a paste.
2. Blend for a few minutes until well processed.
3. Use in green Thai curries.

Note: Red curry paste is the same except use 2-3 red chilies instead; add 1 tablespoon paprika. Red is hotter than the green curry.

Thai Green Curry II

1-2 tbsp. green curry paste
1-1½ cups coconut milk
1 green capsicum cut into strips
2 oz. green peas, fresh or frozen
7 oz. bamboo shoots
1 medium carrot, cut diagonally
3-4 small green squash, sliced
2 tbsp. soy sauce
2 oz. bean shoots

1. Marinate tofu in soy sauce for 20 minutes, drain.
2. Heat 1 tbsp. of oil in a medium saucepan, fry curry paste for 1 minute.
3. Add ¼ cup of coconut milk, tofu and all the vegetables except the peas & bean shoots.
4. Simmer for 5 mins.
5. Add remaining coconut milk, bring to boil, reduce heat and simmer until vegetables are nearly tender.
6. Add peas and bean shoots.
7. Cook for 5 to 10 mins. Serve with rice and chutney.
8. Garnish with chopped shallots.

Thai Red Curry Paste

Makes ½ cup (8 tbsp)

2 or more fresh red chilies, deseeded
5 garlic cloves 2 stalks fresh lemongrass
bottom stems from a large bunch of fresh coriander (cilantro) roots
1x1-inch cube fresh ginger or galangal
1 large shallot or equivalent onion
1 lime, peeled (or 1 tbsp. chopped Kaffir lime peel)
1 tsp. salt
2 tsp. coriander seeds
1 tsp. white or black peppercorns

1. Chop the chilies, garlic, lemongrass, coriander stems, ginger and shallot or onion.
2. Prepare the lime peel by removing as much of the white pith as possible (lay it outside down and slice the pith off with a sharp knife held horizontally) and then chopping. Place all ingredients in the blender and whizz to a fairly smooth paste.
3. The raw ingredients come to about 1 cup, so it's enough to put in most small blenders.
4. Store in a screw-topped jar in the fridge.

Soups

Spicy Sour Soup

3-4 fresh lime leaves, torn into 2 or 3 pieces
2 stalks lemon grass, outer layers removed, cut into 2" sections
5-6 ¼" slices galangal (Thai ginger)
7-8 squirts dark soy sauce
10-12 sliced mushrooms
1 or more fresh chilies
juice of 1 lime
1 tablespoon red chili paste in oil

1. garnish: chopped coriander and green onions
2. Bring 2-3 cup water to boil in heavy pot and add lime leaves, galangal, and soy sauce.
3. Pound lemon grass sections several times with pestle or heavy knife and add.
4. Simmer 5-10 mins to bring out flavor of seasonings.
5. Bring to boil again and add mushrooms and cook 2-3 mins over medium heat.
6. Just before serving, pound chilies a few times with pestle and add.
7. In bottom of serving bowl, combine lime juice and chili paste in oil.
8. Add a little liquid from the soup and stir.
9. Add soup. Sprinkle with garnish.

Thai-Style Pumpkin Soup

Serves 6

2 cans mock chicken broth, (16 ounces)
1 can pumpkin, (15-ounce)
1 can mango nectar, (12-ounce)
¼ cup reduced-fat chunky peanut butter
2 tablespoons rice vinegar
1½ tablespoons minced green onions
1 teaspoon grated peeled fresh ginger
½ teaspoon grated orange rind
¼ teaspoon crushed red pepper
1 garlic clove, crushed
chopped fresh cilantro, (optional)

1. Combine first 3 ingredients in a large Dutch oven, and bring to a boil.
2. Cover, reduce heat, and simmer 10 minutes.
3. Combine 1 cup pumpkin mixture and peanut butter in a blender or food processor; process until smooth.
4. Return mixture to pan. Stir in vinegar and next 5 ingredients (vinegar through garlic).
5. Cook 3 minutes or until thoroughly heated.
6. Ladle into soup bowls. Sprinkle w/cilantro, if desired.

Salads

Glass Noodle Salad

1 bundle glass noodles
7 oz Thai marinated tofu, sliced (optional)
5-6 squirts soy sauce
juice of 2 limes
1 red pepper, sliced thinly
2 tomatoes, cut into small wedges
1 small purple onion, sliced finely
2 or more chilies, finely chopped
1 stalk lemon grass, outer layers removed and finely minced
5-6 bunches coriander, finely chopped
1 green onion, finely chopped

1. Soak noodles in hot water at least 15 mins, then drain. Cut noodle mass into 4 and put in bowl.
2. Add remaining ingredients and mix.

A Taste of Japan
Appetizers, Snacks, Sides

Sushi

1. Cook 2 cups Nishiki or Botan Calrose rice as package directs.
2. Turn cooked rice into large, nonmetal bowl separating kernels.
3. Pour ½ cup Seasoned Rice Vinegar (or ⅓ cup regular rice vinegar mixed with 3 tablespoons sugar and 1½ teaspoons salt) evenly over rice.
4. Gently fold to combine.
5. Let rice cool to room temperature.
6. (I used raw sugar and heated the vinegar, sugar, and salt just till warm to aid in mixing these ingredients.)
7. To roll you can do it two different ways.
8. You can use a bamboo roller (which are fairly cheap) place a sheet of Nori shiny side down on bamboo roller lining up short edge with the bottom of the mat.
9. Moisten hands with water.
10. Place about 1½ cups rice mixture on nori.
11. Press rice to side and bottom to cover about ¾ of the nori leaving edge of nori furthest from you clear.
12. Place filling (I used portabella mushrooms strips, green onions, spinach strips, and pickled ginger) in a line across center of rice.
13. Hold line of ingredients firmly in place with finger-tips.
14. Using thumb, push up and turn mat edge nearest you up and over filling, pressing firmly to enclose filling and lifting mat while rolling to keeping from rolling in sushi roll.
15. Unroll mat and wrap sushi in plastic wrap.
16. The other way is a hand roll which to me was easier.
17. Place half a sheet of Nori shiny side down in the palm of your hand.
18. Spread the sushi rice on half the sheet add your filling.
19. Roll nori, starting at rice covered bottom edge, point the corner edge toward the center, and roll to form a cone.

Nori-Maki-2 / Sushi Rice

3-⅓ cups short grain rice
4 cups water
3 inch piece kombu
5 tablespoons plus 1 teaspoon rice vinegar
5 tablespoons sugar
4 teaspoons salt

1. Put rice in non-stick pot or rice cooker with 4 cups water and kombu.
2. Let boil for 5 minutes.
3. Turn down heat to very low and cook till all water is absorbed (appox. 15 minutes).
4. Then turn off heat and keep covered for another 15 minutes.
5. When rice is almost finished in the above, mix vinegar, sugar, and salt in small saucepan and heat.
6. Stir until all sugar is dissolved.
7. Then quickly cook the mixture by placing in a small metal bowl that sits in a cold water bath.
8. Spread rice out in large baking pan (or similar large container).
9. Using a flat paddle, toss the rice (carefully so as not to break noodles).
10. Fan the rice to cool it quickly and sprinkle on the vinegar mixture as you do this (having two people to do this helps).
11. Rice should end up slightly sticky whole grains with a glossy sheen and very slight sweet-sour taste.

Stir Fried Bell Peppers, Shimeji Mushrooms & Umeboshi

shimeji mushrooms: 1 pack or a large fistful
bell peppers: 2
umeboshi/pickled japanese plums: 2
olive oil: 2 tablespoons
black pepper: to taste
soy sauce, a little
optional spices (chili pepper): to taste

1. Take seed out of umeboshi/pickled Japanese plum and cut to a pulp with a knife.
2. Cut the bell peppers in trips. Make sure you have discarded all the seeds. They are not easily digested.
3. Separate the shimeji mushrooms.
4. Add umeboshi, balck pepper, soy sauce and optional spices. Mix and stir-fry for a few seconds.
5. Serve topped with some fresh green sprouts.

Mount Fuji Trail Mix

Serves 16

4 cups crispy rice or corn cereal squares
3 cups Asian rice crackers
1½ cups dried peas
1 cup chopped walnuts, (optional)
½ cup honey or rice syrup
¼ cup vegetable oil
2 tablespoons margarine
2 tablespoons soy sauce
2 tablespoons brown sugar
½ cup crumbled, dried nori
2 tablespoons black sesame seeds

1. Preheat oven to 250 degrees.
2. In large roasting pan or baking dish, mix cereal, crackers, peas and walnuts.
3. In medium saucepan, combine honey or rice syrup, oil, margarine, soy sauce and sugar.
4. Cook over medium heat, stirring, until margarine melts and mixture is thoroughly heated, about 5 minutes.
5. Pour mixture over dry ingredients in pan; toss to mix.
6. Bake until mixture is crisp, stirring every 15 minutes, about 1 hour.
7. Add nori and sesame seeds during last 15 minutes of baking time.

Entree

Crispy Vegetarian Duck

Serves: 5-6

6 sheets of dried tofu skin (31" x 23")
3 pieces of red fermented beancurd (ang tao joo)
1½ glass water (450ml)
1½ Porcelain spoon fine sugar
1½ Porcelain spoon corn flour
1½ teaspoon sesame oil
¾ teaspoon Five Spice Powder
2 teaspoon pepper
3 Porcelain spoon soy sauce
7 tbsp. sesame seed (slightly fry/roast to golden brown in wok without oil)

Optional:

6 medium Chinese Mushrooms (Soak, sliced and marinate with some ginger juice, soy sauce, sesame oil and pinch of sugar)

Preparation:

1. Take a large bowl, mix all the ingredients thoroughly. Add in the roasted sesame seed last.
2. Place the tofu skin on a large tray or a clean table top length wise.
3. Dampen the right half of the skin (approximately a small ladle full or less depending on your ladle size) and fold into two from left to right.
4. Dampen slightly the folded skin. Fold ⅓ downwards and ⅓ upwards.
5. Dampen slightly again and fold ¼ inwards on both sides.
6. Fold into half and secure with two long bamboo sticks upwards.
7. Heat up a wok with water. When boil, lower fire and place the ready vegetarian duck on a plate and for 10 minutes until bloated up.
8. DO NOT oversteam. You might have to steam many times as the "duck" has to be separated apart when steaming and your wok might not be big enough to fit all.
9. Leave aside to cool down. Make sure they are TOTALLY cool down before frying to ensure the fluffiness.
10. Fry in a wok of hot oil and cut according to your preference.

Bulanglang

1 cup malunggay leaves (if you can't get this, try spinach
-or-
kangkong (swamp cabbage, watercress as a substitute)
1 cup squash, cubed
1 cup upo (gourd), sliced (can substitute with zucchini)
1 cup tokwa (tofu), cubed and fried (don't fry for a lower-fat dish)
½ onion
1 cup water
tomatoes

1. Mix tomatoes, onion, and squash in a deep sauce pan or pot. Add water and boil.
2. After 5 minutes cooking, add tokwa and upo.
3. When the upo is almost tender, add
4. malunggay and cook 2 minutes longer or until malunggay leaves are wilted. Remove from heat.
5. Salt and pepper to taste (or instead of salt, you can add patis, it will give a better flavor).
6. Garnish with fresh tomatoes and cilantro
7. or kinchay (Chinese celery).

Misua

Note: this is an ovo-dish, not entirely vegan.
1 small bundle misua (fine rice vermicelli)
3 eggs
2 cups water
1 tbsp. veg oil
1 clove chopped garlic
1 onion
salt or patis and pepper to taste

1. Sauté garlic in oil until light brown.
2. Add onion and sauté until onion is translucent.
3. Add water, salt or patis and pepper to taste.
4. When the water boils add eggs whole, one at a time.
5. Break misua into 3-inch lengths and add.
6. Remove from heat and serve hot.

Vegetable Hong Kong Style with Fried Noodles

2 onions, each cut into 8 piecesx
1 carrot, cut into thick pieces
8-10 french beans, cut into 1″ pieces
1 cup cabbage, cut into big pieces
4-5 babycorns, cut diagonally into two
2 green or red bell peppers, cut each into 8 pieces
few florets of cauliflower or broccoli
2-3 dry red chilies, tear into pieces
3 crushed garlic flakes or ½ tsp. grated ginger
1 tsp. light soya sauce
1½ tsp. chili sauce
¾ tbsp. vinegar
1 tsp. brown sugar
1½ tbsps corn flour combined in 1 cup water
9-10 cashew nuts or walnuts
Salt and pepper to taste
2 tbsps sesame oil or peanut oil

For fried noodles:
3 cups cooked noodles
½ - ¾ tsp. red chili powder
1 tsp. tomato ketchup
½ tsp. light soy sauce
salt to taste
1 tbsp. oil

1. To parboil vegetables, boil a liter of water with ½ tsp. salt. Add broccoli, carrot, cabbage and beans to the boiling water and cook for 2-3 minutes.
2. Remove from heat, strain and pour cold water over the vegetables and strain again. Keep aside.
3. Heat oil in a large wok and once the oil is hot, add the cashew nuts or walnuts and fry to a golden shade and remove and keep aside.
4. Add garlic or ginger and sauté for a few secs, add red chilies and sauté for few secs. Add the onion and cook on high for a min. Add the parboiled vegetables, baby corn and capsicum and sauté for 5 min.
5. Add soy sauce, vinegar, chili sauce, pepper, sugar and salt and combine well. Add the corn flour along with water and go on stirring continuously till it thickens slightly and coats the vegetables. Remove from heat and keep aside.
6. To prepare fried noodles, heat oil in a wok, add salt, chili powder, soy sauce and tomato sauce and mix. Add boiled noodles and fry till the noodles are browned a bit, approx 2-3 min. Remove from heat.
7. To serve, place the vegetables in the center of the serving plate and surround with fried noodles. Garnish with fried cashew nuts. Serve warm.

Spicy Orange Teriyaki Cutlets

Serves 8

3 boxes silken lite extra-firm tofu
½ cup soy sauce
½ cup brown sugar or honey
2 teaspoons soybean oil
2 cloves garlic, minced
1 teaspoon ginger root, minced
2 tablespoons rice vinegar
¼ cup orange juice
dash dry sherry
dash black pepper, to taste
8 ounces water chestnuts, sliced

1. Slice tofu lengthwise into 3 or 4 slices at least 1 4-inch thick to make "cutlets." Place slices on a baking tray and cover with plastic wrap.
2. Freeze tofu overnight.
3. Additional days in the freezer will result in a meatier texture.
4. Thaw frozen tofu in the refrigerator overnight or place in a bowl covered with hot water until ice crystals melt.
5. Place on paper towel to remove remaining moisture.
6. Combine tamari, brown sugar, oil, garlic, ginger, vinegar, orange juice, sherry and pepper.
7. Pour half the marinade mixture in the bottom of a 9" x 13" glass ovenproof baking dish.
8. Arrange tofu cutlets over marinade.
9. Cover with remainder of marinade.
10. Allow cutlets to marinate 15 minutes or longer.
11. When ready to serve, sauté tofu and water chestnuts in a little of the marinade until brown on both sides or broil 2 to 3 minutes on each side.

Note: Freezing the tofu first gives it a meaty texture.

Teriyaki Seitan and Broccoli

For the Teriyaki Sauce:
¼ cup cooking sherry
¼ cup tamari (or slightly less)
1 clove garlic, pressed
2 tsp. chopped ginger
1 tbsp. vegetable oil
1 tsp. sweetener such as raw sugar

For the vegetable broth:
1 cup hot or boiling water
1 tsp. low sodium vegetable stock powder
for the cornstarch mixture:
¼ cup water
2 tbsp. cornstarch or arrowroot

For the stir fry:
2-3 tbsp. safflower oil
1 tbsp. ginger, minced
8 oz. seitan, traditional flavor
8 oz. mushrooms, sliced
3 stalks broccoli (florettes only*)
1 c snap peas, stems and strings removed
1 tbsp. ginger, slivered
2 cups cooked brown rice
½ cup toasted slivered almonds

Teriyaki sauce:
Mix all ingredients together and set aside.

Vegetable broth:
Mix together and set aside

Cornstarch mixture: Mix together and set aside.

How to make Teriyaki Seitan and Broccoli
1. Heat 2 tablespoons of oil in a wok over medium high heat.
2. Add the minced ginger and cook for a few minutes. Add the seitan and lightly brown.
3. Add the mushrooms and cook for 1 minute.
4. Add 1 tablespoon of oil if the wok is dry.
5. Add the broccoli and cook until it turns bright green, stirring constantly.
6. Stir in the snap peas and the teriyaki sauce, cover and cook for one minute.
7. Add the vegetable broth and the slivered ginger.
8. Cover and cook until the stock boils.
9. Add the cornstarch and cook until thick.
10. Serve over brown rice and garnish with toasted slivered almonds.

Simmered Aubergine (Eggplant) w/ Ginger Sauce (Nasu no Ohitashi)

Serves 2-4 as a side dish

This recipe is slightly adapted from *Good Food from a Japanese Temple*, by Soei Yoneda. The original recipe used 4 x 4-inch aubergines, halved lengthways, but I can usually only find bigger ones. The author recommends using Kikkoman soy sauce for all her recipes; and I agree with her. It's easier to grate the ginger if it's frozen; and this is also the best way to keep it fresh (it doesn't lose its flavor, as frozen garlic can). This dish can be served hot, at room temperature, or chilled. To serve hot, slice and dress the aubergine as soon as it's cooled enough for you to handle. (depending on how many dishes you serve)

1 medium aubergine (eggplant), about 9 oz

Ginger-Soy Sauce:

1 x 1-inch cube fresh ginger, peeled and finely grated
1 tbsp. good-quality Japanese soy sauce (e.g., Kikkoman)

1. Cut the stem end off the aubergine, but don't trim the blunt end.
2. Cut the aubergine in half lengthways, then cut each piece across once so as to make four quarters of roughly the same size; you should cut much nearer the blunt end.
3. Bear in mind that the stem ends seem to lose more size in cooking.
4. In a pan wide enough to take all four pieces in a single layer, bring 2½ cups water to the boil.
5. Add the aubergines, skin side down, and reduce the heat.
6. Simmer for about 5 minutes, turning after about 3 minutes, until soft but not mushy (test by pricking with a fork).
7. Drain the aubergine pieces and cool on a plate, skin side up (don't throw away the remaining liquid; use it to make stock).
8. More liquid will come out as they cool; when cool enough to handle, press gently with your hand to squeeze out water without crushing the aubergine.
9. Avoid squeezing out too much - the aubergine should still be somewhat moist.
10. When cool, slice each piece lengthwise into ⅛ inch pieces.
11. Arrange slices casually on small dishes or saucers.
12. Mix ginger-soy sauce and spread on top of the aubergine.

Sweetened Soy

1 cup Japanese-style soy sauce
⅔ cup sugar (I use about half that)
½ cup sake or sherry
2½ inches long onion, or half a round onion, roughly chopped
1 knob ginger, thinly sliced
2 cinnamon sticks
1 or 2 stars of star anise
1 tbsp dried orange peel

1. Put all ingredients in pan, bring to boil, and simmer over low heat for approximately one hour.
2. Until liquid has reduced to about ⅔.
3. Strain, cool, and store in fridge for up to one month.
4. Use in same quantities as Oyster Sauce.

Kampyo

3 cups water
2 teaspoons salt
1 package dried gourd strips (kampyo), appox. 1.7 oz
1 ⅔ cups dashi (kombu stock, water OK)
4 tablespoons soy sauce
1 teaspoon sugar

1. Mix water and salt in small pot and bring to boil.
2. Add kampyo and boil for a couple minutes.
3. Then rinse and drain the kampyo.
4. Bring dashi, soy sauce, and sugar to a boil.
5. Add softened kampyo and cook for half an hour till most of the liquid is absorbed.
6. Drain and cool kampyo and use as nori maki filling.

Grilled Eggplant with Peanut Miso Sauce

1 medium eggplant, peeled and cut crosswise into 1-inch thick slices
Vegetable oil
Peanut Miso Sauce

1. Brush eggplant slices with vegetable oil.
2. Place slices in center of cooking grate; grill 10 minutes, turn; grill another 5 minutes.
3. Spread sauce on top side of each eggplant slice.
4. Grill 5 minutes or until sauce begins to speckle.

Shingjagaimo No Goma Fumiae

(New Potatoes in Sesame Sauce)

Serves 4

1½ tablespoons soy sauce
1 tablespoon Japanese rice vinegar
½ teaspoon rice syrup
½ teaspoon karashi Japanese mustard
1 teaspoon Oriental sesame oil
2 medium-size new potatoes
2 small cucumbers

1. Start a ¾ full, 3-quart pot of boiling water on the stove.
2. Mix the soy sauce, rice vinegar, rice syrup, mustard, and sesame oil together in a small bowl.
3. Let this mixture stand.
4. Peel and cut the potatoes into ¼ inch julienne strips, 2½ to 3 inches long.
5. Rinse the julienne pieces, then drop them into the boiling water.
6. Make sure all the potatoes are in the boiling water.
7. When the water reboils, count to 10 slowly, then empty the potatoes into a bowl with cold tap water running into it.
8. Wait until the potatoes are cool, then drain and let them sit in a colander.
9. Peel and seed the cucumbers.
10. Cut the trimmed cucumbers into julienne strips the same size as the potatoes.
11. In a bowl, mix the potato and cucumber strips together, then gently pour the sesame sauce all over the vegetables.
12. Let the dish marinate a few minutes.
13. Serve at room temperature or cold.

Kabu No Ichiyazuke
(Quick Turnip Pickles)

Serves 4

Turnip pickles are served with just about every meal in Japanese vegetarian restaurants and monasteries.

5-6 fresh turnips, no more than 2½ inches in diameter
3 teaspoons sea salt

1. Remove the leaves and stems from the turnips.
2. Wash leaves, stems, and turnips carefully, then cut the turnips into ¼ inch rounds.
3. Place on a flat plate, then sprinkle with 2 teaspoons of salt.
4. In a pot, boil the turnip leaves and stems for 1-2 minutes.
5. Cool under running water. Cut into ¼ inch long pieces.
6. Sprinkle on the remaining salt.
7. Spread the cut, salted leaves over the salted turnips in a screw top pickling jar, or place turnips and leaves under a heavy weight.
8. Leave the vegetable to cure overnight.
9. It's a good idea to rinse the turnip pickles slightly before serving, then toss and drain in a colander.
10. Serve cool. Add soy sauce to taste.

Shiitake-Kombu Dashi (Mushroom and Seaweed Seasoning Broth)

Serves 4

4 x 4 inches of kombu seaweed (available in Oriental groceries and health food stores)
4-5 high-quality, dried shiitake mushrooms
4 cups water

1. Wipe the kombu clean with a damp paper towel.
2. Let the kombu soak in the water for at least 3 hours, then heat the water until it is just about boiling.
3. Turn the flame off, remove the kombu, add the shiitake mushrooms, and let stand for 20 minutes.
4. Remove the shiitakes (use them in a stir-fry dish fairly soon). You now have shiitake-kombu dashi.
5. Store the liquid in the refrigerator in a closed container.

Ginataang Talong

Serves 4
1 onion
1 cup coconut cream
salt and pepper to taste
talong – eggplants

1. Roast eggplants in oven or over gas flame.
2. Peel and chop fine.
3. Peel onions and slice crosswise very fine.
4. Heat oil in pan, add onions and fry until translucent.
5. Add eggplants, stir for a couple of minutes.
6. Season with salt and pepper.
7. Remove from heat, add coconut cream, let sit several minutes to develop the flavors.

For 4 people:
1 small Japanese-type talong (eggplant) per person (4 of them then)
1 egg per person
1 onion
salt, pepper to taste
tomato, cilantro or kinchay to garnish

1. Roast the eggplants, either in the oven or over gas flame (latter is preferable) until the outside skin is charred.
2. Peel off the skin and mash the flesh with a fork.
3. Make sure to keep the whole thing as intact as possible.
4. In a skillet, fry the onion until translucent and remove.
5. To prepare one torta, beat an egg in a bowl, then dip the eggplant.
6. Hold the whole thing by the stem and don't dip that part in the egg.
7. Add salt and pepper as you like, and if you really want to, add finely chopped cilantro or kinchay to the egg mixture.
8. Heat oil in a frying pan, then when the oil is hot, add the mixture to the pan and layer some onions to the top of it.
9. Let set then turn over with a spatula.
10. Remove to a plate and garnish with tomato slices and cilantro/kinchay. Serve with rice.

Dumpling Stew with Soba and Wakame

Serves 2
2 quarts water
1 single-serving package Wakame seaweed soup mix
2 cloves garlic, crushed
2 tablespoons sesame seeds
2 tablespoons soy sauce
8 oz. (one bundle) of Japanese Soba (buckwheat) noodles

BBQ Miso Eggplant

1 lb. round Eggplant, cut ½-inch thick

Marinade:
2 oz. shiro miso (white miso paste)
1 oz. sake (Japanese rice wine)
2 oz. sugar (raw if possible or brown)
½ oz. soy sauce
6 oz. water
½ oz. green onion (scallion), chopped
¼ oz. sesame oil

1. Marinate eggplant slices overnight.
2. Drain and grill on a well oiled grill until grill marks are well defined.
3. Serve with reserved marinade.

Ninjin No Amani (Sweet Cooked Carrots)

Serves 4
This carrot recipe makes use of the shiitake mushrooms from the shiitake-kombu dashi.

½ pound peeled carrots
4-5 shiitake mushrooms, soaked in hot water 30 minutes, then sliced ¼ inch thick, or from the shiitake-kombu prepared in the above recipe
1 cup shiitake-kombu dashi
¼ teaspoon sea salt
1 teaspoon rice syrup or other sweetener
1-2 teaspoons mirin (sweet vinegar available in Oriental groceries)

1. Peel the carrots and cut in rounds about ¼ inch thick.
2. Combine all ingredients except carrots and mushrooms in a saucepan and cook together five minutes on low heat.
3. Add the carrots and sliced mushrooms, and simmer 5-10 minutes or until all the liquid is absorbed in the soft vegetables. Serve at room temperature.

Mushinasu (Steamed Eggplant)

Serves 4

Any leftovers can be left in the sauce for one day.

4 or 5 ¾ pound Oriental eggplants (the long, purplish ones) or 2 one-pound European-type eggplants
1 tablespoon soy sauce
1 teaspoon sesame oil
1 tablespoon chopped onions
1 tablespoon rice vinegar
½ to 1 tablespoon rice syrup

1. Cut away the tops and bottoms of the eggplants.
2. Steam them gently 5-7 minutes, or until soft.
3. Test with a toothpick or bamboo skewer.
4. When eggplants are done, let them cool.
5. When they're cool, cut them into quarters, length-wise.
6. Refrigerate until ready to serve, then spread the cool eggplants around a flat plate to form an 8-pointed star.
7. Combine the sauce ingredients and pour all over the eggplants.
8. Serve with hot rice at room temperature.

Soups & Stews

Okura No Nibitashi (Okra Stew)

Serves 4

Another recipe using shiitake-kombu dashi.

20 okra pods
2 teaspoons salt
1 cup shiitake-kombu dashi (see previous recipe)
1 teaspoon usukuchi (light) soy sauce
½ tablespoon mirin (sweet vinegar)
sesame seeds (for garnish)

1. Wash the okra, then cut the stems off.
2. Rub each pod with salt, taking off the okra fuzz on the skin with your fingers.
3. Wash your hands after this operation.
4. Drop the trimmed and cleaned okra into a large pot of boiling water until they soften slightly, about 3-5 minutes.
5. Combine the dashi, usukuchi, and mirin in a 3-quart pot.
6. Bring to a boil, add the okra and let them boil for 1-2 minutes. Remove from the heat.
7. Let the pot stand until it is cool.
8. Arrange on a serving dish, then sprinkle dry roasted sesame seeds over the stewed okra.

Basic Miso Soup with Potatoes and Leeks

Serves 4 (per variation)

4 cups dashi
3 tbsp. miso paste

Heat 4 cups of dashi in a pot. Add whatever ingredients you want, and then add the miso at the end, just before serving. Since the miso paste is refrigerated and quite thick, it takes a while to dissolve in the dashi. Therefore, you must thin the miso in a large soup ladle full of dashi (while it is still partially immersed in the pot), whisking with chopsticks to a smooth consistency first. If you don't follow this step, it is likely that clumps of miso will remain undissolved when serving. A really handy item is a miso koji; a small sieve with a wooden pestle that is made just for this purpose. It works wonderfully and makes quick work of this task, and is a great time saver if you serve miso soup regularly. Miso should not be boiled, because it is said it loses its flavor.

Tofu and Wakame

Cut ½ block of tofu, either kinu-goshi (soft) or momen-goshi (firm), depending on your preference, into cubes the size of dice. Soak ½ cup wakame in lukewarm water for 10 minutes. Rinse the reconstituted wakame, roughly chop it and add it, along with the tofu, to 4 cups of hot dashi. Add 3 tablespoons of white, red, or a combination of the two. Garnish with chopped green onions or chopped mitsuba.

Carrots and Daikon

Cut 1 carrot and a 3 inch piece of daikon into 2 inch long matchsticks. Add to 4 cups of dashi and simmer for 3 minutes, or until tender but not soft. Add 3 tablespoons of white miso.

Potatoes and Onion

Serves 4

Peel and cut 1 potato into half round slices ½ thick. Cut 1 small onion in half, then slice lengthwise into slivers ¼ thick. Add to dashi and simmer for 5 minutes, or until tender. Add 3 tablespoons of white miso.

Nasu (eggplant)

If using a western eggplant, either a half or quarter of an eggplant will be plenty. Peel the skin and cut into quarters, and then into ¼ slices. If using Japanese eggplant, cut one large or 2 small into diagonal slices ¼ thick. Add to dash and simmer for 5 minutes, or until tender. Add 2 table-spoons of red miso and 1 tablespoon of white miso.

Okra

Serves 4

If you like gumbo, you'll like this. The slimy texture of cooked okra makes an interesting (if slightly unorthodox) miso soup. Chop ½ lb of fresh okra into ½ inch slices, or use one cup of frozen okra. Boil for 4 minutes, or until tender. Add 3 tablespoons white or country miso and half a block of cubed kinugoshi (soft) tofu (optional). Garnish with chopped green onion.

Shimeji

Serves 4

Shimeji mushrooms usually come attached to a round and dense "root" base that is pithy, and should be cut and discarded. The mushrooms then separate easily by hand. Saute in 1 tablespoon of butter (not in the traditional recipe) and a touch of salt and pepper. Add 4 cups of vegetarian stock, water or dashi (depending on your preference) and 2 tablespoons of red miso and one tablespoon of white miso. This is an intensely flavored soup and the butter adds a nice touch.

Enoki

Remove the base of the enoki mushrooms and chop into 2 inch lengths. Add to 4 cups of hot dashi. The mushrooms do not need to be simmered, so immediately add 3 tablespoons white miso. Garnish with chopped mitsuba, or if using green onion, add just a few slivers so as not to overwhelm the delicate flavor of the enoki mushrooms.

Traditional Japanese Miso Soup

Serves 4-8

1 Qt. water
8 tbsp. miso (more or less to taste)
2 tsp. dried cut wakame
½ cup chopped daikon (optional; I use mouli, a large white radish)
½ cup carrots (optional)
½ small onion (optional)
tofu, chopped into small cubes (optional)
chopped green onions

Miso Soup II

2 cups water or vegetable broth
2 teaspoons of your favorite bouillon powder (or cubes)
½ tsp. kelp powder (or other sea vegetable powder)
½ tsp. sugar or Sucanat (optional)

1. 2 teaspoons Miso
2. Heat water in saucepan or microwave.
3. Stir in bouillon, kelp, and sugar.
4. Dissolve Miso in a small amount of the hot liquid, then mix this into the rest of the liquid.
5. Serve immediately.

Served with a bowl of rice, this is a very satisfying light meal.

Optional: Add some Tofu, cut into small dice.
Optional: Garnish with scallion shreds.
For Cream of Miso Soup: Add some Rice Milk.

Salads

Japanese Salad

¾ cup red miso
3 tablespoons sugar
3 tablespoons mirin (Japanese rice wine)
2 tablespoons hot water
2 teaspoons light soy sauce
¼ teaspoon sesame oil
1 tablespoon toasted sesame seeds
½ head iceberg lettuce, torn
1 carrot, thinly sliced

1. In a small bowl, combine miso and sugar.
2. Add mirin, water, soy sauce, sesame oil, and sesame seeds. Stir until well blended.
3. Serve over lettuce and carrot slices.
4. Toss to combine.

Zesty Daikon Salad

2 cups peeled and thinly sliced daikon (white radish)
½ cup thinly sliced mild onion
1 cup peeled and chopped apple juice of one lime
Mix all ingredients together and enjoy.

This is incredibly clean and fresh tasting, and is a great accompaniment to more earthy foods. For a sweeter taste, replace the lime juice with orange juice. Prep. time: 10 minutes

A Taste of the Philippines and Pacific Islands
Entrees

Ukoy (Vegetable Fritters)

2 cup flour
1 cup bean sprouts (togue, the fresher the better)
½ cup coriander, chopped chili (the little Thai variety, red or green) to taste
enough water to make a batter (experiment here)
garlic salt, salt and pepper to taste

Alternatively, you can add 1-2 cloves of very finely minced garlic instead of the garlic salt.

1. Combine all ingredients together until you get a nice pancake- like batter.
2. Heat oil in a pan and fry on both sides.
3. Serve with dipping sauce.
4. Possible additions: I've also made this particular variety of ukoy with potatoes, boiled and diced.
5. It dilutes the flavor of the chili but it was still a big hit.
6. If you want the nice reddish-orangish colour, add some atchuete extract (do it yourself from the seeds or buy the readymade stuff from your favourite Oriental market) or red food coloring.

Ukoy II

1 cup all-purpose unbleached white flour
¼ tsp. baking soda
1½ tsp. salt
½ tsp. freshly ground pepper
1 large egg
1 cup cold water
vegetable oil for shallow frying
2 cup peeled and coarsely grated butternut squash
1 cup bean sprouts, washed, drained thoroughly, patted as dry as possible
3 scallions, cut into 2-in pieces and then cut lengthwise into fine strips

1. Make the batter by sifting the flour, baking soda,
2. salt, and pepper together in a large bowl.
3. Beat the egg in a separate smaller bowl and slowly add the water to it.
4. Then slowly add the egg-water mixture to the flour
5. mixture, beating as you do so.
6. Heat ½ inch oil in a skillet over a medium flame.
7. The ideal temperature for frying the fritters is between 350°F and 375°F.
8. Put the grated squash, bean sprouts and scallions into the batter and mix.
9. Remove heaping tablespoons of the fritter mixture and drop gently into the skillet.
10. Fry for about 3 minutes on each side or until fritters are a nice medium-brown colour.
11. If the fritters begin to brown too fast, turn the heat down.
12. Remove fritters with a slotted spoon and drain on paper towels or on a wire mesh rack.
13. Do all fritters this way, putting only as many in the oil as the skillet will hold easily.
14. Serve hot, with small, individual bowls of your choice of dipping sauces.

Note: All Filipino sweets are considered vegetarian.

Adobong Gulay

Gulay = vegetables = talong (eggplant), potato
Adobo is a style of preparation, which in Philippine cuisine is stewing in vinegar and soy sauce.

1 onion
3 cloves of garlic (adjust to your taste)
peppercorn, to taste
2 bay leaves
vegetable oil
potatoes or talong (around 1 lb or so)
soy sauce (¼ c)
sukang Paombong or your favourite
vinegar (¼ c)
pepper and sugar to taste (use a generous dash of pepper and a tiny amount of sugar, to bring out the taste of the rest)

1. Heat oil then add peppercorn and bay leaves.
2. When the bay leaves start to turn brown, add the garlic.
3. Sauté until brown.
4. Then add the onion and fry until translucent.
5. Add the pepper and the sugar, stir briefly to mix, then add the soy sauce and vinegar.
6. Lower heat to medium then add the potatoes or eggplant.
7. Stir briefly then simmer, covered, around 25-30 minutes for the potatoes or around 35-40 minutes for the eggplant.
8. They should be soft but not mushy.
9. Add water if liquid level drops too low.
10. Serve over rice.

Banana Peanut Salad

16 ripe medium-sized bananas
16 tbsp chopped peanuts
mayonnaise
lettuce

1. Slice crosswise and thin 2 bananas for each individual serving and mix with two tablespoons chopped peanuts.
2. Add mayonnaise, mix lightly with a fork and arrange on lettuce leaves before serving.

A Simple Filipino Dipping Sauce

1 tbsp. soy sauce
1 tbsp. vinegar (In the Asian supermarket, sukang paombong is best, but the type you get in Western supermarkets is okay)
2 cloves of garlic, mashed.

1. Combine all and allow to sit.
2. Goes very well with ukoy, lumpia.

Broiled Marinated Vegetables with Noodles

2 small red onions
1 eggplant
2 garlic heads
1 yellow bell pepper (seeded)
4 small zucchini
2 endives
4 ounces egg vermicelli
1 teaspoon olive oil

Marinade:
basil leaves, fennel fronts, cilantro-trimmed and chopped roughly
1 tablespoon chopped ginger root
1 teaspoon chopped green chili
1 tablespoon chopped garlic
1 tablespoon lime juice
8 tablespoons olive oil
½ cup roasted peanuts
1 teaspoon brown sugar
1 teaspoon salt

1. Puree the marinade ingredients in a blender until smooth. Cut zucchini, endive and eggplant lengthwise.
2. Cut the onion and garlic crosswise and yellow bell pepper into quarters.
3. Apply the marinade over the vegetables, sprinkle with olive oil and marinate overnight.
4. Broil the vegetables in a preheated oven for 10-15 minutes brushing with olive oil until tender.
5. Cook the vermicelli and drain. Arrange broiled marinated vegetables over top and serve.

Tofu with Cashews

Serves 4
3 tablespoons peanut oil
2 tablespoons sesame oil
1 tablespoon garlic cloves, chopped
1 tablespoon ginger, chopped
1 teaspoon green chilies
4 scallions
2 cups mushrooms, sliced
½ cup unsalted roasted cashews

Marinade:
14 ounces tofu pressed dry and drained, cut into ½" cubes
4 tablespoons hoisin sauce
1 tablespoon rice wine
1 tablespoon soy sauce
salt and pepper to taste

1. In a bowl, mix the tofu slices with hoisin sauce, rice wine, soy sauce, salt and pepper.
2. Marinate this for two hours. Cut the scallions, separate green and white, make lengthwise shreds. Heat peanut oil in pan.
3. Add ½ teaspoon garlic and ginger, stir fry until garlic turns brown.
4. Add chilies, the green part of scallion, and mushrooms. Stir fry for 2 minutes.
5. Heat the remaining peanut oil in the pan, stir fry the remaining garlic and ginger.
6. Add the marinated tofu and the mushroom-scallion fry.
7. Mix well until the sauce coats well over the mushrooms. Stir in cashews and white part of the scallions.
8. Sprinkle sesame oil on top.

Pansit

Serves 4
6 ounces rice sticks (thin noodles)
4 tablespoons oil
1 inch ginger, chopped fine
1 medium onion, chopped
3 cloves garlic, minced
3 cups shredded bok choy (Chinese chard or cabbage)
½ teaspoon crushed red pepper
2 tablespoons oyster sauce
1 large green onion minced

1. Cook noodles according to directions on package. Heat oil. Add onions, garlic, and ginger.
2. Saute about 2 minutes until onions are brown, stirring occasionally.
3. Add bok choy, oyster sauce, pepper and ¼ cup water. Cook 2 minutes.
4. Place warm noodles on a platter and pour onion bok choy mixture over noodles.
5. Garnish with minced green onions.

A Taste of India
Appetizers, Sides & Small Items

Geeli Khitchri

(Boiled rice, dal and spinach)
1½ cups medium or long-grain rice
2 tsp. salt
2 cloves
1¼ cups mung dal or whole mung beans
1 tsp. turmeric split-peas
¼ tsp. ground nutmeg
8 oz. fresh spinach, washed
quarter cup butter or ghee
stemmed and finely chopped 3 bay leaves
3 tomatoes, chopped
1 tbsp. chopped ginger

1. Wash the dal and rice, soak them for 1 hour, and let them drain. Heat the butter or ghee in a heavy sauce-pan, add the bay leaves, chopped ginger, and cloves, then add the drained rice and dal.
2. Fry for about 8 to 10 minutes, stirring well, until the butter has been absorbed.
3. Stir in enough water to cover the grains by 2 inches
4. Add the salt, turmeric and nutmeg, stir, and boil for 1 minute.
5. Cover lightly and start to cook over medium-low heat. Lower the heat gradually as the grains absorb the water.
6. Cook slowly for about 30 minutes, checking from time to time to ensure that the mixture is always cov-ered with a little water, (if necessary, add a few table-spoons).
7. Then gently stir in the chopped spinach and tomatoes and cover again.
8. Continue cooking for another 15 minutes, or until the grains are well cooked but the mixture is still quite moist. Mix well before serving.
9. Soaking time: 1 hr. Prep. and cooking time: 1hr.

Chapati (Whole-wheat flatbread)

Chapatis, the daily bread of millions of Indians, are cooked first on a dry hotplate, then held directly over a flame, where they swell with steam to the point of bursting.

2½ cups atta or sifted whole-wheat flour
½ tsp. salt
2 or 3 tbsp. melted butter
⅔ cup lukewarm water

1. Combine the flour and the salt in a large salad bowl.
2. Slowly add water, gathering the flour together as you do so, until soft, moist dough is formed.
3. Transfer the dough to a work surface and knead it for 6 to 8 minutes until it is smooth and firm.
4. Sprinkle the ball of dough with water, cover it with a damp cloth, and set it aside for half an hour to two hours.
5. When the dough is ready, place a tava or a heavy cast-iron griddle over a medium heat.
6. With moistened hands, knead the dough again, then shape into 15 equal-sized patties, Dip them into flour and roll them out thin and even on a floured board.
7. Make the m as round as possible and about 5 and half inches across.
8. Keep some plain whole-wheat flour on the side to dust the chapatis as you roll them.
9. Knock the excess flour off a chapati with a few slaps between the hands and place it on a griddle.
10. (You can cook several at a time if the size of your griddle allows.) When small white blisters appear on the surface of the chapati and the edges begin to turn up, turn it over with a pair of flat tongs and cook the other side until the surface bulges with air pockets.
11. Lift the chapati and toast both sides over a direct flame for a few seconds until it puffs up like a ball.
12. A finished chapati should be cooked completely (no wet spots) and should be freckled with brown spots on both sides.
13. Press air out and brush one surface with melted butter.
14. You can also cook a chapati on electric heat.
15. Let it stay on the griddle.
16. Turn it over as many times as it takes for both sides to cook, then gently press the top of the chapati all over with a soft cloth, and the chapatti will swell.
17. Serve the chapatis soon after cooking or wrap them in a cloth.
18. Prep. time: 15 minutes. Standing time: 30 minutes to 2 hours. Rolling and cooking time: 2 to 3 minutes for each chapatti.

Alu Lache (Potato Straws)

4 large potatoes
ice cold water
oil for frying
1 teaspoon salt
½ teaspoon chili powder
½ teaspoon ground cumin
½ teaspoon curry powder

1. Peel potatoes and cut into thin slices.
2. Cut slices in matchstick strips.
3. Soak in ice cold water.
4. Drain and dry on paper towels.
5. Heat oil until very hot and fry the potato straws a handful at a time, When are crisp and golden.
6. Lift out of with a perforated spoon and drain well on absorbent paper.
7. When they are all fried sprinkle with the salt and spices mixed together.

Potato and Broccoli Curry

Serves 1
In A Saucepan, Sauté
1 tablespoon olive oil
1 clove garlic, minced
½ teaspoon ground coriander
½ teaspoon ground turmeric
¼ teaspoon ground cumin
¼ teaspoon ground ginger
⅛ teaspoon dry mustard
1 dash ground red pepper

Add
½ tablespoon olive oil
1 cup water
1 potato, diced (unpeeled ok)
Vegetables
1 cup broccoli, chopped
1 carrot, sliced
¼ teaspoon salt
½ tablespoon curry powder

1. Fry, stirring often to coat potatoes with seasonings.
2. When potatoes are almost tender, add last 4 ingredients.
3. Cover and simmer until broccoli and carrots are tender.
4. Serve with rice or pasta.

Onion Bhajees

Makes 20-25
12 oz. gram (Chick Pea) flour
1-2 teaspoons salt
3 tablespoons curry powder
1 tablespoon of caraway seed
3-4 lb onions
Vegetable Oil for Deep Frying

1. Sieve the gram flour, salt & curry powder into a large mixing bowl and add the caraway seeds.
2. Mix well, Make a well in the centre and add 1 pint of water.
3. Mix with a wooden spoon into a thick batter.
4. Leave to stand whilst preparing the onions.
5. Peel the onions and cut them into quarters.
6. Slice them thinly.
7. Add the onions to the batter and mix until they are all well coated with the batter. Heat a deep fat fryer to 190 degrees cup
8. With two round dessert spoons form balls with the onion mixture and drop them into the oil until the pan is full.
9. After 1 minute use a slotted stainless spoon to make sure that the bhajees are not sticking to the bottom.
10. Continue to fry until the bhajees are a deep golden brown, turning occasionally.
11. Remove the bhajees from the oil, shaking off excess oil.
12. Repeat until all the mixture has been used up.
13. Best served immediately, crisp & fresh or they can be reheated in the oven, under the grill or in a microwave.
14. If they are reheated in a microwave they will lose their crispness but will still be delicious.

Notes: You can use your favourite curry powder, Madras seems to be a good choice. Use less or more according to taste. Serve with a vegetable curry and rice or as part of a buffet. They can also be eaten as a hot or cold snack.

Bombay Palace Piaz Bhujia

(Spicy Onion Tangles)
Serves 6

These crunchy tidbits always leave one wanting to taste just one more. Because of the loose distribution of the whole spices, each bite produces a different delicious explosion of tastes. Ideal as an accompaniment for cocktails.

1 small eggplant, not peeled, sliced into matchsticks
1 large potato, scrubbed but not peeled, sliced into ½ matchsticks
1 large onion, sliced thin, cut into half-rings and separated
¼ pound besan (chick-pea flour)
2 ounces white flour
¼ teaspoon baking soda
1 teaspoon salt
1 teaspoon whole coriander seeds
1 teaspoon whole cumin seeds
teaspoon red chili pepper flakes
½ teaspoon fresh-ground pepper
1 teaspoon cumin powder
1 teaspoon coriander powder
1 teaspoon ground red chili
enough oil to cover bottom of a pan to about ½ inch

1. Prepare the eggplant, potato and onion
2. And mix them well together.
3. Use a large plate or in a shallow bowl.
4. Mix the two flours and the baking soda and salt with all the spices. Add the vegetables to the flour, mixing with your hands to coat them well.
5. Dribble on a bit of water, about ¼ cup, and again using your hands,
6. Blend the bhuji into a loose mass.

Note: This mix should be a bit sticky, but almost dry-- do not make a batter. In a wok or heavy pot, heat the oil and turn flame to medium-high. Dribble in the vegetable mixture a small handful at a time. The coating of spices and flour will bind the vegetables into a loose patty. Turn the buhji cluster several times and cook until it is a dark brown but not scorched, about 5-10 minutes. Set each cluster on paper towels to drain. Serve while still hot and crisp.

*The bhuji can be made ahead of time, well-drained of oil, and then crisped by being put into a preheated 350° F oven for half an hour.

Potatoes with Spices and Sesame Seeds

Serves 4

8 smallish potatoes
2 tsp. whole cumin seeds
¼ tsp. whole fenugreek seeds
2 tsp. whole black mustard seeds
6 tbsp. vegetable oil
2 tbsp. sesame seeds
¼ ground turmeric
2 tsp. salt
black pepper, ground
2 tsp. lemon juice

1. Boil the potatoes (unpeeled), then drain and allow to cool for about 3 or 4 hours.
2. Peel and cut into ¾ inch cubes.
3. Heat the oil in a frying pan.
4. Add the spices one after the other in this order, stirring once after each addition: cumin, fenugreek and black mustard seeds, then the sesame seeds, then the turmeric.
5. Finally add the potatoes.
6. With the heat on medium, fry the potatoes for 5 minutes.
7. Add the salt, a dash of pepper and the lemon juice.
8. Fry for another 5 minutes.

Curry Potato

9-12 oz potatoes
1 shallot (sliced)
2 tsp. curry powder
2 tbsp. fresh coconut juice
a pick of green raisins and minced parsley

Seasonings:
1 cup vegetarian stock or water
½ tsp. salt
2 tsp. light soy sauce
dash of sesame oil

1. Skin potatoes and rinse. Drain. Cut into pieces.
2. Then soak in hot oil and fry until slightly brown.
3. Take out. Heat 2 tbsp. oil and sauté shallot slices and curry powder.
4. Add in potato, sprinkle with wine.
5. Add in seasonings, bring to boil.
6. Turn to med-low heat and braise until ingredients are tender and sauce thickens.
7. Add in coconut juice and green raisins.
8. Stir well. Dish up.
9. Sprinkle with minced parsley and serve.

Onion Chutney

Makes 4 ½ pint jars

6 cup Chopped sweet onions
½ cup Fresh lemon juice
2 teaspoon Whole cumin seed
1 teaspoon Whole mustard seed
½ teaspoon Tabasco sauce
¼ teaspoon Red pepper flakes
2 teaspoon Ground chili pepper
¼ cup Light brown sugar
1 ea Salt to taste

1. Combine all ingredients in heavy saucepan over medium heat.
2. Bring to boil, stirring frequently. When mixture comes to a boil,
3. immediately remove from heat
4. Pack into hot sterilized jars.
5. Vacuum seal.

Bengali-Style Oven-Fried Potatoes

Serves 8

2 lb russet potatoes
olive oil spray
¼ teaspoon turmeric
½ teaspoon cumin
¼ teaspoon cayenne
salt & pepper

1. Preheat oven to 400°F.
2. Remove oven racks & spray them with oil.
3. Wash potatoes & slice them lengthwise into sticks ½" thick or crosswise into rounds ⅓" thick.
4. Transfer to a baking pan & spray well with oil.
5. Add seasonings & toss to coat.
6. Place the rounds in a single layer on the oven racks.
7. Place the racks in the centre of the oven.
8. Bake until the potatoes are tender, with a deep, golden-brown crust, about 20 to 25 minutes.
9. Serve piping hot.

South Indian Potato Curry

curry powder	3 tsp. turmeric
1 tsp. fenugreek	other ingredients
1 tsp. cumin seeds	3 large russet potatoes
1 tsp. coriander seeds	3-4 tsp. vegetable oil
1 tsp. black peppercorns	pinch salt (to taste)
1 tsp. mustard seeds	2-3 Serrano peppers
1 tsp. hot chili powder	(optional)

To make curry powder (enough for 2-3 curries) grind the first 5 ingredients in the curry powder list in a food grinder or mortar, then add the chili powder and turmeric and mix well. Keep a spare coffee grinder which used only for spices – wouldn't suggest using your regular coffee grinder unless you like "curry coffee".

1. Wash the potatoes and scrub a little to remove dirt.
2. Place in just enough water to cover them and boil for 30 minutes.
3. Remove the potatoes and peel off the skins (carefully, they will be hot!).
4. Cut the potatoes into slices, sprinkle liberally with the curry powder. Add salt if desired.
5. Chop up the peppers and add them to the mix.
6. Fry the potatoes in hot oil for around 5 more minutes.

Balti Potatoes and Coriander (Aloo Dhaniya)

Serves 4

9 oz. fresh coriander
2 tablespoons oil
4 ½ oz (½ cup) grated or finely chopped onion
1 teaspoon fresh garlic, ground
½ lb peeled potato, cut into ½ inch cubes
1 teaspoon salt
½ teaspoons red chili powder (omit for milder taste)
½ teaspoons iurmeric
1 teaspoon ground fresh green chilies (optional)
2 tablespoons oil
1 teaspoon grated fresh root ginger

1. To prepare the coriander, take leaves off the stalks, add to a large bowl with plenty of water and soak for 20 seconds, so the silt can settle to the bottom.
2. Gently remove the leaves and chop finely or blend in a food processor.
3. Put the oil in a *karai or deep frying pan, add the onions and fry until transparent.
4. Add the garlic and fry for 1 minute, then add the potatoes, salt, red chili powder and turmeric.
5. Cook on lowest heat setting for 5 minutes, or until potatoes are par-cooked.
6. Add the coriander and fresh chilies (if used) and mix once. Simmer on low heat, for 10 minutes or until potatoes are fully cooked.
7. Stir from time to time to prevent mixture from sticking to the bottom.
8. If the potatoes are cooked but liquid remains, cook uncovered until it evaporates.
9. In a small frying pan add the ghee and grated ginger and cook on low heat for 1 minute or until brown.
10. Pour on top of the vegetables in the *karai; this is called "tarka".
11. Take to the table to serve, without mixing.
12. Serve with warm nan bread or chapattis brushed with some oil, and thin slices of mooli (white radish).

Diced Potatoes with Turmeric and Cumin

Serves 1

1½ pounds new potatoes scrubbed, not peeled
6 tablespoons vegetable oil
⅛ teaspoon asafetida optional
½ teaspoon whole black mustard seeds
½ teaspoon whole cumin seeds
⅛ teaspoon ground turmeric
½ teaspoon ground coriander seeds
½ teaspoon ground cumin seeds
¼ teaspoon cayenne
¾ teaspoon salt

1. Cut the clean potatoes into ½-in diced cubes.
2. Heat the oil in a wok or frying pan over a medium heat.
3. When hot, put in, in quick succession: - First the asafetida. A second later, the mustard seeds.
4. Then the cumin seeds.
5. Now put in the potatoes and stir once or twice.
6. Sprinkle in the turmeric.
7. Continue to stir every now and then and cook for about 15 minutes or until the potatoes are lightly browned and almost done.
8. Sprinkle in the ground coriander, ground cumin, cayenne, and salt. Stir and cook for another 1-2 minutes.

Aloo Calcutta (Indian-style Potatoes)

4 waxy boiling potatoes
2 tbsp. vegetable oil
⅛ tsp. asafoetida powder
½ tsp. whole cumin seed
1 or 2 diced hot red peppers (opt)
½ tsp. turmeric
2 6-oz. cans V8
1 tsp. salt, coriander

1. Boil whole potatoes with the skin until soft.
2. Peel the skin and cut to bite size. In hot oil, put cumin seed, red pepper and asafoetida powder to sizzle.
3. Put in all the potatoes and fry a little, turning. Add salt, turmeric and tomato sauce.
4. Cover and allow to simmer gently 4 to 6 minutes.
5. Asafoetida powder is not your every-day ingredient, but is nearly essential in many Indian dishes.
6. It's considered a flavoring but also a digestive aid.
7. Find it at an Indian or Middle-Eastern grocery, or mail order a small jar.
8. A pinch is usually all that's ever used. A complete modification.
9. First you heat the oil or ghee (or butter) and cook the spices briefly.
10. Throw in some cut green beans for a few seconds and then diced potatoes and some garlic and onion.
11. Let sauté', then add the V-8 (or even plain water) and cover.
12. Cook for as long as it takes to get everything tender, up to 40 minutes or more.

Potato Patties

Serves 6
6 medium-sized potatoes
5 fenugreek seeds
3 tbsp. yellow split peas
2 tbsp. chopped onions
salt
3 tbsp. parsley
2 tbsp. oil
1 fresh hot green chili

1. Two hours before using, boil the potatoes in their jackets. While they are boiling, boil split peas in 3 cups water with a sprinkling of salt for 15 minutes.
2. Remove from heat and drain very well, ensuring that you get rid of all the excess water. Set aside in a covered bowl.
3. In a skillet, add the oil & heat over a medium flame until it is very hot. Add the fenugreek. When they change colour, add onions and fry for 2 minutes, till the onion starts to brown.
4. Add parsley, green chili and stir another 2 minutes. Next, put in the split peas, a little more salt if desired and cook, stirring for 5 minutes or until you are sure that all the water has evaporated.
5. The mixture should become one lump. Cover and set aside. Peel and mash the potatoes with a fork or hand masher, do not use an electric beater otherwise your patties will not hold together when cooked. A few lumps will remain, but get it as smooth as you can. Add some salt and mix thoroughly.
6. Divide the potatoes into 12 balls and do the same with the split pea mixture.
7. Flatten each potato ball in your hand, put one portion of the split pea mixture in the centre. Roll up into a ball again and flatten once more into a patty.
8. Repeat with the remaining ingredients. To cook the patties, you need very little oil and some patience so as not to lose the crust to the skillet when you turn them over.

9. Coat the bottom of the skillet with a small amount of oil. Cook no more than two patties at any one time in each skillet.
10. Cook for 7 minutes, gently turn over and cook for another 7 to 8 minutes. The patties should be reddish brown on each side.
11. Keep the heat fairly low otherwise they will burn. Serve with chutney.

Yellow Curry with...

1 can coconut milk
3-4 squirts soy sauce
1-2 tbsp. yellow curry paste
2 small or 1 large potato, cut into small cubes
10-12 large mushrooms, quartered

1. Heat coconut milk in saucepan until beginning to steam, then add soy sauce and curry paste and cook, stirring, till combined.
2. Add potato, turn heat down to medium, and cook, stirring occasionally, for about 5 mins.
3. When potatoes are beginning to soften, add mushrooms and cook an additional 2-3 mins.

Va-Va-Voom Potatoes (Khas Aloo)

Serves 6
2½ lbs small red potatoes
½ cup tarragon vinegar
¼ cup walnut oil
8 dried red peppers, seeded (optional)
1 tsp. mustard seeds
1 tsp. salt
1½ tsp. dill weed

1. Boil the potatoes in their jackets. Do not overcook them; they should be just firm.
2. Combine the vinegar, oil, peppers, mustard seeds, salt, and dill weed in a saucepan.
3. Drain and halve the unskinned potatoes, mix them with the other ingredients and cook for 10 minutes, covered, over low heat. Serve hot.

Madhur's Indian Potatoes

This recipe, adapted from Madhur Jaffrey, uses only one "mystery ingredient," asafoetida powder (you should find some if you're going to get into Indian cooking at all.) Jaffrey says use two pounds of medium, very waxy boiling potatoes. This recipe uses one pound but leaves everything else the same and is perfect for two hungry people.

5 potatoes
tbsp. olive oil
3 big garlic cloves
½ tsp. ground turmeric
⅛ tsp. ground asafoetida
1 tsp. salt
generous pinch of cayenne pepper or hot powder
1 tbsp. sesame seed (you can get these pre-roasted from a Chinese grocery)

1. Peel potatoes (optional) and cut into long French-fries ⅜-inch square.
2. Dunk in a bowl of cold water for ½ hour. Peel and sliver garlic.
3. Heat the oil in a 9- or 10-inch skillet over medium.
4. Drain and pat dry the potato fingers.
5. Put potatoes in hot oil and turn occasionally for 8 or 10 minutes to partially cook, not brown.
6. Remove potatoes with tongs or slotted spoon to a plate with a paper towel on it.
7. From here on you have to move kind of fast: throw the sesame seeds into the skillet, stir once.
8. Add the garlic, and continue to stir.
9. When it begins to turn brown, quickly add turmeric and asafoetida, and stir once more.
10. After just a couple of seconds put the potatoes back in, with salt and cayenne or hot powder.
11. Reduce heat and cook gently until done. Stir frequently.

Alu Piajer Chorchori
(Dry Curried Potato and Onion)

Serves 4-6

5 medium sized potatoes, cut in half lengthwise and the sliced into ⅛" pcs. crosswise.
4 onions cut in half lengthwise and then sliced thicker than normal.
2 tsp. turmeric paste.
½ tsp. chili paste.
4-6 green chilies washed and slit.
Salt to taste.
2 tbsp. oil.
½ cup water or as required

1. Heat oil.
2. When a blue haze appears, add potatoes and fry for several minutes until potatoes turn opaque.
3. Reduce heat, add onions and continue to fry, stirring now and then for a couple of minutes more.
4. Add the turmeric, chili paste and salt to taste, mixing thoroughly and keep frying.
5. Add green chilies. The potatoes and onions should cook as much as possible in their own juices, but if the curry gets too dry, test to see how much cooking the potatoes need and accordingly add water a little at a time. The cooked dish is dry and therefore adding of water should be judicious.
6. The curry is done when the potatoes are cooked and there is practically no gravy.
7. This curry can be reheated before serving, and is a good accompaniment with rice, luchis, or porota.

Potato Cakes (Aloo Roti)

Serves 6

4 large potatoes
1¼ cups whole wheat flour
1 tsp. salt
3 fresh hot green chili peppers
3 tbsp. chopped fresh coriander leaves
3 tbsp. butter
vegetable oil for frying

1. Boil the potatoes in their skins, drain well and peel. Work in a food processor with the flour, salt, seeded and chopped chili peppers, coriander and melted butter to make a soft dough.
2. Be careful not to over-process to the point of the dough becoming a paste that sticks to the processor bowl.
3. Leave in a warm place for about half an hour.
4. Divide into six portions and roll out each to form a disc about 6 inches in diameter.
5. These breads can either be cooked on an oiled heavy griddle or lightly fried until each side is nicely brown.

Potatoes with Black Pepper (Bengali Aloo)

We take black pepper so much for granted, sprinkling tiny amounts on most foods without much thought. Apart from its taste, black pepper has a very enticing perfume and a delicate tartness as well. You could also stick toothpicks into the potato pieces and serve them with drinks.

Serves 4

5 medium potatoes
4 tbsp. veg. oil
¾ tsp. salt
1 to 1½ tsp. freshly ground black pepper
  (a slightly coarse grind is best)
2 tbsp. very finely chopped fresh coriander -or-
  parsley, optional

1. Boil unpeeled potatoes and allow to cool completely. (Refrigerated day old boiled potatoes work very well for this dish.)
2. Peel potatoes and cut into ¾ inch dice. Heat oil in a frying pan over medium flame.
3. When hot put in potatoes and stir around for a minute.
4. Sprinkle in salt and mix gently.
5. Cover and cook over medium-low flame for about 5 minutes, stirring occasionally.
6. Now add black pepper and mix gently.
7. Cook, uncovered, for another few minutes over a medium flame, stirring now and then and allowing them to brown slightly.
8. Sprinkle in fresh coriander. Mix and serve hot.

White Potato Curry

6 medium potatoes, boiled, cooled and chopped
3-4 tablespoons oil
½ onion, chopped
1 teaspoon garlic
4 curry leaves
½ cinnamon stick
1 teaspoon crushed red pepper
½ teaspoons turmeric
1 teaspoon ground cumin
1 tomato, cut into medium pieces
2 cup coconut milk
1 cup water

1. Heat oil, brown onion and garlic. Add spices and tomato.
2. Fry for a few minutes, stirring occasionally.
3. Add milk and water, boil, add potatoes and cook for 10 minutes.

East Indian Spiced Red Beans and Rice

Serves 6-8

4 cups dry large red kidney beans
⅛ cup coconut oil
⅛ cup panch puran seeds (found at an East Indian -or- Oriental grocery store)
1 medium sized Vidalia onion, diced
1 tbsp. or 5 bulbs fresh garlic, diced
6 roma tomatoes, diced
1 tbsp. Vegesal seasoning
2 tbsp. Spike seasoning
2 tbsp. yellow curry powder
2 tbsp. garam masala
1 tbsp. cayenne pepper

1. Soak beans for 8 hours, or overnight in the refrigerator. Drain and rinse with cold water.
2. Coat the bottom of a large cooking pot with ⅛ cup of coconut oil, and heat on medium heat.
3. Add panch puran seeds and stir. One minute later add fresh onion, garlic, and tomatoes and stir.
4. Add the red kidney beans and stir; then season with Vegesal (vegetable salt), Spike, yellow curry powder, garam masala and cayenne pepper.
5. Mix well, and then add enough water to completely cover the beans.
6. Cook uncovered on medium heat until the beans start boiling.
7. Reduce heat to low, cover and simmer for about 3-4 hours.
8. Once the beans are moderately tender add 2 cups of basmati rice, stir well.
9. Continue cooking on low heat for another hour, checking after 30 minutes to ensure that all of the water hasn't cooked out of the pot.
10. When the water has completely evaporated out of the pot, remove from heat, uncover and let sit for 5 minutes before serving.

From *The Hood Health Handbook: A Practical Guide to Health and Wellness in the Urban Community* also available from Supreme Design Publishing.

Lemon Rice

Serves 4

Here's a unique rice dish.

1 cup long grain white rice
1 teaspoon mustard seeds
1 teaspoon blackgram dal
1 teaspoon split yellow peas
1 green chili
⅛ teaspoon oil
¼ teaspoon fenugreek
1 teaspoon turmeric
¼ teaspoon ginger
¼ teaspoon cumin
6 tablespoons lemon juice
Fresh cilantro to taste
Fresh curry leaves to taste

1. Cook rice in water until done.
2. Fry mustard seeds, blackgram dal, and yellow split peas in oil. Set them aside.
3. Fry chili, fenugreek, turmeric, ginger, and cumin in oil.
4. Add all of them to the cooked rice. Mix thoroughly.
5. Add lemon juice, fresh cilantro, and curry leaves.

Potato and Pea Dry Curry

Serves 6

1 lb. potatoes
1 lb. fresh peas in the pod
2 tbsp. ghee
1½ tsp. panch phora
1 large onion, finely chopped
2 tbsp. chopped fresh mint or coriander leaves
1 tsp. finely grated fresh ginger
1 tsp. ground turmeric
1½ tsp. salt
½ tsp. chili powder, opt.
⅓ cup hot water
1 tsp. garam masala
1 tbsp. lemon juice

1. Peel and dice potatoes. Shell peas.
2. Heat the ghee and fry the panch phora on low heat until seeds start to brown, add onion and fry gently until onion is soft and starts to color.
3. Add chopped herbs and grated ginger and fry for a few seconds, stirring.
4. Add potatoes and peas, stir well and sprinkle with hot water.
5. Turn heat very low, cover saucepan tightly and cook for 20 min., shaking pan occasionally.
6. Sprinkle with garam masala and lemon juice, replace cover and cook for a further 10 min.
7. Serve hot with rice or chapatis.

Vegetarian Korma

1½ tablespoons vegetable oil
1 small onion, diced
1 teaspoon minced fresh ginger root
4 cloves garlic, minced
2 potatoes, cubed
4 carrots, cubed
1 fresh jalapeno pepper, seeded and sliced
3 tablespoons ground unsalted cashews
1 (4 ounce) can tomato sauce
2 teaspoons salt
1½ tablespoons curry powder
1 cup frozen green peas
½ green bell pepper, chopped
½ red bell pepper, chopped
1 cup heavy cream
1 bunch fresh cilantro for garnish

1. Heat the oil in a skillet over medium heat. Stir in the onion, and cook until tender.
2. Mix in ginger and garlic, and continue cooking one minute. Mix potatoes, carrots, jalapeno, cashews, and tomato sauce. Season with salt and curry powder.
3. Cook and stir 10 minutes, or until potatoes are tender.
4. Stir peas, green bell pepper, red bell pepper, and cream into the skillet.
5. Reduce heat to low, cover, and simmer 10 minutes. Garnish with cilantro.

Masaman Tofu Curry

For the curry paste
2 shreds of mace
6 fenugreek seeds (or finely diced garlic)
1 tablespoon of Coriander powder
2 teaspoons of Cumin powder
8 black peppercorn (whole)
3 red chili pepper (soaked in water for 20 minutes)
cayenne pepper to taste
¼ teaspoon of tumeric

For the tofu:
1 carton of tofu – slice ⅛ - ¼ " thick
soy sauce
salt
coconut milk
lemon juice or amchoor powder (powder green mangoes)

1. Gather all the spices and put into frying pan.
2. Turn flame to low and dry-roast the spices without burning them for a few seconds (use a fork to stir them around), the color may darken a bit.
3. Turn off the flame and remove frying pan.
4. Put a 2 teaspoons of lemon juice into spices and turn flame on low again.
5. The lemon juice should evaporate fairly quickly.
6. Remove pan from flame and add one tablespoon of oil to the spices. Put pan on flame again and stir.
7. One should have a wet sticky curry.
8. Add two tablespoons of soy sauce.
9. Let some of the soy sauce get absorbed and then turn flame on medium.
10. Add ⅔ can of coconut milk gradually.
11. Taste the sauce and add salt as desired.
12. When the coconut milk starts to bubble, add the slices of tofu in layers into the pan making sure the sauce covers the tofu.
13. If the sauce doesn't cover all the slices, shift pan side to side until all slices have been covered.
14. Simmer dish until done.

Sauces & Spice

Fiery Onion Relish 2 (Piaz Chatni)

Makes 1 Cup

1 cup chopped onion	1 tsp. cayenne pepper
½ tsp. coarse salt, or to taste	1 tsp. paprika
½ lemon, finely chopped, with peel	½ tsp. chat masala (use a commercial brand, or use recipe below)
1½ tsp. light vegetable oil	

1. Put the onion, salt and chopped lemon in a bowl and toss well. Heat the oil in a small frying pan until very hot. Turn off the heat.
2. Stir in the cayenne and paprika, and immediately pour the oil on the onions, use a rubber spatula to get all of it. Add the chat masala and toss again.
3. Serve cold or at room temperature.
4. Keeps well at room temperature for up to 4 hours; after that, the onions will turn soft and limp.

Fresh Mint and Chile Sauce

Makes about ½ cup

2 teaspoons granulated sugar
½ teaspoon salt
1 tablespoon chopped fresh ginger
1 small serrano chili or jalapeño pepper, with seeds, chopped
1 clove garlic, peeled
2 cups packed fresh mint leaves
2 tablespoons rice wine vinegar, or to taste

1. Place sugar and salt in a blender or mini-food processor.
2. With the motor running, drop ginger, chili, and garlic through the feed tube and process until minced.
3. Add mint and vinegar and pulse until finely chopped, stopping to scrape down sides of work bowl as needed. Transfer to a small serving bowl. Serve within 30 minutes.

Garam Masala "Spice"

Garam Masala is an aromatic spice combination that's delightful in greens.

2 tbsp cumin seeds	1 tsp whole cloves
2 tbsp coriander seeds	½ tsp ground cinnamon
2 tbsp cardamom seeds	1 tsp grated nutmeg
2 tbsp black peppercorns	

1. Add all the spices except the cinnamon and nutmeg to a skillet and toast on medium heat for a few minutes, just until fragrant.
2. Do not burn the spices or you'll have to start over.
3. Add all the spices to a spice mill or coffee grinder and grind into powder. Store in an airtight container.

Entrees

Potatoes, Carrots and Green Beans, Bangalore Style Sopchak

2 medium potatoes, cut into ¼" cubes	½ med. onion, chopped
2 teaspoons olive oil	2 carrots, cut into ¼" pieces
1 tablespoon black mustard seeds	15 green beans, cut into ¼" pieces
¼ teaspoons ginger	½ teaspoons turmeric
¼ teaspoons garlic	½ teaspoons salt
2 green chilies, sliced into ¼" pieces	2 tablespoons coconut
	2 tbsp. lime juice

1. Soak the potatoes in water for 15 minutes.
2. Drain and pat dry. In a large non-stick skillet, heat oil. Add mustard seeds until they crackle.
3. Add ginger, garlic, onion and chilies, stir until onion is translucent.
4. Add carrots, potatoes, green beans, turmeric and salt, stir fry for 3-4 minutes.
5. Add ¼ cup water and boil. Stir, cover and simmer for 5-10 minutes, until vegetables are tender.
6. Remove lid, and cook away any remaining liquid. Add coconut and fry for 2 minutes.
7. Sprinkle with lime juice and serve.

Bell Pepper & Potato Curry

2 medium potatoes	2 tbsp. Kura Podi
2 green bell peppers	1 tablespoon Salt
2 Sun flower oil	1\2 teaspoon

1. Wash potatoes and green bell peppers.
2. Peal the skin off the potatoes.
3. Cut potatoes and bell peppers into small pieces.
4. Fry these cut vegetables with 2 tablespoons of sunflower oil on low fire.
5. While frying, mix them gently now and then so that the pieces at the bottom do not get charred.
6. When it turns light brown add 1 tablespoon kura podi and ½ teaspoon salt.
7. Mix well and fry for another 5 minutes.
8. Gently mix well while frying. Ensure that the vegetables are not charred.
9. The curry is ready for serving with rice.

Above you have a 3-course lunch\dinner. Individually mix the vegetable preparations with rice and eat. Remove the chili pieces while eating, lest they spoil the pleasure of eating something good!

Bread Stuffed with Spiced Potatoes (Aloo Paratha)

Serves 6

3.5 cups whole wheat flour
4 oz. margarine
salt
water to mix
oil and margarine for cooking
6 oz. potatoes
1 fresh hot green chili pepper
¾-inch piece fresh root ginger
½ cup fresh coriander leaves
½ tsp. cayenne pepper

1. To make the filling, boil the potatoes in their skins. Drain well, then peel and mash them. Remove the seeds from the chili pepper and chop finely with the peeled ginger and the fresh coriander.
2. Mix together with the potato and season with the cayenne pepper and salt to taste. In a food processor, mix the flour, salt, and butter together and add a little water, about 1 tbsp., just enough to make a firm dough.
3. Divide into 12 balls and put aside, covered with a damp cloth.
4. On a lightly floured surface, roll out two of the balls to flat discs of about 4 inches in diameter.
5. Place a little of the filling on one disc and cover it with the second disc.
6. Use the rolling pin to gently flatten the bread and seal the edges. The bread will now be about 7 inches in diameter.
7. Heat the tawa, or griddle, brush with oil and cook the bread, turning it once.
8. Traditionally, the bread is only half cooked on the griddle.
9. Then a little butter is melted in a non-stick pan and the paratha are shallow-fried to a crisp finish; however, the frying can be omitted and all the cooking done on the griddle.
10. Continue to make the remaining breads in the same way, keeping them warm in the oven.
11. When all are cooked, serve them hot.

Chat Masala

Makes 1½ tablespoons

1 tsp. ground roasted cumin seeds
½ tsp. cayenne pepper
¼ tsp. asafetida powder
¾ tsp. mango powder
½ - ¾ tsp. garam masala
½ tsp. black salt
1 tsp. coarse salt

Mix all spices and keep in a jar, tightly covered, in a cool place.

Seeni Sambal (Sri Lankan Onions in Coconut Milk)

3 medium yellow onions
¼ cup unsweetened coconut milk
1 tsp. powdered hot red peppers (adjust if necessary)
½-inch cinnamon stick, broken into small pieces
pinch of ground cloves 0.5 tsp. tamarind concentrate dissolved in about 0.25 cup water or 1" dia.
ball of tamarind pulp, extract juice in ¼ cup water
1 tsp. salt or to taste
1 tbsp. sugar
oil

1. Peel the onions.
2. Halve the onions lengthwise and then slice them thin, again lengthwise.
3. Heat a few table spoons of oil in a Dutch oven.
4. Add the sliced onions and fry, stirring frequently, until the onions begin to turn brown.
5. This will take about 10 mins on medium high heat.
6. In a large saucepan (if the Dutch oven above isn't too brown at the bottom you can use that without washing it) combine the rest of the ingredients and simmer gently for about 10 mins.
7. Add the onions, mix well and cook for an additional 10 mins.

Mint Chutney

Process fresh mint leaves, green chili, onion, little bit of ginger (optional), salt, brown sugar, lemon juice and water to get a pesto-like consistency.

Alternatively, use commercial mint sauce and omit lemon juice - experiment a bit.

Potato Masala

4 large potatoes (boiled)
2 large onions (chopped medium size)
4-5 green chilies (slit into long strips)
2 tbsp. channa dhal
1 inch ginger (finely chopped)
salt to taste

1. Heat oil, fry channa dhal until golden brown.
2. Add dash of hing and crackle mustard.
3. Sauté onions and green chilies until golden brown.
4. Add 4 cups of water; ginger, salt, let cook for a while.
5. Mash potatoes and dump into above..and viola!

Masala Dosai

Serves 4
Enjoy this "crepe," with potato stuffing.
½ cup blackgram dal
2 teaspoons fenugreek
1 cup enriched long grain rice
2 tablespoons lime juice (optional)
2 cups water

1. Soak blackgram dal and fenugreek together and rice separately for at least 6 hours.
2. Using a blender, with less than ⅓ cup of water, blend rice first and keep it separate.
3. Next, with less than ⅓ cup of water, blend blackgram dal and fenugreek together.
4. Combine the two mixtures. The batter should not be too thick or too thin. If you take the batter and pour it out of a spoon, the flow from the spoon should be even. Keep the batter in a big pot for at least 12 hours until it ferments and tastes a bit sour.
5. If you do not get a sour flavor, add lime juice.
6. Heat a non-stick pan until it becomes medium hot and wipe the pan with a little oil dipped on a cloth or paper towel.
7. When the pan becomes hot, take a small scoop of batter and pour it on to the pan. Spread it around and make a small circle of batter.
8. Flip it over to the other side when one side is done, that is when air bubbles begin to appear.
9. Reduce the heat to medium before you cook the next one.

Hints:
1. Sprinkle some water on the pan to make the pan cool.
2. Keep the pan hot but not so hot as to burn the dosai.
3. If you find the dosai a bit dry, add ⅛ teaspoon of oil around the edges of the next dosai so as to make it less dry. Flip it and add ⅛ teaspoon of oil.

Aloo Achar (Nepal Potato Salad)

4 medium size waxy boiling potatoes
4 tbsp. ground roasted sesame seeds
3 or 4 tbsp. lemon juice (fresh squeezed)
1 tsp. salt
1 or more hot green chilies, finely minced (*)
4 tbsp. sesame oil
2 tsp. vegetable oil
pinch ground Asafoetida (**)
to 10 whole fenugreek seeds (**)
3 tbsp. cilantro (Chinese parsley) minced

1. (*) Use as many chilies, like jalapenos, as you can stand. If you can't tolerate hot, spicy food, 2 or 3 tbsp. green bell pepper can be substituted.
2. (**) Look for these in an Indian or Middle-Eastern grocery Boil the potatoes in a big pot.
3. Meanwhile, combine the chilies (or green pepper), salt, lemon juice and ground roasted sesame seeds in a non-metallic bowl. (By the way, roasted sesame seeds can be found as "iri goma" in Oriental markets.
4. Add the sesame oil just a little at a time and mix in with a wire whisk.
5. Using a metal ladle or a small butter warmer, heat the vegetable oil by holding it over heat. When quite hot, add the asafoetida powder and fenugreek seeds.
6. The fenugreek seeds will start to darken in the hot oil in just a few seconds... when this happens dump it all into the bowl.
7. Mix well, then add the cilantro (Chinese parsley) and mix some more.
8. Check your seasonings. When the potatoes are done, drain and peel while hot (holding with a fork if you need to.) The peel should slide right off.
9. Cut into 3/4" dice and add to the bowl of dressing.
10. Gently mix to coat all the cubes and finally adjust your seasonings if needed.
11. Let cool, cover and refrigerate. You can eat this after a couple of hours, either cold or room temperature. However, it's supposed to be much better the next day. It keeps for up to 4 days refrigerated. Potato

Masala

Serves 4

Here's a great potato stuffing for Dosai.

3 medium-sized potatoes
⅛ teaspoon oil
1 teaspoon mustard seeds
1 teaspoon yellow split peas
1 teaspoon blackgram dal
3 medium-sized onions
½ cup water
2 cloves garlic
1 tomato
1 teaspoon turmeric
⅛ teaspoon cayenne pepper
½ teaspoon coriander
¼ teaspoon black pepper
¼ teaspoon cumin
⅛ teaspoon ginger
½ teaspoon salt (optional)
1 cup pre-cooked chickpeas
4 teaspoons lemon juice (optional)
cilantro to garnish
4 teaspoons orange juice (optional)

1. Cut potatoes into small cubes. Boil potatoes until tender, drain, and remove the skins.
2. With oil, fry mustard seeds, yellow split peas, and blackgram dal and set them aside.
3. Next, sauté onions in water with chopped garlic and tomato.
4. Add turmeric, cayenne pepper, coriander, black pepper, cumin, and ginger to the onion.
5. Add chickpeas and mix thoroughly. Add cooked potatoes.
6. Add the fried mustard seeds, yellow split peas, and blackgram dal to the potatoes. Mix them all thoroughly.
7. Add lemon juice and garnish the masala with fresh cilantro.
8. If the masala is too spicy for your taste, add orange juice.
9. Put a little masala in the middle of each dosai and roll the dosai.
10. Do the same for the remaining dosai.

Gujar Ka Pullao (Carrot Rice)

Serves 4

1 cup basmati rice
1 cup water
1 large onion
2 tablespoons vegetable oil
1 Bay leaf
½ teaspoon Cumin seeds
2 cloves 1 cardamom pod
½ cinnamon stick; ½ inch
½ teaspoon peppercorns
2 cups carrot, grated to taste

1. Wash the rice under running water, then let soak in 1 cup water.
2. Slice the onion into thin half rounds.
3. In a large, heavy bottom saucepan over medium heat, warm the oil. Add the bay leaf.
4. Cumin, cloves, cardamom pod, cinnamon and peppercorns.
5. Cook until the spices puff up and darken (1 to 2 seconds), then add the sliced onion and sauté until browned (8 to 10 minutes).
6. Add the rice and the soaking water and the salt.
7. Stir gently, cover, increase the heat to high and bring to a boil.
8. Then reduce the heat to very low and cook for 25 minutes without uncovering the pan.
9. Turn off the heat and let the pan stand covered on the burner for 5 minutes.
10. then uncover, fluff up the rice gently and serve.

Suki Bhaji nu Shak
(Dried Potato Vegetable)

Serves 2–3

5 large size potatoes
2 teaspoons jeera seeds (cumin)
2 teaspoons chili powder
½ teaspoon tumeric powder
salt to taste
2 teaspoons dhanna jeeru (a dried powder combination of powdered cumin and coriander seeds)
2 teaspoons sugar or sugar substitute
4 tablespoons oil

¼ cup fresh chopped coriander

1. Wash and peel the potatoes (or you can leave the skin on if it is really nice) Cut the potatoes as if you were making chips but half the size.
2. Wash again if required. Heat a large wok or non stick pan and add the oil.
3. Once oil is hot add the cumin seeds and wait till they pop. Now take of the heat and throw in the potatoes. Place back on the heat and stir, add the salt, tumeric powder and cover the pan.
4. Let the potatoes cook until tender stir every now and again scrape the bits of the bottom as you go along as they taste really nice and crispy!
5. Once the potatoes are tender remove the lid and add the dhanna jeeru. chili powder and the sugar.
6. Turn up the heat slightly so the potatoes start sticking to the bottom and become a little crispy.
7. Once done the potatoes should be crispy on the outside and tender on the inside.
8. Garnish with the chopped coriander and serve with chappattis or even fresh bread slices!

Vegetable Cutlet

Vegetables: Potato, Beans, Carrots, green peas, Beet Root (if preferred)

1. Steam the vegetables in a pressure cooker or a food steamer and mash them into a tight paste.
2. Add grated onions, salt, red chili powder, garam masala powder and ground cinnamon(a pinch).Knead the mixture tightly.
3. Take some rice flour and add water to make it into a slightly watery juice.
4. Make the vegetable mixture into evenly sized balls and roll over the rice flour and then cover it with rawa.
5. Deep fry the balls until they turn golden brown.
6. Side dish: Tomato ketchup

Kicharee

1 cup Split Mung dal
(yellow)
2 Cups White Basmati rice
1 inch Fresh ginger root
1 small handful of cilantro leaves
2 tablespoons. Ghee (clarified butter)
½ tsp. turmeric
½ tsp. coriander powder
½ tsp. cumin powder
½ tsp. whole cumin seeds
½ tsp. mustard seeds
½ tsp. salt (rock salt is best)
1 pinch hing (also called asafoetida)
5-7 cups water (amount of water depends upon climate)

Note: Can use Bragg's Amino Acid for extra flavor after cooking is completed. Also can be used as a replacement for salt.

1. Wash dal and rice together until water runs clear.
2. Heat a large sauce pan on medium heat then add ghee (clarified butter), next mustard seeds, tumeric, hing, whole cumin seeds, cumin powder, and coriander powder.
3. Stir all together for a few minutes.
4. Then add rice, dal and stir again.
5. Now add the water, salt and bring to a boil.
6. Cook for 10 minutes.
7. Next turn heat down to low, cover, and continue cooking until both dal and rice becomes soft.
8. The cilantro leaves can be added before serving.

Carrots, Peas & Potatoes Flavoured with Cumin

Serves 6

2 large carrots
2 small potatoes, boiled & cooled
2 med onions
1 ea scallion
3 tablespoons mustard oil*
1½ tsp cumin seeds
2 ea dried red chilies
1½ cup shelled peas
1 teaspoon salt
¼ tsp sugar

1. Dice the carrots & potatoes.
2. Coarsely chop the onions & thinly slice the scallions.
3. Set aside.
4. Heat oil in a large skillet over medium heat.
5. When hot, add the cumin seeds & let them sizzle for 3 or 4seconds.
6. Add the chilies & stir them for 3 to 4 seconds.
7. Put in theonions & stir & cook for 5 minutes.
8. Add the carrots & peas.
9. Stir themfor 1 minute.
10. Cover. Turn heat to low & cook for 5 minutes.
11. Uncover. Slightly raise the heat.
12. Add the potatoes, salt & sugar.
13. Stir & cook for 3 minutes.
14. Add the scallion, heat for 30 seconds & serve.

*Can be replaced with any vegetable oil.

Dry Potato Sabji

5 red russet potatoes, cubed small
3 tablespoons oil a few jalapenos, cut small mustard seeds
⅓ tsp. cumin seeds
⅓ tsp. coriander powder
½ tsp. turmeric
½ tsp. chili powder, lots
salt (to taste)

1. First make a chaunk.
2. This is done by heating the oil and then putting the mustard seeds and cumin seeds in.
3. Let the seeds start popping.
4. Then also add in the jalapenos.
5. After a while of popping (this roasts the seeds and enhances the flavor) put in the potatoes.
6. Stir for a bit. If it gets sticky, put a little bit of water in, and cover the pot for a while.
7. Make sure you don't scorch it at all.
8. When the potatoes are about half done, put in the coriander and turmeric.
9. Stir and cover. Put it on a low flame for about 5 minutes.
10. It's done when you can easily cut through a potato piece with the back of a knife.

Alu Matar (Potatoes and Peas)

1½ cup peas
2 large potatoes, cut in ½ inch cubes
1 cup chopped tomato
2 cloves minced garlic
½ cup onion, chopped
4 tablespoons oil
1 tsp. salt
¼ tsp. garam masala (spice available in any Indian store)
¼ tsp. tumeric
¼ tsp. ground coriander
1 cup water
¼ tsp. cayenne

1. In heavy frying pan, heat oil over low heat. Add onion and garlic and cook till light brown.
2. Add tomato and all spices except cayenne. Cook for 5 min, continually stirring to form a well blended sauce.
3. Add potatoes and stir for a minute to cover with sauce. Add water and cook covered over med. heat for 10 min.
4. Remove cover and add peas. Lower heat and cook another 15 min. At the end, both vegetables should be done but not too soft or mushy.
5. Taste for seasoning and add cayenne for desired hotness.

Spinach Curry

Serves 4

2 bunch spinach
¼-⅓ cup skimmed milk
2 tbsp. chopped onions
3 medium tomatoes
  (finely chopped)
½ tsp. ginger-garlic paste

1½ tsp. paprika
2 tbsp. sunflower oil
1 pinch of turmeric
1 tsp. salt (or to taste)

1. To make a ginger garlic paste, take equal quantities and grind it to a paste. This can be stored in the refrigerator for around 2 weeks. Take one and half teaspoons of the paste for the curry.
2. Blanche the spinach in boiling water until the leaves become soft enough to puree. It takes about 2 minutes.
3. Now puree the spinach adding milk slowly as needed.
4. Add enough milk to make a thick puree. Depending on the spinach you'll need ¼-⅓ cup of milk
5. Sautee the onions on a medium flame until it turns golden brown.
6. Add ginger-garlic paste and fry for 2 minutes
7. Add the chopped tomatoes. Once the tomatoes become soft add turmeric, salt and paprika.
8. When the mixture becomes uniform, add the pureed spinach and cook for 2 minutes.
9. Your Palak Saag is now ready. It tastes amazing served with Indian breads. You can also eat with regular bread or rice. This makes about 4 half cup servings. You can add some cottage cheese/ tofu along with the tomatoes if you like.

Chops (Alu Ki Tikiya)

Makes 12 "chops"

1½ lb potatoes, boiled & mashed
½ teaspoon salt
1 teaspoon Garam Masala -or- ½ teaspoon ground cumin -and- ½ teaspoon ground coriander
1 tablespoon chopped fresh coriander, (US = cilantro)
1 small onion, very finely chopped
2 green chilies, finely, chopped
½ teaspoon grated fresh ginger root
oil spray for cooking

1. Mix all ingredients (except oil spray) together well.
2. Divide into portions (as many as specified in "yield") and shape each into a thick flat round.
3. Heat a large frying pan (skillet). Spray with a little oil or grease lightly. Cook 3-4 potato cakes at a time, depending on how large the pan is.
4. Do for about 5 minutes on each side until golden - DO NOT disturb them until the 5 minutes is up or you will spoil the crust.
5. When they have been cooking 5 minutes try and lift them gently with a spatula.
6. Lift rather than scrape, and flip over, remembering that they will still be very soft in the middle.
7. If you like, use another spatula placed over the top of the chop to keep it together whilst turning over.
8. Keep them warm in the oven at a moderate heat (375°F) while you cook the others.

Diced Potatoes Cooked With Spinach

Serves 6

5 medium-sized waxy boiling potatoes
  (about 2 lbs.)
1½ tbsp.
plus 1 tsp. salt
1 lb. fresh or 1 package frozen leaf spinach
6 tbsp.veg.
oil or ghee
½ tsp. whole black mustard seeds
1 large onion, peeled and chopped
2 cloves garlic, peeled and minced
1 tsp. garam masala
1/16 to ⅛ tsp. cayenne pepper

1. Bring 2½ qts. water to a boil. Peel potatoes and dice into ¾ inch cubes, then add to boiling water with 1 tbsp. salt. Bring to a boil again.
2. Cover, turn heat to low and cook potatoes until they are just tender- about 6 minutes.
3. Do not overcook. Drain. Spread potatoes out and leave to cool.
4. If using fresh spinach, wash carefully and drop into large kettle of boiling water to wilt. Drain.
5. Squeeze out as much water from spinach as possible and chop fine.
6. If using frozen spinach, follow package directions.
7. Drain, squeeze out liquid, and chop.
8. Set aside. Heat oil in a heavy, 12 inch, preferably non-stick skillet over a medium-high flame.
9. When very hot, put in the mustard seeds. As soon as the seeds begin to pop (this takes just a few seconds), add the onion and the garlic.
10. Turn heat to medium and fry for 3 to 4 minutes. Onions should turn very lightly brown at the edges.
11. Now put in the spinach and keep stirring and frying for another 10 minutes.
12. Add the cooked potatoes, 1 tsp. salt, the garam masala, and the cayenne pepper.
13. Stir and mix gently until potatoes are heated through.

Curried Mushrooms, Potatoes and Peas

Serves 6

1 lb. small white mushrooms
1 lb. small new potatoes
1 cup shelled green peas
1 tbsp. ghee or oil
1 small onion, finely sliced
1 tsp. finely grated fresh ginger
1 clove garlic, crushed - opt.
2 tbsp. finely chopped fresh coriander leaves
1 tsp. ground tumeric
½ tsp. chili powder - opt.
½ cup hot water
1½ tsp. salt
1 tsp. garam masala

1. Wipe mushrooms with a damp paper towel. If mushrooms are large, cut in half or quarters, leaving a piece of stalk on each piece.
2. Wash and scrub potatoes and if large cut into half or quarter. Frozen peas can be used instead of fresh, but add them during the last 15 minutes of cooking.
3. Heat ghee in sauce pan and fry onion over gentle heat for 3 minutes.
4. Add ginger, garlic and coriander leaves and fry for 3-4 min. longer, stirring occasionally.
5. Add turmeric and chili powder, fry for 1 minute, then add mushrooms, potatoes and fresh peas.
6. Add water and salt and stir well. Cover and cook on low heat for 15 min.
7. Uncover, sprinkle with garam masala and stir well. Cover and cook for a further 15 mins. or until potatoes are tender enough to be pierced with a skewer. Serve with rice or Indian bread.

Soups

Carrot-Tomato Soup Nalapaaka Naarayana

4-5 carrots
2 small tomatoes
7-8 whole black pepper
1 onion

1. Chop the onion into fine pieces.
2. In a soup vessel, place 1 tablespoon of butter.
3. Heat on low flame.
4. After the butter melts, put the chopped onions, fry well for 5-6 minutes.
5. Cut the carrots into small pieces, put them in, also cut the tomatoes and put them in.
6. Pour 2 glasses of water, increase the heat.
7. Allow the water to boil well, put whole pepper into it and continue to boil for 5-7 minutes.
8. Switch off heat, allow the semi-boiled carrots and tomato to cool.
9. Transfer the contents to a mixer/grinder, run the mixer for 4-5 minutes, stopping once a minute to check.
10. Take a large metallic juice strainer, slowly pour the contents from the mixer through the strainer, back to the soup vessel. Stir with a spoon.
11. Finally, press with hand to squeeze the liquid portion through the strainer, leaving the pulp above.
12. If there are pieces of carrots left do not worry.
13. Now, transfer the pulp back to the mixer, pour ½ glass of water, run the mixer again and repeat the straining process.
14. Put the soup vessel on a low heat, put enough salt to taste.
15. Heat till the soup is hot but do not allow it to boil.
16. Serve hot in bowls, this one will taste great and provides one serving for 4 people.

Mushroom Korma

Serves 4

1 lb. mushrooms	½ tsp. aniseed (saunf)
2 tbsp. poppy seeds (gasgasalu)	2 cardamom
1 tbsp. coriander seeds	¼ tsp. tumeric
½ tsp. cumin	1 tsp. red chili powder
1 tsp. ginger paste	1 big onion
4 cloves	2 medium tomato
1 inch stick cinnamon	¾ cup oil
	salt to taste

1. Wash mushrooms thoroughly.
2. Slice into halves and keep aside.
3. Crush coriander, cumin, aniseed, poppy seeds, cloves, cinnamon, cardamom into powder and keep aside.
4. Make into a paste ginger, garlic, onion and tomato.
5. Mix mushrooms with all of the above and red chili powder, tumeric and salt to taste.
6. In a deep skillet heat oil on medium and add mushrooms. Stir for two minutes.
7. Add about 1.5 cup water.
8. Lower heat and let cook for 15-17 minutes.
9. Goes well with plain white rice and/or parathas. Prep. time: 30 minutes

Carrot Kheer Samatha Kommana

4 carrots (medium size)
3 cups soy milk
8 cashewnuts (Ground)
3 cardamom
sugar (this depends on your taste)
1 cup water

1. Cook carrots, it's easier in a pressure cooker, otherwise boil in water as you would boil potatoes.
2. Blend cooked carrots to a paste (not too fine).
3. In the meantime heat milk and water, when it begins to boil, lower heat, add carrot paste, sugar and cracked cardamom seeds.
4. Stir constantly, there's a tendency for milk to burn at the bottom of the vessel.
5. When this mixture begins to boil, turn off the stove and add ground cashewnuts.
6. You can have this kheer either hot or cold.
7. Tips: Kheer tends to thicken as it cools.

Microwaved Curried Carrots & Lentils

½ cup dried red lentils
1½ cup water
3 carrots, peeled & cut into 2" pieces
½ cup chopped onion
¼ cup golden raisins
½ tsp. salt
¾ tsp. curry powder
½ tsp. fennel seeds
black pepper, to taste

1. (You can make this the traditional way if you dry-roast the curry & fennel ahead of time, and cook everything over the stove, but this is the quick version).
2. Combine lentils & ½ cup water in a 2-qt microwave-safe casserole.
3. Microwave at full power, covered, for 5 minutes.
4. (If water foams and spills over, add 1-2 tbsp more water.)
5. Stir in carrots & another ½ cup water; cover, and microwave for 5 minutes.
6. Stir in ½ cup water and all the remaining ingredients; cover, & nuke for 5 minutes. Serve.

Note: Intended for 650-700 watt microwave; cook longer if yours is less powerful.

Yellow Mung Dal Soup

1 cups yellow split mung dal
6 cups water
2 tablespoons Ghee (clarified butter)
½ tsp. black mustard seeds
1 tsp. whole cumin seeds
1 pinch hing
2 tablespoons chopped fresh cilantro leaves
½ tsp. salt (rock salt is best)
½ tsp. ground coriander seeds
½ tsp. ground cumin seeds

1. Wash the mung dal until the water runs clear.
2. Heat pot on medium heat, add water and dal.
3. Cook for 30 minutes.
4. Stir occasionally to prevent burning.
5. Then in sauce pan at medium heat add ghee when it is liquid you can add spices (add salt to taste).
6. Then add spicy ghee mix to soap.
7. Before serving garnish with freshly chopped cilantro leaves. Benefits:
8. This dish reduces both Kapha and Vata doshas.
9. With the spices it reduces the Pitta dosha.

Salads

Gujerati Carrot Salad

(Gajar Ka Salad from Madhur Jaffrey's Indian Cooking)
Serves 4
5 carrots, trimmed, peeled, and coarsely grated
¼ tsp. salt
2 tbsp. veg oil
1 tbsp. whole black mustard seeds
2 tsp. lemon juice

1. Toss grated carrots with salt.
2. Heat oil over medium flame until very hot.
3. Add mustard seeds.
4. When they begin to pop, pour contents of pan-oil and seeds-over carrots. Add lemon juice and toss.
5. Serve at room temp or cold.

Dessert

Carrot Halwa

Serves 4
Savor this terrific dessert.

1 cup brown rice syrup
1 cup boiling water
3 cups grated carrots
½ teaspoon ground cardamom

1. Dissolve brown rice syrup in boiling water. Stir until you get a consistent syrup.
2. Add carrots and stir until the mixture becomes semi-solid. Add cardamom. Refrigerate before serving.

Hints:
Add dried fruits for variety. Add 2 teaspoons of chopped cashews and almonds to enhance the flavor (optional).

"Milk" Pudding

Serves 4

Children will love this pudding.

6 cups low fat rice milk
2 bananas, puréed
2 teaspoons apple butter
2 tablespoons brown rice syrup
½ teaspoon ground cardamom

1. Boil rice milk and reduce the heat to low. Stir the milk occasionally.
2. Simmer the milk for about 30 minutes until the milk is reduced by about ⅔ of its volume.
3. Add banana purée and apple butter.
4. Add brown rice syrup and cardamom.
5. Cool and keep in a refrigerator. Serve chilled.

Hints:

Add dried fruits and ¼ teaspoon pistachios or almonds or cashews for variety (optional).

Rice Pudding

Serves 4

Try this great version of rice pudding.

3 cups low fat rice milk
¼ cup long grain rice
¼ cup brown rice syrup
¼ teaspoon ground cardamom

1. Cook rice in rice milk for about 15 minutes.
2. Add brown rice syrup after the rice is cooked.
3. Add cardamom.
4. Allow the rice to cool and refrigerate for a few hours
5. before serving.
6. Hints:
7. Add saffron, chopped cashews, or raisins to enhance taste (optional).

Honey Shrikhand
(Thick flavoured yogurt)

This delicate sweet, an easy-to-prepare guaranteed success, is the perfect dessert with puris, at room temperature or chilled. For an extra treat, put it in dessert bowls and freeze it.

6 cups (1.4l) plain yogurt (or thick yogurt)
½ cup honey
¼ tsp. powdered saffron -or- 5 saffron strands

1. Hang the yogurt in two layers of cheesecloth over a bowl to catch the drippings.
2. Allow to drain overnight, or for at least 5 hours.
3. Then scrape it into a bowl.
4. The drained yogurt should be thick, half its original volume.
5. Add the honey and saffron strand s to the yogurt.
6. Beat with a whisk. If you are using saffron strands, steep them in a little rose-water before adding to the drained yogurt.
7. You may also flavor your shrikhand with half a cup of crushed red berries, crushed pistachio nuts, a few drops of rose-water or ghee, or a teaspoon of finely grated rind of orange or lemon.
8. Draining time: overnight or at least 5 hrs; Prep. time: 10 min.

A Taste of Australia

A Taste of Australia
Appetizers & Side Items

Aubergine Lemon Dip with Tahini

1 large aubergine (eggplant)
4 tbsp. lemon juice
2 tbsp. tahini
1 tbsp. vegetable oil
4 tbsp. chopped parsley
1 clove crushed garlic and seasoning to taste
tomato and lemon slices to garnish

1. Pierce the skin of the aubergine, and bake in the oven at 200*C/400*F for 50-60 minutes, or until the skin is black and the inner flesh very soft.
2. When cool enough to handle, cut the aubergine in half, scoop out the flesh and mash well in a bowl.
3. Add the tahini, lemon juice, vegetable oil, parsley, garlic and seasoning and mix thoroughly to make a smooth paste.
4. This is best done in a blender for a smoother dip.
5. If necessary, thin the mixture with more lemon juice.

Lentil Burgers

1 lb. lentils, cooked
½ cup millet
½ cup sultanas
¼ cup whole meal flour
1 onion, finely chopped
2 tablespoons sunflower seeds
1 tablespoon yeast extract
1 teaspoon basil
soymilk

1. Combine all ingredients, except soymilk, and mix well. Add soymilk until mixture binds.
2. Form into balls and flatten in burgers.
3. Fry in oil or barbeque.

Sliced Potato Roast

4 potatoes, large	2 tsp. rosemary
3 tbsp. oil	1 onion or leek

1. Thinly slice the potatoes.
2. Pour 1 tbsp. oil over base of oven dish and lay half the onion rings or leeks in the dish.
3. Add layers of potato, sprinkling rosemary or basil between each layer.
4. Pour 2 tbsp. of oil over potatoes and spread the remainder of the leeks/onion rings over the top.
5. Bake at 250 degrees cup for 45 minutes covered with foil, then 15 mins uncovered.

Potato Pancakes

6 medium potatoes	half cup soy flour
2 small onions, finely chopped	2-3 tbsp. whole meal flour
4 stalks celery	salt and pepper to taste
1 cup wheat germ	Soy milk

1. Grate potatoes (uncooked) in a shredder.
2. Mix grated potatoes and other ingredients together in a large bowl.
3. Add extra soy flour if needed to make the mixture firmer, then shape into patties about ½ inch thick.
4. Bake at 375°F for 15-20 minutes or fry until golden brown.
5. Delicious with a salad.
6. As an alternative, fried pumpkin fritters are a delicious modification, and can often tempt a child to eat the much underestimated pumpkin! Simply exchange the grated raw potato for a similar quantity of mashed, cooked pumpkin.
7. Prepare and serve in the same way.

Basic Vegetable Kebab

2 large aubergines
½ lb. tiny (pickling) onions
2 green peppers
½ lb. (1 cup) button mushrooms
1 punnet cherry tomatoes
vegetable oil or margarine
1 pack vegetarian sausages
salt
freshly ground pepper

1. Slice the aubergines into ½ inch cubes, sprinkle with salt and place in a colander to drain while preparing other ingredients.
2. Skin the onions and cook them for 10 minutes in boiling water.
3. The rinsed aubergine cubes can also be added for 5 10 minutes of cooking without allowing them to become too soft.
4. Wash and remove the seeds from the peppers, and cut into ½-inch squares.
5. Clean mushrooms and tomatoes.
6. Slice the sausages into ½-inch thick rounds.
7. Skewer all the pieces of sausage and vegetable in attractive, colorful arrangements and baste with the oil.
8. Sprinkle with salt and pepper and cook under the grille or over a medium hot fire or barbecue.
9. Baste with more oil from time to time until ready to serve.

Sauces & Dressings

Basic French Dressing

¾ cup olive oil
⅓ cup cider vinegar (or lemon juice if to be used fresh)
½ tsp. brown sugar
1 tsp. salt
1-2 cloves garlic crushed or finely chopped
1 tsp. worcestershire sauce (check to make sure the ingredients do not include anchovies!)
⅛ tsp. dry mustard or ¼ tsp. mustard paste

1. Place all ingredients in a jar with a tight lid.
2. Shake well before using.

Ginger Salad Dressing

½ cup minced onion
½ cup peanut oil
⅓ cup rice vinegar
2 tablespoons water
2 tablespoons minced fresh ginger
2 tablespoons minced celery
2 tablespoons ketchup
4 teaspoons soy sauce
2 teaspoons sugar
2 teaspoons lemon juice
½ teaspoon minced garlic
½ teaspoon salt
¼ teaspoon black pepper

Combine all ingredients in a blender. Blend on high speed for about 30 seconds or until all of the ginger is well-pureed.

Yogurt Salad Dressing

1 (8 ounce) container plain low-fat yogurt
2 teaspoons lemon juice
1 teaspoon Dijon-style prepared mustard
1 teaspoon chopped fresh parsley
1 teaspoon chopped fresh chives

1. In a small bowl, beat together yogurt and lemon juice until smooth. Stir in mustard, parsley, and chives.
2. Refrigerate until ready to serve.

Vegan Thousand Island Salad Dressing

Just because you're vegan doesn't mean you have to give up on Thousand Island salad dressings, if that's one of your favorites! Just use a vegan mayonnaise to make a homemade vegan Thousand Island dressing. Delish!

1 cup vegan mayonnaise
⅓ cup ketchup
½ tsp. onion powder
dash salt
3 tbsp. sweet pickle relish

Whisk together all ingredients in a bowl.

Fruity Yogurt Dressing

1 cup raspberry or mixed berry yogurt
¼ cup fresh raspberries
¼ cup sliced strawberries
1 tbsp. honey
1 tsp. fresh mint

1. In a blender, combine all ingredients. Cover and blend on high speed about 15 seconds or until smooth.
2. Pour mixture into a serving bowl and serve immediately or refrigerate for up to 3 days for later use.

Try this as an ambrosia dip for fresh strawberries, pineapple chunks, grapes, kiwi and melon slices!

Tahini "Goddess" Dressing

½ cup tahini	3 cloves garlic
½ cup apple cider vinegar	½ cup water
¼ cup soy sauce	2 tbsp. dried parsley
1 tbsp. lemon juice	1 tbsp. sugar
½ tsp. salt	½ cup oil

1. Add all the ingredients, except for the oil to a blender or food processor and puree until smooth and creamy.
2. Slowly add oil until well mixed.
3. Dressing will be thick, but you can always add a bit more water if you prefer a thinner consistency.
4. Enjoy your wonderful homemade goddess dressing!

Vegan Caesar Salad Dressing Recipe

Most recipes for Caesar salad dressings are not vegetarian, as they often contain anchovies. Caesar dressings that you buy at the grocery are almost certainly not vegetarian and unlikely to be vegan! This easy Caesar salad dressing recipe, however, packs in all the flavor without the fish - it is both vegetarian and vegan.

2 cloves garlic
1 tbsp. lemon juice
1 tsp. vegetarian Worcestershire sauce
1 tsp. onion powder
1 tsp. Dijon mustard
½ cup olive oil
dash salt (optional)

1. Place all ingredients except oil in a blender or food processor.
2. Turn the machine on, and slowly add the oil, processing until dressing is smooth and creamy.

Entree

Sweet Potato and Lentil Schnitzels

5 tbsp. lentils
1½ kumera (orange colored sweet potato)
2 medium brown onions, finely chopped
half a stick of celery, finely chopped
2 cloves of garlic, crushed
4 tbsp. parsley, chopped
half a teaspoon dried oregano
quarter teaspoon nutmeg
pinch of salt and pepper
flour for dusting, soy milk, breadcrumbs

1. Cook lentils, drain and let cool.
2. Keep water for stock.
3. Cut kumera into thick slices, steam and let dry.
4. Fry onions with celery until brown.
5. Add garlic, oregano, nutmeg, parsley, salt and pepper.
6. Cook for 1 minute.
7. Mash kumera, stir in onion mixture and lentils and shape into ¼-inch thick flat patties.
8. Dust with flour, dip into soy milk and after draining, dip in breadcrumbs.
9. Fry for a few minutes on either side until golden brown. Drain on paper.

Nut Roast

4 onions, medium
5 tomatoes
2 carrots, medium, grated
3 slices whole meal bread, crumbed
Half a cup vegetable juice
½ cup hazelnuts, ground
½ cup cashews, ground
Fry onions in saucepan for 5 minutes.
Add tomatoes, grated carrot, breadcrumbs, vegetable juice and cook for 15 minutes.
Add nuts and turn out into a loaf tin.
Bake at 375 F for 30 minutes.

Tofu Burgers

1 lb. tofu, mashed
½ cup whole meal flour
¼ cup breadcrumbs
1 teaspoon basil
half teaspoon oregano
1 onion, finely chopped
1 tablespoon soy sauce

1. Combine all ingredients, kneading the mixture to help it hold together.
2. Stand a while to aid binding, then roll into balls and flatten into burgers.
3. Fry in oil or barbecue.

Chickpea Casserole

2 cups chickpeas, dried
1 tin of peeled tomatoes, liquidized
3 medium onions
2 cloves garlic
1 tbsp. vegetable oil or vegetable margarine
1 tbsp. whole meal plain flour or corn flour
half cup chopped fresh parsley
salt and pepper to taste

1. Soak chickpeas overnight.
2. Cook until soft.
3. Sauté onion, garlic until onion is transparent.
4. Add tomatoes, salt and pepper to the pan.
5. Cook on low heat for 10 minutes.
6. Thicken with flour.
7. Combine with chickpeas and cook for another 10 minutes, having strained the chickpeas first.
8. Remove from the heat and add the parsley.
9. May be served hot with other cooked vegetables or cold with salad.

Broccoli and Pine Nuts with Lemon Sauce

1 bunch broccoli, trimmed and cut into florets
2 tbsp. vegetable margarine
½ cup vegetable stock
2 tsp. corn flour
2 tbsp. lemon juice
3 tbsp. toasted pine nuts

1. Place pine nuts on a tray under a medium hot grille and shake tray until nuts are just browned.
2. This happens very quickly so do not leave for long.
3. Steam, blanch or microwave broccoli until bright green, tender, but still firm.
4. Heat margarine and stock in a sauté pan and bring to the boil.
5. Blend the corn flour into the lemon juice and whisk into the margarine/stock mixture a little at a time.
6. Bring back to the boil, whisking well, and simmer for 2 minutes.
7. The sauce should look smooth and glossy.
8. Fold in pine nuts.
9. Arrange broccoli in a heatproof dish, cover with foil and heat in oven for 10 minutes, or cover with plastic and microwave on high for 1 minute.
10. Pour sauce over and wait for the compliments!

Cashew Nut Loaf

2 large onions
2 tablespoons cold pressed vegetable oil
2 medium tomatoes, washed and diced
quarter teaspoon ground ginger
1½ cup unsalted cashew nut pieces
half cup fresh whole meal breadcrumbs
1 teaspoon mixed herbs
half cup of soy flour for binding (more if required)

1. Preheat oven to 375°F.
2. Sauté the onions in oil in a fry pan until tender.
3. Add the tomatoes and ginger to pan and simmer another five minutes.
4. Using a coffee grinder or food processor, grind the cashew nuts into a coarse meal.
5. Combine the whole meal breadcrumbs and herbs.
6. Mix dry ingredients, then add soy flour and stir in.
7. Add the onion and tomato mixture to the large mixture and stir well.
8. Brush vegetable oil around the inside of a loaf dish to avoid sticking and then pack the mixture into the loaf dish, eliminating any air pockets.
9. Bake until cooked through and light brown on top; usually about 45 minutes.
10. Serve with freshly made tomato sauce, and a variety of vegetable dishes.

Salads

Green Salad

1 cup crisp lettuce, torn into small pieces
1 cup chopped chicory
1 cup chopped green capsicum
half cup chopped chives or spring onions
half cup parsley chopped coarsely or broken into small flowers
1 cup chopped cucumber
1 cup small tender silver beet leaves, torn into small pieces
1 2 tomatoes peeled (optional) and diced

1. Mix ingredients in a large salad bowl and sprinkle with a basic French dressing just before serving.
2. This is a very popular, basic salad and one which is accepted easily by Non Vegetarians.

Raw Vegan Red Cabbage Salad

This salad is refreshing on a Summer's day, and can literally be made in 5 minutes

½ head of organic red cabbage
2 bunches of flat leaf Italian parsley
juice of 2 lemons, or more to taste
½ cup extra virgin cold pressed olive oil, or
  more to taste
8 spring (green) onions
cracked pepper and
sea salt to taste

1. Put cabbage, parsley, and onions into the food processor, and pulse quickly just a few times, until chopped roughly.
2. Toss with olive oil and lemon, and season to taste. It is that easy.
3. Treat the quantities as a rough guide – You can use a LOT more olive oil and lemon juice or you might like less.

Colourful Raw Green Superslaw

½ organic red cabbage
½ organic white cabbage
2 bunches continental flat leaf parsley
1 bunch organic kale
2 – 4 organic carrots
8 – 12 green spring onions

Dressing:
1 cup cold pressed extra virgin olive oil
¼ cup raw cashews soaked for about 4 hours
⅛ of fresh lemon juice or more to taste
4 cloves garlic
a pinch of Celtic sea salt

1. Chop up the vegetables individually in your food processor and toss in a salad bowl.
2. Blend the dressing in your high speed blender and toss through the vegetables.
3. Add in more lemon juice, olive oil and sea salt to taste to reach your perfect blend.
4. Serve on its own, or serve with boiled organic eggs or other clean protein.

This salad will keep for a few days in the fridge.

Vegan Cream of Spinach Soup

2 cups raw organic fresh spinach
1 cup organic zucchini (about 1 zucchini)
1 cup chopped red onions (about 1 medium onion)
¼ cup scallions/green onions – (about 6)
¼ cup flat leaf parsley (a handful)
¼ cup celery (1 large stalk)
4 cups strong vegetable broth
1 whole roasted garlic bulb
¼ – ½ cup raw cashews
dash of fresh lemon juice to taste
Celtic sea salt to taste

Place the garlic whole in the oven on about 400°F for about 30 minutes until soft and roasted.
In a saucepan sauté onions and scallions with a pinch of Celtic sea salt to bring out the sweetness until translucent.
Add in spinach, celery, zucchini and parsley and cook for about 5 minutes.
Add in stock and squeeze in roasted garlic pulp and bring to the boil.
Simmer for about 20 minutes until the veggies are cooked through.
Allow to cool slightly and then puree in the blender with the cashews and return to the stove to warm and serve.
Serve sprinkled with parsley and a grain ball. YUM!

Creamy Roasted Sweet Potato Soup

3 tbsp. cold pressed extra virgin olive oil
2 red onions quartered
4 lbs. sweet potato peeled and cut into large chunks
8 cups vegetable broth
½ - 1 cup raw macadamias soaked for 4-6 hours
whole raw macadamias for garnish
chopped cilantro/coriander to serve

1. Peel the sweet potato and cut into rustic chunks with the red onions.
2. Toss the vegetables in olive oil and Celtic sea salt.
3. Roast in a slow oven for about 1 hour so as not to get any burnt black bits.
4. Bring stock to the boil. Add in roasted vegetables and simmer for about 10 minutes.
5. Allow to cool slightly, and then place in batches with the raw macadamias.
6. Return to the stove, and simmer for a further 5 minutes. Season with Celtic sea salt to taste.
7. Garnish with some chopped coriander and some raw macadamias and devour!

Vegan Lemon Asparagus Soup

3 tablespoons of cold pressed virgin olive oil
1 large organic leeks washed thoroughly and thinly sliced
5 large organic red skinned potatoes scrubbed, not peeled and rustically chopped.
3 cups organic asparagus trimmed and chopped.
8 cups vegetable broth
1-2 tsp. Celtic sea salt
juice of 2 lemons – or more to taste
nutmeg to serve

1. Sautee the leeks in oil until soft and translucent.
2. Add the potatoes and the stock, and simmer until the potato is tender, and cooked through.
3. Add in the asparagus, and just blanch for only a couple of minutes until just tender. Be careful not to overcook them.
4. We want to preserve the vibrant green colour, and nutritional value. Allow the soup to cool slightly.
5. Then blend thoroughly, until smooth and creamy, Return to the stove, and reheat.
6. Season with Celtic sea salt, and then pour in the fresh lemon juice gradually – tasting periodically until you achieve your perfect blend.
7. Season with nutmeg and serve with an extra lemon wedge. YUM!

Raw Vegan Avocado Gazpacho

3 cups or 3 large avocados chopped
2 cups cubed cucumbers
1 cup fresh coriander
¼ cup chopped red onion
2 cloves fresh garlic minced
1 tbsp. / ½ small green chili chopped (for a bit of heat)
¾ cup filtered water to thin out to desired consistency.
¼ cup fresh lime juice (juice of 2 juicy limes)
1 tbsp. cold pressed extra virgin olive oil
1 tsp. sea salt

Garnish
1 avocado diced
2 chopped green onions
1 freshly diced tomatoes
¼ cup freshly chopped coriander

1. Place all the ingredients in your blender and puree until smooth.
2. Flavor to taste and chill before serving.
3. Serve with "all the toppings" or on its own in small ramekins or shot glasses.

Desserts

Baked Tofu Cheesecake

As an alternative to a rich cream cheese and egg cheesecake, this cake made with tofu (soy bean curd) is light and nourishing.

Crust:
10 wheat meal biscuits
Three quarters of a cup of vegetable margarine
1 teaspoon of vanilla essence

Filling:
1 tray of tofu
2 tablespoons golden syrup or maple syrup
juice of half a lemon
rind of half a lemon, grated
1 tablespoon tahini
1 teaspoon vanilla essence
half a cup raisins or soaked sultanas (soak in orange or lemon juice)
Cinnamon topping

1. Crush the biscuits finely and mix with melted margarine.
2. Press into cheesecake tin.
3. In a blender, combine the tofu, golden (or maple) syrup, lemon juice and rind, tahini and vanilla.
4. Blend.
5. Add raisins to the filling and spoon over the base.
6. Sprinkle with cinnamon.
7. Bake in a moderate oven for 25-30 minutes.
8. Cool in oven.
9. The cake is firmer if served two hours later.

Banana Ice

½ ripe banana per person

1. Peel bananas and lay them on a tray in the freezer over night.
2. Ensure that the bananas are cut into short lengths if they are curved.
3. When frozen, feed the bananas through a strong juicing machine, such as a "Champion".
4. Serve immediately as an iced dessert.

Holiday Pudding

½ cup currants
½ cup sultanas
½ cup raisins
½ cup chopped candied peel
2 tbsp. almonds, chopped and skinned
½ cup plain whole meal flour
½ tsp. salt
½ tsp. powdered nutmeg
½ tsp. ground ginger
1½ tsp. mixed spice
½ cup raw sugar
½ cup fresh whole meal breadcrumbs
½ cup vegetable suet or margarine
rind and juice of 1 lemon
4 tbsp. soy flour
4 tbsp. soy milk and rum mixed

1. Grease a 1.2 liter pudding basin and have ready a saucepan large enough to hold the pudding basin.
2. Put the fruit into a large bowl with the candied peel and the almonds.
3. Sift the flour, salt and spices on top of the fruit, then add the sugar, breadcrumbs and margarine or suet.
4. Mix well, then stir in the grated lemon rind and juice.
5. Add enough of the soy milk and rum to make a soft mixture which will fall heavily from the spoon when you shake it.
6. Spoon the mixture into the pudding basin, cover with a piece of non stick foil, and tie down.
7. Put the basin into the saucepan and pour into the saucepan enough water to come half way up the bowl.
8. Bring to the boil, then cover the pan and leave the pudding to steam gently for 4 hours.
9. Ensure that the water level remains constant.
10. Cool, then store the pudding in a cool dry place.
11. Steam the pudding again for 3 hours before serving, then turn it out onto a warm serving plate.
12. Flame with brandy if you like, or serve with custard or brandy butter.

Brandy Butter

½ cup vegetable margarine
½ cup soft brown sugar
2 tbsp. of either rum or brandy

Whip all ingredients together until creamy, and serve on top of the warm pudding.

Raw Vegan Ice Cream Bars

This is a raw decadent ice cream bar that tastes heavenly. Makes about 10 small ice cream bars.

Chocolate Pudding Ice cream Base

4 ripe avocados
1 cup raw cacao powder
1 cup agave nectar
½ cup water

Blend everything in a high-speed blender until completely smooth and transfer in ice cream molds. Freeze for at least 8 hours.

White Chocolate Shell

5 oz. raw shaved cacao butter
4 tbsp. raw coconut butter/coconut oil
6 tbsp. coconut milk powder (this is not a raw product, but you can substitute with lucuma, maca or yacon powder)
6 tbsp. agave nectar
½ tsp. ground vanilla powder

1. Place all the ingredients in a double boiler on medium heat and stir until everything melts and comes together.
2. Make sure you don't overheat the chocolate, you should be able to dip your finger in it without burning

To assemble take the ice cream sticks out of the freezer (make sure they are completely frozen) and dip in the chocolate. Hold the stick and let it drip for a few seconds as it hardens. Place on non-stick baking paper until the chocolate sets completely. Repeat until you cover all the ice cream bars. Once you are done, repeat this process again, so that you create a thicker shell. Wrap each ice cream bar in baking paper and store in a container in the freezer.

Vanilla Pudding Ice cream Base

6 young coconuts
½ cup coconut water
½ cup agave nectar
1 tsp. ground vanilla powder

1. Open coconuts and save water for drinking. Scrape out the soft coconut meat.
2. In a high speed blender combine the coconut meat, water, agave and vanilla and blend until you have a rich and smooth cream.
3. Transfer in molds and freeze for at least 8 hours.

Cacao Chocolate Shell

150 gr. raw shaved cacao paste
½ cup coconut butter/oil
½ cup agave nectar (or to taste)

1. Place all the ingredients in a double boiler on medium heat and stir until everything melts and comes together.
2. Make sure you don't overheat the chocolate, you should be able to dip your finger in it without burning!

As you can see from the picture, the chocolate shell is kind of fudgy and not hard like a chocolate shell. That happened because the chocolate seized when adding the agave, but that does not make it any less yummy! To stop this from happening it is safer to put the agave with the cacao paste and melt it together rather than melting the paste and then mixing in the agave. But still, because agave is a liquid there is always a risk that the chocolate will seize. You can also use dry sweeteners like stevia powder or palm sugar. Enjoy!

Drink to

Your Health

Drink to Your Health

by Walasia Shabazz

Whether starting/ending a fast, or just to supplement your meals, there are a number of simple & healthful beverages you can make at home with everyday ingredients in this chapter. Instead of consuming fake juices and sodas full of empty calories and refined sugars, invest in a juicer and/or blender. Along with plenty of water, these delicious drinks will increase your energy, keep your hair and skin glowing healthfully, and above all keep you hydrated.

There is a great debate with regard to sweeteners, but the fewer you use the better off you will be health wise, that's for sure. If you must sweeten, we recommend the use of Turbinado (Raw) sugar, Honey -or- Agave syrup and/or Grade B Maple Syrup if you're vegan. Beware of ingredients like sugar (white/refined), corn syrup, glucose and/or fructose. If you love "sodas" try mixing a sparkling water or club soda with your favorite fresh juice instead.

Water

When you're cleaning up your diet and are used to drinking a lot of sodas, alcoholic beverages and bottled/processed juices it can be tough to train yourself to drink at least 8 glasses of water per day. Try adding fresh mint to your pitcher of water, or slices of citrus – lemon, lime, orange or a combination of all three, or cucumber slices & fresh basil. These "tonics" have little or no calories, no added sugars, and will give a little boost to the taste for those who find water boring to drink.

Juicing

Most juicers come with some recipes, but here are a few combinations to set your juices off right. Fresh is best, but in winter months or cities where fresh fruit is not abundant, break out your blender & use some of the fruits from your frozen fruit aisle (make sure no sugar has been added to the package!) Tasty combinations include:

> From *The Hood Health Handbook: A Practical Guide to Health and Wellness in the Urban Community* also available from Supreme Design Publishing.

Milks & Smoothies
Do-it-Yourself Milk

Rice Milk/Nut Milk

1 cup uncooked organic long grain brown rice
8 cups water for cooking; more water for diluting
1 teaspoon salt
storage container for, glass preferred
   (like a mason jar)
blender
a nut bag (pause) or mesh strainer

Rice Milk – Wash rice. Put 8 cups of water in a pot bringing it to a boil over high heat. Pour in the rice. Cover the pot and lower the heat to let the water simmer. Cook for 3 hours. You will end up with something that looks a bit like a soupy rice pudding. Add the salt. In batches, fill your blender halfway with the rice mixture and halfway with water. Blend until very smooth. Strain twice through a fine mesh strainer into a mason jar. Continue on with the rest of the milk until you're finished, filling jars and screwing the lids on good and tight. Even with the extra water, the homemade rice milk ends up thicker than the product you might be used to. Just add a bit more water until it's the desired consistency. In order to make it more creamy add about 2 tablespoons of some type of oil to the batch (sunflower oil is good for this). Also if you want it slightly sweet add some maple syrup, honey or agave to the mix.

Nut Milk – In order to make nut milk, try using almonds or cashews. You want to soak them night before and use a ratio of one cup of nuts per 2 cups of water. Blend them all together and generally just follow the recipe for rice milk as there is no cooking of anything involved.

> From *The Hood Health Handbook: A Practical Guide to Health and Wellness in the Urban Community* also available from Supreme Design Publishing.

Better Than Cow's Milk

…With much the same results, the amount of water needed for blending will differ according to the oil content of the various nuts, seeds, grains or beans, how finely you grind and strain them, and the humidity that day. The results are best consumed fresh, but may be prepared in advance and will keep well in the refrigerator for a few days. For a quick cold milk substitute, use three or four ice cubes instead of half a cup of the water.

The following recipes are a general guide. You can adjust the sweetness (try adding dates, or use fruit juice instead of water), add flavoring (vanilla essence, ginger, carrots, carob powder, bananas or any fruit in season), or alter the liquid volume to suit your taste.

Basic Nut or Seed Milk Recipe

Use almonds, cashews, coconut, sesame, sunflower, etc. or try combinations.
½ cup nuts (if almonds, remove skins with boiling water).
2 teaspoons maple or other syrup (optional).
2 to 2½ cups water, or sufficient to produce the required consistency and concentration.

1. Blend using a little water to produce a creamy mix, continue adding the remaining water and blend for several minutes before straining through a thin cloth.
2. The remaining pulp can be blended again with a little more water.
3. [NB: straining produces a smoother texture, but also removes the bulk and fiber.]

Cashew Milk

½ cup raw cashew pieces
2 cups water
1 tablespoon maple syrup

Combine cashews with 1 cup water and maple syrup in blender.
Blend on high until thick and creamy.
Slowly add remaining water and blend on high for 2 minutes.
Strain if desired.

Macadamia Milk

1 cup macadmaia nuts, soaked 1 hour or more
3 cups filtered water
3 tablespoons agave nectar
2 tablespoons coconut butter (optional)
2 teaspoons vanilla extract (optional)
pinch of sea salt (optional)

1. In a blender, blend the nuts and water on high speed for about 2 minutes.
2. Add the rest of the ingredients and blend to combine.
3. Strain if you want it super creamy, or drink as is.

Grain Milk

This is less well known, but worth trying.
Rice milk can be made using well cooked rice.
For corn milk, use corn flour.
For oat milk, use rolled oats.
Use well cooked grain, add sweetener and/or flavoring if required and sufficient liquid to produce the right consistency. Blend until smooth. Chill.
Try mixing grains and nuts: e.g., rice and cashew milk.

Soy Milk

There are many good brands available, but this can also be made at home.
Soy milk may be used for hot or cold drinks, but tends to curdle if added to boiling liquid.
Soak 1 cup dry beans overnight.
Drain and blend until very smooth, using 2 to 3 cups of water.
Add the pureed beans to a large pot containing ½ cup of very hot water.

1. Cook on medium heat, stirring constantly to prevent the beans from sticking.
2. When foam suddenly rises, turn off immediately and pour through a thin cloth.
3. Press out the milk.
4. Bring to the boil, stirring constantly to prevent sticking.
5. Reduce heat and simmer for 7 to 10 minutes.
6. Taste and flavor.
7. Serve hot or cold.
8. The pulp remaining after the milk is extracted is called okra and is highly nutritious.
9. It can be used in breads, cakes, veggie burgers, casseroles, soups and pies.

Almonds - Sprouted, Blanched

Some people ask, "How do I sprout my own almonds?", "Why do I have to blanch the almonds?" or "How do you get a sweeter-tasting milk?" We have the answers to those questions right here.

How to Sprout:

When sprouting almonds, first rinse the almonds. Then put them into a bowl and cover with three times as much filtered water and let soak overnight (12 to 15 hours). Next day, drain and rinse the almonds. Put them back into the bowl (without water) and spread the almonds up the sides of the bowl a little. Let them sprout for 1 or 2 days, rinsing them twice a day. You will not be able to see the actual sprout unless you remove the skin, and then you will see it very clearly.

After they are sprouted, you can store them in the refrigerator in filtered water and change the water every two days to prevent fermentation. Keeps for up to a week.

Blanched Almonds:

To blanch almonds (without cooking them), first prepare a large bowl of cold water into which you have added two trays of ice cubes. Then heat up some other water to a boil, turn off the flame, and put in the sprouted almonds for 7 seconds. Time the 7 seconds, and stay with the pot. If you move away to do something else, you might not come back to your almonds in 7 seconds, and then you will have cooked them. Drain the almonds quickly through a colander and plunge the colander into the ice water. This stops the process of cooking immediately. The almond skins will then pop off easily when you push them between your thumb and forefinger.

Why is it necessary to remove almond skins?

Almond skins are not only bitter, but have a high concentration of tannic acid. Research has indicated that tannic acid may interfere with the body's uptake of iron. When you eat a lot of almonds, it might be a good idea to remove the skins. (If you are just having a handful, then you don't need to skin them.)

Raw Almond Milk

Serves 3-4
1 cup sprouted almonds, blanched (see Glossary)
3½ cups filtered water

1. Process almonds in the blender with ½ to 1 cup of water until well blended, then add balance of water and blend again.
2. Pour into a cotton or muslin bag or cloth and squeeze out all the milk.

This milk can be enjoyed as is or flavored in various ways (see suggestions below). Makes almost a quart. Keeps for up to 5 days in the refrigerator.

Nut/Seed Milk

4 cups water
1 cup almonds (soaked overnight)
¼ cup pumpkin seeds (soaked overnight)
1 tbsp. sesame seeds
1 tbsp. flax seeds
1 tbsp. hemp seeds

Blend well and strain through nut bag. Make sure the nuts/seeds are raw and organic!

Sweet Almond Milk

Serves 2-4
The flavored milks keep 1-2 days. After storage, the milk separates, so shake well before using. Save the leftover almond pulp to make cookies.

½ cup almonds
1 tablespoon agave nectar (or sugar)
½ vanilla bean (or ½ teaspoon vanilla extract)
2-5 cups water (2 ½-3 works well)

1. Blend the almonds first.
2. Add the agave, vanilla and water. Blend for a few minutes on high until pretty smooth. Add water, as needed
3. You can drink it like this leaving the fiber in. It is thickish this way though. You can strain yours to get a real milk consistency. Use a little cotton pouch, the texture of a pillowcase, and strain, as desired.
4. It last about 5 days or so in the fridge. You can flavor it with chocolate (cocao), strawberries, use it in smoothies, baking (this can be used in most desserts), ice cream, on a sandwich, in raw breads, in baking, or in raw cookies (or baked).

You can throw in some cocao, maple syrup, and pecans with the pulp, rolled balls of this in coconut flakes, dehydrated for about 2 hours and voila! Brownie cookies! It is so easy to make! You'll never go back to the carton!

Sweet Almond Milk II

1. Take plain almond milk, put into a blender with soaked dates and a little ground vanilla bean and blend well.
2. Make with as many or as few dates as you like.
3. Some people like it sweet and others prefer just a hint of sweetness.

Note: You can also try adding freshly ground lemon rind, pumpkin pie spice, nutmeg or cinnamon, or a combination. With experimentation you will hit upon a flavor combination which will taste delicious to you.

Exotic-Flavored Almond Milk

32 oz. of Sweet Almond Milk
¼ tsp. rosewater*
⅛ tsp. cardamom powder

1. Blend well.
2. Best with food-grade rosewater, with no additives.*

Smoothies & Shakes

Blueberry Greens Smoothie

Serves 1-2
2 cups water
1 cup spinach
1½ cups frozen or fresh blueberries
1 frozen banana
1 tablespoon EFA oil
2 tablespoons agave nectar

1. Put all ingredients into blender.
2. Blend it for about 1 minute or until the spinach is totally obliterated.

If you didn't use frozen fruit this smoothie will not be as thick. You can always add some ice to it if you like it chilled. Great for in the morning or even for dinner. Prep. time: 5 minutes

Sweet Greens Drink (No Bananas!)

1½ to 2 cups fresh apple or pear juice (about 7 apples or pears)
1 teaspoon to 1 tablespoon fresh ginger, minced
2 pears, cored, roughly chopped
1 small lemon or lime, peeled and deseeded
1 stalk celery, roughly chopped
2 large leaves Swiss chard, stalks removed and torn into pieces
2 large leaves of kale, stalks removed and torn into pieces

1. Place juice in a blender. Add all other ingredients and blend until smooth.
2. Makes: 1 to 2 servings, Prep. time: 5 to 15 minutes.

Vanilla Hemp Smoothie

Serves 1
1 crisp red apple, cored and chopped
½ banana
3 tablespoons hemp seeds
1 tablespoon coconut oil
1 teaspoon vanilla flavor
Water, as needed

Add all ingredients to blender and blend. Use enough water to get things moving and add more if you want it thinner. If you are not using a high speed blender, keep it going for a while to fully blend the apple skins.

Simple (No Sugar Added)

Spinach Smoothie

Serves 1
2 cups spinach
½ ripe banana
½ to ¾ cup frozen pineapple
¼ to ½ cup water (depending on desired thickness)

1. Throw everything in a blender and blend for about a minute.
2. If using frozen pineapple, you should make sure that this is closest to the blade so that it blends well.
3. After a while, you'll probably wean yourself off of needing the pineapple. But if you do, you may want to start freezing bananas to get that consistency the frozen fruit adds.

This juice is modified from various ideas. You don't always have to add steva, juice or agave like the other recipes. This is totally sweet enough on it's own.

Purple Power Coconut Water Drink

Makes: 2 to 4 small **wine glasses full**
fresh coconut water from one young Thai coconut
handful blueberries
handful black cherries
handful blackberries
2 pieces fresh Pineapple (optional)

1. Place all ingredients into a blender and blend.
2. The pineapple gives an extra boost of sweetness, however this is a rich and refreshing drink without it.
3. Amazing after a run or bike ride. Play around with the fruit, but the berry one is antioxidant packed!
4. You cut back on some of the fruit combos though and kept it simple: coconut water, blackberries, blueberries. It's sweet enough with just this and a drink this classy can only be consumed from a wine glass..
5. You can always freeze into Purple Power Popsicles! Amazing taste! Prep. time: 10 minutes.

Super Yummy Watermelon Coolie

Serves 1
½ watermelon, seedless and chopped
½ to ¾ cup frozen raspberries

Combine watermelon and blueberries in to a blender. Blend till smooth and enjoy! Prep. time: 3 minutes.

Seedy Coconut Smoothie

Serves 1-2

1 young Thai coconut
1 ounce blueberries, frozen if desired
3 tablespoons raw sunflower seeds
1 tablespoon raw pumpkin seeds
5 tablespoons coconut water
1 to 2 cups raw nondairy milk (or more coconut water)*

Break open your coconut. Drain the juice, scrape out meat making sure to cut off any hard bits. Blend all your ingredients until your desired consistency. Add sweetener if desired.

*You can change up this variation and use 2cups of raw milk, or you may choose to use all coconut water instead.

Cranberry Pineapple Smoothie

2 cups cranberries
1 unpeeled orange
1 cored apple
1¼ cups frozen pineapple
2 large carrots
water, if necessary

1. In a Vitamix or other powerful blender, make a fruity paste by combining the cranberries, unpeeled orange, and cored apple.
2. Blend in the frozen pineapple and carrots for a smoothie. This may require a little water.
3. This juice was inspired just messing around with fruits one day. Prep. time: 10 Minutes.

Vegan Brown Rice Banana Smoothie

2 cups homemade brown rice milk (or any rice milk)
2 organic frozen really ripe bananas
2 tbsp. agave nectar or more to taste
1 tsp. natural vanilla extract
pinch of sea salt

Throw everything in the blender and puree until smooth.

Nothing short of spectacular! OK, so it will be affectionately reserved for the "I don't care about carb overload" responses to future emotional emergencies. But hey, you might just have to pull it out in times of celebration too!

Kickin Kale Smoothie

Serves 1

The chia seeds are great for your skin and kale is a powerhouse of vitamins and minerals, also good for healing.

2 to 3 leaves kale
¾ cup pineapple juice
4 to 5 strawberries, grapes, or 1 small orange
½ banana
2 to 3 pieces of pineapple
1 tablespoon chia seeds, soaked overnight

1. First, blend the pineapple that you are using for your juice, or juice if that's what you are using.
2. Then add the kale by itself to the pineapple juice and blend until smooth.
3. Blending the kale first ensures that you don't get a big chunk while you're sipping later!
4. Add the rest of the ingredients and blend until smooth. Enjoy!

Popeye's Smoothie

Makes 4 cups

This is the easiest way for me to consume raw greens! Don't be turned off by the spinach/fruit combo; the greens cannot be tasted at all. This is a good way to get kids to eat more greens also.

3 cups of raw spinach	2 cups water
1 cup frozen strawberries	2 tablespoons agave nectar
2 frozen bananas	1 tablespoon EFA oil

1. Place all ingredients into a blender and blend it up till the bits of green are teeny tiny and the whole thing is smooth and without chunks.
2. Eating greens has never been easier! Enjoy! Prep. time: 5 minutes.

Delish Green Smoothie

Serves 1
½ cup orange juice
2 big kale leaves
½ banana
½ mango (optional)

Prep. time: 2 minutes.

Raw Cacao Smoothie

Serves 1
A delicious alternative to your regular chocolate shake.

½ banana, frozen
1 heaping tablespoon of cacao powder or nibs
1 heaping tablespoon of hemp seeds
1 to 2 cups almond milk -or-
2 tablespoons almond butter and 1 cup water
½ teaspoon vanilla extract or 1 vanilla bean
1 teaspoon flax seed oil
1 date, pitted

Combine all ingredients in a blender.
Prep. time: 15 minutes

Sunnyside Carotene Smoothie

Among the other great attributes of red grapes are the antioxidants resveratrol and quercetin. They are free radical scavengers and do a wonderful job of sweetening your veggie smoothies.

2 carrots, peeled and chopped
½ cup pineapple
½ banana
½ cup pineapple juice or coconut water
handful of red grapes
1 teaspoon flax oil, flax seeds or soaked chia

1. Chop then liquefy the carrots with the pineapple juice in a blender.
2. Once smooth, add the rest or your ingredients, except the flax oil.
3. Blend until smooth. Add flax and blend again for just a second. ENJOY! Prep. time: 10 minutes.

Strawberry Fields Power Smoothie

Serves 1
5 to 6 medium fresh or frozen strawberries
1 pear or ½ banana (or both)
¼ cup fresh coconut juice (or whatever juice you have on hand or water)
2 big handfuls fresh spinach leaves

1. Place in blender in order shown and blend. It's delicious!!!
2. You can substitute with other greens, and fruit, but this is great.
3. Frozen strawberries taste best.. unless you have really ripe strawberries. Prep. time: 5 minutes.

Living Green and Purple Smoothie

Serves 1

½ cup sprouted organic almonds
1 frozen package of pure acai
½ cup frozen organic blueberries
3-4 stalks of black kale washed and destemmed
½ very ripe banana (spotted with brown, or totally brown is preferable)
2 heaping tablespoons ground flax seeds
¼ cup filtered water
1 tablespoon organic goji berries (optional)

1. Put everything by the goji berries into your blender.
2. Blend until smooth.
3. Top with goji berries and enjoy! Prep. time: 10 minutes.

Almond Fruit Deliciousness

Serves 1
2 oranges
1 slice pineapple
1 cup frozen berries (try a mix of blueberries, strawberries and raspberries)
½ banana
¼ cup almonds/walnuts/pecans (pick one at first!)
Optional: 1 scoop raw protein powder

Just throw all the fruit and nuts into a blender and MIX! It works best to layer the fresh fruit with the frozen fruit and nuts so that the blender has enough liquid to mix it up. If needed, add a dash of water to allow your blender to mix it easier, but don't overdo it on the water, or it will get too watery. Prep. time: 5 minutes

Green Fruit Smoothie

Serves 2 to 4

4 large leaves organic romaine lettuce
1 pint blue berries
2 bananas

1. Place lettuce in blender and blend on high speed.
2. Blend in blueberries; then add the banana and blend.
3. Add spring water to desired thickness and enjoy! Prep. time: 5 minutes.

Super Antioxidant Workout Smoothie

Serves 1

Quick way to put back what you lost while working out or for pre-workout energy.

1 cup raw almond milk
¼ cup frozen blueberries
½ frozen banana
1 scoop raw protein powder mix
(you can use chocolate vega because it's vegan and raw)
1 scoop wheatgrass powder
1 scoop freeze dried acai powder (Sambazon)
ice

1. First blend the almond milk, blueberries and banana until smooth.
2. Next add the 3 powder scoops in. Blend again.
3. Add ice and blend until smooth.
4. You can get a decent texture with around 5 ice cubes.

You can blend everything together but it may be better to do it in three different steps because it prevents clumps of powder in the shake. Prep. time: 5 minutes.

Lemon Lime Shake

Serves 2

1½ Hass avocado, roughly chopped
1 large cucumber, roughly chopped
1½ cup young Thai coconut meat, roughly chopped
4 cup young Thai coconut water
¼ oz. Stevia powder
½ cup lemon juice
¼ cup lime juice
Small pinch of Himalayan salt

Combine all ingredients in a high-power blender such as a Vita Mix and blend well until completely smooth.

Raw Pecan Milk Shake

Serves 1

1 cup raw pecans
2 cups water
1 fresh young coconut, milk and meat removed
raw agave, to taste
½ pinch salt
Cinnamon (optional)

1. Soaking pecans and water in a bowl for 4 to 12 hours.
2. Use enough water to cover pecans plus a little more.
3. Once the pecans are soaked place in the blender.
4. Add fresh coconut milk, coconut meat, salt and cinnamon and blend until smooth.
5. Taste and add agave nectar to taste.
6. To thin the consistency of the shake you can add more water. Enjoy!
7. Prep. time: 10 minutes (excludes soaking).

3 O'clock Green Smoothie

Serves 2

¼ cup raw almonds, soaked in water for 4-8 hours
3 cups water
2 pitted dates
2 roughly chopped peaches
4 large leaves romaine lettuce, chopped
¼ English cucumber, skin on, chopped
4 frozen strawberries
2 tablespoons hemp protein powder
2 tablespoons ground flax seeds

1. Place all ingredients in a blender, and blend until smooth. Makes 2 servings.
2. Fill a glass bottle to leave in the fridge at work until you need an afternoon pick-me-up.
3. Some great additions: cinnamon or fresh mint.
4. Substitutions: use other raw nuts in place of the almonds – cashews would be great!
5. Prep. time: 10 mins.

Island Fantasy Smoothie

Serves 1

⅓ cup coconut milk
½ fresh mango, peeled and cut into slices
¼ fresh papaya, peeled and cut into chunks
6 fresh strawberries
2 dates, pitted and chopped
1 teaspoon pure maple syrup

1. Blend all ingredients together.
2. Feel free to add water or raw almond milk to thin if the smoothie is too thick. Enjoy! Prep. time: 10 min.

Energy-boosting Fruit Juice Smoothie

Serves 2

3 organic carrots
2 organic apples
1 orange
1 organic banana
1 tablespoon organic ground flax meal
1 tablespoon agave nectar or pure maple syrup
½ to ¾ cup frozen pineapple
1 teaspoon pure vanilla extract

1. Juice carrots, apples and orange.
2. Pour juice into blender. Add banana, flax meal, sweetener, pineapple and vanilla.
3. Blend until smooth.
4. Enjoy any time! Prep. time: 8 minutes.

Cherry Apple Sauce Smoothie

Serves 1

1 cup of favorite apple sauce (or try one that comes mixed with other fruits)
1 large banana
½ of strawberries
½ cup blueberries
1 tablespoon of cinnamon

Dice banana for easy blending. Then combine all ingredients into blender, and blend until smoothie quality. That simple. Enjoy! Prep. time: 5 mins.

Carrot, Apple and Beet Milk Shake

Serves 1

½ cup Almond Milk
1 cup of mixed carrot, apple and beet juice

Mix the freshly made carrot, apple and beet juices with the Almond Milk.

The Best Smoothie

Serves 1

1 large banana
1 cup frozen blueberries
2 tablespoons soaked hemp seed
1 tablespoon ground cacao nibs
2 tablespoons carob powder
1 tablespoon maca powder
spring water to desired consistency

1. Please use all organic ingredients and blend until smooth. Enjoy! Prep. time: 5 minutes.

Rejuvenation

Serves 1

½ banana
1 pitted date, chopped
½ Pink Lady apple, peeled and chopped
½ mango
⅓ cup raw coconut cream
papaya nectar or water

1. Blend ingredients until smooth, adding as much papaya nectar or water as needed to achieve desired consistency.
2. Prep. time: 5-10 minutes

Saporific Purple Smoothie

Serves 1

1 Brazilian papaya (the little guy) OR ¼ Caribbean papaya (the big guy), seeded and peeled
½ ripe banana
2 dates, pitted and chopped
1 cup frozen blueberries

1. Throw it all in a blender and blend away until smooth.
2. You may have to "help" the Vita-Mix along with a few prods of the rubber spatula in the blender.
3. Be careful though, or you might end up with chunks of rubber.
4. Also, for an even thicker smoothie, chop the banana and throw it in the freezer for a while, then blend; it becomes almost like sorbet! Prep. time: 5 minutes tops.

Young Alive Green Shake

Serves 2
½ large cucumber
1 oz. lime juice
6 oz. grapefruit juice
1 Hass avocado
½ lb spinach
4 oz. raw coconut milk
1 tsp. Doc Broc's Green Powder
1 tsp. Soy Sprout Powder
10 drops PuripHy pH Drops
4 sprigs of fresh mint
14 cubes purified water ice

Combine all ingredients in a high-power blender such as a Vita Mix and blend well until completely smooth.

Rich Vegan Horchata

⅓ cups long grain Brown rice such as Basmati
½ cup plus 2 tablespoons blanched almonds
A 3-inch piece of cinnamon stick
1¼ cups hot water
½ cup turbinado sugar, plus more to taste
1 cup cold vanilla or plain almond milk
dash of Mexican or Tahitian vanilla extract

1. In a large bowl, combine the rice, almonds, cinnamon stick and water.
2. Cool, cover and refrigerate overnight.
3. Pour into a blender, add sugar and blend on high for several minutes, until the mixture is as smooth as possible.
4. Strain through a sieve or colander lined with cheesecloth, pressing on the mixture until only a dry pulp remains.
5. Pour into a pitcher then add the almond milk.
6. You may add more sweetener or vanilla to taste, if needed. Serve "on the rocks" or chilled.

4 Roads Trini Peanut Punch

28 oz. of chilled soy or almond milk
¾ cup of smooth peanut butter
Turbinado (raw) sugar to taste

1. Blend until peanut butter is evenly distributed.
2. For a spicy punch add a dash of ground nutmeg, cinnamon, allspice and/or ground ginger.

From *The Hood Health Handbook: A Practical Guide to Health and Wellness in the Urban Community* also available from Supreme Design Publishing.

Coconut Water

If you've ever seen the green coconut (still covered with its husk) or "young coconut" in the store & wondered what it was & how to use it, the water inside is fragrant & healthful. Using a large, sharp knife, cleaver or machete, the top of the coconut is hacked off, water poured into the blender, shell cracked in half, inside "jelly" scraped out with a spoon then blended with the water for a unique and delicious treat. Coconut water is full of electrolytes, vitamins and minerals – during the Vietnam conflicts coconut water was even used as a temporary substitute for blood during transfusions while the injured waited for plasma to arrive. The coconut water is cooling, easily digestible, cleanses the urinary tract & bladder, rehydrating, rich in mineral salts and is said to improve mental concentration.

Coconut water can be blended with almond or rice milk and honey or Grade B syrup to relieve fatigue, nervousness, constipation, male sterility, or to protect against osteoporosis. When the water is mixed with lemon juice only, it can prevent nausea or vomiting, loss of appetite, and even eradicate gastrointestinal worms.

Irish Moss

This is a specialty of the Caribbean (especially Jamaica), so if you want to make it yourself, you may have to visit a Caribbean grocery or order the Moss online from an importer. This beverage is said to increase the virility and stamina of men.

½ lb Irish Moss	2 tbsp. Vanilla Extract
½ cup Hemp Oil	½ teaspoon Nutmeg
1 can. Coconut Milk	4 quarts Water
⅔ lb Turbinado Sugar	

1. Wash the moss in the sink to remove sand or foreign matter.
2. Bring water to a boil and then add moss and hemp oil.
3. Let the ingredients simmer at a low temp for about one hour.
4. Strain the liquid into another container and separate the boiled Irish moss from the drink, discard.
5. Add the rest of the ingredients to the mix then allow it to chill in the fridge for at least four hours.

Note: Because the thickness of the drink may vary, you may have to dilute this mixture with more water to suit your liking. Some flavor the drink with peanut butter, strawberry nectar or ground nuts such as cashews. Don't be afraid to experiment with a new combination!

Sorrel (Jamaica)

Brewed from the dried blossoms of red Hibiscus, Jamaica (pronounced Haa-My-Kuh) is a deliciously tart beverage enjoyed in many countries. Mexicans and other Spanish speakers call it Jamaica, while in Jamaica and other Caribbean cultures, it's called Sorrel. The drink was popular in ancient Egypt, even among the Pharoahs.

Today in Egypt and Sudan, the drink is called Karkade and is used to toast at weddings. In Senegal it's called Bissap and is the national beverage. Sorrel or Jamaica is sold in "Hispanic" markets either in bulk or with the packaged spices, or in bulk at Caribbean shops.

1 pound sorrel
2-4 oz. fresh ginger, peeled and grated
2 quarts water
Turbinado sugar to taste
8 allspice grains

1. Wash sorrel thoroughly, using the fingers to lift it from the water so any sediment falls to the bottom.
2. Put into stainless steel container.
3. Scrape the ginger then grate it and add to the sorrel along with the allspice grains.
4. Boil water and pour over sorrel mixture.
5. Allow to sit 4-6 hours. Strain it & discard the sorrel, then sweeten to taste and serve over ice.

Ginger "Beer"

Made popular in the states by the brand "Reeds" ginger beer which is a sparkling Ginger soda sweetened with Pineapple, the original Ginger Beer or Ginger Brew of the islands is a 'flat' beverage but can be mixed with sparkling water to recreate the soda-style if you like.

8 tablespoons of Turbinado sugar
1 pound fresh ginger
2½ quarts water

1. Puree ginger and water in blender. Let it sit for a day.
2. Add sugar to your taste, mix thoroughly then serve over ice.

Earthly Pleasures

We all love fresh juices, but either don't have the time and leave it to the juice bars, or we are just getting started and not sure what juices to go for! To start, juices are a great source of minerals and vitamins. Your produce should be organic and under two days old (locally grown).

One type of juice variation that works miracles are GREEN DRINKS. Green, green, green, we can't get enough of it when healing! Though I have the Samson Juicer, the Breville Juice Fountain Plus is perfect for green drinks. The Vita-Mix is the best blender for blending whole fruits and greens.

Popular Ingredients

Carrots and carrot tops, beetroot and beet greens, ginger, cucumber, celery, lettuce, spinach, parsley, wheatgrass, kale, aloe vera, sweet peppers, cabbage, etc.

How to Prep Vegetables

Clean vegetables and soak in water for a few minutes before juicing. Pour two tablespoons of vinegar into the water to kill microbes and reduce fertilizer impurities.

Chlorophyll cleans and rebuilds our cells quicker than anything!

Chlorophyll [the green molecule in leafy greens] can protect us from carcinogens like no other food or medicine can. It acts to strengthen the cells, detoxify the liver and bloodstream, and chemically neutralize the polluting elements themselves.

The quickest way to break free of addictions is to drink green juices.

What's your addiction? Fried food? Cigarettes? Sugar or alcohol? The bakery? Perhaps the butcher? I'm trusting you're not making it with the candlestick maker... though I have nothing against the candlestick maker. But, test the power of green for yourself, and you may never go back.

Green Juices

Why is GREEN so different?

Because it works in the same way that soap strips oil from your hands. Chlorophyll packages the trash in your tissues into droplets (called micelles) which your blood then washes away. Otherwise this 'unnatural trash' (like pesticides and drugs, even tumors) will choke our cells to death.

We need to juice lots of greens (dark green leaves and wheatgrass) for their chlorophyll to pull toxins, tumors and trash from your tissues. Eating the greens is not enough.

Fountain of Youth

Why age prematurely when you can stay younger longer!

Put through a juicer:
wheatgrass or barley grass, fresh
1 Cucumber
4 Celery stalks
1 Apple
2 inch Ginger
Spinach, at least a handful

All the juicing books agree, these ingredients make the world's finest juices, and they're the quickest of all to prepare! Remember Variety Rules! Blend different fruits and greens each day.

Cucumber, juiced with its high-silica green skin, is for healthy bones, teeth, muscles, skin and all connective tissue.

Celery with its natural sodium is for joints, nerves, and restoring electrolytes after exercise.

Living grasses are so much more powerful in giving energy, focus and a soft skin, than the dead green leaves from the produce store, like spinach.

The grass is cut with scissors seconds before, so it's still GROWING up to the moment of juicing. And nothing to wash. In fact, it's best not to wash fresh greens you pick yourself because chances are they're rich in Vitamin B12, made by microbes living on the greens. Don't wash wild weeds either.

Spinach builds strong bones and a clean colon, but Popeye, scientists and the USDA were quiet about that.

Only wash the small greens like alfalfa and broccoli where you need to rinse the hulls off. These greens are very juicy.

Remember, an ounce of prevention is cure...

All dark green leaves – such as kale, collard, spinach, lettuce – are a good magnesium source because every molecule of chlorophyll has a magnesium atom at its core.

Note: See *The Restorative Power of Fresh Juices* directly behind this section, as well as the Appendix on *The Essential Mineral Guide*, as we share with you ways to build your body with the use of minerals, to reduce risks of dis-EASE associated with heart attack and stroke, combat arrhythmia and angina, and lower your blood pressure.

Lemon Ginger Blast

Put through a juicer:
1 peeled lemon (include the peel if organic)
2" fresh ginger, sliced (add more if you prefer)
1 apple
1 to 2 cups water
1 teaspoon of cayenne pepper (or start with less and increase the amount of Cayenne Pepper over time as you get used to the taste.)

Health Benefits: Lemon has antiseptic qualities and stimulates your liver. It is also full of antioxidants, and we can never get enough of those! Known for its ability to help calm digestive disorders, ginger is a root that has been used in cooking and for medicinal purposes for centuries. Ginger also has anti-inflammatory properties, and helps to lessen cholesterol absorption in the body. This is the sort of healthy habit we need to cultivate, and we should encourage our friends and family to do the same!

Fruits, Vegetables & Leafy Green Juices

Green Healing Properties

Green Smoothies are the first step to end food addiction. How is weight lost? By losing the DESIRE for junk food. What forces you into a bakery or hamburger joint is CRAVING. You've GOT to have it.

When your cells get what they need, and your brain, and emotions, the desire for junk falls away one step at a time – like leaves falling from a tree in autumn. The first to go should be sugar.

Beets the Best!

Serves 3-4
The addition of the sweet fruit and the sweet(ish) carrots make this one not just palatable but supremely delicious!

Juice the following:
1 beetroot (bulb only)
4 medium carrots
3 oranges
6 apples
Small bunch of parsley
4 strawberries (these make all the difference)

Raw V-8 Juice

Celery, tomatoes, red bell pepper, broccoli, carrot, cucumber, parsley, cilantro, spinach, romaine lettuce, lemon, red onion, garlic, ginger, pinch Himalayan salt.

Cantaloupe Strawberry Cooler

Serves 2-3
1 whole cantaloupe, pref. organic and local
   (for juicy freshness!)
2 cup strawberries, cleaned and hulled

If you want a cold drink, have your cantaloupe in the fridge. You may want to freeze the strawberries also.

1. Clean and cut the melon in half. Scoop out the seeds and discard. Using a big spoon, scoop out the flesh and put it into your high-speed blender (Vitamix works great!).
2. Be sure to catch all the juice that comes out when you're scooping and add that to the blender.
3. Place strawberries in next.
4. Place lid on blender and blend on high for about 1 minute, or until the cantaloupe and strawberry have turned to juice.
5. If you have a dryer melon, you might need to add a little water to get it moving.
6. Works best with really ripe cantaloupe and frozen strawberries). Enjoy! Prep. time: 5 minutes.

Super Woman Pomegranate Cranberry Juice (Raw)

Serves 1
1 pomegranate, seeded
1 to 1½ cups fresh cranberries
1 apple (red/gala/pink lady-any sweet variety-not
   grannies; optional)
1 beet (optional)

In a juicer, process pomegranate seeds, then cranberries, then apple, then beet. (The order doesn't really matter, but if you use a beet, add it last to push any pulp through.)

Green Vegetable Cocktail

1 handful spinach leaves
½ cup flat-leaf parsley leaves
1 rib celery
½ cucumber
½ ripe pear
½ green apple
¼ ripe papaya, seeds removed
1 piece (1 inch) ginger

This juice is actually pretty sweet, but you can always add another half an apple and/or pear. Enjoy! Prep. time: 5 to 10 minutes

ABC Energy Booster

Serves 1

1 apple (green for a sour taste, red or yellow for sweet)
1 beetroot
2 carrots

Combine into a juicer and juice away. It is super good, and a pretty color too!!!!

Beet-Carrot-Apple Juice

Serves 1

1 beet, washed & trimmed
2 red delicious apples, washed & stems removed
2 huge (3-4 normal sized) carrots

1. Cut up all produce so it'll fit in your juicer.
2. You can add more carrots or less, depending on your taste. One giant glass of goodness. Enjoy!
3. Prep. time: only a few minutes.

Kale Lemonade

Serves 1

1½ medium sized lemons (remove the rind for a less bitter taste)
2 medium sized apples
4 stalks celery
4 large kale leaves
1 inch ginger (optional)

1. Cut up lemons and apples so they fit into the juicer. Put in ginger first for a bit of zing.
2. Next, add the lemon and apples, followed by the kale.
3. Last, but not least, juice the four stalks of celery and voila! Delicious kale lemonade!
4. Feel free to add more apple if you'd like it sweeter.
5. Prep. time: 5 minutes.

Green "Machine"

Serves 1

½ sweet potato, chopped
1 carrot, chopped
large handful kale, chopped
1 small apple, chopped
½ pear, chopped

Run all ingredients through a centrifugal juicer. It is easiest if you juice "soft" fruits/veggies (the kale and pear) in between "hard".

The resulting juice is absolutely delicious. It tastes vaguely like the green "monster" juice that some companies sell. Prep. time: less than 5 minutes.

The Best Beet Juice!

Serves 1-3

3 beets
6 apples
1-2 inches of ginger
½ to 1 lemon

Juice the beets, apples, and ginger (peeled if you want) and then squeeze the lemon juice in...stir and enjoy!!!

Apple-Carrot-Grape Juice

Serves 1-2

1 cup green grape
2 carrots
2 medium sweet apples (or three small)
water, as needed

1. Wash all produce. Cut the carrot and apple into smaller pieces (carrots in half, apples in quarters for Vita-Mix, smaller for less powerful blenders).
2. Remove the grapes from their stem.
3. Place the grapes, then apples, and finally carrots into the blender.
4. Add enough cold water to cover the grapes.
5. Attach lid and blend on high for 30 seconds to a minute, or under everything is smooth.
6. Add more water, if needed, to help with blending.
7. Pour into a glass and enjoy!
8. The grapes and apples work well to cover up the carrot-veggie flavors, so this would be good for kids.

Green Drink

This is a slightly modified recipe from Dr. Kirschner, who wrote extensively about the health benefits of live, green juices in the 1930s.

1 pineapple, juiced
15 almonds, soaked
4 dates, soaked and pitted
2 heaping tbsp. of soaked sunflower seeds
1–2 large handfuls of fresh green leaves (see below)
½ tsp. kelp powder

1. Juice 1 pineapple, then put into the blender with all the other ingredients and blend well.
2. Makes approximately 1 quart of a delicious and nutritious drink. Best consumed the same day.

Note: The green leaves can be one or a combination of watercress, parsley, spinach, arugula, beet tops, etc. or you can use wild herbs if you can get them. Dr. Kirschner had his own garden of wild edible weeds, such as lamb's quarters, purslane, comfrey, chickweed, filaree, malva, dandelion, etc.

Variation: This drink can also be made with just the pineapple juice blended with the green leaves.

Greens & Apples

Serves 2
2 collard greens leaves
2 kale leaves
handful of spinach
2 stalks of celery
2-3 Granny Smith Apples

Juice all ingredients in a juicer. Pour into a shaker with ice and mix well. Enjoy! Prep. time: 10-15 minutes

Green Drink II

Serves 1-2
1 lemon
½ cup parsley,
chopped 1 rib of celery
2 big handfuls of Spinach
1 pince of peeled ginger
1 medium cucumber
2 apples preferred amount of ice cubes (which is of course, optional)

Variation of Ingredients:
Serves 3-4
2 apples
Juice of ½ lemon
2 cups spinach
2 cups cucumber
1 head of celery
1 bunch parsley
½ inch or teaspoon ginger root
Juice of 1 lime

Alkalizing Lemon ~ Lime Water

Lemon and lime makes it easy to like water. A natural cleanser, containing Vitamin C and Alkaline, lemon and/or lime water daily is the best thing you can do to increase your alkaline intake.

2 lemons, peeled   32 oz. water (alkaline pref)
2 limes, peeled   or as needed
ice cubes

1. Buy fresh lemons and limes and store them in your refrigerator for later use.
2. Fill a pitcher with alkaline water (purified tap water or bottled water if you so desire).

Orange Blossom

Serves 2
2 oranges
½ cantaloupe
2 small golden beets
2 large juicing carrots

1. Put all of the ingredients in juicer.
2. Then, pour the juice in a cocktail shaker to completely mix, and enjoy! Very high in Vitamin A and C.
3. Prep. time: 5-10 minutes.

Raw Fruit Juice

4 medium apples
1 large Valencia orange
1 medium banana
tiny piece of ginger (can omit)

Cut into pieces small enough for your juicer and juice!

Lemonade with Rosemary

1 liter of water
¾ cup of Turbinado (Raw) sugar
1 lemon in slices
12 tbsp. of fresh lemon juice (3 big juicy lemons)
1 little sprig of Rosemary

1. Cut the lemon in slices and put them on a little tray that you put in the freezer.
2. Put the water, together with the sugar, the rosemary and 3 tbsp. lemon juice in a pot and cook for 6-7min.
3. Let cool completely, add the rest of the juice, mix and then filter.
4. Filter in a bottle and let cool in the fridge.
5. Serve with rosemary and frozen lemon slices. Enjoy!

Watermelon Cocktail

half medium watermelon   fresh mint sprigs
1 tbsp. lemon juice   finely sliced orange peel
¼ cup sugar

1. Use a small round scoop to shape the melon flesh into balls.
2. Put them into a bowl and carefully stir in the lemon juice and sugar.
3. Chill for at least half an hour before serving.
4. Serve in individual bowls, garnishing each bowl with mint and some finely sliced orange peel.

Carrot/Vegetable Juice

6 to 8 carrots
1 stalk of celery (cut into 1 inch pieces)
1 or 2 beet(s)
some green leaves from spinach, kale, lettuce or cabbage

1. Run 6 to 8 carrots, celery, beet(s) in addition to some green leaves from spinach, kale, lettuce or cabbage through a juicer.
2. You may vary the number of veggies as well as the quantity to create many different flavors.
3. Find out which combinations you do like best. Enjoy!

Grapefruit & Prune Juice

1 cup grapefruit juice
6 prunes, soaked overnight

Put fresh grapefruit juice into the blender, add pitted prunes and blend well.

Diablo Carrot Beet Juice

8 large carrots
2 large beets
1 hot chili pepper, stem cut off
3 garlic cloves, peeled
3 inches ginger, peeled

1. Wash your carrots and beets.
2. Cut into decent sizes so that they fit into your juicer.
3. Juice all ingredients. Enjoy the taste sensation!
4. Do not drink this too much! The beets and chilies can be quite a dangerous combo if taken too often, if you know what we mean. Prep. time: 5 minutes.

Velvet Ginger Lemon Cocktail

1 whole organic lemon well scrubbed
1 cup freshly squeezed lemon juice
1 cup agave nectar
1 tbsp. of freshly grated ginger, or more to taste
fresh mint leaves
6 – 8 cups of filtered water or sparkling mineral water

1. Place the agave and lemon juice in a saucepan until dissolved. Allow to cool.
2. Place this "syrup" in the blender with the whole lemon and freshly grated ginger and blend until frothy.
3. Stir through the desired amount of water and serve garnished with fresh mint leaves. You could add more freshly grated ginger for an extra punch.

Aloe Vera

You won't need much to get started on your Aloe and juicing journey, just some great fresh fruit and vegetables of your choice, or those we have suggested here, a juicer, an aloe vera plant (bought from a reputable nursery to ensure it is actual Aloe Vera; not that GMO stuff), and you're on your way.

Making the Aloe Gel. Firstly get a nice size Aloe Vera plant from a reputable plant nursery. Cut a few thick fleshy leaves at the base near the stem. Rinse the cut part of the leaf thoroughly, peel off outer layer of skin. Rinse the remaining gel to get rid of any latex residue. Put the gel into a blender and add a little Vitamin C powder or Citric Acid powder to stabilize the gel. If it is too thick to blend, just add a little purified water.

Please take note: for internal use of Aloe Vera make sure you rinse off the brown exudate, called latex, from the open cut of the leaf as well as the gel, as this can have a strong (and usually unwanted) laxative effect. If done properly you shouldn't have a problem. I have been using Aloe Vera for years now, and by being meticulous about rinsing it properly I haven't had an issue with it. Usually keeps in the fridge for a few weeks, depends on your fridge of course.

5 Aloe Vera Juice Recipes That Make You Feel Great

The following 5 recipes are just to get you started, so go ahead and experiment with your own favorite fruits and vegetables and don't forget the Aloe. It's good to juice different fruits and greens each day and if you're in the market for a juicer, Breville Juice Fountain Plus is one of the best and is reasonably priced around $150.

About The Raw Ingredients:

Apples: A good source of Vitamin A in the form of Beta-Carotene, Vitamin C, vitamin K and Folate, plus smaller amounts of Vitamin B1 (thiamine), B2, B3, Biotin and Vitamin E.

A note on Apples Pips/Seeds: Apple pips contain small amounts of Cyanide. While you would need to eat an awful lot of apples to suffer any ill effects, I like to remove the apple cores along with pips when juicing.

Beetroot: A good source of Folic Acid and Vitamin C, plus they contain small amounts of Vitamins B1, B2, B3, and Vitamin A in the form of Beta-Carotene.

Carrots: Very high in Vitamin A - this comes in the safe form of Beta-Carotene which the body is able to convert to Vitamin A as required. Also contains Vitamin K and Vitamin C, plus smaller amounts of the B complex vitamins and Vitamin E.

Cranberries: Rich in Antioxidants and the chemical Quinine which is used to treat arthritis.

Ginger: Stimulates circulation and aids digestion it can also ease motion sickness and nausea.

Oranges: As well as being an excellent source of Vitamin C, orange juice contains Vitamin A, Potassium, Calcium, and Phosphorous. It even contains small amounts of all the essential amino acids which the body can use to make and repair healthy tissue and muscles.

Papaya: Known as "the medicine tree" in Africa, rich in Beta-Carotene and Soluble Fibre, while papain, an enzyme extracted from papaya, aids digestive problems.

Pears: Promote cardiovascular and colon health. The Copper in pears stimulates white blood cells to fight infections.

Pineapple: An excellent source of Vitamin C, Folate, Vitamin A, vitamin K, and B complex vitamins (not B12) and Bromelain which is a powerful digestive enzyme that can destroy bad bacteria and parasites, help digest protein, and may prevent the formation of blood clots. It is also a natural anti-inflammatory and is known to reduce swelling and inflammation in the body, beneficial for arthritis suffers, and to promote healing after injury.

Cranberry Quencher

For those of you lucky enough to have this powerful fruit available to you fresh, we have included this recipe. Genuine cranberry juice is a powerful weapon in fighting colds and flu as well as being renowned for its benefits to kidney function. Fresh cranberry juice is far superior nutritionally to the bottled on-the-shelf variety.

2 handfuls cranberries
2 tablespoons Aloe Vera Gel
freshly juiced apples, to fill the glass

1. Put ingredients though a juicer.
2. Drink immediately.

Carrot-A-Licious

This one is a definite family favourite. Easy to drink, sweet and downright yummy.

2 carrots
2 green apples (or any apples you have)
1 orange (peeled)

Put ingredients though a juicer, add 1 tablespoon aloe vera gel, drink immediately.

Pineapple Paradise

I'm very partial to this combination. I also sometimes add a few tablespoons of Coconut Milk to increase the anti-bacterial and anti-viral content. This is a must-try.

1 to 2 cups fresh pineapple
1 carrot
1 green apple
2 tablespoons aloe vera gel

Put ingredients though a juicer, drink immediately.

Zippy Zinger

If you love the tropics, you'll love this one. Easy on the tummy.

1 piece of ginger (to taste)   2 pears
2 carrots   2 tablespoons aloe vera gel

½ small Red Papaya (known as Pawpaw in Australia)

Put ingredients though a juicer, add 2 tablespoons Aloe Vera Gel, drink immediately.

Beetroot Bliss

A great pick-me-up tonic. If you are unfamiliar with beetroot juice go easy at first, use just a small wedge. It can be a little overpowering. Tastes rich and earthy.

1 qt. small beetroot   1 stalk of celery
2 large carrots   2 tbsp. aloe vera gel

Put ingredients though a juicer, drink immediately.

Mellow Green Juice

Serves 2
½ bunch spinach (just under ½ lb juice)
½ bunch celery (½ lb of juice)
½ large cucumber (⅓ lb juice)
1 bunch romaine lettuce (1 lb romaine lettuce juice)
⅓ bunch parsley (1 oz. fresh juice)

Put ingredients though a juicer, drink immediately.

Young Adult Green Juice

Serves 2
¾ of whole bunch celery (¾ lb juice)
1 whole bunch spinach (just under 1 lb juice)
1 large cucumber (¾ lb juice)

Put ingredients though a juicer, drink immediately.

Organic Herb and Spiced Teas

There are a few herbal remedies every household should have on hand for everyday health troubles. Avoiding aspirin, acetaminophen, products such as Pepto-Bismol etc. will increase your overall health long range Most of these ingredients can be found at your health-food grocery store or you can certainly order the dry herbs online.

Ginger Root (fresh). Prepare with hot water (peel it first) and take as a tea for stomach trouble, nausea, sore throats, flu symptoms & colds. Can be taken with garlic for really tough colds/flu symptoms.

Parsley (fresh). Brewed like tea, helps muscle relaxation.

Raspberry Leaf (dry). Great for pain relief.

Plantain Leaf (dry). Cleanses the urinary tract & bladder for men and women who experience bladder infections or painful urination. (If symptoms persist for this, see a doctor right away!)

Passion Flower (dry). Relaxes the body & helps alleviate insomnia.

Valerian Root (dry). Another sleep aid of the natural kind.

Chamomile (dry). Helps ease stomach ailments, in large quantities it is a sleep aid.

Spiced Anise Tea

4 parts Anise Hyssop   1 part Vanilla Bean
1 part Cinnamon   1 part Cloves

Use about a teaspoon of loose tea per 8 oz. cup.

Aromatic Mint Tea

2 parts Spearmint   1 part Sweet Woodruff
1 part Marjoram   1 part Sage

Note: it's easy to stretch herbal teas by using less and steeping them longer to get the same amount of flavor (they don't get bitter with longer steeping).

Hot Ginger Tea

4 Ginger Aid Tea bags
2 pieces (3" ea) cinnamon
    sticks

8 whole cloves
6 cup boiling water
2 orange slices

Put tea bags, cinnamon sticks, cloves, ginger and sugar into a large teapot. Pour boiling water over and allow to steep 3 minutes. Remove tea bags and steep for 5 minutes. To serve, pour tea into cups and float a quarter slice of orange in each cup.

Black Saffron Tea

4 bags Golden Green tea
6 Green cardamons
4 tsp. Sugar

½ tsp. Saffron threads
4 cups water
4 bags Golden Green Tea
    Black

Add the cardamon, sugar and saffron to the water and bring to a boil. Simmer until reduced by half. Bring to a boil again, add tea bags and steep for 8 minutes. Strain out tea and spices. Serve hot.

Almond Tea

4 tea bags your favorite tea
½ tsp. Lemon zest, finely grated
4 cups Boiling water
½ cup Sugar

2 tbs Lemon juice
1   tsp.   Almond
    extract
¼ tsp. Vanilla

Steep tea and lemon rind in boiling water for about 5 minutes. Stir in sugar, lemon juice, almond and vanilla.

Iced Spiced Tea

Serves 8-10

4 bags of your favorite tea
½ cup (4 oz) sugar
1 cup water
1 stick cinnamon
6 whole cloves
3 cardamom pods (optional)
2 tbsp. tea leaves
4 cups boiling water

juice of 1 large lemon
    and 2 oranges
ice cubes
iced water -or- soda
    water (club soda) to
    taste
orange and lemon slices
    to decorate

1   Boil the sugar, water and spices for 5 mins, then remove from heat.
2   Put the tea bags in a large pot and pour the boiling water over, leave for 5 mins. Strain into large bowl.
3   Add the strained syrup and leave to cool. Stir in the strained lemon and orange juice.
4   Add ice cubes and dilute with iced water or club soda to taste. Decorate with slices of orange or lemon.

Yaa's Green Tea Detox

A perfect blend of nutrients. It's a great aid in undoing the effects of holiday over-indulgence or after being exposed to toxic food. The health benefits of green tea are the high level of cancer-fighting antioxidants, it helps regulate blood sugar levels, lower blood pressure, fights gingivitis and cavities.

freshly-boiled water, enough to fill a teacup or mug
    (filtered, or bottled water preferred*)
1 tsp. loose leaf green tea or 1 tea bag
1 tablespoon Honey (Agave or Grade B maple syrup if
    preferred)
1 squeezed juice of half a lemon
1 dash (⅛ tsp.) cayenne pepper to taste

Note: Loose leaf green teas are generally mild and not overpowering. If your tap water tastes bad, then so probably will your green tea. We recommend fresh water without a lot of minerals for the best tasting tea.

Chai

It's everything our tea should be... comforting, smooth, nourishing, rich, healing and warm. Here are a few we wanted to share with other Chai lovers. Share this tea with friends and family during the fall and winter months. Feel free to play with these recipes to create your own version.

Favorite Chai

4 slices fresh organic ginger root
2 organic cinnamon sticks
8-10 whole organic cloves
8-10 whole organic cardamom pods
¼ tsp. organic whole black or white peppercorns
dash of homemade or organic vanilla extract
2 tbsp. black tea (organic English breakfast, Ceylon, or
    Assam) or, make a decaffeinated version by substituting
    red or honeybush tea
organic honey -or- agave nectar to taste
2 cups water
2 cups organic milk or a milk substitute

1.   Lightly crush Cinnamon sticks and Cardamom Pods.
2.   Bring 2 cups of water to a boil, and add all spices.
3.   Reduce the heat and allow to simmer for 5 minutes or longer, stirring occasionally.
4.   Add milk and allow it to heat up, then remove from the stove and add vanilla and honey. Strain and enjoy!
5.   **Note:** Almost all extracts contain alcohol including organic vanilla extract. None of the nonalcoholic vanillas are organic.

Chai Vanilla Milk Shake

Serves 3-4

3 leveled teaspoons loose tea
4 cardamom pods, bruised or
¼ teaspoon cardamom powder
1 teaspoon fresh grated ginger
3 cups water
2 cups soy ice cream

1. Mix tea leaves, cardamom, ginger, and water in a saucepan and bring to a boil.
2. Reduce heat to a simmer for 10 minutes until the liquid is reduced to 2 cups.
3. Remove from heat and cool to room temperature.
4. Blend vanilla ice cream and cooled tea concentrate in a blender.
5. Pour in tall glasses and serve.

For the Almond Cinnamon Ice Cream:

5 oz rice malt syrup
4 oz raw almond butter
2 tbsp. raw coconut oil
3½ tbsp. unflavored and unsweetened almond milk
¼ cup almond cream, or other GMO-free, unflavored and unsweetened vegetable cream
1 teaspoon cinnamon powder

1. Put all the ingredients in the bowl of a mixer and process until smooth.
2. Transfer the mixture into the fridge for about 30 minutes then pour it into your ice cream maker and process according to the manufacturer's instructions. 40 minutes should be enough to make a creamy, thick ice cream. At the end of the cycle, remove the ice cream from the machine and divide it into bowls.
3. Eat the ice cream right away or keep it in the freezer until serving time.

Instructions for Chai:

1. Mix tea leaves, cardamom, ginger, and water in a saucepan and bring to a boil.
2. Reduce heat to a simmer for 10 minutes until the liquid is reduced to 2 cups.
3. Remove from heat and cool to room temperature.
4. Blend vanilla ice cream and cooled tea concentrate in a blender. Pour in tall glasses and serve.

Note: You can increase the amount of the ice-cream according to your taste.

Vanilla Chai

Serves: 3-4

1 leveled teaspoons loose tea
⅛ teaspoon vanilla essence
⅓ cup water
½ cup soy milk
Sugar or sweetener as per taste

1. Bring water and tea leaves to boil in a saucepan
2. Add milk and bring Chai back to boil
3. Remove from heat and strain into a cup
4. Stir in sugar and vanilla essence
5. Sprinkle a pinch or two of cinnamon powder and serve

Plain Chai

Serves 1

1 teaspoon loose tea   ¼ cup almond milk
1 cup water   Sugar, to taste

1. Mix tea leaves and water in a saucepan and bring to a boil.
2. Reduce heat to a simmer and let tea steep for 2 minutes.
3. Add milk and sugar and bring to boil. Strain Chai in a cup and serve.

Cardamon Chai Tea

Serves 2

1½ teaspoons loose tea
2 cardamon pods, bruised or
⅛ teaspoon cardamon powder
1½ cups water
½ cup almond milk
sugar, to taste

1. Mix tea leaves, cardamon, and water in a saucepan and bring to a boil.
2. Reduce heat to a simmer and let tea and cardamon pods steep for 2 minutes.
3. Add milk and sugar and bring to boil.
4. Strain Chai in cups and serve.

Dr. Sunyatta Amen's Favorite Chai Blends: "The Remix"

Having experimented with Dr. Sunyatta's Chai, we've come up with a few more combinations we think you'll enjoy.

In these hot remixes we have 3 different loose tea bases at work, each one resulting in amazing, tasty, healing chai. In most parts of Africa and Asia the word Chai simply means tea. So many of the ingredients in Chai are aphrodisiac that the aroma alone is said to put one in the mood for love. So whether you're jump starting your day or just engaging your endorphins, try these remixes and discover the healing abilities and magic of exotic spices.

Stirred but not Shook

For a comforting mellowed out Chai:

3 teaspoons African Redbush (this is not caffeinated)
Exhale and snuggle in!

High Karate

3 teaspoons Darjeeling, Ceylon, Assam Bukhial or even green tea.

For a morning that kicks! This has caffeine but not at the level of coffee... so it's perfect to replace that coffee that has been killing your adrenals, metabolism and nerves.

Digestive Chai

Serves 2

1½ teaspoons loose tea	3-4 black peppers
¼ teaspoon fresh grated ginger -or- ⅛ teaspoon ginger powder	1½ cups water
	¾ cup almond milk
	agave, to taste

1. Mix tea leaves, ginger, peppers, and water in a saucepan and bring to a boil.
2. Reduce heat to a simmer and let tea and spices steep for 4 minutes. Add milk and sugar and bring to boil.
3. Strain Chai in cups and serve.

For more of Dr. Sunyatta's Exotic SiTea Blends, check her out online. SiTea features organic exotic teas, spices and seasoning blends fairly traded from the world over.

Bush Doctor

For an extra boost of healing to your already power-ful Chai use:

3 teaspoon of Purple Lapacho "Pau D'arco"
(Grown in Central America, Caribbean and South America, this amazing herb was serious medicine to the ancient Caribbeans, Incas and Aztecs.)
3 teaspoon of your choice from aforementioned REMIX descriptions
½ in. slice fresh ginger (use vegetable peeler)
1 2 in. cinnamon stick (break it in ½ inch pieces to release the oils)

1 dash ground white pepper	3 tablespoons agave syrup -or- 3 tablespoons of Stevia powder
3 whole cloves	
3 pods of cardamom	2 cups water
2 dashes of cayenne	2 cups almond milk

1. Bring 2 cups of water to a boil and toss in everything except tea, milk and sweetener. Boil for 10 minutes.
2. Reduce heat and add tea, milk and agave. Simmer about 5 minutes stirring occasionally.
3. Turn off and strain through strainer. Serve hot or in a tall glass filled with ice.
4. Refrigerate unused portion – the spices will have even more time to cavort with one another - to the delight of your taste buds!
5. To reheat, you may either warm in a pot or froth with cappuccino maker.
6. Dust with a hint of fresh nutmeg. Drink Deeply.

Dr. Sunaya's Green Tip: Save the used strained herb mix in a covered glass bowl in fridge... it can be used with more great tea. "It's sexy to make a smaller footprint by reusing great ingredients." **Excerpted from The World's Sexiest Cookbook by Dr. Sunyatta Amen.**

Ultimate Juice Cleansers

If only water and fruit juices were strong enough to clean our toxic tissues of today. Decades after a pesticide is banned, it still persists in our waterways. If the oceans and rivers can't break down the pesticide, how can a glass of water or distilled water in fruit juices do so?

A juice fast is great way to nurture your body, rebuild your immune system and restore yourself to a healthy way of living. Raw fruit and vegetable juice contains many cleansing elements such as minerals, vitamins, enzymes and antioxidants to heal and detoxify the body safely. Little energy is used by your digestive system during the cleanse, allowing the body to focus on rebuilding, renewing and healing. You might be surprised by how much energy you have after the first few days!

Ginger/Lemon Cleanse

1-inch slice fresh ginger root
1 fresh lemon
6 carrots with tops
apple
water

Stomach Cleanser

1 bunch grapes
1 basket strawberries
3 apples
4 sprigs fresh mint
water

Constipation Cure

1 firm papaya
¼-inch slice ginger root
1 Pear
water

Skin Cleanse

1 cucumber with skin
½ bunch fresh parsley
1 4-oz. tub alfalfa sprouts
4 sprigs fresh mint
water

Blood Builder (Iron-enriched)

2 bunches grapes
6 oranges
8 lemons peeled
¼ cup honey or Agave nectar
water

Blood Builder Vegetable Juice

This juice is a popular one for breakfast as it gives your energy levels a boost, wakens your digestive system whilst giving your body a nutrition, yet gentle start to the day.

Serves 2
1 cucumber
2 large handfuls spinach
handful parsley
1 stick celery
handful of kale

1. Simply wash all of the ingredients thoroughly, roughly chop and juice!
2. To give it more of a fruity, less veggie flavor squeeze fresh lime or lemon in at the end.

Kidney Cleanser Juice

Here are three great kidney cleanse recipes. Just throw it all together in the juicer, then drink! You can also use a blender if you want it to be more like a smoothie.

Recipe 1
4 stalks celery
3 sprigs parsley*
1 cucumber
½ lemon
water

Recipe 2
2 apples
4-6 slices watermelon
water

Recipe 3
3 celery stalks
2 tomatoes
1 lemon, peeled
2 carrots
water

Note: Parsley detoxifies the kidney by flushing toxins out, and is beneficial in the treatment and prevention of kidney stones. Parsley contains a compound named Apoil, which has now been isolated and used in medication to treat kidney ailments and kidney stones.

Carrot Juice (Respiratory Cleanse)

A primary function of a respiratory cleanse is to remove the accumulated mucus from the bronchi and lungs. Meat, dairy products, wheat and sweets may increase the amount of mucus buildup in the respiratory system. Homemade carrot juice is helpful in cleaning out mucus.

Parsley Tea (Kidney Cleanser)

1. Place 2 cups of water and 2 tablespoons of chopped parsley into a pot with the lid on.
2. Heat the water to almost boiling, then turn off the heat.
3. Let it sit for fifteen minutes, then strain the parsley out and enjoy the tea.

Blood Builder

2 apples
1 carrot
1 stick celery
1 large handful of mixed green leaves (kale, parsley, spinach and whatever other green leafy vegetables that is available)
¼ cucumber
½ broccoli stem
1 small handful of alfalfa sprouts
1 unpeeled raw beetroot
¼ small piece of lemon
½ inch slice of ginger

1. Place one apple in the chute followed by all the other ingredients, finishing it off with the other apple.
2. You then simply put the machine on the higher speed and push through. Pour over ice.

This juice is packed with vitamin A, which not only helps maintain healthy skin, eyes and bones, but also boosts the immune system. Beetroot is one of nature's best blood builders, as well as being rich in carotenoids. A true anti-cancer king! Well deserving the crown.

Top 10 Juice Fast Recipes for Liver Detox

Detox, or detoxification, is the removal of potentially toxic substances from the body. Special diets, supplements, herbs and other methods help remove environmental and dietary toxins from the body. To make your own juice at home, buy an inexpensive juicer with cutting blades and a centrifugal spin. If possible, you want to look for a juicer that operates a lower speeds to avoid heating and thereby damaging nutrients, adding oxygen to the juice and eliminating impact shock to the fruit or vegetable. Otherwise, you can press juice or squeeze juice by hand or using a presser.

If you have been diagnosed as a chronic alcoholic or drug addict, the following recipes might help you restore balance to your internal organs and systems. Please consult with a medical doctor before using any of the recipes to be sure that your body is prepared for the cleansing nature of these juices.

Carrot, Beet Juice

4-5 carrots
3-4 small beets

This is one of the most detoxifying juices for the body and specifically for the kidneys. If you are new to juicing, you may want to start with half a dose at first just to test for dizziness, when detoxification starts.

Carrot, Beet Juice Plus

| 1 carrot | 1 stick celery |
| ½ beet | 1 cucumber |

This is a great breakfast drink and is very effective in liver cleansing.

Citrus Blend

1 small lemon
2-3 oranges
1 grapefruit

Feel free to add 1 teaspoonful of agave nectar or honey (if you don't have agave), if the juice is too bitter. As with many other juices, this treatment works best if you drink it in the morning before breakfast.

Cabbage Juice Plus

2 pears or 2 carrots
½ small cabbage
2 sticks celery
handful watercress

Raw cabbage juice tastes a little sharp to say the least but it aids digestion and prevents fluid retention and constipation. Cabbage also contains compounds that help the liver function properly as well as protecting against cancer. Celery, watercress, pears or carrots are also powerful intestinal cleansers and contribute to the detoxification process. You can modify this liver detox juice recipe by adding more watercress, spinach or even pear to balance the bitterness.

Wheatgrass Juice

You must purchase a special wheatgrass extractor (looks like a meat grinder) in order to correctly juice wheatgrass. Wheatgrass is high in chlorophyll which can clean the body, works as a natural antiseptic, neutralize toxins and even slows the aging process.

Fruit Liver Cleanse

2 apples
1 bunch grapes
½ beet
¼ grapefruit
¼ lemon

Super Green

2 celery sticks
1 cucumber
2 handfuls spinach
handful lettuce
handful kale
handful parsley

TIP: Add the celery and cucumbers last, as these vegetables will help flush the fibers of the other leafy greens from the juicer.

Carrot Apple Cleanser

4 carrots
2 apples
1 lemon
handful dandelion leaves

This is a good detox juice recipe that uses dandelion.

Alkaline Liver Cleanse

2 grapefruit
4 lemons
2 cloves garlic, grated
2 inches ginger, grated
2 tbsp. flax oil
1 tsp. acidophilus
dash of cayenne (optional)

1. Juice the lemon and the grapefruit, then add the other ingredients to the juice.
2. This is said to be a cure for a hangover, but contains all of the most potent liver cleansing ingredients.
3. The alkaline liver cleanse gives your liver a gentle flush and the opportunity to heal itself.

Extreme Liver Cleanse

1 grapefruit
½ cup extra virgin olive oil
3 cups water
4 tbsp. Epsom salt

Health Advisory: Medical supervision is suggested for the more extreme juices with cleanses, as it's good to watch blood pressure, sugar levels, etc. during a cleanse.

Ginger Fireball

2 oranges, medium
1½ juice of lemon juice
1 inch ginger
½ tsp. cayenne pepper
oil of oregano*

Oil of oregano is an anti-microbial helpful with indigestion and building immunity. It is an anti-oxidant and is an amazing defense against food borne pathogens. Cayenne increases white blood cell count and is a fat burning metabolizer; also high in essential vitamins. Ginger is an anti-inflammatory and is another amazing defense against cold and flu symptoms. Try drinking daily.

Dr. Green Juice

Serves 1-2
⅓ pineapple, medium
2 apple, medium
1½ lemon
¼ ginger
4 kale leaves

Juice ⅓ pineapple before putting it into the blender with all the other ingredients and blend well.

Amazing flavor, Drink as much of this as you can! This is just what the doctor ordered when replacing highly and mostly artificial/imitation manufactured foods, from which nutritious matter has been removed, to prolong self life, which is advocated mostly by those who are interested most in sales. What's removed from over processed fruit and vegetable juices is what is most advantageous to modify our digestive canal.

How Much Does It Take: Conversion for Cooking, Weights & Measures

U.S. to Metric, Cooking Measurement Equivalents – Pt. 1 of 2

Cups

⅛ cup	=	30 mL
¼ cup	=	60 mL
⅓ cup	=	80 mL
½ cup	=	120 mL
⅔ cup	=	160 mL
¾ cup	=	180 mL
1 cup	=	240 mL
1¼ cups	=	300 mL
1-⅓ cups	=	320 mL
1½ cups	=	360 mL
1⅔ cups	=	400 mL
1¾ cups	=	420 mL
2 cups	=	480 mL
2¼ cups	=	540 mL
2½ cups	=	600 mL
3 cups	=	720 mL
1 quart	=	.95 L
4 cups (1 quart) =		.95 L
4 qrts./1-gal.	=	3.78 L

Weight

1 gram = .035 ounce
100 grams = 3.5 ounces
454 grams =1 pound
500 grams = 1.10 pounds
1 kilogram = 2.205 pounds
1 kilogram = 35 oz.

Ounces (Oz.)

1 oz. / 2 tbsp. = 30mL/31.05 grams
1 pint / 16 fluid oz. = 453.6 grams (1 lb.)
28 fluid ounces = 828 mL

Pints

1 pint = 454 grams / .475 L
2 pints = 1 quart / .95 L
4 quarts = 1 gallon / 3.78 L

Dry Measures

1 ounce = 28.35 grams
1 pound/16 ounces = 453.6 grams
2.2 pounds = 1 kilogram
2.3 1.035 = 1 gram

16 cups = 128 fluid ounces = 4 quarts =
1 gallon = 3.78 liters

Healthy Substitutions

1 cup (240 mL) sugar =
¾ cup (180 mL) honey/agave

1 cup (240 mL) butter or margarine =
⅞ cup (210 mL) vegetable oil

2 eggs = 1 egg + 2 egg whites or
2 tablespoons (30 mL) oil
Plus 1 tablespoon (15 mL) water

1 cup (240 mL) white flour =
¾ cup (180 mL) whole-wheat flour

Teaspoons

⅛ tsp.	=	1 mL / 1.035 grams
¼ tsp.	=	2 mL / 2.07 grams
½ tsp.	=	3 mL / 3.11 grams
¾ tsp.	=	4 mL / 4.14 grams
1 tsp.	=	5 mL / 5.175 grams
1¼ tsp.	=	7 mL / 7.25 grams
1½ tsp.	=	8 mL / 8.28 grams
2 tsp.	=	10 mL / 10.35 grams

Tablespoons

1 tablespoon=		15 mL / 10.35 grams
1½ tbsp.	=	23 mL / 15.53 grams
2 tbsp.	=	30 mL / 23.81 grams
2½ tbsp.	=	38 mL / 31.05 grams
3 tbsp.	=	45 mL / 39.33 grams
3½ tbsp.	=	53 mL / 54.86 grams

Butter/Margarine to Olive Oil

1 teaspoon	¾ teaspoon
1 tablespoon	2¼ teaspoons
2 tablespoons	1½ tablespoons
¼ cup	3 tablespoons
⅓ cup	¼ cup
½ cup	¼ cup + 2 tbsp
⅔ cup	½ cup
¾ cup	½ cup + 1 tbsp
1 cup	¾ cup

U.S. to Metric, Cooking Measurement Equivalents – Pt. 2 of 2

Liquid Measures				½ fl oz. =	1 tbsp. =	3 tsp
		⅛ cup	1 fl oz	2 tbsp	6 tsp	⅛ cup
		¼ cup	2 fl oz	4 tbsp	12 tsp	¼ cup
		½ cup	4 fl oz	8 tbsp	24 tsp	½ cup
	¼ qt	½ pt	1 cup	8 fl oz		
	½ qt	1 pt	2 cups	16 fl oz		
¼ gal	1 qt	2 pt	4 cups	32 fl oz		
½ gal	2 qt	4 pt	8 cups	64 fl oz		
1 gal	4 qt	8 pt	16 cups	128 fl oz		

Metric to U.S.

1 millimeters = ⅕ teaspoon
5 ml = 1 teaspoon
15 ml = 1 tablespoon
34 ml = 1 fluid oz.
100 ml = 3.4 fluid oz.
240 ml = 1 cup
1 liter = 34 fluid oz.
1 liter = 4.2 cups
1 liter = 2.1 pints
1 liter = 1.06 quarts
1 liter = .26 gallon

Temperature Conversions

Fahrenheit		Celsius
250°	=	120°
275°	=	135°
300°	=	149°
325°	=	162°
350°	=	176°
375°	=	190°
400°	=	204°
425°	=	218°
450°	=	232°

(To convert F to C: subtract 32°, multiply by 5, and divide by 91 [F-32°] x5/9=C)

Tablespoons to Cups

16 tablespoons = 1 cup
12 tablespoons = ¾ cup
10 tablespoons + 2 teaspoons = ⅔ cup
8 tablespoons = ½ cup
6 tablespoons = ⅜ cup
5 tablespoons + 1 teaspoon = ⅓ cup
4 tablespoons = ¼ cup
2 tablespoons = ⅛ cup
2 tablespoons + 2 teaspoons = ⅙ cup
1 tablespoon = 1/16 cup
2 cups = 1 pint
2 pints = 1 quart
1 tablespoon = 3 teaspoons
48 teaspoons = 1 cup

Common Abbreviations:

tsp. = teaspoon	c = cup	ml = millimeter	60 drops = 1 tsp
tbsp. = tablespoon	pt = pint	l = liter	1 dash = ⅛ tsp
oz = ounce	qt = quart	g = gram	a few grains = less than ⅛ tsp
fl oz. = fluid ounce	gal = gallon	lb = pound	

Conversion for Fruits, Veggies, & More

How many folks actually cut up a pineapple to measure its juice or to find out how many cups you can get out of it? Or how many pounds of carrots should you buy if you need two cups of slices or juice? Here's that answer and lots more.

Fruits

Apples (diced or sliced)	1 lb. = 3 med. = 2 ¾ cups (1 apple = shy 1 cup)
Apples (for juice)	42 oz. weight = 20 juice = 2½ cup
Apricots, dried	1 lb. = 3 cups = 4 ½ cups cooked
Apricots, fresh	1 lb. = 5 to 8 med. = 2-¼ cups sliced
Bananas	1 lb. = 3 to 4 med. = 2 cups sliced, 1-⅓ cups mashed
Berries (except strawberries)	1 lb. = 2 cups
Blueberries (for juice)	8 oz. weight = 2 oz. juice = ¼ cup
Cherries, canned	1 lb. = 1¾ to 2 cups
Dates (pitted)	1 lb. = 2½ cups
Grapes, seedless	1 lb. = 2½ cups
Lemon, juice	3 med. lemons = 4 oz. juice = ½ cup juice
Lemon (zest/grated)	1 lemon = 2 to 3 teaspoons
Lime, juice	4 med. limes = 4 oz. juice = ½ cup juice
Melon (for juice)	22 oz. weight = 10 oz. juice = ¼ cup
Orange (for juice)	3 oranges = 20 oz. weight 8 oz. juice = 1 cup
Orange (zest/grated)	1 orange = 1 tablespoon
Papaya, juice	8 oz. weight = 1 cup juice (high speed)
Peaches (canned/sliced)	16-ounce can = 1¾ to 2 cups
Peaches (fresh/sliced)	1 lb. = 4 med. = 2 cups
Pears (fresh/sliced)	1 lb. = 4 med. = 2 cups
Pears, juice	19 oz. weight = 6 oz. juice = ¾ cup
Pineapple (canned/chunks/crushed)	20-ounce can = 2½ cups
Pineapple (canned/slices)	20-ounce can = 10 slices
Pineapple (fresh/cubed)	2 lb. = 1 med. = 3 cups
Pineapple (for juice)	40 oz. weight = 16 oz. juice = 2 cups
Prunes (dried/pitted)	1 lb. = 2¼ cups = 4 cups cooked
Raisins	1 lb. = 2¾ cups (1 cup = 6 ounces)
Rhubarb (fresh/diced)	1 lb. = 3½ cups = 2 cups cooked
Strawberries	1 lb. = 1¾ cups sliced

Note: Weight of lemons, melons, oranges, and pineapple includes skin or peel and tops, all of which are not juiced.

Vegetables

Asparagus, fresh	1 lb. = 16 to 20 spears = 2 cups cooked
Asparagus (fresh/for juice)	8 oz. weight = 4 oz. juice = ½ cup
Beans (green/fresh/cut)	1 lb. = 3 cups = 2½ cups cooked
Beans, dry	1 lb. = 2½ cups (1 cup dry = 2¼ cups cooked)
Beans (green/frozen)	9-ounce pkg. = 1⅔ cups
Beans (green/canned)	15 ½ ounce can = 1⅔ cups
Beans, dried	5 oz. solid = 2 oz. strained = ¼ cup
Beats (fresh/for juice)	24 oz. weight = 8 oz. juice = 1 cup
Broccoli (fresh/cut)	2-inch lengths 1 lb. = 6 cups (incl. 4 cups florets)
Broccoli (fresh/chopped)	1 lb. = 4½ cups
Broccoli (fresh/for juice)	13 oz. weight = 3 oz. juice = ⅜ cup
Cabbage (fresh/shredded)	1 lb. = 4 cup; med. head is 2 lb.s
Cabbage (fresh/for juice)	23 oz. weight = 8-oz juice = 1 cup

Vegetables (Cont'd)

Carrots, sliced	1 lb. = 8 to 9 large = 4 cups sliced (2 large carrots = 1 cup)
Carrots (for juice)	6 med. = 32 oz. weight = 14 oz. juice = 1¾ cup
Cauliflower, fresh	1 lb. = 1½ cups
Cauliflower, frozen	10 ounces = 2 cups
Celery, chopped	1 rib = ¾ cup
Celery (for juice)	30 oz. weight = 16 oz. juice = 2 cups
Cilantro (for juice)	1 bunch = 2 oz. juice = ¼ cup
Cucumbers (for juice)	2 med. = 16 oz. weight. = 8 oz. juice = 1 cup
Garlic, minced	1 med. clove = ½ teaspoon
Ginger (root/peeled/chopped)	2 ounces (.13 lb.) = 5 tablespoons
Ginger (for juice)	2 oz. weight = 2 tbsp. juice
Greens (fresh/leafy)	8 oz. = 3-6 oz. juice = ⅞ cup
Mushrooms	8 ounces = 3 cups sliced = 1 cup sliced sauteed
Onions, green	cut in 1-inch lengths 4 onions (½ bunch) = 1 cup
Onions, coarsely chopped	1 lb. = 3 large = 2½ cups (1 cup = 1¼ large)
Parsley (for juice)	1-bunch = 2-3 oz. weight = ½ cup juice
Parsley, chopped	1 bunch = 1⅓ to 1½ cups chopped (¼ cup = 6 or 7 stems)
Pepper (for juice)	5 oz. weight = 2 oz. juice = ¼ cup
Peas (fresh/in pod)	1 lb. = 1¼ cups shelled.
Peas, frozen	10 ounces = 2 cups
Spinach (for juice)	12 oz. weight = 1½ juice
Tomato (for juice)	2 med. = 16-oz. weight = 10 oz. juice = 1⅛ cup
Pepper green, diced	1 med. = 1 cup
Potatoes	1 lb. = 3 med. = 2¼ cup cooked, 1¾ cups mashed
Pumpkin, canned	16-ounce can = 2 cup
Radish, fresh	2 med = 9-oz. solid = 2-3 oz. juice = ⅓ cup
Root, solid (3 medium)	16-oz. = 10 oz. juice = 1¼ cup
Shallots, chopped	1 med. = 3 to 3½ teaspoon
Spinach, fresh	12-ounce bag, stems removed = 5 cups = ½ cup chopped & cooked.
Spinach (frozen/chopped)	10-ounce pkg. = 1-⅛ cups
Tomatoes (canned whole/chopped)	28-ounce can = 1-⅓ cups tomatoes, lots of liq.
Tomatoes (fresh/chopped)	1 lb. = 3 med. = 3 cups
Water chestnuts (canned/sliced)	8-ounce can = 1 cup
Zucchini, sliced	4 (bratwurst size) = 4 cups

Grain — Flour, Cereal

Bread crumbs from day-old bread	2 slices = 1 cup
Bread crumbs canned dry	10-ounce can = 2½ cups
Cornmeal	1 lb. = 3 cups (1 cup uncooked = 4 ½ cups cooked)
Crackers graham	1 lb. box = 66 singles or 33 doubles; 16 singles = 1 cup crumbs
Crackers saltine	28 singles = 1 cup crumbs
Flour all-purpose (unsifted/spooned)	1 lb. = 3½ cups
Flour all-purpose, sifted	1 lb. = 4 cups
Flour cake, sifted	1 lb. = 4¾ cups
Flour whole wheat (unsifted/spooned)	1 lb. = 3⅓ cups
Oatmeal (uncooked)	1 lb. = 5½ cups; 1 cup uncooked = 1¾ cups cooked
Pasta	1 lb. uncooked = 4 to 5 cups uncooked = 8 cups cooked
Rice brown	14-ounce pkg. = 2 cups = 8 cups cooked
Rice quick-cooking or converted	14-ounce pkg. = 2 cups = 8 cups cooked
Rice regular	1 lb. = 2¼ cups raw = 6¾ cups cooked (1 cup raw = 3 cups cooked)
Rice wild	1 lb. = 3 cups raw = 11 to 12 cups cooked

Dessert Ingredients

Chocolate chips	1 cup = 6 ounces
Cocoa powder unsweetened	8-ounce can = 3 cups
Coconut flaked or shredded	7-ounce bag = 2⅔ cups
Honey	1 lb. = 1⅓ cups
Sugar brown, packed	1 lb. = 2¼ cups
Sugar raw/granulated	1 lb. = 2¼ cups
Almonds slivered	4-ounce bag = ¾ cup (1 cup = 5⅓ ounces
Pecans chopped	2-ounce bag = ½ cup
Pistachios	4 ounces (1 cup) with shells = ½ cup shelled
Walnuts chopped	2-ounce bag = ½ cup

Emergency Substitutions

If you don't have _____, substitute _____

1 cup sifted cake flour	1 cup minus 2 tablespoons sifted all-purpose flour
1 tbsp. cornstarch	2 tablespoons flour
1 cup light corn syrup	or 1¼ cups sugar plus ⅓ cups liquid. honey
1 clove garlic	¼ teaspoon garlic powder
1 tablespoon fresh herbs	1 teaspoon dried herbs
¼ cup chopped onions	1 tablespoon dried minced onion or 1 teaspoon onion powder
½ cup wine (in desserts)	½ cup fruit juice
½ cup wine (in cooking)	½ cup broth

Note: Numbers above are approximate, but much better than guessing.

Grain, Flour, Cereal

Bread crumbs from day-old bread	2 slices = 1 cup
Bread crumbs canned dry	10-ounce can = 2½ cups
Cornmeal	1 lb. = 3 cups (1 cup uncooked = 4½ cups cooked)
Crackers graham	1 lb. box = 66 singles or 33 doubles
Crackers graham,	16 singles = 1 cup crumbs
Crackers saltine,	28 singles = 1 cup crumbs
Flour all-purpose (unsifted/spooned)	1 lb. = 3½ cups
Flour all-purpose, sifted	1 lb. = 4 cups
Flour cake, sifted	1 lb. = 4¾ cups
Flour whole wheat (unsifted/spooned)	1 lb. = 3⅓ cups
Oatmeal (uncooked)	1 lb. = 5½ cups; 1 cup uncooked = 1¾ cups cooked
Pasta	1 lb. uncooked = 4 to 5 cups uncooked = 8 cups cooked
Rice, brown	14-ounce pkg. = 2 cups = 8 cups cooked
Rice, quick or converted	14-ounce pkg. = 2 cups = 8 cups cooked
Rice, regular	1 lb. = 2¼ cups raw = 6¾ cups cooked (1 cup raw = 3 cups cooked)
Rice, wild	1 lb. = 3 cups raw = 11 to 12 cups cooked

Dessert Ingredients

Chocolate chips	1 cup = 6 ounces
Cocoa powder unsweetened	8-ounce can = 3 cups
Coconut flaked or shredded	7-ounce bag = 2⅔ cups
Honey	1 lb. = 1⅓ cups
Sugar brown, packed	1 lb. = 2¼ cups
Sugar granulated	1 lb. = 2¼ cups

All The Other Stuff You Need To Know

In the following pages, you'll find tons of resources to help you along your journey, including helpful guides to vitamins, minerals, nutritional deficiencies, and animal ingredients, and dozens of other things you'll want to use, possibly just to show off how smart you are. Whatever works for you!

The Healing Power of Fruits

by SUPREME UNDERSTANDING, from THE HOOD HEALTH HANDBOOK

The following list is a sampling of the health benefits of fruits. Some of them might really surprise you.

Apples: There's a reason they say that an apple a day keeps the doctor away. Apples contain a variety of essential nutrients and vitamins that may help protect the body from certain illnesses, including the common cold. Apple juice may also help improve brain function, protect the heart, and inhibit various types of cancer.

Apricots: Contains plenty of fiber, vitamin C, iron, boron, silica, and potassium. Which means it helps your heart, fights fatigue, prevents infection, improves your skin, hair, and nails, regulates your blood pressure, and keeps your digestion moving smoothly, all in only about 16 calories. Apricots, rich in beta carotene, can also cleanse your system of nicotine leftovers. This is one case where fresh is not the best. Dried apricots have three times the amount of fiber and vitamins.

Avocadoes*: Avocadoes are known to prevent birth defects, lower cholesterol, benefit arteries, dilate blood vessels, and lower blood pressure. Yes, they're high in fat, but half of it is heart-healthy monounsaturated oleic acid. One of the richest source of glutathione, a powerful antioxidant, shown to block thirty different carcinogens and to block proliferation of the aids virus in test tube experiments. And they're a good source of vitamin E.

Bananas: High in fiber and contain lots of vitamin C, B6, and folate as well as the minerals potassium and magnesium. The nutrients found in bananas help fight cancer, heart disease and a long list of other ailments. Banana peels make excellent fertilizer, but also contain a compound that may shift the immune balance of your skin to help relieve warts. People have claimed to heal warts by pressing the inside of a peel against their skin. Why not?

Blackberries: Interferes with the metalloproteinases that contribute to skin wrinkling. Also acts as an antibiotic by blocking the attaching of bacteria that cause urinary tract infections. Contains chemicals that curb diarrhea. Also

has antiviral activity and high in natural aspirin.

Blueberries: Blueberries help prevent and treat bladder infections by making it hard for bacteria to stick to urinary tract walls.

Cantaloupes: One cup of cantaloupe provides about 103.2% of the daily value for beta carotene. Because of its high vitamin C, it also fights infection, and stimulates white blood cells. Its folate content is very important in the production of new cells, especially during pregnancy. Green and yellow (cantaloupe and honeydew) have anticoagulant blood-thinning activity.

Cherries: A good source of perillyl alcohol, which helps prevent cancer. Heart-protective anthocyanins give cherries their color.

Cranberries: May treat urinary tract infections and bladder infections.

Eggplants*: Contains a host of vitamins, minerals, and phytonutrients. An anthocyanin phytonutrient found in eggplant skin called nasunin is a potent antioxidant and free radical scavenger that has been shown to protect cell membranes from damage.

Elderberries: May speed the recovery from type A and B influenza.

Figs: Helps to prevent cancer. Both extract of figs and the fig compound, benzaidehyde, have helped shrink tumors in humans. Also laxative, anti-ulcer, antibacterial and antiparasitic powers.

Grapes: Contains many antioxidant and anticancer compounds. Red grapes (not the white or green grapes) are high in antioxidant quercetin, and are antibacterial and antiviral. Grape seed oil also raises good type HDL cholesterol. Purple grapes (especially the skins) and juice offer three heart-guarding compounds: flavonoids, anthocyanins and resveratrol. (Green grapes are not rich in them)

Kiwis: Kiwi consumption has been linked to a decrease in respiratory-related health problems among children, including asthma. Enjoying just two kiwifruit daily may significantly lower your risk for blood clots and reduce the amount of fats (triglycerides) in your blood, therefore helping to protect cardiovascular health. Kiwis also contains more vitamin C than oranges.

Mangoes: A single mango has your entire recommended

daily amount for beta-carotene, 57 mg of vitamin C, and plenty of cancer-fighting antioxidants and heart-healthy carotenoids.

Noni: Used in the Pacific and Caribbean islands for the treatment of inflammation and pain. Human studies indicate it may help prevent cancer.

Oranges: One orange provides an impressive 50 g to 70 g of vitamin C, 40 mcg of folic acid, 52 mg of calcium, as well as beta carotene and Vitamins B1, B2, B3, and fiber. Tangerines provide similar benefits.

Papayas: Called "the fruit of the angels" by Christopher Columbus, who noticed that the natives (who ate them daily) were strong and had few health problems (if any). The nutrients in papaya promote heart health, boost immune systems, increase male fertility, aid digestion, prevent emphysema, and protect against colon cancer. Papaya contains the digestive enzyme, papain, which is used like bromelain, a similar enzyme found in pineapple, to treat sports injuries, wounds, other trauma, skin disorders, and allergies.

Peaches: Though low in calories (one cup of sliced peaches has only 60 calories) and composed of 80% water, peaches are packed with fiber, vitamins, minerals, and carotenoids. The dose of fiber in peaches acts as a gentle laxative, aids digestion, and may also help combat cancer. A study in China found that men and women who ate peaches more than two times per week had less risk of developing cancers of the mouth than those who did not eat peaches.

Pears: Pears are high in fiber, particularly lignin, an insoluble fiber that helps to move cholesterol out of the body, and pectin, a soluble fiber which binds to cholesterol, also causing it to be removed from the body. The insoluble fiber also helps reduce the risk of colon cancer. Pears also contain a mineral, boron that play an important role in keeping bones strong.

Pomegranates: Contains tons of phytochemicals like potassium, which is great for lowering your blood pressure. Studies also suggest that pomegranates, which contain the most cancer-fighting ellagitannins out of any common fruit, can inhibit cancer cell growth, slow the progression of prostate cancer and reduce the risk of atherosclerosis (See "Heart Disease").

Prunes (Dried Plums): Because of their high fiber, prunes are famous for their laxative effect. Prunes are known for normalizing blood sugar levels, protecting against many ailments (heart disease, breast cancer, colon cancer, etc.), and helping with weight loss.

Raspberries: High in fiber, as well as vitamin C, natural aspirin, ellagic acid and anthocyanins. They appear to have anti-viral and anti-cancer properties, with studies suggesting they may have a role in preventing oral cancer.

Squash*: Very high in vitamin A. Also contains fiber, vitamins C, B6, B1, potassium, folate, and other phytonutrients which may help prevent cancer, heart attack, stroke, and high blood pressure. The copper found in summer squash is also helpful for reducing the painful symptoms of rheumatoid arthritis.

Strawberries: Contain high levels of ellagic acid and anthocyanins, and are rich in vitamin C and fiber. Strawberries also display anti-viral and anti-cancer activity, particularly against liver cancer. In one study, strawberries topped a list of eight foods most linked to lower rates of cancer deaths among elderly people. Those eating the most strawberries were three times less likely to develop cancer compared to those eating few or no strawberries. Strawberries also protect against macular degeneration and rheumatoid arthritis.

Tomatoes*: A major source of lycopene, an antioxidant and anti-cancer agent that intervenes in devastating chain reactions of oxygen free radical molecules. Tomatoes are linked to lower rates of pancreatic cancer and cervical cancer. Lycopene – even as found in ketchup – may also lower the risk of cardiovascular disease. Organic ketchup (which is darker) contains up to 60% more lycopene per gram than regular brands. Researchers have also found that organic ketchup has the highest levels of vitamins A, C, and E.

Watermelons: Contains high amounts of lycopene and glutathione, antioxidant and anti-cancer compounds, and also displays mild anti-bacterial, anti-coagulant activity. Watermelon boosts energy production, while preventing erectile dysfunction, macular degeneration, and prostate cancer.

*Note: Fruits that are often thought of as vegetables.

The Healing Power of Vegetables

by SUPREME UNDERSTANDING, from THE HOOD HEALTH HANDBOOK

The following list is a sampling of the health benefits of vegetables.

Alfalfa: One of the most popular sprouts, Alfalfa is a good source of vitamins A, B, C, D, E, F, and K and is rich in many minerals, as well as many enzymes needed for digestion. Alfalfa sprouts are high in phytoestrogens – known to have preventive elements for cancer, heart diseases, menopausal symptoms, and osteoporosis.

Artichokes: High in fiber, as well as a flavonoid that has been shown to reduce skin cancer. May also reduce cholesterol levels.

Arugula: This green contains cancer-preventative compounds known as isothiocyanates.

Asparagus: High in the antioxidant glutathione, which appears to lower cancer risk.

Beets: Beta-cyanin, which gives them their reddish-purple color, is a disease-fighting antioxidant. Beets are richer than spinach in iron and other minerals. Helpful in cases of anemia, tuberculosis, constipation, poor appetite, obesity, tumors, gout, and pimples. Also helpful in the elimination of irritating drug poisons.

Beans: (Including legumes, navy, black, kidney, pinto, soybeans, black-eyed peas and lentils) One-half cup of cooked beans daily reduces cholesterol an average 10% and regulates blood sugar levels. An excellent food for diabetics. Linked to lower rates of certain cancers. Very high in fiber.

Broccoli: Abundant in antioxidants, including quercetin, glutathione, beta-carotene, vitamin C, lutein, glucarate, sulforaphane. Extremely high in cancer fighting activity, particularly against lung, colon and breast cancers. Like other cruciferous vegetables, it speeds up removal of estrogen from the body, helping suppress breast cancer. Rich in cholesterol reducing fiber. Has anti-viral, anti-ulcer activity. High in chromium, which helps regulate insulin and blood sugar. Cooking and processing destroys some of the antioxidants and anti-estrogenic agents, such as indoles and glutathione. Most protective when eaten raw or lightly cooked.

Brussels Sprouts: Possesses some of the same powers as its relatives, broccoli and cabbage. Anti-cancer, estrogenic and packed with various antioxidants (including plenty of Vitamin C) and cancer-fighting indoles.

Cabbage: (including Bok Choy) Contains numerous anti-cancer and antioxidant compounds. Speeds up estrogen metabolism, is thought to help block breast cancer and suppress growth of polyps, a prelude to colon cancer. Eating cabbage more than once a week cut men's colon cancer odds by 66%. As little as two daily tbsp. of cooked cabbage protected against stomach cancer. Has anti-bacterial and anti-viral powers. Some of these important compounds are destroyed by cooking. Raw cabbage, as in cole slaw, appears to have stronger overall health value. Raw cabbage juice helps heal ulcers in humans.

Carrots: High in beta carotene, with powerful anticancer, artery-protecting, immune-boosting, infection-fighting, antioxidant qualities. A carrot a day slashed stroke rates in women by 68%. The beta carotene in one medium carrot cuts lung cancer risk in half, even among formerly heavy smokers. Also reduces odds of degenerative eye diseases (cataracts and macular degeneration as well as chest pain (angina). The high soluble fiber depresses blood cholesterol and promotes regularity. Cooking can make it easier for the body to absorb carrot's beta carotene.

Cauliflower: Another great source of anti-cancer indoles, fiber, and vitamin C. Cauliflower provides special nutrient support for three body systems that are closely connected with cancer development as well as cancer prevention: (1) the body's detox system, (2) its antioxidant system, and (3) its inflammatory/anti-inflammatory system. To preserve these anti-cancer nutrients, raw is best, steamed is second best.

Celery: A remedy for high blood pressure. Also has a mild diuretic effect. Contains eight different families of anti-cancer compounds, such as phthalides and polyacetylenes, that detoxify carcinogens, especially cigarette smoke.

Cucumbers: Good for fevers, constipation, skin eruptions, high blood pressure, rheumatism, obesity, acidosis and is a mild diuretic.

Green beans: Contains a variety of antioxidant carotenoids, including beta-carotene, lutein and zeaxanthin.

Greens: (Including collard, kale, mustard, turnip) These greens are packed with anti-cancer, antioxidant compounds (lutein, zeaxanthin, and isothiocyanates), beta carotene, vitamin C, and 93 to 226 mg of calcium per cup. Like other green leafy vegetables, these are all associated with low rates of all cancers.

Kale: A rich source of various anti-cancer chemicals. Has more beta carotene than spinach and twice as much lutein, the most of any vegetable tested. Kale is also a member of the cruciferous family, endowing it with indoles that help regulate estrogen and fight off colon cancer.

Leek: Effective on diarrhea and back pain.

Onions: An exceptionally strong antioxidant. Thins the blood, lowers cholesterol, raises good-type HDL cholesterol, wards off blood clots, fights asthma, chronic bronchitis, hay fever, diabetes, atherosclerosis and infections. Anti-inflammatory, antibiotic, antiviral, thought to have diverse anti-cancer powers. The onion is the richest dietary source of anti-cancer quercetin (in shallots, yellow and red onions only – not white onions). Specifically linked to preventing human stomach cancer.

Okra: Originating in Africa, okra is a low-calorie source for many nutrients, effective for the prevention of neural tube defects in developing fetuses, mainly due to its high content of vitamin B6, calcium, fiber, and folic acid. Unlike fiber from grains, okra's fiber is easy on the stomach. It can ease digestion and constipation, help irritable bowel syndrome, sooth the gastrointestinal track, and can help to heal ulcers. Okra can also help prevent heart disease, cancer, and diabetes, and help treat asthma and sun stroke.

Peas: A good source of the carotenoids lutein and zeaxanthin – both of which help protect against age-related eye disease.

Peppers (chili, hot): Capsaicin (which makes peppers "hot") helps dissolve blood clots, opens up sinuses and air passages, breaks up mucus in the lungs, acts as an expectorant or decongestant, and helps prevent bronchitis, emphysema and stomach ulcers. Also a potent painkiller, alleviating headaches when inhaled, and joint pain when injected. Antibacterial, antioxidant (anti-cancer) activity.

Pepper (green): Bell peppers have been shown to be protective against cataracts, blood clot formation, and the risk of heart attacks and strokes, probably due to their vitamin C, capsaicin, carotenoids and flavonoids.

Peppers (red, sweet): An improved version of the green pepper, with twice the vitamin C content and more vitamin A.

Potato (white): When eaten with the peel, provides 5g of fiber, 43% of the day's vitamin C requirement, anticancer protease inhibitors, and a major dose of potassium, which may help prevent high blood-pressure and strokes.

Pumpkin: Extremely high in beta carotene, the antioxidant reputed to help ward off numerous health problems, including heart attacks, cancer, cataracts.

Radishes: Chewing activates the heat-producing but healthy indoles and isothiocyanates.

Lettuce: (Including Romaine and other dark lettuce) The darker the green, the more carotenoids. There's also 40% of the RDA for folic acid in 2 cups of Romaine. Iceberg lettuce contains much less nutrients.

Seaweed: Seaweed contains the broadest range of minerals of any food – the same minerals found in the ocean and in human blood, such as potassium, calcium, magnesium, iron, and iodine. Seaweed also contains vitamin C, fiber, beta-carotene, and pantothenic acid and riboflavin – two B-vitamins needed for your body to produce energy. Sea vegetables have been shown to cleanse the body of toxic pollutants, improve hair growth, enrich the bloodstream, and enhance metabolism.

Spinach: Contains many antioxidants and cancer fighters, containing about four times more beta carotene, more than half the RDA for folic acid, and three times more lutein than broccoli. Rich in fiber that helps lower blood cholesterol. Some of its antioxidants are destroyed by cooking. Eat raw or lightly cooked.

Squash (Winter, Butternut, Summer): Due to their carotene properties, winter squash exert a protective effect against many cancers, particularly lung cancer. Summer squash is less nutritious, but studies have shown that juice made from them is equal to juice made from pumpkins, leeks, and radishes in their ability to prevent cell mutations. Summer squash are most helpful during the summer due to their higher water content. They protect against dehydration and the carotenes help protect against UV damage from the sun.

Turnips: Turnips are root vegetables known to lower the risk of obesity, high blood pressure, diabetes, and cancers of the stomach, pancreas, bladder, and lung diseases, as well as cataracts. Turnip greens are more nutrition dense than the root. The greens provide an excellent source of vitamins A, B6, C, E, folic acid, calcium, copper, fiber, and manganese.

Watercress: One of its compounds detoxifies a major carcinogen in tobacco and as such may help prevent lung cancer. Also contains carotenoids.

Yams (Sweet Potatoes): Yams, also native to Africa, supply elements that are important for optimal glandular function and benefit the respiratory, urinary and nervous systems. Their sugar content is absorbed slowly, so they actually help maintain blood sugar levels as well as blood pressure. In addition, due to their high fiber content, yams help control the body weight, by the uniform distribution of weight without transferring extra weight to the hip area or the waistline.

Are You Eating Enough Fruits and Vegetables?

from THE HOOD HEALTH HANDBOOK

It's been recommended that you eat at least 5 servings a day of fruits and vegetables. And if you have a healthy, plant-based diet, you'll probably be eating more than that (about 9 to 11, or more). But are you?

Circle the fruits and vegetables you have eaten in the last week. Give yourself a point for every serving. (A serving is defined as 1 cup of raw leafy vegetables; ¾ cup of 100% fruit or vegetable juice; ½ cup cut–up-fruit or cooked vegetables; 1 medium whole fruit; ½ cup cooked beans or other legumes or ¼ cup dried fruit.)

Count the produce in the chart below then read the following table for your score.

Applesauce	**Dates**	**Dried Fruit**	**Asparagus**
Baked Potato	Peppers	Carrots	Papaya
Steamed Vegetables	**Pears**	**Cantaloupe**	**Berries**
Kale/Collards	Grapes	Cauliflower	Apples
Green Salad	**Pineapple**	**Mushrooms**	**Garlic**
Squash/Zucchini	Grapefruit	Onions	Avocado
Strawberries	**Salsa**	**Eggplant**	**Tomatoes**
Tropical Fruit	Bananas	Spinach	Spinach
100% Fruit Juice	**Oranges**	**Sprouts**	**Beans**
Bean or Pea Soup	Cabbage	Cucumbers	Broccoli

Scoring

35 or more: Healthy	**You're eating at least 5 servings a day of fruits and vegetables. Unless you're also eating 30 servings of ribs a day, you probably have a pretty healthy diet.**
20-34: Not Bad.	You're almost there, so you should try to increase the variety and servings of fruits and vegetables you eat, starting today. Consider fruits and vegetables you liked as a child, but haven't incorporated in your meals in a while.
10-19: Um, no.	**It's time you visit the produce department right away. That's the place on the side of the supermarket with all the colorful round things. Pick up some fruits and vegetables and cook something better, starting tonight.**
9 or less: Your diet sucks.	I know, it's harsh. Maybe the table just didn't list those "special" fruits and vegetables you DO eat, but I'm more willing to bet that you really don't eat any fruits or vegetables beyond the toppings at Pizza Hut. It's time for a change. I guarantee your health is suffering, perhaps silently, but it's suffering.

The Restorative Power of Fresh Juices

The Keyword is "FRESH". Fresh juices gives life. It is the gift given by Mother Nature to nourish the healthy and to nurse the sick back to health! Therefore, it is not just an excellent source of vitamins, minerals, enzymes, purified water, proteins, carbohydrates and chlorophyll. When it is in liquid form, it supplies nutrition that is not wasted to fuel its own digestion as it is with whole fruits, vegetables, and grasses. Therefore, the body can quickly and easily make maximum use of all the nutrition that fresh juice offers.

What's Ailing You?	Fresh Vegetables/Juices and their Preventive Effect
Acidity (body)	Raw potato, wolfberry (Goji) juice
Acne	Carrot, cucumber, fenugreek sprout, wheatgrass
Aging (premature)	All fresh juices
Anemia	Alfalfa sprout, asparagus, bean sprout, beetroot, buckwheat green, lettuce, parsley, spinach, watercress, wheatgrass, Breuss formula
Arthritis	Bean sprout, carrot, celeriac root, cucumber, fennel, kale, pepper, raw potato, sunflower green, turnip, wheatgrass
Asthma	Cabbage, cabbage sprout, carrot, celery, elderberry, parsnip, radish, radish sprout, scallion, sunflower green, wheatgrass
Bladder disorders	Beetroot, cabbage, cabbage sprout, carrot, fenugreek sprout, parsley, sunflower green, tomato, watercress, wheatgrass
Blood Cleanser	Celeriac root, wolfberry (Goji) juice
Blood Pressure (High or Low)	Beetroot, cabbage, cucumber, spinach, wheatgrass
Blood sugar regulation (including diabetes and hypoglycemia)	Artichoke, bean sprout, carrot, kale, spinach, wheatgrass
Bone Disorders	Alfalfa sprout, bean sprout, carrot, tomato, wheatgrass
Brain Circulation	Sauerkraut, carrot
Bronchitis	Celery, elderberry, fennel, wheatgrass
Cancer	Asparagus, bean sprout, beetroot, Breuss formula, carrot, parsley, spinach, sunflower green, wheatgrass, juice fast and detoxification is very beneficial.
Cholesterol reduction	Buckwheat green
Colitis	Cabbage, spinach, wheatgrass
Constipation	Sauerkraut, carrot, celeriac root
Diarrhea	Carrot
Digestion	Sauerkraut, digestive, carrot, bilberry
Eczema	Cucumber, radish, radish sprout, sauerkraut
Eye disorders (including cataracts and fatigue)	Alfalfa sprout, asparagus, beetroot, bilberry, blueberry, grape, beet green, carrot, parsley, pepper, sunflower green, wheatgrass, wolfberry (Goji) juice
Fatigue	Alfalfa sprout, bean sprout, beetroot, beet green, wheatgrass, Breuss formula
Fever	Cucumber, water melon with skin, Biotta Vita 7 fruit juice
Fluid retention	Bean sprout, celeriac root, cucumber, fenugreek sprout, potato juice
Goiter	Sauerkraut

What's Ailing You?	Fresh Vegetables/Juices and their Preventive Effect
Gout	Asparagus, carrot, celery, celeriac root, fennel, tomato, Breuss formula
Hair Loss	Alfalfa sprout, cabbage, cabbage sprout, cucumber, kale, pepper, wheatgrass
Headache	Sauerkraut, carrot, and plenty of plain water
Heart Burn	Raw potato juice, sauerkraut juice
Heart disease	Beetroot, beet green, buckwheat green, fenugreek sprout, pepper, scallion, spinach, sunflower green. Supplementation of EPA (fish oil) or flaxseed oil is highly recommended.
Hemorrhoids	Sauerkraut
Infection	Sauerkraut, raw potato, Goji juice
Immune Support	Sauerkraut, raw potato, beetroot, Breuss formula, wolfberry (Goji) juice
Impotence	Alfalfa sprout, kale, wheatgrass, Breuss formula, Goji juice
Insomnia	Breuss formula, celery, lettuce, carrot
Jaundice	Beetroot, beet green
Joint Support	Carrot, celeriac root
Kidney disorders	Alfalfa sprout, asparagus, beetroot, beet green, cabbage, carrot, sauerkraut, cabbage sprout, celery, cucumber, wolfberry (Goji) juice
Liver disorders	Alfalfa sprout, beetroot, beet green, carrot, celery, lettuce, parsnip, sauerkraut, radish, spinach, sunflower, tomato, wheatgrass, Goji juice
Menopause	Beet root, beet greens, Breuss formula
Menstrual problems	Beetroot, beet green
Nervousness	Celeriac root
Night blindness	Carrot, bilberry, wolfberry (Goji) juice
Poor digestion	Sauerkraut, spinach
Pregnancy and delivery	Alfalfa sprout, bean sprout, beetroot, beet green, carrot
Prostate disorders	Asparagus, parsley
Psoriasis	Cucumber
Radiation damage	Beetroot, cranberry
Respiratory tract and lungs	Elderberry, carrot
Rheumatism	Asparagus, aloe vera, a mix of cucumber and carrot juice, raw potato juice, fresh carrot juice with 1-2 tablespoon of lemon juice
Scurvy	Sauerkraut
Skin problems	Sauerkraut, beetroot, carrot, celeriac root, pomegranate
Sore throat (tonsillitis)	Celeriac root, Vita 7 (fruit juice rich in vitamin C), several drops of Propolis liquid extract
Toxemia	Celeriac root
Ulcers (peptic)	Raw potato, sauerkraut
Urinary tract	Cranberry, parsley

What's Ailing You?	Fresh Vegetables/Juices and their Preventive Effect
Weight loss	All the greens
Worms	Sauerkraut

Words of caution: Fresh juices are contra-indicative for some diseases.

If you have peptic ulcer, gastritis or pancreatitis exacerbation, then don't drink the following juices: lemon, orange, apple, currant, cranberry, because they might increase gastric acidity, can cause heartburn and pain attacks. If you are diabetic, restrict the grape juice consumption. It contains too much glucose and calories. It is also undesirable to drink too much grape drinks, if you have irritated bowels syndrome.

Many fresh fruit juices are depletive in nature. So if you suffer from diarrhea, you should dilute them with water beforehand and drink little by little. You don't need to drink liters of them to reap the benefits. 2 to 3 glasses of juices per day are all it takes. Try to include some of the roughage from the juicing process, the fiber serves as a buffer for slowing down the uptake speed of glucose into the blood stream.

Quick Vegetarian Cooking Tips

by SUPREME UNDERSTANDING, from THE HOOD HEALTH HANDBOOK

Smaller = Quicker. Instead of trying to cook one large solid item, cut it or break it into very small pieces. (Instead of a baked potato, try potato cubes!) Likewise, thin spaghetti will cook faster than thick.

Frozen, not fresh. Sure, fresh is better, but often, you may not have made the time to prepare fresh vegetables. Frozen veggies can be stored for long periods and microwaved quickly in small portions on an "as needed" basis. They may not be as crunchy or as nutritious, but it's better than NO veggies!

Work vegetables into everything. Even an "ordinary" sandwich or burger could be improved by throwing in some spinach leaves or mushrooms. And adding green and yellow/orange veggies (most of which are easy to freeze and store) to a meal is always good nutritionally.

Saute Substitute. You can heat chopped onions, green peppers, etc. for a slight time in the microwave to "soften." Also, fresh mushrooms can be "cooked" when microwaved in a small dish of water or diluted marinade.

Eat your leftovers. You can take leftovers from a stir-fry and turn them into a sandwich, or take unused vegetables from another recipe and throw together a quick soup. Waste not, want not…saves time and money.

Beans and Rice Ideas

Bulk beans, grains, and rice are always really cheap. Unfortunately, they often take a while to make. But, fortunately, they also are easy to keep once made. With that in mind, always make yourself a double, triple, or more batch and freeze the rest. In the long run, you'll save lots of money and lots of time.

Vegetarian Baked Beans. Use baked beans that are specifically labeled "vegetarian." Bush's are great. Eat with whole wheat bread, small potato, and side of steamed vegetable.

Vegetarian Chili. Start with canned or pre-cooked beans (experiment with different beans, including kidney beans, black beans, pinto beans, etc.). Things to add: spice (chili powder, cayenne Pepper, etc.), sautéed onions, green pepper, garlic, canned tomatoes or tomato paste, salsa or barbecue sauce, macaroni or other pasta, Bac-O's or other fake bacon/ham bits, crumbled veggie burger (or try veggie ground beef like Ground Meatless from Morningstar)

Refried Beans for Burritos. There are lots of great low/no fat types. Microwave beans and tortillas separately. Add your favorite veggies, sauces, etc. Chunky salsa is quick when short on time.

Steamed Vegetables or Squash on Rice. Topping ideas: a little grated cheese, lemon pepper, oregano, ground black pepper, salsa and other sauces (For a quicker version than steaming your veggies, you can take refrigerated, pre-cooked rice and microwave frozen veggies on top) Brown rice instead of white will increase the nutrition value of the rice and is just as cheap, but takes a little longer to cook.

Black Beans and Rice. Cheaters version: heat can of beans in a pan, add garlic powder, onion powder, salt and pepper serve over rice. Non-cheaters: Saute real onions and garlic, then add beans.

Red Beans and Rice. Saute a can (or two) of red beans in some oil with onions, garlic, and salt add two cups rice 4 cups water and a heaping teaspoon of fake veggie broth powder. Cover and let cook 20 mins. Serve with salsa. (You can add veggies to this too.)

Refried Beans and Rice. Take a can of no-fat refried beans and add an equal amount of salsa. Add a 10 oz. package of frozen peas or fresh veggies. Put in pan and cook until hot. Serve over rice or toast.

Pasta Ideas

"Pre-sauce" pasta will store for a few days in the fridge if you keep it in a closed container. So just like beans, rice, and grains, cook extra pasta and then microwave for a quick pasta meal a few days later.

Spaghetti. Cook frozen mixed veggies and serve them over pasta w/ canned sauce or your own. Note: Traditional Hunt's in a can is always the cheapest and best. Consumer Reports rated it as tasty as sauces costing 2 or 3 times more. No sugar added too!

Mac and Cheese. Topping ideas: broccoli, mushrooms, garlic, oregano, green pepper, cayenne pepper, shreds of veggie meat or veggie bacon bits.

Egg Drop Ramen with Veggies. Boil water, add Ramen, add fresh or frozen veggies (like green onions and frozen peas) and an egg or two. Stir till Ramen is done

Tomatoes and Chiles Pasta. Add a can of tomatoes and chilies to your favorite pasta shape. Possible garnishes/seasonings: salt and pepper, fresh lime juice, coriander leaves, basil leaves, mint leaves, chives, garlic, curry powder (but not much!)

Pizza Ideas

Dough ideas. Storebought pizza crust (ready made), storebought pizza dough (the kind in a tube), French bread, bagel halves, English muffins, tortillas (the kind used for quesadillas), pita bread.

Sauce ideas. If you can't make your own or buy pizza sauce, just use spaghetti sauce (or tomato slices/paste) and spices instead.

Topping Ideas. Mushrooms, garlic, cheeses, bell peppers, onions, veggie meat, veggie bacon bits, sundried tomatoes, spinach, artichoke, eggplant, jalapenos, whatever you can imagine (from pineapples to zucchini)

Salad Ideas

Make salads easy by making them in advance. Pre-cut your lettuce and carefully choose toppings for easy salad making. Cut, wash and dry lettuce on Sunday before the work week. If the lettuce was freshly bought, it should last until Friday. This is where a salad spinner comes in handy. Choose toppings that don't need to be cut or are hardy. Don't pre-dress salads – they will get soggy. Pre-make salad dressing and put into a travel-size bottle. A vinai grette won't spoil if left on your desk from morning until lunch. Lemon and lime wedges also make a great salad dressings.

Base Ideas: Start with leafy greens, such as lettuce (not Iceberg though!), cabbage, spinach, kale, field greens, etc.

Topping Ideas. Slices or shreds of veggie cheese, feta cheese crumbs, hard-boiled eggs, boiled potato chunks, sliced tomatoes, canned beans, canned or marinated artichoke hearts, pimientos, peperoncini (and other hot peppers), veggie meat or fake bacon bits, croutons, Chinese noodles, cashews, pecans, walnuts, sunflower seeds, pumpkin seeds, flax seeds, radishes, onions, raisins, cranberries, grapes, cherry tomatoes or grape tomatoes, sundried tomatoes, and any other vegetables you have lying around (like broccoli, carrots, asparagus, green, red, and yellow peppers, cucumbers, etc.). Sprinkle the whole thing with some dressing or vinaigrette.

Sandwich Ideas

Start with whole grain bread (Try to find "good" heavy bread made from whole grains rather than the bleached/processed white flour variety. It's worth it.)

"Meat" Ideas. Sliced mushrooms (dry or marinated), grilled tempeh, veggie patties/veggie burgers (If you're not shopping at a health foods store, veggie burgers are still available in most supermarkets. They are usually found in the frozen food section next to the Egg Beaters, bagels, and waffles), veggie deli meat (also usually available near the produce section), refried beans, veggie chili, marinated/sautéed vegetables.

Other Ingredient Ideas. Lettuce, spinach leaves, other leafy things, jalapeno slices, pickles, sprouts, potato chips, Chinese noodles, hummus, veggie bacon bits, veggie cheese (you really can't taste the difference), garlic powder, cayenne pepper, dill, lemon pepper, tomatoes, mushrooms, onions, pickles, green pepper, barbecue sauce, mustard, ketchup, mayonnaise, salsa.

Stir Fry Ideas

You can stirfry (or sauté) your way into some very easy (and healthy) Asian-inspired dishes. (See "Basic Cooking Techniques") This is a way to get lots of vegetables into your diet.

"Base" ideas: Rice, couscous, lo mein noodles (you can use spaghetti noodles stirfried with some onion and soy sauce), any starchy product (from bread to pasta)

Topping ideas. Chopped up fresh or frozen veggies (anything you can imagine, depending on the flavor you're going for) veggie meat chunks, eggs (add egg or two, fry rice until egg is done), onions, scallions, mushrooms, soy sauce, hoisin sauce, sesame seeds, teriyaki sauce, salsa, peanut sauce (peanut butter, soy sauce, garlic, and crushed red pepper), peanuts.

Other Ideas

Baked Potatoes (microwaving can work if your time is short). Topping ideas: salsa, barbecue sauce, ketchup, mustard, spaghetti sauce, spice/seasoning (cayenne pepper, garlic powder, black pepper, etc.), broccoli chunks, stir-fried veggies, homemade chili, cheese (colby, swiss, parmesan) or veggie cheese alternative, veggie bacon bits, sour cream and chives, and anything else you can imagine.

Omelets. Topping ideas: cheese, veggie meat shreds, onions, jalapenos, diced tomatoes, spinach, vegetables.

Hash browns. Topping ideas: cheese, veggies, mushrooms, onions, spices.

Quinoa, millet, or other grain with veggies. Saute grain in oil. Add water, simmer, and add small pieces of veggies. Cook until done

Couscous with veggies or spaghetti sauce. Put couscous in boiling water for 5 min. with a little tamari, salt, onion, and curry.

Soup. Saute onions, garlic, etc. in oil. Then add canned tomatoes, more water, celery, carrot, basil, bay leaf, other vegetables, dried beans, barley, grains, potato, etc. Throw it all in a pot and cook for 1-3 hours. Not a 15 minute meal, but if you make a bunch, it will pay off.

Spending Less To Feed More

by SCIHONOR DEVOTION, from THE HOOD HEALTH HANDBOOK

In this day and time, food is expensive. For those of us who have children, grocery bills could really add up. Some of us have larger households than others, so here are some ideas to help shop for healthy foods on a budget.

Determine a Budget. Make sure it is compatible with all your other household needs. Consider your light bills, travel expenses, phone bill, etc. It may be a good idea to look back at old receipts and do some calculating to see how much you spend on these bills, determine what is unnecessary (and can be cut) and how much you can spend on food. Remember that food is a necessity, while cable TV is not. Don't forget to include all of your non-food items like toothpaste, soap, shampoo, feminine hygiene products, paper towel, toilet tissue, cleaning supplies, etc. Also, don't compare your spending habits to friends with smaller families or those who eat different types of things than you do. Instead compare your spending habits with a family who is similar to yours. Compare notes with them to see if they have any money-saving ideas that can help your budget while still keeping you healthy.

Plan Ahead. Make a meal plan for the next 2 weeks. This will help you to find out what ingredients you need to shop for. Scan your cabinets, refrigerator and freezer to see if you already have the things you need, so that you don't spend money unnecessarily. After you've made a meal plan, make your shopping list. Keep the list on the refrigerator so that if something runs out, you can add it to the list and remember to pick it up with your next shopping trip. Tell the children to add to the list when they've finished something.

Look for Savings. Cut coupons. I know you don't feel like sitting there cutting coupons like an old woman, but hey, you gotta do what you gotta do. Get to clipping. Keep the coupons organized (perhaps clip them to your list), and don't cut coupons for products that you don't use. You'll end up spending money on something you don't need, just because it's on sale. But returning to the last tip, plan your meals around what's on sale. If what you buy usually doesn't have a coupon in the Sunday paper, check the store circulars. Buying store brands can be more affordable and just as healthy, if not more healthy, than getting name brands. It's also a good idea to invest in reusable grocery bags (often sold at the register for about $1), since some stores are charging for disposable bags now. Some stores offer discounts on cases of items, such as rice milk or water. Some have a scanner guarantee program where if an item comes up at the wrong price at the register, you could get it for free. Ask around. Read the signs. Their policies may even be listed. Also, many health food stores now accept EBT/food stamp cards.

Shop at Wholesale Clubs. The cost of membership is well worth it when you calculate all of your savings. You can buy things in bulk there and the prices are usually really good. If your family is not big enough to take advantage of the bulk quantities they offer, you can find a partnering family to go half with you. You could split the cost of membering (and even the products). I do this with a good friend of mine. We split aluminum foil (which comes in a pack of 2), toilet paper, paper towels, and even produce.

Travel. Another way to look for savings is to travel to different stores. I know this may seem time-consuming, but it could be well worth it if the stores are not really far away from each other. On the street where I do a lot of my shopping, there is a Whole Foods, a Trader Joes, and a Stop and Shop. I've been to them all so many times that I know which ones offer the best deals on which products. So, when I go shopping, I organize my list by store and section. This makes it much easier. I go to the furthest store and have to pass the others to get home, so I'm not wasting gas either. Sometimes, I even carpool with that same friend I mentioned earlier.

Stick to Your Script. When you go to shopping, stick with the items on your list. Many stores place more expensive items on the shelves that are at eye level. Don't get got. Look high and low for savings, literally. Be sure to not only check the nutritional value of the items but also the unit pricing. It's usually listed on the shelves below the item. This will tell you how much you are paying for each ounce or pound of that particular item. You can compare costs easily this way. Bring cash and only spend the cash that you bring. Don't use your credit cards unless you absolutely have to. You'll end up going way over budget and you'll be charged finance charges on top of that. If you must, bring a calculator and add things up as you go along. I usually write the cost of my items next to the item on the list as I shop and add each section up as I go along. This way, I know if I have to put something back before I actually get to the register and look really bad. That's not a good look. But hey, it's reality and most of us have had to do that before.

Farmer's Markets. Check out local farmers' markets when they are in town. Also, check out CSA's (Community Supported Agriculture). CSA's provide delivery of produce sometimes weekly to its members. For example, you may pay a certain amount for membership for a certain amount of produce in pounds. Whatever is harvested for that season is what you get. You may pay, let's say, $40 each month and twice a month, you may receive, 3 pounds of plums, 5 pounds of nectarines, 2 pounds of grapes, 3 pounds of tomatoes, and 2 pounds of broccoli and 1 pound of cauliflower. Now, this is just an example since you may not know exactly what you will get since you will get whatever is harvested and in season. Farmers Markets are good because you support your local farmers and you usually get fresh fruits and vegetables. Some farmers even offer affordable organic produce which is great. Sometimes the farmers also sell breads,

handmade soaps, honey, and other things that you may need. Then again you can always grow your own fruits and vegetables. Hey, if certain "herbs" can be grown in a closet, why can't we get creative and grow our produce right at home?

Food Co-ops. Food co-ops are like grocery stores except that they are basically owned and operated by their members. So, if you join a food co-op, you will be able to get some good deals on food, but, you will be required to work in the store in some capacity. Don't worry. It's not like a full time job. You may have to do something like 6 hours a week. Oh and the good thing is that anyone in your household can do the shift for you. So, if you have a large family, send one of the children who are old enough to do the shift. It'll be good for them. No, seriously.

Don't eat out. It costs way too much, whether you have a large family or a small one. I know you're probably used to just grabbing something quick on the way to work, on the way home, or during your lunch break, but that adds up. Just add up what you spend every week that way and you'll see.

I suggest that you wake up earlier than you usually do, cook at home for breakfast, and bring your own lunch from home as well. Leftovers that wouldn't make a full meal for your family may be good to bring for lunch.

Or you can cook all day Sunday and freeze your meals so that you'll just have to worry about salad of some vegetables when you get home from work. And when I say cook, I mean from scratch. You will need to get used to taking more time to prepare meals, but as always, involve the children in the preparation. This will be good for them too.

Alright! I hear you yelling at me through the pages… "Yeah right!" "What does she think this is?" "Now how the heck am I supposed to do that?" Dag! I hear yall. Just bear with me so I can explain the cost savings. Now, one box of instant potatoes is about $3. A 5 pound bag of potatoes is about $3 too. Which one do you think will feed most of you for the longest period of time? Of course the bag of potatoes. You can make mashed potatoes, baked potatoes, home fries for breakfast, potato pancakes, homemade French fries, Sheperd's pie, or even your own hash browns. You can make a ton of meals with that bag and only a side of a meal with that box. Not to mention all of that stuff they might have added to that box to make your potatoes instant. But that's another story. You get my point. You can make dry beans, pasta, stews, soups or casseroles with hearty vegetables for economical meals.

Want to spend quality time with your children? Make peanut butter or oatmeal raisin cookies together. Make pancakes from scratch and add berries and bananas. Make muffins and add berries, nuts, and bananas. Children will love this. You can even invest in a bread machine to make your own bread (though you can also do it by hand). Either way, it's much cheaper than buying loaves of bread.

Other Things to Try

There are many things that you can try in order to cut back on spending and to make sure that your family is getting the nutritious meals that you all need. Here are some…

- ☐ Get a water filter – This way, you don't have to worry about always buying bottled water.

- ☐ Learn to eat new healthy things like cauliflower, cabbage, squash, zucchini, eggplant, and other things besides the popular veggies like broccoli, peas, string beans, and carrots.

- ☐ Avoid soda – it is not only unhealthy, but it is expensive and if you have children can be contributing to headaches, behavioral problems, and other issues.

- ☐ Drink more water – Our bodies are made of water. If you don't put water in it, you will get dehydrated and will be suffering, maybe without even realizing until it's too late. Did I mention that water is cheaper than juice or soda? It may even be free if you have a good filter. Get hood and add a drop of liquid chlorophyll to the gallon to be sure that every family member is getting iron. Chlorophyll also detoxifies the liver, cleans the digestive tract and more.

- ☐ To save time, make larger amounts of each meal and freeze some for a day when you don't feel like cooking. If you have a large family, invest in a deep freezer. This will allow you to shop for many items at once and freeze unused items for a later time.

- ☐ Don't get stuck on buying colored sugar water. There is barely no nutrition in this and it is full of artificial color and flavor. Buy 100% juice and not the 2% they give you in prison. Think about it. If the bottle only has 2% juice in it, what's the other 98% made up of? When you do buy 100% juice, dilute it in an empty gallon bottle with half a gallon of water. This is good because it will reduce your sugar intake and it will stretch the juice to feed more people. You can make a half gallon of 100% juice into a whole gallon of juice.

- ☐ Use smaller plates, cups and bowls. We tend to overeat in this country. By cutting back on plate size, don't worry. You will not cheat your family of their needed nutrition.

- ☐ If you can't afford fresh vegetables, buy frozen. You must have some sort of vegetables in your diet each day. Especially if you are going by S.A.D. (Standard American Diet). It is sad that the small amount of vegetables they suggest is often left out since it can easily be forgotten. If your family has members with low iron, don't be afraid to have spinach for breakfast.

- ☐ Keep Food Fresh – Be sure that when you close packages or containers, you get rid of the air in it first. Air is a breeding ground for bacteria to grow. Use the green bags made to keep produce fresher longer. They may sell them in your produce section.

- ☐ Keep onions away from other produce. The natural sulphur in them will ripen your stuff too soon. Keep produce in the fridge if you have room. Give preference to softer fruits (as opposed to apples, oranges, etc. that may last longer than some others). Don't put bananas in the fridge. They will go bad faster.

- ☐ If you buy spoiled food, don't hesitate to return it. I've held on to stuff for 2 weeks just so I could get a replacement or get a credit or my money back when I returned it. Food is too expensive to literally just throw away.

- ☐ Shred your own cheese and peel your own carrots. It may be a little more work, but it's cheaper and the carrots will last longer with the peels on.

- ☐ Hot cereals are cheaper than cold cereals. Make a big pot in the morning. Get creative like they do in jail and add some peanut butter to a nice pot of oatmeal for extra protein. Add cinnamon, raisins, nuts, or dried fruits, etc.

- ☐ Avoid canned foods. But if you do get them, wash the cans with warm, soapy water, then rinse the food after you've opened the can. Rinsing will get all the added salt and sugar from syrup off of the food before you eat it.

- ☐ Eat less meat. Don't be fooled. Our bodies don't need as much protein as we've been told. Eat protein rich foods that are more affordable like apricots, grapes, bananas, beans, nuts, figs and avocados. Guacamole is good with some crackers for a snack or even in a wrap with veggies for lunch. If you do eat eggs, stretch them but adding a little milk like my parents and grandparents did. You can use organic eggs, egg white, rice milk, soy milk, hemp milk, almond milk too. Try it. You may like it.

- ❏ Don't waste food! If fruits look like they are going bad, make a smoothie for the family or a fruit salad. You could also just cut them up and add them to the side of your meals. Use leftover meat from dinner to make sandwiches for lunch if it isn't enough to fill everyone for dinner.

- ❏ If you make burgers or some sort of patties, you can add things to it to bulk it up like oatmeal, beans, rice, cornmeal, cream of wheat, chopped vegetables, and

other things laying around that will give it some weight.

- ❏ Don't eat out of the box or bag. You will probably eat more than if you just pour some out in your hand.

- ❏ Eat slowly. Be sure your family knows how to chew? They should be chewing enough to break the food down so that as it goes through the system, you can absorb what you need and get rid of the rest easily.

Finally, the following provides advice on saving money by storing and reheating food safely at www.EatDrinkBetter.com, Rachel Fox, RD in Food Safety:

- ❏ Keep stored food cold. The bacterial danger zone is between 41-140 degrees Fahrenheit. Purchase a refrigerator thermometer to double check your temperature.

- ❏ Travel safely. If you need to bring your lunch to work, keep it in a cooler while in transit to your workplace. Maintaining the cold temperature is important in preventing bacterial growth.

- ❏ Don't save food forever. Leftover food should be kept in the refrigerator for 7 days or less. If you need to, put date labels on storage containers.

- ❏ When in doubt, throw it out! If your food looks funny, smells funny or feels funny…it's probably time to pitch it.

- ❏ Reheat thoroughly. Your reheated food should be too hot to eat for 2 minutes after cooking. If you can eat your leftovers right out of the oven (toaster oven/microwave) you have not heated it hot enough to kill harmful bacteria.

- ❏ Cook low and slow. For "solid" foods (meat, casserole, lasagna, quiche, etc) cook at a lower temperature for a longer period of time. This will prevent

the outside from cooking too much while leaving the inside too cold.

- ❏ Stir or turn halfway through. "Non-solid" foods (pasta, rice, chopped veggies, etc) can be stirred easily. Stir these foods halfway through cooking to ensure the whole meal is cooked through. If you can't stir it, flip it.

- ❏ Don't reheat in plastic! Ever wonder why reusable containers turn red after heating tomato sauce? The sauce is melted into the container and yes the container melts into the sauce. Don't heat your plastic containers anymore; reheat in glass/ceramic.

- ❏ Leftovers make for easy lunch planning and are a life saver when you have no time to make dinner. Remember these eight tips when enjoying your leftovers. The summer season provides us with bountiful farmer's markets and overflowing gardens. An easy way to save food dollars is to cook in batches. You can pre-portion meal servings and refrigerate/freeze them for later.

When All Else Fails: Healthy Fast Food?

by SUPREME UNDERSTANDING, from THE HOOD HEALTH HANDBOOK

We understand that it's unlikely you'll cook EVERY meal at home, and will eventually have to eat out at some point. This can be a daunting task for vegetarians. In many cities, vegetarians have the option of dining at a number of exclusively vegetarian restaurants or establishments that are especially vegetarian-friendly. To find out what's in your city, we suggest the online guide to vegan, vegetarian, and veg-friendly establishments at

www.happycow.com. You may even find a few that only serve raw and living foods. But what about when your budget or time constraints make those options unlikely? Or what about when you're brought along on a lunch or dinner date to a place you'd never expect to find healthy food? We understand those concerns, so we've created the following guide to vegetarian dining at non-vegetarian food franchises. Keep in mind, though, that simply picking vegetarian items at fast food spots does NOT mean you're eating healthy. I recommend avoiding fast food spots as much as possible, because even the vegetarian items at many of these places are unhealthy. If you can't imagine why, just read this book's articles on Fast Food. If you asked me to name the "healthiest" fast food chain that you can find in just about any city, I'd say Subway. When my family does road trips, that's where we go. Again, that's not the BEST place to eat, but it's certainly better than the alternatives available in Cooter County, West Virginia. Before we begin, there are a few things you should be mindful of at ANY place where you eat:

Is this place clean? Does it have a good rating from the Health department? Will my meal be free of any "unwanted" particles? Do they cook meatless items separately? Or is everything cooked on the same grill (or the same wok) and cut with the same knives? Do they clean the grill or wok for meatless dishes? Is this enough for me? Does the server appear knowledgeable about which items contain animal products? Do I need to ask a manager? Does the manager need to call *her* manager?

Finally, can I replace the meat in an entrée with extra vegetables? And are meals discounted when meat is eliminated? For example, Burger King charges less for a Veggie Whopper (a Whopper without the beef patty), but McDonald's charges the same price for a burger with or without the meat! tablespoonsG.I.Fridays normally takes $2-3 off entrees without meat, but Johnny Carino's charges full price. With that said, the following information should help you make an informed choice when eating out.

Burger Joints

There are several popular establishments where you can now order veggie burgers. These include: Backyard Burgers, Bennigan's, Burger King, Cheeburger Cheeburger, Cheers, Claim Jumper, Coco's, Denny's, 5 and Diner, Flamer's Grill, Hard Rock Café, Hard Times Café, Harvey's, Houston's, John Harvard's, Johnny Rockets, Kelsey's, Mimi's Café, Pyramid Brewery, Rainforest Café, Ruby Tuesdays, Shari's, and Village Inn franchises. Many of these restaurants also offer side items such as cooked vegetables, in additional to the traditional carb-heavy French fries.

Bagel/Bread/Breakfast Shops

Most restaurants catering to breakfast food, whether it's bagels or pancakes, have a decent selection of items fit for vegetarians. Again, be aware of how and where these items are prepared. At places like Einstein Bros. and Manhattan Bagels, nearly all the bagels are vegan, except for the cheese and egg varieties. At some shops, like Einstein Bros., hummus is offered as a healthy (and tasty) alternative to cream cheese. At Manhattan Bagels, the Manhattan Grille and Vegetable Garden sandwiches can be made on a bagel, a roll, or a tortilla, and are vegan if you omit the spreads and cheese. Panera Bread has a wide selection of soups and sandwiches, but many of their soups are made with a chicken stock, and our readers have reported difficulty with getting straight answers from the people who work there. Be careful about uninformed workers! Just because the big girl with the gold tooth told you its "vegitaranian" doesn't mean there's not chunks of chicken waiting for you to discover (many people don't think chicken or fish, or animal by products, are the same as "meat")

IHOP and Waffle House are gradually becoming more mindful of the needs of vegetarians, but you should still ask if your eggs and hash browns will be cooked on the same grill as items prepared with meat. Denny's vegan foods include oatmeal, English muffins, bagels, grits, applesauce, fresh fruit, vegetable plates, seasoned French fries, baked potatoes with several vegetable toppings, garden salads with light Italian or oil-and-vinegar dressing, and sandwiches that can be made with several vegetable options.

East Asian Restaurants

Asian restaurants, like the continent of Asia itself, are not homogenous in any way. In spite of the great diversity between, for example, Thai eateries and Japanese Steak and Sushi joints, there are some things to look for wherever you go. For beginners, many East Asian cultures are familiar with sects of Buddhism that avoid eating meat entirely, or at least for particular periods of time. Thus, most servers will understand your request for vegetarian food. However, with Japanese food, you should also be clear that you are not interested in katso bushi, or the fish stock/powder that makes it into a great deal of their otherwise "vegetarian" dishes. Out of the East Asian countries, Vietnamese and Mongolian cuisine rely heaviest on meat dishes, and are thus least likely to have cookware set aside for vegetarian fare. Chinese restaurants may offer more tofu (sometimes called bean curd) and vegetable dishes, but depending on the size and quality of the restaurant, your food may be cooked in the same wok as the meat dishes. If you're at a place called "Mr. China King, home of the $2 Lunch Special," I would think twice before ordering. Finally, Thai food is often one of your best bets for good vegetarian food, as Thailand has a long-standing vegetarian (Buddhist) tradition, recognized everywhere in the country. This is reflected in Thai restaurants, nearly all of which offer some sort of "tofu curry" dish.

Ethiopian Restaurants

Most Ethiopian restaurants offer vegetarian entrees like Allicha Kik and Meser Wot, wonderfully seasoned lentil or vegetable dishes that are sopped up in the traditional Injera flatbread.

Greek/Middle Eastern Food

There's much more at these places than lamb gyros. Most of the side items, like the tabbouleh, baba ghanoush, hummus, cous cous, and stuffed grape leaves, are vegetarian (and in most cases vegan). You can assemble a full meal from these items or order a falafel wrap (or veggie wrap) as your entrée.

Indian Restaurants

With a population of nearly 1 billion, and recognized by many as its own "subcontinent," India is also home to great diversity in both culture and cuisine. For beginners, North Indian cuisine is much more reliant on meat than South Indian cuisine, and Hindu-owned eateries are more mindful of vegetarians than their Muslim-owned counterparts. With this in mind, it is still good to know that most servers will understand your request for a meatless dish, and nearly all Indian restaurants will have something to satisfy you.

Jamaican/Caribbean Restaurants

Because of Rastafarian influence on the cuisine and culture of many Caribbean islands, one can usually find some vegetarian items at any Caribbean restaurant. While some only offer baked patties filled with spinach, callaloo (a plant similar to collard greens), broccoli, or mixed vegetables, others offer entrees based around curry tofu and the like.

With vegetable sides however, it is best to ask what kind of stock they've been cooked in. In fact, if you're not at the type of place that serves tofu, it's best to ask about the status of any item, especially if you're vegan. One of the few Caribbean food franchises, Pollo Tropical, offers several vegan options such as the Vegetarian TropiChop entrée, the Balsamic Tomatoes and Bananas Tropical. The chain's black beans, French fries, white rice, yellow rice, boiled yucca, and corn are vegan too.

Mexican Restaurants

Many Mexican restaurants can substitute beans for meat on their items, but it is important to know what the beans and tortillas were cooked with, because in more traditional restaurants, it may have been lard. This is less common in franchises, particularly those restaurants that serve somewhat Americanized versions of Mexican fare. Many such franchises, Chili's for example, offer vegetable quesadillas, burritos, and fajitas on their menu. Other's, like Moe's or Willie's Mexicana Grill, offer tofu as a meat substitute. Chipotle offers a vegetarian fajita burrito, but be sure to order it with black beans–the pinto beans are cooked with bacon.

Finally, Taco Bell may not seem like a healthy choice for a vegetarian, but they now offer the opportunity to make any item "vegetarian" simply be requesting it as such. They will then replace any meat in the item with refried beans, which – like everything else at Taco Bell – is now cooked without lard.

Pizza Places/Italian Restaurants

Though it isn't the healthiest option, cheese pizza is a common resort for new vegetarians. Enjoying pizza can be a little more complicated if you are vegan. However, both the pizza sauce and dough at Chuck E. Cheese, Little Caesars, and Papa John's are vegan. Pizza Hut uses vegan sauce, and only its Thin & Crispy and dessert crusts are vegan. Thus, by omitting the cheese and choosing your favorite vegetable toppings, you can easily make a delicious vegan pizza. With Cici's you should ask about the vegan status of each item on your pizza, but they also offer a pasta-and-salad buffet with many vegan options.

Regarding Italian restaurants in general, it's usually pretty easy to order a vegetarian meal featuring pasta, vegetables, and sauce (just make sure the sauce is meatless). Ordering vegan requires that the noodles aren't made with egg and the sauce isn't made with dairy, but a knowledgeable server should be able to assist you. A number of popular Italian-based franchises are vegetarian-friendly. Macaroni Grill has several vegetarian options, including all the pastas with garlic and oil (vegan), the Capellini Pomodoro (vegan), and many options including dairy, such as the Tomato Bruschetta and Penne Arrabbiata. Vegans can ask for these dishes without cheese. As a side note, pizza (and most pastas) are actually not traditional Italian innovations, but are actually "borrowed" from China.

Sub/Sandwich Shops

Vegetarian subs, sandwiches, and wraps are available nearly everywhere nowadays, including: Blimpie, Cousin's Subs, Firehouse Subs, Jason's Deli, Jersey Mike's Subs, Quizno's Subs, Roly Poly, Subway, and World Wraps. You can also make a vegetarian subway sandwich "meatier" by purchasing vegetarian "lunchmeat" and putting a few slices into your sandwich.

In fact, most supermarkets with a deli counter can prepare a vegetarian sandwich, and a trip to the nearby health food aisle should provide you with the "meat" to put inside. For people trying to avoid "fake meat," extra mushrooms can also provide the substance and texture of a traditional sandwich or sub. Keep in mind that it's typically the sauce that gives the sandwich its flavor. With this in mind, however, also remember that "vegetarian" doesn't always mean "vegan" and many sauces contain dairy products.

Miscellaneous Fast Food

At Arby's, vegans can have the hash browns, baked potato, garden salad or side salad with Italian dressing, and an apple or cherry turnover. Burger King has the BK Veggie (which you can have "your way" – that is, with mushrooms, Buffalo sauce, etc.). Just ask how it is prepared. Some places run it through an oven, others microwave it, and a few others fry it with the meat! You can also order a Veggie Whopper, which is a Whopper minus the meat, for about $1.49 at most places. At Carl's Jr., the french fries, hash-brown nuggets, breadsticks, English muffins, and CrissCuts are all vegan. In the restaurant, there is an all-you-can-eat salad bar that offers a variety of fresh vegetables and a three-bean salad. They also offer baked potatoes, which can be ordered with all-vegetable margarine.

McDonald's, as you know, secretly used beef powder and beef fat on their French fries for years, until vegetarians complained. So they stopped, but the fries weren't as "flavorful" (meaning addictive), so they secretly snuck beef powder back in until a vegetarian association launched a huge lawsuit against them. Now they've stopped, but considering their corporate practices throughout the world, as well as the chemicals in their food, they're hard to recommend for anybody trying to eat healthy or vegetarian. In fact, McDonald's website now says that NONE of their items can be guaranteed 100% free of animal ingredients. You can learn a lot more about McDonald's elsewhere in this book.

Years back, Taco Bell also sold a Vegetarian Fajita that was made with clam and oyster sauce. However, since then, Taco Bell has made a significant transition in meeting the needs of vegetarians. You can now order any item at Taco Bell "vegetarian," which, as said earlier, simply involves them replacing the meat on an item with vegan refried beans. At Wendy's, vegans can have the plain baked potato, the Deluxe Garden Salad with red Italian dressing and no cheese, or French fries. You can also ask for a veggie sandwich, which is pretty much the same deal as Burger King's Veggie Whopper.

To reiterate my first point however, being healthy is not JUST about "avoiding meat." You can avoid meat and still eat at Mickey D's every day and damn near die like dude on SuperSize Me, except you'll be experiencing the vegan version of fast food death. So think of fast food as a last resort. This guide is provided to help you learn how to make the best of that last resort.

There IS another alternative, however. According to Dr. Joe Esposito:

> Yes, healthy fast food does exist…and not only fast food, but "traveling fare" is also at your fingertips…There is the obvious, (or maybe not so obvious), healthy choices such as fruit bars and trial mix. These are usually my first choices, they are inexpensive, don't need to be refrigerated and will help keep you healthy while under the stress of traveling…Sesame sticks made with wheat or spelt are always a hit. Dried pineapple or dried papaya are high in digestive enzymes and will satisfy your sweet tooth. Dried ginger has been shown to help with motion sickness, is great for circulation, and has been claimed to be an aphrodisiac (so be careful with this one!) What if you want something a bit more exotic and more like a meal? Dried, packaged hummus is a great choice. Just add water and you have hummus! How about dried, packaged tabouli? Again, just add water and eat them as they are or put them on a baked chip or baked cracker. If you don't mind your "traditionally hot foods" a little on the cool side, how about dried refried beans… just add water. A can of room temperature baked beans, no meat chili, soups, rice and beans or even a can of organic veggies are good choices. If you are going camping or on an overnight trip and you want a "traditional" breakfast, bring along powdered soy milk and dry, healthy, organic cereal or granola, add water to the powdered soy milk and enjoy your All American breakfast of cereal and milk. These ideas are quick, light weight, healthy and will save you a bundle on restaurant bills. Not to mention the convenience of having your choice of quality food where you want it and when you want it.

The Essential Vitamin Guide

from THE HOOD HEALTH HANDBOOK

"God, in His infinite wisdom, neglected nothing and if we would eat our food without trying to improve, change or refine it, thereby destroying its life-giving elements, it would meet all requirements of the body." – Jethro Kloss

Why do we eat food? Not just to get full. In fact, we don't actually eat to get full at all, so if you're doing that, you've got other health issues we can't even talk about here. We eat for sustenance. Meaning we eat to live. Food provides our body with the fuel it needs to function. And because our body is so complex and multi-layered, there are different things we need from the food we eat. That is, we need more than just calories and carbohydrates for energy. We also need the vitamins and minerals that keep every system in our body, large or small, fine-tuned. Yes, that's what food's really here for. To provide us with health. Nothing wrong with good flavor, but flavor without nutrition is like the wagon without the horse (or a fresh paint job without the car, for you modern folks who never heard of folk sayings).

What are Vitamins?

"The human body heals itself and nutrition provides the resources to accomplish the task." – Roger Williams Ph.D.

Vitamins are organic substances which help change the food we eat into skin, muscles, nerves, and other parts of our bodies which a basic, balanced diet provides. Certain vitamins lacking in our diet causes deficiency diseases. On the same note, vitamins in excess of what the body needs may actually produce illness rather than increase health and wellbeing. Many scientific studies have shown that a high dietary intake of vitamins is associated with health and a low dietary intake of vitamins is associated with disease.

Unfortunately, many of the vitamins in our foods are often rendered inactive before we get a chance to consume them. Loss of vitamin content occurs in food products because of all the methods used to "treat" our food before it gets to us, including: overheating, processing, preservation, pasteurization, irradiation, and genetic modification. Thus, the best sources for vitamins are found in raw and fresh fruits and vegetables, the peels of fruits and vegetables (and the outer covering of some grains), and the hearts of many grains, seeds, and fruits. It's also clear that the nutrients in food work best in conjunction with each other, rather than isolated in supplements.

"Nutrition can be compared with a chain in which all essential items are separate links. We know what happens if one link of a chain is weak or is missing. The whole chain falls apart." – Patrick Wright, Ph.D.

Our bodies need at least 13 vitamins to function, which fall into two specific vitamin groups:

Fat-soluble (stored in the body's fatty tissue and the liver)	Water soluble (not stored so they must be taken into the body every day)	
Vitamin A	Vitamin B1	Vitamin B7
Vitamin D	Vitamin B2	Vitamin B9
Vitamin E	Vitamin B3	Vitamin B12
Vitamin K	Vitamin B5	Vitamin C
	Vitamin B6	

Vitamin A (Retinol in animal foods/Beta-carotene in plant foods)

Functions: Helps you see normally in the dark and promotes the growth and health of all body cells and tissues. It also protects against infection by keeping healthy the skin and tissues in the mouth, stomach, intestines and respiratory and uro-genital tract.

Deficiency problems: Night blindness and other eye problems; dry, scaly skin, problems with reproduction, poor growth.

Food sources: Beta-carotene can be found in brightly colored fruits and vegetables such as apricots, pumpkins, and carrots, as well as leafy green vegetables, squash and melon.

Excess amounts: Can lead to birth defects, headaches, vomiting, double vision, hair loss, bone abnormalities and liver damage.

Vitamin B1 (Thiamin)

Functions: Converts bloods sugar into energy, and is involved in key metabolism. Promotes growth and is a tonic for the nerves. There is some evidence that vitamin B1 may help to improve IQ/ memory and it may help to control diabetes.

Deficiency problems: Alcoholics are frequently low in thiamin and suffer fatigue, weak muscles and nerve damage as a result. Depression, irritability, withdrawal, and schizoid tendencies can also be symptoms of deficiency.

Food sources: Whole grains, potatoes, nuts and legumes. Legumes include beans, lentils, peas, and peanuts.

Excess amounts: In very high doses (usually only possible with supplements), excessive thiamin can be toxic. But excessive natural intake of thiamin is expelled in the urine.

Vitamin B2 (Riboflavin)

Functions: Helps all body cells produce energy. Riboflavin is an antioxidant, also involved in the production of red blood cells and maintaining a healthy heart.

Deficiency problems: Severely malnourished people may suffer eye disorders (such as cataracts), dry and flaky skin, and a sore red tongue.

Food sources: Milk and other dairy products (particularly yogurt), whole grain products, eggs, green leafy vegetables, nuts, mushrooms, leafy green vegetables and yeast extracts.

Excess amounts: No known toxicity.

Vitamin B3 (Niacin)

Functions: Helps the body use sugars and fatty acids, and helps all body cells produce energy. It also helps enzymes function in the body, aids the nervous system, helps digestion, and maintains healthy skin.

Deficiency problems: Symptoms include diarrhea, mental disorientation (including anxiety, confusion, fatigue, and depression) and skin problems.

Food sources: Some niacin is produced in the body. Foods high in protein, such as peanut butter and legumes, whole grains, nuts and yeast extracts are also usually good sources.

Excess amounts: Excessive intake of nicotinic acid (a form of niacin), which usually only occurs with supplements, may cause flushed (reddish, itchy) skin, liver damage, stomach ulcers and high blood sugar.

Vitamin B5 (Pantothenic Acid)

Functions: Helps all body cells produce energy by helping metabolize protein, fat and carbohydrate in food. It also aids in healing wounds, fights infections, strengthens the immune system and helps build cells.

Deficiency problems: Rare in healthy people who eat a balanced diet.

Food sources: All vegetables and many other foods, including whole grain cereals, oats, dried fruits and nuts.

Excess amounts: May cause occasional diarrhea and water retention.

Vitamin B6 (Pyridoxine)

Functions: Helps the body make proteins, which are then used to make body cells. It's required for the functioning of more than 60 enzymes, aids the nervous system, protects against certain types of cancer, and helps produce other body chemicals such as insulin, hemoglobin and antibodies to fight infection.

Deficiency problems: Depression, nausea, mental convulsions in infants and greasy, flaky skin.

Food sources: Legumes, eggs, whole grains, nuts, yeast extract, soybeans and bananas.

Excess amounts: Can cause nerve damage.

Vitamin B7 (Biotin)

Functions: Helps all body cells produce energy. It also helps metabolize protein, fat and carbohydrates in food.

Deficiency problems: Heart abnormalities, appetite loss, fatigue, depression and dry skin.

Food sources: Peanuts and peanut butter, almonds, eggs, yeast breads and cereals.

Excess amounts: No known toxicity.

Vitamin B9 (Folate, Folacin or Folic Acid)

Functions: Plays an essential role in the metabolism of sugar, the manufacture of antibodies, the normal function of the nervous system, red blood cell formation in bone marrow, and for the normal production of DNA and RNA, which determines hereditary patterns.

Deficiency problems: Impaired cell division and growth, a type of anemia, and, during the first trimester of pregnancy, increased risk of delivering a baby with neural tube defects including spina bifida.

Food sources: Brewer's yeast, green leafy vegetables, oranges, bananas, red fruits, nuts, avocado, and whole grains.

Excess amounts: May interfere with medications and cause convulsions in people with epilepsy. It can also mask vitamin B12 deficiencies, which can lead to permanent nerve damage.

Vitamin B12 (Cobalamin)

Functions: Forms and regenerates red blood cells, serves in body cells as a vital part of many body chemicals, helps the body use fatty acids and some amino acids, increases energy, improves concentration and maintains the nervous system.

Deficiency problems: Anemia, fatigue, nerve damage, a smooth tongue, very sensitive skin. B12 deficiencies may be hidden when extra folate is taken to treat or prevent anemia. Strict vegans who eat no animal byproducts (and their infants) are the most likely to develop vitamin B12 deficiencies.

Food sources: Plant products do not contain B12. Non-vegans can get B12 from eggs or dairy, and strict vegans can get B12 from certain yeasts and some fortified foods.

Excess amounts: No known toxicity.

Vitamin C (Ascorbic Acid)

Functions: Helps the body absorb iron out of food made from plant sources. Vital for healthy skin, bones, muscles, healing and protection from viruses, toxins, drugs, infections and allergies. Necessary for cholesterol metabolism.

Deficiency problems: Scurvy, a disease that causes loose teeth, Excessive bleeding, swollen gums and improper wound healing. Scurvy is rare in the United States.

Food sources: Citrus fruits and many other fruits and vegetables, including berries, melons, peppers, leafy herbs and many dark-green leafy vegetables, potatoes and tomatoes.

Excess amounts: May cause kidney stones, gout, diarrhea and stomach cramps in excess

Vitamin D (Calciferol)

Functions: Promotes the absorption of calcium and phosphorus and helps deposit these minerals in bones and teeth to make them strong.

Deficiency problems: Greater risk of osteoporosis and osteomalacia (softening of the bones). Children can develop rickets or defective bone growth.

Food sources: Vitamin D is known as the "sunshine" vitamin, because your body can produce it after sunlight or ultraviolet light hits the skin. Food sources include cheese, eggs, and some fish (such as salmon).

Excess amounts: Can lead to kidney stones or kidney damage, weak muscles and bones, excessive bleeding and other problems. Excessive amounts usually come from supplements, not food or overexposure to sunlight.

Vitamin E (Tocopherol)

Functions: An antioxidant essential for absorption of iron and metabolism of essential fatty acids, protection of the circulatory system and cells, and slowing the aging process. May have a possible role in protecting against illnesses such as heart disease and some types of cancer.

Deficiency problems: Nervous system problems. Deficiencies are very rare, as vitamin E is abundant in foods. Premature, very low birthweight babies and people who do not absorb fat normally may have deficiency problems.

Food sources: Nuts, seeds, eggs, whole grains, unrefined oils, leafy vegetables, avocados and soybeans.

Excess amounts: May interfere with vitamin K action and enhance the effect of some anticoagulant drugs.

Vitamin K

Functions: Vitamin K, also known as Phylloquinone or Phytomenadione from vegetable sources (and Menaquinone or Menatetrenone from animal sources), helps blood to clot and stop bleeding.

Deficiency problems: Thin blood that does not adequately coagulate.

Food sources: Intestinal bacteria produce some of the vitamin K you need. The best food sources include green leafy vegetables such as kale, parsley, spinach and broccoli. Smaller amounts are found in milk and other dairy products, eggs, whole grains, molasses, fruits and other vegetables.

Excess amounts: No known toxicity.

Recommendations

Vitamins can be lost from foods during preparation, cooking, or storage. To prevent loss of vitamins:

❑ Serve fruits and vegetables raw whenever possible.

❑ Steam, boil, or simmer foods in a very small amount of water, or microwave them for the shortest time possible.

❑ When you boil vegetables, use the water (which contains a lot of the nutrients) to make a vegetable juice or broth.

❑ Cook potatoes in their skins. Be sure to wash the dirt off the outside.

❑ Refrigerate prepared juices and store them for no more than 2 to 3 days.

❑ Store cut, raw fruits and vegetables in an airtight container and refrigerate—do not soak or store in water. Vitamin C will be dissolved in the water.

The Essential Mineral Guide

from THE HOOD HEALTH HANDBOOK

Dietary minerals are the chemical elements required by living organisms, other than the four common elements found in our cells (carbon, hydrogen, nitrogen, and oxygen). The trace minerals group includes over 50 chemical elements, all of which can be found in our bodies, but all of which are not essential to our health. Scientists group these minerals into three categories:

❑ **The essential trace minerals.** These are minerals that are required in the diet for full health, and when

the intake is insufficient, symptoms of deficiency will arise.

❑ **The toxic trace minerals.** The term is used for minerals that cause health problems even at levels that may be encountered normally in the environment. With these, the greater danger is getting too much instead of too little. This category changes from time to time, but generally includes aluminum, arsenic, cadmium, lead, mercury, and tin. Actually, too much of ANY nutrient can be toxic; how much is too much depends on the nutrient.

☐ **Everything else.** These are all the other minerals that are present in the body but are not essential in our diet or particularly toxic.

Like vitamins, minerals can also be lost from food due to processing and cooking. And just as with vitamins (except perhaps more so), minerals have been called a double-edged sword because too much of a mineral can be just as harmful as not enough. Malnutrition is the number one cause for mineral deficiencies. But mineral deficiencies can also be caused by anemia, cancer, colitis, constipation, convulsions, diabetes, dysentery, eczema, heart disease, intestinal diseases, menstruation disorders, paralysis, infantile paralysis, rickets, scurvy, tuberculosis, tumors and skin eruptions.

Our bodies need at least 15 minerals to function:

Calcium	Phosphorus	Magnesium
Copper	Fluoride	Iodine
Manganese	Molybdenum	Selenium
Chloride	Potassium	Sodium
Chromium	Iron	Zink
		Nickel*

Calcium

Functions: Calcium builds bones, both in length and strength, and helps slow the rate of bone loss as you age. It helps muscles contract, plays a role in normal nervous system function, and helps blood clotting and blood pressure regulation. It's necessary for the body to metabolize iron and absorb vitamin B12, to keep the heart beating and for the release of neuro-transmitters in the brain. Calcium also has been shown to reduce the risk of cardiovascular disease in postmenopausal women.

Deficiency problems: Affects bone density and increases the risk of osteoporosis.

Food sources: You don't have to drink milk to get your calcium. Other good sources include dark green leafy vegetables (kale, broccoli, bok choy), nuts, root vegetables, broccoli and tofu.

Excess amounts: Too much calcium over a prolonged period can cause constipation, kidney stones and poor kidney function. It may also interfere with the absorption of other minerals, such as iron and zinc. But excess amounts are only consumed via supplements.

Phosphorus

Functions: Phosphorus helps body cells produce energy and acts as a main regulator of energy metabolism in body organs. It is a major component of bones and teeth, and makes up part of DNA and RNA.

Deficiency problems: Rare, but symptoms include bone loss, weakness, loss of appetite and pain.

Food sources: Protein-rich foods are the best sources. Legumes and nuts rank next. Bread and baked goods also contain phosphorus.

Excess amounts: Too much phosphorus may lower calcium levels in the blood and increase bone loss if calcium intake is low.

Magnesium

Functions: Repairs and maintains body cells; required for hormonal activity; required for most body processes, including energy production, and the action of our muscles. Magnesium is also important for bone development and growth.

Deficiency problems: Lack of magnesium absorption can lead to irregular heartbeat, nausea, weakness and mental derangement. Magnesium deficiency has also been linked to asthma.

Food sources: Magnesium is found in all foods in varying amounts. Legumes, nuts, whole grains, brown rice, soybeans, brewer's yeast, bitter chocolate and green vegetables are good sources.

Excess amounts: Too much can cause nausea, vomiting, low blood pressure and heart problems. Excess amounts from food are unlikely to cause harm, unless kidney disease prevents magnesium from being excreted.

Chromium

Functions: Chromium works with insulin to help the body use glucose (blood sugar).

Deficiency problems: Symptoms may resemble diabetes, including impaired glucose tolerance and nerve damage.

Food sources: Good sources include whole grains, brewer's yeast, molasses, mushrooms, eggs, cheese, and nuts.

Excess amounts: The effects of too much chromium are still being studied.

Copper

Functions: Copper is needed for the absorption, storage, and metabolism of iron. Copper helps make hemoglobin, which carries oxygen in the blood. It's also a part of many body enzymes and helps all body cells produce energy.

Deficiency problems: Rare, except from genetic problems or consuming too much zinc, which can hinder copper absorption. The symptoms of a copper deficiency are similar to iron-deficiency anemia.

Food sources: Unless you like eating liver, I'd say you can get enough from nuts and seeds. Cooking in copper pots also increases the copper content of foods.

Excess amounts: Too much copper can cause nausea, vomiting, diarrhea, coma and liver damage.

Fluoride

Functions: Fluoride helps harden tooth enamel, protecting teeth from decay. It may also protect against osteoporosis by strengthening bones.

Deficiency problems: Causes weak tooth enamel.

Food sources: Tea (especially if made with fluoridated water) and fish with edible bones, such as canned salmon. Many communities add fluoride to the water supply.

Excess amounts: Too much fluoride can mottle or stain otherwise healthy teeth. It can also lead to brittle bones, increasing the frequency of bone fractures.

Iodine

Functions: Iodine is part of thyroxin (thyroid hormone), which regulates the body's rate of energy use.

Deficiency problems: Interferes with thyroxin production, slowing the rate at which the body burns energy. Symptoms include weight gain and goiter (enlarged thyroid gland). Use of iodized salt has virtually eliminated iodine deficiency as a cause of goiter in the United States.

Food sources: Found naturally in saltwater fish and foods grown near coastal areas. Iodine is added to table salt.

Excess amounts: Too much iodine may also cause goiter, but not at levels usually consumed in the United States.

Iron

Functions: Iron is an essential part of hemoglobin, which carries oxygen to body cells.

Deficiency problems: Anemia, fatigue and infections. Deficiencies are more common among women with regular menstrual periods.

Food sources: Dark chocolate, molasses, dark green leafy vegetables.

Excess amounts: Adult iron supplements can be harmful to children, but naturally occurring iron (from food) is not likely to do much harm beyond causing constipation.

Manganese

Functions: Manganese is part of many body enzymes. It's necessary for the functioning of the brain; proper metabolism and normal functioning of the thyroid gland.

Deficiency problems: Rare.

Food sources: Whole grain products, nuts, root vegetables, brown rice, legumes, tea, and some fruits and vegetables, such as pineapple, kale and strawberries.

Excess amounts: Consuming harmful levels of manganese from food is very rare.

Molybdenum

Functions: Molybdenum works with riboflavin to incorporate iron into hemoglobin for red blood cells. It is also part of many body enzymes.

Deficiency problems: Rare with a normal diet.

Food sources: Milk, legumes, breads and grain products.

Selenium

Functions: Selenium works as an antioxidant with vitamin E to protect body cells from damage that may lead to cancer, heart disease and other health problems. It also aids cell growth. Selenium also improves liver function, maintains healthy eyes and eyesight, maintains healthy skin and hair, and may impede the aging process.

Deficiency problems: May affect the heart and immune system.

Food sources: Whole grains, nuts, seeds, brown rice and legumes contain selenium, but the amount can depend on the type of soil in which they were grown.

Excess amounts: Toxic in large doses, usually only possible with supplements.

Zinc

Functions: Zinc is essential for growth. It promotes cell reproduction, tissue growth, repair and wound healing. It forms part of more than 70 body enzymes and helps the body use carbohydrate, protein and fat. Zinc is also an excellent immune booster. Allergies have also responded to zinc.

Deficiency problems: Birth defects and retarded growth during childhood. Appetite loss, decreased sense of taste and smell, skin changes and reduced resistance to infection are also symptoms.

Food sources: Sunflower seeds, peanuts, whole grains, and soybeans are good sources.

Excess amounts: Excess zinc intake comes from supplements and can cause gastrointestinal irritation, vomiting, reduced HDL ("good") cholesterol and can interfere with copper absorption and immune function.

Chloride

Functions: Chloride helps regulate fluids in and out of body cells. It forms part of stomach acid to help digest food and absorb nutrients. It also helps transmit nerve impulses.

Deficiency problems: Rare, as chloride is found in table salt. Heavy, persistent sweating, chronic diarrhea or vomiting, trauma or kidney disease may cause deficiencies.

Food sources: Sea salt, seaweed, rye, tomatoes, lettuce, celery, and olives.

Excess amounts: Excess chloride may be linked to high blood pressure in chloride-sensitive people, but more study is needed.

Potassium

Functions: Potassium helps regulate fluids and mineral balance in and out of body cells. It also helps maintain normal blood pressure, water balance, the proper synthesis of protein, as well as nerve and muscle function.

Deficiency problems: Prolonged vomiting, diarrhea, laxative use or kidney problems can result in deficiencies of potassium. Symptoms include weakness, appetite loss, nausea and fatigue.

Food sources: Fruits and vegetables will give you all you need. Particularly good sources include apricots, avocados, bananas, cantaloupe, honeydew, kiwi, oranges, prunes, strawberries, potatoes, tomatoes, dried fruits, leafy green vegetables, nuts, and molasses.

Excess amounts: Excess potassium is usually excreted. If this doesn't happen, as in people with some types of kidney disease, heart problems or ulceration of the small intestine can occur.

Sodium

Functions: Sodium helps regulate movement of fluids in and out of body cells. It also helps transmit nerve impulses, regulate blood pressure and relax muscles.

Deficiency problems: Unlikely, except with chronic diarrhea, vomiting or kidney problems. Symptoms include nausea, dizziness and muscle cramps.

Food sources: Processed foods account for about 75% of the sodium we eat. Another 25% comes from table salt. Only a small amount occurs naturally in food.

Excess amounts: Healthy people excrete excess sodium, but some kidney diseases interfere with sodium excretion, leading to fluid retention and swelling. Sodium-sensitive people may experience high blood pressure eating a daily diet that contains high levels of sodium.

Meat, liver and seafood are often considered good sources of minerals like iron, zinc and selenium, but then you have to worry about what else they contain. Fortunately, nuts, seeds, and dark green vegetables typically contain enough of such minerals, so that if you're eating a healthy diet (which requires a significant amount of such foods), you don't have to worry about missing out on essential minerals, even if your diet is "missing" meat.

Animal / Non-Animal Derived Ingredients

from THE HOOD HEALTH HANDBOOK

Companies use animal ingredients because they're cheaper, not better. They're cheaper because slaughterhouses (and other industries involving animals) have to get rid of their leftovers, so they might as well make a profit in the process. Rendering plants process the bodies of millions of tons of dead animals every year, transforming decaying flesh and bones into profitable animal ingredients.

Some animal ingredients don't wind up in the final product but are used in the manufacturing process. For example, in the production of some refined sugars, bone char is used to whiten the sugar. And in some wines and beers, isinglass (from the swim bladders of fish) is used as a "clearing" agent.

The following list of animal ingredients (and alternatives) can help you avoid the many (often hard to detect) animal ingredients in food, cosmetics, and other products. This list is not all-inclusive. There are thousands of technical and patented names for ingredient variations. Not only that, but many ingredients can come from an animal, vegetable, or even synthetic source. In fact, some of the items listed below are commonly being made from synthetic (chemical) sources nowadays.

Adding to the confusion over whether an ingredient is of animal origin is the fact that many companies have removed the word "animal" from their ingredient labels to avoid putting off consumers. For example, rather than use the term "hydrolyzed animal protein," companies may use another term such as "hydrolyzed collagen." If you have a question regarding an ingredient in a product, call or write the manufacturer. Many companies are used to responding to questions like this, so you can expect an accurate reply.

Ingredients Derived from Animals:

A

Acetylated Hydrogenated Lard
  Glyceride
Acetylated Lanolin
Acetylated Lanolin Alcohol
Acetylated Lanolin Ricinoleate
Acetylated Tallow
Albumen
Albumin
"Amerachol"(TM)
Ammonium Hydrolyzed
  Protein
Amniotic Fluid
AMPD Isoteric Hydrolyzed
  Animal Protein
Amylase
Animal Collagen Amino Acids
Animal Keratin Amino Acids
Animal Protein Derivative
Animal Tissue Extract,
  Epiderm Oil R
Arachidonic Acid

B

Batyl Alcohol
Batyl Isostearate
Beeswax
Benzyltrimonium Hydrolyzed
  Animal Protein
Brain Extract
Buttermilk

C

C30-46 Piscine Oil
Calfskin Extract
Cantharides Tincture, Spanish
  Fly
Catharidin
Carmine, Cochineal
Carminic Acid, Natural Red
  No. 4
Casein
Castor, Castoreum (not Castor
  Oil)
Ceteth-2, Poltethylene (2)
  Cetyl Ether
Ceteth-2, -4, -6, -10, -30
Cholesterol
Civet
Cochineal
Cod-Liver Oil
Coleth-24
Collagen
Cysteine, -L-Form
Cystine (or Cysteine)

D

Dea-Oleth-10 Phosphate
Desamido Animal Collagen
Desamidocollagen
Dicaployloyl Cystine
Diethylene Tricaseinamide
Dihydrocholesterol
Dihydrocholesterol Octylede-
  canoate
Dihydrocholeth-15
Dihydrocholeth-30
Dihydrogenated Tallow
  Benzylmoniumchloride
Dihydrogenated Tallow
  Methylamine
Dihydrogenated Tallow
  Phthalate
Dihydroxyethyl Tallow Amine
  Oxide
Dimethyl Hydrogenated
  Tallowamine
Dimethyl Tallowamine
Disodium Hydrogenated
  TallowGlutamate
Disodium Tallamido Mea-
  Sulfosuccinate
Disodium Tallowamino-
  dipropionate
Ditallowdimonium Chloride
Dried Buttermilk
Dried Egg Yolk

E

Egg
Egg Oil
Egg Powder
Egg Yolk
Egg Yolk Extract
Elastin
Embryo Extract
Estradiol
Estradiol Benzoate
Estrogen
Estrone
Ethyl Arachidonate
Ethyl Ester of Hydrolyzed
  Animal Protein
Ethyl Morrhuate, Lipineate
Ethylene Dehydrogenated
  Tallowamide

F

Fish Glycerides
Fish Oil

G

Gelatin (not Gel)
Glucuronic Acid
Glyceryl Lanolate
Glycogen
Guanine, Pearl Essence

H

Heptylundecanol
Honey
Human Placental Protein
Human Umbilical Extract
Hyaluronic Acid
Hydrogenated Animal
  Glyceride
Hydrogenated Ditallow
  Amine
Hydrogenated Honey
Hydrogenated Laneth-5, -
  20, -25
Hydrogenated Lanolin
Hydrogenated Lanolin
  Alcohol
Hydrogenated Lard
  Glyceride
Hydrogenated Shark-Liver
  Oil
Hydrogenated Tallow Acid
Hydrogenated Tallow
  Betaine
Hydrogenated Tallow
  Glyceride
Hydrolyzed Animal Elastin
Hydrolyzed Animal Keratin
Hydrolyzed Animal Protein
Hydrolyzed Casein
Hydrolyzed Elastin
Hydrlyzed Human Placental
  Protein
Hydrolyzed Keratin
Hydrolyzed Silk
Hydroxylated Lanolin

I

Isobutylated Lanolin
Isopropyl Lanolate
Isopropyl Tallowatelsopropyl
  Lanolate

Isostearic Hydrolyzed Animal
  Protein
Isostearoyl Hydrolyzed Animal
  Protein

K

Keratin
Keratin Amino Acids

L

Lactic Yeasts
Lactose, Milk Sugar
Laneth-5 through -40
Laneth-9 and -10 Acetate
Lanolin, Wool Fat; Wool Wax
Lanolin Acid
Lanolin Alcohols, Sterols;
  Triterpene Alcohols; Ali-
  phatic Alcohols
Lanolin Linoleate
Lanolin Oil
Lanolin Ricinoleate
Lanolin Wax
Lanoinamide DEA
Lanosteral
Lard
Lard Glyceride
Lauroylhydrolyzed Animal
  Protein
Leucine
Liver Extract
Lysine

M

Magnesium Lanolate
Magnesium Tallowate
Mammarian Extract
Mayonnaise
MEA-Hydrolyzed Animal
  Protein
Menhaden Oil, Pogy Oil;
  Mossbunker Oil
Milk
Mink Oil
Minkamidopropyl Diethyl-
  amine
Muscle Extract
Musk
Musk Ambrette
Myristoyl Hydrolyzed Animal
  Protein

N

Neat's-Foot Oil

O

Oleamidopropyl Dimethyl-amine Hydrolyzed Animal Protein
leostearine
Oleoyl Hydrolyzed Animal Protein
Oleth-2, and 3
Oleth-5, and 10
Oleth-10
Oleth-25 and 50
Oleyl Alcohol
Oleyl Arachidate
Oleyl Imidazoline
Oleyl Lanolate
Ovarian Extract

P

Palmitoyl Hydrolyzed Animal Protein
Palmitoyl Hydrolyzed Milk Protein
PEG-28 Glyceryl Tallowate
PEG-8 Hydrogenated Fish Glycerides
PEG-5 through -70 Hydro-genated Lanolin
PEG-13 Hydrogenated Tallow Amide
PEG-5 to -20 Lanolate
PEG-5 through -100 Lanolin
PEG-75 Lanolin Oil and Wax
PEG-2 Milk Solids
PEG-6, -8, -20 Sorbitan Beeswax
PEG-40, -75, or -80 Sorbitan Lanolate

PEG-3, -10, or -15 Tallow Aminopropylamine
PEG-15 Tallow Polyamine
PEG-20 Tallowate
Pentahydrosqualene
Perhydrosqualene
Pigskin Extract
Placental Enzymes, Lipids and Proteins
Placental Extract
Placental Protein
Polyglyceryl-2 Lanolin Alcohol Ether
Potassium Caseinate
Potassium Tallowate
Potassium Undecylenoyl Hydrolyzed Animal Protein
PPG-12-PEG-50 Lanolin
PPG-2, -5, -10. -20, -30 Lanolin Alcohol Ethers
PPG-30 Lanolin Ether
Pregnenolone Acetate
Pristane
Progesterone
Purcelline Oil Syn

R

Royal Jelly

S

Saccharide Hydrolysate
Saccharide Isomerate
Serum Albumin
Serum Proteins
Shark-Liver Oil
Shellac
Shellac Wax
Silk Amino Acids
Silk Powder

Sodium Caseinate
Sodium Chondroitin Sulfate
Sodium Coco-Hydrolyzed Animal Protein
Sodium Hydrogenated Tallow Glutamate
Sodium Laneth Sulfate
Sodium Methyl Oleoyl Taurate
Sodium n-Mythyl-n-Oleyl Taurtate
Sodium Soya Hydrolyzed Animal Protein
Sodium Tallow Sulfate
Sodium Tallowate
Sodium / TEA-Lauroyl Hydrolyzed Animal Protein
Sodium / TEA-Undecylenoyl Hydrolyzed Animal Protein
Sodium Undecylenate
Soluble (Animal) Collagen
Soya Hydroxyethyl Imida-zoline
Spleen Extract
Squalene
Stearyl Alcohol, Stenol

T

Tallow
Tallow Acid
Tallow Amide
Tallow Amidopropylamine Oxide
Tallow Amine
Tallow Amine Oxide
Tallow Glycerides
Tallow Hydroxyethal Imidazoline
Tallow Imidazoline
Tallowmide DEA and MEA

Tallowmidopropyl Hydroxy-sultaine
Tallowminopropylamine
Tallowmphoacete
Talloweth-6
Tallow Trimonium Chloride, Tallow
Tea-Abietoyl Hydrolyzed Animal Protein
Tea-Coco Hydrolyzed Animal Protein
Tea-Lauroyl Animal Collagen Amino Acids
Tea-Lauroyl Animal Keratin Amino Acids
Tea-Myristol Hydrolyzed Animal Protein
Tea-Undecylenoyl Hydrolyzed Animal Protein
Testicular Extract
Threonine
Triethonium Hydrolyzed Animal Protein Ethosulfate
Trilaneth-4 Phosphate

W

Wood Fat
Wool Wax Alcohols

Y

Yogurt

Z

Zinc Hydrolyzed Animal Protein

The Following Ingredients MAY be Animal-Derived:

A

Acetaldehyde, Ethanal
Acetic Acid
Acetic Anhydride, Acetyl Oxide; Acetic Oxide
Acetoin, Acetyl Methyl Carbinol
Acetylated Sucrose Distearte
Acetylmethylcarbinol
Alanine
Alcloxa, Aluminum Chlorohy-droxy Allantoinate
Aldol
Allantoin
Allantoin Acetyl Methionine

Allantoin Ascorbate
Allantoin Biotin
Allantoin Calcium Pantothen-ate
Allantoin Galacturonic Acid
Allantoin Glycyrrhetinic Acid
Allantoin Polygalacturonic Acid
Allantoinate
Aluminum Acetate, Burow's Solution
Aluminum Chorhydroxy Allantoinate
Aluminum Distearate
Aluminum Isostea-rates/Laurates/Stearates

Aluminum Isostea-rates/Myristates
Aluminum Isostea-rates/Palmitates
Aluminum Lactate
Aluminum Myris-tates/Palmitates
Aluminum Salts (Aluminum Acetate, Aluminum Lanolate, Aluminum Stearate,
Aluminum Tristearate)
Aluminum Stearates
Aluminum Tripalmi-tate/Triisostearate
Aluminum Tristearate

Ammonium C12-15 Pareth Sulfate, Pareth-25-3 Sulfate
Ammonium Isostearate
Ammonium Myristyl Sulfate
Ammonium Oleate
Ammonium Stearate, Stearic Acid; Ammonium Salt
Amphoteric
Amphoteric-2
Ascorbyl Stearate
Asparagine
Aspartic-Acid, DL & L Forms; Aminosuccinate Acid

B

Basic Voilet 10
Beheneth-5, -10, -20, -30
Behenic Acid, Docosanoic Acid
Behenic Acid, Docosanol
Beta-Carotene, Provitamin A; Beta Carotene
Betaine
Biotin, Vitamin H; Vitamin B Factor
Brilliantines
Burow's Solution
Butyl Acetate, Acetic Acid; Butyl Ester
Butyl Glycolate
Butyl Oleate
Butyl Palmitate
Butyl Phrhaly Butyl Glycolate
Butylrolactone, Butanolide

C

C18-36 Acid
C29-70 Acid, C29-70 Carboxylic Acids
C18-36 Acid Glycol Ester
C18-36 Acid Triglyceride
C9-11 Alcohols
C12-16 Alcohols
C14-15 Alcohols
C12-15 Alcohols Benzoate
C12-15 Alcohols Lactate
C21 Dicarboxylic Acid
C15-18 Glycol
C18-20 Glycol Palmitate
C8-9, C9-11, C9-13, C9-14, C10-11, C10-13, C11-12, C11-13, C12-14, C13-14, C13-16, and C20-40 IsoParaffins
C11-15 Pareth-12 Stearate
C11-15 Pareth-40
C12-13 Pareth 3-7
C14-15 Pareth-7, -11, -13
C10-18 Triglycerieds
Calcium Stearate
Calcium Stearoyl Lactylate
Caproamphoacetate
Caproamhodiacetate
Capryl Betaine
Caprylamine Oxide
Caprylic / Capric / Stearic Triglyceride
Caprylic Acid
Caprylamphoacetate
Caprryloamphodiacetate
Carbamide
Cetearalkonium Bromide

Ceteareth-3, Cetyl/Stearyl Ether
Ceteareth-4, -6, -8, -10, -12, -15, -17, -20, -27, -30
Ceteareth-5
Cetaryl Alcohol
Ceteth-1
Cetyl-
Cetyl Alcohol
Cetyl Ammonium
Cetyl Arachidate
Cetyl Betaine
Cetyl Esters
Cetyl Lactate
Cetyl Myristate
Cetyl Octanoate
Cetyl Palmitate
Cetyl Phosphate
Cetyl Ricinoleate
Cetyl Stearate
Cetyl Stearyl Glycol
Cetylarachidol
Cetylpyridinium Chloride
Cetyltrymethylammonium BromideChitin
Cloflucarbon

D

Deceth-7-Carboxylic Acid
Decyl Betaine
Diacetyl
Diazo-
Diazolidinyl Urea, Germall II (TM)
Dicetyl Adipate
Dicetyl Thiodipropionate
Diethyl Asparate
Diethyl Palmitoyl Apartate
Diethyl Sebacate
Diethylaminoethyl Stearamide
Diethylaminoethyl Stearate
Diglyceryl Stearate Malate
Dihydroxyethyl Soyamine Dioleate
Dihydroxyethyl Stearamine Oxide
Dihydroxyethyl Stearyl Glycinate
Dimethyl Behenamine
Dimethyl Lauramine Oleate
Dimethyl Myristamine
Dimethyl Palmitamine
Dimethyl Stearamine
Dimethylaminopropyl Oleamide
Dimethylaminopropyl Stearamide
Dimethylol Urea
Dimyristyl Thiodipropionate
Dioleth-8-Phosphate

Direct Black 51
Direct Red 23, Fast Scarlet 4BSA
Direct Red 80
Direct Violet 48
Direct Yellow 12, Chrysophenine

G

Disodium Cetaeryl Sulfosuccinate
Disodium Isostearamino Mea-Sulfosuccinate
Disodium Monooleamidosulfosuccinate
Disodium Monoricinoleamido Mea-Sulfosuccinate
Disodium Oleamido MIPA-Sulfosuccinate
Disodium Oleamido PEG-2 Sulfosuccinate
Disodium Oleyl Sulfosuccinate
Disodium Stearmido MEA-Sulfosuccinate
Disodium Stearminodipionate
Disodium Stearyl Sulfosuccinate
Distearyl Thiodipropionate
DI-TEA-Palmitoyl Asparate
Dodecanedionic Acid; Cetearyl Alcohol; Glycol Copolymer
Dodecyltetradecanol

E

Enfleurage
Enzyme
Ethyl Aspartate
Ethyl Oleate
Ethyl Palmitate
Ethyl Serinate
Ethyl Stearate
Ethyl Urocanate
Ethylene Dioleamide
Ethylene Distearamide
Ethylene Urea
Ethylhexyl Palmitate

F

Fatty Alcohols, Cetyl; Stearyl; Lauryl; Myristyl
Folic Acid
Fructose

G

Gel (not Silica gel)
Glucose Glutamate
Glyceryl Caprate
Glyceryl Caprylate

Glyceryl Caprylate/Caprate
Glyceryl Dioleate
Glyceryl Distearate
Glyceryl Hydrostearate
Glyceryl Hydrostearate
Glyceryl Hydroxystearate
Glyceryl Isostearate
Glyceryl Monostearate
Glyceryl Myristate
Glyceryl Oleate
Glyceryl Palmitate Lactate
Glyceryl Stearate SE
Glyceryl Trimyristate
Glycol Stearate SE
Glycyrrhetinyl Stearate
Guanidine Carbonate
Guanosine

H

Hexanediol Distearate
Histidine
Hydrogenated Fatty Oils
Hydroxylated Lecithin
Hydroxyoctacosanyl Hydroxyastearate
Hydroxystearmide MEA
Hydroxystearic Acid

I

Imidazlidinyl Urea
Indole
Isobutyl Myristate
Isobutyl Palmitate
Isobutyl Stearate
Isoceteth-10, -20, -30
Isocetyl Alcohol
Isocetyl Isodecanoate
Isocetyl Palmitate
Isocetyl Stearate
Isocetyl Stearoyl Stearate
Isoceteth-10 Stearate
Isodecyl hydroxystearate
Isodecyl Myristate
Isodecyl Oleate
Isodecyl Palmitate
Isohyxyl Palmitate
Isopropyl Acetate
Isopropyl Isostearate
Isopropyl Myristate
Isopropyl Palmitate
Isopropyl Stearate
Isostearamidopropalkonium Chloride
Isostearamidopropyl Betaine
Isostearamidopropyl Dimethylamine Glycolate
Isostearamidopropyl Dimethylamine Lactate

Isostearamidopropyl Ethyldimonium Ethosulfate
Isostearamidopropyl Morpholine Lactate
Isostearamidoporopylamine Oxide
Isosteareth-2 through -20
Isostearic Acid
Isostearoamphoglycinate
Isostearoamphopropionate
Isostearyl Alcohol
Isostearyl Benzylimidonium Chloride
Isostearyl Diglyceryl Succinate
Isostearyl Erucate
Isostearyl Ethylimidonium Ethosulfate
Isostearyl Hydroxyethyl Imidazoline
Isostearyl Imidazoline
Isostearyl Isostearate
Isostearyl Lactate
Isostearyl Neopentanoate
Isostearyl Palmitate
Isostearyl Stearoyl Stearate

L

Lactic Acid
Lauroyl Sarcosine
Lauryl Isostearate
Lauryl Palmitate
Lauryl Stearate
Lauryl Suntaine
Lecithin
Lithium Stearate

M

Magnesium Myristate
Magnesium Oleate
Magnesium Stearate
Methyl Gluceth-10 or -20
Methyl Glucet-20 Sesquistereate, Glucamate
Methyl Glucose Sesquioleate
Methyl Glucose Sesquistearate
Methyl Hydroxystearate
Methyl Lactate
Methyl Myristate
Methyl Oleate
Methyl Palmitate
Mixed Isopropanolamines
Myristate
Morpholine Stearate
Myreth-3
Myreth-3 Caprate, Myristic Ethoxy Caprate
Myreth-3 Laurate
Myreth-3 Myristate
Myreth-4

Myristamide DEA, Myristic Diethanolamide
Myristamide MIPA
Myristamidopropyl Betaine
Myristamidopropyl Diethylamine
Myristamidopropylamine Oxide
Myristamine Oxide
Myristaminopropionic Acid
Myristate
Myristic Acid
Myristimide MEA
Myristoamphoacetate
Myristoyl Sarcosine
Myristyl Alcohol
Myristyl Betaine
Myristyl Hydroxyethyl Imidazoline
Myristyl Isostearate
Myristyl Lactate
Myristyl Myristate
Myristyl Neopentanoate, Ceraphyl
Myristyl Propionate
Myristyl Stearate
Myristyleicosanol
Myristyleicosyl Stearate
Myristyloctadecanol

N

Nonyl Acetate

O

Octododecanol-2, Octyl Dodecanol
Octododeceth-20, -25
Octododecyl Myristate
Octoxyglyceryl Behenate
Octyl Acetoxystearate
Octyl Hydroxystearate
Octyl Palmitate
Octyl Stearate
Octyldocecanol
Octyldodecyl Stearate
Octyldodecyl Stearoyl Stearate
Oleamide, Oleylamide
Oleamide DEA, Oleic Diethanolamide
Oleamide MIPA
Oleamine Oxide
Oleic Acid
Oleoyl Sarcosine
Oleth-3 Phosphate
Oleth 20
Oleth-20 Phosphate
Oleyl Betaine
Oleyl Myristate
Oleyl Oleate

Oleyl Stearate
Orotic Acid, Pyrimidecarboxylic Acid

P

Palmamamidopropyl Betaine
Palmitamide DEA, MEA
Palmitamidopropyl Betaine
Palmitamindopropyl Diethylamine
Palmitamine
Palmitamine Oxide, Palmityl Dimethylamine Oxide
Palmitate
Palmitic Acid
Panthenyl Ethyl Etheracetate
Pareth-25- 12
PEG-9 Caprylate
PEG-8 Caprylate / Caprate
PEG-6 Caprylic / Capric Glycerides
PEG-6 to -150 Dioleate
PEG-3 Dipalmitate
PEG-2 through -175 Distearate
PEG-5 through -120 Glyceryl Stearate
PEG-25 Glyceryl Trioleate
PEG-6 or -12 Isostearate
PEG-20 Methyl Glucose Sesquistearate
PEG-4 Octanoate
PEG-2 through -9 Oleamide
PEG-2 through -30 Oleamide
PEG-12, -20, or -30 Oleate
PEG-3 through -150 Oleate
PEG-6 through -20 Palmitate
PEG-25 through -125 Propylene Glycol Stearate
PEG-8 Sesquioleate
PEG-5 or -20 Sorbitan Isostearate
PEG-3 or -6 Sorbitan Oleate
PEG-80 Sorbitan Palmitate
PEG-40 Sorbitan Peroleate
PEG-3 or -40 Sorbitan Stearate
PEG-30, -40, or -60 Sorbitan Tetraoleate
PEG-60 Sorbitan Tetrastearate
PEG-2 through -150 Stearate
PEG-66 or -200 Tryhydroxystearin
Pentaerythrityl Tetraoctanoate
Pentaerythrityl Tetrastearate and Calcium Stearate
Phospholipids, Phosphatides
Polyglycerol

Polyglycerol-4 Cocoate
Polyglycerol-10 Decalinoleate
Polyglycerol-2 Diisostearate
Polyglycerol-6 Dioleate
Polyglycerol-6 Distearate
Polyglycerol-3 Hydroxylauryl Ether
Polyglycerol-4 Isostearate
Polyglycerol-3, -4 or -8 Oleate
Polyglycerol-2 or -4 Oleyl Ether
Polyglycerol-2 PEG-4 Stearate
Polyglycerol-2 Sesquiisostearate
Polyglycerol-2 Sesquioleate
Polyglycerol-3, -4 or -8 Stearate
Polyglycerol-10 Tertraoleate
Polyglycerol-2 Tetrastearate
Polysorbate 60 and Polysorbate 80
Potassium Apartate
Potassium Coco-Hydrolyzed Protein
Potassium DNA
Potassium Oleate-Oleic Acid
Potassium Salt
Potassium Myristate
Potassium Palmitate
Potassium Stearate, Stearic Acid
Potassium Salt
PPG-3-Myreth-11
PPG-4-Ceteareth-12
PPG-4-Ceteth-1, -5 or -10
PPG-4 Myristyl Ether
PPG-5-Ceteth- 10 Phosphate
PPG-6-C12-18 Pareth
PPG-8-Ceteth, -5, -10, or -20
PPG-9-Steareth-3
PPG-10-Ceteareth-20
PPG-10 Cetyl Ether
leyl Ether
PPG-11 or -15 Stearyl Ether
PPG-26 Oleate, Polyxypropylene
2000 Monooleate; Carbowax
PPG-28 Cetyl Ether
PPG-30 Cetyl Ether
PPG-30, -50, Oleyl Ether
PPG-36 Oleate, Polyoxypropylene (36) Monooleate
PPG-Isocetyl Ether PPG-3-Isosteareth-9
Proline
Propylene Glycol Myristate
Protein Fatty Acid Condensates

Proteins
Pyridium Compounds
Pyroligneous Acid

R

Retinyl Palmitate
Ribonucleic Acid, RNA

S

Sarcosines
S-Carboxy Methyl Cysteine
Sebactic Acid , Decanedioic
   Acid
Serine
Skatole
Sodium Aluminum Chloroy-
   droxyl Lactate
Sodium C12-15 Pareth-7
   Carboxylate
Sodium C12-15 Pareth-Sulfate
Sodium Cetearyl Sulfate
Sodium Cetyl Sulfate
Sodium Cocyl Sarcosinate
Sodium DNA
Sodium Glyceryl Oleate
   Phosphate
Sodium Isosteareth-6
   Carboxylate
Sodium Isosteroyl LacrylatE
Sodium Myreth Sulfate
Sodium Myristate
Sodium Myristoyl Isethionate
Sodium Myristoyl Sarcosinate
Sodium Myristyl Sulfate
Sodium Oleth-7 or -8
   Phosphate
Sodium Palmitate
Sodium Pareth- 15-7 or 25-7
   Carboxylate
Sodium Pareth-23 or -25
   Sulfate

Sodium PCA
Sodium PCA Methylsilanol
Sodium Ribonucleic Acid,
   SRNA
Sodium Sarcosinate
Sodium Soap
Sodium Stearate
Sodium Steroyl Lactylate
Sodium Urocanate
Sorbeth-6 Hexastearate
Sorbitan Diisoseate
Sorbitan Dioleate
Sorbitan Fatty Acid Esters
Sorbitan Isostearate
Sorbitan Oleate, Sorbitan
   Monooleate
Sorbitan Palmitate, Span 40
   (TM)
Sorbitan Sesquioleate
Sorbitan Sequistearate
Sorbitan Triisostearate
Sorbitan Tristearate
Spermaceti, Cetyl Palmitate
Stearalkonium Bentonite
Stearalkonium Chloride
Stearalkonium Hectorite
Stearamide
Stearamide DEA, Stearic Acid
   Diethanolamide
Stearamide DIBA Stearate
Stearamide MIPA Stearate
Stearamide MIPA
Stearamide Oxide
Stearmidopropalkonium
   Chloride
Stearamidopropyl Dimethyl-
   amine
Stearamine
Stearamine Oxide
Stearates
Steareth-2
Steareth-4 through -100

Stearic Acid
Stearic Hydrazide
Stearmidoethyl Diethylamine
Stearoamphoacetate
Stearoamphocarboxyglycinate
Stearoamphodiacetate
Stearoamphohydroxypropysul-
   fonate
Stearoamphopropionate
Stearone
Stearoxy Dimethicone
Stearoxytrimethylsilane
Stearoyl Lactylic Acid
Stearoyl Sarcosine
Steartrimonium Chloride
Steartrimonium Hydrolyzed
   Animal Protein
Stearyl Acetate
Stearyl Betaine
Stearyl Caprylate
Stearyl Citrate
Stearyl Erucamide
Stearyl Erucate
Stearyl Ghycyrrhetinate
Stearyl Heptanoate
Stearyl Hydroxyethyl Imida-
   zoline
Stearyl Lactate
Stearyl Octanoate
Stearyl Stearate
Stearyl Stearoyl Stearate
Stearyldimethyl Amine
Stearylvinyl Ether/Maleic
   Anhydride Copolymer
Steroids
Sterol
Sucrose Distearate
Sucrose Laurate
Sucrose Stearate
Synthetic Spermaceti

T

TEA-Lauroyl Sarcosinate
TEA-Myristate
TEA-Oleate, Triethanolamine
   Oleate
TEA-Palm-Kernel Sarcosinate
TEA-Stearate
Terpinyl Acetate
Tetramethyl Decynediol
TIPA-Stearate
Tridecyl Stearate
Tryhydroxy Stearin
Triisostearin
Trimethylopropane Tri-
   isostearate
Trimyristin-Glyceryl Tri-
   myristate
Trioleth-8 Phosphate
Trioleyl Phosphate
Tristearin
Tristearyl Citrate
Tryptophan
Tyrosine

U

Undecylpentadecanol
Urea, Carbamide
Urease

V

Valine

W

Waxes

Z

Zinc Stearate, Zinc Soap

Ingredient Sources and Uses

The following are some of the major ingredients, with more detailed backgrounds.

Ingredient	Source	Use	Status
Acetic Acid	Plant juices, milk, oil petroleum and some-times muscles	It is the final product of many aerobic fermentation	When it is from petroleum, it is vegetarian
Agar Agar	Seaweed	A substitute for gelatin (cream and in confectionery items)	Vegetarian
Albumin	Blood (serum albumin), milk (dairy), eggs	Coagulant and stiffener in baked goods	Questionable*
Alginate (calcium alginate, alginic acid, sodium alginate, propylene glycol	Seaweed	Thickening and stabilizing agent in pastry, jelly, ice cream, cheese, candy, yogurt, canned	Vegetarian

aginates)		frosting, whipped cream, and beer	
Alginic Acid	See alginate		
Alpha Amylase	Hog pancreas	In flour to breakdown any starches	Not vegetarian
Alum Aluminum Sulfate (Also known as cake alum or patent alum)	Earth	Clarifying oils and fats	Vegetarian
Ambergris	Whale intestine	Flavoring (also used in perfume)	Not vegetarian
Anise	Fruit of an herb (in the parsley family)	Flavoring foods in beverages	Vegetarian
Argot (See also cream of tartar and tartaric acid)	Sediment in wine casks during fermentation and storage	In the manufacture of tartaric acid and vinegar from malt	Vegetarian
Ascorbic Acid (vitamin c)	Synthetic or corn	Nutrient	Vegetarian
Ascorbate Palmitate	Synthetic and palm oil	Preservative	Vegetarian
Benzoic Acid	Synthetic	Preservative	Vegetarian
BHA (Butylated Hydrox-anisole)	Synthetic	As an antioxidant in cereals, stabilizers, shortenings, and potato flakes and granules	Vegetarian
BHA (Butylated Hydrox-toluene)	Synthetic	As an antioxidant in beverages, desserts, cereals, glazed fruits, dry mixes for beverages, and potato flakes and granules	Vegetarian
Calcium Alginate	See alginate		
Calcium Carbonate	Limestone	Tooth powder and in removing acidity of wine	Vegetarian
Calcium Chloride	Synthetic	In canned goods and in cottage and cheddar cheeses as a preservative	Vegetarian
Calcium Citrate	See citric acid		
Calcium Disodium (EDTA)	Synthetic	Flavor retention in canned soda and canned white potatoes; as a preservative in dressings, egg products, oleomargarine, potato salad, lima beans, mushrooms, pecan pie filling, and spreads	Vegetarian
Calcium Propionate	Synthetic	Preservative	Vegetarian
Calcium Stearate (See Stearic Acid)	A compound of calcium and stearic acid	Anticaking ingredient in some spices (especially garlic salt and onion salt) and extensively in tablets	Questionable*
Calcium Sorbate	Synthetic	Preservative	Vegetarian
Calcium Sterol Lactylate	Milk or soybeans	Instant mashed potatoes	Questionable*
Calcium Stearoyl Lactylate	Chemical reaction of stearic acid and lactic acid	As a dough conditioner, whipping agent and as a conditioner in dehydrated potatoes	Questionable*
Caprylic Acid	Palm oil or coconut oil	Preservative and flavoring	Vegetarian
Carbon Black	Synthetic	Black coloring in confectionery	Questionable*

Carmine (Cochineal)	Insect (a crimson pigment derived from a Mexican species of scale insect (coccus cacti))	Coloring in red apple sauce, fruit cocktail, confections, baked goods, meats, and species	Not vegetarian
Carrageenan	Seaweed and fresh moss	As a substitute for gelatin (an emulsifier, stabilizer, and food thickener)	Vegetarian
Caramel	Sugar or glucose	Coloring foods, beverages, and confectionery items	Vegetarian
Casein	Milk, hence dairies	Stabilizer for confectionery, texturizer for ice cream and sherbets, or as a replacement for egg albumin	Because it is precipitated by acid or by animal or vegetable enzymes, questionable*
Catalase	Cow liver use	Coagulant	Questionable*
Choline Bitartrate	Animal tissue	Nutrient (b complex vitamin)	Questionable*
Citric Acid	Fruits and vegetables, molasses and grain	Antioxidant, sugar solubitizing in ice cream and sherbet, fruit juice drinks, and canned and jarred products, including jelly, cheese, candy, carbonated beverages, instant potatoes, wheat, chips, potato sticks, wine	Vegetarian
Civet, Absolute	Cats	Flavoring for beverages, ice cream, ices, candy, baked goods and chewing gum	Not vegetarian
Cocoa Butter	Cocoa bean	Chocolate coatings	Vegetarian
Coconut Oil (see Oil)	Coconut	In the manufacture of edible fats, chocolate, and candies; in baking in place of lard	Vegetarian
Confectionery Glaze	See resinous glaze and shellac		
Corn Starch	Corn		Vegetarian
Cream of Tartar (Tartaric Acid)	Argot, the stony sediment of wine casks	In a variety of confections and in the preparation of baked goods	Vegetarian
Cysteine - L form	An amino acid, human and horse, or synthetic (sometimes from deceased women)	Nutrient in bakery products	Questionable*
Dextrin	Starch	Prevents caking of sugar in candy, encapsulates flavor oils in powdered mixes, thickener	Vegetarian
Dextrose (corn syrup)	Starch	Sweetener, coloring agent in beverages, ice cream, candy and baked goods	Vegetarian
Dilauryl Thiodiproprionate	Synthetic	Preservative	Vegetarian
Dough Conditioners	Calcium stearoyl~2 lactylate, or animal fat	To improve the texture of bread	Because it often will contain mono and diglyc-erides, ques-

			tionable*
Emulsifiers	Fats (animal or vegetable, synthetic.) Use	Binding oils and water, thickening, a preservative in baked goods, reducing ice crystals and air bubbles in ice cream	Questionable*
Erythrobic Acid	Synthetic	Preservative	Vegetarian
Eschalots (shallot)	An onion like plant	Bulbs used like garlic for flavoring	Vegetarian
Ethyl Vanillin	Synthetic, bark of spruce tree, or wine alcohol	As a flavor instead of vanilla or to fortify it	Vegetarian
Fats	Animal or vegetable	Substances that are solid at room temperature are fats; those that are liquid at room temperature are oils	Questionable*
Fatty Acids Source	Animal or vegetable fats	Emulsifiers, binder, lubricants	Questionable*
Filberts	A type of hazelnut		Vegetarian
Gelatin	Derived from the collagen in cow or pig bones	To give substances a gelatinous or chewy texture. Generally, "Kosher gelatin" is also made from pig bones.	Not Vegetarian
Glucose	Fruits and other plants such as potatoes and corn (see dextrose)	Sweetener, coloring agent	Vegetarian
Glyceride	See mono and diglyc-erides		
Glycine	Gelatin, animal or vegetable oil, sometimes used in cereals	Also as a flavor enhancer	Questionable*
Glycerol Monostearate	Glycerol monostearate may be of animal origin		Questionable*
Glycerin	Beef fat, petroleum, or vegetable	As a solvent or humectant (maintains the desired level of moisture)	Questionable*
Gum Arabic, Gum Acacia	Trees	Thickening agent, emulsifier, stabilizer	Vegetarian
Gum Base	Trees (chicle, natural rubber, etc.) Synthetic butyl rubber, paraffin, polyethylene, vinyl, resin, glycerin, glycerol monostearate	In the manufacture of chewing gums	Questionable*
Gum Guaiac	Trees	Antioxidants	Vegetarian
Guar Gum	Plants	Extender for pectin, stabilizer and thickener for spreads, syrups, sauces, salad dressing and licorice	Vegetarian
Gum Tragacanth	Shrubs (herb derived from green leaves or herbaceous part of the plants)	Thickening agent	Vegetarian
Invert Sugar (inversol nulomoline colorose)	Cane sugar	Sweetener	Vegetarian

Invertase (invertin)	Yeast	Preparation of invert sugar from sucrose	Vegetarian
Lactic Acid	Molasses, corn starch, glucose, molasses	Preservative, flavoring (can also be produced from whey, in which case it is dairy, but its use is restricted to ice cream and cream cheese)	Vegetarian
Lactose (milk sugar)	Whey	Sweetener, humectant, and nutrient	Vegetarian (not vegan)
Lauric Fats	Coconut, palm oil	With or instead of cocoa butter	Vegetarian
Lecithin	Soybeans, corn oil	Emulsifier and preservative, especially in chocolate	Vegetarian
Lipids	Animal or vegetable fats	Shortening, flavoring, thickener	Questionable*
Lactalbumin	See albumin		
Lysine, L and DL Forms	Casein, fibrin, blood	Usually synthesized	Questionable*
Magnesium Stearate	Stearic acid (from tallow, vegetable oils or synthetic)	Anti caking agent	Questionable*
Malt Syrup	Malt and barley	Emulsifier and starch dissolving	Vegetarian
Mannitol	Fungi	Sweetener	Vegetarian
Methylparaben	Synthetic	Preservative	Vegetarian
Methyl P Hydroxy Benzoate	See methylparaben		
Mono and Diglycerides (do not necessarily have to be listed in the ingredients)	Animal and vegetable	Stabilizer, emulsifier, softener, preservative	Because most are animal byproducts, questionable*
Monosodium Glutamate	Sugar, plants, beets and corn	Flavor enhancer	Vegetarian
Musk	Deer glands, synthetic	In flavorings, for beverages, ice cream, candy, baked goods, and chewing gum	Usually produced synthetically, but questionable*
Natural fruit flavors	Concentrated under vacuum or freeze dried	Concentrated fruit pulp that is used in confectionery usually requires fortification with some synthetic flavor	Vegetarian
Oil of Lemon	Lemon peel		Vegetarian
Oil of Rose	Distilled from fresh rose petals	Comes mostly from bulgarian damask rose	Vegetarian
Oil of Caraway	Seeds of carum carui	Flavoring for chocolate and coatings	Vegetarian
Oil of Cardamon (grains of paradise)	Alleppy cardamon, trees from India	Enhance the flavor of ground coffee, butter, chocolate, liquor, spice and vanilla	Vegetarian
Oil of Cassia (Cassia Bark)	Leaves and twigs of the Chinese cinnamon	For cocoa flavor in biscuits, cakes, ice cream and beverages	Vegetarian
Oil of Celery	Celery plant	Usually as flavoring for cocoa, chocolate, and other confections	Vegetarian
Oil of Cinnamon	Under the bark of the cinnamon zeylanicum tree	To enhance fruit flavorings	Vegetarian

Oil of Peppermint	Dried plant leaves	Flavoring	Vegetarian
Oleic Acid	Fats and oils (animal or vegetable)	Defoaming, flavoring	Questionable*
Oxysterins	Glycerides, stearic acid	Prevents oil from clouding	Questionable*
Ox Bile	Ox bile	Preservative and emulsifier in dried egg whites	Questionable*
Ox Gall	See ox bile		
Pepper Cream	Herb	Spice (requires diglycerides or other emulsifiers to mix)	Vegetarian
Pepsin	Enzyme, usually extracted from hog stomachs, but can be synthetic	Coagulant in cheese	Questionable*
Polyglycerol Esters of Fatty Acids	Fats and oils, animal or vegetable		Questionable*
Polysorbate 60, 65, 80	Stearic acid (also called tween)	Emulsifiers, especially in "non-dairy" products	Questionable*
Potassium Bisulfite	Synthetic	Preservative	Vegetarian
Potassium Caseinate	Milk	Stabilizer and texturizer	Questionable*
Potassium Metabisulfite	Synthetic	Preservative	Vegetarian
Potassium Sorbate	Berries or synthetic	Preservative	Vegetarian
Propionic Acid	Synthetic or may be made from cheese	Mold inhibitor, preservative	Questionable*
Propyl Gallate	Synthetic or from nuts produced by insects	Preservative	
Proplyene Glycol (Alginate)	Synthetic	Emulsifier, stabilizer, solvent	Vegetarian
Propylparaben	Synthetic	Preservative	Vegetarian
Release Agents (These need not be listed in the ingredients)	Oils, mineral oil, mono glycerides or synthetic	Keeps heated foods from sticking to equipment, utensils, and packaging	Questionable*
Resinous Glaze	Insect secretion	Coating candies and pills	Vegetarian (not vegan)
Rennet	Animal enzymes (derived from the lining membranes of the stomach of suckling calves)	Coagulant and curdling agent especially in cheese and other dairy products	Not vegetarian
Serum Albumin	Blood	See albumin	Not vegetarian
Rennin	See rennet		
Shellac (See Resinous Glazes)	Insect secretion	In glaze for confectionery products and in chocolate panning	
Shortenings	Oil	To make baked goods light and flaky (factories often make both animal and vegetable shortenings on the same equipment)	Questionable*
Sodium Alginate	Seaweed or kelp	As a stabilizer	Vegetarian
Sodium Ascorbate	Synthetic	Preservative	Vegetarian
Sodium Benzoate	Synthetic origin	Preservative	Vegetarian
Sodium Bisulfite	Synthetic	Preservative	Vegetarian
Sodium Casinate	Milk and cheese	Texturizer in "non dairy" creamers and instant mashed potatoes	Vegetarian (not vegan)

Sodium Citrate	Synthetic	Emulsifier and buffer in processed produce	Vegetarian
Sodium Lauryl Sulfate	Synthetic	Detergent, whipping agent, an emulsifier (in egg products) and surfactant (in beverages)	Vegetarian
Sodium Meta Bisulfate	Synthetic	Preservative	Vegetarian
Sodium Propionate	Synthetic origin or rarely it is made from cheese	Mold preventative	Vegetarian (not vegan)
Sodium Nitrate	Synthetic	Preservative	Vegetarian
Sodium Sorbate	Synthetic or from corn	Preservative	Vegetarian
Sodium Sulfite	Synthetic	Preservative	Vegetarian
Softeners	Animal or vegetable	In chewing gum	Questionable*
Sorbic Acid	Berries, corn or synthetic	Mold inhibitor	Vegetarian
Sorbitan Monostearate	Stearic acid	Emulsifier, defoamer, flavor disperser	Questionable*
Span	See polysorbate		
Spearmint Oil	The herb mentha viriais	Primarily as flavoring in chewing gum	Vegetarian
Sperm oil	Whale	Release agent and lubricant in baking pans	Not vegetarian
Spices	Dried vegetable product derived from any part of the plant, whether rot, stem, bark, fruit, bud or seed		Vegetarian
Stannous Chloride	Synthetic	Preservative	Vegetarian
Stearic Acid	Animal or vegetable oil	In butter and vanilla flavoring, softener in chewing gum	Questionable*
Stearyl Lactylic Acid	Fats and oils	Emulsifier	Questionable*
Sulfur Dioxide	Synthetic gas	Preservative	Vegetarian
Tartars Acid	See cream of tartar		
Tween and Span	See polysorbate		
Thiodipropionic Acid	Synthetic	Preservative, or from cheese	Vegetarian (not vegan).
Tocopherols	Synthetic, or soybeans	Preservative, nutrient (vitamin e)	Vegetarian
Tricalcium Phosphate	Synthetic	Anti caking agent, bleaching agent	Vegetarian
Turmeric	Herb	Spice (often used in its oleo resin form for use in pickling brine and mustard with glycerides added)	Normally vegetarian
Vanilla	Bean	Flavoring, it may be processed with glycerine	Questionable*
Vanillin	Bark of spruce tree	Flavoring	Vegetarian
Vegetable Shortening	See shortening		
Vegetable Oil	See oil		
Vegetable Gums (Also see gum)	Substitute for gelatin in desserts and candies		Vegetarian
Whey	Milk, hence dairy	Binder and flavoring agent	Vegetarian (not vegan).

THE HOOD HEALTH HANDBOOK

A PRACTICAL GUIDE TO HEALTH AND WELLNESS IN THE URBAN COMMUNITY

How can you attain optimum health with minimum resources? This book shows us how, in plain English. *Hood Health* is an anthology of health experts from urban communities throughout the Americas, offering practical health solutions. Over 50 health experts contributed to this handbook. The contributors include fitness gurus, dieticians, personal trainers, and holistic practitioners from around the country. The text was edited by C'BS Alife and Dr. Supreme Understanding and supervised by a panel of licensed physicians.

Featuring articles from **Wise Intelligent** (of Poor Righteous Teachers), **Supa Nova Slom**, **Stic.man** (of Dead Prez), **Dr. Scott Whitaker** (author of *MediSin*), **Dr. Vernellia Randall** (author of *Dying While Black*), **Bryant Terry** (author of *Vegan Soul Kitchen*), **Afya Ibomu** (author of *Vegan Soulfood Guide to the Galaxy*), and over 40 others, as well as a Foreword from the world-renowned **Dick Gregory**.

TOPICS INCLUDE

- Fast Food vs. Real Food
- Weight Loss without Crash Diets
- Raising Healthy Children
- Exercise and Fitness without a Gym Membership
- Eliminating the Chemicals in our Homes
- Avoiding the Chemicals in Food
- Holistic/Herbal medicine
- Home Remedies that Work

- Traditional Medicine vs. Western Medicine
- Psychological Wellness
- Natural Hair and Skin Care
- Treating ADHD, Depression, and Drug Addiction
- Food Budgeting and Preparation
- Preventing and Treating Diabetes, Cancer, and Heart Disease
- Beating Drug and Alcohol Addiction
- Urban Survival and First Aid

FROM POVERTY TO POWER

THE REALIZATION OF PROSPERITY AND PEACE

BY JAMES ALLEN

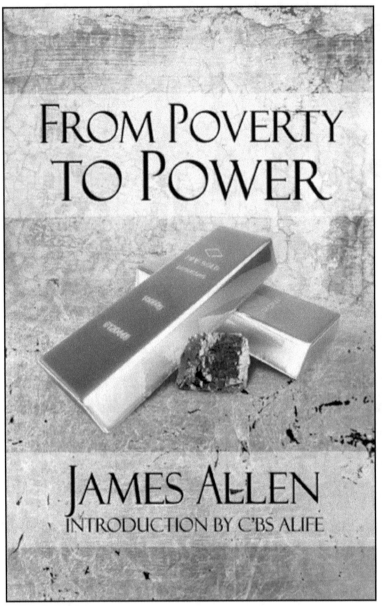

"It matters everything what you are within, for everything without will be mirrored and colored accordingly." – p. 17

With the current abundance of motivational coaches, talk shows, self-help books, and "positivity" seminars, it's easy to think you've heard it all. You haven't. Before "affirmations" and "visualization" became a part of our everyday language, a man by the name of James Allen blazed the trail you now see others following.

"And as we clothe both events and objects with our own thoughts, so likewise do we clothe the souls of others in the garments of our thoughts." – p. 21

Allen is most widely known for his seminal book, *As a Man Thinketh*, which teaches readers the immense power of the conscious mind. *From Poverty to Power*, his first book, explores the same concepts, but focuses on recovering from adversity. Considering our society's present conditions, the message of this book is especially relevant. Allen explores the power of the conscious mind in transforming the conditions of one's life and how one can harness all of their innate powers.

"Most people will admit that selfishness is the cause of all the unhappiness in the world, but they fall under the soul-destroying delusion that it is somebody else's selfishness, and not their own." – p. 62

This edition is further enhanced with an introduction by C'BS ALife that firmly sets the context of this writing by James Allen in time and space. Readers will understand how and why the message of James Allen arose when it did, how this message remains unique even in today's atmosphere of "positive thinking," and – most importantly – how we can put them into practice now.

A Sucker Born Every Minute

A Guide to Avoiding Scams, Cons, Frauds and Rip-Offs

The essential guide to every common scam, con, fraud, and trap out there! Take advantage of this book or find yourself taken advantage of!

Are you tired of getting losing your money, wasting your time, and wondering how you fell for the con? This book covers hundreds of popular scams, cons, and cheats, and simple tactics on how to avoid them. Cash for Gold, the Black Money scam, Ponzi schemes, multi-level marketing, college scholarship scams, predatory lending, gambling cheats, used car sales scams, counterfeiting, conversational cons, Internet fraud, identity theft, chain letters, religious and political frauds, little-known hustles, and even online dating sites are explained.

AFTER READING THIS BOOK, YOU'LL NEVER WASTE ANOTHER PENNY!

Heritage Playing Cards

The Whole World in the Palm of Your Hand

Why bother with a dull deck of plain cards when there's Heritage Playing Cards?

Not only is this deck perfect for any game you can think of, it's also an amazing conversation starter and an incredible educational tool! Featuring 54 hand-painted images of indigenous people from every corner of the globe, this deck is like a world tour in a box!

In any given hand, you might find an Egyptian pharaoh sharing the company of a Chinese merchant, a Pawnee chieftain, a Mayan priest and an Indian folk dancer!

The enclosed booklet offers details on the cultures represented on every card, a history of how playing cards came to be, and a selection of traditional card games from around the world! This deck can be used to teach number concepts, world cultures, geography, history, and multicultural education.

WITH HERITAGE CARDS, YOU'VE FOUND TREMENDOUS VALUE IN A TINY BOX!

DARKWATER

VOICES FROM WITHIN THE VEIL

BY W.E.B. DU BOIS

"While *Souls of Black Folk* deserves its praise, Du Bois' *Darkwater* merits wider recognition."

DARKWATER
VOICES FROM WITHIN THE VEIL
W.E.B. DU BOIS

Originally published in 1920, *Darkwater* makes Du Bois' previous work, including the ever-popular *Souls of Black Folk*, seem tame and conservative by comparison. That's why you haven't heard of it! *Darkwater* is revolutionary, uncompromising, and unconventional in both its content and style of presentation, addressing topics ranging from the plight of Black women to the rise of a Black Messiah, from a critical analysis of white people to the need for outright revolution.

"People will wish that this book had not been written. Actually it is a book so skillfully put together, so passionately felt, so lyrically expressed, that it will be read widely. May it also be read wisely!"

– R. Foerster, *The Survey* (1920)

"There is, to my mind, no better example of Du Bois's critical engagement of the dialectics of colonialism and capitalism, and racism and sexism, and the interlocking, intersecting and inter-connecting nature of each of the afore-mentioned than his 1920 monumental pièce de résistance, *Darkwater*."

– Dr. Reiland Rabaka, *Jouvert* (2003)

"Like *Souls of Black Folk*, Du Bois's masterpiece *Darkwater* is filled with brilliant ideas and experimental methodology. Beginning with autobiography and ending with a chilling science fiction story about the destruction of Manhattan, Du Bois provides pathbreaking sociological analysis."

– Historian J.R. Feagin (2003)

FIND OUT MORE AT

WWW.DUBOISDARKWATER.COM

MAIL-IN ORDER FORM

Want to order copies of this book for the people in your life who need it? Or are you interested in the rest of our catalog? Either way, the process is easy. Simply mail in this order form (or a photocopy or written note) with a money order. We cover the tax. The best part is: Shipping is NOW a FLAT RATE, meaning no matter HOW MUCH you buy, you only pay $4 for shipping.

QTY.	TITLE	COST	SUBTOTAL (QTY x COST)
	How to Hustle and Win, Part 1	$15	
	How to Hustle and Win, Part 2	$15	
	Knowledge of Self	$10	
	Hood Health Handbook, Vol. 1	$20	
	Hood Health Handbook, Vol. 2	$20	
	La Brega (HHW en Español)	$10	
	Real Life is No Fairy Tale	$15	
	Heritage Playing Cards	$7	
	Black Rebellion	$13	
	From Poverty to Power	$13	
	365 Days 2011 Wall Calendar	$15	
	Darkwater by W.E.B. Du Bois	$13	
	Call of Duty	$15	
	Locked Up, but Not Locked Down	$15	
	T-Shirt (Size: S M L XL 2X 3X) Which Book Cover:	$15	
	SHIPPING (FLAT RATE)	$4	4.00
	TOTAL		$

Make sure your math is accurate, or it may keep you from getting your order in a timely manner! Send in your completed order form with an official money order (made out to Supreme Design, LLC.) for the total amount. Don't forget to provide your mailing address.

Your address:

_____

_____

_____

Total amount enclosed:

$_____

Send to: Supreme Design, LLC.
PO Box 10887
Atlanta, GA 30310

You can also order online at www.SupremeDesignOnline.com
There, you can also order larger quantities at bigger discounts.
If you have questions, email us at info@supremedesignonline.com

Index of Recipes

CPSIA information can be obtained
at www.ICGtesting.com
Printed in the USA
BVHW060753061021
618236BV00006B/43